P9-BZK-766

Windows®
8.1
BIBLE

Windows® 8.1
BIBLE

Jim Boyce

Jeffrey Shapiro

Rob Tidrow

WILEY

Windows® 8.1 Bible

Published by
John Wiley & Sons, Inc.
10475 Crosspoint Boulevard
Indianapolis, IN 46256
www.wiley.com

Copyright © 2014 by Jim Boyce, Jeffrey Shapiro, and Rob Tidrow

Published by John Wiley & Sons, Inc., Indianapolis, Indiana

Published simultaneously in Canada

ISBN: 978-1-118-83531-9

ISBN: 978-1-118-83518-0 (ebk)

ISBN: 978-1-118-83527-2 (ebk)

Manufactured in the United States of America

10 9 8 7 6 5 4 3 2 1

No part of this publication may be reproduced, stored in a retrieval system or transmitted in any form or by any means, electronic, mechanical, photocopying, recording, scanning, or otherwise, except as permitted under Sections 107 or 108 of the 1976 United States Copyright Act, without either the prior written permission of the Publisher, or authorization through payment of the appropriate per-copy fee to the Copyright Clearance Center, 222 Rosewood Drive, Danvers, MA 01923, (978) 750-8400, fax (978) 646-8600. Requests to the Publisher for permission should be addressed to the Permissions Department, John Wiley & Sons, Inc., 111 River Street, Hoboken, NJ 07030, (201) 748-6011, fax (201) 748-6008, or online at http://www.wiley.com/go/permissions.

LIMIT OF LIABILITY/DISCLAIMER OF WARRANTY: THE PUBLISHER AND THE AUTHOR MAKE NO REPRESENTATIONS OR WARRANTIES WITH RESPECT TO THE ACCURACY OR COMPLETENESS OF THE CONTENTS OF THIS WORK AND SPECIFICALLY DISCLAIM ALL WARRANTIES, INCLUDING WITHOUT LIMITATION WARRANTIES OF FITNESS FOR A PARTICULAR PURPOSE. NO WARRANTY MAY BE CREATED OR EXTENDED BY SALES OR PROMOTIONAL MATERIALS. THE ADVICE AND STRATEGIES CONTAINED HEREIN MAY NOT BE SUITABLE FOR EVERY SITUATION. THIS WORK IS SOLD WITH THE UNDERSTANDING THAT THE PUBLISHER IS NOT ENGAGED IN RENDERING LEGAL, ACCOUNTING, OR OTHER PROFESSIONAL SERVICES. IF PROFESSIONAL ASSISTANCE IS REQUIRED, THE SERVICES OF A COMPETENT PROFESSIONAL PERSON SHOULD BE SOUGHT. NEITHER THE PUBLISHER NOR THE AUTHOR SHALL BE LIABLE FOR DAMAGES ARISING HEREFROM. THE FACT THAT AN ORGANIZATION OR WEBSITE IS REFERRED TO IN THIS WORK AS A CITATION AND/OR A POTENTIAL SOURCE OF FURTHER INFORMATION DOES NOT MEAN THAT THE AUTHOR OR THE PUBLISHER ENDORSES THE INFORMATION THE ORGANIZATION OR WEBSITE MAY PROVIDE OR RECOMMENDATIONS IT MAY MAKE. FURTHER, READERS SHOULD BE AWARE THAT INTERNET WEBSITES LISTED IN THIS WORK MAY HAVE CHANGED OR DISAPPEARED BETWEEN WHEN THIS WORK WAS WRITTEN AND WHEN IT IS READ.

For general information on our other products and services please contact our Customer Care Department within the United States at (877) 762-2974, outside the United States at (317) 572-3993 or fax (317) 572-4002.

Wiley publishes in a variety of print and electronic formats and by print-on-demand. Some material included with standard print versions of this book may not be included in e-books or in print-on-demand. If this book refers to media such as a CD or DVD that is not included in the version you purchased, you may download this material at http://booksupport.wiley.com. For more information about Wiley products, visit www.wiley.com.

Library of Congress Control Number: 2013954190

Trademarks: Wiley and the Wiley logo are trademarks or registered trademarks of John Wiley & Sons, Inc. and/or its affiliates, in the United States and other countries, and may not be used without written permission. Microsoft and Windows are registered trademarks of Microsoft Corporation. All other trademarks are the property of their respective owners. John Wiley & Sons, Inc. is not associated with any product or vendor mentioned in this book.

Credits

Executive Editor
Steve Hayes

Project Editor
Elizabeth Kuball

Technical Editor
Todd Meister

Copy Editor
Elizabeth Kuball

Editorial Assistant
Annie Sullivan

Sr. Editorial Assistant
Cherie Case

Project Coordinator
Ana Carrillo

Cover Image
iStockphoto.com / Aleksandar Velasevic

About the Authors

Jim Boyce has authored and co-authored over 50 books on computers and technology, covering operating systems, applications, and programming topics. He has been a frequent contributor to Microsoft.com, TechRepublic (`www.techrepublic.com`), and other online publications. Jim has written for a number of print publications, including *Windows IT Pro, WINDOWS Magazine, InfoWorld*, and others, and was a contributing editor and columnist for *WINDOWS Magazine*.

Jim has been involved with IT in various capacities for nearly 30 years. He has been a CAD system administrator and trainer, college instructor, independent IT consultant, ISP owner, and practice director for managed services practices in a global environment. Today, Jim is a Support Practice Manager for Microsoft in its Premier Support organization and a former Microsoft MVP.

Jeffrey Shapiro has worked in IT for more than 21 years. He has published more than 20 books on IT, network administration, and software development, and has written for numerous publications. Some of his books include the *Windows Server Bible* (from version 2000 to 2008), *Building High Availability Windows Server Solutions,* and numerous books on Microsoft's server technologies, Visual Studio, and the .NET programing languages.

Jeffrey works for MISIQ (`www.misiq.com`) an organization that specializes in IT infrastructure and software architecture, systems, and development for large companies. MISIQ caters to cloud-based infrastructure, high-performance software for large web and line-of-business solutions, and Windows Server and Windows 8.x migration strategies.

Rob Tidrow has authored and co-authored over 35 books on computers and technology. He specializes in operating systems, social media tools, live video technologies, office suite applications, web technologies, and networking. Some of his books include *IBM Lotus Symphony For Dummies, Teach Yourself Visually Microsoft Windows Vista, Teach Yourself Visually Wireless Networking,* and *Master Visually Windows XP SP2*. Rob has been guest speaker at several industry events, including Blog Indiana, Hoosier Educational Computer Coordinators (HECC) Conference, and the RCS TechExpo.

Today, Rob is Technology Coordinator for Richmond Community Schools in Richmond, Indiana (`www.werrichmond.com`), where he leads the IT department, serving over 6,000 students and staff. He lives in Richmond with his wife, Tammy, and two sons, Adam and Wesley. Follow him on Twitter (@robtidrow) and Facebook (`www.facebook.com/robtidrow`).

Acknowledgments

We want to recognize Steve Hayes and Carole McClendon for bringing us this opportunity. This project would not have stayed on track without Elizabeth Kuball pushing and pulling us. Finally, we offer our appreciation and thanks to Todd Meister for his technical review of the manuscript.

It was a great experience.

Contents at a Glance

Contents

Contents

Contents

Contents

Contents

Contents

Contents

Contents

Contents

Introduction

Welcome to *Windows 8.1 Bible*. If you're familiar with Windows, you might know that the Windows operating system has existed for over two decades. In that time, it has transformed in many ways as computer hardware has changed dramatically.

Windows 8.1 is the latest edition in the Windows family and builds on the usability and performance improvements in Windows 7. One of the biggest differences, however, is the shift in support in Windows 8 for tablet and handheld devices. The streamlined, tile-based Windows 8.1 interface is designed from the ground up for tablet devices, and Windows 8.1 provides a consistent user experience across a range of devices from cellphones to PCs.

Although we've tried to cover as many of the features and capabilities as Windows 8.1 offers, some naturally fall through the cracks because we have only so much space in this book. With a good understanding of the key features, however, you're well on your way to getting the most from your Windows PC.

Whom This Book Is For

Not everyone wants to be a computer expert, and few have the time to become one. Most people just want to use a computer to get things done, or even just to have some fun. This should come as no surprise. After all, not everyone who drives a car wants to be a professional mechanic. Not everyone who uses a cellphone wants to be an electrical engineer. So, why should everyone who uses a computer want, or need, to be a computer expert? They shouldn't. Some people just need to be computer *users*, people who use the computer without being total nerds about it.

This book is for the computer users — the people who just want to use their computers to have some fun and get some things done. It might seem like an awfully big book for such an audience. The only reason it's such a big book is because there are *so many* things you can do with Windows 8.1.

Most of us prefer to learn by discovery, by exploring and trying things out. It's a lot more fun that way and typically much more effective. However, a couple problems are evident with that approach. For one, you can get yourself into a bind from time to time. For another, when you get to a place where you don't know what's going on, sometimes you need to fill in some gaps before you can move on and continue learning by discovery.

A book can help with that by covering all the stuff everyone else assumes you already know. Especially if that book is divided up into sections and chapters that deal with one topic at a time, so you can focus on just the thing you need to know, when you need to know it. Which brings us to ....

How to Use This Book

A book that supports learning by discovery needs to have some elements of a tutorial and some elements of a reference book. We guess you could say it has to be a reference book divided into multiple mini-tutorials, so you can learn what you need to know about one topic, whenever it becomes important to you. To that end, this book is divided into ten major parts, each of which covers a large topic.

Each part, in turn, is divided into multiple chapters, each chapter covering a smaller topic. Chapters are divided into sections and subsections, all designed to help you find the information you need, when you need it. The table of contents in the front of this book covers all the specifics. The index at the back of the book helps you find things based on a keyword or topic. The only thing missing is a high-level view of just the parts. So, that's what we'll provide here:

Part I: Getting Started, Getting Secure: How you get started with Windows 8.1 depends on where you're coming from. This part covers all fronts. If you're an experienced Windows user, you probably want to know what's new. Chapter 1 covers that turf. Chapters 2 and 3 cover important "getting started" topics for everyone, and help you learn to navigate the Windows 8.1 environment. Chapters 4 and 5 touch on security and safety. Chapter 6 provides solutions to common problems with getting started.

Part II: Personalizing Windows 8.1: We all like to tweak things to suit our personal needs, taste, and style. That's what this part is all about. But it's not just about changing the look and feel of things. It's about really making the computer a useful tool for whatever your work (or play) requires.

Part III: Beyond the Desktop: Just about everyone who uses a computer also uses the Internet. And Windows 8.1 has many tools to make that possible. The chapters in this part cover social networking features, using computers remotely, and synchronizing your data in the cloud.

Part IV: Pictures, Music, and Movies: The Internet isn't the only place to have fun with a computer. You can have a lot of fun offline with pictures, music, and movies. The chapters in this part tell you how.

Part V: Managing Your Content: We all have to make some effort to get our stuff organized and keep it organized. Otherwise, we spend more time looking for stuff than actually doing things. This part covers all the necessary housekeeping kinds of chores to help you spend less time looking for things and more time doing things.

Part VI: Printing and Managing Printers: Sometimes, you just have to get a thing off the screen and onto paper. That's what printing is all about. This part covers printing and managing printers.

Part VII: Installing and Removing Programs: Hot topics here include downloading programs, installing programs from CDs and flash drives, getting older programs to run, controlling access to programs, getting rid of unwanted programs, and dealing with problem programs and processes. After all, what good is a computer without some programs to run on it?

Part VIII: Hardware and Performance Tuning: *Hardware* is the computer buzzword for physical gadgets you can hold in your hand. As the years roll by, hardware just keeps getting smaller, better, faster, cheaper, and, well, cooler. This part covers everything you need to know about adding and removing hardware and troubleshooting hardware problems.

Part IX: Networking and Sharing: Whether you have 2 PCs or 20, eventually you may want to link them all together into a single private network so they can share a single Internet account and printer, or perhaps several printers. And if you've been wasting time transferring files via CDs or some other removable disk, you may want to replace all that with simple drag-and-drop operations on your screen. This part tells you how to make all that happen.

Part X: Appendixes: Rounding out the book are four appendixes, where you'll find information on how to install a clean copy of Windows 8.1 or upgrade an existing Windows 7 or Windows 8 installation. You'll also find details on Windows gestures and hotkeys.

That's a lot of topics and a lot to think about. But there's no hurry. If you're new to Windows, or your experience is limited to things like e-mail and the web, Chapters 2 and 3 are probably your best first stop. If you have more extensive Windows experience, you might want to hop over to Chapter 1 for a quick look at things that are new in Windows 8.1.

Part I

Getting Started, Getting Secure

IN THIS PART

What's New in Windows 8 and Windows 8.1

IN THIS CHAPTER

New platforms

The Windows 8.1 Interface

The Windows store

Cloud synchronization

Messaging

Other new features

In some ways, Windows 8.1 is a radical departure from Windows 7, as well as the other versions of Windows that preceded it. In other ways, Windows 8.1 isn't much different from Windows 7. Both possibilities are good ones, both from a technology standpoint and for the user. The differences mean an expanded set of features, richer experience, broader platform support, performance improvements, and much more. The similarities mean that if you're familiar with previous versions of Windows, you can put Windows 8.1 to work right away without a steep learning curve.

In this chapter, we focus not on those familiar features, but rather on many of the new and changed features in Windows 8.1. You'll find an overview here of those features, with deeper explanation in other chapters. We can't cover every new feature here, but we hope to give you a good overview of the key features and conceptual changes introduced in Windows 8 and Windows 8.1.

In this chapter, we also focus on Windows 8 as a whole, rather than Windows 8.1 specifically. So, if you're looking for information on how Windows 8 is different from Windows 7, you'll find it in this chapter. We also highlight the differences and improvements in Windows 8.1 versus Windows 8. So, you get a holistic view of the Windows 8 family in this chapter.

Now, whip out that new Windows 8.1 tablet or PC, start reading, and start taking advantage of the great new features that Windows 8 and Windows 8.1 have to offer.

New Platforms

One of the most significant additions to Windows 8 is its support for platforms other than the traditional PC. Windows 8 moves beyond the Intel and AMD x86 processor family to support System on a Chip (SoC) devices from both the x86 and ARM architectures. Windows 8.1 naturally also supports the ARM architecture.

ARM, which stands for Advanced RISC Machine, was developed by the company now known as ARM Holdings. Although you might never have heard of them, ARM processors are found extensively in consumer electronics devices, including tablets, cellphones, MP3 players, gaming consoles, computer peripherals, and much more.

While the traditional PC portable form factor continues to shrink with ultra-light tablets and notebooks, SoC support for Windows 8 generally means the capability to provide a Windows experience on small form-factor tablets, cellphones, and smaller handheld devices, in addition to the generally larger (albeit typically more powerful) traditional PC platforms. For ARM devices, the result is a new opportunity for device manufacturers to provide a new selection of handheld devices running a Windows operating system (dubbed *Windows on ARM,* or WOA) with support for applications like those in the Microsoft Office suite.

For users, it means a consistency of user experience across a broad range of devices. For example, your experience could be largely the same between your notebook, your tablet, and your cellphone. Support for ARM also opens up some interesting possibilities for embedding Windows in a vast array of consumer electronic devices. It's quite likely that someday soon your TV will be running Windows and give you, for example, the same, consistent experience streaming movies on your TV as on your PC.

An important distinction to understand about the ARM platform, however, is that applications written for your desktop PC or notebook won't necessarily run on an ARM device. For example, none of the applications in existence today, built for the x86 Windows 7 and earlier operating systems, will work on ARM-based devices. However, that roadblock doesn't exist for Windows 8–specific applications.

Microsoft's Visual Studio development environment makes it relatively easy to compile an ARM version of an application at the same time you compile one for the x86 platform. This means that developers can create one code set for their application and publish it for both platforms. When you download an application from the Windows Store, that app will run on the Windows 8 "traditional" devices, as well as ARM-based Windows 8 devices. You can install the app on up to five devices in any mix of x86- and ARM-based devices. The app will provide the same experience on all of them.

What about Office applications, you ask? Excellent question! Microsoft includes four Office applications with WOA devices, including Word, Excel, PowerPoint, and OneNote. These versions of the Office applications don't provide the same level of features as the regular version, but they provide a means for users to work with their data across multiple types of devices. For example, if you sync your OneNote notebooks to SkyDrive, you can view them in OneNote on your WOA device. Or when someone e-mails you a spreadsheet as an attachment, you can view it in Excel on the WOA device.

Although there are many new devices being introduced near Windows 8.1's release, Windows 8.1 does not represent a platform shift from Windows 8. Windows 8.1 will run on the same two platforms as Windows 8 (x86- and ARM-based devices).

> **NOTE**
>
> In this chapter, the term *Windows 8* is used to denote the Windows 8 family that includes Windows 8 and Windows 8.1. So, a discussion of "Windows 8 apps" describes apps designed to run on both Windows 8 and Windows 8.1 devices.

The Windows 8.1 Interface

As with many previous versions of Windows, Windows 8 introduced a new user interface, and Windows 8.1 fine-tunes that interface. Unlike many previous versions, Windows 8's new interface is radically different from what we've come to know as the "traditional" Windows user interface. Clearly designed with the tablet and handheld market in mind — at least in large part — Windows 8 and Windows 8.1 give you a simplified, clean user experience with tiles providing access to applications.

> **NOTE**
>
> The Windows 8 UI look isn't just about tablets and small form-factor devices. To Microsoft, the new UI is really as much an aesthetic concept as it is a user interface. It's about uncluttering the desktop, websites, and PowerPoint decks almost as much as it's about uncluttering the Windows user interface.

The Start screen

Figure 1.1 shows the Windows 8.1 Start screen, a key component of the new Windows 8.1 interface. You'll learn how to navigate the new Windows 8.1 interface in Chapter 2. For now, understand that the tiles on the Start page, like icons on the traditional Windows desktop, give you quick access to your programs and documents. Tap the Internet Explorer tile, for example, and Internet Explorer opens. Likewise, click or tap the Photos tile, and the Photos app opens, enabling you to view the photos stored on your computer, or in SkyDrive, Facebook, Flickr, and other locations.

FIGURE 1.1

The Windows 8.1 Start screen.

A key difference between Windows 8.1 tiles and desktop icons, however, is that tiles can be live, showing data that changes dynamically. The Mail tile, for example, shows a preview of new messages in your Inbox. The Calendar tile shows a preview of meetings and events in your Calendar, the Finance tile shows stock prices (as shown in Figure 1.1), and so on. The advantage is that the tiles can give you information at a glance that you would otherwise have to open a program to view.

The Windows 8.1 UI isn't just about the Start page or its tiles, however. Windows 8 apps generally follow the same clean, streamlined look as the Windows 8.1 interface itself. For example, Figure 1.2 shows the Finance application. There is no window border, no controls in the title bar, and no visible menu. While a Windows 8 app can include any number of interface features specific to the application, in general the interface will be simple and streamlined like the Finance app, if not more so.

FIGURE 1.2

A Windows 8 app typically has a clean, simplified interface.

Although the Windows 8.1 interface is a departure from the traditional Windows desktop, the combination of live tiles, clean look, and capability to put your most frequently used apps and documents in one area for quick access makes Windows 8.1 a winner, particularly for tablets and handheld devices.

The Lock Screen

The Windows 8.1 Lock Screen appears when the computer is locked (see Figure 1.3). The Lock Screen shows the current day and time, battery status, and network status, all on a photo background. The Lock Screen can also display notifications from applications. To display the logon screen, slide the Lock Screen up.

FIGURE 1.3

The Lock Screen.

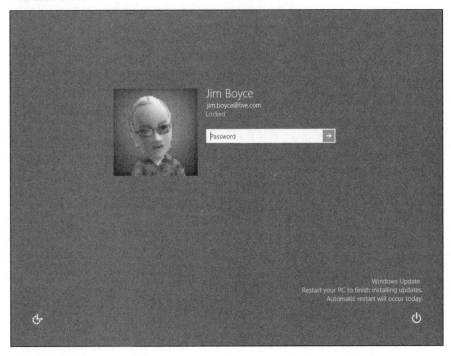

The Charms Bar

The Charms Bar appears at the right edge of the display (see Figure 1.4) when you move the mouse to the bottom-right or upper-right corner of the display. You can also display the Charms Bar by swiping in from the right edge of the display.

The Charms Bar gives you quick access to Search, Settings, and other options and features.

The Windows Store

If you're familiar with the iPad, iPod, or Android devices (not to mention a handful of other types), you're familiar with the concept of an app (application) store. As you might expect, given the expansion of Windows 8 in the tablet and handheld market, Windows 8 added its own app store, called the Windows Store, shown in Figure 1.5.

FIGURE 1.4

The Charms Bar.

The great thing about the Windows Store, like its counterparts for other devices and platforms, is quick access to a vast collection of applications from games to productivity tools to multimedia apps. As long as your device is connected to the Internet, you can open the Windows Store, browse for and quickly locate the app you need, and typically, in less than a minute, have the app installed and running on your device. Many apps are free; others have some cost. Many give you the capability to try the app for free before you buy it.

Cloud Synchronization

With the likelihood that many people will have multiple Windows 8 devices, it's no surprise that Windows 8 introduced some great cloud-synchronization features that are carried over to Windows 8.1. For example, Windows 8.1 can integrate with your Windows account (formerly called Windows Live accounts) and SkyDrive to give you access to documents and photos from multiple devices. You can save, open, and view files from SkyDrive from a variety of devices, including a Mac or iPad, your Windows Phone, or your iPhone.

FIGURE 1.5

The Windows Store.

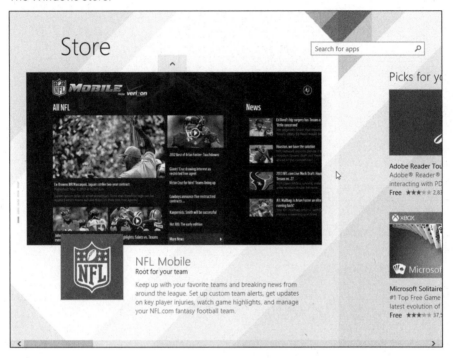

Many Windows 8 applications integrate with SkyDrive directly. For example, the Photos app lists not only the photos you have on your computer, but also those in SkyDrive (as well as Facebook and Flickr). If you have a domain account, you can associate your domain account with your Windows account and enjoy that same cloud experience.

Other applications also support SkyDrive. For example, you can get a free OneNote app for your Windows Phone, iPhone, or Android device that enables you to view OneNote notebooks that are synced to SkyDrive. So, if you create a note on your PC, it can automatically sync to SkyDrive, and from there it can be viewed from your mobile phone. This is a great feature for taking your work notes, shopping list, or other notes with you wherever you go.

> **TIP**
> Office Web Apps, introduced with SharePoint Server 2010, are included with SkyDrive, enabling you to view and edit Word, Excel, OneNote, and PowerPoint documents from a web browser without having Office installed on a device.

Integrated Messaging

A lot of great new apps are included with Windows 8.1, but one deserves particular mention here. The new Mail app included with Windows 8 combines a sleek interface with the capability to integrate e-mail accounts into a unified mailbox (see Figure 1.6). Bringing all your mail into one app can be a great timesaver and can eliminate the need for multiple mail applications or the need to open multiple web browsers to check your mailboxes.

NOTE
You can use Mail to connect to almost any mail service.

FIGURE 1.6

The Mail app.

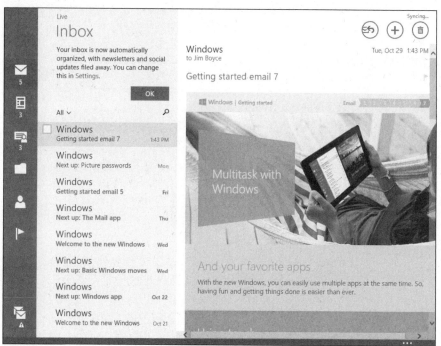

Social Networking Integration

Windows 8.1 provides social network integration in a handful of ways to make it easier for you to work with your friends and contacts across those services.

For example, the People app lets you integrate contact information from Hotmail (Windows Live), LinkedIn, Twitter, Exchange, and Google. So, all your contacts from all those services can appear in the People app. The People app also provides social updates about your friends within the People app, so you can, for example, see what status updates your friends have posted on Facebook.

File Explorer

The ribbon interface made its appearance in Office 2007 and, since then, has expanded in the 2010 and 2013 editions of Office and SharePoint. Now, you'll find the ribbon interface in File Explorer. Figure 1.7 shows an example of an Explorer window's ribbon.

FIGURE 1.7

The ribbon interface in Explorer.

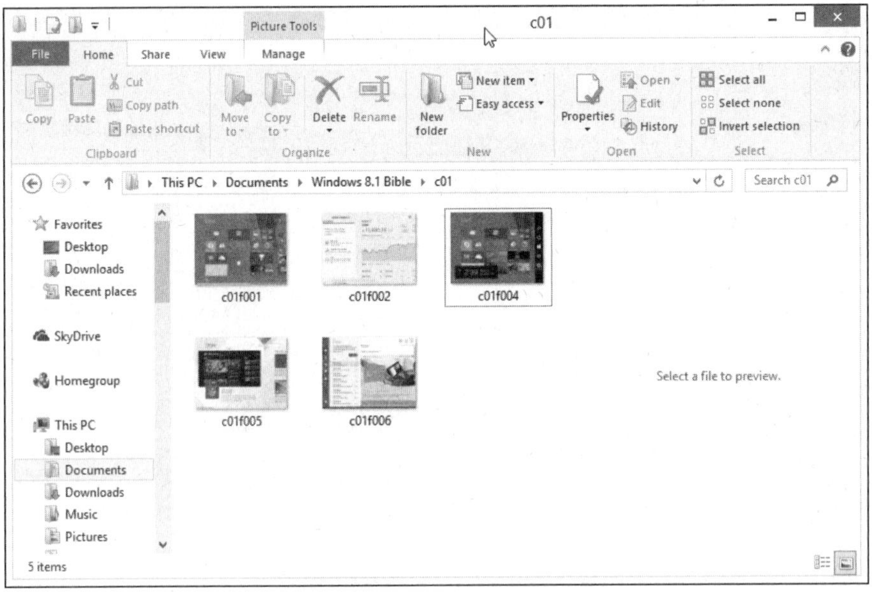

As you might expect, the ribbon in Explorer groups has commands for working with and sharing files and folders, changing how items display in the window, and in the case of media files, playing the files.

1

TIP

You can click the up arrow near the top right of the ribbon to minimize it. The arrow changes to a down arrow, which, when clicked, expands the ribbon.

Another great addition in File Explorer is the capability to easily mount CD images and virtual hard drive images right in Explorer. Once you mount an ISO image, for example, the image appears in File Explorer as CD, just as if you had a physical CD inserted in your CD drive. Although you could mount these images in Windows 7, File Explorer makes it much easier.

Search

Windows 7 integrated search within the operating system to enable you to quickly locate files, e-mail messages, and other items on your computer. Windows 8.1 enhances that dynamic search capability and includes a great new interface for search that categorizes results. Figure 1.8 shows an example of a search in Windows 8.1 Search.

FIGURE 1.8

The new Windows 8.1 Search screen showing results for Apps.

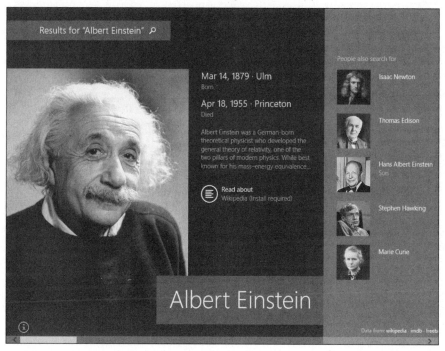

Search categorizes your search results so you can quickly find the item you're looking for. The categories are listed on the right, and clicking on a category displays the results for that category at the left. By default, the App category is selected, so Search automatically shows all apps on your computer. To find a specific app, document, e-mail, or other item, just type an appropriate search word or term in the text box. Then click a category to view the items in that category that meet your search criteria.

You can use natural language query syntax, such as "Find all files where the filename starts with Goober and the size is greater than 10MB." You can also use the Advanced Query Syntax (AQS) available in Windows 7 to search, such as `filename:Goober size:>10MB`.

Spell Check and AutoCorrect

Windows 8.1 extends spell check across the operating system to any application that uses standard text controls. This means, for example, that you can use spell check in Lync or other applications that don't have their own spell-check feature.

Enterprise Features

Windows 8 and Windows 8.1 include a selection of features that will only be available to enterprise users via the Windows 8/8.1 Enterprise editions. This section explores the major features that are exclusive to Windows 8 and Windows 8.1 Enterprise.

Windows to Go

Windows to Go enables you to boot and run Windows 8 from a USB flash drive. This means you can take your operating system, applications, and documents with you from one device to another. This capability also offers administrators a means of restricting access for specific types of users, such as contingent workers, consultants, or visitors.

DirectAccess

DirectAccess allows remote users to access the corporate network without the need for a virtual private network (VPN) connection. Unlike a VPN connection, which the user must establish manually, DirectAccess establishes a bi-directional connection automatically for the user. The result is that users can gain access quickly and simply to internal network resources such as messaging services, file servers, printers, collaboration tools like SharePoint, and more. Think of DirectAccess as an automatic VPN that just happens for the user; users don't need to do anything to initiate the secure connection to the corporate network. DirectAccess authenticates the computer, which means the computer can connect to the network before the user logs on. DirectAccess can also authenticate the user and supports two-factor authentication using smart cards. The end result is a very seamless VPN experience for users, with simplified deployment and management for the IT team.

BranchCache

BranchCache in Windows Server 2012 and in Windows 8 caches web, file, and other application content, enabling users to access that cached content locally from the locan area network (LAN) rather than retrieve it from the wide area network (WAN). BranchCache, therefore, can potentially eliminate a large amount of external network traffic, which can be particularly important for organizations with relatively low-bandwidth WAN links. For security, BranchCache encrypts the content both on the caching server(s) and on the client computers.

AppLocker

AppLocker enables administrators to control which applications and processes users can run on their computers, including executable files, Windows Installer files, DLLs, scripts, packaged applications, and packaged application installers. Controlling applications in this way can improve security and adherence to processes by blocking unapproved applications and ensuring licensing compliance, and also helping to ensure process compliance. Administrators can define rules based on attributes such as application publisher, product name, filename, version, and others. Rules can be assigned to individuals as well as security groups, providing flexibility and the ability to implement exceptions.

VDI enhancements

Virtual Desktop Infrastructure (VDI) provides the capability to deliver a desktop computing experience to users from virtual clients running in a datacenter. The VDI features in Windows 8 support a rich client desktop experience, including host-side rendering to support for graphics-intensive applications; GPU Virtualization, which enables multiple clients to share a graphics processing unit (GPU) on the Hyper-V server; intelligent screen capture and compression to improve user graphics experience and reduce network bandwidth requirements; and USB device redirection. All these features combine to enable a rich desktop user experience to a broad range of devices, including lower-cost devices.

Windows 8 app deployment

The Enterprise edition of Windows 8 includes the capability for PCs and tablets that are domain joined to side-load internal apps. This feature gives administrators an easy means for deploying these apps across the enterprise.

Internet Explorer 11

Internet Explorer 11 (see Figure 1.9), included with Windows 8.1 and also available as a download for Windows 7 and Windows 8, includes some great new features that build on its predecessor, Internet Explorer 10. Internet Explorer 11 now supports the Web Graphics Library (WebGL) standard, adding features for interactive content, graphics performance, and other features for rich content experiences. IE 11 also offers great performance overall, and browsing feels faster thanks to web page caching, prefetch, and prerender features. HTML 5 support is also strengthened in IE 11.

FIGURE 1.9

Internet Explorer 11's Windows 8.1 look.

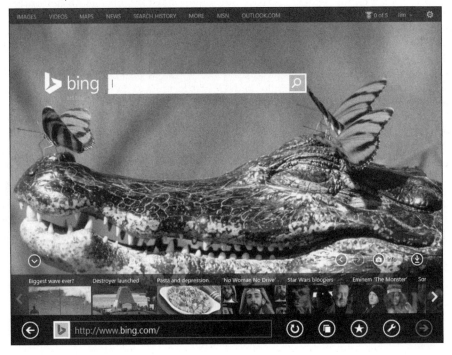

IE 11 also offers new features for the tablet market, offering better touch-based interaction, gyroscope input, and display orientation lock. As with IE 10, there are two versions of IE 11, one a Windows 8–style app and the other running on the desktop. The desktop version supports touch-based navigation, just like the Windows 8 version.

There are several new features in IE 11 designed with the user in mind. These include enhanced pinned sites, which enable IE to update content dynamically using live tiles; the capability to sync your open IE tabs across multiple devices, better Skype integration, and more.

IE 11 also offers new features for the IT administrator. These include security improvements for enhanced protected mode, which prevents pages from accessing protected parts of the operating system. Adobe Flash is included with IE 11 on Windows 8.1, and can be updated through Automatic Updates and group policy. There are also several new group policy settings to help administrators more closely manage the user experience and control security with IE 11.

Client Hyper-V

Although not enabled by default, Windows 8.1 includes the Hyper-V client, enabling you to run virtual machines (VMs) within the Hyper-V platform. For example, you might run a VM of Windows XP to support an application that isn't compatible with later versions of Windows. Or maybe you need to run Linux, but you don't want to dual-boot between them. Hyper-V on Windows 8.1 is a great solution.

Client Hyper-V on Windows 8.1 offers more capabilities and power than its predecessor, Virtual PC. Client Hyper-V supports both 32- and 64-bit client operating systems, although Client Hyper-V only runs on 64-bit PCs running the 64-bit version of Windows 8.1. It requires a minimum of 4GB of RAM on the host PC and processors that support Second Level Address Translation (SLAT), although most of today's PCs provide that support.

> **TIP**
> To enable Hyper-V on your computer, open the Programs and Features object in the Control Panel and click Turn Windows Features On or Off.

BitLocker

BitLocker has been around for a while, but Windows 8.1 improves performance and includes features for disk encryption. For example, when you turn on BitLocker to encrypt a drive, you have the option to only encrypt sectors on the drive that have data stored on them, instead of encrypting the entire drive. As space gets used on the drive, BitLocker encrypts that data. Windows 8.1 BitLocker also adds the capability to deploy Windows 8.1 to an encrypted state, instead of encrypting the drive after installation.

Additional Windows 8 BitLocker features include the capability for users to change the BitLocker PIN or password, with support for password and PIN complexity through group policy; a Network Unlock feature that enables automatic unlocking of operating system volumes at system reboot when those systems are connected to the corporate network; and support for Encrypted Hard Drives, which offload the encryption process to the storage controller on the hard drive.

Smart Cards

Windows 8.1 includes a handful of features for smart card users and simplifies smart card deployment and management for administrators. For example, Windows 8.1 supports virtual smart cards (VSC) on systems that support the Trusted Platform Module (TPM). Virtual smart cards can be deployed to users' systems with no cost for physical cards.

Other smart card changes in Windows 8.1 include improvements in the smart card sign-on process, making it easy for users to choose a different authentication option after they insert their smart card, and system-level changes for the way the Smart Card Service starts and stops, enabling the service to run only when it's needed, improving overall system performance.

Task Management

The Task Manager, which lets you view and manage running applications and processes, received a facelift in Windows 8 that carries through to Windows 8.1. The Task Manager simplifies the default display to show only a list of running applications (see Figure 1.10). You can click an application in the list and click End Task to end it.

If you want to see additional information about running applications and processes, click More Details to expand the Task Manager, as shown in Figure 1.11. This more-familiar interface provides multiple tabs to view performance data, application history, and other details.

FIGURE 1.10

The Windows 8.1 Task Manager.

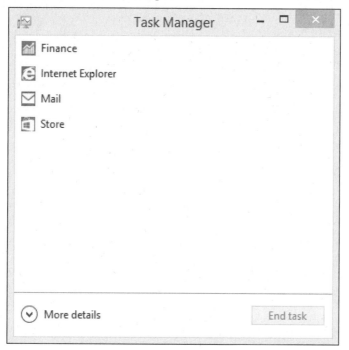

Proximity and Wi-Fi Direct

Wi-Fi Direct is a peer-to-peer connectivity technology that allows Wi-Fi devices to interact directly with one another without going through a wireless access point/router. Wi-Fi Direct is a bit like Bluetooth, but with a stronger signal and further range.

One of the advantages to the capability for devices to detect one another (Proximity) through Wi-Fi Direct is that you can easily make connections to printers, headsets, and other devices that support Wi-Fi Direct. In addition, Windows 8 applications that support Wi-Fi Direct can discover and communicate with each other across devices easily. This capability opens up a broad range of new features and interesting scenarios for social networking, gaming, and data sharing.

FIGURE 1.11

Task manager's expanded view.

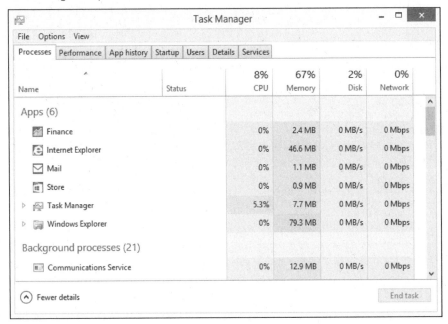

Refresh/Reset

Windows 8.1 offers two features to help you restore your Windows 8.1 device to a known, good state. The first of these is Refresh Your PC, which reinstalls Windows 8.1 without losing your data, Windows 8 apps, and settings. Refresh Your PC also maintains your network and mobile broadband configurations, BitLocker settings, drive assignments, and so on. Refresh Your PC doesn't keep all your applications, however. Although Windows 8 apps are retained, traditional Win32 applications are not. Refresh Your PC creates an HTML list on your desktop to let you know what applications were removed. The second feature is Reset Your PC, which reinstalls Windows 8.1, removing your data, apps, and settings (essentially, a complete reset to "factory condition").

Changes and Updates Specific to Windows 8.1

The previous sections of this chapter offered a holistic overview of many of the key changes introduced in Windows 8 and Windows 8.1. Naturally, there are changes that are specific to Windows 8.1.

For example, the Start button has returned to the desktop (see Figure 1.12), although it is functionally different from the Start button in Windows 7. In Windows 8.1, clicking the Start button takes you to the Start screen. Right-clicking the Start button displays the Quick Links menu shown in Figure 1.12).

Many users complained that they had to boot to the Start screen in Windows 8, so Windows 8.1 adds a feature that lets you start at the desktop instead. In addition, as explained in Chapter 11, you can control other desktop and Start screen behaviors, such as having Windows display the desktop when you close all apps (including Windows 8 apps).

Windows 8.1 adds new interface features to give you more flexibility for tile sizing, color options, and animated backgrounds. Windows 8.1 also offers a new all apps view of the Start screen to help you more easily access all your installed apps. Where Windows 8 supports two Windows 8 apps displayed side-by-side, Windows 8.1 enables you to work with four apps at one time.

FIGURE 1.12

The Windows 8.1 Start button displays The Quick Links menu.

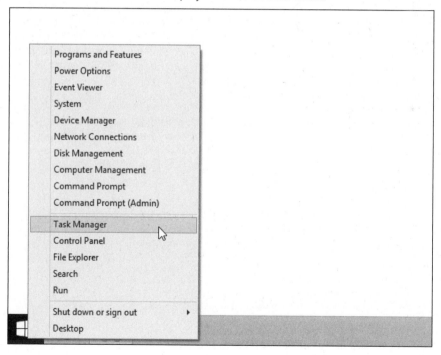

Search has also been improved in Windows 8.1 with the addition of Bing Smart Search. You don't need to open a browser to search; you can search right from the Start screen and quickly navigate to resulting sites, open documents, play songs, and more. Results are delivered in a clean, graphic view to help you quickly identify results.

The Messaging app is gone, replaced by Skype. All the bundled Windows 8 apps have been updated for Windows 8.1, some significantly. The Music app, for example, has been completely revamped. New apps have been added, including Calculator, Alarms, Health & Fitness, and Food & Drink. The new Reading List app lets you save links, e-mail messages, snippets from news apps, and other items as a to-do reading list.

Input is improved, also. The onscreen keyboard implements an auto-suggest feature that not only suggests matches for the word you are currently typing, but also uses a linguistic model to suggest the next word.

There are many other subtle changes in Windows 8.1 in addition to those described here. The following chapters explore these new features and changes in detail.

Wrap-Up

There are literally thousands of changes in Windows 8 and Windows 8.1 from previous versions of Windows, so this chapter naturally doesn't cover them all. Many of the bundled applications have been updated, new applications have been added, the interface has been changed (and not just for Windows 8 apps), and so on. You'll find explanations of many of these changes in the following chapters.

Because the interface potentially has the most impact on the way you use Windows and your Windows apps, that's the best place to start getting familiar with the changes in Windows 8.1. So, move on to Chapter 2 to learn how to navigate through and use the new Windows 8.1 interface.

Navigating the Windows 8.1 Interface

IN THIS CHAPTER

Introducing the Windows 8.1 interface

Using the Start screen

Using the Charms Bar

Using the taskbar

Working with Windows 8 apps

Getting to the desktop

I f you've been using previous versions of Windows for a while, you're no doubt familiar with the Windows desktop and how to work with Windows and Windows applications. Even so, you might find the Windows 8.1 interface very different. Gestures such as swipe, tap, tap and hold, slide, and so on might be foreign concepts. Fortunately, Windows 8.1 uses many of the same general gestures and actions you'll find on other touch-based devices. So, the Windows 8.1 interface should feel familiar to you.

If you don't have much experience with touch interfaces, this chapter will get you up to speed. You'll learn to navigate through the Windows 8.1 interface, use Windows 8 apps, and even get to that familiar Windows desktop! Armed with some basic concepts, you'll be navigating the Windows 8.1 interface like a pro in no time.

If you've been using Windows 8 for a while and are new to Windows 8.1, this chapter will also help you understand the changes that Microsoft introduced in Windows 8.1 to address some user angst over the Start menu (or lack thereof) and make the interface even easier to use.

Introducing the Windows 8 Interface

The new interface introduced in Windows 8 and fine-tuned in Windows 8.1 represents a shift toward touch-based interaction with the operating system and applications, driven in large part by the growth of the tablet and handheld device markets. But the Windows 8.1 interface is not just about touch; it's also about simplification and putting data and applications within easy reach. As you grow comfortable using the Windows 8.1 interface, you'll no doubt come to appreciate both the simplicity of using it and its clean look.

Figure 2.1 shows the Windows 8.1 Lock screen, which you use to log into the device. Although Chapter 4 explains how to log in and out of Windows, we cover it briefly here. To log in, *slide* the display up. To slide on a touch device, move your finger from the bottom of the display toward the top. With a mouse, click anywhere on the Lock screen. Windows will display the list of user accounts available on the device (see Figure 2.2). Tap (touch or click) on a user tile to enter the password for that user account, and then press Enter or tap (or click) the arrow icon to the right of the password field.

FIGURE 2.1

The Windows 8.1 Lock screen.

FIGURE 2.2

Choose an account with which to log in.

After you log in, you'll see the Windows 8.1 Start screen, shown in Figure 2.3. The Start screen serves much the same function as the Start menu in previous versions of Windows. Square or rectangular tiles give you quick access to apps, external resources such as SkyDrive, folders, and even the desktop.

The key goal for the design of the Windows 8.1 interface is simplicity. From the Start screen with its simple tile metaphor, to Windows 8.1 apps with no borders or traditional window elements such as menu bars and close buttons, the Windows 8.1 interface takes a minimalist approach to how you interact with Windows, your apps, and your data.

Before we dig deeper into the Windows 8.1 interface and its elements, let's take a look at the gestures and actions you'll use within the interface.

FIGURE 2.3

The Windows Start screen.

Gestures and Mouse Actions

There are a handful of touch-based gestures you'll use with Windows 8.1, along with mouse-based alternatives for use on non-touch devices (or when you have a mouse connected to a touch device). The following list summarizes Windows 8.1 gestures, along with corresponding mouse actions.

- **Tap/Left-click:** Touch a finger to the object you want to select, and then remove your finger from the screen. With a mouse, left-click the object (point to it, click the left button, and then release the button).

- **Tap and hold/Click and hold:** Put a finger on the object you want to select, and hold your finger there. Tap and hold is typically followed by another gesture, such as sliding. For example, to relocate a tile on the Start screen, you tap and hold the tile, and after a check mark appears at the top right of the tile, you can slide it to a new location. The equivalent mouse action for tap and hold is left-click and hold.

- **Swipe:** Slide your finger across the display, left, right, up, or down. For example, to view the tiles at the right side of the Start screen if they're off-screen, swipe from right to left.

- **Slide (drag)/Click and drag:** After you've selected an object, you can slide it on the display. Tap and hold to select the object, and then simply slide your finger across the screen to move the object. The mouse equivalent is to click and drag the object.

- **Swipe from the edge of the screen inward:** There are a handful of tasks you can accomplish by swiping from the edge of the display in toward the middle of the screen. For example, swiping from the left edge lets you switch between apps. Swipe from the right edge to display the Charms Bar. Slide up from the bottom or down from the top to view options for the current app. The mouse equivalent varies depending on the task. To view options for the app, right-click the app. To open the Charms Bar, hold the mouse at the bottom right or top right of the screen.

- **Pinch:** Place two fingers on the screen and move them apart or toward each other to zoom in or out, respectively.

Using the Start Screen

Now that you know some basic gestures and their corresponding mouse actions, you're ready to start navigating around the Windows 8.1 interface, starting with the Start screen, previously shown in Figure 2.3. Use any of these actions to open the Start screen:

- Press the Windows key on the keyboard.
- Use the mouse to place the cursor at the bottom-left corner of the screen, and then click the resulting Start screen icon.
- Open the charms and tap the Start charm.
- Press Windows + Tab to open the Task Switcher and select the Start icon.

To move around the Start screen on a touch device, simply swipe the display left or right to view additional tiles. Then, tap a tile to open its associated app. Or, in the case of the Desktop tile, tap the tile to open the Windows 8.1 desktop.

You'll find that tiles on the Start screen can be *live*, meaning they can dynamically display information. For example, after you add an account to the Mail app, it will show a preview of messages in your Inbox. The Weather tile is also live; it shows the current weather conditions (assuming your device is connected to the Internet). Other tiles show similar dynamic data. Figure 2.4 shows some examples of live tiles.

FIGURE 2.4

Live tiles on the Windows Start screen.

If you're working in an app or on the desktop and you want to return to the Start screen, the easiest method is to push the device's Windows button. On a device without a Windows button (such as a PC with a traditional keyboard), press the Windows key on the keyboard. You can also click or tap the Start icon at the bottom left of the display (see Figure 2.5).

> **TIP**
>
> On a touch device, swipe from the left edge of the screen, hold, and then move slowly back to the left to display a graphic list of the running applications. Then, tap the Start icon to open the Start screen. Or, tap another icon to return to the associated app. You can also open the charms and tap the Start icon.

FIGURE 2.5

Use the Start icon to open the Start screen.

Using the Charms

Charms, shown in Figure 2.6, give you access to Devices, Settings, Search, sharing options, and the Start screen. To display the charms, swipe in from the right edge of the screen. Or, place the mouse at the bottom right or top right of the screen. When the charms appear, click the charm you want to use. To close the charms, simply tap or click any other area of the screen.

TIP
You can press Windows + C to open the charms.

FIGURE 2.6

Access Settings and Devices with charms.

Clicking Settings opens a menu similar to the one shown in Figure 2.7. The top portion of the menu is in the context of the current app. For example, if you tap or click Devices with the Start screen displayed, you'll see menu items that pertain to the Start screen. If you have Internet Explorer open, you'll see settings for Internet Explorer. The menu behaves similarly for other apps, showing settings for that app.

The bottom portion of the menu provides system-wide options, including the current network connection status, sound and brightness indicators, a Notifications icon that lets you turn on or off notifications, a Power icon for turning off or suspending the device, and a language icon for selecting the current language. You can click Change PC Settings to open the new Windows 8 PC Settings app, shown in Figure 2.8.

The charms include the following:

- **Search:** Tap or click Search to open the Search screen, where you can search for apps, documents, and other items.

  See Chapters 22 and 23 for more details on using Search in Windows 8.1.

- **Share:** Tap or click Share to open the Share menu, which you can use to share content from the current app (if it supports sharing) to other apps. For example, if you open a website in Internet Explorer (IE) and then open the charms and tap Share, the resulting menu enables you to e-mail a link and synopsis of the currently displayed page. A new mail page appears with the content already in the message, and all you have to do is enter an e-mail address and tap Send. You don't have to leave IE to share the content; it remains open while you create and send the e-mail.

- **Start:** Tap or click Start to open the Start screen.

- **Devices:** Tap or click Devices to open the Devices menu, where you can view and set options for devices such as secondary displays, printers, and other devices.

- **Settings:** Described earlier in this section, tapping or clicking Settings opens a Settings menu that lets you specify settings for the current app (or for Windows 8.1 in general, if the Start screen is open when you tap Settings).

FIGURE 2.7

The Settings menu.

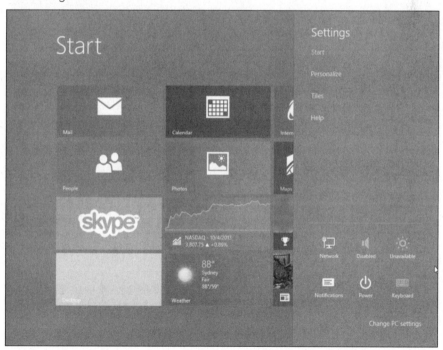

FIGURE 2.8

Use the PC Settings app to change a variety of settings.

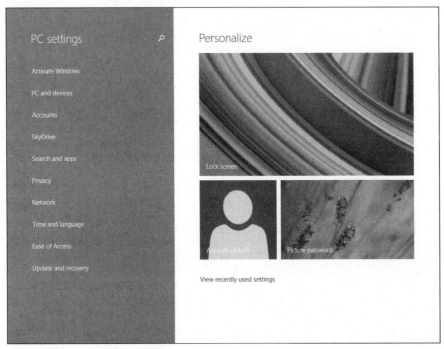

Working with Windows 8.1 Apps

If you're working on a traditional PC with Windows 8.1 installed, some (potentially many) of your apps will be "traditional" Windows apps running on the desktop. But, as more and more Windows 8.1 apps are published, you'll no doubt have several favorite Windows 8.1 apps. On touch devices such as tablets and smaller handhelds, many of your apps will probably be Windows 8.1 apps.

In general, working with a Windows 8.1 app should be fairly intuitive. The gestures and actions you use to work with the Start screen and other Windows 8.1 screens are the same for apps. For example, to move back and forth between visited pages in IE, swipe left or right in the IE app.

Rather than focus on specific Windows 8.1 apps, this section of the chapter focuses on actions and methods you'll use in general to work with Windows 8.1 apps.

Opening and using a Windows 8.1 app

Opening a Windows 8.1 app couldn't really be any easier. Just open the Start screen, locate the app's tile, and tap or click the tile. If you're working on a non-touch device, and you have a mouse with a scroll wheel, you can use the wheel to scroll through the Start screen's tiles. Scroll down to move to the right, or scroll up to move to the left. Then, just click the tile for the app you want to open.

How you work in a Windows 8.1 app depends entirely on the app, but will rely on the standard touch gestures and mouse actions described earlier in this chapter. To open a Windows 8.1 app's app menu (see Figure 2.9), swipe up from the bottom or down from the top of the screen. Or, right-click in the app. The app menu offers options for the current app.

FIGURE 2.9

Use an app's menu to configure the app or set options.

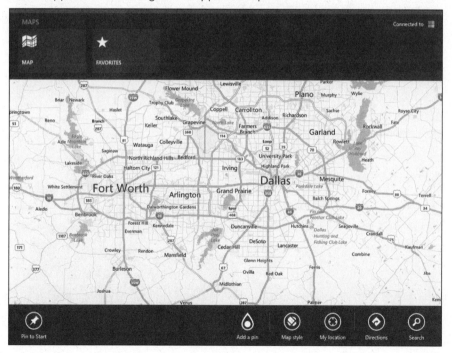

2

Snapping apps on the screen

At first, it might seem that you can view and work with only one Windows 8 app at a time, but you can actually snap two apps to the screen at once and easily switch between them. You can even view the desktop and any running apps there side-by-side with a Windows 8.1 app.

To snap two Windows 8.1 apps to the screen, follow these steps:

1. Open the two Windows 8.1 apps.

2. Switch to the app you want to be "primary," and consume most of the screen space.

3. Open the app thumbnails and drag the app to the left or right side of the screen. Either action snaps the second app to the left or right of the screen.

> **TIP**
>
> Your device must be configured for a minimum resolution of 1366 x 800 pixels to snap apps on the screen. If your resolution is lower than this, dragging another app in causes it to become the foreground app.

Figure 2.10 shows two Windows 8.1 apps snapped side-by-side.

FIGURE 2.10

Two Windows 8.1 apps snapped side-by-side.

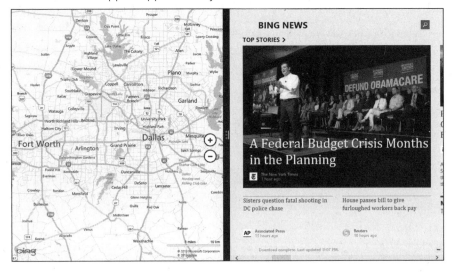

As we hinted at above, you can snap a Windows 8.1 app beside the desktop, enabling you to see and work with a traditional Windows app on the desktop while also using a Windows 8.1 app. For example, Figure 2.11 shows the Windows 8.1 Finance app snapped beside the desktop.

FIGURE 2.11

The desktop and a Windows 8 app snapped side-by-side.

To snap the desktop and a Windows 8.1 app, open the Windows 8.1 app and the desktop from the Start screen. If you want to work with a desktop app, open it from the desktop. With either app in the foreground, open the app thumbnails and drag the other app to the left or right side of the screen. If you look closely at Figure 2.11, you'll see a drag handle between the two apps. Drag this handle to resize the apps, shrinking the primary app and expanding the secondary app. Drag the handle in the other direction to change the primary and secondary again.

If the desktop is primary, dragging the handle to resize the Windows 8.1 app causes the desktop to appear at the edge of the screen as a set of thumbnails showing the running desktop apps. You can switch to a desktop app simply by tapping or clicking its thumbnail. It then becomes primary and the Windows 8.1 app shrinks to become secondary. To show only one app on the screen, drag the handle to move the unwanted app off the screen.

NOTE

Removing an app from the screen in this way doesn't close the app; it simply brings the other app to the foreground. The other app continues to run until you close it.

Switching between apps

Experienced Windows users will be happy to learn that the methods you've used in the past to switch between apps are still available in Windows 8.1. For example, you can press Alt + Tab to view a list of running apps (see Figure 2.12) and select one to bring to the foreground. You can also press Windows + Tab to open a task switcher at the left of the screen showing thumbnails of your running apps (see Figure 2.13). Continue pressing Windows + Tab until the desired app is highlighted; then release the keys to switch to that app.

FIGURE 2.12

Use Alt+Tab to switch between apps.

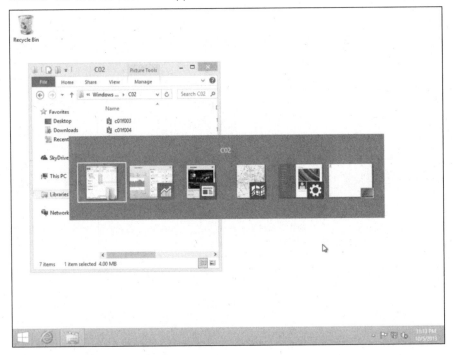

FIGURE 2.13

Use Windows+Tab to switch between apps.

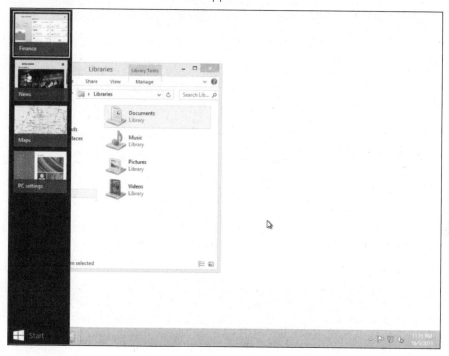

Thanks to the touch-based nature of Windows 8.1, you also have some new ways to switch applications on touch devices:

- Swipe in from the left edge of the screen and release to cycle between running apps. The desktop and all apps running on the desktop are treated as a single app for the purpose of switching in this way.

- Swipe in from the left edge, hold, and then move your finger back to the left until the app thumbnails appear. Then, tap the app you want to use.

- Move the mouse cursor to the top left of the screen, and then move the mouse down to display the app thumbnails. Or, simply click in the upper-left corner of the screen to switch to the next app.

- Move the mouse cursor to the bottom left of the screen, and when the Start screen icon appears, move the mouse up to display the app thumbnails.

Closing a Windows 8.1 app

It's easy to close a Windows 8.1 app, although you might not have figured it out on your own. Just grab the app at the top and drag it down to the bottom of the display.

This method isn't all that intuitive, but it's the easiest way to close a Windows 8.1 app, once you know the method exists. When using a mouse, just move the cursor to the top of the app until the pointer changes to a hand; then click and drag the app to the bottom of the screen. When using a touch device, swipe down from the top to the bottom of the screen. The app should close.

Getting to the Desktop

If you're like most people, you haven't left behind your legacy desktop-based Windows apps in favor of all Windows 8.1 apps. That will, no doubt, change over time as more Windows 8.1 apps become available and as desktop versions are updated to support the Windows 8 interface. Fortunately, Windows 8.1 still supports those desktop apps and makes it easy to get to them from the Start screen. To open the desktop, just tap or click the Desktop tile on the Start screen.

> **NOTE**
> Windows RT, the version of Windows designed for the ARM processor, does not support legacy Windows desktop apps.

If you're working in a Windows 8.1 app and you want to switch to the desktop, you can access it from the app thumbnails. Just open the thumbnails and tap or click the desktop thumbnail. Or, you can press Alt + Tab or Windows + Tab to open the desktop.

Using the Taskbar

Although not technically a part of the Start screen or the new Windows 8.1 interface, the Windows taskbar nevertheless deserves mention here, if for no other reason than you probably want to pin apps to the taskbar so you can get to them quickly from the desktop.

Figure 2.14 shows the taskbar at the bottom of the desktop with a small selection of apps pinned to it. As in previous versions of Windows, you can open or switch to an app by tapping or clicking its icon on the taskbar.

Although you can't pin Windows 8.1 apps to the taskbar, you can pin your other Windows apps there, as well as app resources such as File Explorer. To pin an app to the taskbar, open the Start screen or search for the app in the Search screen, right-click or tap and hold the app's tile, and in the app menu, tap or click Pin to Taskbar.

FIGURE 2.14

The taskbar remains an important fixture in the Windows 8.1 interface.

Wrap-Up

Although there are some significant improvements and new features in Windows 8.1 geared toward the enterprise and traditional desktop user, some of Windows 8.1's biggest impact will be in the tablet and handheld market. Windows 8.1 and its interface are clearly designed to tackle that market. The clean Windows 8.1 look is well suited to tablets and smaller devices, uncluttering the display.

Some of the gestures and actions you use to work in the Windows 8.1 interface aren't exactly intuitive, but most of them are, and you should have little trouble getting the hang of the new interface. If you're new to Windows, turn to Chapter 3 to learn how to navigate through the desktop and work with desktop apps.

Getting Around the Windows Desktop

IN THIS CHAPTER

Logging in

Using the Windows desktop

Using the Start screen

Using programs

Shutting down the computer

In today's busy world, few people have the time to sit down and learn to use a computer. Many books and online tutorials don't really help because they assume you already know all the basic concepts and terminology. That's a big assumption because the truth is that most people don't already know those things. Most people don't know a file from a folder from a megabyte from a golf ball. These just aren't the kinds of things we learned about in school or from our day-to-day experiences.

This chapter is mostly about the kinds of things everyone else assumes you already know. It's for the people who just bought their first computer and discovered it has this thing called Windows 8 on it. Or the people who were getting by with an older computer but now have a new Windows 8 computer and really want to know more about how to use it.

We often refer to the skills in this chapter as "everyday skills" because they're the kinds of things you'll likely do every time you sit down at the computer. In this chapter, we point out the name and purpose of many elements you'll see on your screen. Together, these bits of information provide a foundation of basic knowledge of how you use a computer, in general, to get things done. And it all starts with logging in.

Terminology for Things You Do

If you're new to computers, the first step is to learn a little terminology about actions you perform to operate the computer. We assume you know what the *mouse* is. When you move the mouse, the *mouse pointer* on the screen moves in whatever direction you move the mouse. Most mice have two buttons. The button on the left is the *primary* or *left* mouse button. It's referred to as the primary button because clicking it always makes an action occur directly.

When you rest your hand comfortably on the mouse, the left mouse button should be under your index finger. You don't want to hold the button down, however. Just rest your index finger on it lightly.

> **TIP**
>
> If you're left-handed, you can switch the orientation of the buttons using the Mouse applet in the Control Panel. To open the Mouse applet, swipe in from the right to open the Charms Bar, tap or click Settings, and then tap or click Control Panel.

The button on the right is the *secondary* or *right* mouse button. In contrast to the primary mouse button, clicking the secondary mouse button usually doesn't make an action take place directly; instead, it shows you various actions you can take.

 Windows 8 includes new terminology for new mouse and touch-based gestures. Those terms are covered in detail in Chapter 2, where you learn more about the new Windows 8 interface.

Mouse terminology

Everyone uses some specific terms to refer to actions you perform with the mouse. These terms include *point, click, double-click, right-click,* and *drag.*

Point

The term *point,* when used as a verb, means to touch the mouse pointer to an item. For example, "point to the Desktop tile" means to move the mouse pointer so that it's positioned over top of the Desktop tile (the tile named Desktop that, by default, is at the lower-left corner of the Start screen). If the item you want to point to is smaller than the mouse pointer, make sure you get the tip of the mouse pointer arrow on the item. Whatever the tip of the mouse pointer is on is the item to which you're pointing.

The term *hover* means the same thing as "point." For example, the phrase "hover the mouse pointer over the Desktop tile" means the same as "point to the Desktop tile."

When you point to an item on the Windows desktop, the item's name typically appears in a *tooltip* (a small box that appears, telling what you're pointing to). For example, if you point to a date and time on the notification bar on the Windows desktop taskbar, the day and date appear in a tooltip near the mouse pointer. The tooltip tells you the name of the item you're pointing to. Figure 3.1 shows an example of a tooltip when pointing to the desktop calendar.

> **TIP**
>
> You can learn the name and purpose of many items on your screen just by pointing to the item and reading the tooltip that appears near the mouse pointer.

FIGURE 3.1

The tooltip that appears when pointing to the Windows desktop calendar on the notification bar.

Click

The term *click* means to point to an item and then tap the left mouse button. Don't hold down the left mouse button. Just *tap* (press and release) it. It makes a slight clicking sound when you do. For example, the phrase "click the Desktop tile" means "put the mouse pointer on the Desktop tile on the Start menu and tap the left mouse button." When you do, the Windows desktop appears.

Double-click

The term *double-click* means to point to an item and then tap the left mouse button twice, quickly. Don't hold down the button and don't pause between clicks. Just tap the left mouse button twice. You use double-clicking to *open* items represented by icons on your screen.

Right-click

The term *right-click* means to point to an item and then tap the right mouse button. Again, don't hold down the mouse button, and don't use the left mouse button. Whereas clicking an item usually takes an immediate action, right-clicking presents a shortcut menu of things you can do with the item. You'll see many examples throughout this book.

Drag

The term *drag* means to point to an item and hold down the left mouse button while you're moving the mouse. You typically use dragging to move and size things on the screen. You can see examples a little later in this chapter.

 As you discover in Chapter 21, you can also use dragging to move and copy files from one location to another.

Keyboard terminology

It should go without saying that the computer keyboard is the thing that looks like a typewriter keyboard. The keys labeled F1, F2, and so forth across the top are *function keys*. The keys with arrows and names such as Home, End, PgUp (Page Up), and PgDn (Page Down) are *navigation keys*.

Tab, Enter, and Spacebar

The Tab key has two opposing arrows pointing left and right. That key is usually to the left of the letter Q. The Enter key (also called the Return key) is located where the carriage return key is on a standard typewriter. It may be labeled Enter or Return, or it may just show a bent, left-pointing arrow. The Spacebar is the wide key centered at the bottom of the keyboard. When you're typing text, it types a blank space.

If in doubt, Escape key out

The Escape key is labeled Esc or Escape (or maybe even Cancel). It's usually at the upper-left corner of the keyboard. It's a good one to know because it often allows you to escape from unfamiliar territory.

The Help key (F1)

The Help key is the F1 function key. That's a good one to know because it's the key you press for help. Not the kind of help where someone appears and helps you along. Unfortunately, it's not possible to get that kind of help from a computer. Instead, pressing Help opens a help window.

The ⊞ key

If you have a Windows keyboard, you also have a *Windows key*, which shows the Windows logo. It's usually near the lower-left corner of the keyboard. The Windows key might also show the word *Start* because you can tap it to show and hide the Windows 8 Start screen.

Shift, Ctrl, and Alt

The keys labeled Shift, Ctrl (Control), and Alt (Alternate) are *modifier keys*. There are usually two of each of those keys on a keyboard, near the lower left and lower right of the main typing keys. The Shift key may be labeled with a large, up-pointing arrow. One Shift key is located to the left of the Z key, the other to the right of the question mark (?) key. They're called modifier keys because they usually don't do anything by themselves. Instead, you hold down a modifier key while pressing some other key. For example, when you hold down the Shift key and press the *A* key, you get an uppercase *A* rather than a lowercase *a*.

Shortcut keys

The term *press* always refers to a key on the keyboard rather than something you do with the mouse. For example, the statement "Press Enter" means to press the Enter key. When you see an instruction to press two keys with a plus sign in between (*key* + *key*), that means "hold down the first key, tap the second key, release the first key." For example, the instruction "Press Ctrl + Esc" means "Hold down the Ctrl key, tap the Esc key, release the Ctrl key."

You will see the following several times in this book: Press Windows + X while on the Windows desktop. This displays the Windows 8.1 Quick Link menu. It displays in the same location that the Start menu in previous versions of Windows (including Windows 7, Vista, XP, 98, and 95) displayed. The Quick Link menu includes several key menu options to help you locate system apps and programs, such as the Control Panel, Event Viewer, and so on.

You'll often see the term *shortcut key* used to refer to *key* + *key* combinations. The "shortcut" part refers to the fact that the keystroke is an alternative way of doing something with the mouse. (It may not seem like much of a shortcut, however, if you can't type worth beans!)

Much as we all hate to learn terminology, knowing the terms and keyboard keys we just described is critical to learning how to use a computer. All written and spoken instructions assume that you know what those terms mean. If you don't, the instructions won't do you any good.

Okay, let's move on to using the computer and to the names of things you'll do, see, and use often.

Logging In

Obviously, the first step to using a computer is to turn it on. Shortly after you first start your computer, the Windows 8 Lock screen appears (see Figure 3.2). To log in, *slide* the display up. To slide on a touch device, move your finger from the bottom of the display toward the top. With a mouse, click and drag the display toward the top, or press the spacebar. Windows displays the list of user accounts available on the device. You learn more about user accounts in Chapter 4, but for now, all you need to know is that if you see user account icons shortly after you first start your computer, you have to click one in order to use the computer. Tap (or click) on a user tile to enter the password for that user account, and then press Enter or tap (or click) the arrow icon to the right of the password field.

FIGURE 3.2

The Windows Lock screen.

 You also can use a new Windows 8 feature called Picture Passwords to log in to Windows. The Picture Passwords feature is covered in Chapter 4.

TIP

The blue circle near the lower-left corner of the logon screen provides Ease of Access options for the visually impaired. The button at the lower-right corner lets you turn off the computer rather than log in.

If the user account isn't password protected, the Windows Start screen appears automatically. If the user account you clicked is password protected, a rectangular box appears instead. You have to type the correct password for the account to get to the Windows Start screen. The letters you type won't show in the box by default. Instead, you'll see a dot for each letter you type, as in Figure 3.3. This prevents others from learning your password by looking over your shoulder as you type it on the screen. To temporarily see the characters you enter, press and hold the eye icon on the right side of the password box. This toggles on the characters so you can see that what you typed is what you intended to type.

FIGURE 3.3

Typing a password.

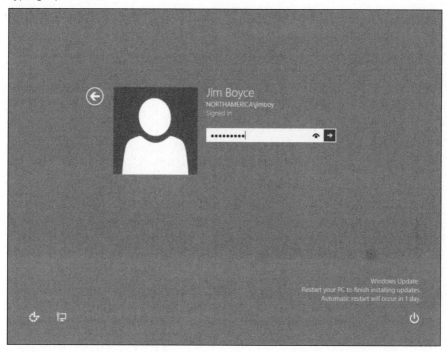

After you type the password, press Enter or click the arrow to the right of the password box.

After you've successfully logged in, the Windows Start screen appears.

Windows Start Screen

After you log on, you'll see the Windows 8.1 Start screen, shown in Figure 3.4. The Start screen serves much the same function as the Start menu in previous versions of Windows. Square or rectangular tiles give you quick access to apps, external resources such as SkyDrive, folders, and even the desktop. The Start screen shows the look of the new Windows 8 interface. We don't focus on the Start screen in this chapter because it was discussed in detail in Chapter 2.

FIGURE 3.4

The Windows Start screen.

Using the Windows Desktop

The Windows desktop is the electronic equivalent of a real desktop. It's the place where you keep stuff you're working on right now. Every program that's currently open is usually contained within some program window. When no programs are open, the desktop and all your desktop icons are plainly visible on the screen.

What's on the desktop

Users upgrading from previous Windows versions are familiar with the *Windows desktop,* the primary place for users to start their work in earlier versions of Windows. You work with programs on the Windows desktop in much the same way you work with paper on an office desktop. With Windows 8.1, the Start screen is intended to replace the desktop as the primary work environment. However, the Windows desktop is still very much a part of Windows, and it's the environment in which you run legacy Windows applications.

The desktop is accessed from the Start screen by clicking the Desktop tile. The desktop may get covered by program windows and other items, but the desktop is still under there no matter how much you clutter the screen. It's the same as a real desk in that sense. Although your real desktop may be completely covered by random junk, your desktop is still under there somewhere. You just have to dig through the mess to get to it.

The two main components of the Windows desktop are the desktop itself and the taskbar. The desktop is where everything that you open piles up. The taskbar's main role is to make it easy to switch from one open item to another. Everything you'll ever see on your screen has a name and a purpose. Virtually nothing on the screen is there purely for decoration (except the wallpaper). Figure 3.5 shows the main components of the Windows desktop and other items. Your desktop might not look exactly like the picture and might not show all the components. But don't worry about that. Right now, you want to focus on learning the names of the most frequently used elements.

FIGURE 3.5

The desktop, taskbar, and other items.

Here's a quick overview of what each component represents.

> **TIP**
>
> You learn to personalize your desktop in Chapter 10. But here's a quick hint: Virtually everything you'll ever see on your screen, including the desktop, is an object that has properties. To customize any object, right-click that object and choose Properties.

- **Desktop:** The desktop itself is everything above the taskbar. Most programs you open appear in a window on the desktop.

- **Desktop icons:** Icons on the desktop provide quick access to frequently used programs, folders, and documents. You can add and remove desktop icons as you see fit.

- **Quick Link menu:** The Quick Link menu provides access to commonly used Windows programs and apps. To see it, right-click the Start button at the bottom-left side of the screen, or press Windows + X.

- **Taskbar:** A task is an open program. The taskbar makes switching among all your open programs easy. Right-clicking the clock in the taskbar provides easy access to options for customizing the taskbar and organizing open program windows.

- **Notification area:** Displays icons for programs running in the background, often referred to as *processes* and *services*. Messages coming from those programs appear in speech balloons just above the notification area.

- **Clock:** Shows the current time and date.

That's the quick tour of items on and around the Windows 8.1 desktop. The sections that follow examine some of these items in detail.

About desktop icons

Desktop icons represent a *closed* object that you can *open* by double-clicking the icon. Most desktop icons are shortcuts to files and folders. They're shortcuts in the sense that they duplicate icons that are available elsewhere, such as on the Start screen.

Rules always have exceptions. When it comes to desktop icons, the Recycle Bin is the exception. The Recycle Bin icon exists only on the desktop, and you won't find it anywhere else. The role of the Recycle Bin is that of a safety net. Whenever you delete a file or folder from your hard drive, the item is actually just moved to the Recycle Bin. You can restore an accidentally deleted item from the Recycle Bin back to its original location.

In addition to the Recycle Bin, you have other built-in desktop icons from which to choose. If you want to take a shot at adding icons, you have to get to the Personalization page and make some selections. To get to the Personalization page, use one of the following methods:

- Show the charms, click Search, and type **pers.** Click Settings and then click Personalization on the Settings screen.

- Right-click the desktop and choose Personalize.

NOTE

If you don't see Personalize when you right-click the desktop, that means you didn't right-click the desktop. You right-clicked something that's covering the desktop. You learn to close and hide things that are covering the desktop a little later in this chapter.

The Personalization Control Panel applet opens. In its left column, click Change Desktop Icons. You see a *dialog box* like the one in Figure 3.6. It's called a "dialog" box because you carry on a sort of dialog with it. It shows you options from which you can pick and choose. You make your choices and click OK. You'll see menu dialog boxes throughout this book.

To make an icon visible on your desktop, select (click to put a check mark in) the check box next to the icon's name. To prevent an icon from appearing on the desktop, click the check box to the left of its name to deselect it (remove the check mark). In the figure, we've opted to show just the Recycle Bin.

FIGURE 3.6

The Desktop Icon Settings dialog box.

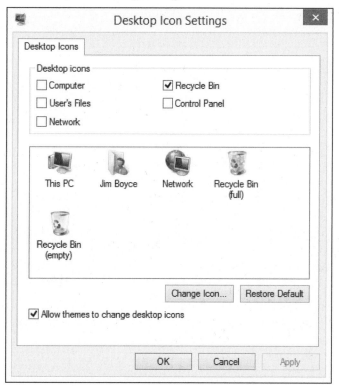

You can choose a different picture for any icon you've opted to show on the desktop. Click the icon's picture in the middle of the dialog box. Then click the Change Icon button. Click the icon you want to show and then click OK. If you change your mind after the fact, click Restore Default.

Click OK after making your selections. The dialog box closes, and the icons you choose appear on the desktop. However, you might not see them if that part of the desktop is covered by something that's open. Don't worry about that. You learn about how to open, close, move, and size things on the desktop a little later in this chapter.

If nothing is covering the desktop, but you still don't see any desktop icons, they might just be switched off. We cover this topic in the next section.

Arranging desktop icons

As you discover in Chapter 10, there are many ways to customize the Windows 8 desktop. But if you just want to make some quick, minor changes to your desktop icons, right-click the desktop to view its shortcut menu. Items on the menu that have a little arrow to the right show submenus. For example, if you right-click the desktop and point to View on the menu, you see the View menu, as shown in Figure 3.7.

FIGURE 3.7

Right-click the desktop.

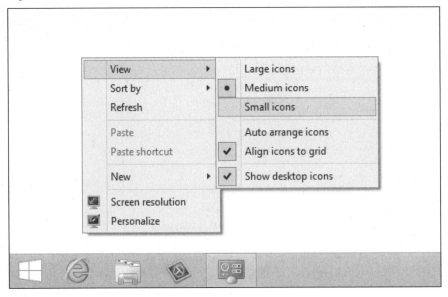

The last item on the View menu, Show Desktop Icons, needs to be selected (checked) for the icons to show at all. If no check mark appears next to that item, click the item. The menu closes, and the icons appear on the desktop. When you need to see the menu again, just right-click the desktop again.

The top three items on the menu — Large Icons, Medium Icons, and Small Icons — control the size of the icons. Click any option to see its effect. If you don't like the result, right-click the desktop again, choose View, and choose a different size.

> **TIP**
>
> If your mouse has a wheel, you can also size icons by holding down the Ctrl key as you spin the mouse wheel. This gives you an almost endless range of icon sizes from which to choose. Use one of the three items in the View menu to get them back to one of the three default sizes.

The Sort By option on the desktop shortcut menu enables you to arrange desktop icons alphabetically by Name, Size, Item Type, or Date Modified. However, no matter how you choose to sort icons, the built-in icons are sorted separately from those you create.

 You learn more about personalizing your desktop in Chapter 10.

Using Jump Lists

Jump lists were a new feature of Windows 7 that enhance the usefulness of the icons and pin items on the taskbar. Windows 8.1 continues to use Jump Lists. Jump Lists add the most recently used objects from the application to a pop-up menu. Just right-click the icon to view the Jump List (see Figure 3.8).

You don't need to do anything to set up Jump Lists — they happen automatically. Whenever you want to use a Jump List, just right-click a taskbar icon and choose from the list the item you want to open.

Running Programs and Apps

You can start any program or app that's installed on your computer by finding the program's icon on the Start screen or by searching for it using the Search app, and then clicking that icon. There are other ways to start programs as well. For example, if you see an icon for the program pinned to the taskbar, you can click that. If you see a shortcut icon to the program on the desktop or pinned to the taskbar, you can click (or double-click) that icon to start the program.

FIGURE 3.8

A Jump list for Internet Explorer.

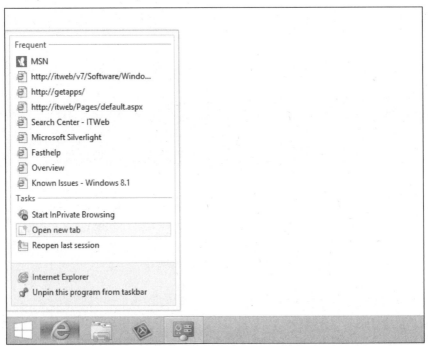

 Whether you need to single-click or double-click a desktop icon to open it depends on how you've configured Windows 8. See Chapter 20 for details.

Every time you start a program or app, an *instance* of that program opens in a program window. No rule exists that says you can have only one program open at a time. Some programs even enable you to open multiple copies of the same program. (New Windows 8 apps, however, limit you to running only one copy of that app at a time.) You can have as many programs open simultaneously as you can cram into your available memory (RAM). Most programs allow you to run multiple instances. The more memory your system has, the more stuff you can have open without much slowdown in performance.

> **NOTE**
>
> When it comes to using programs, or apps, the terms *start*, *run*, *launch*, and *open* all mean the same thing — to load a copy of the program into memory (RAM) so that it's visible on your screen. You can't use a program or app until it's running.

Most programs you open show their own names somewhere near the top of the program window. Figure 3.9 shows Microsoft PowerPoint open on the desktop. You see its name in the title bar at the top of the window, appearing either by itself or as part of a string of items.

FIGURE 3.9

Sample title bar and taskbar button.

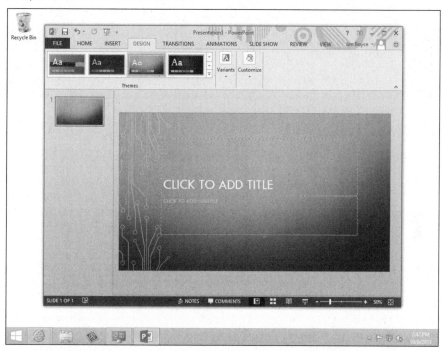

> **NOTE**
>
> Windows 8 apps don't follow the same window conventions that regular Windows programs do. For example, many apps, such as the Weather app, don't show a title bar or status bar. Also, you don't resize their windows as you can conventional Windows programs.

> You learn more about Windows 8 apps in several chapters of this book, including Chapters 2 and 9.

Most items that you open also have a taskbar button. The name in the taskbar button matches the name of the item. For example, the taskbar button for the open PowerPoint program also shows the name of the PowerPoint presentation we're editing on the taskbar. You can click the PowerPoint taskbar button to make the open window appear and disappear. That's a good thing to know because sometimes you want to get something off the screen temporarily so that you can see something else on the screen.

When you have multiple program windows open, they stack up on the desktop the way multiple sheets of paper on your real desktop stack up. When you have multiple sheets of paper in a pile, you can't see what's on every page. You can see only what's on the top page because all the other pages are covered by that page.

It works the same way with program windows. When you have multiple program windows open, you can see only the one that's on the top of the stack. We call the program that's on the top of the stack the *active window*.

> **NOTE**
>
> Some programs have an option called "Always on Top" that makes them display on top of the stack even when they aren't active. So, a program could be active but not necessarily on top of the stack. For the purposes of this chapter, however, assume that the active window is always the one on top of the stack.

The active window

When two or more program windows are open on the desktop, only one of them can be the active window. The active window has some unique characteristics:

- The active window is usually on the top of the stack. Any other open windows will be under the active window so that they don't cover any of its content. The exception is a window configured for Always on Top, as described previously.
- The taskbar button for the active window is highlighted with a brighter foreground color.
- Anything you do at the keyboard applies to the active window only. You can't type in an inactive window.

Switching among open programs

Whenever you have two or more programs open at the same time, you want to be able to easily switch among them. You have several ways to switch among open programs, as discussed in the sections that follow.

> **NOTE**
>
> The taskbar shows a miniature version of the window by default. Pointing to a taskbar button reveals a tooltip with the name of the window or program. You can set the size of the icons used by the taskbar through the properties for the taskbar.

Switching with taskbar buttons

As mentioned, almost every open program has a button on the taskbar. When you have multiple open programs, you have multiple taskbar buttons. To make any one particular program active, click its taskbar button. If you're not sure which button is which, point to each button. You see the name and a miniature copy of the program that the button represents, as in Figure 3.10. You also see a full-size preview of the window.

> **TIP**
> If any portion of the window you want to bring to the top of the stack is visible on the screen, you can just click that visible portion of the window to bring it to the top of the stack.

FIGURE 3.10

Pointing to a taskbar button.

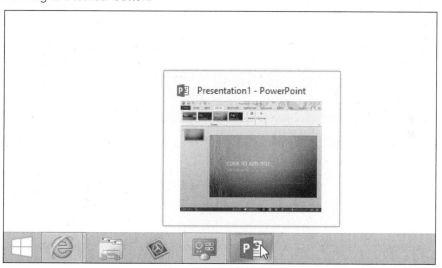

Switching with the keyboard

If you prefer the keyboard to the mouse, you can use Alt + Tab to switch among open windows. Hold down the Alt key and then press the Tab key. You see a thumbnail image for each open program window, as in the example shown in Figure 3.11. Keep the Alt key pressed down and keep pressing Tab until the name of the program you want to switch to appears above the icons. Then release the Alt key.

> **TIP**
> The Tab key shows two arrows pointing in opposite directions and is usually just to the left of the letter Q on the keyboard.

The last (rightmost) item in the Alt + Tab window represents the desktop rather than an open program. If you release the Alt key with that selected, all windows are minimized to the taskbar. But you can still bring up any open program by clicking its taskbar button.

FIGURE 3.11

Alt+Tab window.

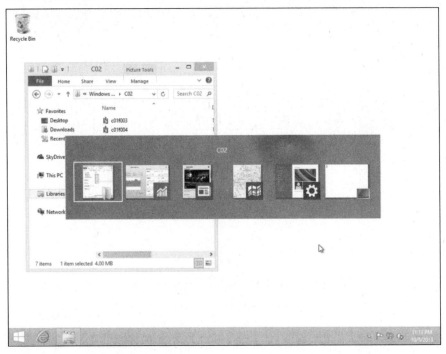

Arranging program windows

You can use options on the taskbar shortcut menu to arrange all currently open program windows. To get to that menu, right-click an empty portion of the taskbar, or right-click the clock in the lower-right corner of the screen. Figure 3.12 shows the options on the menu.

The four options that apply to program windows on the desktop are similar to the options you get when you right-click a taskbar button that represents multiple instances of one program:

- **Cascade Windows:** Stacks all the open windows like sheets of paper, fanned out so that all their title bars are visible, as in Figure 3.13.

- **Show Windows Stacked:** Arranges the windows in rows across the screen, or as equal-sized tiles.

FIGURE 3.12

Taskbar shortcut menu.

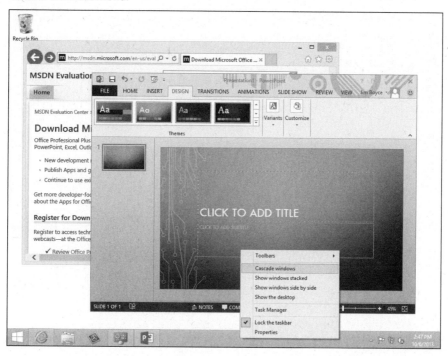

- **Show Windows Side by Side:** Arranges the windows side by side. As with the preceding option, if you have too many open windows to show that way, they'll be displayed in equal-sized tiles.

- **Show the Desktop:** Minimizes all open windows so that only their taskbar buttons are visible. You can see the entire desktop at that point. To bring any window back onto the screen, click its taskbar button. To bring them all back, right-click the clock or taskbar again and choose Show Open Windows.

The only way to truly appreciate these options is to try them out for yourself. Open two or more programs. Then try each of the options described to see their effects on your open program windows.

FIGURE 3.13

Cascaded program windows.

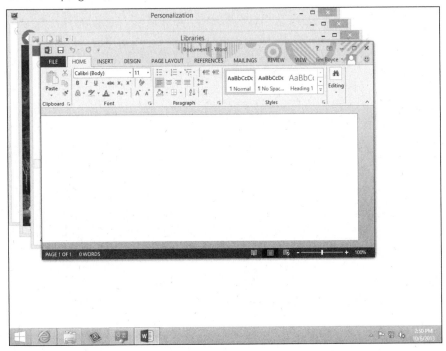

Sizing program windows

As a rule, program windows can be any size you want them to be, but this rule has a few exceptions. For example, the tiny Calculator program can't be sized at all. Some programs, such as Windows Media Player and Windows Media Center, will shrink down only so far. But in general, most open program windows can appear in three categories of sizes:

- Maximized, in which the program fills the entire screen above the taskbar, covering the desktop
- Minimized, in which only the program's taskbar button is visible, and the program window takes up no space on the desktop
- Any size in between those two extremes

Often, you'll want to work with two or more program windows at a time. Knowing how to size program windows is a critical skill for doing so, because working with multiple program windows is difficult if you can't see at least some portion of each one.

Maximize a program window

A maximized program window enlarges to its greatest window size, which in many cases causes it to fill all the space above the taskbar. This makes it easy to see everything inside the program window. If a program window isn't already maximized, you can maximize it in several ways:

- Click the Maximize button in the program's title bar (see Figure 3.14).
- Grab the title bar and move the window to the top of the screen. Pause for a moment and then release the mouse button.
- Double-click the program's title bar.
- Click the upper-left corner of the window you want to maximize and choose Maximize. Optionally, right-click anywhere near the center top of the window and choose Maximize.

TIP

Few buttons on the screen show their name. But you can find out a button's name just by touching the button with the tip of the mouse pointer to display a tooltip.

FIGURE 3.14

The Maximize button in a title bar.

3

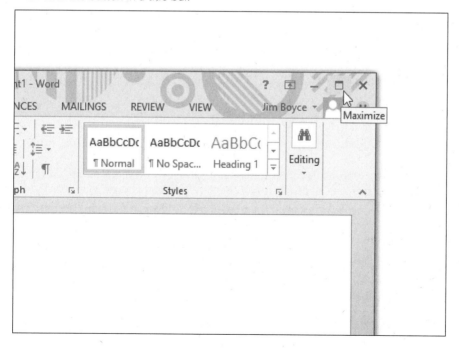

Minimize a program window

If you want to get a program window off the screen temporarily without losing your place, minimize the program window. When you minimize the program window, the program remains running. However, it takes up no space on the screen, so it can't cover anything else on the screen. When minimized, only the window's taskbar button remains visible. You can minimize a window in several ways:

- Click the Minimize button in the program's title bar (see Figure 3.15).

FIGURE 3.15

The Minimize button in a title bar.

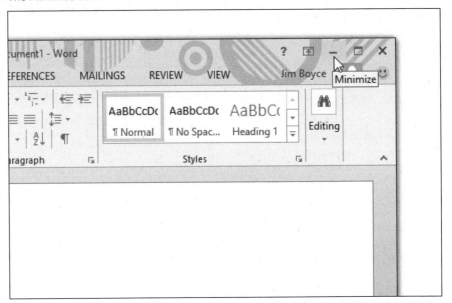

- Click the upper-left corner of the window you want to minimize (or right-click anywhere near the center top of the window) and choose Minimize.
- Click the program's taskbar button once or twice. (If the program isn't in the active window, the first click just makes it the active window. The second click then minimizes the active window.)
- Right-click the program's taskbar button or title bar and choose Minimize.

Size at will

Between the two extremes of maximized (hog up the entire desktop) and minimized (not even visible on the desktop), most program windows can be any size you want them to be. The first step to sizing a program window is to get it to an in-between size so that it's neither maximized nor minimized. You can do that in one of two ways:

Minimize versus Close

Everything that's "in your computer," so to speak, is actually a file on your hard disk. The stuff on your hard disk is always there, whether the computer is on or off. When you open an item, two things happen. The most obvious is that the item becomes visible on the screen. What's not so obvious is the fact that a copy of the program is also loaded in the computer's memory (RAM).

When you minimize an open window, the program is still in memory. The only way you can tell that is by the fact that the program's taskbar button is still on the taskbar. When you want to view that program window, you just click its taskbar to make it visible on the screen again. It shows up looking exactly as it did before you minimized it.

When you close a program, its window and taskbar button both disappear, and the program is also removed from the RAM (making room for other things you might want to work with). The only way to get back to the program is to restart it from its icon. However, this new program window will be an entirely new instance of the program, unrelated to how things looked before you closed the program.

- If the program window is currently minimized, click its taskbar button to make it visible on the screen.

- If the program window is currently maximized, double-click its title bar or click its Restore Down button to shrink it down a little. Figure 3.16 shows the tooltip that appears when you point to the Restore Down button. Optionally, use the Cascade Windows option described earlier to get all open program windows down to an in-between size.

After the program window is visible but not hogging up the entire screen, you can size it to your liking by dragging any edge or corner. You have to get the tip of the mouse pointer right on the border of the window you want to size so that the pointer turns into a two-headed arrow, as in Figure 3.17.

When you see the two-headed arrow, hold down the left mouse button without moving the mouse. After the mouse button is down, drag in the direction you want to size the window. Release the mouse button when the window is the size you want.

You can also size a program window using the mouse and the keyboard. Again, the program window has to be at some in-between size to start with. Also, note that you always begin the process from the program window's taskbar button. Follow these steps:

1. Click the program window's control menu button (upper-left corner of the window) and choose Size.

2. Press the navigation arrow keys (←, →, ↑, ↓) until the window (or the border around the window) is the size you want.

3. Press the Enter key.

FIGURE 3.16

The Restore Down button in a maximized program window.

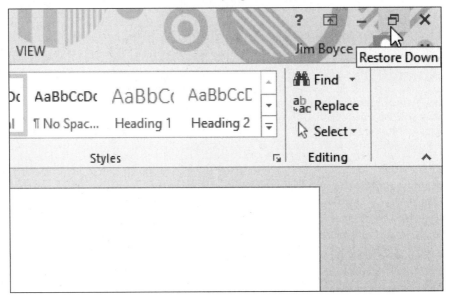

FIGURE 3.17

The mouse pointer positioned for sizing a window.

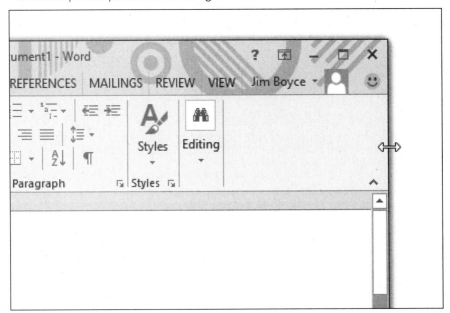

Moving a program window

You can easily move a program window about the screen just by dragging its title bar. However, you can't start with a minimized window. You have to get the program window to an in-between size or maximized size before you even get started. Then just get the mouse pointer somewhere near the top center of the window you want to move, hold down the left mouse button, and drag the window around. Release the mouse button when the window is where you want it on the desktop. This works for both in-between sized and maximized windows.

Dialog boxes work the same way. You can't size or minimize a dialog box, and dialog boxes don't have taskbar buttons. But you can easily drag a dialog box around the screen by its title bar.

Moving and sizing from the keyboard

As you've seen, most of the techniques for moving and sizing program windows rely on the mouse. There are some keyboard alternatives, but they're not available in all program windows. The only way to find out whether these work in the window you're using at the moment is to press Alt + Spacebar and see whether a system menu drops down from the upper-left corner, as in Figure 3.18.

FIGURE 3.18

A system menu from a program window.

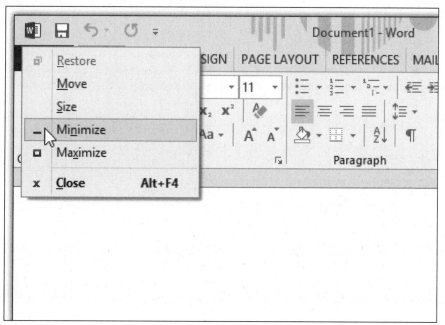

If you see the menu, you just have to press the underlined letter from the menu option you want to select. For example, press the letter *x* to Maximize or *n* to Minimize. If you press *m* to Move or *s* to Size, you can then use the arrow keys ($\leftarrow$, $\rightarrow$, $\uparrow$, $\downarrow$) to move or size the window. Then press Enter when the window is positioned or sized to your liking.

> **TIP**
>
> Sometimes, a window can be outside the viewable area of the desktop. This can happen if you extend your Windows desktop onto another monitor but that monitor isn't connected or turned on. If you can press Alt+Tab and determine that a program is running, but you can't see it on the desktop, press Alt+Tab and select the program (make it active). Then press Alt+Spacebar, press M, and use the arrow keys on the keyboard to move the window into a viewable area of the desktop.

Closing a Program

When you're finished using a program, you should close it. Every open program and document consumes some resources, mostly in the form of using memory (RAM). The computer also uses *virtual memory,* which is basically space on the hard disk configured to look like RAM to the computer.

RAM has no moving parts and, thus, can feed stuff to the processor (where all the work takes place) at amazing speeds. A standard hard disk has moving parts and is much, much slower. Newer solid state drives do not rely on moving parts, but you still have speed differences between RAM and solid state drives. As soon as Windows has to start using virtual memory, everything slows down. So, you really don't want to have a bunch of stuff you're not using anymore open and consuming resources.

There are many ways to close a program. Use whichever of the following techniques is most convenient for you, because they all produce the same result — the program is removed from memory, and both its program window and taskbar button are removed from the screen:

- Click the Close (X) button in the program window's upper-right corner.
- Right-click the title bar across the top of the program window and choose Close.
- Choose File ➪ Exit from the program's menu bar, if the program provides a File menu.
- Right-click the program's taskbar button and choose Close Window.
- If the program is in the active window, press Alt + F4.

> **TIP**
>
> You can close a Windows 8 app by grabbing the top of the app window until the mouse pointer changes to a hand. Then drag the window down to the bottom of the screen.

If you were working on a document in the program and you've made changes to that document since you last saved it, the program should ask in a message box like the example in Figure 3.19 whether you want to save those changes.

FIGURE 3.19

Save changes to a document before closing the app.

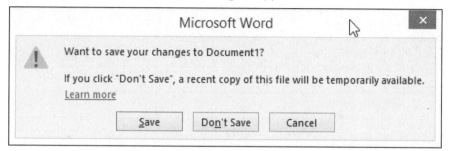

Never take that dialog box lightly because whichever option you choose is final, and there's no going back and changing your mind. Your options are as follows:

- **Save/Yes:** The document is saved in its current state; both the document and the program close.
- **Don't Save/No:** Any and all changes you made to the document since you last saved it will be lost forever. Both the document and the program close.
- **Cancel:** The program and document both remain open and on the screen. You can then continue work on the document and save it from the program's menu bar (choose File ⇨ Save).

Using the Notification Area

Over on the right side of the taskbar is the notification area (also called the *system tray* or *tray*). Each icon in the notification area represents a program or service that's running in the background. For example, antivirus and antispyware programs often show icons in the notification area so that you know they're running.

To conserve space on the taskbar, Windows 8 gives you the option of hiding inactive icons. When inactive icons are hidden, you see a button with up and down arrows on it at the left side of the notification area. Click the button to see icons that are currently hidden.

As with any icon or button, you can point to an icon in the notification area to see the name of that icon. Right-clicking an icon usually provides a context menu of options for using the item. Clicking or double-clicking the icon usually opens a program window that's associated with the running background service.

NOTE

A *context menu* is a menu that offers commands that are in the context of the selected item. In other words, the commands apply specifically to the selected item, not to other items. To open a context menu, right-click an item (such as an icon).

For example, the Volume icon provides a simple service: It lets you control the volume of your speakers. To change the volume, you click the icon and then drag the slider (shown in Figure 3.20) up or down. Optionally, you can mute the speakers by choosing the button at the bottom of the slider. Click it again to remove the mute. The Mixer option opens a window in which you can control the volume of different kinds of sounds independently.

FIGURE 3.20

The volume control slider.

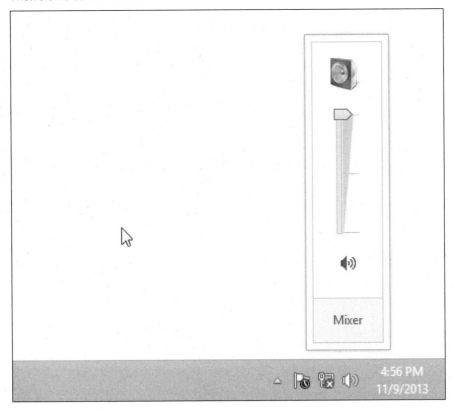

The icons in the notification area don't represent programs that you *can* run. They represent programs that *are* running. The icon simply serves as a notification that the program is running, although in most cases, the icon also provides options for closing the program or changing how it runs. Different computers have different notification area icons. The following are some common examples:

- **Network Connections:** You might see an icon that lets you disconnect from the network, view and connect to wireless networks, and open the Network and Sharing Center.

- **Security programs:** Programs that protect your system from malware (such as viruses and spyware) often display icons in the notification area.

- **Updates:** An icon notifies you when updates are available for downloading or installing.

- **Safely Remove Hardware:** If you have a USB device connected to your computer, the Safely Remove Hardware icon lets you disable the device before removing it, which you do to make sure that the device doesn't disconnect while it's still in use.

Showing/hiding notification icons

You can choose for yourself which notification area icons you do and don't want to see at any time. You rarely need to see them all, so you can hide some if you prefer. To make choices about those icons, right-click the clock or blank area of the tray and choose Customize Notification Icons. The Notification Area Icons dialog box, shown in Figure 3.21, opens.

FIGURE 3.21

The Notification Area Icons dialog box.

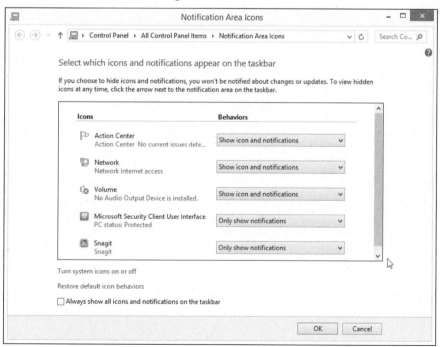

The Notification Area Icons dialog box lists items that are currently active, as well as inactive items that were active in the past. You can choose if and how you want to display an icon by selecting a choice from the Behaviors drop-down list to the right of an item's name. Here are your options:

- **Show Icon and Notifications:** The item is always visible in the notification area.
- **Hide Icon and Notifications:** The item is always hidden.
- **Only Show Notifications:** The icon is visible only when it's active and serving some purpose.

As always, what you choose to show or hide is entirely up to you. Just make your selections and click OK in each of the open dialog boxes.

If you always want all notification area icons to be visible, follow these steps:

1. Right-click the current time in the lower right of the screen and choose Customize Notification Icons.
2. In the Notification Area Icons dialog box that opens, select the Always Show All Icons and Notifications on the Taskbar check box.
3. Click OK.

 Chapter 13 discusses additional techniques for customizing the desktop, taskbar, and notification area.

Responding to notification messages

Icons in the notification area may occasionally display messages in a speech balloon. Many messages just provide some feedback and don't require any response from you. These kinds of messages generally fade away on their own after a few seconds. But you can also close the message by clicking the Close (X) button in its upper-right corner.

Icons or messages that show a red X icon, like the one in Figure 3.22, are security related. You can click the balloon or message title to get more information about the items.

 Chapters 9, 10 through 11 discuss security in some depth.

Using scroll bars

Scroll bars appear in program windows whenever the window contains more information than it can fit. You may not see any on your screen right now. But don't worry about that. The trick is to recognize them when you do see them, to know what they mean, and to know how to work them. Figure 3.23 shows an example of a vertical scroll bar and a horizontal scroll bar.

FIGURE 3.22

A security warning from the notification area.

When you see a scroll bar, it means that there's more to see than what's currently visible in the window. The size of the scroll box (the bit inside the scroll bar area that looks like a long button) relative to the size of the scroll bar tells you roughly how much more there is to see. For example, if the scroll bar is about 10 percent the size of the bar, it means you're seeing only about 10 percent of all there is to see.

To see the rest, you use the scroll bar to scroll through the information. You have basically three ways to use scroll bars:

- Click a button at the end of the scroll bar to move a little bit in the direction of the arrow on the button.
- Click an empty space on the scroll bar to move the scroll box along the bar toward the place where you clicked. That moves you farther than clicking the buttons would.
- Drag the scroll box in the direction you want to scroll. To drag, place the mouse pointer on the button and hold down the left mouse button while moving the mouse in the direction you want to scroll.

If your mouse has a wheel, you can use that to scroll as well. If the window shows a vertical scroll bar, spinning the mouse wheel scrolls up and down. If the window shows only a horizontal scroll bar, spinning the mouse wheel scrolls left and right. Some mice have a horizontal scroll button (or wheel) that you can push left or right to scroll horizontally.

FIGURE 3.23

Examples of scroll bars.

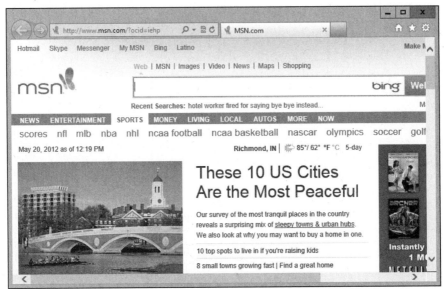

You can also use the keyboard to scroll up and down. But understand that the scroll bars work only in the active window (the window that's on the top of the stack). If necessary, first click the window or press Alt + Tab to bring it to the top of the stack. Then you can use the up and down arrow keys (↑ and ↓) to scroll up and down slightly. Use the Page Up (PgUp) and Page Down (PgDn) keys to scroll up and down in larger increments. Press the Home key to scroll all the way to the top (or all the way to the left). Press the End key to scroll all the way to the end.

Using Back and Forward buttons

Back and Forward buttons help you navigate through multiple pages of items. As with scroll bars, they appear only when useful, so don't expect to see them on your screen right now, or all the time. At times, they may be *disabled* (dimmed), as at the top of Figure 3.24. At other times they are *enabled* (not dimmed). Also, you won't find Back and Forward buttons in every program window.

A disabled button isn't broken. When an item is disabled, it's just not appropriate at the moment. For example, when you first open a window, both buttons may be disabled because you have no page to switch to yet. When you click a link that takes you to another page, the Back button is then enabled because now you *do* have a page to go back to (the page you just left). After you go back to the previous page, the Forward button is enabled because now you have a page to go forward to — the page you just left.

When a button is enabled, you just click it to go back or forward. When a button is disabled, clicking it has no effect.

FIGURE 3.24

Disabled Back and Forward buttons.

Logging Off, Shutting Down

Here's a question a lot of people ask: "Should I shut down my computer if I won't be using it for a while, or should I just leave it on?" Everybody has an opinion about this. So here's ours: It doesn't matter. It's fine to leave your computer running. Many people shut down their computers only when they need to, such as when installing certain types of hardware. Aside from that, their computers are on, and online, 24 hours a day, 7 days a week. With today's green PCs, turning off the computer every day isn't as important as it once was. Perhaps more important, leaving the computer on means you can start working with it almost right away, instead of waiting for it to boot.

> **NOTE**
>
> Windows 8.1 provides a much quicker startup process than previous versions of Windows. In some cases, the boot-up time is less than 8 seconds, which is substantially quicker than Windows 7.

The Power button in Windows 8.1 is located on the Charms Bar. But you also can access the power commands from the Quick Link menu. Figure 3.25 shows the power commands in the Quick Link menu. Figure 3.26 shows the Power button in the Charms Bar.

NOTE

Understand that turning off a PC isn't quite the same as turning off a TV or radio. You usually don't want to just hit the main power switch to shut down while you have things open and unsaved. You want to close all of your documents and apps first. Then click the Power button and choose Shut Down.

FIGURE 3.25

The power commands available while on the desktop.

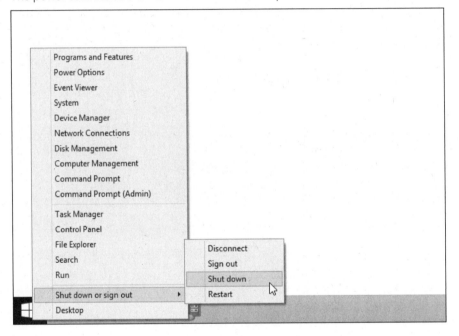

Although shutdown is much faster in Windows 8.1 than previous versions, don't expect the computer to turn off immediately. It takes a few seconds for Windows to get everything closed up and ready to shut down. On most computers, you don't have to do anything else. The computer will eventually shut itself down completely.

FIGURE 3.26

The Power button available from the Charms Bar.

Wrap-Up

That about wraps it up for the main terminology and basic skills. Much of what you've learned in this chapter is the kind of stuff most people assume you already know. You may have to read the chapter a few times and practice things before it all sinks in. Use the Windows Help for more information and for hands-on practice.

Here's a quick summary of the most important points covered in this chapter:

- The Windows desktop is the primary place you'll do your work.
- Unless you have a touchscreen device (such as a mobile phone or tablet), you'll use your mouse and keyboard to operate the computer.
- Most of your work will involve opening and using programs and apps.

- You can start any program that's installed on your computer from the Start screen.
- Each open program appears in its own program window on the desktop. Program windows stack up like sheets of paper.
- Each open program window has a corresponding taskbar button. The taskbar buttons help you switch from one open program window to another.
- You can move and size program windows to see exactly what you need to see, when you need to see it.
- When you finish using your computer and want to shut it down, don't go straight for the main power switch. Instead, click the Settings item from the Charms Bar, choose Power, and then click Shut Down.

That's enough for now about the desktop and programs. These days, with just about everyone using a computer to access the Internet, security is a major issue. So, we begin to address that topic in Chapter 4 with a discussion of user accounts and how they relate to computer security.

Sharing and Securing with User Accounts

IN THIS CHAPTER

E very person who uses your computer is called a *user,* and each user should have his or her own *user account* on the computer. Giving each person a user account is a lot like giving each person his or her own separate PC, but a lot cheaper. Each user can personalize the desktop and other settings. Each person can have his or her own separate collection of pictures, music, videos, and other files. Each user can also set up his or her own separate e-mail account.

User accounts allow parents to create and enforce parental controls in Windows 8.1. This is a great tool for parents who can't always monitor when and how children use the computer. Parental controls allow you to control and monitor children's computer use 24 hours a day, 365 days a year, even when you're not around to do it yourself.

User accounts also add a level of security to your computer. Many security breaches occur not because of a problem with the computer or Windows, but because the user is in an account that grants malware (bad software) *permission* to do its evil deeds. Of course, people don't realize that they're granting permission because the program doesn't ask for permission. It gets its permission automatically from the type of user account you're currently logged into.

Creating and managing user accounts is easy. But before getting into the specifics of all that, let's take a look at how you, as a user, experience user accounts.

Logging In and Out of User Accounts

When you start your computer, Windows 8.1 presents you with the Lock Screen. This screen shows a background picture and can run background apps such as a calendar app or mail app before you log in. To advance beyond the Lock Screen, click a mouse button, gesture down (press the down arrow on your keyboard), press the spacebar or press Enter. You're shown the login screen. At this screen, the last user logged in at that computer will display. If you have multiple user accounts on your computer, you can choose to log in using the previous user account (if that's you) or select a different user.

To log in, enter the password for the chosen account and press Enter or click the arrow at the right end of the password text box. If you want to log in using a different login name, click the left arrow to see a list of all the users who have logged into this computer. Select the user you want to log in as, and then enter that user's login credentials to start Windows 8.1.

For accounts that don't have an associated password, simply click the name for that user, and Windows loads to the Windows 8.1 Start screen.

Where am I now?

To see the name of the user account you're currently logged into, look at the top-right corner of the Windows 8.1 Start screen. In Figure 4.1, the user account name is Jeffrey, but it could be any username set up on your computer. If Windows 8.1 came pre-installed on your computer, it might be a generic name, such as Owner or User.

Switching accounts

You have a few different ways to switch from the account you're currently logged into to another account (assuming that you have more than one user account on your computer already).

The quickest way is to display the Start screen and then click your account name at the top of the screen. Figure 4.2 shows an example of a list of users. You can use the following methods to change users:

- **Click Sign Out.** This option logs you out of Windows and sends you to the Windows startup screen. Press Enter, slide the screen up, or roll the mouse button down to display the sign on screen. Select a username by clicking the back arrow to display all users set up on this computer.

- **Click a username.** When you click your username at the Start screen, all user accounts for your computer appear. Click the name you want to switch to. Windows suspends the current user and displays the login screen for the selected name. Enter the password for that username to continue.

Why Switching Users Can Be Bad

When you switch users, instead of signing out the original user, all the programs and documents on your desktop remain open and in memory. This is useful if you need to leave your computer in a hurry and don't need to shut down all the stuff you're working on; however, it leaves less working memory for other users in their accounts.

If multiple users consistently switch users to leave their accounts, you end up with an enormous amount of memory tied up all the time. The likely result is that the computer will run much slower for everyone.

Ideally, every user should save all open files, exit all programs, and sign off from his or her account when finished using the computer.

FIGURE 4.1

Username on the new Windows 8.1 Start screen.

4

FIGURE 4.2

Available users who can log into the current computer.

You also can change users by using the Power options. Click the Settings Charm button and then click the Power icon. Three menu options appear, as shown in Figure 4.3. The options are described in the following list:

- **Sleep:** This option saves the system state to disk and powers down the computer, but the computer can be restored more quickly than shutting down and starting up.

- **Hibernate:** This option saves all active data to the hard drive and then shuts down all the electronics that are no longer needed. The state is similar to sleep because very little power is used; however, it takes longer to start back up because the active data needs to be loaded back into RAM from the hard drive.

- **Shut Down:** This option closes all open programs and shuts down the computer. Press the power button to restart the computer and show the login screen. The Power Options\System Settings applet allows you to decide what the power button does when you press it. You may need to change your computers BIOS configuration as well.

- **Restart:** This option closes all programs, shuts down the computer, and then restarts the computer to the login screen.

FIGURE 4.3

Windows Power options.

> **CAUTION**
>
> If your user account isn't password-protected, other people aren't really locked out of your account. Anyone can come along, click your user account name, and be at your desktop. Also, once someone is at your desktop, he can use the Accounts screen to set up a password of his own. Unless he gives you that password, you can be locked out of your own account. In most cases, particularly when your computer is shared with another user or has the potential to be available to others, take precautions and set up a password for your account.

Sign-in Options

Windows 8.1 provides you with four sign-in options, available from a new link in the Account area in PC Settings. To access the options, click the Settings Charm button and then click the Change PC Settings link at the bottom of the page.

The four options are:

- **Password:** This link takes you to the page where you can create and manage your passwords (see the next section).

- **Picture password:** This link takes you to the page where you can create and manage a picture password (see Picture Passwords later in this chapter).

- **PIN:** Clicking this link prompts you for your password, after which you can enter and confirm a number to log on with.

- **Password policy:** This link toggles the option to force Windows 8.1 to request a password when the PC wakes up.

The Sign-in Options page is shown in Figure 4.4.

FIGURE 4.4

Windows sign-in options.

Creating Strong Passwords

We talk about techniques for creating, managing, and password-protecting user accounts, but before we get into the details, it might be worthwhile to talk about passwords in general. Not just passwords for user accounts, but for all types of accounts you create, including online accounts.

A password that's easily guessed is a weak password. A strong password is one that's not easily guessed and is immune to *password-guessing attacks.* The two most common forms of password-guessing attacks are the *dictionary attack* and the *brute-force attack.* Both types of attacks rely on special programs that are specifically designed to try to crack people's passwords and gain unauthorized entry to their user accounts.

The dictionary attack tries many thousands of passwords from a dictionary of English terms and commonly used passwords. The brute-force attack tries thousands of combinations of characters until it finds the right combination of characters needed to get into the account.

Admittedly, both types of attacks are rare in a home PC environment. They're also easily frustrated by common techniques such as forcing a person to wait several minutes before trying again after three failed password attempts. Nonetheless, the general guidelines used to protect top-secret data from password-guessing attacks can be applied to any password you create. A strong password is one that meets at least some of the following criteria:

- It is at least eight characters long.
- It does not contain your real name, user account name, pet name, significant date (such as birthday), or any name that's easily guessed by other family members or co-workers.
- It does not contain a word that can be found in a dictionary.
- It contains some combination of uppercase letters, lowercase letters, numeric digits, and symbols (such as !, &, ?, @, and #).

Again, we realize that few people need Fort Knox–style security on their personal PCs. You don't want to come up with a password that's difficult to remember and a pain to type. But any steps you take to make the password less easy to guess are well worth the effort. Some websites offer *password checkers*, programs that analyze a password and tell you how strong it is. See `www.microsoft.com/security/pc-security/password-checker.aspx` for an example. Or go to any search engine, such as `www.google.com`, and search for "password checker."

Remembering passwords

The most common problem with passwords is forgetting them after the fact. When you set up a password for a website, you can usually be reminded what the password is just by clicking an "I forgot my password" link at the sign-in page. But there is no such link for passwords that protect your Windows user accounts. Therefore, it's extremely important that you *not* forget your Windows passwords!

Before you password-protect a user account, take the time to come up with a password that you (or the user) can remember. Make sure you use exactly the same uppercase and lowercase letters that you'll be typing. Windows passwords are always case sensitive, which means uppercase and lowercase letters count!

For example, say you jot down your password as Tee4me!0 (where that last character is a zero). But later you type it in as tee4Me!o (with the last character being the letter *o*). Still later, you forget the password and dig out the sheet of paper. The tee4me!o you wrote down won't work, because the password is actually Tee4Me!0.

> **CAUTION**
>
> On a typewriter, the number 0 is basically the same as an uppercase letter *O* and the number 1 is basically the same as a lowercase letter *l*, but that is *not* true of computers. You must use the 1 and 0 keys near the top of the keyboard or on the numeric keypad to type 1 (one) and 0 (zero).

Devising a password hint

With Windows passwords, you can specify a password hint to help you remember a forgotten password. But still, it's tricky. Anyone who uses your computer can see the password hint. So, the hint shouldn't be so obvious that it tells a potential intruder what the password is. By the same token, the hint might trigger your basic memory of the password. But perhaps not the exact uppercase and lowercase letters you used.

Writing down your passwords isn't a good idea, because other people may be able to access them. But if you need to keep track of multiple passwords, consider using a password-protected Excel spreadsheet to store all your passwords. Then, you only need to remember one — the password for the Excel file. There are also password-keeper applications available that achieve the same result.

> **TIP**
>
> If you decide to store your passwords in an Excel file, make a copy you can open on another computer in case your computer crashes or you forget the password to log on. Better still, get a secure password storage program you access from your computer or telephone.

The bottom line on remembering passwords is simple: You're allowed no margin for error. A password that's "sort of like" the one you specified is not good enough. It must be *exactly* the one you specified. You must treat passwords as though they are valuable diamonds. Keep them safe and keep them secure, but don't keep them so safe that even *you* can't find them!

Okay, that's enough general advice about passwords. Next, you need to find out about types of user accounts.

> **TIP**
>
> As long as your account is an administrator account, or you have a separate administrator account that you can access, you can always reset someone's password on the computer if needed. You don't have to go through a password recovery process — just reset the password.

Picture Passwords

Picture passwords were introduced in Windows 8, and Windows 8.1 extends this new way to log into your computer. Picture passwords are designed to be used with touchscreen PCs and tablets so you don't have to type in characters. Instead you choose a picture, draw a combination of three gestures on the picture that become your "password," and then save those combinations with that picture. You use those gestures to gain access to your computer, much like what happens when you type in a password on your keyboard.

Creating a picture password

You set up a picture password through the Accounts area in PC Settings. Click on the Sign-in options link and then click Add to display the Create a Picture Password dialog box (shown in Figure 4.5). Type your user password and click OK to verify your password. You're now ready to select a picture and set up gestures to create the picture password.

Click Choose Picture and select a picture you want to use. Click Open to see the picture. Figure 4.6 shows an example of a picture that can be used for setting a picture password.

FIGURE 4.5

Creating a picture password

FIGURE 4.6

Use any picture, like the ones shown here, for your picture password.

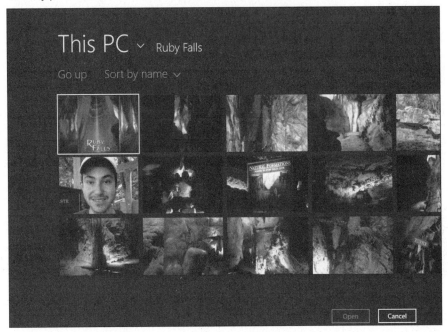

It's time to draw the gestures to create the combination you want to use for the password. You can draw any combination of these three gestures: taps, circles, and straight lines. Figure 4.7 shows the screen for setting up your gestures. You'll want to remember the following when you set up the gestures:

- Position of the gestures
- Size of the gestures
- Direction of the gestures
- Order in which you make the gestures

For example, on a picture of the flag of the United States, the following are suggested gestures:

- Draw a circle around three stars on the flag
- Tap the lowest white strip
- Draw a straight line from the top-right corner of the blue border down to the bottom of the lower red stripe

FIGURE 4.7

Set a picture password using a combination of three gestures.

As you draw each gesture, Windows does two things. First, it shows each gesture using a white outline arrow for straight lines, a white circle outline for circles, and a white dot for taps. Second, it shows the sequence of each gesture as 1, 2, or 3.

If you make a mistake, click Start Over and restart the gestures.

After you complete the gestures once, you must confirm them before they're saved. Simply repeat your three gestures. If you forget one, click Start Over and redraw the gestures — and be sure to remember your gestures this time!

When you successfully redraw the gestures in their correct order, click the Finish button. You're returned to the Users screen of PC Settings.

Testing your picture password

After you create a picture password, it's a good idea to test it soon to commit the gestures to memory. To do this, return to the Windows Start screen and sign out. Sign back into your account, this time using the gestures on the picture that displays. After you draw the correct gestures of your picture password, you're presented with the Windows Start screen.

Types of User Accounts

Windows 8.1 offers five basic types of user accounts: the built-in Administrator account, user accounts with administrative privileges, standard accounts, the Guest account, and the new Child account, which is set up in the Family Safety features of Windows 8.1. They vary in how much privilege they grant to the person using the account.

 Family Safety and child accounts are discussed in Chapter 5.

With Windows 8.1, you also have the choice of setting up the user accounts as local or Microsoft accounts. You can read about these types of accounts in the following sections.

Microsoft accounts

With Microsoft accounts, you have the greatest flexibility for taking advantage of many of the newest Windows 8.1 features. To set up a Microsoft account, you must use a valid e-mail address. You can use an existing account, such as one you use at your office or a third-party account such as Gmail, Yahoo! Mail, or something similar. If you don't have one, you can set up an e-mail account during the Windows 8.1 user account setup.

A Microsoft account provides the following features:

- Allows you to log in to a computer on which you haven't previously set up a user account. (Conversely, with local accounts, you must set up a local account on each computer on which you want to log in.)
- Provides access to Microsoft services like Xbox Live, Windows Phone accounts, and SkyDrive.
- Enables you to download apps from the Windows Store.
- Syncs settings across multiple computers. For example, if you work on two or more computers, logging in with the same Microsoft account on each one will enable you to keep your favorites, history, sign-in info, and languages synced between the two computers.
- Enables you to access your files and photos from multiple computers.

Local accounts

Local accounts are used when you do not need to keep computers synced. When you use local accounts, you set up accounts for each user that will be using a computer. If you need to set up one account that can be used on multiple Windows 8.1 computers, you must set up Microsoft accounts.

Local accounts are also limiting in that you cannot use them to access the Windows Store to download apps, or services like SkyDrive. Again, to access Windows Store apps, you must set up and use a Microsoft account.

The built-in administrator account

A single user account named Administrator is built into Windows 8.1. This is not the same as an administrative account you create yourself or see on the login screen. This account is hidden from normal view. It doesn't show up on the usual login screen.

The built-in Administrator account has unlimited computer privileges. So, while you're logged in to that account, you can do anything and everything you want with the computer. Any programs you run while you are in that account can also do anything they want. That makes the account risky from a security standpoint, and very unwise to use unless absolutely necessary.

In high-security settings, a new computer is usually configured by a certified network or security administrator who logs in to the Administrator account to set up the computer for other users. There, the administrator configures accounts on the *principle of least privilege,* where each account is given only as much privilege as necessary to perform a specific job.

When the administrator is finished, he or she typically renames the built-in Administrator account and password-protects it to keep everyone else out. The account is always hidden from view, except from other administrators who know how to find it. All this is standard operating procedure in secure computing environments, although hardly the norm in home computing.

In Windows 8.1, you really don't need to find, log in to, and use the built-in Administrator account unless you're an advanced user with a specific need, in which case you can get to it through Safe Mode. As a regular home user, you can do everything you need to do from a regular user account that has administrative privileges.

 Experienced users who need access to the built-in Administrator account can get to it through Safe Mode. We talk about that in Chapter 11. But if you're not a professional, we suggest you stay away from that and use an administrative account, discussed in the next section.

Administrative user accounts

Most of the time when you hear reference to an Administrator account in Windows 8.1, that reference is to a regular user account that has administrative privileges. This is an account that has virtually all the power and privilege of the built-in Administrator account. But it also has a lot of security built in to help thwart security threats that might otherwise abuse that account's privileges and do harm to your computer.

Ideally, you want to create one user account with administrative privileges on your computer. If you intend to implement parental controls, you'll need to password-protect that account to keep children from disabling or changing parental controls.

4

Standard accounts

A standard user account is the kind of account everyone should use for day-to-day computer use. It has enough privilege to do day-to-day tasks such as run programs, work with documents, use e-mail, and browse the web. It doesn't have enough privilege to make changes to the system that would affect other people's user accounts. It doesn't have enough privilege to allow children to override parental controls. And most important, it doesn't have enough privilege to let malware such as viruses and worms make harmful changes to your system.

If you use a standard account all the time, and use a built-in administrative account only when absolutely necessary, you'll go a long way toward keeping your computer safe from Internet security threats.

Guest account

The optional Guest account exists to allow people who don't regularly use your computer to use it temporarily. Basically, it lets them check their e-mail, browse the web, and maybe play some games. It definitely won't let them make changes to your user account or anyone else's. Its limited privileges also help protect your system from any malicious software they might pick up while online.

Creating and Managing User Accounts

The best way to handle user accounts is for one person to play the role of administrator, even if that person isn't a professional. In a home environment, it would most likely be a parent who needs to define parental controls. It's best to log into a user account that already has administrative privileges to get started. If you have only one user account, or you're taken straight to the desktop at startup, then that account probably has administrative privileges.

As with most configuration tasks, you create and manage user accounts through the Control Panel. There are several pages you can use, and several ways to get to them. As always, there is no right way or wrong way. No good way or bad way. You just use whatever is easiest and most convenient for you at the moment. Here are a couple of ways to navigate to options for managing the user account you're logged into at the moment:

- Display the Charms Bar, click Search, select Settings from the drop-down link, type **user** in the search box, and click Change User Account Control settings.
- Display the Charms Bar, click Search, click Settings, type **user** in the search box, and click Make Changes to Accounts.

A Control Panel applet appears that lets you make changes to an account as shown in Figure 4.8.

FIGURE 4.8

The User Accounts Control Panel applet.

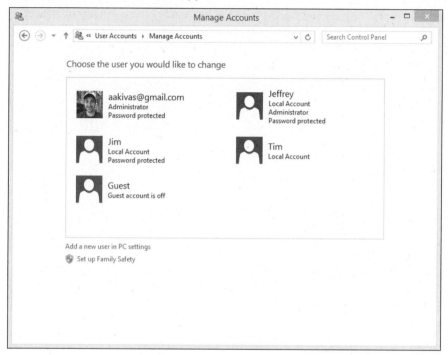

To create a new user account from this applet, click Add a New User in PC Settings. If you're in a standard account on a computer that already has a password-protected administrative account, you'll have to enter the password for the Administrator account. Or, if the administrative account doesn't have a password, press Enter to leave the password box empty. You end up in the Manage Accounts page. (You can also get to accounts management options from the Accounts page in PC settings.) There, you see an icon for every user account on your system. You can also see each account's type. Figure 4.9 shows an example with three administrative accounts and one standard account (the Guest account icon also appears, but it's disabled on this computer).

Creating a Microsoft user account

Creating a new Microsoft user account is easy. You should have one standard account for your day-to-day computing, plus one standard account for every other person who will use your computer. Microsoft accounts require passwords, so you must set up a password when you create a new Microsoft account.

Keep in mind that each user account has its own collection of files, Xbox Live, SkyDrive, Windows Phone information, apps, and various other settings and services from Microsoft.

FIGURE 4.9

The User Accounts page.

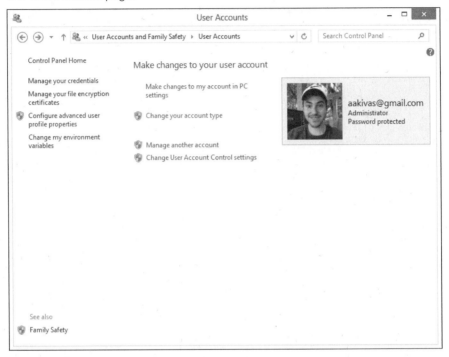

TIP

If you've been using your administrative account for a while, you may not want to create a new standard account from scratch. Better to create a new administrative account from scratch and then change your current account from an administrative account to a standard account. That way, you won't have to move files from your current account to the new account.

To create a new Microsoft user account, display the Charms Bar, click Settings, click Change PC Settings, click Accounts, and then click Other Accounts. The Manage Other Accounts page is shown in Figure 4.10.

Click Add an Account and you arrive at the sign-in option screen shown in Figure 4.11. Enter an e-mail address for the user account. If you don't have an e-mail address, see the next section.

FIGURE 4.10

Manage other account.

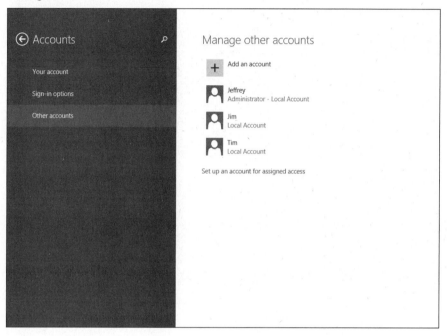

After you type an e-mail address, click to complete the account creation process. You can repeat the process to create as many user accounts as you wish.

Creating a new e-mail address for a new user account

If you don't have an e-mail address, you can set one up as you create a new Microsoft user account. To do this, click the Manage Other Accounts link on the Accounts page, and then click the Sign Up for a New Email Address link (see Figure 4.12 for this link). The Create a Microsoft Account page appears, as shown in Figure 4.12.

Windows 8.1 enables you to set up a new outlook.com, hotmail.com, or live.com e-mail address. Enter an e-mail address and then select one of the options from the drop-down list. Enter a new password (re-enter the password), your first and last names, your country, and your ZIP code. Click Next to show the general and security information pages, as shown in Figure 4.13. Here you can enter mobile phone information, an alternate e-mail address, and a secret question/response in case you need to recover your password. You must provide at least two of the three verification methods to continue.

4

FIGURE 4.11

The sign-in option page.

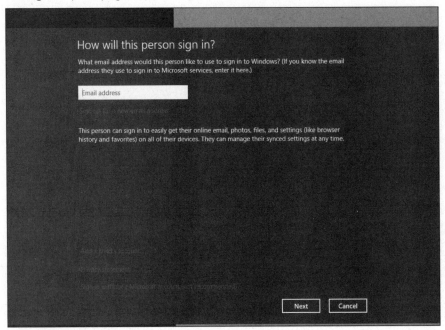

Enter your birth date, gender, and a list of characters and/or words to ensure that a human is filling out the Microsoft account page. Click Next to display the Communication preferences page, as show in Figure 4.14, and then click Finish to complete the new Microsoft account setup procedure. After some final communications options, you're returned to the previous Manage Accounts page or the Users Settings page, where you see that the new user account has been added to the system.

Creating a local account

If you don't want to set up a Microsoft account to sign in to Windows, you can set up a local account. To set up a local account, click Other Accounts from the Accounts page (refer to Figure 4.10), and then click Add an Account on the Manage Other Accounts page and then click the Sign In without a Microsoft Account link at the bottom of the page. The Add a User page appears.

Click Local Account to display the Add a User page. Enter a username, type a new password, re-type the password, and enter a password hint, such as a word or phrase that will help jog your memory in case you forget your password later. With a local account, you aren't required to enter a password, but we recommend that you do. Click Next to create the user and then click Finish to return to the Manage Other Accounts page.

FIGURE 4.12

Fill out the information to set up a new e-mail address for your Microsoft account.

Changing user accounts

When you create a user account, you're just giving it a name and choosing a type. After you've created a user account, you can change it to better suit your needs. Use the Accounts applet page shown in Figure 4.8 or the Accounts screen shown in Figure 4.10 to make changes to accounts.

> **CAUTION**
>
> When you delete a user account, you might also delete all the files in that account if you're not careful. Read the section "Deleting User Accounts," later in this chapter, before you delete an account so that you don't end up deleting photos or other documents that could be difficult or impossible to recover.

Changing a user account type

You can change an Administrator account to a standard account, or vice versa, from the main Accounts page. For example, if you've been using an administrative account for your day-to-day computing since buying your computer, you might want to change it to a standard account for the added security that a standard account provides. At least one user account must have administrative privileges, so you can make this change only if you have at least one other user account on the system that has administrative privileges.

FIGURE 4.13

Fill out security information when setting up a new e-mail address for your Microsoft account.

To change an account's type, click the account's icon or name on the Accounts page. First, you're taken to the Change an Account page. As you can see in Figure 4.15, that page lets you change the account in a number of ways, or even remove the account.

Click the Change the Account Type link to change the account from an administrative account to a standard account or child account, or vice versa. To change the account type, click OK after making the selection.

Password-protecting an account

You have the option to set up local accounts without password protection (Microsoft accounts require passwords). If you share your computer with other people, chances are, you'll want to keep some people out of the Administrator account. Likewise, you'll want to keep some users from having administrative privileges. This is especially important with parental controls. If the administrative account isn't password-protected, it won't take long for the kids to figure out how to bypass any controls you impose.

FIGURE 4.14

Fill out the Communication preferences page when setting up a new e-mail address for your Microsoft account.

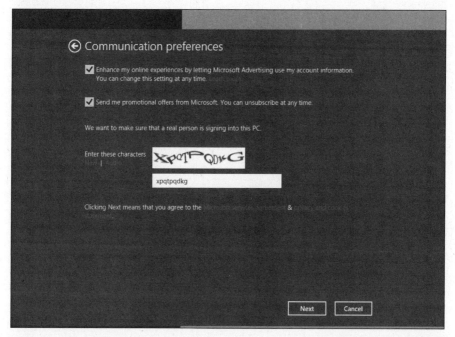

CAUTION

Don't forget the password you set on the administrator account if it's the only administrator account; otherwise, nobody will have administrative privileges, and that will cause a world of headaches. So, think up a good password and password hint, and make sure you enter the password correctly while you're setting it.

To password-protect a user account, go to the main page for the user account. For instance, if you're on the Accounts page, click the user account you want to password-protect and then click Sign-in Options. You're taken to the page that lets you change the password. Or you can open the Create Password applet like the one in Figure 4.16. If you've been using the account for a while without a password, heed the warnings. If it's a brand-new account, you don't have anything to worry about.

4

FIGURE 4.15

Change an Account page.

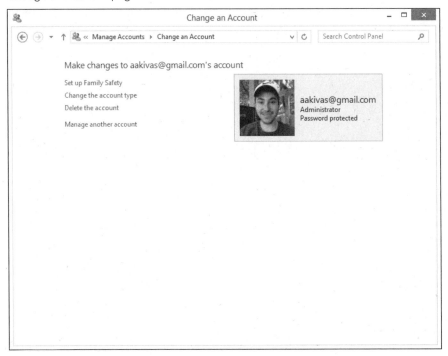

To password-protect the account, type your password in the New Password text box. Then press Tab or click the Confirm New Password text box and type the same password again. You won't see the characters you type, just a placeholder for each character.

> **TIP**
>
> When you type passwords, the characters are always hidden to prevent shoulder surfing. *Shoulder surfing* is a simple technique for discovering someone's password just by watching over the person's shoulder as he or she types it.

Next, enter a password hint in the Type a Password Hint text box. The hint should be something that reminds you of the forgotten password, but not a dead giveaway to someone trying to break into the account. Click Create Password after you've filled in all the blanks.

If you see a message indicating that your passwords don't match, you'll have to retype both passwords. Make sure you type the password exactly the same in both boxes. Then click the Create Password button. You'll be taken back to the main page for the user account when you've successfully entered the password in both boxes and provided a password hint.

FIGURE 4.16

Password-protecting an account.

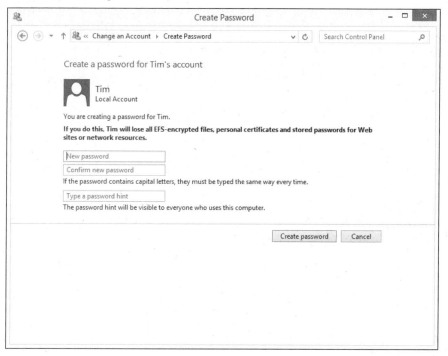

You can repeat the process to password-protect as many accounts as you wish. If you're creating user accounts for people other than yourself, set a default password for the account and then let them manage their own passwords. In our opinion, every account should have a password.

> **TIP**
>
> Why have a password on all local accounts? First, it's basic security. Second, if you have more than one child using a shared computer, having a password for each child will help prevent a younger child from using an older child's account to potentially bypass parental restrictions.

Changing the account picture

Every user account has an associated picture. The picture is like an icon, giving you a quick visual reference without having to read the name. The picture you choose can be any one of several built-in pictures, or it can be a picture of your own choosing.

If you decide to use your own picture, try to avoid using one that comes straight from a digital camera. The file size on such pictures is really too large for a user account picture.

Your best bet would be to crop out a section from a photo, and size it to about 100 x 100 pixels. The picture you choose must be a JPEG, BMP, GIF, or PNG file type.

> **TIP**
>
> If you don't know enough about pictures to meet all the requirements, you can use built-in pictures. Then, after you've acquired some of the skills covered in Chapter 18, you can create a suitable user account picture and apply it to any user account.

To change the picture for a user account, use the new Windows 8.1 User Settings by displaying the Windows Charm and clicking Settings. Next, click Change PC Settings to display the PC Settings page, which is shown in Figure 4.17.

Click Accounts and then click Your Account. Figure 4.18 shows the Account Picture, which is the current picture of the selected user (or the default image if you didn't select one). Click Browse and then select the area on your computer to locate a new picture. For example, click This PC, and then Pictures to display your Pictures folder. Click the picture you want to use and then click Choose Image as shown in Figure 4.19.

You also can use an attached webcam to snap a picture or a five-second video to use as an account picture. To do this, you must have a webcam connected to your computer. On the same page, under Create a Picture, click Camera to start your camera (of course, this won't work if you don't have a camera or webcam working on your computer):

FIGURE 4.17

PC Settings page with a user account picture.

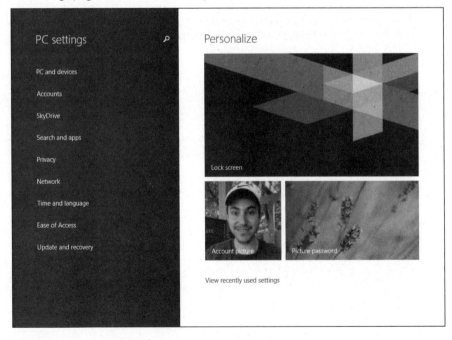

FIGURE 4.18

Your Account Picture from the Accounts page.

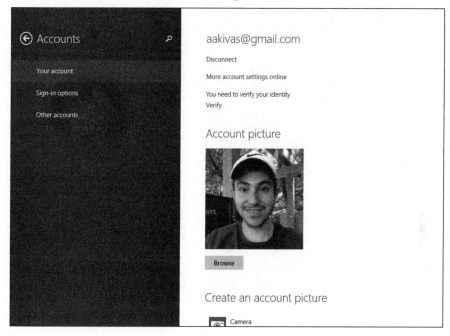

- To snap a still picture, click the screen. Use the cropping and resizing tools to select the portion of the picture to use. Click OK to save that picture as your new account picture.

- To take a five-second video, click Video Mode and click the screen to start the video. Click the screen again to stop the video and to review the video. Click Retake if you aren't satisfied with the video. Click OK when you want to keep the video and to set it as your account picture.

The picture or video you selected replaces the original picture.

Enabling or disabling the Guest account

The Guest account is for anybody who might need to use your computer on a temporary basis. For example, with a home computer, you might set up a Guest account for houseguests so that they can check their e-mail, browse the web, and such. The Guest account has very limited privileges, so you don't have to worry about guests messing things up while using your computer.

FIGURE 4.19

Choosing an account picture.

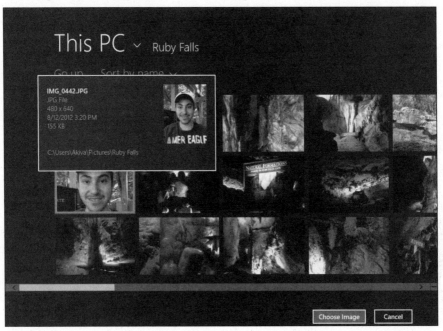

The Guest account is turned off by default. You can keep it that way until you actually need it. To activate the Guest account, go to the Manage Accounts Control Panel page and click the Guest Account icon. Then choose Turn On. Likewise, should you ever need to disable the Guest account, click its icon on the Manage Accounts page and then click Turn Off the Guest Account.

Navigating through user account pages

In Windows 8.1, user account management involves using two environments, including the Control Panel and PC Settings page. You can use the Control Panel to complete almost all user account tasks described earlier, even those that use the new PC Settings page. When you get to a task, it's largely just a matter of choosing options and reading text that's right on the screen. Windows provides links to advance to configuration screens. Some links are blue text (standard web hypertext color), while others use new Windows 8.1 buttons to display new settings or options for a task. You can use Back and Forward buttons to get around from page to page. You can click the Manage Another Account link on the User Accounts page as shown in Figure 4.20.

FIGURE 4.20

The Manage Another Account option is highlighted using the Windows 8.1 applet interface.

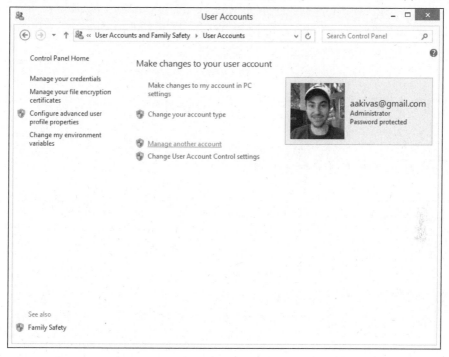

Cracking into standard user accounts

If a local standard user forgets his or her password, you can use an account that has administrative privileges to reset the standard user's password. If you're an administrator and you just want to see what a standard user is up to, you can use this same technique to change the password and get full access to its folders.

> **CAUTION**
>
> This approach will cause the standard user to lose access to encrypted files and e-mail messages created in an e-mail program such as Windows Live Mail.

To change the password for a local standard user account:

1. Log in to a user account that has administrative privileges.
2. Go to the Manage Accounts page (press Windows Key + X and choose Control Panel, click User Accounts, and click Manage Another Account).

3. Click the password-protected account for which the user has forgotten the password.

4. Click the Change the password link.

5. Enter a new password, and then enter it again to confirm it.

6. Type a password hint.

7. Click Change Password to save the new password.

The local standard user account will now have a new password. Be sure to share this password with the user so he or she can sign into Windows.

Deleting User Accounts

An administrator can easily delete user accounts. If nobody has ever used a user account, then deleting the account is no big deal. But if someone has used the account, the decision to delete it is more complicated. When you delete a user account, you also delete all e-mail messages downloaded to the computer, Internet favorites, music, pictures, and videos. You could also delete all of that user's saved files if you're not careful. Doing this by accident would be a disaster because there's no way to undo the deletion.

> **CAUTION**
>
> Deleting a user account can have very serious consequences. Don't do it unless you fully understand the ramifications.

If you want to save the user's e-mail messages and Internet favorites, export them to that user's Documents folder first. Read the Windows online Help for more information on exporting Internet Explorer favorites. Also, refer to your e-mail program's help for information on saving e-mail messages to a local drive, such as to your Documents folder.

So let's assume you understand the consequences and have no intention of deleting an account just for the heck of it. Only administrators can delete user accounts. So if you're in a standard account, you at least need to know the administrative password to delete a user account. You also need to log in to any account except the one you intend to delete. Then follow these steps:

1. Display the Control Panel, click User Accounts, and click Manage Another Account.

2. Click the account you want to delete.

3. Click Delete the Account and read the resulting message. Then click one of the following buttons:

   - **Delete Files:** Click this button only if you intend to delete *everything* associated with the account, including all files that the user has created and saved.

   - **Keep Files:** Click this option to save the user's files. You will still lose the user's saved e-mail messages, Internet favorites, and user account.

4. Read the next page to make sure you understand the consequences of your choice. Then click Cancel if you change your mind, or click Delete account if you're sure you know what you're doing.

If you choose Delete account, the user's account will no longer exist. If you choose Keep Files, the user's saved files (those from his account's profile) will be in a folder on the desktop. That folder will have the same name as the user account you just deleted. Otherwise, nothing of the user's account, not even his or her saved files, will remain. (If you choose Cancel in Step 4, the entire account remains intact and unchanged.)

If you create a new user account with the same name as the one you just deleted, the new account is still an entirely new account. It won't inherit any files or settings from the account you previously deleted.

> **NOTE**
>
> If the user's Documents folder contains no documents, Windows won't create a copy of the folder on your desktop when you delete the account (because there is nothing to save).

Using User Accounts

As mentioned at the start of this chapter, each user account is like its own separate PC. Every user has his or her private Documents, Pictures, Music, and Video folders for storing files. Each user account can have its own Windows apps, e-mail account, and Internet favorites. Each user can customize the desktop, Start screen, and other settings to that user's own liking.

When you first start your computer, the Windows lock screen appears. Press Enter, swipe up (on a tablet or touch screen), hit the spacebar or roll the mouse wheel up to display the sign in screen. You also see the sign on screen when you sign out of your user account. If you click a user account that isn't password-protected, you're taken straight into the account. But if you click the picture for a password-protected account, a password prompt appears.

To get into the account, you need to enter the appropriate password. If you enter the wrong password, a message appears letting you know that the user account name or password is incorrect. You can click OK to try again. You can't get into the user account until you've entered the correct password for the account.

The first time you or someone else logs in to a new user account, it's just like starting Windows 8.1 on a brand-new PC. The desktop has the default appearance. All the document folders in the account are empty. There are no e-mail accounts, no Internet favorites, and no Windows apps installed. To use e-mail, the user needs to set up the account with an e-mail account, preferably an account used only by that user.

The user does have access to all the programs installed on the computer (except for rare cases in which someone installed a program for personal use only). The user will likely have Internet connectivity through the same network or Wi-Fi as all other user accounts.

4

If the user account is a standard account, there are some limitations to what the user can do. For one, Windows settings are not synced with other devices, such as a Windows Phone or tablet. Also, the user can't make any changes to the system that would affect other users. That's where Windows 8.1's User Account Control security comes into play.

Understanding User Account Control

User Account Control (UAC) is the general term for the way administrative and standard user accounts work in Windows 8.1. As you browse around through various pages in the Control Panel, you'll notice that many links have a shield icon next to them.

Items that have a shield icon next to them require administrative approval. Items without a shield icon don't. For example, any user can change his or her Windows password, with or without administrative approval.

Options that do have a shield icon next to them require administrative approval. But you don't necessarily need to be logged in to an administrative account to use those options. You just have to prove that you have administrative privileges. You do that by entering the password for an administrative account. To prove you have administrative privileges on this computer, enter the password for the administrative user account and click Submit (or OK in some dialog boxes).

Of course, when someone who doesn't know the administrative account password encounters the User Account Control dialog box, he or she is stuck. Users who don't know the password can't go any further. This prevents the standard user from doing things that might affect the overall system and other people's user accounts. It also prevents children from overriding parental controls. (You learn how to set up parental controls in Chapter 6.)

Privilege escalation in administrative accounts

If you happen to be logged in to an administrative account when you click a shielded option, you don't need to enter an administrative password. After all, if you're in an administrative account, you must already know the password required to get into that account. You don't need to prove that you know that password again. But, by default, you'll still see a prompt telling you that the program you're about to run makes changes to the system. You have to click Continue to proceed.

It might seem odd (and irritating) that you still have to click something to get to the item you clicked. But it works that way for a reason. The dialog box lets you know that the program you're about to run is going to make changes to the overall system. You expect to see that dialog box after you click a shielded option. And with time and experience, you'll learn to expect it when you do other things that affect the system as a whole, such as when you install new programs.

Sometimes it occurs when you don't expect to see it. For example, when opening an e-mail attachment, you wouldn't normally expect to see that message. After all, opening an e-mail attachment should just show you the contents of the attachment, not make a change to the system as a whole. Seeing the warning in that context lets you know that something fishy is going on, most likely something bad in the e-mail attachment. You can click Cancel to *not* open the attachment, thereby protecting your system from whatever virus or other bad thing lies hidden within the e-mail attachment.

On a more technical note, UAC operates on a principle of least privilege. When you're in an administrative account, you actually run with the same privileges as a standard user. This is done to protect your system from malware that would otherwise exploit the privileges of your administrative account to make malicious changes to your system.

When you enter a password or click Continue in response to a UAC prompt, you temporarily elevate your privileges to allow that one change to be made. After that change is made, you're back to your more secure standard user privileges. This is how things have been done in high-security settings for years, and it's considered a security best practice.

Turning UAC on and off

If at all possible, you should follow standard best practices and keep UAC active on your own computer. But if it proves to be impractical, you can turn off UAC.

Even though it is much improved from Windows Vista and Windows 7, UAC is not always a very popular Windows 8.1 feature. After all, nobody wants a feature that makes them do more work, even when the extra work is nothing more than an occasional extra mouse click. Furthermore, sometimes UAC is just impractical. For example, if you give your kids standard user accounts, they can't install their own programs. But if you give them administrative accounts, you can't institute parental controls.

 See Chapter 5 for setting up Child accounts.

Before you turn off UAC, we recommend that you first ensure that all the other security measures discussed in Part II of this book are installed and working on your PC. UAC is just one component of an overall security strategy. The more components you have on and working, the better.

> **NEW FEATURE**
>
> UAC in Windows 8.1 follows similar functionality that was used in Windows 7 to make it less obtrusive to the user. In contrast to how it functioned in Windows Vista, and even in ways it worked in Windows 7, in which UAC was an on or off feature, UAC in Windows 8.1 offers a range of settings to tailor the end-user experience.

Changing UAC settings is a simple process. From the Windows 8.1 interface, display the Charms Bar and click Search, choose Settings from the drop-down list and enter **User** in the text field. Or from the Start menu, select Control Panel, click User Accounts and Family Safety, and then click User Accounts. Or from the desktop, press Windows + W and click Control Panel. Click User Accounts and Family Safety and then click User Accounts. Click Change User Account Control settings and then, if prompted to do so, enter an administrative password to get to the dialog box shown in Figure 4.21.

4

FIGURE 4.21

User Account Control Settings dialog box

You can choose from the following options:

- **Always Notify:** Windows will notify you if programs try to install software or make changes to the computer, or if you make changes to Windows settings.

- **Notify Me Only When Apps Try to Make Changes to My Computer (Default):** Windows will not notify you when you make changes to your computer, but it will notify you, by dimming the desktop and displaying a warning, if programs attempt to make changes.

- **Notify Me Only When Apps Try to Make Changes to My Computer (Do Not Dim My Desktop):** Windows will not notify you when you make changes to your computer, but it will notify you when programs attempt to make changes. However, Windows will not dim the desktop; instead, it will just display a message.

- **Never Notify:** Windows will not notify you of changes (this turns off UAC). The only safe time to use this option is when you need to install a program that doesn't work with UAC. Turn off UAC, install the program, and then turn on UAC again.

To turn UAC off, drag the slider down to Never Notify. Or, if it was already off and you want better security, drag the slider up to the desired level. Then click OK.

If you turned off UAC, when you click a shielded option you'll receive no prompting for credentials or status checking. Things will basically be as they were in Windows XP and other earlier versions of Windows.

Creating and Using Password Reset Disks

A password reset disk is an important part of any password-protected PC. It's the only method of password recovery that allows you to retain all data in an account in the event of a forgotten password. Advanced features such as EFS (Encrypting File System) encryption, personal certificates, and stored network passwords can be recovered only by using a password reset disk.

The trick is that you need to create the password reset disk *before* you forget the password. You can't do it after you've forgotten the password. Keep that disk in a safe place where you can find it when you need it, but where others can't find it to gain unauthorized access to the administrative account.

A USB flash drive or memory card works equally well. However, a memory card will work only if your computer has slots for inserting a memory card.

Choosing a memory device for the password reset

A *USB flash drive* (also called a *jump drive*) is a small device that plugs into a USB port on your computer and looks and acts like a disk drive. A *memory card* is a storage device commonly used to save pictures in digital devices, like cameras or smartphones. If your computer has slots for such cards, you can slide a card into the slot and treat the card just as you would a USB flash drive.

To see examples and get an idea of cost, check out some online retailers. Then search the site for *flash drive, jump drive,* or *memory card reader* to view available products. If you're looking at memory card readers, the kind that plug into a USB port will be the easiest to install. Many retail department stores that sell computer or office supplies also carry flash drives.

Creating the password reset disk

To create a password reset disk, log in to the password-protected administrative account you created. Connect a jump drive to a USB port, or put a spare memory card in a memory card slot. Launch the Password Reset Wizard by going to the Windows Start screen, pressing Windows + W, and typing **Password Reset** into the search field. Click the Create a Password Reset Disk item. Then follow these steps:

4

1. Read the first page of the wizard that opens and click Next.

2. Choose the drive letter that represents the jump drive or memory card; then click Next.

3. Type the password for the administrative account you're currently logged into and click Next.

4. When the progress indicator is finished, click Next and then click Finish.

Keep the drive or card in a safe place. If you use a jump drive that you also use for other purposes, make sure you don't erase the userkey.psw file. That's the file needed for password recovery.

Using the password reset disk

If you ever need to use the password reset disk to get into the administrative account, first start the computer and click the administrative account for which you created the password reset disk. Take a best guess at the password and press Enter.

If the password is rejected, insert the USB flash drive or memory card you created as a password reset disk. Wait a few seconds for Windows to recognize and register the item. Then click Reset Password under the password hint on the login screen.

Follow the instructions presented by the wizard that opens. You won't be required to remember the original password. Instead, you create an entirely new password and hint for the account. Use that new password whenever you log in to the account from that point on.

Running Programs as Administrator

Most newer programs work with UAC's privilege escalation on-the-fly. But sometimes a program won't work, especially with older programs. You can run many programs with administrative privileges by right-clicking its startup icon and choosing Run as Administrator, as in the example shown in Figure 4.22.

If the option to run the program as an administrator is not available, then one of the following is true:

• The program doesn't require administrative privileges to run.

• You're already logged into an administrative account.

• The program is always blocked from running with elevated privileges.

FIGURE 4.22

Run a program as administrator.

Add the Built-in Administrator Account to the Login Screen

The built-in Administrator account is intentionally hidden to discourage users who don't have sufficient knowledge to understand the risks involved in using such an account. Typically, the only way to get to it is by starting the computer in Safe Mode. If you're an advanced user and you want to be able to get to that account from the sign-on screen, you just have to enable the account. Here's how:

1. Log in to an account that has administrative privileges.

2. At the desktop, press Windows + X and click Computer Management.

3. In the left column of the Computer Management tool that opens, click Local Users and Groups.

4. In the center column, double-click the Users folder.

5. Right-click the Administrator account and choose Properties.

6. Clear the check mark beside Account Is Disabled and click OK.

7. Close the Computer Management window.

When you log out of your current account, you'll see the Administrator account on the sign-on screen. It will also appear there each time you start the computer.

Stop Entering Password on Lockout

If you leave the computer for a few minutes without logging out, you're taken to a lock screen that shows your user account information. If your user account is password protected, you need to enter your password to get back to the desktop. This prevents other people from using your account while you're away. But this makes sense only in a work environment. In a home environment, it may be overkill. You can reconfigure Windows 8.1 so that you don't have to reenter your password to get back to your desktop. Here are the steps:

1. At the desktop, press Windows + X and click Power Options.

2. In the left column, click Require a Password on Wakeup.

3. Click Change Settings That Are Currently Unavailable. Then elevate your privileges by clicking Continue or entering the password for an administrative account.

4. Choose Don't Require a Password.

5. Click Save Changes.

Advanced Security Tools

IT professionals and highly experienced users can also use Local Users and Groups and Local Security Policy consoles for more advanced security configuration. Detailed instructions on using these security configuration tools are beyond the scope of this book and not the kind of thing the average user wants to mess with. However, if you want to access the Local Users and Groups tools, at the desktop press Windows + X and click Computer Management. Then click Local Users and Groups in the left column.

To get to Local Security Policy, press Windows + X, click Search, type **local**, and click Local Security Policy. To find the new settings related to UAC, expand Local Policies in the left column and then click Security Options. The new UAC settings are at the bottom of the list in the content pane.

Using Credential Manager

Credential Manager (see Figure 4.23) enables you to manage your usernames and their associated passwords (collectively called *credentials*) for servers, websites, and programs. These credentials are stored in an electronic virtual vault. When you access a server, site, or program that requests a password, Credential Manager can submit the credentials for you so that you don't have to type them yourself. If your password cache has dozens of sets of credentials in it, you'll be more than happy to put Credential Manager to work for you.

FIGURE 4.23

Store usernames and passwords in Credential Manager.

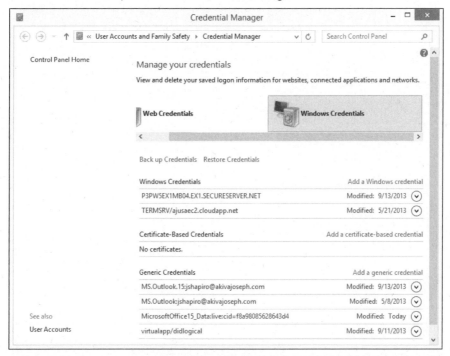

NOTE

Credential Manager can't interact with every website that requests credentials. For example, when you log in to your online banking site, the site probably displays a form in which you enter your credentials. Credential Manager can't store this type of form-based credential, but you can have Internet Explorer remember the credentials for you.

Although you can add credentials to your vault directly, you don't need to do so in most cases. Instead, you can let Windows do it for you. To do so, navigate to a server or other computer on your network, or to a web server that prompts you for credentials. Enter the username and password in the Windows Security dialog box, select Remember My Credentials, and click OK. Windows stores the credentials in Credential Manager.

You can add credentials to your vault directly if you want to. For example, if you have lots of credentials you use with multiple servers or sites, you might want to prepopulate your credential vault so that you don't have to wait to enter them until the next time you visit that resource.

To add credentials directly, open the User Accounts and Family Safety item in the Control Panel and then click Credential Manager. Click the Windows Credentials icon and then click Add a Windows Credential and in the resulting form (as shown in Figure 4.24), and enter the following:

FIGURE 4.24

Manually add a Windows credential.

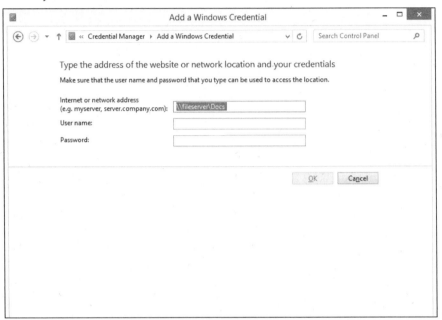

- **Internet or Network Address:** Type the path to the resource. For example, enter **fileserver\Docs** to specify the Docs share on a server on the network named fileserver. Or, you would enter **portal.mycompany.com** if your company intranet portal was located at `https://portal.mycompany.com`.

- **User Name:** Enter the username you want to use to log on to the specified service.

- **Password:** Enter the password associated with the username.

You can also add a certificate resource, which associates a network resource with a security certificate that is already installed in the Personal certificate store on your computer. In this case, verify that you've already installed the certificate, click Add a Certificate-Based Credential (see Figure 4.23), type the resource URL, and click Select Certificate to select the certificate.

The final type of credential you can add is a generic credential, which are credentials used by applications that perform authentication themselves instead of relying on Windows to perform the authentication. As with a Windows credential, you specify the URL, username, and password for a generic credential.

> **TIP**
> You can specify a port number in the resource path, if needed. For example, if an application is connecting to a SQL Server at `sql.mydomain.tld` on port 1433, you would specify `sql.mydomain.tld:1433` in the Internet or Network Address field in Credential Manager.

Managing Profile Properties and Environment Variables

From the earliest days of DOS, the PC operating system we old computer geeks used before Windows came along, *environment variables* have been used to store information used by the operating system. For example, the TMP and TEMP variables tell Windows where to store temporary files. The PATH variable tells Windows where to look for programs if it can't find them in the current directory. A number of other system and user variables serve similar purposes.

In most cases, you shouldn't need to change environment variables. But if you do — such as when adding a folder to the PATH variable — you can do so through your user account properties. Open the User Accounts object in the Control Panel and click Change My Environment Variables. In the Environment Variables dialog box (see Figure 4.25), click the user variable that you want to change, click Edit, modify as needed, and click OK. You can also click New and then add a new user environment variable.

FIGURE 4.25

The Environment Variables dialog box.

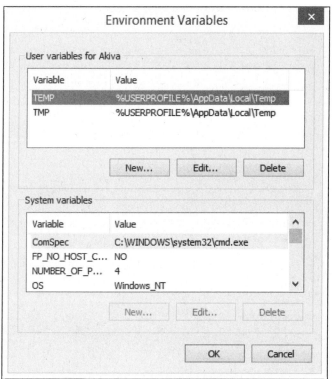

4

NOTE

Only the built-in Administrator account can modify the system environment variables.

Wrap-Up

When two or more people share a computer, user accounts enable each person to treat the computer as though it was his or her own. Users can personalize settings to their liking and keep their files separate from other users. Windows 8.1 Microsoft Accounts provide an account structure that enables multiple devices (Windows computer, Windows Phone, Windows tablets, and so on) to sync settings, apps, and other personalized items.

User accounts also work in conjunction with parental controls. A parent can set up a password-protected administrative account and then use that account to set up parental controls. You can create standard accounts for children and allow them to log in to their own accounts only.

 The parental controls in the Family Safety options are covered in Chapter 5.

User accounts also add security to your system by requiring all users to have limited privileges. The general term for security through user accounts is User Account Control (UAC). Some key points to keep in mind:

- At least one person should play the role of administrator for the computer. That person should create a password-protected user account with administrative privileges.

- The administrator should also create a standard account for himself or herself and one for each person who shares the computer.

- All users (including the administrator) should use their standard accounts for day-to-day computing.

- All accounts should have strong passwords.

- All the tools for creating and managing user accounts are accessible from User Accounts and Family Safety in the Control Panel.

Using Windows 8.1 Family Safety

IN THIS CHAPTER

Setting up Windows 8.1 Family Safety

Setting limits to computer usage, games, and apps

Controlling web browsing

Viewing activity reports

K eeping kids safe online isn't always easy for parents — especially for the parent who hasn't exactly been riding the crest of the tech wave in recent years. Parental safety controls are a great first step to keeping children safe online. You don't need to be a computer guru to set parental controls using the Microsoft Family Safety features of Windows 8.1. After you've set up standard user accounts for the children, the rest is fairly easy. In this chapter, you see just how easy it is to set up controls using the Windows 8.1 Family Safety tool and how to view reports and options online.

 For more on setting up user account for children, turn to Chapter 4.

Before You Get Started

To use the Family Safety features in Windows 8.1, your computer must be set up with at least one password-protected administrator user account. If you set up multiple user accounts with administrative privileges, make sure that they're all password protected. And make sure the kids don't know the password. Otherwise, the kids can easily go in and change any parental controls you import.

With Windows 8.1, each child is given his or her own child user account. Creating and configuring a child user account is easy to do. Here are the steps:

1. Log into Windows with a user account that has administrative privileges.

2. Open the Other Accounts page from PC Settings, Accounts as described in Chapter 4 in the "Creating and Managing User Accounts" section and Figure 4.11. Click Other accounts and then click Add an Account. At the bottom of the page, click the Add a Child's Account link. This will bring you to the first page to create your child's account.

3. On the first page decide if your child is going to use e-mail with the account. If an e-mail address is needed, enter the e-mail address in the address field, as shown in Figure 5.1 and click Next.

FIGURE 5.1

Add an e-mail address.

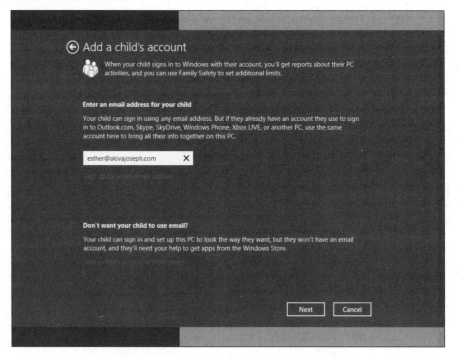

4. The page to enter personal details required for a Microsoft account appears as shown in Figure 5.2. This information is mandatory. Fill in the details and click Next.

5. The page to enter Security information appears. This information is also mandatory. Fill in the information for the account and click Next.

6. The next page that appears requests mandatory communication information. It's the same page as the one shown in Chapter 4 in Figure 4.14. Provide the information and click Next to view a summary of the information that will be used to create the account.

7. The final page that appears (shown in Figure 5.3), gives you the opportunity to create and add the child account and apply family monitoring to it. Click Finish to complete the process.

FIGURE 5.2

Enter personal details.

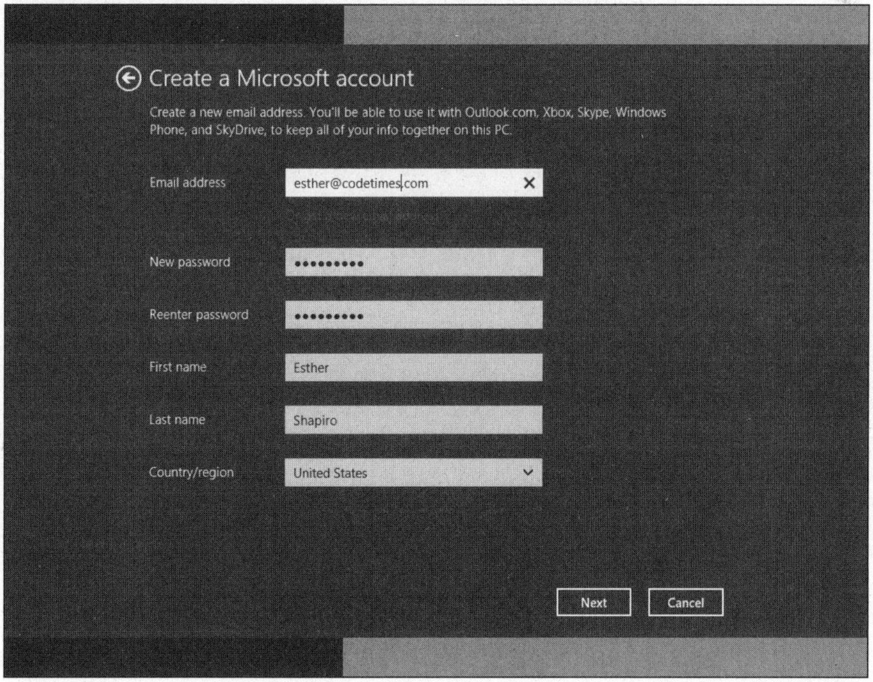

FIGURE 5.3

Click Finish to create the account.

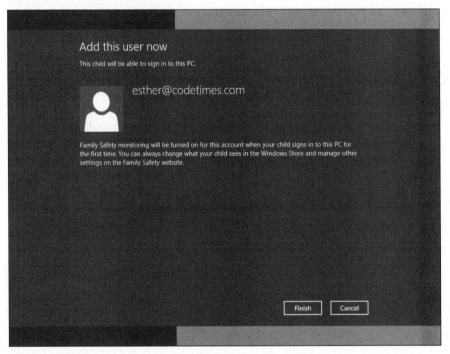

The child account is now added, as shown in Figure 5.4.

NOTE
You can change a child account back to a standard account at any time by clicking Edit on the page shown in Figure 5.4.

FIGURE 5.4

The account is now created as shown here.

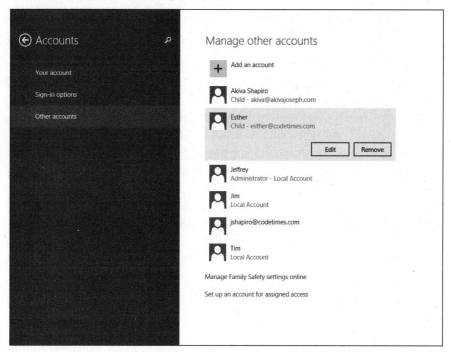

Setting Up Windows 8.1 Family Safety

With Family Safety, Windows 8.1 provides four options for controlling how your children (or anyone) can use the computer:

- **Windows Web Filters:** Specify the type of content that the child is allowed to view.
- **Time Limits:** Specify the hours during each day that the child can use the computer.
- **Windows Store and Game Restrictions:** Specify whether the child can access the Windows Store and if the child can play games on the computer. You can also set the rating and content types that are allowed.
- **App Restrictions:** Select which apps and programs the child can run.

Family Safety setting can be saved on the Microsoft Family Safety website or locally on the computer the child will actually use. The following section manages and stores the Family Safety data on the computer the child will use.

Getting to the Family Safety page

Fortunately, you don't need to be a computer guru to set up parental controls in Family Safety. After you've set up appropriate user accounts, the rest is easy. Here are the steps:

1. Log into Windows with a user account that has administrative privileges.

2. Do whichever of the following is most convenient for you at the moment:
   - At the Windows Start screen, press Windows + W. Type **fam** in the search box, click Settings, and click Family Safety.
   - At the Windows desktop, press Windows + X, and choose Control Panel, click User Accounts and Family Safety, and then click Family Safety.

3. A page appears that shows the name and picture for each user account you've created, as in the example in Figure 5.5. Click the Child user account for which you want to set up parental controls.

Now you're in the parental controls page shown in Figure 5.6. Any options you choose are applied to the account shown in the page. For example, in Figure 5.6, we're setting up Family Safety options for a user named Esther.

FIGURE 5.5

Click a Child user account to create parental controls.

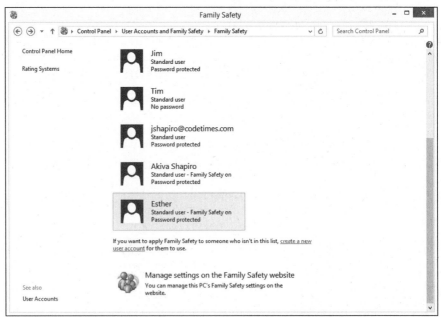

FIGURE 5.6

Setting up Family Safety options for a user.

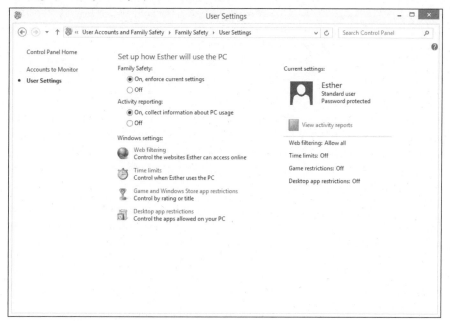

To activate Family Safety for the account, choose On, Enforce Current Settings under the Family Safety heading. After you turn on these parental controls, you can choose which controls to apply for the selected user.

Setting Web Filtering

To control which websites a child can view, click the Web Filtering link. You can allow or block access to specific websites, or specify that Windows should block web content automatically. Figure 5.7 shows the Web Filtering page. If you use the former feature, manually specify which sites can be visited (for example www.disney.com) and which are blocked (for example, sites that are suspected as being adult-related sites). If you use this feature, you can limit your child's web activity only to those sites you specify in the Allowed list. This provides you absolute control over the sites your child can view.

> **CAUTION**
>
> We need to point out that when you use Family Safety, your child's browsing history is maintained on a Microsoft website (http://familysafety.microsoft.com). This can be handy because you have access to the browsing history from any location, such as at work. However, it is a potential privacy risk. If you don't like the idea of your child's Internet usage history being stored on a public server, even if it's secured to prevent others from browsing the history, consider not using Windows 8.1's Family Safety feature. You also have the option of disabling the gathering of browsing history at the http://familysafety.microsoft.com page.

5

FIGURE 5.7

Use the Web Filtering page to set which websites a user can visit.

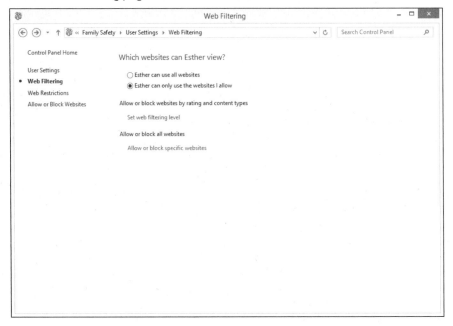

Click the option < *username* > Can Only Use the Websites I Allow to be able to set web fil-tering options. Click Set Web Filtering Level to choose the web restriction levels. The Web Restrictions page (shown in Figure 5.8) opens. On this page, you can select the Allow List Only option, which enables you to specify a list of sites that a user can access. All other sites on the web, including suspected adult sites, are blocked.

The other options on the Web Restrictions page relate to content areas that Family Safety monitors automatically. If you choose to let Windows block web content automatically, you have the following categories from which to choose:

- **Allow List Only:** Allows all websites that are in the list. All other sites are blocked. This is the most secure option because it allows you to explicitly include only the websites that you have cleared for access.
- **Designed for Children:** Blocks suspected adult-related websites. Allows your child to view sites on the Allow list and in this category. When your child visits popular search engines — such as Google, Bing, and Yahoo! — the SafeSearch setting is automatically enabled, limiting the types of search results your child will see and blocking adult images.
- **General Interest:** Blocks suspected adult-related websites. Allows your child to view child-friendly sites, general interest sites, and those specified on the Allow list. When your child visits popular search engines — such as Google, Bing,

and Yahoo! — the SafeSearch setting is automatically enabled, limiting the types of search results your child will see and blocking adult images.

- **Online Communication:** Blocks suspected adult-related websites. Allows your child to view child-friendly sites, general interest sites, social media sites, web chat, web mail, and those specified on the Allow list. When your child visits popular search engines — such as Google, Bing, and Yahoo! — the SafeSearch setting is automatically enabled, limiting the types of search results your child will see and blocking suspected adult images.

- **Warn on Adult:** Does not block suspected adult-related websites, but does display a warning if the site contains adult-related material. All other sites are available. When your child visits popular search engines — such as Google, Bing, and Yahoo! — the SafeSearch setting is automatically enabled, limiting the types of search results your child will see and blocking adult images.

- **Block File Downloads:** This check box prevents files from being downloaded by the user to the PC, intentional and unintentional.

To edit the Allow List Only option, click Allow List Only and then click the Click Here to Change Allow List link. The Allow or Block Websites page appears. Figure 5.9 shows an example of this page, with some sample websites listed in the Allowed Websites and Blocked Websites lists. On the Allow or Block Websites page, enter the web address of a site you want to block or allow. Click the appropriate button — Allow or Block — for the site you enter. The site will appear in the Allowed Websites or Blocked Websites list.

FIGURE 5.8

Use the Web Restrictions page to specify a web restriction level.

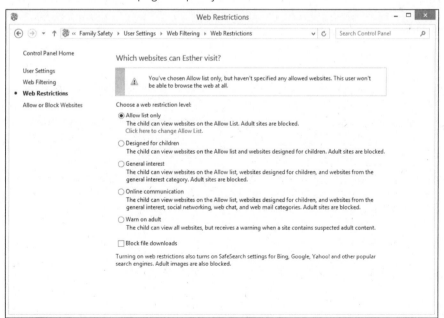

FIGURE 5.9

Enter the sites you want to specifically allow and/or specifically block.

Click the back button at the top right of the window when you finish. This returns you to the Web Restrictions page.

Click the User Settings breadcrumb on the address bar to return to the User Settings page when you're finished setting Web Restrictions.

Setting time limits

To specify times when the child is allowed to use the computer, click Time Limits on the User Settings page (refer to Figure 5.6 to see what the User Settings page looks like). The Time Limits page (shown in Figure 5.10) opens. This page has the following two options:

- **Set Time Allowance:** Enables you to specify if a user can use the computer all day, or only for a specified number of hours and/or minutes per day. For example, you might allow your child to use the computer one hour a day on weekdays, but then allow her three hours a day on weekends.

- **Set Curfew:** Enables you to specify times during the day when your child can use the computer.

FIGURE 5.10

The Time Limits page.

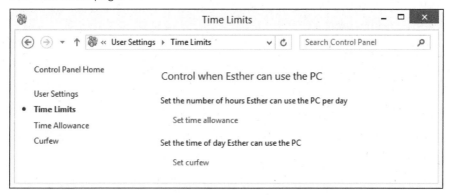

Use the Following steps to set a time allowance for a user:

1. Click the Set Time Allowance link to view the Time Allowance page.

2. Click the *< username >* Can Only Use the PC for the Amount of Time I Allow link (Figure 5.11 shows an example of weekday and weekend time limits).

FIGURE 5.11

The Time Allowance page.

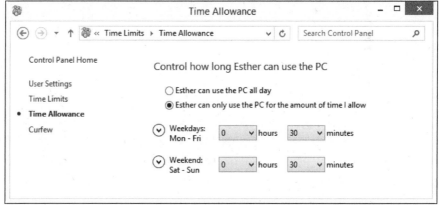

3. To set the same time amount for every weekday, use the Hours and Minutes drop-down lists to the right of the Weekdays: Mon–Fri label to indicate how many hours and minutes to allow this user to use the computer. Do the same for the Weekend Sat–Sun setting.

4. If you want to specify different time limits for each day, however, click the down arrow to the left of the Weekdays: Mon–Fri label or Weekend: Sat–Sun label. You are shown options for each day of the weekday and weekend.

5. Click the back button at the top left of the page when you finish.

Another way to regulate user access on a computer is to specify the actual time of day a user can be on the computer. Family Safety provides the Set Curfew option to control time-of-day access. Click Set Curfew on the Time Limits page to set a computer curfew.

In Figure 5.12, you can see the Curfew page. On this page, you see a grid of days and times. Initially, all squares are white, meaning there are no time restrictions. You can click any time slot for which the child isn't allowed to use the computer to turn it blue. Blue indicates that the time is blocked and the specified user (in our example, Esther) is not allowed to be on the computer during that time. You also can drag the mouse pointer through a longer stretch of time to block more time.

Optionally, you can place the mouse pointer in the upper-left corner of the grid and drag down to the lower-right corner to block all times. Then drag the mouse pointer through the times that the child is allowed to use the computer. For example, in Figure 5.13, the user is allowed to use the computer from 10:00 a.m. to 7:00 p.m. on Sunday; 3:00 p.m. to 7:00 p.m. on Monday, Tuesday, Wednesday, and Thursday; 3:00 p.m. to 9:00 p.m. on Friday; and 10:00 a.m. to 9:00 p.m. on Saturday.

FIGURE 5.12

The Curfew page.

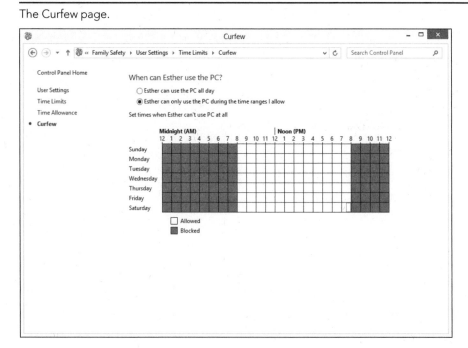

FIGURE 5.13

White squares indicate when your child is allowed to use the computer.

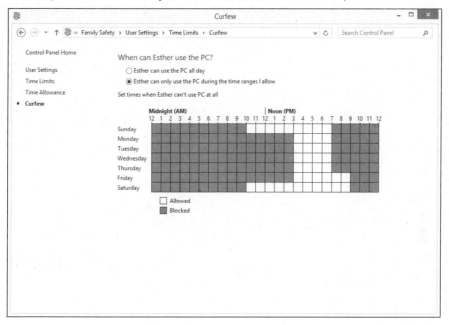

Click the back button after setting allowable times. You can change those settings at any time by clicking Time Limits. For example, if the child needs a "time out" from the computer, you can block out all the times so that the child can't use the computer at all!

Controlling Windows Store and game play

Family Safety enables you to control access to the Windows Store and to downloading and/or playing games on a computer.

To control access to the Windows Store and to the type of apps that can be downloaded, return to the User Settings page and click the Game and Windows Store Restrictions link. Click the *< username >* Can Only Use Games and Windows Store Apps I Allow option. Figure 5.14 shows the Game and Windows Store Restrictions page after selecting that option.

5

FIGURE 5.14

The Game and Windows Store Restrictions page.

To allow or block games and Windows apps that can be downloaded by the selected user, follow these steps:

1. Click Set Game and Windows Store Ratings. The Rating Level page appears, as shown in Figure 5.15.

2. To specify the ratings that are okay for the user, click one or more of the ratings (such as Early Childhood, Everyone, and so on) that you want to allow the user to access. As you select a rating, a blue box appears around the rating name and description. To unselect a rating, click it again. Notice that as you go down the list of ratings and select a rating, all ratings above it are selected as well. That is, you cannot select a rating lower on the list, such as Teen, without also automatically selecting a rating higher on the list, such as Early Childhood.

3. Click the back button when you finish selecting the games and apps ratings you want to allow.

To control the child's game play, return to the Game and Windows Store Restrictions page and click Allow or Block Specific Games. Doing so opens a page for controlling if your child is allowed to play games on this computer. If you don't want the child to use the computer for game play at all, choose No; otherwise, choose Yes.

> **NOTE**
> ESRB stands for Entertainment Software Rating Board, an independent third party that rates games for age appropriateness and specific content. The ratings are similar to movie ratings, but specific to computer games. To find out more about the ESRB rating system, click the ESRB logo on the Rating Level page. Windows connects you to the Entertainment Software Rating Board website, which provides information about ESRB.

FIGURE 5.15

The Rating Level page.

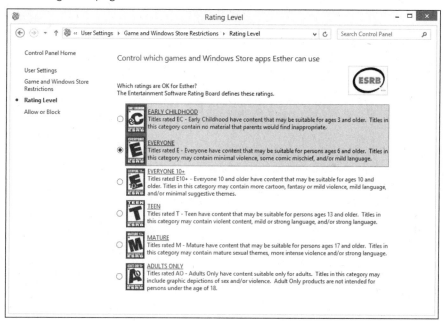

If you want to allow or block games that are installed on your computer, click the Allow or Block Specific Games link on the Game and Windows Store Restrictions page. The Allow or Block Games page appears. Then you can scroll down the page and block more games based on content type. To block games based on content, select the type of content you want to block. When you get to the bottom of the list and have blocked all the content that you feel is inappropriate, click the back button.

Blocking and allowing Apps

With Family Safety, you can control the apps and programs that a user can run on the computer. Clicking Desktop App Restrictions on the User Settings page displays the App Restrictions page. By default, all users have access to run all apps. To limit the apps that a user can run, click the < *username* > Can Only Use the Apps I Allow link. When you do this, as shown in Figure 5.16, a message appears that indicates that the selected user can run only the apps and programs needed by Windows. Also, after a few moments, a list of apps and programs appear at the bottom of the page, which shows all installed apps and programs.

You use the list of apps to specify which apps are allowed by the selected user. Select the apps that you deem OK for the user to use. After you select the first app, notice that the warning called This Person Can Only Run Apps Needed by Windows disappears.

FIGURE 5.16

The App Restrictions page.

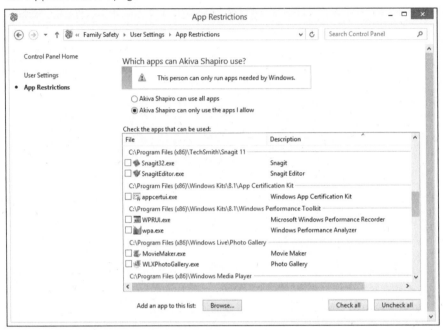

If you don't see an app or program that you know is installed on your computer, click the Browse button next to Add an App to This List. You then can navigate to the app or program file (programs usually are .exe files), select it, and click Open. That app or program will be listed in the Check the Apps That Can Be Used list.

> **TIP**
>
> If you want to allow a user to use all apps and programs but a few, consider clicking the Check All button. This selects all the apps and programs in the Check the Apps That Can Be Used list. Then find the individual apps or programs you want to restrict access to and click its check box to deselect it. Continue this until your list appears the way you want it to.

When you finish with the App Restrictions page, click the back button to return to the User Settings page.

Viewing Family Safety Activity Reports

Windows 8.1's Family Safety tool provides user activity reports. User activity reports provide a summary of user activity as it relates to Family Safety settings, including the following items:

- Most Popular Websites
- Latest Blocked Page
- PC Time Used
- Most Used Apps and Games

To see this report, click the View Activity Reports on the User Settings page.

Viewing Family Safety Online Reports

A feature available with the Windows 8.1 Family Safety tool is access to an online Family Safety website. This website includes additional reports about Family Safety settings and allows you to modify Family Safety settings. To access the Family Safety online site, follow these steps:

1. Click the Manage Settings on the Family Safety website link on the main Family Safety page. Internet Explorer launches.

2. If prompted, enter your Windows Live sign-in credentials, which you need to have to use the online Family Safety features. If you don't have a Windows Live account, click the Sign Up button on the left side of the screen and follow the onscreen instructions. If you logged into Windows 8.1 using a Microsoft account, you can use those credentials as your Windows Live username and password.

3. Once at the Activity Reporting website, use the links on the left side of the page to view Family Safety activities and features. Most of these links mirror those found on the Family Safety pages that we already covered. However, if you click the Request link, you see those pages that a user has requested to view. Click one of the links to visit that site and to determine if you want to unblock its access.

4. Select an option from the Response drop-down list, such as Allow for This Account Only, to specify the type of access you want to give, if any.

5. Click Save to save any changes to settings you might make.

The changes you make online will copy down to your local version of Family Safety. The next time you open the User Settings page for a user, your online changes should be reflected.

You can view these online reports and options for any user at any time as long as you have Internet access. This comes in handy if you're away from your home computer and you want to view your child's online activity and see if any requested sites have been added to the Requests page.

When you sign onto Family Safety online, Microsoft starts sending you e-mails with tips, additional information about Family Safety, and a link to the Family Safety website. You can opt out of these e-mails by clicking the Change Email Frequency link on the top of the Microsoft Family Safety e-mail. This connects you to the Family Safety website, on which you can change the frequency in the Email Notifications area. You might want to keep these notifications turned on until you become more familiar with Family Safety.

5

Other Online Safety Resources

Technical approaches to online safety, such as parental controls, are a good thing. But they can't cover all possible risks. Kids can get involved with instant messaging and chats in which people aren't always who they claim to be.

Children should be taught some basic ground rules. For example, children should never give out personal information, such as where they live or go to school. If anything makes them feel uncomfortable, they should report it to their parents. They should never agree to meet with anyone you don't know.

As a parent, you have many online resources for sharing your concerns with others and getting advice. You don't need to be a technical whiz to take advantage of these sites. Here are some you might want to add to your Favorites:

- **CyberAngels:** www.cyberangels.org
- **GetNetWise:** www.kids.getnetwise.org
- **Microsoft Safety & Security Center:** www.microsoft.com/security/family-safety/childsafety-internet.aspx
- **SafeKids.com:** www.safekids.com

Wrap-Up

The Internet is here to stay. Today's children will likely use it as their main source of information and communication throughout their lives. The Internet is also very much a public place, a direct reflection of the world at large. Although most people online are perfectly normal, the Internet has its share of wackos, just as the real world does.

Knowledge is a parent's best defense against Internet dangers. A parent who has been out of the loop in terms of technical advances over recent years will feel some helplessness and insecurity about keeping kids safe online. Setting up user accounts and parental controls is a great way to get started in taking control of kids' computer use. Monitoring their activity is another. Here's a quick wrap-up of the main points covered in this chapter:

- A parent should set up at least one password-protected administrative user account to take control of the computer.
- Each person who uses the computer can have a standard account, which offers greater security than an administrative account.
- The person with the administrative account can use parental control features of Microsoft Family Safety to set limits on Internet and computer usage for people using standard accounts.
- The administrator can also use activity reports to monitor standard users' activities.
- Parents can find support and stay up-to-date through many websites dedicated to online safety.

Troubleshooting Startup Problems

IN THIS CHAPTER

The computer won't start

The computer takes too long to start

Resources for troubleshooting startup problems

When programs won't start

E ach major part in this book ends with a troubleshooting chapter like this one. The trouble-shooting chapters provide quick solutions to common problems. That's about it. You won't catch us yammering on for paragraph after paragraph in these troubleshooting chapters!

The Computer Won't Start

If the computer does absolutely nothing when you first turn it on, your first move is to check all cable connections. Make sure the power plug on every device that plugs into the wall is firmly plugged in. Also, make sure the mouse, keyboard, and all other devices are firmly plugged into their slots.

If it's a desktop computer, look for a 0/1 power switch on the back of the computer and make sure it's on (flipped to the 1 position).

If it's a laptop computer or tablet device, make sure your battery is connected correctly. You might also ensure that the AC adapter is plugged in on your device.

Turn on the computer again and, as it is powering up, push the button on the CD or DVD drive. If there is a disk in the drive, remove it.

If the computer sounds as though it's starting up but you don't see anything on the screen, make sure all plugs to the monitor are firmly seated. If it's a desktop computer, make sure the monitor's power cable is firmly attached to the monitor and wall socket, and that the cable connecting the computer to the monitor is firmly attached at both ends of the cable. Make sure the monitor is turned on. Then restart the computer.

Non-system disk or disk error message

This type of message appears when the computer attempts to boot from a disk on which Windows is not installed. If a floppy disk is in the floppy drive (there are still computers that have floppy disk drives), remove it. Likewise for any disk in the CD drive or DVD drive, or any drive that's connected to the computer through a USB port. Press any key to continue startup. If that doesn't work, press Ctrl + Alt + Del or restart the computer with the main on/off switch.

Computer starts but mouse and keyboard don't work

If the computer starts but doesn't respond to the mouse and keyboard, turn off the computer. Unplug both the mouse and keyboard from the computer. For USB mice and keyboards, unplug each and re-connect them. Ensure each USB connection is tight and secure. If the plug is round and green, make sure you plug it into the PS/2 port for the mouse (usually colored green). Make sure nothing is resting on the keyboard and holding down a key. Then firmly plug in the keyboard. If the plug is round and purple, plug it into the PS/2 port for the keyboard. Check *all* cable connections to the computer one more time. Then restart the computer.

Screen turns blue during startup and then stops

This is commonly referred to as the "blue screen of death." It doesn't mean your computer is permanently broken. A frequent cause of this problem is a device driver for a hardware device that doesn't work with Windows 8. If you recently connected or installed a new hardware device, disconnect or uninstall it. Then start the computer again. That's your best bet.

If you still get the blue screen of death, you'll likely have to boot to Safe Mode and disable the device through Device Manager. This is not the sort of thing the average user normally does. This is more the kind of thing that a professional handles. But if you want to take a shot at fixing it yourself, see this chapter and Chapter 37.

If the error persists, look for an error number on the blue screen of death page. It will most likely start with the characters 0x. Jot down that number on a sheet of paper. Then, if you can get online through another computer, go to Microsoft's site (http://search. microsoft.com) or your favorite online search engine (such as Google or Bing) and search for that number. You might find a page that offers an exact solution to your problem.

If you can get online through another computer, you might also consider posting a question at the Windows Communities site (http://answers.microsoft.com/en-us/windows). Be sure to include the error number in your post. You might find someone who has already experienced and solved that very problem.

Computer Takes Too Long to Start

On most systems, Windows 8 is optimized to decrease boot time from many seconds (or minutes) to just a handful of seconds. For example, a laptop might take approximately 35 seconds to boot to Windows 7. With Windows 8, the boot time is only about 8 seconds. You may or may not see that large of a decrease in wait time, but you should pay attention if the boot time takes longer and longer each time you start your computer.

When the computer takes much longer to start than it used to, the problem is usually caused by too many programs trying to auto-start. Consider uninstalling any programs you don't really use, as discussed in Chapter 30. Configure the remaining programs so that they don't start automatically (see Chapter 13).

Many things that prevent a computer from starting have nothing to do with Windows 8. It often takes even seasoned pros many hours to diagnose and repair startup problems. But before you resort to the repair shop, here are some other things you can try.

Restore system files to an earlier time

The Windows 8 Advanced Startup options (described later, in the "Advanced Startup" section) include a System Restore item that enables you to restore your system to a previous state. Windows 8.1 creates restore points automatically, and you can also create a restore point any time you want using the Recovery item in the Control Panel. To recover your system to a previous state, boot using the Advanced Startup options as explained later in this chapter, and then choose System Restore from the Advanced Options screen. Follow the prompts to choose a restore point from which to restore.

Open the Control Panel, open the Restore item, and click Open System Restore.

If you can get the computer to start in Safe Mode, you can also use System Restore to restore your PC. Boot to Safe Mode and then open the Control Panel. Then use the Restore item to choose a restore point and start the restore process.

Windows 8.1 Automatic Repair Mode

If Windows 8.1 automatically detects an issue with your startup, you see a light blue window (not the blue screen of death) that says "Automatic Repair." This is the Windows 8 Automatic Repair Mode. The screen informs you that Windows could not start properly and that a System Restore point can be used to attempt to repair the issue.

 Chapter 24 discusses the System Restore process and how you should consider keeping this feature activated for situations like the one you're experiencing.

System Restore turns back the clock to a previous setup when Windows was working correctly. During the System Restore process, you don't lose any personal data that you added to the system. Instead, programs and apps that were installed after the latest System Restore point and time are uninstalled from your computer. The assumption is that a program or app may have damaged your computer to the point that it won't boot. By removing the programs and apps, Windows may be able to start properly.

If you decide to choose to restore, the process cannot be undone. You have the option of canceling, but you must do it from this initial screen; don't try to cancel after you start the restore process. If you decide to cancel, click the Cancel button now.

To continue, click the Restore button and work through the onscreen prompts.

Repair Windows 8 Install

If you have the DVD with Windows 8.1 on it, you can boot from that disk and do a repair installation. Put that disk in the DVD drive and start the computer. Watch the screen for the message "Press Any Key to Boot from CD or DVD" (or a similar message); then press Enter or the Spacebar.

If the option to boot from the CD or DVD never appears, and the computer won't boot from that disk, you need to change your BIOS options to boot from the CD/DVD drive. How you do that varies from one computer to the next. Typically, you start the computer and then immediately start pressing the F1, F2, or Del key (perhaps all three, if you don't know which is required) repeatedly as the computer is starting. This should take you to the BIOS Setup options where you can configure the computer to try booting from the CD/DVD before it tries booting from the hard drive. Close and save the new settings. The computer will restart, and this time you should be able to boot from the Windows DVD.

If you're able to boot from the DVD, the first screen you see will likely ask about your language and locale. Make any necessary changes and click Next. On the next page, click Repair Your Computer (not the Install Now option). Then just follow the onscreen instructions to do a repair install of Windows 8.1.

Advanced startup

If you can boot into Windows 8.1, but you're having issues with the boot process, consider using Windows 8.1's Advanced Startup tool. This tool does assume you can boot into Windows and navigate to the PC Settings area.

To use this tool, perform the following steps:

1. Display the Charms Bar and choose Settings.
2. Click Change PC Settings.
3. Click the Update and Recovery item.
4. Click Recovery, and then click Restart Now in the Advanced Startup group, as shown in Figure 6.1.
5. After Windows 8.1 restarts, it displays a screen similar to the one in Figure 6.2.
6. Click Troubleshoot.

7. Click one of three options (see Figure 6.3) and work through the onscreen prompts:

   - **Refresh Your PC:** Use this option to refresh your copy of Windows but not to destroy any of your files. This is similar to the Automatic Repair Mode discussed previously in this chapter. This is a good option because you don't lose your file and you get a "fresh" version of Windows.

   - **Reset Your PC:** Use this option to completely remove all files (including files you've created) and to reinstall Windows 8. This will destroy all files you have created or saved to the computer.

CAUTION

You should *not* use this option until you've made a backup of your critical files and you should use it only as a last resort — when all other troubleshooting tasks fail.

   - **Advanced Options:** Provides additional tools for fixing startup problems.

FIGURE 6.1

Advanced startup option in the Update and Recovery settings.

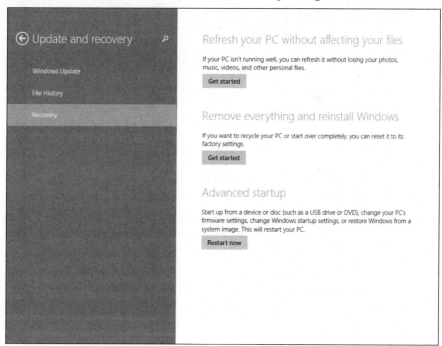

FIGURE 6.2

Troubleshoot startup problems.

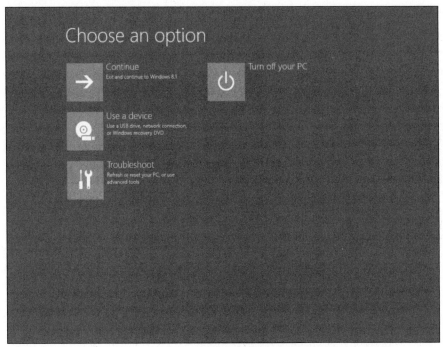

Start in Safe Mode

For many experienced Windows users who have dealt with faulty Windows startups, Safe Mode has become a close friend. Safe Mode offers a way to start Windows in a barebones setup. That is, Windows starts with just enough system files, programs, and services to allow it to run so you can diagnose issues, remove programs, and perform other tasks that can be done only at the graphical user interface level.

To enter Safe Mode in Windows 8, access the Advanced Startup options as described in the previous section. Click Troubleshoot, click Advanced Options, and click Startup Settings. On the resulting page, click Restart.

Figure 6.4 shows the options you can choose to start Windows and to diagnose and/or repair Windows from the resulting menu. Figure 6.5 shows the Safe Mode Windows desktop. Although this looks like a normal version of Windows, many programs and features do not work. It is simply a place where you can modify system settings, such as those for Device Manager, MSCONFIG, the Windows Registry, Control Panel applets, and the like. You cannot, for example, start some Windows 8 apps or other programs.

After you finish repairing Windows, shut down Safe Mode and restart normally.

FIGURE 6.3

Advanced options for troubleshooting startup problems.

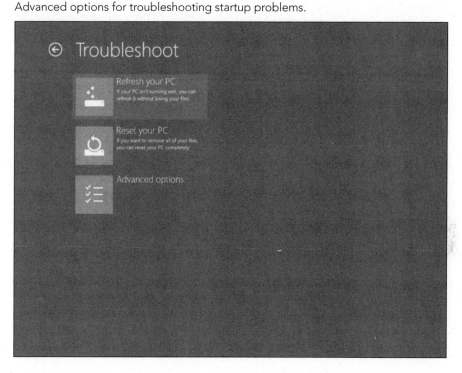

Another way to boot into Safe Mode is to set Windows to do it automatically. To do this, press Windows + X and choose Run. Type **MSCONFIG** in the Open dialog box and click OK. The System Configuration dialog box appears (see Figure 6.6).

Select the Boot tab and click the Safe Boot option. Click Apply and then OK. You're prompted with a dialog box that has Restart or Exit without Restart buttons. Click Restart so that Windows reboots. When it restarts, you're in Safe Mode, as shown in Figure 6.5. Use Safe Mode to diagnose or repair Windows.

When you want to leave Safe Mode, you need to undo the Safe Boot option in the System Configuration tool. To do that, press Windows + X, choose Run, and enter **MSCONFIG**. On the Boot tab of the System Configuration dialog box, clear the Safe Boot option and click Apply; then OK. Click Restart to shut down and restart Windows into its normal view.

The instruction manual that came with your computer

Most computer manufacturers provide some means of helping you troubleshoot and repair startup problems. Be sure to look through whatever documentation you have for your computer manufacturer's recommendations. That could be your best bet because all computers are unique in some ways. The manual that came with your computer provides information that's specific to your exact make and model of computer.

FIGURE 6.4

Windows 8.1 boot options.

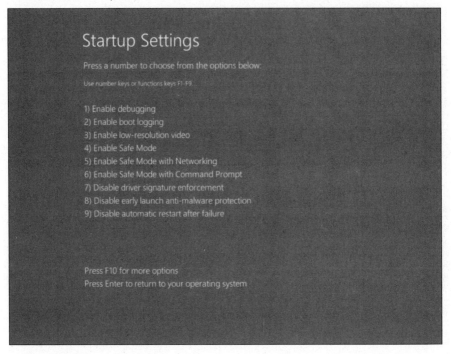

Resources in this book

We've thrown a lot of technical terms and concepts at you in this chapter. But when it comes to solving startup problems, there's no way around that. Here are some additional resources within this book that might help you solve a startup problem:

- **Restoring from previous file versions:** If you've backed up your entire hard disk using File History, see Chapter 24 for information on restoring from that backup.

- **Restoring to an earlier time:** For information on restoring your computer to an earlier time, see "Using System Protection" in Chapter 24.

- **Removing programs:** If you think a faulty program might be preventing your computer from starting, you can uninstall the program using techniques described in Chapter 30 (assuming that you can get to Safe Mode so that you have access to that program).

- **Removing hardware:** When faulty hardware or drivers are preventing Windows 8 from starting, techniques described under "Removing Hardware" in Chapter 34 might help.

- **Troubleshooting hardware:** Startup problems are often hardware problems. See Chapter 37 for more information on troubleshooting hardware.

FIGURE 6.5

Windows 8.1 Safe Mode desktop view.

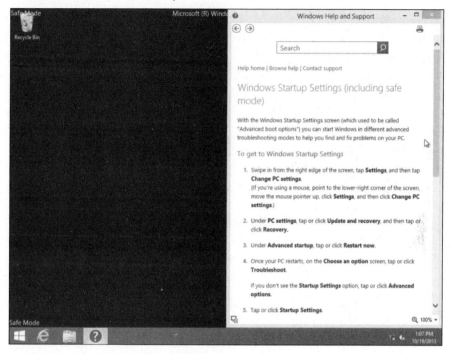

Resources in Windows Help

If you can start the computer in Safe Mode, you can get to Windows Help, too. In fact, the Help window should open automatically as soon as you enter Safe Mode. If it doesn't, click the Start button and choose Help and Support. Then search using the keywords "Safe Mode" for additional information on using Safe Mode to troubleshoot startup options.

Online resources

If you can start in Safe Mode with Networking, you can access online resources. You might try searching Windows Communities (which you can get to from Windows Help) for words related to the startup problem you're having, or you can post a question describing the problem in as much detail as possible.

You can also search Microsoft's website for words that describe the problem you're having. Be sure to include the number 8 in your search. Otherwise, the search result will likely include other irrelevant Microsoft products. Starting your search from `http://search.microsoft.com` or `http://support.microsoft.com` will help limit the search to Microsoft, rather than include the entire web. If that doesn't help, you can try searching the entire web from `www.bing.com`, `www.google.com`, or whatever search engine you prefer. If you're not a technical person, don't expect it to be easy. As we said, startup problems can be difficult to troubleshoot, even for the pros. If all else fails, you may have to take the system to a repair shop to get the problem resolved. Or call a mobile service that will send a computer geek to your home or office.

FIGURE 6.6

Windows 8 Safe boot options in the System Configuration tool.

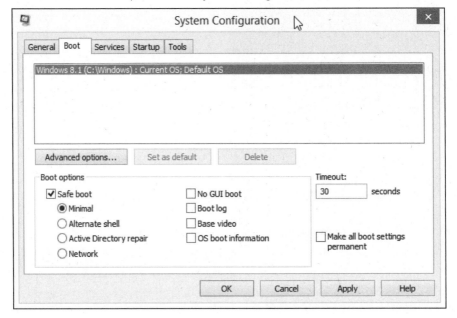

Programs Won't Start

If a favorite old program won't start, it's most likely an incompatibility issue. Try right-clicking the startup icon for the program and choosing Run as Administrator. If that doesn't help, try the program compatibility features.

 See Chapter 29 for more information on getting older programs to run with Windows 8.1.

Wrap-Up

This chapter discussed ways to troubleshoot your computer when you're experiencing problems. Some fixes to problems are easy, while others may require you to reinstall Windows 8.1. If the steps and methods described in this chapter don't help, refer to the other chapters described above for tips on additional troubleshooting steps you can take.

Part II

Personalizing Windows 8.1

IN THIS PART

Protecting Yourself with Windows Firewall

I f you use the Internet, a firewall is a must-have security tool. It's not the only tool you need, but it's an important one. It protects your computer from hackers and worms. Hackers are people who would attempt to access your computer through the Internet without your knowing it. Worms are programs, such as viruses, that are usually written to do intentional harm.

Windows 8.1 comes with its own built-in firewall. If you didn't know about it before going online, relax. It's enabled by default. So, most likely, it's been protecting you since the very first moment you went online. (Plus, your Internet service provider protects you from most invasions.) In this chapter, you learn how the firewall works and how to configure it for maximum protection.

How Firewalls Work

To understand what a firewall is, you need to first understand what a network connection is. Even though you have only one skinny set of wires connecting your computer to the Internet (through a DSL phone line or cable outlet), that connection actually consists of 65,535 ports. Each port can simultaneously carry on its own conversation with the outside world. So, theoretically, you could have 65,535 things going on at a time. Of course, nobody ever has that much going on all at one time. A handful of ports is more like it.

The ports are divided into two categories:

- **TCP (Transmission Control Protocol):** This is generally used to send text and pictures (web pages and e-mail), and includes some error checking to make sure all the information that's received by a computer matches what the sending computer sent.

- **UDP (User Datagram Protocol):** This works more like broadcast TV or radio, where the information is just sent out and there is no error checking. UDP is generally used for real-time communications, such as voice conversations and radio broadcasts sent over the Internet.

Each port has two directions: incoming (or *ingress*) and outgoing (or *egress*). The direction is in relation to stuff coming into your computer from the outside — namely, the Internet. It's the stuff coming into your computer that you have to watch out for. But you can't close all ports to all incoming traffic. If you did, there'd be no way to get the good stuff in. But you don't want to let everything in, either. You need a way to separate the wheat from the chaff, so to speak.

Anti-spyware and antivirus software are good tools for keeping out viruses and other bad things that are attached to files coming into your computer. But hackers can actually sneak worms and other bad things in through unprotected ports without involving a file in the process. That's where the firewall comes into play. A *stateful* firewall, such as the one that comes with Windows 8.1, keeps track of everything you request. When traffic from the Internet wants to come in through a port, the firewall checks to make sure the traffic is something you requested. If it isn't, the firewall assumes this is a hacker trying to sneak something in without your knowing it and, therefore, prevents the traffic from entering your computer. Figure 7.1 illustrates how it works.

FIGURE 7.1

A stateful firewall.

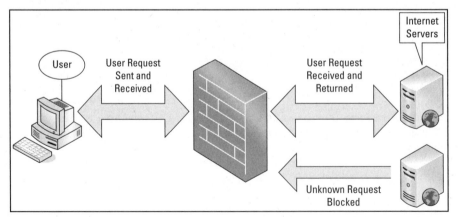

What a Firewall Doesn't Protect Against

It's important to understand that a firewall alone is not sufficient protection against all Internet threats. A firewall is just one component in a larger defense system. Specifically:

- Windows Firewall *doesn't* protect you from spyware and viruses.
- Windows Firewall **doesn't** protect you from attacks based on exploits. Automatic updates (see Chapter 8) provide that protection.
- A firewall *doesn't* protect you from pop-up ads.
- A firewall *doesn't* protect you from phishing scams.
- Windows Firewall *doesn't* protect you from spam (junk e-mail).

So, a firewall isn't a complete solution. Rather, it's an important component of a larger security strategy.

So, there's really more to it than just having a port open or closed. It's also about *filtering* — making sure that data coming into an open port is something you requested and not some rogue, uninvited traffic sent by some hacker. Many of the worms that infected so many computers in the 1990s did so by sneaking in undetected through unfiltered ports. These days, you really want to make sure you have a firewall up whenever you go online to prevent such things.

> **NOTE**
>
> Note that in the preceding list, we indicated that Windows Firewall doesn't provide certain types of protection, such as spam or virus blocking. Many hardware firewalls *do* provide this type of protection. This is sometimes referred to as *perimeter protection* because it protects your network from threats at the perimeter of your network. These types of firewalls can cost from several hundred to several thousands of dollars, so they aren't always the best bet for a home network. They can be extremely valuable, however, for business networks.

Introducing Action Center

Before you explore Windows Firewall, take a look at the Action Center. This is a single point of notification for most of your PC's security. You can open the Action Center in several ways. Use whichever is most convenient for you:

- From the Windows Start screen, show the Charms Bar and click Search Control Panel. Click Control Panel, click System and Security, and then click Action Center.
- On the desktop, right-click the flag icon in the notification area and choose Open Action Center.
- On the desktop, press Windows + X, choose Control Panel, click System and Security, and then click Action Center.

Whichever method you use, the Action Center opens. Figure 7.2 shows an example. We clicked the arrow button to the right of each heading so that you can see the descriptive text under each heading. You can click that button to show or hide the same descriptive text.

FIGURE 7.2

Action Center.

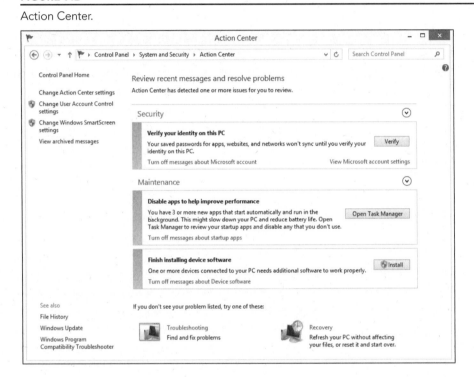

How you know Windows Firewall is on

By default, Windows Firewall is turned on and working at all times, so your Action Center should show "On" beside the Firewall item, as in Figure 7.2 (and you see only the Network Firewall item in Action Center if you click the arrow beside the Security heading). If your version of Figure 7.2 shows Off or Not Monitored, you may have a third-party firewall program running in place of Windows Firewall. Many such programs are available, such as McAfee, Symantec, and Check Point. If your firewall is turned off and you don't know why, it would be good to find out the reason — perhaps from your computer manufacturer or a support person who worked on your computer. If you don't have any firewall up, you should definitely turn on Windows Firewall.

> **NOTE**
> There is no advantage to having two or more firewalls running simultaneously. In fact, more than one firewall is likely to cause unnecessary problems.

Turning Windows Firewall on or off

To turn Windows Firewall on or off, you must have administrative privileges. In the System and Security Control Panel window, click Windows Firewall. You should see the current firewall status in the right pane, and options for controlling the firewall in the left pane. Click Change Notification Settings or Turn Windows Firewall On or Off in the left pane to see the options shown in the foreground of Figure 7.3.

> **TIP**
>
> Use the Block All Incoming Connections check box only to temporarily disable exceptions when connecting to public Wi-Fi networks. You can find more on that topic in the sections that follow.

If you have a third-party firewall that you feel is more secure than the Windows Firewall, you can choose the Off option to turn off Windows Firewall. Just make sure you have a firewall up when you go online. Otherwise, you won't have anything to stop uninvited traffic on your network connection after the traffic gets by your Internet service provider.

7

FIGURE 7.3

Settings for Windows Firewall.

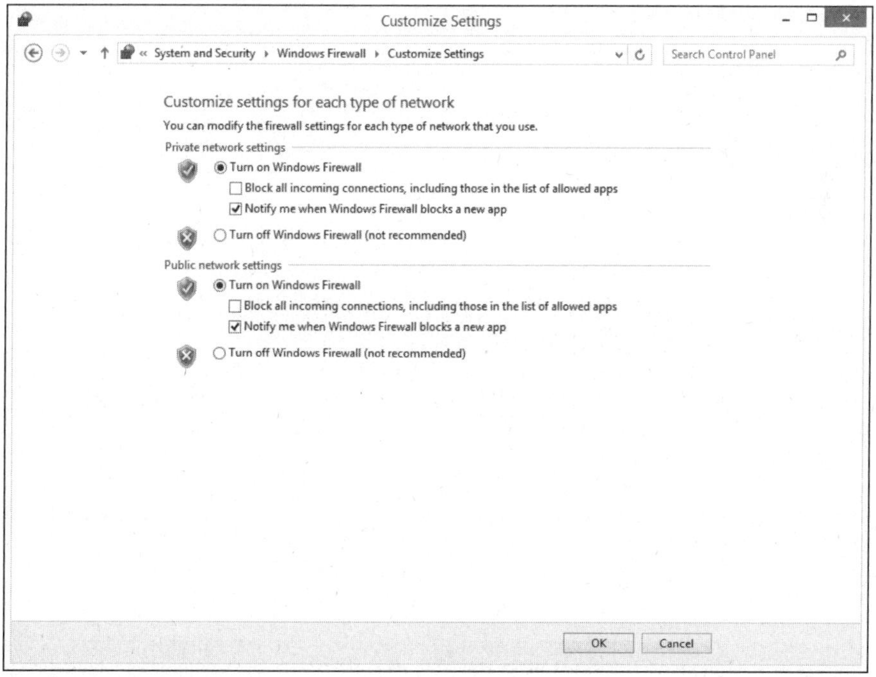

> **TIP**
>
> If you have a firewall at home, such as a wireless access point (WAP) or a cable or DSL modem that provides firewall features, and those features are turned on, you can safely turn off Windows Firewall. However, there usually is no downside to leaving Windows Firewall turned on even when an upstream firewall is in place. The exception is when you are trying to play multiplayer games or accomplish networking with other computers on the network and can't get the ports right in Windows Firewall to make it work. In these situations, just turn off Windows Firewall on the computers.

Making Exceptions to Firewall Protection

When Windows Firewall is turned on and running, you don't really have to do anything special to use it. It will be on constant vigil, automatically protecting your computer from hackers and worms trying to sneak in through unprotected ports. Ports for common Internet tasks such as e-mail and the web will be open and monitored so that you can easily use those programs safely.

Internet programs that don't use standard e-mail and web ports may require that you create an *exception* to the default firewall rules for incoming traffic. Examples include instant messaging programs and some online games. When you try to use such a program, Windows Firewall displays a security alert like the one in Figure 7.4.

FIGURE 7.4

Windows Firewall security alert.

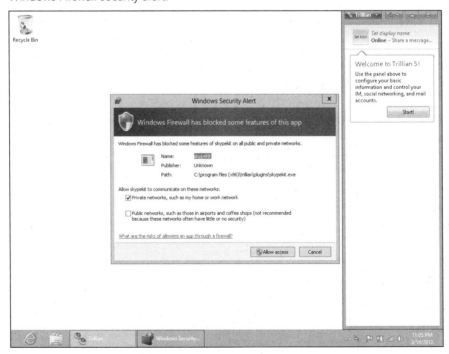

The message doesn't mean that the program is "bad." It just means that to use the program, the Firewall has to open a port. If you don't recognize the program name and publisher shown, click Cancel. If you want to use the program, first decide for which networks the exception will be allowed. For example, if the traffic is coming from another computer on your local network, select the Private Networks option. For traffic coming from the Internet, select Public Networks (you can select either or both, as needed). Then, click Allow Access. Allowing access for a program doesn't leave the associated port wide open. It just creates a new rule that allows that one program to use the port. You're still protected because the port is closed when you're not using that specific program. The port is also closed to programs other than the one for which you unblocked the port. If you change your mind in the future, you can always reblock the port, as described in the next section.

Manually configuring firewall exceptions (allowed apps and programs)

Normally, when you try to use a program (or an app) that needs to work through the firewall, you get a message like the example shown in Figure 9.4. Occasionally, you might need, or want, to manually allow or block a program through the firewall. If you have administrative privileges, you can do that via the Allowed Apps page shown in Figure 7.5. To open that page, click Allow an App through Windows Firewall in System and Security (by the Windows Firewall item in the Control Panel).

FIGURE 7.5

Windows Firewall Allowed Apps and Features.

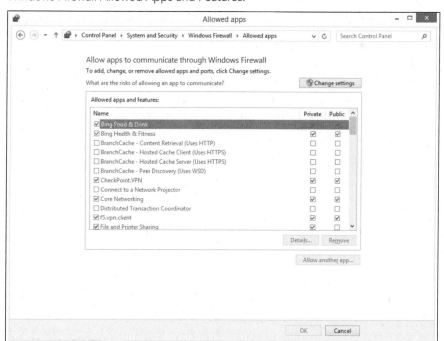

Items on the list with a check mark beside them represent apps that work through the firewall. You'll also see any exceptions you created in response to a security alert.

You probably aren't familiar with most of the apps and programs listed in the Allowed Apps and Features list, so you should not select or deselect a box just by guessing. But you don't need to guess, either. If you just leave things as they are, everything will be fine. If you later decide to use one of the listed features, you'll be prompted at that point to allow access for the app or program if it's necessary to do so.

Adding an app exception

You can unblock ports for apps and programs that aren't listed under Allowed Apps and Features. You would do this only if specifically instructed to do so by an app or program manufacturer you know and trust.

If the app or program for which you want to create an exception isn't listed under Allowed Apps and Features, you can do the following:

1. Click Change Settings and then click the Allow Another App button. When you do so, you see a list of installed programs that might require Internet access, as shown in Figure 7.6.

FIGURE 7.6

Add an App dialog box.

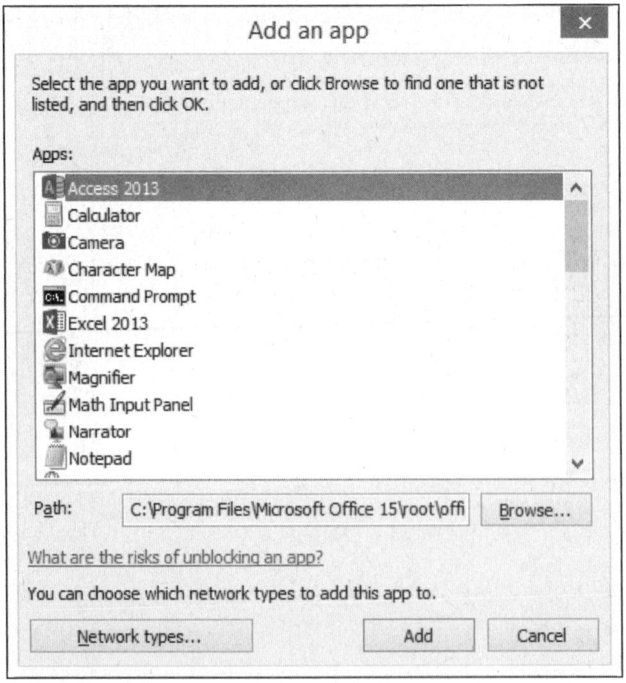

2. Click the app or program that you want to add to the list. Optionally, if the program isn't listed, but you know where it's installed, you can use the Browse button to get to the main executable for that program (typically the .exe file).

3. Clicking the Network Location Types button lets you define the addresses from which any unsolicited traffic is expected to originate. For example, if you're using a program that provides communications among programs within your local network only, you wouldn't want to accept unsolicited traffic coming to that port from the Internet. You'd want to accept unsolicited traffic coming only from computers within your own network. When you click Network Types, you see the options shown in Figure 7.7. Your options are as follows:

   - **Private:** For home or workplace networks. If the program in question has nothing to do with the Internet, and is for your home or business network only, choose this option to block Internet access, but allow programs within your own network to communicate with each other through the program.

   - **Public:** For public networks, such as those in an airport or coffee shop. If you want the program to be able to connect to the Internet, choose this option.

4. Click OK to save your settings.

FIGURE 7.7

The Choose Network Types dialog box.

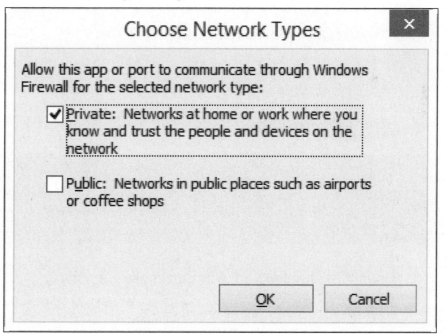

7

Tip

You can choose the scope for the program within the Allowed Programs and Features list just by placing a check mark in the Private or Public columns for the program.

Disabling, changing, and deleting exceptions

The check boxes in the Allowed Apps and Features list indicate whether the exception is enabled or disabled. When you clear a check box, the exception is disabled, and traffic for that program is rejected. This makes it relatively easy to enable and disable a rule for a program on an as-needed basis because the program name always remains in the list of exceptions.

To change the scope of an exception in your exceptions list, click the check box in the Private or Public column, as needed. To remove a program from the exceptions list, and stop accepting unsolicited traffic through its port, click the program name and then click the Remove button.

Tip

You can't remove the default programs from the list — only those you've added.

Advanced Firewall Configuration

The rest of this chapter goes well beyond anything that would concern the average home computer user. It's for more advanced users and network and security administrators who might need to configure Windows Firewall to comply with an organization's security policy. All these options require administrative privileges. We don't go into great detail on what the various options mean because we assume you're working to comply with an existing policy.

Caution

If you're not a professional administrator, it's best to stay out of this area altogether. You certainly don't want to guess and hack your way through things just to see what happens. Doing so could alter the Windows Firewall configuration such that it's wrong, causing you to be unable to connect to the Internet at all, or leaving you exposed to outside attacks by hackers.

Open Windows Firewall with Advanced Security

To get to the advanced configuration options for Windows Firewall, first open Windows Firewall from the System and Security item in the Control Panel. Then click the Advanced Settings link in the left pane. The firewall console, shown in Figure 7.8, opens.

IP Addresses on Home/Office Networks

When you set up a network using the Network Setup Wizard described in Part IX of this book, each computer is automatically assigned a 192.168.0.*x* IP address, where *x* is unique to each computer. For example, if the computers are sharing a single Internet connection, the first computer may receive the 192.168.0.1 address, and the subsequent computers will also have addresses in that same address space.

All computers will have the same subnet mask of 255.255.255.0. The subnet mask just tells the computer that the first three numbers are part of the *network address* (the address of your network as a whole), and the last number refers to a specific *host* (computer) on that network. The 192.168 … addresses are often referred to as *private addresses* because they can't be accessed directly from the Internet.

To see the IP address of a computer on your local network:

1. Go to that computer, display the desktop, press Windows+X, and choose Command Prompt.

2. At the command prompt, type **ipconfig /all** and press Enter. You see the computer's IP address and subnet mask listed along with other Internet protocol data.

As you can see in the figure, you have three independently configurable profiles to work with:

- **Domain Profile:** This is active when the computer is logged in to a network domain, such as in a corporation or business setting.

- **Private Profile:** This applies to computers within a local, private network.

- **Public Profile:** This protects your computer from the public Internet.

FIGURE 7.8

The Windows Firewall with Advanced Security console.

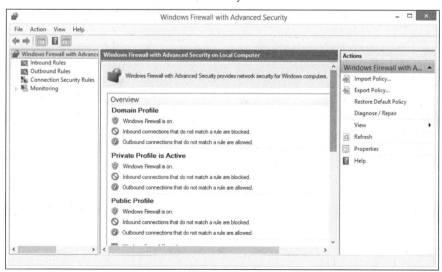

Changing firewall profile properties

Clicking the Windows Firewall Properties link near the bottom of the console (or the Properties item in the Actions pane) takes you to the dialog box shown in Figure 7.9. Notice that you can use tabs at the top of the dialog box to configure the Domain, Private, and Public settings. The fourth option applies to IPsec (IP Security), commonly used with virtual private networks (VPNs), which are described a little later in this section. By default, Inbound Connections are set to Block and Outbound Connections are set to Allow. You can change either setting by clicking the appropriate button.

Firewall alerts, unicast responses, local administrator control

Each profile tab has a Customize button in its Settings section. Clicking that button provides an option to turn off firewall notifications for that profile. Administrators can also use options on that tab to allow or prevent unicast responses to multicast and broadcast traffic. There's also an option to merge local administrator rules with rules defined through group policy.

FIGURE 7.9

Windows Firewall advanced properties.

Security logging

Each profile tab also offers a Logging section with a Customize button. Click the Customize button to set a name and location for the log file and a maximum size, and to choose whether you want to log dropped packets, successful connections, or both. You can use that log file to review firewall activity and to troubleshoot connection problems caused by the firewall configuration.

Customizing IPsec settings

The IPsec Settings tab in the firewall properties provides a way to configure IPsec (IP Security). Clicking the Customize button under IPsec Defaults reveals the options shown in Figure 7.10. The Default settings in each case cause settings to be inherited from a higher-level group policy object (GPO). To override the GPO, choose whichever options you want to apply to the current Windows Firewall instance. When you override the default, you can choose key exchange and data integrity algorithms. You can also fine-tune Kerberos V5 authentication through those settings.

FIGURE 7.10

The Customize IPsec Defaults dialog box.

Clicking OK or Cancel in the Customize IPsec Defaults dialog box takes you back to the IPsec Settings tab. There you can use the IPsec Exemptions section to exempt ICMP from IPsec, which may help with connection problems caused by ICMP rules.

> **NOTE**
>
> IPsec is a set of cryptographic protocols for securing communications across untrusted networks. It is commonly associated with tunneling and VPNs.

That covers the main firewall properties. You can configure plenty more outside the Properties dialog box. Again, most of these go far beyond anything the average home user needs to be concerned with, so we're being brief here. Advanced users needing more information can find plenty of information in the Help section for the firewall.

Inbound and outbound rules

In the left column of the main Windows Firewall with Advanced Security window shown back in Figure 7.8, you see Inbound Rules and Outbound Rules links. These provide very granular control over Windows Firewall rules for incoming and outgoing connections. Figure 7.11 shows a small portion of the possibilities there. Use the scrollbars to see them all.

FIGURE 7.11

Advanced outbound exceptions control.

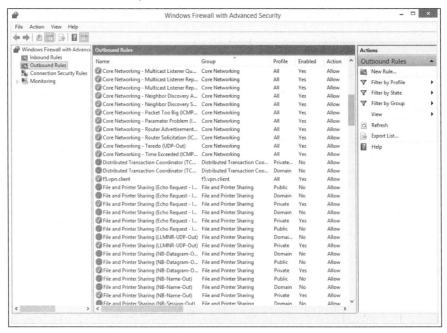

Why Outbound Connections Are Set to Allow

Contrary to some common marketing hype and urban myths, having outbound connections set to Allow by default does not make your computer more susceptible to security threats. Firewalls are really about controlling traffic between trusted and untrusted networks. The Internet is always considered untrusted because it's open to the public and anything goes. It's necessary to block inbound connections by default so that you can control exactly what does, and doesn't, come in from the Internet.

Things that are already inside your computer (or local network) are generally considered "trusted." That's because, unlike the Internet, you do have control over what's inside your own PC or network. Your firewall and anti-malware programs also help to keep out bad stuff. Therefore, you shouldn't need to block outbound connections by default.

There are exceptions, of course. In a secure setting in which highly sensitive data is confined to secure workstations in a subnet, it certainly makes sense to block outgoing connections by default. That way, you can limit outbound connections to specific hosts, programs, security groups, and so forth. You can also enforce encryption on outbound connections.

7

Here we're getting into security matters that go beyond the scope of this book. But we think it will be easy for any professional administrator to figure out what's going on there. Options (and the Help link) in the Actions column on the right tell all. You can also change any exception in the center column by right-clicking and choosing Properties.

Wrap-Up

A firewall is an important component of a larger overall security strategy. Windows 8.1 comes with a built-in firewall that's turned on and working from the moment you first start your computer. The firewall is automatically configured to prevent unsolicited Internet traffic from getting into your computer, thereby protecting you from worms and other hacking attempts. The Windows 8.1 firewall also provides advanced options for professional network and security administrators who need more granular control over its behavior. In summary:

- A firewall protects your computer from unsolicited network traffic, which is a major cause of worms and other hack attempts.
- A firewall will not protect your computer from viruses, pop-up ads, or junk e-mail.
- You don't need to configure the firewall to use standard Internet services such as the web and e-mail. Those will work through the firewall automatically.
- When you start an Internet program that needs access to the Internet through a closed port, you'll be given a security alert with options to Unblock, or Keep Blocking, the port. You must choose Unblock to use that program.
- Windows Firewall is one of the programs in the Security Center. To open Security Center, press Windows + X and choose Control Panel⇨Security⇨Security Center.

- To get to Windows Firewall configuration options, from the Windows Start screen, open the Charms Bar and choose Search. On the Search page, click Control Panel⇨Security⇨Security Center.

- Exceptions in Windows Firewall are programs that are allowed to work through the firewall.

- Professional network and security administrators can configure Windows Firewall through the Windows Firewall with Advanced Security console in Administrative Tools.

Automatic Updates as Security

IN THIS CHAPTER

Using automatic updates

Activating automatic updates

Configuring updates

Using Data Execution Prevention (DEP)

Internet security is a never-ending cat-and-mouse game between the security experts and the hackers who seem to have endless amounts of time to search for new ways to exploit the basic programmability of PCs. It seems that every time the good guys find a way to patch some security hole that the bad guys have learned to exploit, the bad guys find two more holes to exploit.

Windows 8.1 is certainly the most secure Windows version ever, by a long shot. But there is no such thing as a 100 percent secure computer because people can always find a way to take something good and turn it into something bad. So, in addition to the security features discussed in the preceding chapters, you need to keep your computer up to date with security patches as they become available. That's what Windows Update and this chapter are all about.

Understanding Automatic Updates

Many people are afraid of Windows Update — they're afraid that the updates will break something on their system that they can't fix. It's certainly true that any change to your system could create a problem. But it's unlikely that keeping up with updates will cause any significant problems — certainly nowhere near as many problems as you expose yourself to by *not* keeping up with updates. In addition, Windows Update creates restore points before installing many updates (but not for all updates), so you have the added security of being able to restore the system to a point prior to the update.

Other people fear that Microsoft will somehow exploit them through automatic updates. That's not the way it works. Microsoft has tens of millions of customers and tens of billions of dollars. It doesn't need to exploit anybody to be successful. Desperate people (and companies) do desperate, exploitive things. Microsoft is as far from desperate as you can get. Microsoft is also a publicly held company on the stock exchange, which means it's subject to constant scrutiny. Such companies aren't the ones that distribute malware. Most malware comes from e-mail attachments and free programs from unknown sources. When it comes to knowing who to trust and who not to trust, large publicly held companies are by far the most trustworthy, if for no other reason than that they can't afford to be untrustworthy.

A third common fear of automatic updates centers around the question "What's this going to cost me?" The answer to that is simple: Absolutely nothing. This brings us to the difference between *updates* and *upgrades*.

Some Hacking Lingo

The hacking world is replete with its own terminology. A *zero day exploit* is one that exploits a problem in software before the software vulnerability is known by the software company. A *black hat* is a bad guy who has sufficient technical knowledge to find and publish exploits. A *script kiddie* is someone (sometimes simply an inexperienced programmer who doesn't have enough skills to create or discover his own exploits) who runs scripts and malware created by more experienced hackers. A *white hat* is one of the good guys — the security experts who find ways to thwart the efforts of black hats and script kiddies.

Updates versus upgrades

People often assume that the terms *update* and *upgrade* are synonymous. We certainly use the terms interchangeably in common parlance. But in the computer world, there is a big difference. Upgrades usually cost money and involve a fair amount of work. For example, upgrading from Windows 7 to Windows 8.1 will cost you some money and take some time. You might even need to hire someone to verify that the upgrade will work and do the upgrade for you.

Updates are much different. Updates are small, simple, and free of charge. Some people turn off automatic updates because they're afraid they'll get some mysterious bill for something they downloaded automatically without realizing it. That will not happen. Turning on and using automatic updates won't cost you a penny.

Why updates are important

Automatic updates are an important part of your overall security. Many forms of malware, especially viruses and worms, operate by exploiting previously unnoticed flaws in programs. The term *exploit,* when used as a noun in computer science, refers to any piece of software that can take advantage of some vulnerability in a program in order to gain unauthorized access to a computer.

Some hackers actually publish, on the Internet, exploits they discover, which is both a good thing and a bad thing. The bad thing is that other hackers can use the exploit to conjure up their own malware, causing a whole slew of new security threats. The good thing is that the good guys can quickly create security patches to prevent the exploits from doing their nefarious deeds. Automatic updates keep your system current with *security patches* that fix the flaws that malware programs attempt to exploit.

Enabling Automatic Updates

Automatic updates are the best way to keep up with security patches. In fact, chances are, they're already enabled on your system. To find out, open Windows Update. As you know from previous chapters, you can use any technique that follows to open Windows Update:

- At the desktop, press Windows + X and choose Control Panel ➪ System and Security ➪ Windows Update.
- At the Windows Start screen, show the Charms Bar and choose Search, and type **Control Panel** in the text box. Click Control Panel ➪ System and Security ➪ Windows Update.

Figure 8.1 shows the Windows Update applet. To determine Windows Update's status, click the Change Settings link in the left pane. The Important Updates drop-down list shows the current setting.

FIGURE 8.1

Windows Update.

If automatic updates are turned off, seriously consider turning them on. To do so, click the Change Settings link in the Windows Update applet, and then choose from one of the four options that enable Windows Update.

Managing Updates

Automatic updates related to security require little or no effort on your part. But sometimes you may be faced with optional updates. These updates aren't security related. Instead, they're new versions of drivers, fixes for minor bugs, or some other type of update. They're optional because your computer is secure whether you install the update or not.

Managing optional updates

To manage optional updates and tweak some settings, use the Windows Update applet in the Control Panel. To get to that applet, do one of the following:

- At the desktop, press Windows + X and choose Control Panel ⇨ System and Security ⇨ Windows Update.
- At the Windows Start screen, show the Charms Bar and choose Search, and type **Control Panel** in the text box. Click Control Panel ⇨ System and Security ⇨ Windows Update.

Figure 8.1 shows the Windows Update applet.

If there are any optional updates, click the Optional Updates link to see what they are. The name of each will be listed next to an empty check box (see Figure 8.2). You have three options for dealing with each one:

- If you want to download and install the update, select its check box.
- If you want to hide the item so it doesn't show up in the future, right-click it and choose Hide Update. (It won't go into hiding until you leave the current window.) Right-click and choose Restore Update to restore a hidden update.
- If you want to get more information about the item before you decide, click its name and view more information about the update in the right pane.

If you selected optional updates to install, click Install to return to the Windows Update window and start the download and installation process. If you don't want to install any optional updates, simply close Windows Update.

> **TIP**
>
> To restore updates that have been previously hidden, open Windows Update and click Restore Hidden Updates in the right pane.

Changing how updates work

You can modify the times when Windows updates are downloaded to your computer. For example, what if your computer isn't turned on and online at 2:00 in the morning? Will you miss out on something important? Not at all. For one thing, there is no time limit on updates. After an update is posted, it stays posted forever, so you can download and install it at any time.

FIGURE 8.2

Optional updates.

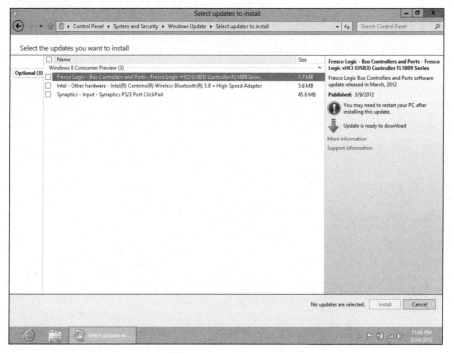

To change how automatic updating works, follow these steps:

1. In the left column of the Windows Update page, click Change Settings. The Choose Your Windows Update Settings page appears, as shown in Figure 8.3.

2. Click Updates Will Be Automatically Installed during the Maintenance Window link to see when automatic updates are downloaded. Figure 8.4 shows the preferred time, which has Windows checking for critical updates daily at 2:00 a.m.

3. Use the Run Maintenance Tasks Daily At drop-down list to select a different update time.

   If your computer isn't online at 2:00 a.m.:

   - Your computer will check for updates and download them in the background (in other words, without interfering with whatever you want to do yourself) as soon as you do go online.

   - If you shut down the computer before the scheduled time, Windows will offer to check for updates before you shut down. So, you don't have to worry about missing out on anything important.

FIGURE 8.3

The Windows Update Settings page.

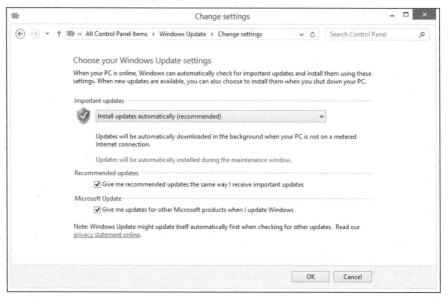

- You also can click the Allow Scheduled Maintenance to Wake Up My Computer at the Scheduled Time option, which will turn on your computer and download the updates automatically.

- You can choose a different schedule if you prefer, such as weekly at noon.

4. Click OK after you make changes to the Automatic Maintenance options and to return to the Change Settings screen.

On the Change Settings windows, you can modify the types of updates that are downloaded. As an alternative to fully automatic updates, you can choose one of the other options shown on the Important Updates drop-down list. For example, you can:

- Have Windows download the updates but ask your permission before actually installing them.

- Have Windows alert you to available updates. You can then choose whether you want to download or install them.

- Turn off automatic updating altogether. If you choose that option, the only way to get updates is to click Check for Updates at the left side of the Windows Update page.

By default, important and recommended updates are downloaded and installed. An important update is one that's needed to protect your computer against current Internet threats. Choosing Give Me Recommended Updates the Same Way I Receive Important Updates on the Change Settings screen extends that to less-critical updates that aren't directly related to security. Recommended updates are usually things such as minor bug fixes or improvements to Windows and other Microsoft products.

FIGURE 8.4

Windows Updates automatically runs at a specific time.

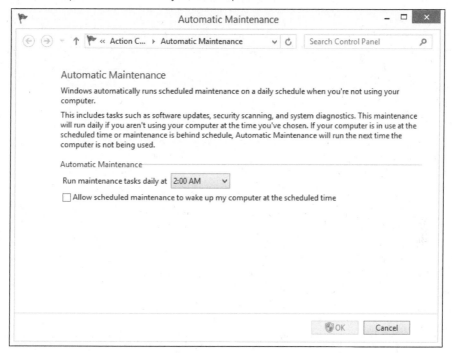

Click OK after making any changes to your settings, or click Cancel to leave all settings in their original state.

Reviewing and removing updates

The fact that well over 200,000 hardware and software products are available for Windows means that, once in a while, an update could cause problems with a particular device or program. Typically, you fix that problem by going to the product manufacturer's website and finding out what it recommends. If the manufacturer hasn't fixed the problem yet, and you need immediate access to the device or program, you might want to temporarily remove the conflicting update, especially if it isn't a critical security update.

To review your history of installed updates, follow these steps:

1. Click View Update History in the left column of the Windows Update window.

2. If you need to remove any installed updates, you can do so through the Uninstall A Program item in the Control Panel. Open the Control Panel and click Uninstall A Program.

3. Click View Installed Updates.

4. Right-click the update you want to remove and then click Uninstall.

5. If necessary, you can reinstall the update later by clicking Check For Updates in the left column of the Windows Update page.

> **TIP**
> For more information and general troubleshooting, click the help question mark on the right side of the Windows Update page.

Thwarting Exploits with Data Execution Prevention

Thwarting malware attacks that exploit software vulnerabilities is the most important element of automatic updates. But Windows 8.1 offers a second way of thwarting such attacks. It's called *Data Execution Prevention* (DEP). You don't want to use DEP as an alternative to other techniques described in this part of the book. Instead, you want to use it in addition to other techniques.

Many malware attacks use a technique called *buffer overflow* (or *buffer overrun*) to sneak code (program instructions) into areas of memory that only the operating system (Windows) should be using. Those areas of memory have direct access to everything on your computer. So, any bad code that sneaks into that area can do great damage.

More Security Tricks up Its Sleeve

Some malware techniques rely on well-known memory locations to exploit system vulnerabilities. Windows 8.1 has a surprise for those programs, too. It doesn't load essential programs to well-known, predictable locations. Instead, it uses Address Space Layout Randomization (ASLR) to load things in a random location each time you start your computer. So, malware writers can't really know in advance where a particular exploit resides in memory, making it much more difficult to exploit those memory addresses.

DEP is a security antidote to such attacks. It monitors programs to make sure they use only safe and appropriate memory locations. If DEP notices a program trying to do anything sneaky, it shuts down that program before it can do any harm.

By default, DEP is enabled for essential Windows programs and services only. When coupled with antivirus protection, that setting is usually adequate. You can crank it up to monitor all programs and services. But if you do, you might also have to individually choose programs that are allowed to bypass DEP. Knowing when that's okay may require technical expertise that goes beyond the scope of this book.

To get to options for DEP, follow these steps:

1. Open the System window. Or at the desktop, press Windows + X and choose System. You end up in the System window.

2. In the left column, click Advanced System Settings. That takes you to the System Properties dialog box.

3. Select the Advanced tab, click the Settings button on the Performance heading, and then select the Data Execution Prevention tab. At last, you see the options shown in Figure 8.5.

FIGURE 8.5

Data Execution Prevention options.

4. By default, the option to apply DEP only to essential Windows programs and services is selected. For stronger protection, you can turn on DEP for all programs and services. If you choose that option, DEP may sometimes shut down a program to prevent it from running.

> **NOTE**
>
> Many modern processors offer *NX technologies,* which prevent buffer overflows at the hardware level. When buffer overflows do occur, Windows supports that hardware-based DEP. For processors that don't have hardware DEP, Windows uses DEP software to achieve the same result.

If DEP does shut down a program you need, you have a couple choices:

- Contact the program manufacturer to find out whether there's a version of the program that runs under DEP.
- If you trust the program, you can add it to the list of programs that are allowed to bypass DEP. To accomplish that, you need to click the Add button and then navigate to and double-click the executable file (typically, such a file has the extension `.exe`) that DEP is shutting down.

Wrap-Up

When it comes to general computer security, the "big three" items are a firewall, malware protection, and automatic updates. Chapters 7 and this chapter cover those topics. Comprehensive malware strategy is beyond the scope of this book. But don't forget that running under a Standard user account (see Chapter 4) counts, too. Furthermore, you have less technical "social" threats to consider, such as phishing scams and pop-up ads.

The main points for this chapter are as follows:

- Automatic updates provide a quick and simple way to protect your computer against current software exploitation malware.
- Unless you have some compelling reason to do otherwise, you should allow Windows 8.1 to automatically download and install updates daily.
- Data Execution Prevention (DEP) offers another layer of protection against threats that work by sneaking errant code into sensitive parts of system memory.

Personalizing the Windows 8.1 Interface

IN THIS CHAPTER

The Windows 8.1 interface

Working with tiles

Working with tile groups

Customizing the contents of the Start screen

Clearing tile data

The Windows 8.1 interface presents a clean, streamlined way to interact with your apps, data, and documents, but like the traditional Windows desktop interface, the new interface is just a starting point. You can customize the organization of tiles and tile groups on the Start screen, change the picture on the Lock screen, and much more.

This chapter explores how you can change all these elements of the Windows 8.1 interface and customize it to suit the way you work and play.

Customizing the Start Screen

Although the Lock screen might be the first thing you see when you start Windows 8.1, you'll certainly spend a lot more time working on the Start screen, so that's where we'll start our tour of the tools and settings you can use to customize the interface.

Rearranging tiles

Figure 9.1 shows a portion of a typical Windows 8.1 Start screen. As the figure shows, the tiles on the Start screen are grouped. You can rearrange the tiles on the Start screen, moving them within a group, moving them to other groups, or even creating new groups.

FIGURE 9.1

Tiles on the Windows 8.1 Start screen.

Moving tiles within a group is easy. If you're using a touch device, tap and hold the icon until a check mark appears near the upper-right corner of the tile; then simply drag it into its new position. If you're using a mouse, right-click the tile to make the check mark appear, and then left-click and drag the tile to its new position.

> **TIP**
>
> If the group where you want to place the tile is not shown on the display, just drag the tile in the direction of the target group. The screen will automatically scroll.

Adding and removing tiles

You can customize the tiles that appear on the Start screen, adding and removing tiles as desired. For example, you might add the documents or websites you use most often, and remove the apps you seldom or never use. The following sections explain how to add and remove tiles from the Start screen, as well as the Windows taskbar.

> **TIP**
>
> The Start screen includes a button near the bottom left (a down-facing arrow in a circle) for accessing all installed apps. Click the button to show all installed apps.

Adding tiles

Apps that you add from the Windows Store are automatically pinned to the Start screen. When you install other apps, Setup generally adds one or more tiles to the Start screen for those, as well.

If you've removed a tile and you want to add it back, or you need to add a tile for an app that wasn't added automatically, you can easily do so. To add an app using the mouse, right-click the Start screen to show the App Bar, and then click All Apps. With a touch device, slide up from the bottom of the display and then tap All Apps.

TIP

You can also open Search and click or tap Apps in the results list to show all apps.

Locate the app that you want to add to the Start screen, and then either right-click or swipe down on the icon. When the App Bar appears (see Figure 9.2), click or tap Pin to Start. If you also want to add the app to the Windows taskbar, open the App Bar again for the app and click or tap Pin to Taskbar. Note that you can pin only legacy Windows apps to the Taskbar.

FIGURE 9.2

Pin items to the Start screen using the App Bar.

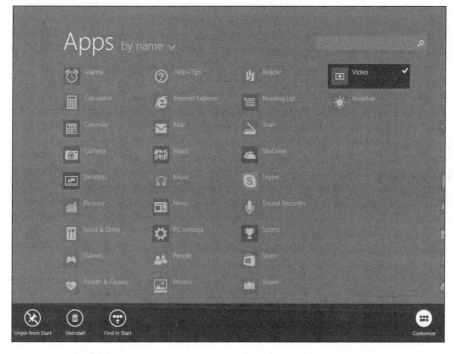

> **TIP**
>
> To swipe down on a tile or icon, touch it, slide it down slightly, and then release it. A check mark should appear in the upper-right corner, and the App Bar appears.

Removing tiles

As mentioned earlier, Setup typically adds tiles to the Start screen when you install an app. Over time, the Start screen gets cluttered with apps you probably use seldom, if at all. You can certainly uninstall apps you don't need, but in some cases you might prefer to simply remove the app's tile(s) from the Start screen. For example, maybe it's a utility app that runs in the background that you never need to open.

Removing a tile is easy. If using a mouse, right-click the tile and then, in the App Bar, click Unpin from Start. If using a touch device, swipe down on the tile to open the App Bar, and then tap Unpin from Start.

Resizing tiles

Although some tiles have a fixed size, you can change others from small to large, or vice versa. This is particularly handy for live tiles for which you want to provide more space to display their live data. To change the size of a tile, right-click or swipe down on the tile to open the App Bar. Click Resize, then click Small, Medium, Large, or Wide, as appropriate.

> **NOTE**
>
> In general, tiles for non–Windows 8 apps will be fixed at the smaller, square size. For some apps, Windows 8.1 will not offer the Wide option for the tile size.

Working with live tiles

In the Windows 8.1 interface, live tiles are ones that display data dynamically. Examples include the Weather, Mail, and Finance tiles. For example, Finance shows stock price information for stocks that you've added to your watch list.

You can control whether a live tile–capable app shows data on the Start screen. For example, if you don't use the Weather app much, you might not want it showing data. To turn live tiles on or off, right-click or swipe down on the tile to open the App Bar. Then click or tap either Turn Live Tile Off or Turn Live Tile On (see Figure 9.3), depending on the current state of the tile.

Working with groups

You've already seen that the Start screen groups tiles and that you can move tiles from one group to another. Groups enable you to group together tiles on the Start screen in whatever way makes sense to you. For example, you might group your Office apps together in one group, and other items that you use less often into another group.

FIGURE 9.3

Use the App Bar to turn live tiles on or off.

The "Rearranging tiles" section, earlier in this chapter, explained how to move tiles from one group to another, or within the same group. But there are other actions you can take in regards to groups, including creating new groups and naming them.

Creating groups

To create a new group, simply drag a tile to the vertical space between two groups, or to the left or right edge of the Start screen. Windows displays a translucent vertical bar to indicate that it's going to create a new group when you release the tile. Release the tile, and then drag other tiles as desired into the group.

Rearranging groups

You can also change the order of groups on the Start screen. To work with a group as a whole, you first need to zoom out to see the entire Start screen. To do so with a mouse, click the Summary View icon at the bottom right of the display. On a touch device, simply pinch the Start screen to zoom out and view the Summary view (see Figure 9.4). With the Start screen at the Summary view, click or tap on a group and then drag it to the desired location.

FIGURE 9.4

Use the Summary view to manage tile groups.

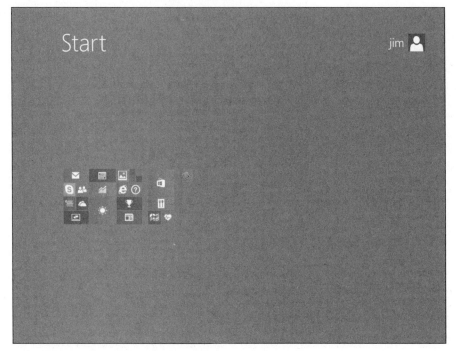

Clearing live data

Over time, as you use live tiles to display data, you might want to clear the data the tiles show. For example, if you're working in a public place such as on an airplane, you might not want your data displayed on the Start screen. Windows 8.1 makes it easy to clear that data.

Display the Start screen, and then open the Charms Bar and click or tap Settings. Click Tiles in the resulting Settings menu, and then click or tap Clear (see Figure 9.5).

Allocating storage for Tile updates

Live tiles display data, and as you might expect, that data needs to be stored somewhere. The more live tiles you use, the more data is created. By default, Windows 8.1 will store up to 50MB of live tile data, and when that storage is used, your live tiles will let you know there are updates available but won't display them. To increase the amount of storage allocated for live tile data, open the Charms Bar, click or tap Settings, and then click or tap Tiles on the Settings menu. Use the Data Used for Tile Updates drop-down to specify the amount of storage allocated for live tile data.

FIGURE 9.5

The Tiles menu.

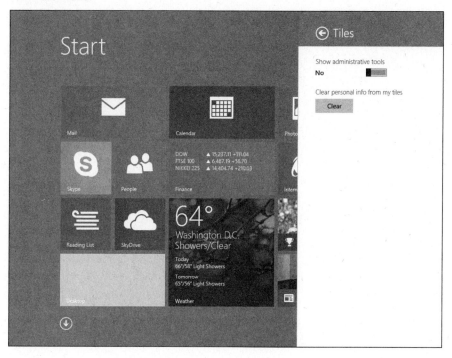

Adding administrative tools to the Start screen

One final change you might want to make to the Start screen is to add the Windows 8.1 administrative tools to it. These tools include Performance Monitor, Task Manager, Optimize Drives, and other tools for managing your device. If you use these tools often, or simply want quick access to them, you can add them to the Start screen. To do so, open the Charms Bar, click or tap Settings, click or tap Tiles in the Settings menu, and set the Show Administrative Tools option to Yes.

Changing the Start Screen Background and Color

Another change you can make to the Start screen is to change the background color and/or choose a background for the Start screen. To change either of these properties, open the Charms Bar, click or tap Settings, and then click or tap Personalize.

In the Personalize menu, choose a background from the options provided, or choose the solid color if you prefer no background image. Use the color selector to choose a color for the Start screen (see Figure 9.6).

FIGURE 9.6

Use the Personalize menu to choose a color and background image.

Customizing the Lock Screen

Although you probably don't spend a lot of time on the Lock screen, you might still want to customize the way the Lock screen looks and functions. For example, maybe you want to change the picture displayed on the Lock screen. Or maybe you want to choose the apps that run in the background and display information on the Lock screen (such as the Mail app, showing how many unread e-mails you have). Only apps written to do so can display status on the Lock screen. Depending on their design, some apps can display basic information, while others can display detailed status. The Calendar app is an example of an app that can display detailed status.

To customize the Lock screen, open the Charms Bar, click or tap Settings, and then click or tap Change PC Settings. In the PC Settings app, click or tap PC and Devices and then click or tap Lock Screen to display the options shown in Figure 9.7.

Windows 8.1 provides a small number of stock images from which you can choose for the Lock screen. Just click an image to set it as the background for the Lock screen, or click Browse to choose a photo or other image stored on your device.

FIGURE 9.7

Use the Personalize item to set Lock screen options.

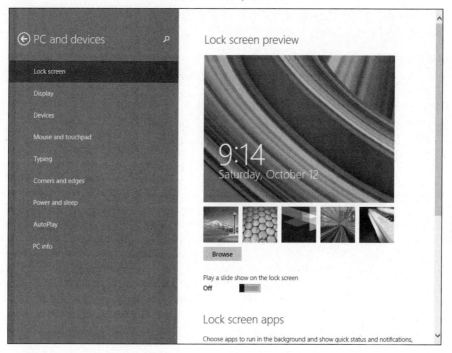

The Lock Screen Apps section of the Lock Screen page lets you choose which apps display status updates on the Lock screen. By default, the Skype, Mail, Calendar, and Alarms apps are selected to display their status, with the Calendar app set to display detailed status. To add an app, click or tap one of the available boxes (with the plus sign in the middle) and choose an app from the resulting pop-up menu. To change which app displays detailed status, click or tap the detailed status icon and choose the desired app. If you prefer not to have detailed status on the Lock screen, click or tap Don't Show Detailed Status on the Lock Screen.

Changing Your Account Picture

One final change you'll probably want to make that affects both the Lock screen and the Start screen is your account picture. For example, maybe you want to use your Xbox avatar as your account picture.

> **NOTE**
> If you've linked your Microsoft account (formerly Windows Live ID) to your Windows account, the picture associated with your Microsoft account is used automatically for your account picture. If you change the account picture in Windows 8.1, that change also updates your Windows account picture.

After you have the image you want to use as your account picture, open the Charms Bar, click or tap Settings, and click or tap Change PC Settings to open the PC Settings app. Click or tap Accounts. The Account Picture page shows your currently assigned picture, if any. To choose a different one, click or tap Browse, choose an image, and click or tap Choose Image to apply the new image.

> **TIP**
>
> If you want to use your Xbox avatar for your Microsoft or Windows account image, go to http://live.xbox.com/en-US/ AvatarEditor, click Gamer Picture, and then create and save your gamer pic. After your gamer pic appears beside your account name on the Xbox.com site, you can right-click the image and choose Save Background As to save the image to your computer.

Wrap-Up

In previous versions of Windows, you had a considerable amount of control over what the Windows interface looked like, and to a lesser degree, over how it functioned. With the introduction of the Windows 8.1 interface, you have fewer options for customizing the interface because of the nature of that interface — it's more streamlined, so there is less to customize. Even so, Windows 8.1 gives you a fair amount of flexibility over the position and grouping of tiles on the Start screen, its background and color, and other properties. You learned how to change those properties in this chapter.

The Windows desktop hasn't gone away, however, and you'll no doubt want to do at least a little customization of the desktop interface. To learn more about the available customization options, check out Chapter 10.

Personalizing the Desktop

IN THIS CHAPTER

Personalizing your screen, mouse, and keyboard

Personalizing your taskbar

Using Windows gadgets

O
n a touch device, the Start screen is probably where you'll spend most of your time. On a more traditional PC, however, the Windows desktop is probably your main workplace. Or maybe "play place," depending on how you use your computer.

We all like to set up our own desktops and work environments in unique ways. What works best for one person isn't necessarily great for someone else. Fortunately, the way things look and work on your Windows 8 desktop aren't set in stone. You can personalize your desktop and features in a variety of ways to make them look and work the way you like. That's what this chapter is all about — having your Windows environment set up your way.

Most of the options described in this chapter apply only to the user account you're currently logged in to, so any changes you make to your own desktop apply only to you (assuming that you're logged in to your own user account). This means that all users of a computer can have their settings just the way they want them without stepping on each others' toes.

Using the Personalization Page

Many options for personalizing the look and feel of Windows 8.1 are on the Personalization page, shown in Figure 10.1. As with most aspects of Windows 8.1, there are many ways to get to the Personalization page. Use whichever is most convenient for you at the moment:

- Right-click the desktop and choose Personalize.
- Open the Control Panel and choose Appearance and Personalization ⇨ Personalization.

The following sections look at how you can use the various options on the page to fine-tune the look and feel of Windows 8 on your screen.

FIGURE 10.1

The Personalization page.

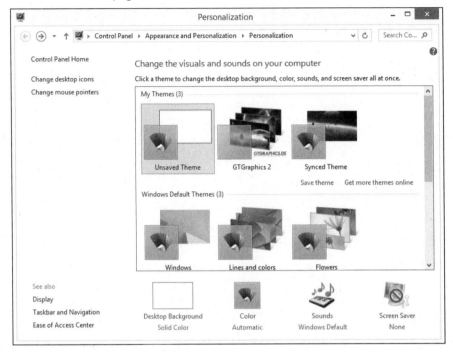

Choosing a theme

A theme is a collection of appearance settings that determine how things look on your screen. For example, Figure 10.2 shows how Windows 8.1 looks with the default theme selected. Figure 10.3 shows how it looks with the GT Graphics 2 theme downloaded from the Microsoft website.

To choose a theme, open the Personalization window from the Control Panel. You see a selection of themes from which to choose. A good way to personalize your screen is to choose a theme that looks most like how you'd like your screen to look. You can certainly modify it to your preferences or even create your own custom themes. Using a predefined theme that has many of the characteristics you like, however, is a good way to get started.

To try a theme, just click the theme in the Personalization page. The theme is applied to your desktop. If you don't like the results, just click another theme or your previous theme.

Feel free to try out as many themes as you like. If you plan to further customize things, click Save Theme, a link located on the Personalization page. Then enter a name for the theme and click Save.

FIGURE 10.2

The Windows 8.1 theme.

TIP

You can create as many custom themes as you like. Just remember to give each one a unique name when you save it.

Personalizing your desktop background

You can *wallpaper* your desktop with any picture or color you like. In the Personalization window, click Desktop Background to open the Desktop Background page, shown in Figure 10.4.

Click the drop-down button and choose Solid Colors to choose a solid-color background for the desktop, or choose Pictures Library to view pictures from your own Pictures folder (see Figure 10.5) and from the shared Public Pictures folder. Of course, if these folders are empty or don't contain any compatible picture types, you won't see any pictures after making your selection. After you choose a category, point to or click any picture to see it applied as your desktop background.

10

FIGURE 10.3

The GT Graphics 2 theme.

The Top Rated Photos option lets you choose from photos in your own Pictures folder or in the Public Pictures folder that have a rating of 4 or higher.

If you have pictures in some folder other than the Pictures folder for your user account or the Public Pictures folder, click Browse. Navigate to the folder that contains those pictures. Then click (or double-click) the picture you want to use as your desktop background. All pictures from that folder will appear in the Desktop Background window. Click whatever picture you want to use.

If the desktop is covered, hover the mouse over the Show Desktop button at the lower-right corner of the screen to make all windows invisible and show the desktop. Try out different pictures until you find one you like.

You might have noticed that you can choose more than one picture for your desktop. The Change Picture Every option lets you choose how often Windows displays a new desktop picture. Enable the Shuffle option if you want the photos to be shown randomly from the selected group.

FIGURE 10.4

The Desktop Background page.

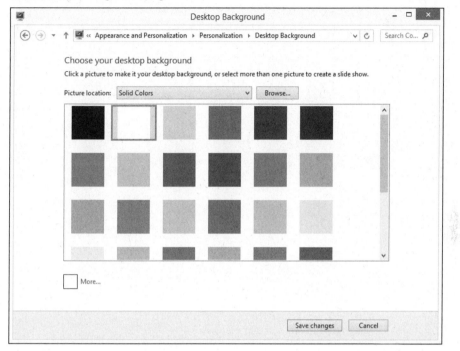

Try the options under Picture Position to view it in different ways. The options have little or no effect on large pictures. But if you choose a small picture of your own, the Tile option shows it repeatedly, like tiles. The Center option shows it centered on the screen. If you choose the Center option, you can click Change Background Color to color the desktop surrounding the picture.

If you don't want a picture on your desktop, choose Solid Colors from the drop-down list. Then click whatever color you like, or click More for a wider selection of colors. When you've found and chosen a picture or color you like, click Save Changes.

Personalizing your color scheme

To choose a basic color scheme for your screen and selected theme, click Color in the Personalization window (see Figure 10.6).

Most of the options are self-explanatory. Click any color sample to apply that color to your windows. Use the Color Intensity slider to adjust the amount of color used.

FIGURE 10.5

Choose a desktop background.

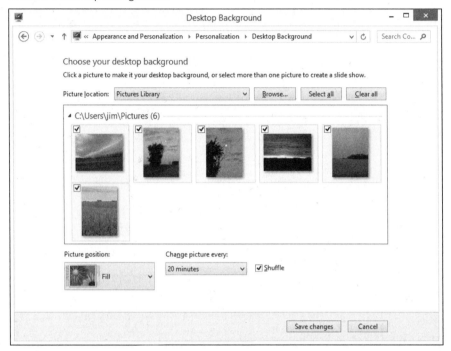

If you want to create your own colors, click any color selection other than Automatic, and then click Show Color Mixer to see the additional sliders shown in Figure 10.7. You can use those to create your own color.

Before you start creating a color, you might find it useful to drag the Intensity slider to the middle or far-right end of the bar and deselect the Enable Transparency check box. Also, drag the Saturation and Brightness sliders to the middle. Doing so will make it easier to see your color selection on the window's border.

Drag the Hue slider along the rainbow bar until you find a color you like. Move the Saturation slider to adjust, deepen, or fade your selected color. Use the Brightness slider to brighten or darken the color. Just keep playing around with things until you get a color you like.

Making text sharper with ClearType

ClearType is a technology that makes fonts look clearer and smoother on a display. ClearType is particularly effective for LCD displays but can have some effect on CRT displays as well. Windows 8 supports ClearType.

FIGURE 10.6

Change your color scheme.

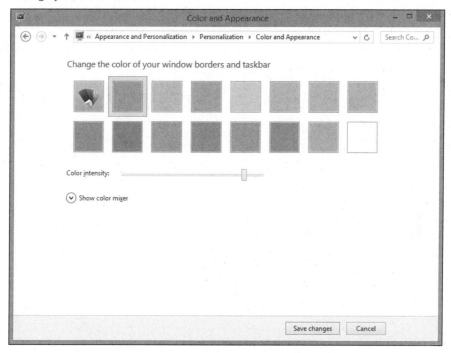

To adjust ClearType on your Windows 8.1 computer, first open the Control Panel. Then click Display and click Adjust ClearType Text. The ClearType Text Tuner appears (see Figure 10.8).

The ClearType Text Tuner is a wizard that steps you through a couple of settings to fine-tune font display on your computer. Select the Turn On ClearType check box and then click Next. Windows 8 checks your computer's display resolution and offers to change resolution to the display's native resolution or keep the current resolution. Choose the desired option and click Next. Windows 8 then displays four pages with different text samples, prompting you to choose the ones that look the best to you. Click Finish when you're satisfied with your selections.

Personalizing sound effects

You might have noticed some little beeps and whistles as you do things in Windows 8. Those are called *sound effects,* and you can customize them from the Personalization window. Just click Sounds in the Personalization window to open the Sound dialog box, shown in Figure 10.9.

10

FIGURE 10.7

The color mixer sliders.

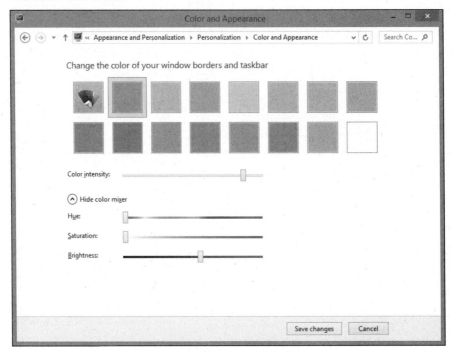

If you don't want to assign sound effects one at a time, you can choose a predefined sound effects scheme from the Sound Scheme drop-down list. Choose No Sounds if you don't want any sound effects.

The Program Events list shows different events to which you can assign sounds. Items that have a speaker icon to the left already have a sound effect associated with them. To hear one, click any program event that shows a speaker icon. The Sounds drop-down menu below the list shows the filename in which the sound effect is stored. Click the Play button to the right of the sound effect name to hear that sound effect.

Sound effects play only when your computer has a sound card with speakers plugged into the correct jack. If the speakers have their own power switch, they must be turned on. Likewise, if the speakers have their own volume control, the volume must be turned up high enough. And if the speakers have a Mute button, it must be turned off. Likewise, the volume control in the notification area must have its volume set to a level you can hear and must not be muted, as in Figure 10.10.

In the Sound dialog box, you can assign any sound effect you like to any program event. First, click the program event to which you would like to assign or change a sound effect. Then click the drop-down button under Sounds to see a list of built-in sound effects. Click the sound effect you'd like to assign. Then click the Play button to hear that sound effect.

FIGURE 10.8

The ClearType Text Tuner.

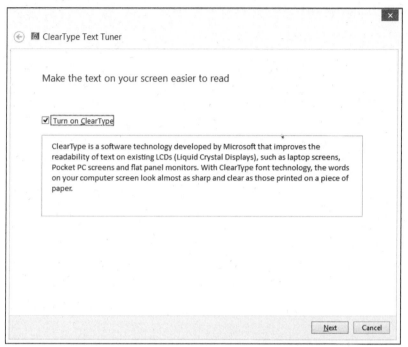

If you have your own sound effect to assign to a program event, click the Browse button and navigate to the folder that contains your sound effects. Then double-click the sound effect you want to assign to the program event.

If you change the sound effects associated with program events, you'll want to save all that work as your own sound scheme. Click the Save As button and give the scheme a name.

Personalizing your screen saver

A screen saver is a moving picture or pattern that fills the screen after a period of inactivity. The name "screen saver" harkens back to the earlier days of computing when leaving a fixed image on the screen for too long a time could cause permanent damage to the screen. This type of burn-in can still be a problem with CRT displays but isn't generally a problem with LCD and LED displays, so a screen saver is typically optional nowadays. Still, it's a nice way to have your screen do something entertaining when the computer is on but nobody is using it. Plus, it can be a way to protect your computer from prying eyes when you walk away from it. Better still, lock your workstation before you leave.

10

FIGURE 10.9

The Sound dialog box.

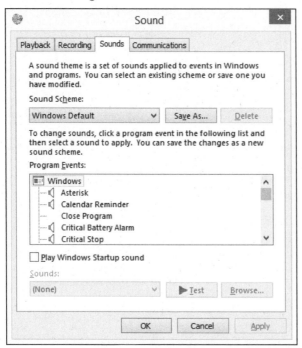

In the Personalization window, click Screen Saver. The Screen Saver Settings dialog box shown in Figure 10.11 opens. Click the drop-down button to see a list of screen savers from which you can choose. Click any name in that list to get a sneak peek at how it will look if you apply it.

Some screen savers are customizable. Click the Settings button to see whether the screen saver you selected has optional settings you can change. If it does, you'll see those options in a dialog box. Choose whatever options look interesting.

If you have pictures in Photo Gallery, choose Photos from the drop-down button. The screen saver will be a slide show of pictures from your gallery. If you choose Photos from the drop-down list, you can also click the Settings button to see the options shown in Figure 10.12.

 For the goods on photos and Photo Gallery, drop by Chapter 17.

As you can see in Figure 10.12, the default setting is for the screen saver to show all pictures and videos from your Pictures library, which includes your own Pictures folder and the Public Pictures folder. You can click Browse to choose a different location, if desired.

FIGURE 10.10

Windows volume control.

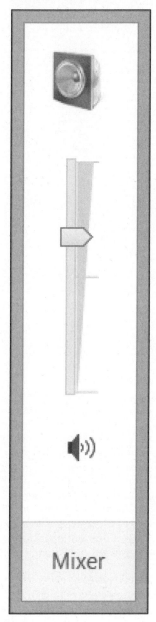

FIGURE 10.11

The Screen Saver Settings dialog box.

Use the Slide Show Speed drop-down button to choose the slide show speed, and choose the Shuffle Pictures option to have Windows randomize the photo selection. Click Save after making your choices.

Regardless of which screen saver and settings you choose, the small preview window in the dialog box shows you how it will look. For a larger view, click the Preview button. Your selected screen saver will play full screen. To make it stop, just move your mouse.

After you've chosen your screen saver, specify how many minutes of inactivity are required before the screen saver starts playing. A period of inactivity means that nobody has touched the touchscreen, mouse, or keyboard. So, if you set the Wait option to five minutes, the screen saver kicks in after the computer has been unused for five minutes. The screen saver plays until someone moves the mouse or presses a key on the keyboard.

Choosing On Resume, Display Logon Screen causes the screen saver to show the login page rather than your desktop when someone moves the mouse. If you're using a password-protected user account, showing the login page prevents that other person from accessing your desktop. It also means that when *you* want to start using the computer again, you have to enter your password to get back to your desktop. Your programs will still be running so this isn't the same as logging out and logging back in again.

FIGURE 10.12

Photo slide show options.

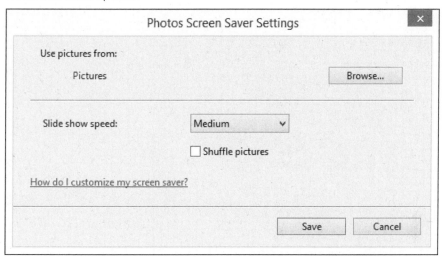

The screen saver won't kick in at all if your power options are set to turn off the monitor before the screen saver kicks in. The Change Power Settings link in the dialog box lets you check, and optionally change, when the monitor goes off.

For example, the Power Save plan turns off the monitor after 20 minutes. If you set the screen saver to kick in after 21 or more minutes, you'll never see the screen saver because the monitor will be off. If you prefer the screen saver to an empty screen, make sure to set the screen saver timeout to a shorter time period than your screen power-off setting.

 See Chapter 36 for more information on using power options.

When you're happy with your screen saver selections, click OK. Remember that the screen saver won't actually play until you've left the computer alone and untouched for the number of minutes you specified in the Wait box on the Screen Saver Settings dialog box.

Personalizing desktop icons

In the left column of the Personalization window, you see a link titled Change Desktop Icons. Click that link to see the dialog box shown in Figure 10.13. Select the check boxes for any icons you want to see on your desktop. Clear the check box for any icon you don't want to see. As always, choosing icons is purely a matter of personal taste. Also, you can change the icons you see on your desktop at any time. Click OK after choosing the icons you want to see.

10

FIGURE 10.13

The Desktop Icon Settings dialog box.

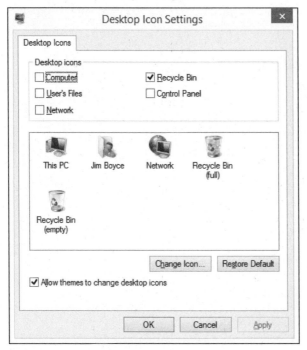

Creating your own desktop icons

The Desktop Icons Settings dialog box shows only the few desktop icons built into Windows 8.1. Many programs you install create other desktop icons. You're also free to create your own desktop icons. Most desktop icons are actually just *shortcuts* to other places or programs.

Shortcut icons are unique in a couple of ways. For one, they show a little curved arrow like the example in Figure 10.14. For another, deleting a shortcut icon has no effect on the item that the shortcut opens. Instead, deleting a shortcut icon deletes only the icon. The program or folder to which the icon referred still exists. You can still open that item through a non-shortcut method.

If you often go through a series of clicks or steps to open some item, creating a desktop shortcut will make opening that item quicker and easier. Get to the icon you normally click (or double-click) to open a program, folder, or document. Then right-click that icon and choose Send To ➪ Desktop (Create Shortcut).

FIGURE 10.14

A sample shortcut icon.

Sizing, arranging, showing, and hiding desktop icons

You can size and arrange desktop icons as you see fit. First, minimize or close all open program windows so that you can see the entire desktop. Then right-click any empty area on the desktop and hover the mouse over the View menu.

The View submenu, shown in Figure 10.15, contains several options for arranging icons. An item on that menu that has a check mark is currently selected and active. An item without a check mark is deselected and inactive. Clicking an item selects it if it's not already selected, or deselects it if it's selected. Here's what each option does:

- **Large Icons:** Shows desktop icons at a large size.
- **Medium Icons:** Shows desktop icons at a medium size.
- **Small Icons:** Shows desktop icons at a smaller size, similar to earlier Windows versions.

TIP

If your mouse has a wheel, you can make desktop icons almost any size by holding down the Ctrl key as you spin the mouse wheel.

FIGURE 10.15

The View submenu.

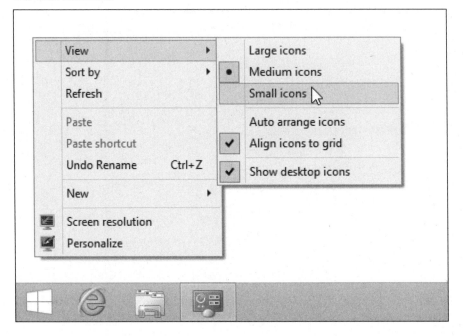

- **Auto Arrange Icons:** Choosing this option keeps icons neatly arranged near the left side of the desktop. If you clear this option, you can put desktop icons wherever you like. Just drag any icon to wherever you want to put it on the desktop.

- **Align Icons to Grid:** Choosing this option keeps icons aligned to an invisible grid, to make the spacing between them equal.

- **Show Desktop Icons:** If this option is selected (checked), desktop icons are visible. Clearing this option makes the desktop icons invisible. It doesn't delete them, however. They'll come back into view when you choose this option again.

The Sort By option on the desktop shortcut menu lets you quickly sort icons by name, size, file extension, or date modified. Regardless of which option you choose, built-in icons are always listed first, followed by your own custom icons in whatever order you specified.

The remaining options are similar to their counterparts in folders. The Refresh option ensures that icons on the desktop are up to date with changes you may have made elsewhere in the system. If you accidentally delete a shortcut icon, you can choose Undo Delete (or press Ctrl + Z) to bring it back. The New option lets you create a new folder or document on the desktop. Personalize opens the Personalization page (refer to Figure 10.1).

Customizing icons

To change a built-in icon, open the Desktop Icon Settings dialog box (refer to Figure 10.13). Then click the icon you want to customize, and click Change Icon. To change the appearance of a shortcut icon, right-click it and choose Properties ➪ Change Icon. The Change Icon dialog box opens, displaying possible alternative icons. Figure 10.16 shows a general example.

> **NOTE**
>
> Not all programs offer optional icons. If the Change Icon button is disabled, that means you can't change that particular icon.

If you have your own .ico files and would prefer to use one of those, click the Browse button in the Change Icon dialog box. Navigate to the folder that contains the .ico file and choose the icon you want to use. Note that some .dll and .exe files also contain icons you can use.

FIGURE 10.16

The Change Icon dialog box.

> **TIP**
> To explore programs that let you create your own icon pictures, search the web for "icon maker." To find pre-made icons that you can download, search the web using the keywords "download Windows icons."

Choosing a screen resolution

One of the changes you might want to make in Windows is to adjust your screen resolution because your screen resolution determines how much stuff can fit on your screen. Resolution is measured in *pixels,* with each pixel representing a tiny, lighted dot on the screen. The higher the resolution, the smaller everything looks, and the more stuff you can get on the screen. To choose a resolution, right-click the desktop and choose Screen Resolution. Doing so opens the Screen Resolution page shown in Figure 10.17.

There is no right or wrong setting for the screen resolution. A high resolution is good because you can see more stuff on your screen. But a high resolution isn't good if things are so small on your screen that you can't see them. On the Screen Resolutions page, click the Resolution drop-down list and then move the slider from one resolution to the next. As you move the slider, you can see a sample of the *aspect ratio* of the current selection. You can't really judge how small things will look on your screen as you move the slider, so it may take a little trial and error to get things just right. But let's stop a second to talk about that *aspect ratio* term here.

FIGURE 10.17

The Screen Resolution page.

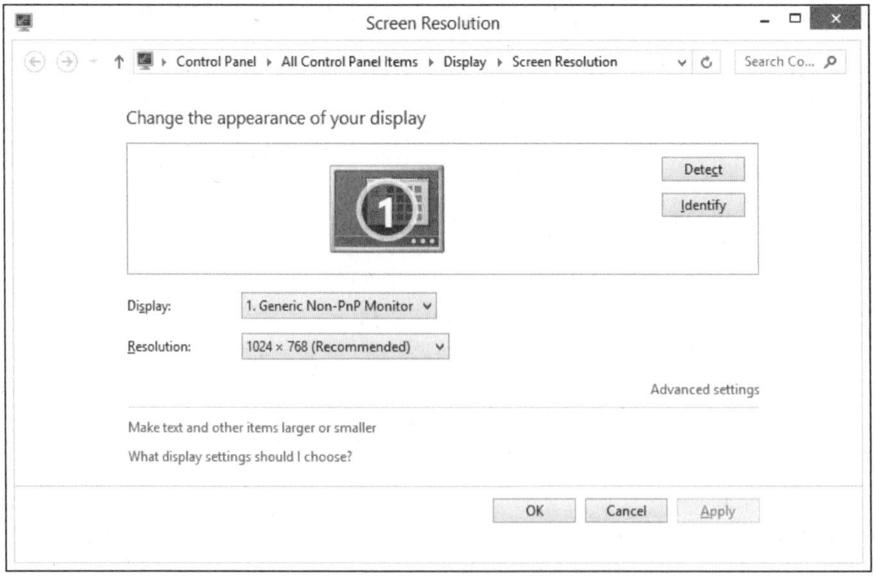

There was a time when all computer monitors had a 4:3 aspect ratio, which meant that for every 4 pixels of width, you got 3 pixels of height. These days, you'll come across other aspect ratios including 5:4 and the 16:9 ratio found on widescreen TVs. There are some others, too. You can check the manual that came with your monitor or notebook computer for your screen's exact aspect ratio, or just choose a resolution that looks good on your screen (and is supported by the computer's video adapter). Table 10.1 lists some common aspect ratios and resolutions that fit them.

Other Ways to Size Onscreen Elements

The resolution you choose sets only a basic default size for items on the screen. There are countless other ways to adjust the size of text, icons, and pictures on your screen, and they work no matter what resolution you choose. For example, holding down the Ctrl button while spinning your mouse wheel affects icon size. In Internet Explorer, you can click the Page button and choose Zoom or Text Size to change the size of pictures and text on your screen.

Many programs have a View option in their menus that lets you zoom in and out of things to make them larger or smaller. DPI scaling and the Accessibility Settings described later in this chapter offer many options for making items larger and easier to see onscreen.

TABLE 10.1 Common Aspect Ratios and Resolutions

Aspect Ratio	Resolutions that Fit
4:3	800 x 600, 1024 x 768, 1152 x 864, 1600 x 1200
5:4	1280 x 1024, 1600 x 1280
16:9	1088 x 612, 1280 x 720, 1900 x 1080

So, the trick here is to move the slider to a resolution (for example, 1024 x 768) and then click the Apply button. The new resolution is applied to your screen. If the screen goes blank, don't panic: You just chose a setting that won't work. The setting will be undone automatically in about 15 seconds and everything will be okay again. To try a different resolution, move the slider to another setting and click Apply again. If you find a setting you like, you can click OK and be done with it.

Using multiple monitors

Windows 8.1 supports the use of multiple monitors in a variety of configurations. In many cases, adding a second monitor is a simple matter of connecting to the external monitor and turning it on. If the display supports Extended Display Identification Data (EDID), Windows will detect it and adjust the resolution automatically.

10

If the external monitor is a television set, you may need to connect, turn on the TV, and then use the Input Select or TV/Video button on the TV or remote control to select the external input (often shown as AV1, PC, or Component on the TV screen). You can also add multiple video cards to the PC and connect a monitor to each one. Many newer display adapters support multiple monitors, so you can use a single adapter to drive more than one monitor.

After you connect to an external monitor and configure it to show input from the plug to which you connected the computer (if necessary), you can configure settings in Windows for the displays. Right-click the desktop and choose Screen Resolution to display the Screen Resolution page shown in Figure 10.18.

FIGURE 10.18

Display settings with three monitors working.

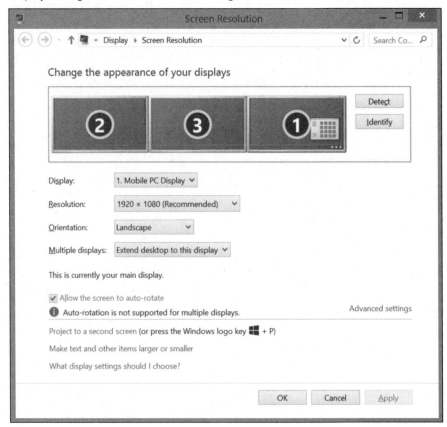

> **TIP**
> You can specify multiple monitor configurations from the Start screen as well. Open the Charms Bar, tap Devices, and then tap Second Screen.

The Screen Resolution page will show the additional displays after you connect the other displays to the computer. The displays are identified by numbers. The graphics on the displays indicate which is primary (that is, where the Start menu will appear) and which are secondary. Click the Identify button to have Windows display a large number on the display to help you identify which is which.

The following list explains the controls on the Screen Resolution page:

- **Display:** Use this drop-down button to choose a display to configure.
- **Resolution:** Select the display resolution from this slider button.
- **Orientation:** Choose between Landscape and Portrait modes, as well as Landscape (Flipped) and Portrait (Flipped) modes (which rotate the display).
- **Multiple Displays:** Choose Duplicate These Displays to display the same information on both displays. Choose Extend These Displays to extend the desktop across both displays. The other two options show the desktop only on display 1 or 2, depending on which you select.
- **Make This My Main Display:** Select this option to make the display number selected in the Display button the main display where the Start menu will appear.
- **Detect:** Click this button to have Windows detect the new display.
- **Identify:** Click this button to display an identifying number on the displays so that you can tell which is which.
- **Make Text and Other Items Larger or Smaller:** Click this link to open a Display page, where you can choose the font size to use on the displays.

> **TIP**
> Extending Microsoft Excel across two monitors enables you to see twice as many columns!

You can also display content on the second monitor only, leaving the first monitor black. If you're using a mobile computer on batteries, this option conserves battery power.

Regardless of how you set things in the New Display Detected window (or even if it doesn't appear at all), you can use the Display Settings dialog box to configure the second monitor. Open Display Settings as described at the top of this section. Then click the second monitor's box (with the number 2 in it). If that second monitor is grayed out, choose Extend My Desktop onto This Monitor. If the second monitor still doesn't light up, click Apply.

10

More Stuff You Can Do with Monitors

Your monitor attaches to a graphics card or graphics chip inside your computer. That card or chip defines the full range of your visual display. Windows 8.1 might not give you access to the full range of settings available to you, even after you click the Advanced Settings button.

To take full advantage of your graphics card's (or chip's) capabilities, you may want to use the configuration program that came with that device. There are hundreds of such devices on the market and no rule that applies to them all. To fully understand the capabilities of your graphics card and the programs for using it, refer to the manual that came with the card or your computer.

> **NOTE**
>
> If you can't get the second monitor to work, make sure it's properly connected and turned on. If the second monitor is a TV, make sure you choose the right input setting using Input Select or TV/Video on the TV or its remote control.

You can arrange the squares in the dialog box to match the arrangement of the monitors. For example, if monitor 2 is to the left of monitor 1, drag the 2 square to the left of the 1 square. If the monitors are stacked with 1 on top of 2, drag the 1 square so that it's above the 2 square.

Reducing monitor flicker

If a monitor seems to flicker, adjusting its refresh rate can help. You shouldn't change the refresh rate just for the heck of it, however. Do so only to reduce flicker. First, click the Advanced Settings link. Then select the Monitor tab in the dialog box that opens. Use the drop-down under Screen Refresh Rate to try a higher setting.

After you choose a new refresh rate, click Apply. The monitor might go blank for a few seconds. When it comes back on, see whether the situation has improved. If not, you can try another refresh rate (followed by a click on the Apply button) until you find an optimal setting. When you find the best setting, click OK to close the Advanced Settings dialog box.

Don't forget to click OK after adjusting settings in the Display Settings dialog box. Remember that the settings you choose aren't set in concrete. You can re-open that dialog box and change things any time you like.

Adjusting the font size (dpi)

Windows 8.1 lets you change the size of text and other items on the display, which can be particularly useful for high-resolution displays, making the screen more readable (which becomes more important the older we get!). To change text size, open the Display item from the Control Panel. Or right-click the desktop, choose Screen Resolution, and then click Make Text and Other Items Larger or Smaller. Figure 10.19 shows the resulting page, where you can change the size of all items (choose a custom DPI size). Just drag the slider control left or right to change the overall size.

> **NOTE**
>
> Be careful to increase the current percentage value only slightly. Otherwise, you might make things so huge that hardly anything fits on the screen.

The new setting will be applied after you log out and log back in again. If the items on your screen are too large, repeat the preceding steps, choosing a smaller size.

Adjusting the font size dpi isn't the only way to enlarge text on the screen. Many programs offer a Zoom option on their View menus that enables you to resize text. The Accessibility options described later in this chapter also offer some alternatives.

You can also change a scaling level for all your displays. To do so, click the check box labeled Let Me Choose One Scaling Level for All My Displays. The dialog box changes as shown in Figure 10.20.

FIGURE 10.19

The Display page.

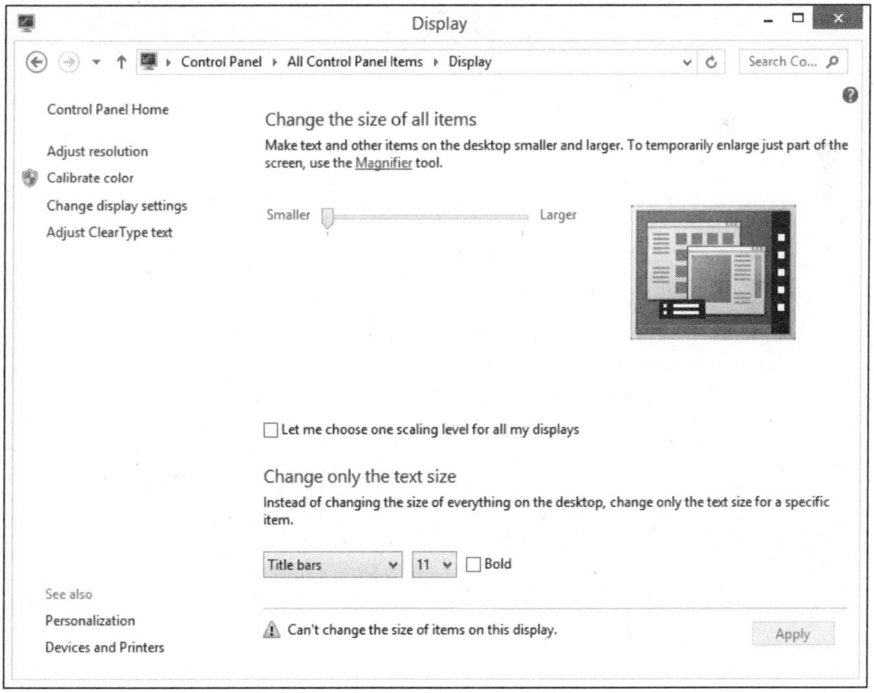

FIGURE 10.20

Choose a scaling level for all displays.

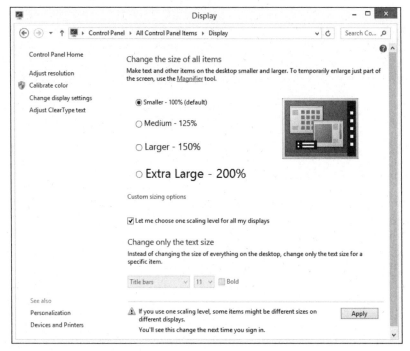

Personalizing your mouse

If you grow tired of the same old mouse pointer, or you need to make your mouse pointer easier to see, click the Change Mouse Pointers link in the Personalization window. You see the Mouse Properties dialog box with the Pointers tab selected, as shown in Figure 10.21.

To change your mouse pointers, choose a scheme from the drop-down menu. The list under the Customize heading shows you how the pointers in that scheme look. You can keep all the mouse pointers in the scheme by clicking OK, or you can assign a mouse pointer of your own. Double-click the pointer you want to change, or click it and click the Browse button. Clicking Browse takes you to a folder named Cursors, which contains all the built-in Windows 8 mouse pointers.

> **TIP**
>
> After you click Browse, you can enlarge the mouse pointer icons in the Browse dialog box for a better look. Hold down the Ctrl key and spin your mouse wheel, or click the Views button and choose Medium icons or a larger size.

FIGURE 10.21

The Pointers tab in the Mouse Properties dialog box.

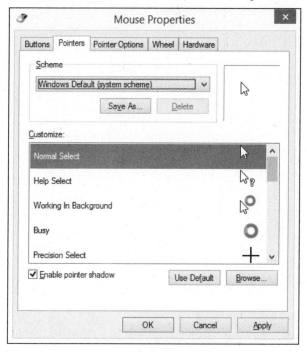

If you do assign mouse pointers on a case-by-case basis, click the Save As button to save your selections as a theme with any name you like.

TIP

Don't forget that most dialog box options aren't actually applied until you click the Apply or OK button.

Mice for lefties

If you're left-handed and you want the main mouse button to be below your left index finger, you need to reverse the normal functioning of the buttons. Generally, the left mouse button is the primary button, and the right mouse button is the secondary button. To reverse that setup, first select the Buttons tab in the Mouse Properties dialog box so that you see the options shown in Figure 10.22. Then select the Switch Primary and Secondary Buttons check box.

10

FIGURE 10.22

The Buttons tab in the Mouse Properties dialog box.

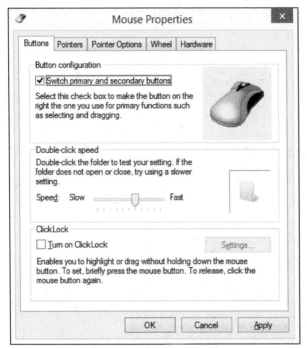

If you do reverse your mouse buttons, you have to adjust all the standard mouse terminology accordingly. Table 10.2 shows how the various mouse terms apply to right-handed and left-handed settings.

TABLE 10.2   Mouse Terminology for Righties and Lefties

Standard Terminology	Righties	Lefties
Primary button	Left button	Right button
Secondary button	Right button	Left button
Click	Left button	Right button
Double-click	Left button	Right button
Drag	Left button	Right button
Right-click	Right button	Left button
Right-drag	Right button	Left button

Adjusting the double-click speed

To double-click an icon, you have to tap the primary mouse button twice very quickly. Otherwise, it counts as two single clicks. If you have trouble tapping the button quickly enough, or if you're so fast that two single clicks are being interpreted as a double-click, adjust the Double-Click speed slider on the Buttons tab of the Mouse Properties dialog box.

> **TIP**
>
> To do away with the need to double-click anything, open the Folder Options applet from the Control Panel, and choose the option Single-Click to Open an Item.

To test your current setting, double-click the folder icon. If the closed folder doesn't change to an open one (or vice versa), you didn't double-click fast enough. Move the slider box toward the slow end of the scale and try again. When the slider is at a place where it's easy to open/close the little folder next to the slider, that's a good setting for you.

Using ClickLock

If you find it difficult to select multiple items by dragging the mouse pointer through them, you may want to try activating the ClickLock feature. Enabling that feature lets you select multiple items without holding down the mouse button. First you need to choose Turn On ClickLock on the Buttons tab of the Mouse Properties dialog box. Then use the Settings button to specify how long you need to hold down the primary mouse button before the key is "locked."

For example, say that you turn on ClickLock and set the required delay to about one second. To drag the mouse pointer through some items, you position the mouse pointer to where you plan to start selecting and hold down the mouse pointer for one second. Then you can release the mouse button and move the mouse pointer through the items you want to select. Those items will be selected as though you were actually holding down the left mouse button.

When you've finished selecting, just click some area outside the selection. The mouse pointer returns to its normal function, and the items you selected remain selected.

Speed up or slow down the mouse pointer

Selecting the Pointer Options tab in the Mouse Properties dialog box reveals the options shown in Figure 10.23. The first option, Select a Pointer Speed, controls how far the mouse pointer on the screen moves relative to how far you move the mouse with your hand. If you find it difficult to zero in on small things on your screen, drag the slider to the slow end of the scale. If you feel you have to move the mouse too much to get from one place to another on the screen, move the slider toward the fast end of the scale.

10

FIGURE 10.23

The Pointer Options tab in the Mouse Properties dialog box.

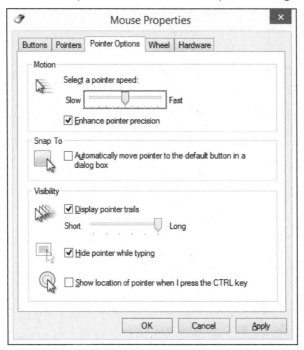

Selecting Enhance Pointer Precision makes it easier to move the mouse pointer short distances. It's especially useful if you move the pointer speed slider to the Fast side of the scale.

Making the mouse pointer more visible

If you keep losing sight of the mouse pointer on your screen, the remaining pointer options can make it easier to find, as follows:

- **Snap To:** If selected, this causes the mouse pointer to jump to the default button (typically the OK button) automatically as soon as the dialog box opens.
- **Display Pointer Trails:** If selected, this causes the mouse pointer to leave a brief trail when you move it, making it easier to see the pointer.
- **Show Location of Pointer When I Press the CTRL Key:** If you select this option, you can easily locate the mouse pointer on your screen by holding down the Ctrl key.

TIP

When you use a projector to give a demonstration onscreen, turn on the pointer trails to make following the mouse across the screen easier for your audience.

Yet another way to make your mouse pointer more visible is to use a large or animated mouse pointer.

Changing mouse wheel behavior

The Wheel tab in the Mouse Properties dialog box lets you control how far you scroll when spinning the mouse wheel (if your mouse has one). The default is usually three lines per notch. But you can change that to any value from 1 to 100 lines. Optionally, you can configure the wheel to move an entire page with each notch.

> **NOTE**
>
> The Hardware tab in the Mouse Properties dialog box shows information about your mouse and provides a means for manually updating the mouse driver should the need ever arise.

Don't forget to click OK after making your selection in the Mouse Properties dialog box.

That wraps it up for options in the Control Panel's Personalization page. But as you'll see in the following sections, there are many more things you can do to tweak Windows 8 to better suit your needs and tastes.

Personalizing the Keyboard

There are a few things you can do to change how the keyboard works. Some are in the Keyboard Properties dialog box, which we cover here. Others come under the heading of accessibility and are set using the Ease of Access Center in the Control Panel (not covered in detail in this book). To get to the Keyboard Properties dialog box, open the Keyboard item from the Control Panel (see Figure 10.24).

The options in the Keyboard Properties dialog box are as follows. As always, there is no right or wrong setting. It's all a matter of choosing settings that suit your typing style:

- **Repeat Delay:** Determines how long you have to hold down a key before it starts autotyping (repeating itself automatically).

- **Repeat Rate:** Determines how fast the key types automatically while you're holding it down.

- **Cursor Blink Rate:** Determines how rapidly the cursor blinks in a document.

If your keyboard offers programmable buttons, you may not see any options in the Keyboard Properties dialog box for defining those keys. More likely, you'll need to install and use the program that came with the keyboard to define the keys. There is no "one rule fits all" for that sort of thing. The only places to get the information you need are from the instructions that came with the keyboard and the keyboard manufacturer's website.

10

FIGURE 10.24

The Keyboard Properties dialog box.

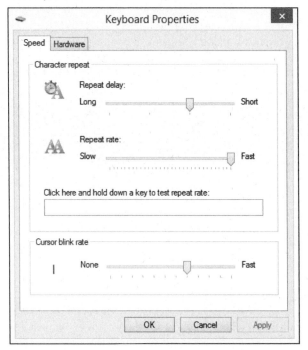

Customizing the Taskbar

The taskbar, which by default is at the bottom of your screen, is one of the most useful tools in Windows. It contains a button for each open desktop program window, icons for any programs that you've pinned to the taskbar, and the notification area. It can also contain some toolbars, such as the Address toolbar, which provides an easy way to open websites, drives, folders, or other items by their path or URL. You can customize the taskbar in many ways, so don't worry about what you see on yours right at this moment.

Some options for customizing the taskbar are in the Taskbar Properties dialog box. To open that dialog box, use whichever of the following techniques is easiest for you:

- Right-click any empty spot on the taskbar and choose Properties.
- Tap the Windows key, type **task**, and click Taskbar and Navigation.
- In the Control Panel, choose Appearance and Personalization ➪ Taskbar.

In the dialog box, select the Taskbar tab to see the options shown in Figure 10.25. The options on that tab are as follows:

- **Lock the Taskbar:** If you select this option, you lock the taskbar, which prevents you from accidentally moving or resizing it. If you want to move or resize the taskbar, you first need to deselect this option to unlock the taskbar.

- **Auto-Hide the Taskbar:** If you select this option, the taskbar automatically slides out of view when you're not using it, thereby freeing the little bit of screen space it takes up. After the taskbar hides itself, you can rest the tip of the mouse button on the thin line at the bottom of the screen to bring the taskbar out of hiding.

- **Use Small Taskbar Buttons:** Shows small icons rather than the larger, default-size icons for taskbar items.

- **Taskbar Location on Screen:** Choose on which edge of the display the taskbar will appear.

- **Taskbar Buttons:** Choose whether Windows combines similar items on the taskbar (such as documents for the same program), and whether it combines icons all the time or only when the taskbar is full.

- **Notification Area:** Click the Customize button to specify which items appear in the notification area of the taskbar (tray).

- **Use Peek to Preview the Desktop:** Choose this option to hide all applications and show the desktop when you hover the mouse over the Show Desktop button at the far bottom right of the display.

FIGURE 10.25

The Taskbar tab in the Taskbar and Navigation Properties dialog box.

Click OK after making your selections from the dialog box. There are some other things you can do outside that dialog box to customize the taskbar, as described next.

Locking and unlocking the taskbar

The taskbar doesn't have to be at the bottom of the screen. And it doesn't need to be a specific height, either. When the taskbar is unlocked, you can move and size it at will. If the taskbar is unlocked, putting the tip of the mouse pointer at the top of the taskbar changes the pointer to a two-headed arrow. Also, if you have any toolbars on the taskbar, you'll see a *dragging handle* (columns of dots) next to each toolbar. When you right-click an empty area of the taskbar or the current time, the Lock the Taskbar option on the menu is deselected (see Figure 10.26).

FIGURE 10.26

An unlocked taskbar.

If the taskbar is locked, just right-click an empty portion of the taskbar or the current time and click Lock the Taskbar to unlock. The option is a toggle, so you can use the same procedure to lock the taskbar when it's unlocked.

Moving and sizing the taskbar

When the taskbar is unlocked, you can dock it to any edge of the screen as follows:

1. Place the tip of the mouse pointer on an empty portion of the taskbar (not in a toolbar or on a button).
2. Hold down the left mouse button, drag the taskbar to any screen edge, and release the mouse button.

To change the height of the taskbar, put the tip of the mouse pointer on the top of the taskbar so that it changes to a two-headed arrow. Then hold down the left mouse button and drag up or down until the bar is at a height you like. The minimum height is one row tall. The maximum is about a third of the screen.

> **TIP**
> If you have any problem getting the taskbar back to the original one-row tall size, close all open toolbars. Then size the taskbar to the height you want and choose which toolbars you want to view.

If you want to hide the taskbar altogether, select the Auto-Hide the Taskbar option in the Taskbar and Start Menu Properties dialog box, described earlier in this chapter. The taskbar stays hidden until you move the mouse pointer to the edge of the screen where you placed the taskbar.

Showing toolbars on the taskbar

Windows 8 comes with some optional toolbars you can add to the taskbar or allow to float freely on the desktop. To show or hide a toolbar, right-click the clock in the lower-right corner of your screen or an empty part of the taskbar and choose Toolbars. You see the names of toolbars shown in Figure 10.27 and summarized here.

FIGURE 10.27

Show or hide optional toolbars.

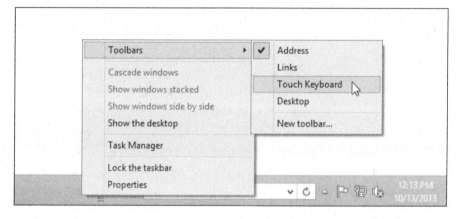

- **Address:** Displays an Address bar like the one in your web browser. Typing a URL into the bar opens your web browser and the page at the URL.

- **Links:** Displays the contents of Internet Explorer's Links folder as a toolbar. See "Using the Links toolbar (Favorites Bar)," later in this chapter, for more information.

- **Touch Keyboard:** Displays the touch keyboard/handwriting recognition window used with tablet PCs. Add this toolbar to your taskbar if you routinely work from the Windows desktop on a touch device.

- **Desktop:** Shows all the icons from your desktop in a condensed toolbar format, along with Libraries, Computer, Network, Control Panel, and your user profile folder.

TIP

Add the desktop toolbar to your taskbar to give you quick access to many of the items previously included in the Windows Start menu.

10

- **New Toolbar:** Create a custom toolbar containing icons from any folder you wish. For example, after choosing this option, click Documents under Libraries in the New Toolbar dialog box and click OK. The new toolbar that appears will provide quick access to all your folders and documents in your Documents folder.

On the Toolbars menu, any toolbar that has a check mark next to its name is "on" and visible in the taskbar. Any toolbar whose name isn't selected is hidden. Click a name to hide, or show, the toolbar.

When you first choose a custom toolbar, there may not be room for it on the taskbar, especially if the taskbar is already loaded up with buttons or other toolbars. The next section explains ways to deal with that.

Sizing and positioning taskbar toolbars

There isn't a lot of room on the taskbar, so it gets crowded if you add too many items to it. If you use a lot of optional toolbars on your taskbar, consider making it taller so that it can show more items. Try moving it to the side of the screen to see whether that helps.

When you have more items on a toolbar than it can show, you see the > > symbol at the right side of the toolbar. Clicking that shows the items that don't fit onscreen on the toolbar. If you have more open program windows than space for taskbar buttons, use the up and down arrows to the right of the visible taskbar buttons to see additional buttons.

> **TIP**
> You can also switch from one open program window to the next by pressing Alt+Tab.

When the taskbar is unlocked, you see a dragging handle at the left side of each toolbar. You can drag those handles left and right to move and size toolbars. You can also show or hide the toolbar titles. Figure 10.28 shows an example of the titles, a handle, and taskbar button scrolling arrows.

FIGURE 10.28

Taskbar and toolbar handles, titles, text, and buttons.

To show or hide the title or text, right-click the toolbar's title or dragging handle. Then choose Show Title to show or hide the toolbar's title. Click Show Text to show or hide text for icons on the toolbar.

> **NOTE**
>
> Text always appears next to icons when you click >> on a toolbar. The Show Text option has no effect on that. To change the text that appears next to an icon, right-click that text, choose Rename, type the new name (or edit the existing name), and press Enter.

Using the Links toolbar (Favorites Bar)

The Links toolbar offers easy, one-click access to favorite websites. In fact, the Links toolbar shows the contents of your Internet Explorer Favorites Bar. Just understand that Links on the taskbar is actually your Internet Explorer Favorites Bar.

You can make the Favorites Bar visible in Internet Explorer, the taskbar, or both. It's easiest to add links to the toolbar from Internet Explorer. If you don't see that toolbar in Internet Explorer, right-click the Internet Explorer window's title bar and choose Favorites Bar. The rest is easy:

- To create an icon for the page you're currently viewing, click the Add to Favorites Bar button at the far left of the Favorites Bar.

> **TIP**
>
> As with any toolbar, when there are more links than space, you see >> at the end of the toolbar. Click that symbol to see hidden links.

- To create an icon for a link on the current page, drag the link from the page onto the Favorites Bar.
- To remove an icon from the Favorites Bar, right-click the item and choose Delete.
- To rearrange items on the Favorites Bar, drag the item's icon to a new location on the toolbar.

Any changes that you make to the Favorites Bar in Internet Explorer are automatically reflected in the Links toolbar on the taskbar.

Customizing the Notification Area

The notification area (also called the system tray) appears at the right side of the taskbar. It contains icons for programs and services that are running in the *background,* which means it's a program that typically doesn't have a specific program window or taskbar button associated with it. Icons in the notification area represent features such as your antivirus software, volume control, network connection, and Windows Sidebar. Pointing to an item displays its name or other information.

To conserve space on the taskbar, nonessential or inactive icons can be hidden. When you have hidden items, you see a small up-facing arrow at the left side of the notification area, as shown in Figure 10.29. Click the arrow button (labeled Show Hidden Icons) to see the hidden items.

10

FIGURE 10.29

The notification area.

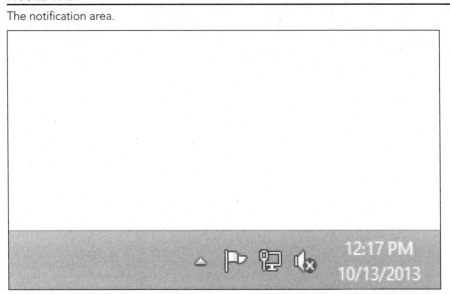

To customize the notification area icons, right-click the taskbar and choose Properties. Then click Customize in the notification area group and click the Turn System Icons On or Off link near the bottom of the window to see the options shown in Figure 10.30.

Use the drop-down buttons to show or hide the Clock, Volume Control, Network, Power, Action Center, and Input Indicator icons. Any items that are disabled (dimmed) aren't relevant to your system, so don't worry about those.

> **NOTE**
>
> As always, the items you turn on or off aren't affected until you click Apply or OK.

Getting rid of notification area icons

You cannot delete a notification area icon by right-clicking and choosing Delete. Unlike toolbars, its icons are not shortcuts for opening programs. Icons in the notification area represent programs that are already running — albeit in the background, with nothing showing on the screen.

There is no single, simple step you can perform to get rid of a notification area icon. There are hundreds of programs on the market that can run in the background. To keep such a program from showing up in your notification area, you might need to prevent that program from auto-starting with your computer, or you might need to remove the program from your system altogether. Then again, you might need only to get to the program's Options dialog box and deselect the check box that makes it show a notification area icon.

FIGURE 10.30

The Notification Area Icons window.

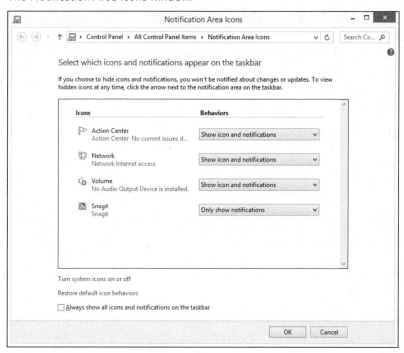

One thing's for sure: You don't want to delete anything from the notification area unless you know exactly what you're deleting and why. For example, an icon could represent your virus or spyware protection. You wouldn't necessarily want to delete such programs, or prevent them from auto-starting, because they need to be running in the background to keep your computer secure.

To see what options are available for a notification area icon, right-click the icon. Some programs that run as icons in the notification area can show up on the screen in a program window. Double-clicking its notification area icon will usually open that program window. From there, you can learn more about the program that the icon represents. If it has a menu bar, choosing Tools ⇨ Options might take you to a dialog box where you can prevent the program from auto-starting, or prevent it from showing up in the notification area.

If the notification area icon represents a program you don't want on your system at all, you can remove the program through Control Panel. Just make sure you don't remove a program you actually need and cannot replace.

 See Chapter 32 for tips on removing programs.

If you want to keep a program but also want to prevent it from auto-starting and can't find a way to do that from within the program, there are still a couple other ways to do that. If the program has an icon in your Startup folder, you can just remove that icon from that

10

folder. Or you can use the System Configuration tool in the Administrative Tools folder to disable auto-starting of specific programs.

Tweaking the clock

The clock in the lower-right corner of the screen doesn't look like much, but you can do quite a few things with it. If you point to it, you see the current date. If you click it, you see the current date marked on a calendar and the time on a clock. If you right-click the time and choose Adjust Date/Time, you come to the dialog box shown in Figure 10.31. There you can do several things with the clock.

FIGURE 10.31

Date and time properties.

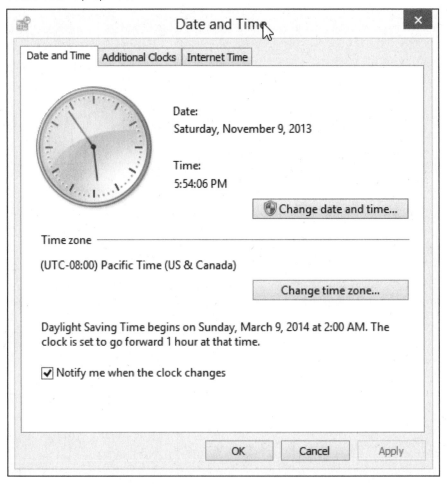

> **NOTE**
>
> You need administrative privileges to change some aspects of the date and time. That might sound silly, but in a home environment, it keeps the kids from getting around parental controls that limit when they can use the computer.

First, you want to make sure your clock is set to the time zone you're in. Click Change Time Zone and choose your time zone. If you're in an area that honors daylight saving time, check the option that allows that change to be handled automatically.

If the date or time is wrong on your clock, you can click Change Date and Time and manually enter the correct information. Or select the Internet Time tab and click Change Settings. Then click Update Now to synchronize your calendar and clock with the "official time" on the Internet.

> **NOTE**
>
> You might see a message that the Windows Time service is not running when you select the Internet Time tab. You can still click Change Settings and click Update Now to set the time. Windows will start the Time service for you.

You can also make the clock show the current time for up to three time zones. Click Additional Clocks. Then just follow the onscreen instructions to add one or two more times to your clock. Click OK after adjusting all your time settings.

Back on the desktop, the current time in the notification area will be accurate. Likewise when you point to the time to see more information. If you set up multiple time zones, you'll see them all when you point to the current time. Clicking the time shows times for all time zones in the form of clocks, as in Figure 10.32.

FIGURE 10.32

Clocks for multiple time zones.

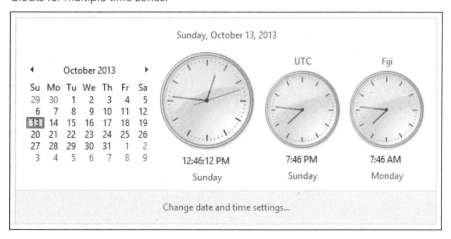

10

Wrap-Up

This chapter has been all about the many ways you can customize the Windows desktop, Start menu, and taskbar to set up your screen in a way that works for you. You have many options. The important thing to keep in mind is that they are *options,* and there is no right or wrong way to do things. It's all about making choices that work for you. Here's a quick recap of the essentials:

- The Windows desktop is basically your entire screen — the place where you do all your work.
- Most tools for personalizing your system are in the Personalization page of the Control Panel. To get there quickly, right-click the desktop and choose Personalize.
- To personalize your taskbar, right-click the taskbar and choose Properties.
- To add or remove taskbar toolbars, right-click the clock and choose Toolbars.
- To show or hide notification area icons, right-click the clock and choose Customize Notification Icons.

Customizing Startup Options

Your computer already has many programs and apps installed on it, and many thousands more that you can add to it. Many are programs that you can start at will from icons on the Start screen or desktop. Some programs start automatically when you log in. Often, these programs run in a window, as an icon on the taskbar, or both.

Another type of program starts automatically as soon as you start your computer. These are referred to as *services,* and services are most often part of the Windows operating system itself or programs that control hardware or other underlying functions. Services generally don't have program windows or have taskbar buttons on your desktop. In fact, you would likely never know that services existed unless you went looking for them.

This chapter is about controlling exactly which programs and services do, and don't, start automatically when you first start your computer and Windows. By controlling these programs, you can streamline the Windows startup and fix problems with performance or function. We don't cover new Windows 8 apps too much in this chapter because they're covered in more detail in other chapters. Instead, this chapter focuses primarily on legacy Windows programs that run in the desktop environment.

First Things First

First, we need to make a distinction between application programs and services. For the purposes of this chapter, an application program (or *application*) are programs that, when open, usually have a program window on your desktop and a rectangular button in the taskbar. Typically, you open and use such a program to perform some specific task, such as browse the web or perform spreadsheet tasks. Then you close the program when you've finished that task. To close such a program, you can typically click the Close (X) button in the program's upper-right corner or right-click the program's taskbar button and choose Close. You can reopen the program at any time by clicking its icon on the Start screen. Windows 8 apps can be closed by grabbing the top edge of their window and dragging down until the app resizes to a small rectangle. Release the mouse button and the app closes.

Even though most application programs run in a window and live on the taskbar, not all do. Windows 8 apps run as standalone programs that do not show up on the Windows taskbar. They are accessible as tiles from the Windows 8.1 Start screen. Many utility applications appear as icons on the notification area (tray). The Ultramon program, for example, runs as an icon on the tray and provides special features for using multiple displays. Typically, when you rest the mouse pointer on a tray icon such as Ultramon's, a tooltip appears, showing the name of the program that the icon represents. Clicking or double-clicking such an icon often opens a dialog box or similar window. Right-clicking such an icon often displays a list of things you can do with the program.

 In many cases, you can control whether a program's icon appears in the tray. You can also control which of the Windows 8 tray icons appear in the tray. See Chapter 10 to learn how to customize the taskbar and tray.

Services are also application programs, but services generally don't provide any means for the user to interact with them. Many services are actually included as part of the operating system. For example, the Windows Time service provides time synchronization functions for Windows, enabling it, for example, to set the computer's time from a remote time server. The DHCP Client service is another example of a service. It is responsible for (among other things) obtaining an IP address for your computer when the computer starts up, enabling your computer to participate on the network.

Neither the Windows Time service nor the DHCP Client service provides any means for you to interact with them; they do their thing in the background with no input from you. In contrast, the Windows Firewall service does provide a means for you to interact with it. Even so, Windows Firewall is still a service, and most of the time, you don't interact with it. Services such as this that provide a means for user interaction are by far the exception rather than the rule.

Why are we telling you about services and how they differ from other programs? In most cases, you won't need to manage services or control their startup, but in some situations, doing so is necessary. Most of the time, you'll be more concerned with which application programs start automatically. But it's important for you to understand the difference so that you can make an educated decision as to how to handle services. One of the main focuses of this chapter is to help you understand how to make programs start automatically that normally don't do so, how to stop certain programs from starting automatically, and why you would want to do either. Let's start with how you make programs start automatically.

Starting Programs Automatically

If you always use a certain program when you start your computer, you can configure Windows to start that program automatically. For example, maybe you use Microsoft Outlook 2013 all the time for your e-mail and want it to open as soon as you log in to the computer so that you don't have to start it yourself.

> **CAUTION**
>
> Be aware that some programs provide an option during the program setup wizard to turn on or off auto start features. For many programs that rely on constant network and/or Internet connectivity, you can almost bet that the program will need to auto start each time Windows starts. You may not need other programs, such as graphics tools, to start every time Windows launches, so consider de-selecting the option to have the program start when Windows starts.

Using the Startup folder

You have a couple of ways to make programs start automatically when you log in. In previous versions of Windows (for example in Windows 7), you could access the Start menu from the Start button and All Programs menu. Windows 8.1 does not provide this type of access to it. Similarly, you cannot use Search to directly find the Startup folder.

Fortunately, you can pin the Startup folder to the Start screen so you can quickly add or remove programs from it. To do that, use these steps:

1. Press Windows + X and then click Run.

2. Type **shell:startup** and click OK. File Explorer opens so you can see the contents of the Startup folder. Click the Programs folder in the Address bar to go back one subfolder so you can see the Startup subfolder listed in the main Explorer window. Figure 11.1 shows an example Startup folder. You also can enter the following path, using your user profile name in place of <username>:

FIGURE 11.1

The Startup folder.

225

```
C:\Users\<username>\AppData\Roaming\Microsoft\Windows\Start Menu\
   Programs
```

3. Right-click the Startup folder and choose Pin to Start on the context menu, as shown in Figure 11.2. A shortcut of the folder appears in the current folder view.

FIGURE 11.2

Pin the Startup folder to the Start screen.

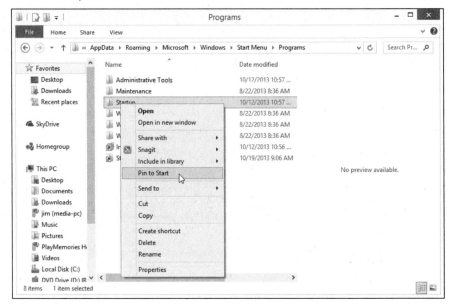

4. Display the Start screen by pressing the Windows Key or showing the Charms Bar and clicking Start.

5. Scroll to the far right to see the Startup folder pinned to the Start screen, as shown in Figure 11.3.

You can now open the Startup folder to view and manage programs that start when you boot up Windows. If you want a program to start automatically for you, put a shortcut for the program in your Startup folder. If you want a program to start automatically for everyone, you can instead put it in the Startup folder for all users.

FIGURE 11.3

The Startup folder pinned to the Start screen.

If you're already logged in to your user account, the steps to open your own Startup folder are easy:

1. Display the Start screen.

2. Scroll over until you see the Startup folder tile on the screen.

3. Click that Startup folder tile. The folder opens as a folder on the desktop.

To make an application program auto start, right-drag (drag with the right mouse button) an icon for that program into Startup folder and drop it there; then choose Create Shortcuts Here.

CAUTION

Keep in mind that the more programs you add to the folder, the longer it will take for your computer to start. So don't get carried away and put all your favorite programs in there. One or two shouldn't slow down the system.

When you've finished, close the Startup folder. Windows Defender may show a message alerting you to the fact that your startup options have changed. No cause for alarm. In this case, the message is superfluous because you intentionally changed your startup programs. Defender doesn't know that, however. It's just doing one of its many jobs, which in this situation is to keep you informed of changes to your startup options.

TIP

To add a program's shortcut to the Startup folder for all users so that it starts for everyone, use the same process as described previously, except drag the icon to the All Users Startup folder rather than your personal Startup folder.

Using the Task Manager Startup tab

You can use the Windows 8.1 Task Manager to help you manage and monitor running programs and services. Chapter 32 discusses Task Manager in detail, but it's worthwhile to mention now that you can view and disable properties of programs in your Startup folder with the Startup tab.

Figure 11.4 shows an example of a Startup tab (click More Details to view this tab). Notice the Status column. It tells you if a program is enabled or disabled. To disable a program, right-click the row on which it appears and click Disable. You also can click a program and click the Disable button at the bottom of the Task Manager window.

FIGURE 11.4

The Startup tab of Task Manager.

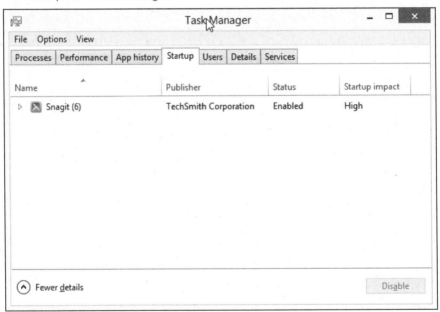

An interesting part of the Startup tab is the Startup Impact column. That column shows you the relative impact on your system when Windows starts a program automatically.

11

Stopping auto start applications

Should you ever change your mind about auto start applications, you just need to reopen that Startup folder for your user account. Then delete the shortcut icon for any program you don't want to auto start. Or, if you moved it from another location, move it back (out of the Startup folder). However, not all programs that auto start will be in the Startup folder for your user account. Some may be in the Startup folder for all users. (Still others will be in other locations.)

To view, and optionally remove, programs that start automatically in all user accounts, you need to get to the all users Startup folder, found at the following hidden location:

```
C:\ProgramData\Microsoft\Windows\Start Menu\Programs
```

You may need administrative privileges to make changes to that folder, so be prepared to enter an administrative password if you're working from a standard account. Figure 11.5 shows an example of the Startup folder for all users. You can open the Startup folder from within this folder view.

FIGURE 11.5

Open the Startup folder for all user accounts.

The Startup folder for all users works just like the Startup folder for a single user account. If you want a program to auto start in all user accounts, drag that program's icon into the folder. If you want to stop a program from auto starting in all user accounts, delete its icon from that Startup folder. But again, stick with programs you know. Removing programs from the Startup folder for all users at random could have unpleasant consequences that you weren't expecting.

Using the System Configuration Tool to Control Startup

One tool that has existed in multiple versions of Windows that lets you control program startup is the System Configuration program. That program is also available in Windows 8.1. To open System Configuration, open the Control Panel, click Large Icons or Small Icons from the View By drop-down list, and click Administrative Tools. Double-click the System Configuration shortcut.

If you're at the Windows Start screen, type **MSCONFIG**. Click the Msconfig icon in the Apps window.

Figure 11.6 shows the System Configuration program window.

FIGURE 11.6

The System Configuration program window.

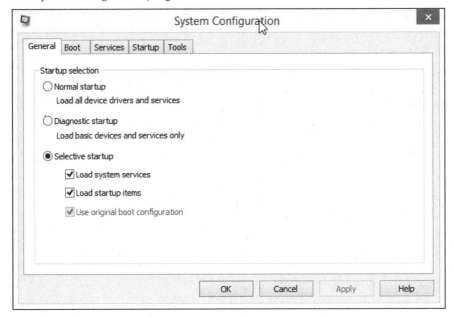

The General tab, shown in Figure 11.6, offers three options for controlling startup:

- **Normal Startup:** Start Windows normally. All items that normally start automatically are started.

- **Diagnostic Startup:** Load only basic device drivers and operating system services but not other services or programs. Use this option to troubleshoot problems with Windows startup that might be caused by a third-party service, device driver, or program.

- **Selective Startup:** Choose which types of items to start automatically. Start Windows with basic devices and services, and optionally other system services and startup programs.

The Boot tab, shown in Figure 11.7, lets you control how Windows boots. The large list box lists all the operating system boot selections. If Windows 8.1 is the only operating system on the computer, it will be the only one listed in the text box. If you have a dual-boot system (for example, with Windows 7 and Windows 8.1 on the same computer in different partitions), those additional operating system instances will also be listed. Click an instance and then click Set as Default to make that operating system boot by default when the computer starts.

FIGURE 11.7

The Boot tab.

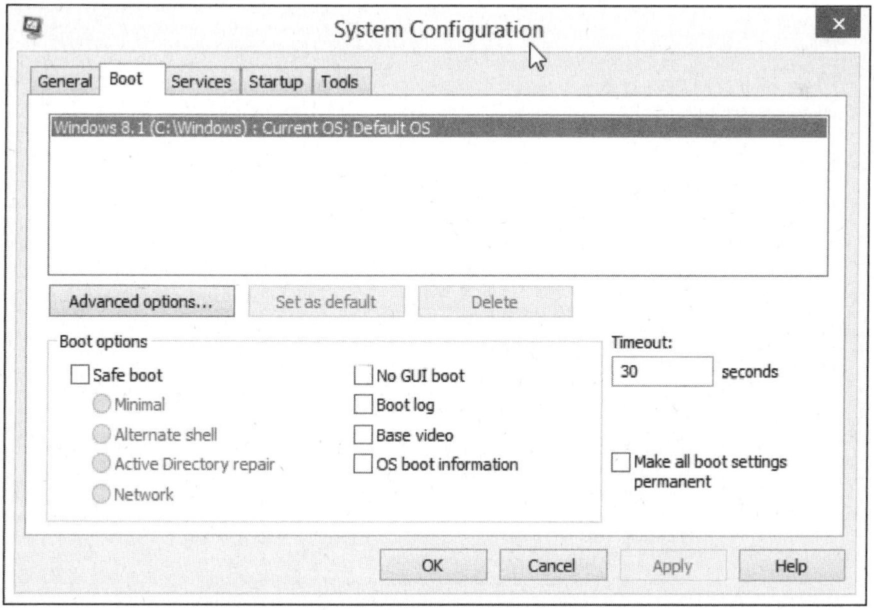

The other options under the Boot Options group enable you to configure options for a safe boot so that the next time you start Windows, it boots with the specified safe boot option. You can also set other boot options. Because you likely will use these options rarely, if ever, we point you to the Help content rather than cover them here. Just click the Help button on the Boot tab to view an explanation of these options.

> **NOTE**
>
> Use the option Make All Boot Settings Permanent to have the settings apply every time you boot the computer.

The Services tab (shown in Figure 11.8) gives you a means to disable services so that they don't start when Windows boots. This tab also shows the current state of the services on the computer. Selecting the check box beside a service indicates that the service is enabled. You can disable a service by clearing its check box. If you want to view only third-party services, select the Hide All Microsoft Services check box. This helps you identify services that are not part of the Windows 8 operating system.

FIGURE 11.8

The Services tab.

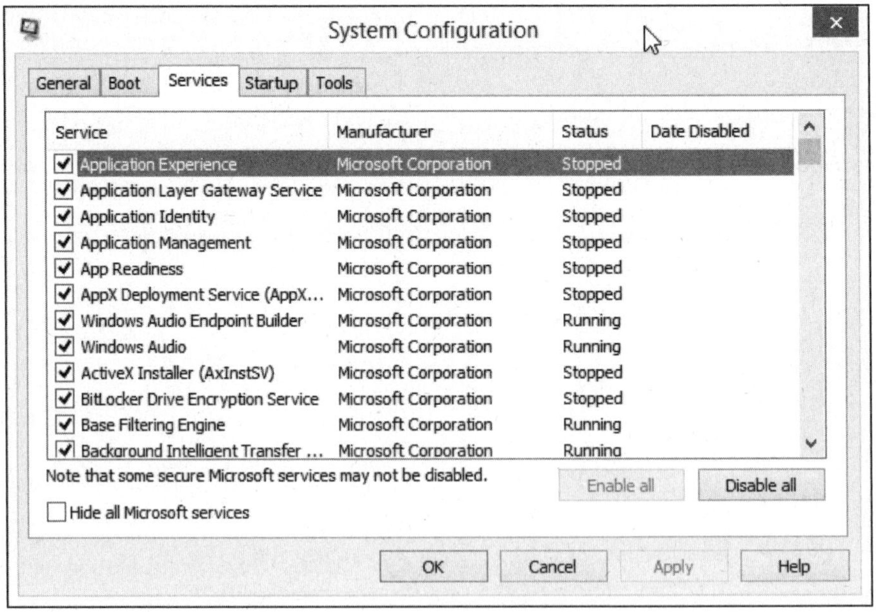

In general, you should avoid disabling services unless you know exactly what the service does and what the consequences of disabling it will be. Usually, you want to disable a service only if a tech support engineer or some troubleshooting documentation has directed you to do so.

The Startup tab is pretty useless in Window 8.1. It simply has a link (see Figure 11.9) to the new and improved Task Manager's Startup tab, which was discussed earlier in the chapter (refer to Figure 11.5).

FIGURE 11.9

The Startup tab.

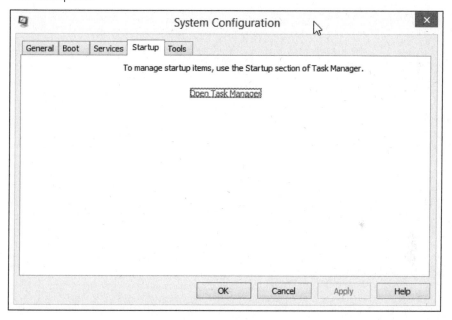

Often, program developers design their programs to start from the registry instead of the Startup folder when they don't want the user to be able to turn off the program without uninstalling it. This is typical for antivirus programs and other utility programs. If you're trying to turn off a program and you don't find it in one of the Startup folders, there is probably an entry for the program in the registry that causes it to start automatically.

The Tools tab (see Figure 11.10) gathers a selection of useful tools for troubleshooting problems with your computer and compiling more information about programs. Just click a tool and click Launch to open the tool.

FIGURE 11.10

The Tools tab.

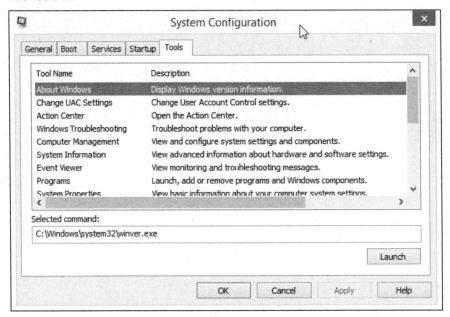

After you make changes to configuration settings in the System Configuration tool, you need to click OK and then restart the computer to make the changes take effect.

Services Snap-In

Windows 8.1 includes a system management framework tool called the Microsoft Management Console (MMC). The MMC provides access to various *snap-ins,* with each snap-in providing options for different configurations or an interface to manage items such as policies, accounts, and so on. One of these snap-ins is named Services.msc. It's not a user-friendly program; instead, it's designed for professionals. Beginners and casual users are better off sticking with the Startup folders to work with auto start programs. Even so, beginners can start to understand how some of the underlying pieces of Windows work by looking through the Services console and checking out what some of the services do.

> **NOTE**
>
> If you want to make any changes in the Services snap-in, log out of any standard accounts and in to an account that has administrative privileges. Or right-click Services and choose Run as Administrator.

To start the Services snap-in, press Windows + X on the desktop, click Run, and type **SERVICES.MSC**. Click OK. When the Services snap-in is open, use the View menu options to choose how you want to view icons. Figure 11.11 shows how things are displayed in the Detail view. The toolbar contains a couple of buttons for showing and hiding optional Console Tree and Action panes. (Both are shown in Figure 11.11.) Extended and Standard tabs are near the bottom of the window. Both tabs show the same information, but the Extended tab shows additional information about the selected service, with links for starting and stopping the service. The figure shows how things look in the Extended tab.

> **TIP**
>
> You can also start the Services console by opening it in the Administrative Tools folder of the Control Panel. Another way is to type SERVICES.MSC while at the Windows Start screen, and click View Local Services in the Apps window.

FIGURE 11.11

The Services snap-in.

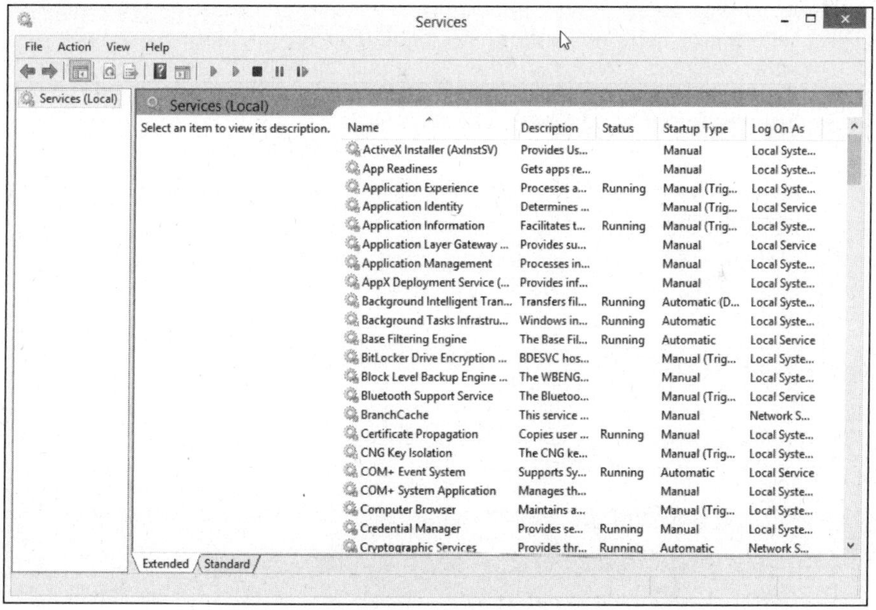

Selecting the Extended tab opens a new pane at the left side of the program window that shows detailed information about any service name you click. It also provides options to start a service that's not running, or to stop or restart the service if it's not running correctly.

> **NOTE**
>
> Because of enhanced security in Windows 8 and Windows 8.1, you don't have as much leeway in starting and stopping services as you did in earlier Windows versions. Some services can't be stopped at all if you don't have administrative privileges.

If you scroll through the list of services, you'll probably see quite a few. Exactly which services are listed will vary from one computer to the next. Few, if any, of the services will have any meaning to the average computer user. These things are really only of use to professional programmers, network administrators, support technicians, or other experienced professionals. What follows is mainly for those folks. We don't summarize what each service does because doing so would eat up several pages and only repeat the information that's already in the Description column.

The Status column shows Running for those services that are currently running. It shows nothing for services that aren't running. The Startup Type column shows whether the service is configured to run automatically, if at all. Common settings are as follows:

- **Automatic (Delayed Start):** The service starts automatically, but only after a delay in time to enable other dependent services to start.
- **Automatic:** The service starts automatically when the computer starts or when a user logs in.
- **Manual:** The service doesn't start automatically. You can start the service, however, by right-clicking the service name and choosing Start or by choosing Start from the Action menu.
- **Disabled:** The service is disabled and must be enabled from the Properties dialog box before it can be started.

To get more information about a service or change its Startup type, right-click the service name and choose Properties. You see a dialog box like the one in Figure 11.12.

> **WHAT DOES THE DNS CLIENT DO?**
>
> IP addresses are what *routers* (networking hardware that move data around) use to locate devices such as servers on the Internet and send traffic back and forth between devices. The DNS client service is called a *DNS resolver* and is critical for networking because it resolves hostnames such as `www.wiley.com` to IP addresses such as `208.211.179.146`. When you type a URL into your web browser and press Enter, the DNS service contacts a Domain Name Server and gives it the hostname (in this example, `www.wiley.com`), and the name server responds with the IP address (or addresses) that corresponds to the hostname. Then the traffic (in this case, the request for the specified website) gets routed on the Internet to the server based on its IP address. Of course, you can browse the web for the rest of your life without knowing anything about DNS or IP addresses.

FIGURE 11.12

Properties for the DNS client service.

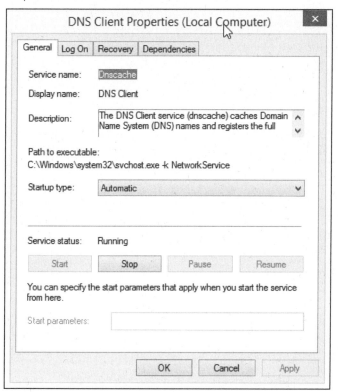

The options you see in Figure 11.12 are typical of the items listed in the Services snap-in. The Description text box provides a description of the services and tells what will happen if you disable or stop the service. The Path to Executable text box shows the location and name of the program that provides the service. The Startup Type option provides the Automatic, Manual, and Disabled options.

The buttons let you stop, pause, resume, or start the service. Some programs accept parameters, which you can add to the Start Parameters text box.

The Log On tab provides options for granting rights to services that need permissions to run. The Recovery tab provides options for dealing with problems when a service fails to start.

The Dependencies tab (see Figure 11.13) is one of the most important of the bunch because it specifies which services the current service depends on (if any) and which services depend on the current service. For example, DNS is a TCP/IP thing (which is the protocol used by the Internet and most modern local networks). If a service isn't starting and you can't figure out why, seeing what services the current one depends on might provide a clue. If the dependent service isn't running, the original one you're looking at can't start, so you need to go to its dependent service and make sure it's starting.

FIGURE 11.13

The DNS Client service Dependencies tab.

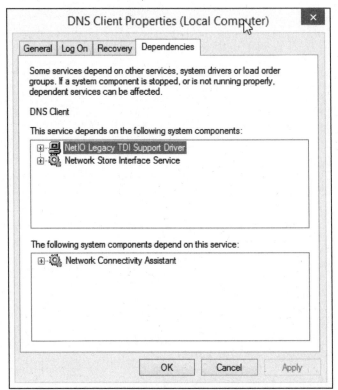

If you're interested in learning more about TCP/IP and how the Internet works, any book on TCP/IP or networking, or any book or course that prepares you for Microsoft Certified Systems Administrator (MCSA) or Microsoft Certified Systems Engineer (MCSE) certification, would explain all that in depth. For broader technical coverage of services, consult a technical reference such as Microsoft TechNet at http://technet.microsoft.com.

For more information on Microsoft certifications, see www.microsoft.com/learning/en-us/default.aspx.

Bypassing the Login Page

This is one of those little Windows secrets everyone likes to know about but should be cautious about using. It lets you bypass the login screen and start up Windows 8.1 in a specific user account automatically. Although it does save you one click at startup, it means anyone who sits at your computer can just turn on the power switch and have full access to everything in your user account. So don't do this if you want to keep other people out of your user account.

This trick requires administrative privileges. So, you need to know the password or you need to log in to an administrative account first. Here are the steps:

1. Press Windows + X, click Run, and enter **netplwiz**. Or you can open the Charms Bar, click Search, and enter **netplwiz**. Click the Netplwiz application on the Apps screen. The User Accounts dialog box appears, as shown in Figure 11.14.

FIGURE 11.14

The User Accounts dialog box.

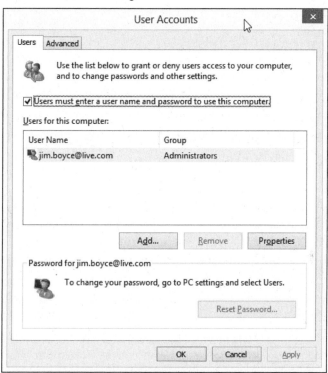

2. Grant permission or enter an administrative password if prompted.

3. Clear the Users Must Enter a User Name and Password to Use This Computer check box.

4. Click Apply.

5. In the dialog box that opens, type the name of the non-administrative user account to which you want to log in automatically.

6. If that user account requires a password, type the password once in the Password box and then again in the second box for confirmation. If the user account isn't password protected, leave both boxes empty.

7. Click OK in each open dialog box.

That's it. The next time you restart your computer, there will be no login page. You're taken directly to your user account. If there are other user accounts on the computer, and you want to let another user log in, log out of your account (click the Start button, the arrow next to the lock symbol, and choose Log Off). You're taken to the login page, which works normally. For example, if you want to get into a password-protected administrative account, you'll still click that account's icon and you'll have to enter the correct password.

If you ever change your mind about doing this, just repeat Steps 1 and 2 in the preceding list. This time, however, select the Users Must Enter a Username and Password to Use This Computer check box and click OK.

Troubleshooting Startup

Many things can prevent Windows from starting properly. There is no simple solution to the problem because too many things might be wrong. Typically, you need a professional to fix such problems. But we can tell you a few things that even the average user might try to get things going again.

Get rid of disabled devices

If your computer contains a hardware device that Windows 8.1 can't use, you should still be able to get to the desktop. But each time you do, you'll see a notification message about a device being disabled. That can get tiresome. If you manually disable the device through Device Manager, you won't see that message anymore. Also, it should take a little less time for Windows 8 to start.

> **CAUTION**
>
> Don't take wild guesses here. If you disable a hardware device you really need, you might not be able to start Windows 8.1 at all! If in doubt, it's better to take the computer into a repair shop and let the pros figure it out.

To disable a device, you need to first log in to a user account that has administrative privileges. Then press Windows + X and click Device Manager on the Power menu. Expand the category to which the device belongs. If you're not sure which category to look in, try the Other Devices category. You'll be looking for a device whose icon shows an exclamation point in a tiny yellow triangle. After you find the device, right-click its name and choose Disable.

When you've disabled the device, the yellow icon changes to a white downward-pointing arrow. That means the device is disabled and Windows 8 won't try to reinstall it on future boot-ups, which should mean a slightly quicker boot-up time and no irritating message about the disabled device.

When Windows won't start at all

If Windows won't start at all, try to start Windows 8 in Safe Mode. This is a special mode in which Windows 8 loads only the minimum services, drivers, and programs it needs to get going. Getting to Safe Mode isn't always easy. Read Chapter 6 on how to enable Safe Mode in Windows 8 and how to boot into it once it's enabled.

Start Screen versus the Desktop

Most of the negative press about Windows 8 and Windows 8.1 has little or nothing to do with the technical features in Windows, but rather focuses on the design shift from the desktop to the Start screen. Rather than focus on the capabilities and improved performance of the operating system, many so-called Windows "pundits" decry the fact that Windows 8 boots to a Start screen rather than the desktop. Most of them ignore the fact that the Windows desktop is just a click away. All a user has to do is click the Desktop tile to switch to the familiar desktop.

To address these complaints, Microsoft has introduced some additional features in Windows 8.1 to enable you to control whether Windows 8.1 opens the Start screen or the desktop when you log on. You can also configure additional settings that control how Windows 8.1's Start screen and desktop work together.

To access these settings, open the desktop, right-click the Taskbar, and choose Properties. Then select the Navigation tab (see Figure 11.15).

FIGURE 11.15

The Taskbar and Navigation Properties dialog box.

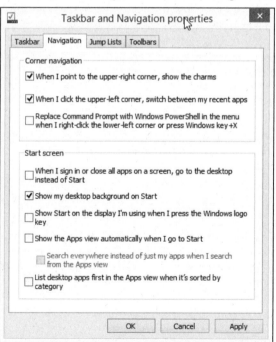

The first three options on the Navigation tab let you control what happens when you move the pointer to or click in the upper-left, upper-right, and lower-left corners of the desktop:

- **When I Point to the Upper-Right Corner, Show the Charms:** When this option is enabled, Windows 8.1 displays the Charms Bar when you move the pointer to the upper-right corner of the display.

- **When I Click the Upper-Left Corner, Switch between My Recent Apps:** When this option is enabled, Windows 8.1 cycles through the currently running apps when you click in the upper-left corner of the display.

- **Replace Command Prompt with Windows PowerShell in the Menu When I Right-Click the Lower-Left Corner or Press Windows + X:** Enable this option if you want Windows 8.1 to show a link for Windows PowerShell in the desktop's Start menu rather than the Command Prompt.

The options in the Start Screen control group let you control how and when Windows displays the Start screen:

- **When I Sign In or Close All Apps on a Screen, Go to the Desktop instead of Start:** Enable this option if you want Windows 8.1 to start on the desktop rather than the Start screen when you log in. This option, when enabled, also causes Windows 8.1 to display the desktop after you close a Windows 8 app.

- **Show My Desktop Background on Start:** Enable this option if you want Windows 8.1 to display the same background on the Start screen as you have on your desktop.

- **Show Start on the Display I'm Using When I Press the Windows Logo Key:** If your computer has multiple displays attached, enabling this option causes Windows 8.1 to display the Start screen on the currently active display when you press the Windows logo key. When this option is disabled, Windows 8.1 shows the Start screen on the primary display.

- **Show the Apps View Automatically When I Go to Start:** Enable this option if you want Windows 8.1 to shows the Apps view of the Start screen (see Figure 11.16), rather than the default Start screen view.

- **Search Everywhere instead of Just My Apps When I Search from the Apps View:** Enable this option to have Windows 8.1 search everywhere (for example, including the Internet) instead of just your installed apps when you search from the Apps view.

- **List Desktop Apps First in the Apps View When It's Sorted by Category:** Enable this option if you want Windows 8.1 to show your installed desktop apps first in the Apps view of the Start screen (when shown by category). Enabling this option helps you locate your desktop apps more quickly when using the Start screen.

FIGURE 11.16

The Apps view of the Start screen.

Wrap-Up

This chapter has covered all the different ways you can control which programs do, and don't, automatically start when Windows first starts up or when you first log in to your Windows user account.

- Some programs have their own built-in options for choosing whether the program starts automatically and appears in the notification area.

- You can start any application program automatically, or even open a folder automatically, by adding a shortcut for the program to the Startup folder.

- The full set of services that can be started and stopped automatically is listed in the `Services.msc` snap-in.

- The `Services.msc` snap-in is an advanced tool designed for professional Information Technology workers and network engineers. As such, it contains very little information that would be useful to the average computer user.

- You can use `netplwiz` to bypass the login page and go straight to any user account you wish.

- Safe Mode provides a means of starting Windows 8 with the fewest drivers and services. It helps you get the system started so that you can diagnose and repair the problem that is preventing normal startup.

- Use the Navigation tab of the Taskbar and Navigation Properties dialog box to control how and when Windows 8.1 displays the Start screen and desktop.

Part III

Beyond the Desktop

IN THIS PART

Windows 8.1 and Windows Live

IN THIS CHAPTER

Understanding Windows Live

Uploading files to SkyDrive

Using Office web apps

Windows Live is a web-based portal you can use to communicate and collaborate with others using Office web apps and shared files in SkyDrive. SkyDrive, which was introduced in 2007, has undergone multiple revisions and enhancements, is now fully integrated with Windows 8.1.

 See Chapter 16 for more on cloud technology.

With a free account to Windows Live, you have access to free online versions of Microsoft Office programs, including Word, Excel, PowerPoint, and OneNote. You also have a minimum of 7GB of free storage space using the SkyDrive service. This chapter shows you how to set up a Live account, use Office web apps, and upload files to SkyDrive.

Windows Live

Windows Live is an online, web-based portal (also known as the "cloud") for storing files that you want to access from the cloud. Windows Live is free and is hosted by Microsoft. Here are some of the Windows Live features available to users:

- **Outlook:** Free e-mail from Microsoft.
- **SkyDrive:** 7GB of free file storage.
- **Office web apps:** Access to online versions of Microsoft Office applications, including Word, Excel, PowerPoint, and OneNote.
- **Calendar:** For setting schedules, event reminders, and to-do lists. You can share your calendar with other users.

- **Contacts:** Where you can use Microsoft Messenger to chat with friends and manage your Hotmail contacts.
- **Photos:** An online place for posting photos and videos. You also can create slideshows to share with others.

Figure 12.1 shows an example view of the Windows Live website.

FIGURE 12.1

The Windows Live online portal.

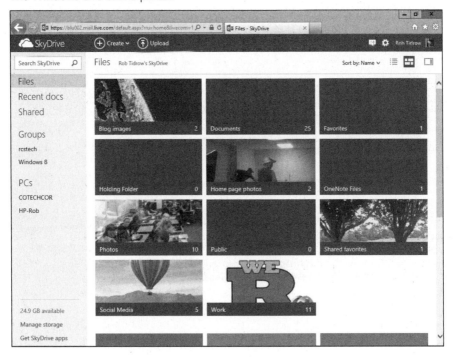

Creating a Windows Live Account

To begin using Windows Live, you must create an Outlook.com e-mail account. Visit www.outlook.com to see the screen shown in Figure 12.2. Click the Sign Up Now link to access the Microsoft Account form, as shown in Figure 12.3. Fill out the following information to create your Outlook.com account, which provides access to Windows Live.

FIGURE 12.2

Signing up for a Windows Live account is free.

- **Name:** Fill in your first and last names.

- **Birth Date:** Specify your birthdate.

- **Gender:** Select Male, Female, or Not Specified.

- **Microsoft Account Name:** Enter a name that you want to use as your e-mail address. The domain name will be @outlook.com.

- **Password:** Create a password with a minimum of eight-characters and enter it again in the Reenter Password field.

- **Phone Number:** Enter a phone number so Microsoft can send you a text message if you forget your password in the future.

- **Alternate Email Address:** In case you need to reset your password, fill in a second e-mail address you have. Or click the Or Choose a Security Question link to choose a security question to set up for any future password resets that are needed. You must provide at least two ways (phone number, alternate e-mail address, or security question) for Microsoft to confirm who you are in case you lose your password in the future.

- **Country/Region:** Select the country you reside in.

- **ZIP Code:** Fill in your ZIP code.

FIGURE 12.3

When you create an Outlook.com account, you can access Windows Live tools as well.

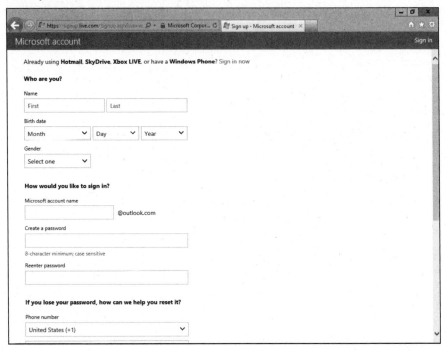

Once you finish, click I Accept. The Help Us Make Sure You're Not a Robot area appears. To continue, enter the CAPTCHA characters shown on the screen to prove that you aren't a robot.

The Outlook.com website appears. A message describing Outlook.com features displays. Click Continue to Inbox to see your new e-mail inbox.

Before you continue, you may want to know how to return to Windows Live or Outlook. com without setting up a new account. That is easy. The next time you visit Windows Live, you can go to www.outlook.com and then enter your Windows Live credentials.

Using Windows Live

When you first connect to Windows Live by using Outlook.com, you may wonder what else besides e-mail is available. To see additional services of Windows Live, use the Windows Live top menu. To access this menu, hover the mouse over the word *Outlook* on the top left of the screen. A down arrow appears, as shown in Figure 12.4.

FIGURE 12.4

Click the down arrow next to the Outlook label to see other Windows Live tools.

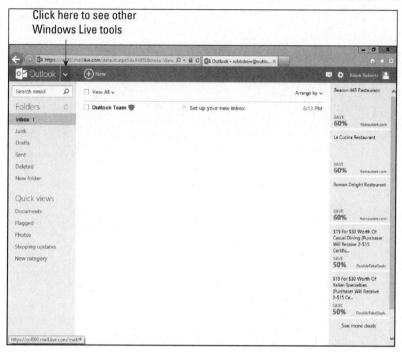

Click the down arrow to display the additional Windows Live tools (see Figure 12.5), which are described in the following list:

- **Mail:** Provides access to the Outlook.com Inbox area.

- **People:** Provides access to the Windows Live People area. This area enables you to follow your social media accounts, including Facebook, Google contacts, LinkedIn, and Twitter.

- **Calendar:** Provides access to your Outlook.com calendar.

- **SkyDrive:** Provides access to Microsoft SkyDrive (cloud-based storage) and Microsoft Office web apps. SkyDrive is discussed in the "Saving Files in SkyDrive" section next. Also, see the "Using Office Web Apps" section on using Office web apps.

For a more advanced discussion of SkyDrive see Chapter 16.

FIGURE 12.5

Windows Live includes more than just Outlook.com.

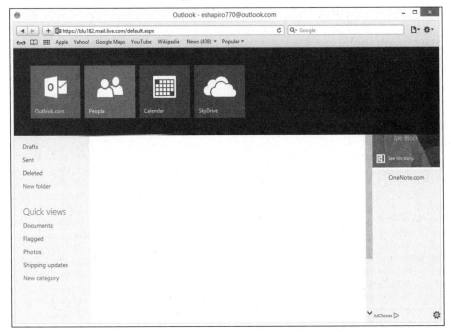

Saving Files in SkyDrive

SkyDrive is a cloud-based storage area available with your Windows Live account. You can upload files from your computer into the SkyDrive area on Windows Live to be accessible from other devices that have Internet access. For example, you can store files from your work computer on SkyDrive that you can access from home using your home computer, iPad, or smartphone. SkyDrive is now fully integrated into Windows 8.1 and looks like any hard drive attached to your computer.

To save a file to SkyDrive, click SkyDrive in Windows Explorer (see Figure 12.6). SkyDrive also shows up as an optional location in all your apps that can open, save, and delete files, such as Microsoft Word.

 Read Chapter 16 for more information on using SkyDrive as a Windows 8.1 app and as a Windows 8.1 application.

FIGURE 12.6

Saving files to SkyDrive through Windows Explorer.

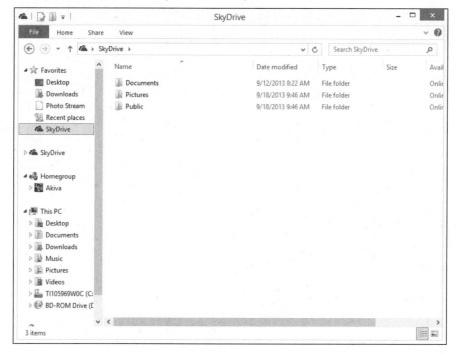

To upload a file from apps that are not integrated with SkyDrive, click the Upload link in Windows Live to display the Choose File to Upload dialog box. Select a file to upload to SkyDrive and click Open. SkyDrive uploads the file into your SkyDrive area.

Using Office Web Apps

Windows Live includes Office web apps, which are free online versions of Microsoft Word, Microsoft Excel, Microsoft PowerPoint, and Microsoft OneNote applications. The Office web apps are not full-featured versions of the Microsoft Office suite of programs. However, Office web apps provide many of the most common commands and options found in their non–web-based versions.

The idea is that you may need to make some minor edits to Office files while you're away from a computer that has Microsoft Office installed on it. If that's the case, you can upload your file to SkyDrive and then open that file in the Office web page in which it was created. Similarly, if you aren't able to access a computer with Office installed on it and you want to create a new document, spreadsheet, note, or presentation, you can do so with the Office web apps.

To use these apps, select the SkyDrive tool from the Windows Live top menu. Click the Create drop-down menu (see Figure 12.7) and select one of the following choices. For each of the choices, you need to enter a filename for the new file you want to create. Click Create to continue onto the editing screen of the Office web app you choose.

FIGURE 12.7

Use the Create drop-down menu to access Office web apps.

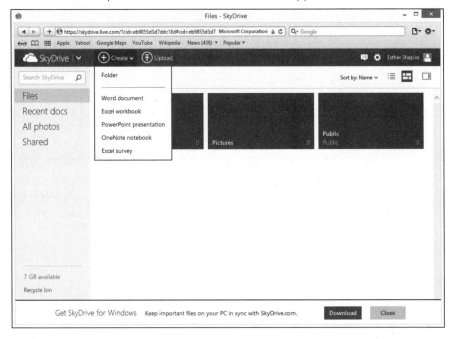

- **Word Document:** Launch the Word web app for creating a word processing document, as shown in Figure 12.8.

FIGURE 12.8

Create a new Microsoft Word document in the Word web app.

- **Excel Workbook:** Launch the Excel web app for creating a spreadsheet file, as shown in Figure 12.9.
- **PowerPoint Presentation:** Launch the PowerPoint web app for creating a presentation file, as shown in Figure 12.10.

FIGURE 12.9

Create a new Microsoft Excel spreadsheet in the Excel web app.

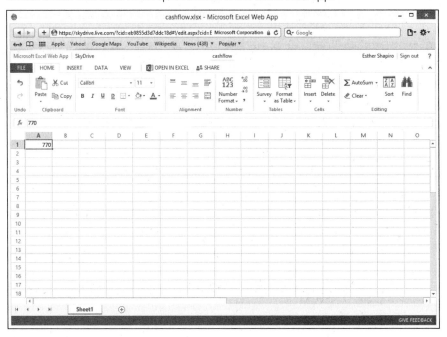

FIGURE 12.10

Create a new Microsoft PowerPoint presentation in the PowerPoint web app.

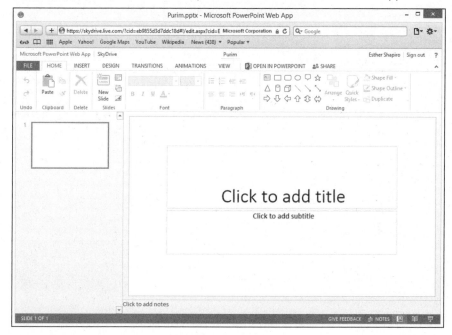

- **OneNote Notebook:** Launch the OneNote web app for creating a new note in OneNote, as shown in Figure 12.11.

If you have copies of Microsoft Office 2010 installed on your computer, or if you regularly use it, you may notice how the web apps look very similar to the ones installed on your computer. This is done on purpose so users can get comfortable using the online or installed version and be able to transfer those skills to the other version. No relearning is required.

Files you create using the web apps don't have to be explicitly saved. Once you create the file, Windows Live automatically saves your files as you work on them in the Web App area.

> **TIP**
>
> Office web app files can be shared with other users. To do this, create or open a web app document. Click the File menu and choose Share. Type the e-mail address of a person you want to share the document with, enter a quick note about the file, and click Send. To share with people on Facebook, click the Post to Facebook link.

FIGURE 12.11

Create a new Microsoft OneNote note in the OneNote web app.

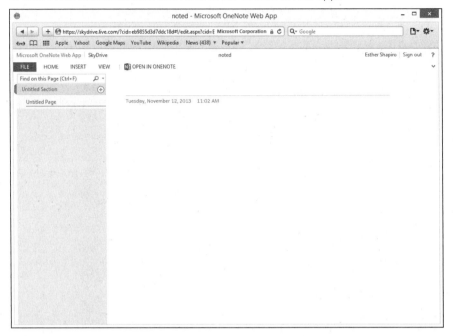

The web app files can be downloaded to your computer and opened in full versions of their corresponding Office application. For example, you can click the Open in Word tool on the Word Web App screen to download and open an online version of a Word file you're working on.

Wrap-Up

Windows 8.1 works well by itself or with online tools such as Windows Live. With Window Live, you can extend your workspace to allow you to store files in the cloud, use e-mail, and create files in Office web apps.

In summary:

- Access Windows Live at www.outlook.com.
- SkyDrive is now fully integrated into Windows 8.1. To save a file on SkyDrive, use Windows Explorer or Save As from any Windows App, or use the Add Files link on the SkyDrive screen.
- You can create Word, Excel, PowerPoint, and OneNote files using the Office web apps.

Social Networking with Windows 8.1

IN THIS CHAPTER

Using the People app

Setting up social media accounts

Viewing social media activity

Navigating the People app

O ne of the most popular activities online is communicating using social media programs, such as Facebook, LinkedIn, Twitter, Google +, and YouTube.

The updated Windows 8.1 People app lets you integrate your contacts and updates from multiple social network sites such as Windows Live, Facebook, and Twitter into one single location for that person. For Windows users, at least, it has now become the de facto hub for all your social media accounts. Also, the Mail and Messaging apps rely on the People app for selecting contacts to send e-mail and instant messages.

This chapter explores how to access various social media programs in Windows 8.1, including using the People app to consolidate many of your favorite social media communications into one app.

Using the People App

The Windows 8.1 People app is provided on the Windows Start screen when you install Windows 8.1. Figure 13.1 shows the People live tile. This tile displays information, updates, status changes, and photo changes for contacts you follow on different social media tools. For example, the information shown in Figure 13.1 shows Facebook friends.

FIGURE 13.1

The People app has a live tile on the Windows Start screen.

Setting up a social media account

You won't see any live updates on your People app if you haven't set up any social media accounts under Windows 8.1 yet. To do that, follow these steps:

1. Show the Windows Start screen.

2. Click the People app. The People app screen appears. (See Figure 13.2.)

3. To add accounts to People, click the Me link and click the OK button under the Go to Settings to Add Your Social Networks and Social Accounts link. Click a social media tool to set up your account information for it (see Figure 13.3).

4. Click Connect to connect Twitter to your Microsoft account. The Connecting to a Service screen appears.

FIGURE 13.2

The People app screen.

5. Enter your Twitter username and password to authorize Microsoft to use your account to read tweets, see whom you follow, and perform other tasks as they relate to using the Twitter service (see Figure 13.4). A similar screen appears for the other social media services you set up with the People app.

6. Click Remember Me if you want the People app to store your username and password.

7. Click Authorize App. After a few moments, you are shown the You're Ready to Go screen, shown in Figure 13.5.

8. Click Done.

NOTE

When authorizing Microsoft to use your social media accounts, you should note that Microsoft can't access your direct messages, nor can it see your password.

FIGURE 13.3

Setting up Twitter to work with the People app.

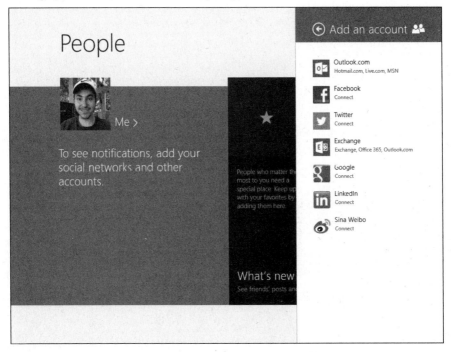

After you set up one account, return to the main People app screen. You can choose to set up other accounts, such as Exchange or Google accounts from the Add People to Your Contact List area. You can click the Add More Accounts link to see additional accounts you can set up.

Viewing social media activity

The People app is currently designed to allow you to view activity of your contacts and see their social media messages, status updates, and photos. It's divided into three main areas: People, What's New, and Me. By default, the People view shows you a list of your favorite contacts and then a list of your contacts from Twitter, Exchange, Google, Facebook, LinkedIn, and Hotmail accounts.

FIGURE 13.4

You must authorize Microsoft to use your Twitter or other social media tool account.

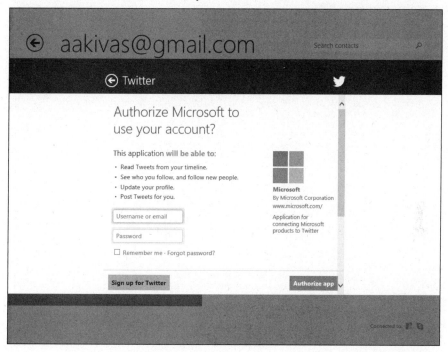

Figure 13.6 shows an example of the first screen of the People app. This screen is set up to include Favorites on the left side, with a list of contacts to the right. Figure 13.7 shows how contacts are listed in the People app.

To view a contact's current information and postings, click that person's tile. A contact card like the one shown in Figure 13.8 appears. On that card, you can do the following:

- View a current photo of the contact.
- Send a message.
- Get a Bing map of the contact's location.
- View the contact's profile information. Click the down arrow and click More Details to see additional profile information, such as full address if available.
- Like and comment on Facebook comments, and retweet and reply to tweets (on Twitter).

FIGURE 13.5

The You're Ready to Go screen displays after you set up a social media account.

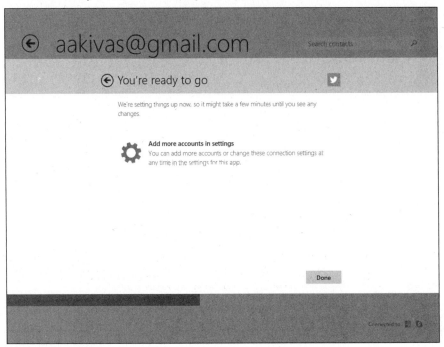

The All Updates button shows an expanded view of photos, uploads, status changes, postings, and so forth. Photos shows profile pictures, albums, and other photographic features posted by the contact.

When you return to the first screen of your People app, the second main area is What's New (see Figure 13.9). When you click What's New, you're shown the latest posting by people in your list of contacts. By looking at the bottom of each posting, you can see which social media tool was used to post that message.

FIGURE 13.6

The People app provides a complete view of your contacts in one place.

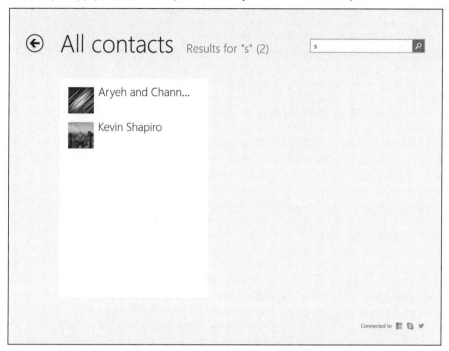

The final main area is the Me area (see Figure 13.10). Me shows the contact card set up for you, any recent updates and postings you've made, updates, and notifications. The notification area shows messages sent to you or comments made on one of your Facebook posts. The photos section shows photos you've posted and profile pictures. Right-click and choose Edit to display your profile for you to edit.

FIGURE 13.7

The People app showing a list of contacts.

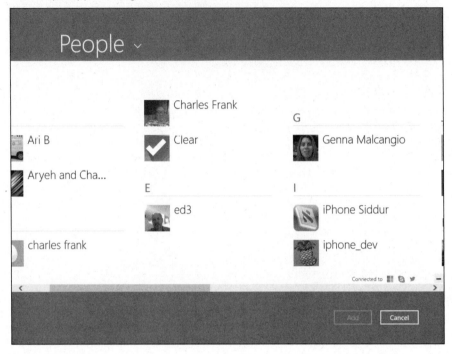

Navigating the People app

The People app is fairly easy to navigate by using your mouse or touchscreen actions (such as swiping to the left or right). You can display the People app menu by right-clicking. Contextual commands for the items you're currently viewing display in that menu. Also, the People button returns you to the main People app screen when you click it.

FIGURE 13.8

Viewing a contact card in the People app.

All Contacts

The All Contacts screen lets you easily find the name of the contact you're looking for. The letter grid lets you jump to the first letter of the person's name you're looking for. When you click a contact, you're shown all the posts and photos your contact has recently posted.

FIGURE 13.9

What's New collects the posts from all your contacts across all social services and brings them to one place.

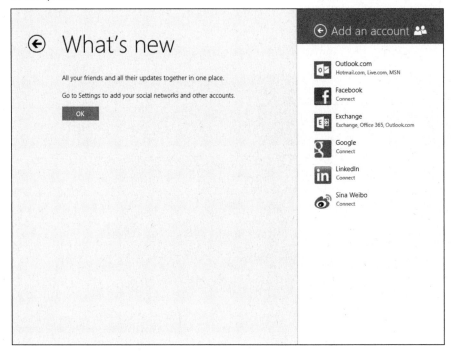

FIGURE 13.10

The Me area shows information about you, notifications, your latest posts, and photos you've posted.

Wrap-Up

Social networking is one of the most popular shared activities in the world. Windows 8.1 makes it easy to follow all your contacts in one central location using the People app.

Here's a quick summary of the main points presented in this chapter:

- You use the People app to follow your contacts' activities in social media tools.
- The People app supports many social media forums like Facebook, Twitter, Google, LinkedIn, Exchange, and Hotmail.
- The People app is divided into three main areas: People, What's New, and Me.

Using Computers Remotely

Remote Assistance lets you turn control of your computer over to a trusted expert for advice, troubleshooting, or general support. Remote Desktop allows you to control a remote computer from whatever computer you happen to be using. Both of these topics are covered in this chapter.

Using Remote Assistance

Remote Assistance is a way to give control of your computer to a trusted expert. A trusted expert is any computer expert you know well enough to trust not to damage your computer or steal any personal information. It might be someone from Desktop Support at your place of business. It may be a friend or relative who just happens to be a computer expert. Whoever it is, you have to find that person yourself. Remote Assistance provides you only the *ability* to let a trusted expert operate your computer from afar — it doesn't provide the trusted expert.

Remote Assistance and Firewalls

If you have any trouble using Remote Assistance, make sure that it's listed as an exception in Windows Firewall. To do so, open Windows Firewall from the Control Panel. Click the Allow an App or Feature through Windows Firewall link. Select Remote Assistance and click OK. Note that to send e-mail requests for Remote Assistance, you must enable Windows Remote Assistance for Public connections. In addition, if your computer sits behind a perimeter firewall (DSL router, wireless access point, or other hardware firewall), both your local firewall and the remote firewall must support Universal Plug and Play (UPnP) to support Remote Assistance without any special configuration. Or, if the firewall in front of the system requesting Remote Assistance doesn't support UPnP, you need to use port forwarding to get the incoming Remote Assistance traffic to the computer. How you set up port forwarding depends entirely on the type of firewall you have. Essentially, you need to create a rule in the firewall to forward incoming traffic for port 3389 to the computer that needs Remote Assistance. For additional information, contact your local ISP or contact your network administrator.

Setting up Remote Assistance

Before you try to use Remote Assistance, make sure that it's enabled in your user account. This requires administrative privileges. You find options for enabling and disabling Remote Assistance in the System Properties dialog box. Here's a quick and easy way to get to those options:

1. At the Windows Start screen, start typing the word **assistance**. The Allow Remote Assistance Invitations to Be Sent from This Computer link will appear in the results area and clicking this option will open the System Properties dialog box direct to the Remote tab. (You can also open Remote Assistance through Control Panel via the classic Start button location.) Choose the Allow Remote Access to Your Computer option in this dialog.

2. If prompted, enter an administrative password. The Remote tab of the System Properties dialog box, shown in Figure 14.1, opens.

FIGURE 14.1

The Remote tab of the System Properties dialog box.

3. If you want to allow the computer to be used in Remote Assistance sessions, select the Allow Remote Assistance Connections to This Computer check box. Otherwise, the computer cannot be used for Remote Assistance.

4. Optionally, click the Advanced button. Then, to allow trusted experts to control the computer remotely, select the Allow This Computer to Be Controlled Remotely option.

5. Optionally, set a time limit on how long Remote Assistance invitations remain open. Also, you can limit Remote Assistance to other computers running Windows Vista or later versions of Windows.

6. Click OK.

7. Click OK again.

The next section assumes that you've allowed Remote Assistance in the preceding steps.

Requesting Remote Assistance

Before you allow a trusted expert to take over your computer online, you need to agree on a time and a password. For security reasons, it would be best to agree on a password over the phone or in person.

If you know the e-mail address of an expert you can trust to help with your computer, follow these steps to send a Remote Assistance request:

1. Show the Charms Bar.

2. Choose Settings.

3. Click Help and enter **RemoteAssistance**.

4. The Windows Help and Support Screen loads with information on how to request Remote Assistance. You can also access this screen by opening the Control Panel. Click on System and Security in Control Panel. The Remote Access features are available under the System section.

5. Click the link Tap or Click to Open Windows Remote Assistance in the Help screen or click the link Launch Remote Assistance in the System section of Control Panel. The Windows Remote Assistance screen shown in Figure 14.2 loads.

14

FIGURE 14.2

The Windows Remote Assistance screen.

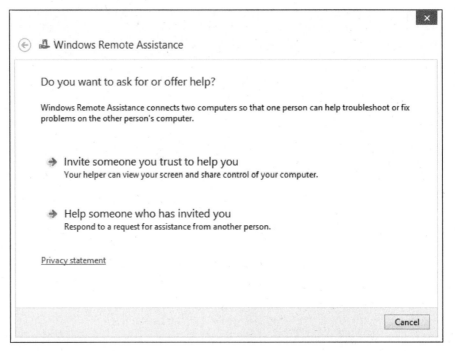

6. Click Invite Someone You Trust to Help You. A window like the one shown in Figure 14.3 appears.

How you proceed from there depends on how you use e-mail. If you use Windows Mail or another e-mail client that's compatible with Windows 8.1, follow these steps:

1. Click Use E-Mail to Send an Invitation.

2. Type the expert's e-mail address in the To box and click Send.

3. If your e-mail client isn't configured to send mail immediately, open that program and perform a Send/Receive.

FIGURE 14.3

Creating an invitation for someone to help you solve a problem on your computer.

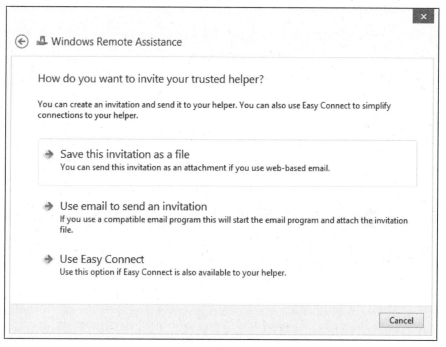

If you use web mail, follow these steps instead:

1. Click Save This Invitation as a File.

2. Choose a location in which to save the file and click Save.

3. Compose an e-mail message to the expert and attach the Invitation (or `Invitation.msrcincident`) file to that message using the standard method for your e-mail service. Then send the message normally.

4. Compose a second message to the expert and enter the Remote Assistance password that shows on your screen. Send the message.

TIP

If you don't know how to attach files to messages, search your e-mail service's support using "Attach" as the keyword, or ask your trusted expert.

The e-mail message is sent to the trusted expert. You then see the Windows Remote Assistance window, shown in Figure 14.4.

FIGURE 14.4

The Windows Remote Assistance window.

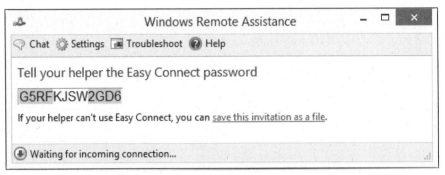

> **NOTE**
>
> If you close the Windows Remote Assistance window, your invitation will expire and the expert won't be able to connect. You'll need to repeat the previous steps to create a new invitation.

The trusted expert needs to receive your e-mail and open the attached file. Remember to also provide the password in the Remote Assistance window to your trusted expert. Remote Assistance doesn't send that password in the e-mail so you need to send it to the other person in a separate e-mail or by phone. Then the trusted expert can enter the password in the Remote Assistance window on his or her end.

After your expert has done all that, you see a new message on the screen (like the one shown in Figure 14.5), asking whether you're willing to allow your helper to connect to your computer. Choose Yes.

When connected, the trusted expert sees your screen and options for chatting, requesting control of the computer, sending a file, and starting a voice conversation. To operate your computer from afar, the expert needs to take control of your computer, which she can do by clicking Request Control at her end. Depending on the computer that the trusted expert is using (such as Windows Vista), you may see another message asking if you're willing to share control (shown in Figure 14.6). Again, you have to choose Yes.

FIGURE 14.5

Allowing someone to connect to your computer.

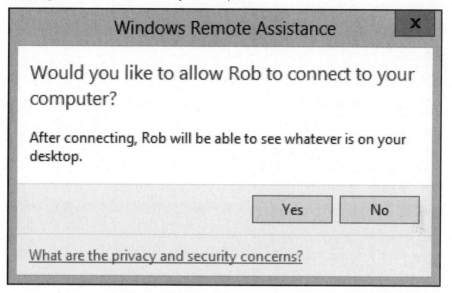

FIGURE 14.6

Allowing someone to control your computer remotely.

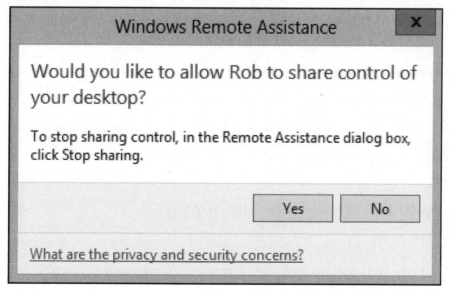

14

You'll be able to see everything the expert is doing while she has control of your computer. On the expert's computer, the following icons represent the main actions that can be performed in the Remote Assistance window for actions:

- **Disconnect:** Terminates the connection. The expert loses all access to your computer.

- **Request Control:** Allows the expert to take control of your computer from a remote location.

- **Stop Sharing:** Keeps the expert connected visually, but the expert can't operate your computer.

- **Pause:** Temporarily breaks the expert's connection to your computer. Click Continue to reestablish the connection.

- **Fit to Screen:** Resizes the display of the remote computer so it fills the entire screen.

- **Settings:** Takes you to a Settings dialog box, where you can control some optional Remote Assistance settings. (Click "What do these settings do?" in that dialog box for details.)

- **Chat:** Opens a chat window so that you and the expert can communicate during the session.

- **Send File:** Lets you send one or more files to the expert.

- **Help:** Opens Windows Help and Support.

At any time, you can click the Stop Sharing button on your screen to take back control of your computer. Similarly, the expert on the other end can click Stop Sharing to stop the sharing session and give you back control of your computer.

While the expert has control of your computer, she can use your computer just as you can. As the expert moves around your computer, opening applications, setting options, or displaying the Windows 8.1 interface, you can sit back and watch. This is one way in which you can learn new troubleshooting steps or application procedures if you're stumped on how to make something work or improve Windows performance.

When the expert has finished working or if you want to stop sharing your desktop, click the Stop Sharing button and close the Remote Assistance window. The expert can click the Disconnect button to end the session.

Using the Remote Desktop App

The Remote Desktop app allows you to control a computer from a remote location. It's often used to access computers on a corporate network from a home PC or vice versa. It's also very commonly used by system administrators to remotely manage Windows servers.

Remote Desktop is different from Remote Assistance in that, with Remote Desktop, you're remotely logging on to a computer and controlling it remotely as a single user. With Remote Assistance, the session includes the local user and the remote expert.

Before you can connect to a remote computer on your office network, a network administrator on the corporate side needs to set up that capability, enabling Remote Desktop Connection inbound to the network (or providing a VPN connection to the remote network for the user). Likewise, if you want to connect to your home computer from the office, you need to configure your home firewall to forward port 3389 to the home computer you want to manage. How you configure the firewall depends on the firewall, so we can't give you specific steps. At this point, we assume that whichever direction you're going, the necessary network and firewall changes are in place to make it possible.

> **TIP**
>
> If you're connecting to another computer on the same network segment as the one your computer is on, no firewall configuration is needed other than having Remote Assistance in Windows Firewall enabled.

To connect to the remote computer, you need to know either the hostname of the computer or its IP address. If the computer is on your local network segment, you can use the computer name. To connect to a computer on a remote network segment, you need to use either the fully qualified domain name (FQDN) of the remote computer, a private IP address on a private network or its externally (public) facing IP address. This IP address is the public address that is mapped in the firewall to the private address assigned to the computer. The computers you connect to must be set up to allow Remote Desktop connectivity.

> **NOTE**
>
> An FQDN is a name in the common `host.domain.tld` format.

When you have the information you need, making the connection should be easy. You have to be online, of course. If the company requires connecting through a virtual private network (VPN), make that connection as specified by your company's network administrator. With Windows 8.1, you also have the option of using a Remote Desktop Gateway server, if your company allows it. With the Remote Desktop Gateway server, a VPN is not required to be set up.

Next, open Remote Desktop by clicking the Windows 8.1 Remote Desktop icon in the Windows Accessories section of Apps. The Remote Desktop app opens, as shown in Figure 14.7. If you can't find the Remote Desktop app for some reason, you need to connect to Windows Store and search for Remote Desktop App and install it (don't confuse this app with the classic Remote Desktop app, which is built into Windows 8.1). The screen in Figure 14.7 appears.

14

FIGURE 14.7

The Remote Desktop app.

In the field at the bottom of the Remote Desktop app window, type the name of the PC to which you want to connect. Click Connect or press Enter.

If the remote computer is password protected, the Enter Your Credentials window appears, which looks like the one shown in Figure 14.8. Enter credentials that will allow you access to the remote computer. If you don't have an account on the remote computer, or you don't know the username and password of a user on that remote computer, you won't be allowed to connect to it.

After you enter the credentials, you can click the Remember My Credentials check box to store those credentials for the remote computer. This will enable you to connect to the remote computer next time without entering credentials. Click Connect.

FIGURE 14.8

Enter credentials to connect to the remote computer.

If the identity of the remote computer cannot be verified using a security certificate, the Can't Verify the Identity of the Remote PC window appears (see Figure 14.9). For our example, we know the identity of the remote computer is valid. Before continuing, you might first want to select Don't Ask Me Again for Connections to This PC if you plan on connecting to this computer again in the near future. To continue, click Connect.

14

FIGURE 14.9

The Remote Desktop app cannot verify the identity of the remote computer.

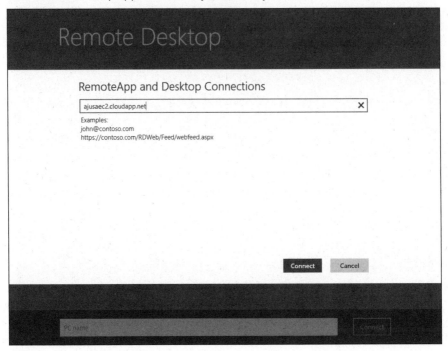

Allowing remote connections on a home network

You can also use Remote Desktop to control your Windows 8.1 PC from any other PC within your home network. For example, say you have a notebook computer that you use for work and a home computer that you use for personal use. You no longer need to hook up a monitor, keyboard, or mouse to the home computer; instead, you can simply open a Remote Desktop Connection to it any time you need to use it. Likewise, you can connect to the other computers in the house when you need to fix something on them.

> **NOTE**
>
> Remote Desktop is not required for normal home networking tasks such as sharing folders, files, and printers. Nor is it required to access those shared resources. You use Remote Desktop only if you want to operate the remote computer from the screen, keyboard, and mouse on another computer in the network.

Because the notebook computer has a wireless connection to your home network, you can use your personal PCs from anywhere in the house, even outside on the deck when the weather is nice.

To set up this type of remote connection, you first need a home network. The computer you want to control remotely needs a version of Windows that offers Remote Desktop, including all versions of Windows 8, Windows 7, Windows Vista, and Windows XP. Finally, you can log in only to password-protected accounts on the Windows 8.1 computer. It can be a standard account, but it has to be password protected.

The remote computer also needs to have a edition of Windows that supports Remote Desktop. Home editions of Windows, such as Windows 8.1 Home, do not include Remote Desktop capability that would allow you to connect to them remotely, but they include a client that enables them to connect to other computers that do support it.

Assuming that you have all the hardware and software to meet the requirements, the first step is to set up the Windows 8.1 computer to allow remote connections. Doing so requires administrative privileges and the following steps:

1. On the Windows 8.1 computer, log in to an account that has administrative privileges.

2. Display the Desktop.

3. Press Windows + X.

4. Choose Control Panel.

5. Choose Large Icons or Small Icons from the View By drop-down list.

6. Choose System.

7. Click Remote Settings under the System section of Control Panel.

8. On the Remote tab, under the Remote Desktop heading, choose the Allow Remote Connections to This Computer option.

> **NOTE**
> The last option in the list of Remote Desktop choices, NLA (Network Level Authentication), provides more-secure Remote Desktop connections but isn't available in older Windows versions. For more information, click the Help Me Choose link.

9. Click the Select Users button.

10. Use the Add button to add usernames of people who are allowed to connect remotely. The administrator is added to the list automatically. In Figure 14.10, we've added the username Jeffrey as the second person who can connect remotely.

11. Click OK in each open dialog box.

14

FIGURE 14.10

Added user as a Remote Desktop user.

Make sure you know the computer name or IP address of the Windows 8.1 computer. You can see the name to the right of the Computer Name label on the main page of System Properties. To find the IP address of the computer, log in to the computer you want to control remotely. On the desktop, press Windows + X and choose the Command prompt. Then type **ipconfig** in the command console window and press Enter. The IP address appears on the IPv4 Address line and is in the form similar to the following: 192.168.2.12.

Connecting from a remote home network PC

To connect remotely to the Windows 8.1 PC from another network in your local area network (LAN), open the Remote Desktop app on your local computer.

In the window that opens, enter the remote computer's IP address or computer name and click Connect. If the user account name of the computer at which you're sitting is different from the user account on the Windows 8.1 computer, click Use Another User. Type in the username and password for the user account on the Windows 8.1 computer and click OK or press Enter.

Depending on the display settings you used for the connection, the remote computer's screen either appears in a window or fills your local display. If you're running the connection in full-screen mode, move the mouse to the top of the screen to access the connection bar, which you can use to minimize, restore, or close the connection. From the local computer, you use the remote computer exactly as you would if you were sitting at that computer. When you've finished with your remote session, log out of the remote user account. That is, click the connection bar and click the close button. If you're connecting remotely to an earlier version of Windows, such as Windows 7 or Windows Vista, click the Start button on the remote computer and choose the Log Off option.

For more information, check the Remote Desktop Help on both computers that you intend to use in your own local network.

Using Classic Remote Desktop

Although the new Windows 8.1 Remote Desktop app provides a Windows 8.1 interface and is easy to use, you may be more comfortable using the previous version of Remote Desktop Connection. If so, you can still run it, but you must launch it from its executable filename: MSTSC.EXE. Follow these steps to launch it:

1. Display the Charms Bar.
2. Click Search.
3. Type **MSTSC** and press Enter. The Remote Desktop Connection window appears (see Figure 14.11).

FIGURE 14.11

The classic Remote Desktop Connection window.

14

Before you connect to a remote computer, you might want to click the Show Options button and take a look at the options on the various tabs. The only required option is the name or IP address of the computer to which you're connecting. The following sections describe the tabs and options.

Display

Use the Display Configuration settings on the Display tab (shown in Figure 14.12) to specify the screen resolution for the Remote Desktop Connection. If you have multiple monitors connected to the local computer, you can select the option Use All My Monitors for the Remote Session to span the Remote Desktop session across your multiple monitors.

FIGURE 14.12

The classic Remote Desktop Connection Display tab.

Use the Colors drop-down list to specify the color depth for the remote session. A lower color depth provides faster response for the remote session.

The Display the Connection Bar When I Use the Full Screen option, if enabled, causes Remote Desktop to display a connection bar at the top of the display when the remote session is using full-screen mode. Moving the mouse to the top of the display shows the connection bar, which then enables you to minimize, restore, or close the remote session window.

Local Resources

The settings on the Local Resources tab (shown in Figure 14.13) enable you to configure how Remote Desktop uses local and remote resources. For example, click the Settings button in the Remote Audio group to open a dialog box that enables you to specify whether Remote Desktop plays audio from the remote computer at the remote computer, brings it to your local computer, or does not play the sounds. You can also specify similar settings for remote recording.

FIGURE 14.13

The classic Remote Desktop Connection Local Resources tab.

Use the drop-down list in the Keyboard group to specify how Remote Desktop treats Windows key combinations such as Alt + Tab — sending them to the local computer or remote computer, or sending them to the remote computer only when using full-screen mode.

The Local Devices and Resources group lets you specify how local resources such as your printers, Windows Clipboard, ports, disk drives, and other resources are made available during the remote session. This capability can be extremely useful. For example, by enabling the drives on your local computer for the connection, you make them accessible in the File Manager on the remote computer. This means that you can easily drag and drop files between the two systems. By enabling the Clipboard, you can cut and paste between the systems.

Programs

On the Programs tab (shown in Figure 14.14), you can specify a program to start on the remote computer. Only the program you specify runs on that remote computer. You can exit the session, which closes the program, or you can close the session and leave the remote program running.

FIGURE 14.14

The classic Remote Desktop Connection Programs tab.

Experience

The options on the Experience tab (see Figure 14.15) help you control the performance for the remote session. You can choose an option from the drop-down list, which determines which options in the list below the drop-down are enabled. You can also simply select which options you want to use.

FIGURE 14.15

The classic Remote Desktop Connection Experience tab.

Advanced

The Advanced tab (shown in Figure 14.16) offers options that control authentication alerts and Remote Desktop Gateway. The drop-down list on the Advanced tab lets you specify what action Remote Desktop Connection takes when you connect to a remote computer that doesn't satisfy the security requirements as defined by your local system security policy. You can choose to have Remote Desktop Connection drop the connection, warn you so that you can choose the action to take, or connect without warning you.

FIGURE 14.16

The classic Remote Desktop Connection Advanced tab.

The Settings button opens the RD Gateway Server Settings dialog box (see Figure 14.17), which lets you specify how Remote Desktop Connection works with a Terminal Services Gateway Server, now called Remote Desktop Gateway Server. RD Gateway acts essentially as an intermediary between your computer on the Internet and remote computers behind a firewall, such as at your office. RD Gateway uses SSL (port 443) rather than the usual port 3389 used by Remote Desktop Connection. RD Gateway, therefore, makes connecting to remote computers possible without having a VPN or opening port 3389 in the firewall. What's more, it enables connection to multiple back-end computers, rather than just the one that would otherwise be possible with a hole in the firewall for port 3389.

FIGURE 14.17

The RD Gateway Server Settings dialog box.

Remote Desktop Connection can detect the RD Gateway server settings automatically, or you can specify them manually. The first two options on the RD Gateway Server Settings dialog box let you specify which method to use. If you choose to specify the settings yourself, you can enter the server name, login method, and whether to bypass the gateway for computers on your local network. If you enter the settings manually, you also have the option of specifying that Remote Desktop Connection will use your RD Gateway credentials to authenticate on the remote computer to which you are connecting.

TIP

In most cases, you can open a remote session in Remote Desktop Connection without changing any options.

Wrap-Up

Remote Assistance and Remote Desktop Connection both provide a means to view and remotely control other computers. Key points of this chapter are as follows:

- If you know a trusted computer expert who can help with your computer, use Remote Assistance to get live help online.
- Some corporations allow employees to connect to a corporate network from home using Remote Desktop Connection.
- If you have a home network and suitable versions of Windows, you can use Remote Desktop to control one PC on the network from another PC in the same network, or from the Internet.

Managing Names and Addresses

IN THIS CHAPTER

Using your Contacts folder

Creating and managing contacts

Creating contact groups

Importing and exporting contacts

You've no doubt seen and tried out the new People app, which lets you integrate your contracts and updates from multiple social network sites such as Windows Live, Facebook, and Twitter. The Mail app relies on the People app for selecting contacts to send e-mail and instant messages.

 If you haven't tried out the People app, have a look at Chapter 13.

Windows 8.1, like Windows 8 and Windows 7 before it, offers an alternative you can use from the desktop to manage contacts — the Contacts folder. Each file in that folder is a contact, someone with whom you communicate. It doesn't have to be only people you contact online. You can store anybody's contact information in your Contacts folder. As with pictures, songs, videos, and other documents, each user account has its own Contacts folder. So, each person who has a user account can have his or her own collection of names and addresses.

> **NOTE**
>
> ...ep in mind that the Windows Contacts folder and the contacts in it are separate from the contacts in your e-mail program. For ...ample, if you opt to download and use Windows Live Mail as your e-mail program, it has its own set of contacts. Although you ...n import your Windows Contacts into Windows Live Mail, the contacts are not synchronized. So, if you import your Windows ...ntacts into Windows Live Mail and then make a change to one of your Windows Contacts, that change will not show up in ...dows Live Mail because there are actually two separate contacts. Likewise, there is no synchronization between the Contacts ...der and the People app.

Why use Windows Contacts? If you're one of the few people who use a computer but don't use e-mail, the Windows Contacts folder provides a place for you to keep your own address book for letters, a phone list, and so on. Or you might use Windows Contacts to store your personal contacts and your e-mail program to store your business contacts. Whatever the case, you can use your Windows Contacts for addressing e-mail, as described later in this chapter.

> **TIP**
>
> The Contacts folder does not offer social networking integration like the People app does. However, if the Mail app is set as your default e-mail program, you can click a contact's e-mail address to open a new e-mail message in Mail addressed to that address. If you use social networking sites, and you've previously used the Contacts folder, consider switching to the People app. Unfortunately, there is currently no way to export existing contacts from the Contacts folder and import them into the People app.

Opening Contacts

To create or manage contacts, open your Contacts folder using whichever of the following methods is most convenient for you:

- Open Windows Explore and navigate to the Users folder. Find your name in the Users folders and expand the folder. The Users folder is accessible with your other user folders, such as Documents and Music.

- If you're already in a folder, click your username in the breadcrumb trail, and then click (or double-click) the Contacts folder icon.

If you've never used your Contacts folder before, it will likely be empty. Figure 15.1 shows a sample Contacts folder with a few contacts already in place.

FIGURE 15.1

A sample Contacts folder.

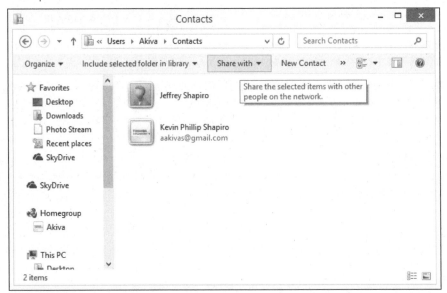

Changing how you view contacts

Because Contacts is a folder, you can control how things look using the standard techniques described in Chapter 20. For example:

- To show or hide the Preview pane, click Organize and choose Layout ⇨ Preview Pane.

- To show or hide the Navigation pane, click Organize and choose Layout ⇨ Navigation Pane.

- To show or hide the menu bar, press the Alt key or click Organize and choose Layout ⇨ Menu Bar.

- To change the size of icons, click the arrow next to the Change Your View button and choose an icon size, or hold down the Ctrl key while spinning your mouse wheel.

- To sort or group contacts in Details view, point to any column heading and click the arrow that appears.

Making shortcuts to contacts

Before we go any further with Contacts, we want to point out some easy ways to create shortcuts to your Contacts folder. These make opening the folder in the future easier. You don't have to create any of these shortcuts, of course. They're entirely optional. But if you use your Contacts folder often, you'll probably find them handy.

First, click your username in the breadcrumb menu so that you're in the main folder for your user account. Right-click the Contacts icon, as shown in Figure 15.2, and choose Send To ⇨ Desktop (Create Shortcut). Then drag the shortcut from the desktop to the taskbar and release it to pin it to the taskbar.

> **TIP**
>
> Here's an easy way to open your user folder to get at your Contacts. Open Windows Explorer from the taskbar. In the Address bar, click the arrow to the left of the word *Libraries*. Then click your username in the resulting drop-down menu. You'll see your Contacts folder, along with the other folders that are part of your profile.

To add a shortcut to the Favorites pane in the Navigation bar, open your user folder and drag the Contacts folder into the Favorites box.

Creating a contact

Creating a contact is simple. First, open your Contacts folder if you haven't already. Then click the New Contact toolbar button, or right-click some empty space in your Contacts folder (not on an icon) and choose New ⇨ Contact.

An empty, fill-in-the-blanks form opens. (The blanks are called *fields.*) It's divided into multiple tabs. You don't have to fill in everything for a contact. Fill in only as much information as you need or want for the contact. Here are some tips for filling in a contact:

15

FIGURE 15.2

Right-click Contacts.

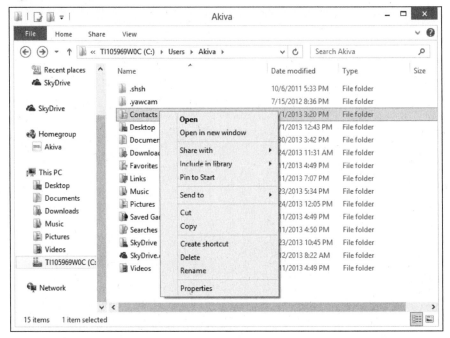

- After filling in a field, press the Tab key to move to the next one, or click the next blank you want to fill.

- After filling in the first and last names, click the Full Name drop-down button to choose how you want the name displayed for alphabetizing.

- To add an e-mail address, type it into the E-mail text box and click Add. If the contact has several e-mail addresses, repeat the process to add each one. Then click the e-mail address you use most often for that person and click Set Preferred.

- To add a picture, click the picture box and choose Change Picture. Then navigate to the folder that contains the picture you want to add and click (or double-click) the desired picture. The picture becomes the contact's icon in the Contacts folder.

- If this is a personal contact, use the Home tab to fill in the person's home address.

- Use the Work tab to fill in the work address and other information.

- Use the Family tab to fill in personal information such as birthday, anniversary, spouse, children, and so forth.

- Use the Notes tab to fill in any miscellaneous information you desire.

- The IDs tab shouldn't require any intervention on your part. It gets filled in automatically when you receive a digitally signed message from the person.

- When you've finished entering the contact, click OK.

Opening and editing contacts

To open a contact, double-click its icon (unless you're using single-clicks, in which case you just have to click it once). You see a Name and E-Mail tab that contains name, e-mail, and other basic information, as in the example in Figure 15.3.

FIGURE 15.3

The Name and E-Mail tab of a sample contact.

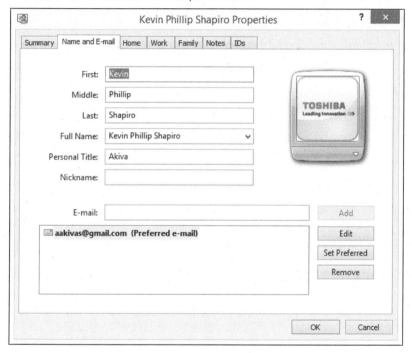

The contact's information can be changed as follows:

- To send the person an e-mail, click the e-mail address.
- To visit that person's website (if any), click the URL.
- To add, remove, or change the picture, select the Name and E-mail tab, click the picture, and click either Change Picture or Remove Picture.
- To see or change any other information, select the appropriate tab.

15

NOTE

Each contact you create in your Contacts file is stored as a `.contact` file. The extension, however, is visible only if you deselect the Hide Extensions for Known File Types check box on the View tab in the Folder Options dialog box.

Tips for Contact Pictures

For best results, you'll want to create copies of pictures appropriately sized and cropped for contacts. You might want to create a subfolder, perhaps named Contact Pix, in your Pictures folder just for those pictures. That will make them easy to find.

If you want to use a photo you took with a digital camera, start with a copy of the photo so that you don't compromise the original. Try to crop out a perfect square around the person's face. Then size that cropped image to about 250 × 250 pixels. Save it in BMP, JPEG, TIFF, or PNG format. If you're using a logo or icon rather than a photo, you can use the GIF or ICO extension. For picture-editing tools and techniques, see Chapter 17.

Create a "Me" contact

It's a good idea to create a contact for yourself, filling in as much information as you want to share with others. You can e-mail that contact to folks so that they don't have to type your contact information themselves. After you create a contact for yourself, right-click its icon and choose Set As My Contact. The menu option then changes to This Is Me. You can click This Is Me to direct Windows to use your Windows user account picture for the contact or to change the picture in the contact to your current Windows user account picture.

> **TIP**
> To use a different contact as your own, simply create the contact, right-click it, and choose This Is Me.

If you want to e-mail your contact information to others who aren't using Windows 7, Windows 8, or Windows 8.1, attach a .vcf file to an e-mail message. To do that, right-click your Contact icon and choose Send Contact. A new message window opens with the card already attached as a .vcf file. Fill in the To and Subject lines. Fill in the body of the message informing the recipient that your contact information is attached.

Creating Contact Groups

A *contact group* is any collection of contacts that have something in common. It could be people who go to the same church as you, members of the same club, work colleagues, or just pals. You might also think of a contact group as a mailing list (or distribution list). The beauty of a contact group is that you can send or forward an e-mail message to everyone in the group in one fell swoop.

> **TIP**
> Contact groups make sending and forwarding messages to multiple recipients easy.

Visually, a contact group is just a collection of contact names. For example, Figure 15.4 shows a contact group named Friends.

FIGURE 15.4

A sample contact group.

To create a contact group in your Contacts folder:

1. Click the New Contact Group toolbar button.

2. In the Group Name box, enter any name that describes the group.

3. Add members using any of the following methods:

   - To add existing contacts, click Add to Contact Group. Click the first person who should be in the group. Then hold down the Ctrl key as you click everyone else who belongs in the group. Then click Add.

   - To add a new person to the group, as well as create a contact for that person, click Create New Contact. Fill in contact information for that person and click OK.

   - To add a person's name and e-mail address without creating a contact icon for that person, fill in the Contact Name and E-mail boxes near the bottom of the window and click Create for Group Only.

4. Optionally, click the Contact Group Details tab and fill in details about the group. For example, if you're all members of the same club or church, you can add address and phone information for the building where you meet.

5. Click OK.

15

The group window closes and appears as an icon in the Contacts folder. You can use and treat the group in much the same way as you do an individual contact:

- To send an e-mail to the group, right-click the group icon and choose Action ⇨ Send E-mail.
- To change the group, double-click the group's icon in Contacts.
- To delete the group, right-click its icon and choose Delete. Contacts within the group will remain. Only the group icon and noncontacts are deleted.

Don't forget that you have much leeway in how you view the contents of folders. For example, to view and organize your contacts as a list or table, choose View ⇨ Details. To choose columns to display, right-click any column heading, as shown in Figure 15.5. If the drop-down menu doesn't show a column you want to include, click More for a more complete list.

FIGURE 15.5

Choose columns to display.

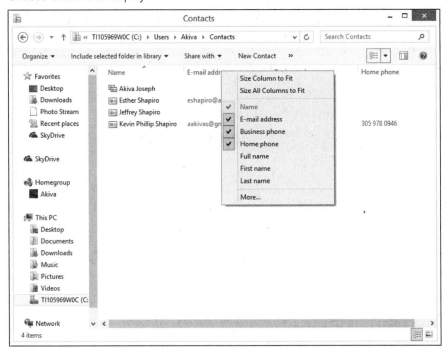

After you've selected the columns you want to view, you can arrange them however you like. Just drag any column heading left or right to place it where it's easy to see.

You can sort, group, and filter contacts as you would files in any folder. For more information on how that works, see Chapters 21–23.

Printing Contacts

Printing contact information is easy. If you want to print only certain contacts, select their icons using any of the standard techniques, such as Ctrl + click. Then click the Print toolbar button. If that button isn't visible, click > > at the end of the toolbar and then click Print. The Print dialog box opens, looking something like the example in Figure 15.6.

FIGURE 15.6

Print options for contacts.

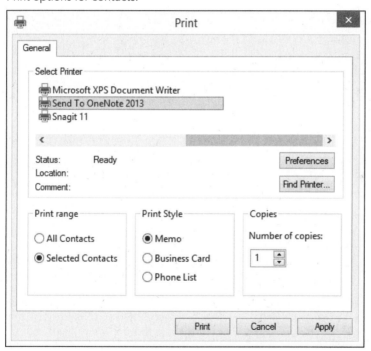

To print all contacts, choose All Contacts under Print Range. To print only selected contacts, choose Selected Contacts. Then choose a print format:

- **Memo:** Prints most business and address contact information
- **Business Card:** Prints business, address, and phone information
- **Phone List:** Prints phone numbers

If you have multiple printers, click the one you want to print with. Then click the Print button.

If none of the available print formats fits what you need, you can export contacts to a file. Then import those contacts into some other program that gives you the flexibility you need to print as you see fit.

Importing and Exporting Contacts

Importing allows you to copy contacts from external programs into your Contacts folder. Exporting lets you copy contacts to another program or a format that's compatible with an outside program. We start this section with importing.

Importing people to your contacts folder

You can import names and addresses from the following formats into your Windows Contacts folder:

- **CSV (Comma-Separated Values):** This is a generic format to which many programs can export data. You start in the other program by exporting names and addresses to a CSV file. Then you open your Contacts folder and import the CSV file you created from the original program.

- **LDIF (LDAP server):** Use this format to import contacts from a directory server that uses Lightweight Directory Access Protocol (LDAP).

- **vCard (VCF file):** This format is used by many programs to store virtual business card data. In contrast to other options described here, you might use this format to import a single contact whose data is stored in a `.vcf` file.

- **WAB (Windows Address Book):** This format imports contacts from the `.wab` file used by Windows Address Book and Outlook Express in earlier versions of Windows. Typically, you find that file in the `x:\Documents and Settings\ UserName\Application Data\Microsoft\Address Book` folder, where x is the disk drive and `UserName` is the name of the user account.

If the data you want to import isn't already in one of these formats, open the program that you normally use to manage those contacts. Then search its Help for "export" to see whether you can export to CSV or another compatible format.

When the data you want to import are in an appropriate format and you know the location of the file, follow these steps to import the data to your Contacts folder:

1. Open Windows Contacts.

TIP

If you plan to import from Application Data or another hidden folder, click the Organize button and choose Folder and Search Options. Select the View tab and then click Show Hidden Files, Folders, and Drives and then click OK. Doing so ensures that all folders and files are visible in the steps to follow.

2. Click the Import toolbar button.

3. Click the format in which the data to be imported are stored; then click Import.

4. Navigate to the drive and folder in which the data to be imported are stored; then click (or double-click) the file to import. Click Next.

5. If importing from a CSV file, in the CSV Import dialog box, verify the field mapping to use for the import. To change a field, click the field, click Change Mapping, choose the field you want to map to, and click OK.

6. When you're satisfied with the mapping, click Finish.

You should see an icon for each imported contact.

Exporting contacts to vCards

Many programs store contact information in virtual business cards, where each contact is a file with a .vcf extension. Before you get started, you might want to create a folder to store the exported data. That way, all the exported contacts will be together in a single folder.

To export contacts in vCard format:

1. Open Windows Contacts.

2. Click the Export toolbar button.

3. Click vCards (folder of .vcf files).

4. Click Export.

5. Navigate to the folder in which you want to place the exported vCards.

6. Click OK.

7. When the export is complete, click OK.

To verify the export, open the folder to which you exported. You should see an icon for each exported contact. The contacts won't show any pictures because the vCard format doesn't support the use of pictures.

Exporting to a CSV file

You can export contacts to a single comma-separated values (CSV) file for later import to another program. For example, after exporting contacts to a CSV file, you can open them in Microsoft Excel, import them to a Microsoft Access table, or use them for a Microsoft Word mail merge. With Word and Access, you can print form letters, mailing labels, and envelopes from the CSV file.

To export contacts to a CSV file, open Windows Contacts as you normally would. Then follow these steps:

1. Click the Export toolbar button.

2. Choose CSV (Comma-Separated Values) ➪ Export.

15

3. Type a name for the exported file. Or click the Browse button, navigate to the folder in which you want to store the file, enter a filename, and click Save.

4. Click Next.

5. Select (check) the fields you want to export and click Finish.

6. Click OK when the export is complete.

To verify the export, open the folder to which you exported the file. To view the contents of the file using Notepad, right-click its icon and choose Open With ⇨ Notepad. That will show you the file in its raw form. But in actual practice, you'll likely import it into whatever program you want to use.

Searching for Contacts

If you have a lot of contacts in your Contacts folder, you can use the Search Contacts box in the upper-right corner of the Contacts window to quickly locate a contact. Click in the Search Contacts box and type a few characters from the person's name. The contact list shrinks to contain only the people whose names contain those letters, and highlights the search text in the contact information (such as name or e-mail address). When you see the person you want, double-click the name to open. To remove the filter and see all contacts again, click the X at the right side of the Search Contacts box.

Sharing Contacts on a Network

If your computer is part of a network, you can share a contact with other Windows 7, Windows 8 or Windows 8.1 computers in that network. The process is the same as that for sharing any other file. Right-click the contact and choose Share With. Choose the people with whom you want to share, and set permission levels.

 For more information on sharing contacts on a network, see Chapter 38 and Chapter 39.

Wrap-Up

Names and addresses are easy to manage in Windows 8.1, thanks to the Contacts folder. Here's a summary of all the things you can do:

- To view contacts, open your Contacts folder.
- To create shortcuts to your Contacts folder, first open Windows Explorer. Click the arrow to the left of Libraries in the breadcrumb and choose your username. Then drag the Contacts folder to the Favorites branch in the Navigation pane, or to the desktop, depending on where you want to place shortcuts.

- To create a new contact, click the New Contact toolbar button in your Contacts folder.

- To open or change a contact's information, open the contact icon.

- To identify a contact as yourself, right-click your own contact icon and choose Set As My Contact.

- To create a mailing list, click New Contact Group in the toolbar.

- To send an e-mail to a contact group, right-click the group icon and choose Action ➪ Send E-mail. Or from a new message or forwarded message, click To in the address field and choose the group as the recipient.

- To print contacts, click the Print toolbar button.

- Click Import or Export on the toolbar to import contacts from an external source, or copy contacts to an external file.

- To quickly find a contact without opening your Contacts folder, type a few characters of the name in the Search Contacts box.

15

Working in the Cloud

I n 2005, Microsoft introduced an online web portal for users to store files, get their e-mail, communicate with other users, and share files. This web portal is collectively known as Windows Live and is discussed in more detail in Chapter 12. In this chapter, however, you learn about working in the cloud with Microsoft SkyDrive, an online file sharing and file storage tool. To go to SkyDrive using a browser simply open `https://skydrive.com` or `https://skydrive.live.com` in your web browser.

Microsoft SkyDrive provides an area online for you to store and share photos, presentations, and other files. With Windows 8.1, an app is available to help you manage and add files to SkyDrive. This chapter shows you how to use the SkyDrive app Windows syncing application.

In previous versions of Windows, SkyDrive was an app you downloaded and installed. In Windows 8.1, SkyDrive functionality is fully integrated with the operating system and the service appears as a separate drive or device to all applications.

Even if you aren't connected to the Internet, you can still use SkyDrive locally and use its features to sync your files with the online portal and share files with other applications that are SkyDrive aware.

Synchronizing files between all your devices is as simple as setting up your devices to support and sign in to SkyDrive with your Microsoft account. You can copy files to each local drive or simply access and work with a single instance of your file.

Understanding the Cloud

Computer users have been limited in the way in which they can access files on disparate systems. Traditionally, users store their files on a local hard drive (such as the `C:` drive) or on a network drive at work. To use those files on a different computer, that computer must have a network connection to that user's network drive, or the user must transfer files using a removable drive such as a floppy drive, flash drive, or similar.

With cloud technology, the user just has to have access to the Internet in order to work on files. Microsoft SkyDrive is Microsoft's cloud-based technology that provides access to users' files from any location at any time. The advantage with cloud technologies is that you aren't limited to a company network location or to a removable drive strategy. Storing files in the cloud also provides a more flexible way for users to share files with other users. You no longer have to rely on the network administrator in your organization to establish shares for your teams, colleagues, or other people with whom you might want to share files.

> **NOTE**
>
> As with most systems, there are some disadvantages to working with cloud-based systems. First, you must have an Internet connection to access files. Second, your company may have rules against storing files in a cloud-based system because of confidentiality and/or file security regulations. Finally, your files may be subject to terms and conditions imposed by the cloud company that gives it (the cloud company) rights to read and access your files. Currently, Microsoft SkyDrive does not indicate that it has those rights, but you should be aware of that possibility as you decide to store your photos, documents, videos, and other items in the cloud.

Microsoft has a vision that every user should have access to his or her files anytime and anywhere they want them (with Internet connectivity, of course). In addition, not only should users have access to files at any time and any location, but the device you use to access them should be irrelevant. Users should, for example, be able to access files using a personal computer, a tablet device with Wi-Fi connectivity, a smartphone, or a laptop. In fact, with Microsoft SkyDrive, any user who has an Apple iPhone, iPad, or iPod Touch or a Google Android–based tablet or smartphone (using a non-Microsoft SkyDrive app) can access SkyDrive files as well.

In addition to Microsoft SkyDrive, other cloud-based file-storage services do exist. This chapter focuses on Microsoft SkyDrive, but you're welcome to learn more about other services to see which is best for you and/or your organization. The following are a few of the most popular online storage services:

- **Google Drive:** http://drive.google.com
- **Sugar Sync:** www.sugarsync.com
- **Dropbox:** www.dropbox.com
- **Box:** www.box.com
- **InSync:** www.insynchq.com
- **Cubby:** www.cubby.com

Setting Up a SkyDrive Account

SkyDrive has been available for users in the Microsoft Live family of products for several years. With SkyDrive, you can store many types of files online, including word processing documents, spreadsheets, text files, photos, presentations, and videos.

To begin using SkyDrive, you need a Windows Live account. This chapter assumes you have a Windows Live account. To ensure you can start using SkyDrive, read Chapter 12 to see how to set up an account and to ensure you can log into Windows Live. Also refer back to Chapter 4, which shows you how to create a Microsoft account that syncs you both into your PC account and the Microsoft Cloud resources like SkyDrive.

Signing into your computer with a local account will only let you use the SkyDrive app to browse your PC. You won't be able to access your files unless you also login to SkyDrive.com.

Accessing SkyDrive Files

With Windows 8.1, you have three primary ways to access files stored in your SkyDrive environment:

- **SkyDrive Device:** SkyDrive appears as a drive to File Explorer and all applications. Simply click on it as you would your C: drive or any other storage device. This option is shown in Figure 16.1.

FIGURE 16.1

You can access SkyDrive using File Explorer.

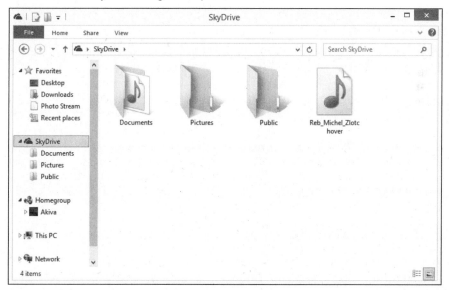

- **Web-based:** You can navigate to Windows Live from Microsoft Internet Explorer and access files from the SkyDrive menu. Figure 16.2 shows an example of this approach. You can also navigate to `https://skydrive.live.com`, which will automatically re-route you to the Window Live website.

FIGURE 16.2

You can access SkyDrive using a web browser, such as Safari.

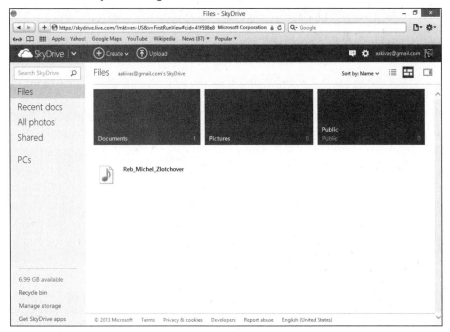

- **SkyDrive Windows 8.1 app:** The built-in app lets you view, manage, and add files to your SkyDrive account. The Windows 8.1 app also provides sharing between some other Windows 8.1 apps, such as the Photos app and Peoples app. The app is shown in Figure 16.3.

Using SkyDrive

As you've read, SkyDrive is now a folder on your computer. Files and folders you put into your SkyDrive folder get synced with the SkyDrive (Windows Live) web portal and will sync with other devices that are running SkyDrive apps.

FIGURE 16.3

Accessing SkyDrive using the built-in app.

> **TIP**
>
> If you have an Apple iPad or iPod Touch, consider downloading the free SkyDrive app from the Apple iTunes Store. The SkyDrive app enables you to view your SkyDrive files, delete them, move them to different folders, add folders, send photos or videos to SkyDrive, and open files (if you have a support app for that file type).

The following section describes the use of the SkyDrive app.

Using SkyDrive

SkyDrive is available on the Windows Start screen. Click it now to start using it.

When the app first appears, if you don't have a Microsoft account on your local PC, you'll be prompted to enter your Microsoft Live login credentials. Do so now to continue with the initial setup process. You can view SkyDrive items in one of two ways. In the SkyDrive app or from File Explorer. To access your SkyDrive folders from the app, simply open the app from the Start page. The screen in Figure 16.3 opens. You can click the view icon to change the view:

- **Details:** Displays filename, modification date and time, and file size of each file. Figure 16.3 shows files in the SkyDrive view using the Details view.
- **Thumbnails:** Shows each file as a thumbnail icon. Figure 16.4, for example, shows the SkyDrive in thumbnail view.

FIGURE 16.4

SkyDrive app in Thumbnails view.

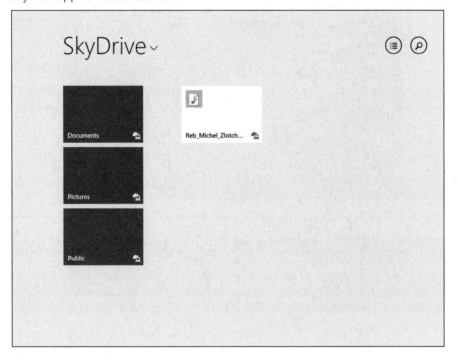

Adding files to SkyDrive

One of the tasks that you can perform with the SkyDrive app is to add files to your SkyDrive folders. You can add files from your computer to SkyDrive by using the following steps:

1. From the SkyDrive app, right-click at the bottom of the app and click the Add files button. The SkyDrive app lets you browse folders and select files.

2. Navigate to your folders and select a file or a collection of files. Selecting files is shown in Figure 16.5.

FIGURE 16.5

Select files to add to SkyDrive.

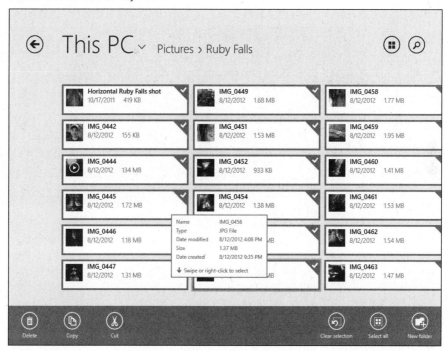

3. Click Copy to SkyDrive. If the file you want to add is shown in the folder that displays (in our example, the Documents folder displays), click that file. However, in some cases you may want to locate files in other folders. To do this, click the Up arrow to go up to the next folder.

The SkyDrive app uploads the files to your SkyDrive account and displays those files in your SkyDrive folder. Figure 16.6 shows an example of what this looks like.

Copying or moving files to SkyDrive using File Explorer is as easy as moving files around on your local hard drive. Clicking the SkyDrive icon in File Explorer gives you access to the remote folders, as shown in Figure 16.7. The beauty of working with SkyDrive is that you can use the full functionality of Windows drag and drop with SkyDrive.

FIGURE 16.6

The new files are added to SkyDrive.

FIGURE 16.7

The new files are added to SkyDrive using File Explorer.

Sharing files using SkyDrive

One of the most powerful uses of SkyDrive is the capability to share files with other users. With the SkyDrive app, you can share files using the Shared folders in SkyDrive, or use the Charms Bar Share tool to share using supported Windows 8.1 apps. For example, you can choose to share files from SkyDrive to people you have listed in your People app. The following steps show you how to do this:

1. Open SkyDrive to the file you want to share.

2. Right-click the file to select it. A check mark appears on the file.

3. Display the Charms Bar.

4. Click Share, as shown in Figure 16.8.

FIGURE 16.8

Share from the Charms Bar to share SkyDrive files with others.

5. Click the service you want to share to, such as People or e-mail.

6. Select where you would like to share the file. In our example, we are sharing with e-mail (see Figure 16.9).

7. Enter the e-mail address of the recipient of the file.

8. Click the Send button.

FIGURE 16.9

We're sending a file from SkyDrive to someone using e-mail.

Configuring SkyDrive

To configure your SkyDrive, access the Charms Bar while the SkyDrive app is open and select Settings. Select Options as shown in Figure 16.10, and then click the Open PC Settings link to access more SkyDrive options.

FIGURE 16.10

The SkyDrive Options screen.

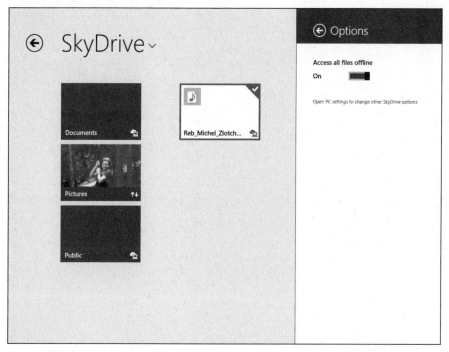

16

Wrap-Up

Windows 8.1 provides a good platform for using the Microsoft SkyDrive cloud service. You can use a web browser (such as Internet Explorer), use the SkyDrive for Windows application, use the SkyDrive app, or File Explorer to access and manage your SkyDrive files.

In summary:

- SkyDrive is a cloud-based file storage and sharing tool.
- The SkyDrive for Windows application can be downloaded from `https://apps. live.com/skydrive`.
- SkyDrive Windows app provides a way to view and share your SkyDrive files.

Part IV

Pictures, Music, and Movies

IN THIS PART

Working with Pictures

IN THIS CHAPTER

Getting pictures into your computer

Using your Pictures folder

Using Photo Gallery

Fixing your photos

Understanding picture types

In the computer world, the terms *picture, photo, image, graphic image,* and *digital image* all refer to the same thing — a still picture. Windows 8.1 offers lots of great tools for organizing, editing, printing, and e-mailing pictures.

Today's hard disks have room to store many thousands of photos. The Photo Gallery, an optional add-on for Windows, provides an easy way to organize and find photos based on keywords called *tags*. The Edit tab in Photo Gallery makes common tasks such as cropping and red-eye removal a breeze.

Much of this chapter focuses on Photo Gallery as the primary tool for managing photos. You can download Photo Gallery from `http://explore.live.com/windows-live-photo-gallery` and click the Photo Gallery link to be taken to the page where you can download Photo Gallery.

Getting Pictures into Your Computer

You can acquire pictures to use in your computer in several ways. You can store pictures in any folder you like. If you don't have a preference, use the Pictures folder for your user account. You can always move or copy the pictures to another location later, should the need arise.

Getting pictures from a digital camera

Before we tell you how to get pictures from a digital camera, you should understand that we're talking about the digital cameras that connect through a USB cable and appear as a USB mass storage device, or your camera's SD card that you can insert into a compatible SD slot on your computer. If the method described doesn't work for your camera, see the manual that came with that camera for details. You may have to install and use the software that came with your camera to get pictures from it, but the following steps will work with most modern digital cameras:

1. Use a USB cable to connect your camera to your computer and turn on the camera.

2. Wait a few seconds, and then:

   - If you see an auto start dialog box like the one in Figure 17.1, click Import Photos and Videos. Then skip to Step 4.

FIGURE 17.1

AutoPlay options for a digital camera.

If nothing happens within a minute or so of connecting and turning on your camera, open Photo Gallery. Choose File ⇨ Import Photos or Videos. Then click the icon for your camera and click Import.

3. In the dialog box shown in Figure 17.2, click Import All New Items Now and enter a *tag* (keyword) that will later help you identify pictures. For example, enter the event, location, or subject of the photos.

17

TIP

Entering a tag is optional but very useful. Try to think of keywords that describe the pictures you're importing. You can add, change, or delete tags at any time. So, don't knock yourself out trying to find a word that applies to every picture.

FIGURE 17.2

Importing pictures from a camera phone.

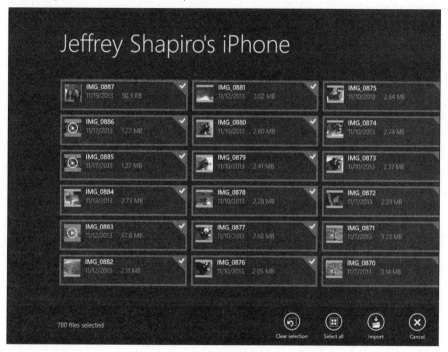

4. Click Import.

5. The next dialog box keeps you apprised of the progress.

6. When copying is finished, turn off and disconnect the camera.

TIP

If you miss the opportunity to erase pictures after importing, you can still erase those using buttons on your camera. Or open the camera from your This PC folder and delete the pictures using standard techniques described in Chapter 21.

Depending on your camera and the types of pictures (and videos) you imported, Photo Gallery might open and display thumbnails of your pictures. However, the pictures aren't actually stored in Photo Gallery, so don't worry if you don't see them there. The pictures are actually in your Pictures folder as described in the section "Using your Pictures folder" later in this chapter.

Getting pictures from a memory card

If you have pictures on a memory card, and your computer has slots for those cards or a card reader attached, you can copy pictures directly from the card. Once you've inserted a memory card into a slot, the card is basically the same as any external disk drive. You can use all the standard techniques discussed in Chapter 21 to move, copy, and delete files as you see fit.

Exactly what happens on your screen after you insert a memory card depends on your auto start settings for cards. See Chapter 31 for more information on auto start. Regardless of what happens after you first insert a card, you can always get to its contents through your Computer folder. Here's how:

1. Press Windows + X, click File Explorer, and then click This PC.

2. If necessary, scroll down through your removable drives. If you have multiple card slots, look for the one that shows a specific name. For example, in Figure 17.3, drive F: is a slot that contains a memory card labeled Photos.

FIGURE 17.3

Drive F: contains a memory card.

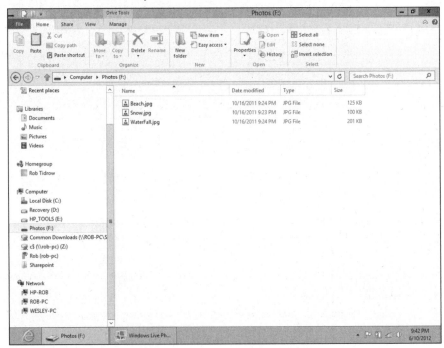

3. Open the card's icon. Then navigate through folders on the card until you find the icons that represent pictures.

4. Select the icons for the pictures you want to copy, or choose Home ⇨ Select All (or press Ctrl + A) to select them all.

5. Drag or copy and paste the selected icons to your Pictures folder and ignore the following steps. Optionally, use the following steps to copy without dragging or using the copy-and-paste method.

6. Display the ribbon. Choose Edit ⇨ Copy from the menu (or Cut if you want to delete the pictures from the memory card).

7. Open the destination folder for the images and press Ctrl + V to paste them into the folder.

> **Tip**
>
> *After* (not before) you've verified that pictures have been copied, you can delete them from the memory card. Select all the icons in the card as in Step 4. Then press Delete (Del) or right-click any selected icon and choose Delete.

The pictures are copied to the destination folder. You can close the folder that's open and remove the memory card. Open the destination folder to see the copied pictures.

No Memory Card Slots?

If your computer doesn't have slots for memory cards, you can easily add them by purchasing and connecting a card reader. Go to any online site that sells computer accessories. Then search for "memory card reader." If you're not interested in installing hardware inside your computer, choose a product that connects through a USB port. Make sure you know what physical size card you need to read and get an appropriate reader. Or choose a reader that works with all types of memory cards.

Getting pictures from a CD or DVD

You can store pictures and copy them in many ways on CDs and DVDs. If someone sends you a CD or DVD that contains only pictures, you'll likely see a prompt on the screen shortly after you put the disk into your drive. A simple way to import the pictures from that prompt is to click Import Using Windows Picture and Video Import. Then just follow the instructions that appear on the screen. If you're prompted to enter a tag, just type in any word or short phrase that describes the pictures. All the pictures will be copied (imported) to your Pictures folder, where you can access them at any time without using the CD or DVD. But you should keep that disk as a backup.

> **Tip**
>
> You can also copy pictures from a CD using the standard techniques described in Chapter 21.

Some commercial CDs might automatically launch some program when inserted. That might leave you wondering how in the heck you're going to copy pictures from the disk to your computer. The trick is to simply close that program and get to the CD's contents directly. The process goes something like this:

1. Insert the disk into your CD/DVD drive and wait a few seconds. Then:

   - If an auto start dialog box asks what you want to do with the disk, click Open Folder to View Photos and go to Step 3.

   - If some program opens automatically to show the pictures, close that program and go to Step 2.

   - If nothing at all happens within a minute or so of inserting the disk, continue with Step 2.

2. Open File Explorer and right-click the icon that represents your CD/DVD drive and choose Open.

3. Now you're viewing the contents of the CD. If necessary, navigate through any folders you find until you find icons for the pictures.

4. Select the icons for the pictures you want to copy. Select the Home tab and click Select All, or press Ctrl + A to select them all.

5. Drag or copy and paste any selected icon to the Pictures folder in the Navigation pane. Make sure you get the mouse pointer right on that Pictures folder icon so that you see Copy to My Pictures near the mouse pointer. Then release the mouse button.

6. Wait for all the pictures to copy and then remove the CD from the drive.

You won't need the CD to access those pictures anymore. You'll be able to access them directly from your Pictures folder. But keep the CD as a backup, in case you accidentally delete or destroy any of the copied pictures.

Getting pictures from a scanner

To get photographs on paper into your computer, you use a scanner. Optionally, you can use a film scanner or slide scanner to get pictures from film or slides, but those are a bit more expensive than traditional paper scanners.

The first step is, of course, to install the scanner and any required software as per the instructions that came with the scanner. The second step is to read the instructions on how to work your scanner. The steps we provide here work with most, but not all, scanners and there may be differences among different products. So, if all else fails here, read the instructions that came with *your* scanner to understand the product you own.

The standard operating procedure for more modern scanners goes like this:

1. Turn on the scanner and put in the picture you want to copy.

2. Start Photo Gallery from Apps or launch it from Search results.

3. Click the File toolbar button and choose Import.

4. In the Import Photos and Videos dialog box that opens, click the scanner's icon and click Import.

5. Select the scan settings from the options provided as summarized in the following list:

> **TIP**
>
> If you previously saved settings in a scan profile, click Select Profile and then click the profile you want to use.

- **Paper Source:** Select the type of scanner you have (flatbed, feeder, or film scanner).
- **Paper Size:** If you're using an automatic document feeder to scan multiple items, select the size of the paper you're scanning. Otherwise, leave this empty.
- **Color Format:** Choose Color, Grayscale, or Black and White.

> **NOTE**
>
> For a black-and-white photo, choose Grayscale. The Black and White option provides only black and white with no shades of gray. Black and white, in this context, is best used only for typewritten documents (black ink on white paper).

- **File Type:** Choose a file format. Bitmap Image offers the highest quality at the cost of a large file size. Also, bitmap is an older format that doesn't support tagging and metadata as well as newer formats. You're better off using JPEG or PNG for a photo. Use Microsoft Document Imaging File only for typewritten documents, not photos.
- **Resolution (DPI):** Select your resolution dots per inch (DPI). The larger the DPI, the better the quality of the scanned image, but the larger the file will be. Your best bet for color photos is 300 DPI. Use 75 DPI only for black-and-white text documents. The 150 DPI setting is okay for photos you don't intend to print. You can't change resolution after scanning, but you can rescan the item.
- **Brightness and Contrast:** Use these, if necessary, to enhance the picture's brightness and contrast. You'll need to do a preview scan to see the effects of any changes you make.

   Optionally, if you plan to scan more pictures at the current settings, click Save Profile and give your profile a name.

6. Click Scan.

When the scan is complete, the picture appears in the Photo Gallery. The actual picture file is in your Pictures folder.

Using pictures you get by e-mail

Pictures that are embedded in, or attached to, e-mail messages you receive won't show up in Photo Gallery at first. You need to save the picture(s) to your Pictures folder if you want to access and edit them using techniques described in this chapter.

Exactly how you save attachments and embedded pictures depends on your e-mail program. For most e-mail clients, it's a simple matter of right-clicking the attachment's icon and choosing Save As. In the case of a picture that's visible in the body of the message, right-click the picture and choose Save Picture As. However, do keep in mind that all e-mail clients and systems are different. If you can't figure out how to save attachments or pictures in your e-mail, search your ISP or e-mail provider's e-mail support for **attachment**, or contact its technical support.

Copying pictures from websites

Needless to say, billions of pictures exist on the Internet. You can often find just the picture you're looking for by going to a site like `http://images.google.com` and searching for an appropriate word or phrase.

If you find a picture you can use (and you're not infringing on anyone's copyright in the process), you can store a copy of the picture in any folder of your choosing. If the picture you see on the screen is a link to a larger copy of the image, click to get to the larger copy of the picture. Then use whatever options your web browser provides to save a copy of the picture. Here are the steps for Internet Explorer, the web browser that comes with Windows 8.1:

1. In Internet Explorer, right-click anywhere on the picture you want and choose Save Picture As (see Figure 17.4).

FIGURE 17.4

Saving a picture.

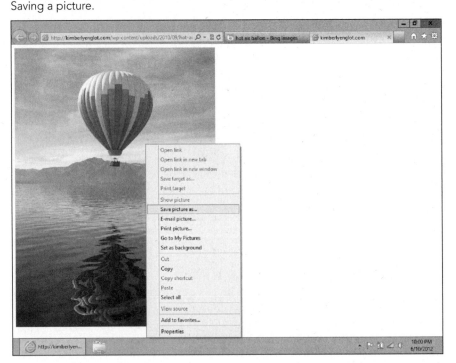

2. Click Pictures in the Navigation pane. Of course, you can choose some other folder if you prefer. For example, double-click any subfolder icon in the main pane to store the picture in that subfolder. You can also perform other tasks, including the following:

- To put the picture in a subfolder of the folder you just opened, double-click that subfolder's icon.

- Change the filename of the picture to a filename of your own choosing.

- Click to the right of the Save As Type label and choose a format. (JPEG works best if you plan to use Photo Gallery.)

3. Click Save.

A copy of the picture is saved in whatever folder you specified in Step 2.

 For more information on saving files, see Chapter 20.

Copy and paste pictures

You can copy an open picture from just about any document to any document that accepts pictures. For example, you can copy and paste a picture from a web page to a Microsoft Word document. You just have to make sure the picture is open (not just an icon or thumbnail). To copy and paste an open picture:

1. Right-click the picture and choose Copy.

2. Right-click where you want to put the picture and choose Paste.

You can use the same technique to make a copy of a picture within a folder or Photo Gallery. Right-click the icon or thumbnail of the picture you want to copy and choose Copy. Then right-click some empty place within the folder (perhaps after the last icon) and choose Paste. The copy will have the same filename as the original, followed by –Copy.

Taking screenshots

CAUTION

The Snipping Tool lets you take a screenshot and also annotate it with your own text. For information on using the Snipping Tool, see the Windows 8.1 online help.

A screenshot is like a photo of something you see on your screen. Most of the pictures in this book are screenshots. You can create screenshots in Windows 8.1 in two ways. One is to use the Snipping Tool. The other is to use the Print Screen key.

The Print Screen key gets its name from the early days of computers where pressing it actually printed whatever was on your screen at the moment to paper. It hasn't worked that way in a long time. Today the Print Screen key takes a snapshot of the screen and puts it in the Windows Clipboard where it just sits waiting for you to paste the Clipboard contents (or until you copy or cut something else to the Clipboard). You can use the Print Screen key in three ways:

- **Print Screen:** Takes a snapshot of the entire screen.

- **Alt + Print Screen:** Takes a snapshot of the active window only.

- **Windows + Print Screen:** Takes a snapshot of the entire screen, saves it to the Picture\Screenshots folder, and names it using the format `Screenshot.png`, `Screenshot (2).png`, `Screenshot (3).png`, and so on.

> **NOTE**
> The Print Screen key may be labeled Prnt Scrn, PrtScn, or something similar on your keyboard.

To make a screenshot, get the screen looking the way you want. Then follow these steps:

1. Press Windows + Print Screen, Print Screen, or Alt + Print Screen.

2. Open your favorite graphics program. If you don't have one, use Search and type **Paint** to open Paint (which comes with Windows 8.1).

> **NOTE**
> You can paste the snapshot into a document (like a Word document). But if you do, you won't be able to treat it like a normal editable picture that is saved separately on disk. It's a good idea to paste it into Paint or some other graphics program and save it as a JPEG or PNG file. You can't paste the snapshot into a folder or Photo Gallery.

3. Choose your program's Paste command (usually located in the Edit menu, or for Paint, on the Home toolbar), or press Ctrl + V. The screenshot is pasted into the program.

4. Exit Paint or your graphics program by clicking the Close (X) button.

5. When you see a message asking if you want to save your changes, click Yes. The Save As dialog box opens.

6. In the Save As dialog box, type a filename of your own choosing.

7. The Save location should already be your Pictures folder (for example, `C:\Users\Your User Name\Pictures`). If it's not, navigate to your Pictures folder (or the folder in which you want to store screenshots).

My Print Screen Key Doesn't Work

If the Paste option on Paint's Home toolbar is disabled (dimmed), that means there is nothing on the Clipboard. That might happen for a couple reasons. You might have forgotten to press Windows+Print Screen, Print Screen, or Alt+Print Screen. Or perhaps you copied something else to the Clipboard after pressing Print Screen. And that "something else" isn't a picture.

The second possible problem is that your keyboard works differently. For example, on some keyboards, you have to press Shift+Print Screen or Shift+Alt+PrintScreen. On some laptop computers, you have to click Fn+Print Screen. On other keyboards, you have to make sure the F Lock key is turned off before pressing the Print Screen key.

If you can't find the right combination of keystrokes for your system, see if you can find the information in the manual that came with your computer, or contact your computer manufacturer and see if they can help.

8. Set the Save as Type option to PNG or JPEG unless you have a good reason for using a different format.

9. Click the Save button.

You won't see anything on your screen. But rest assured, the screenshot is saved as a file in whatever folder you specified in Step 7, with whatever filename you specified in Step 6. If you chose your Pictures folder in Step 7, you'll find the file when you open your Pictures folder, described next.

Using Your Pictures Folder

As its name implies, the Pictures folder is the place to store pictures. Many of the techniques described in the preceding section put pictures in that folder automatically. To view pictures, just open your Pictures folder using whichever technique is most convenient at the moment:

- Using Search, type **pictures** and click Pictures in the Search screen (see Figure 17.5).

FIGURE 17.5

The Pictures options from Search.

17

- Click Pictures in File Explorer's Navigation pane (see Figure 17.6).

FIGURE 17.6

The Pictures link in the Navigation pane.

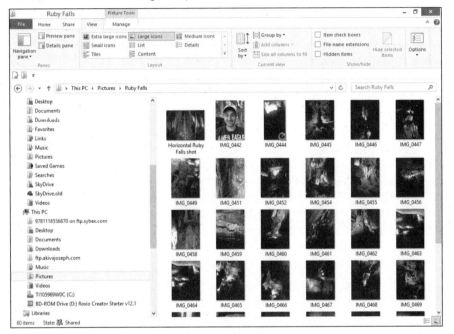

- Click your username in a breadcrumb menu and choose Pictures (see Figure 17.7).

Your Pictures folder opens in File Explorer and is no different from any other folder. You can use all the tools and techniques described in Chapters 20 and 21 to size and arrange icons, hide and show panes, and so forth.

Pictures that you copied from a camera or scanner will likely be stored in subfolders. The name of the subfolder will be the same as the date on which you acquired the pictures, followed by any tag word you added. Figure 17.8 shows an example.

When you open a subfolder that contains pictures, you'll see a thumbnail icon for each one. The size of that thumbnail and the amount of textual information shown with each depends on where you place the Views slider in the toolbar. If the Preview pane is open, pointing to a thumbnail displays an enlarged copy of the thumbnail. Figure 17.9 shows an example. To choose which panes you want to show or hide, click the View toolbar and make your selections in the Layout area.

FIGURE 17.7

The Pictures link from a breadcrumb menu.

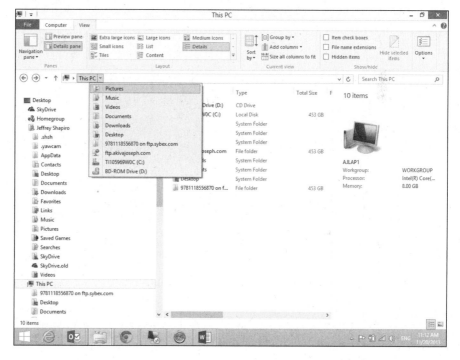

17

FIGURE 17.8

The Pictures folder.

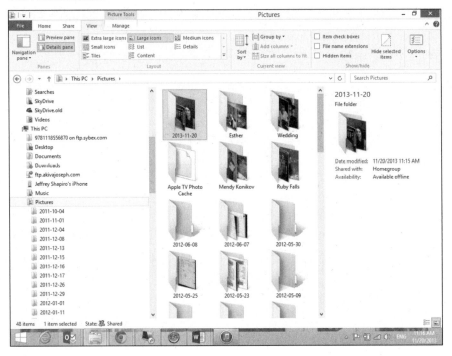

Pictures folder quick tips

Here are some quick tips that apply to most folders, with a few things that are unique to your Pictures folder:

- If your mouse has a wheel, hold down the Ctrl key while spinning the wheel to size thumbnails and change views.

- Drag the inner border of the Navigation or Preview pane to widen or narrow the pane.

- To open a subfolder, click (or double-click) its icon. To leave a subfolder, click the Back button or press Backspace.

> **TIP**
>
> Whether you need to click or double-click depends on settings in Folder Options. Click the View toolbar and choose Options. Make your selection under Click Items as Follows and click OK.

- To rotate a picture, right-click its thumbnail and choose Rotate Right or Rotate Left.

FIGURE 17.9

Folder of pictures.

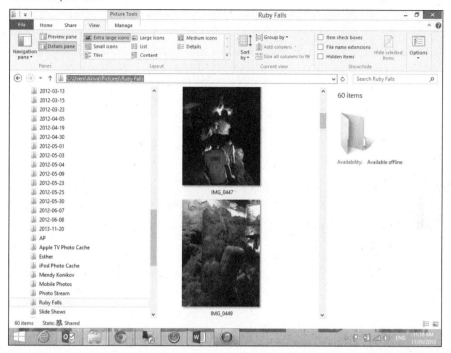

NOTE

If the Rotate options are disabled or missing, the picture's file type can't be rotated in Windows, but you can open and rotate it in many graphics programs.

- To preview a larger version of a picture, click (or double-click) its thumbnail.
- To view all the pictures in the folder as a slide show, click the Slide Show toolbar button on the Manage tab.
- Right-click any thumbnail icon for a shortcut of things you can do with that item.
- Use standard techniques described in Chapter 28 to select multiple icons that you want to print, copy, and so forth. To select all icons, choose Home ➪ Select All or press Ctrl + A.
- To e-mail pictures using a default e-mail program installed on your computer, select their thumbnail icons. Then click the E-mail toolbar button on the Share tab.

NOTE

The E-mail button isn't visible until you select one or more icons in the folder. Also, it doesn't work with all e-mail programs.

- Click Burn to Disc to copy all pictures in a folder to a writable CD or DVD. To copy only specific items, select their icons and click Burn.

> **NOTE**
>
> Copying to CD and DVD isn't like copying to other media. Chapter 20 provides the full story.

- Right-click any column heading in Details view to choose which columns you want to show or hide.
- Click any column heading to sort thumbnails into ascending or descending order by Name, Date Taken, Rating, or any other heading.
- Click the arrow next to any column heading, as in Figure 17.10, or right-click empty space between icons to arrange or sort by Name, Date, Type, Size, or Tags.

> **TIP**
>
> See "Using Photo Gallery," later in this chapter, for more information on tags. See Chapter 22 for more info on grouping, stacking, and filtering.

FIGURE 17.10

Grouping options.

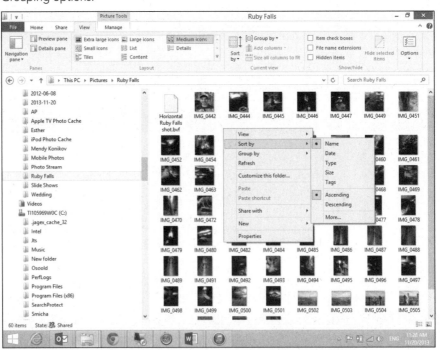

- When the Details pane is open, you can use it to add a tag or title to any selected pictures or multiple selected pictures.

- If you have multiple programs that can open a picture type, right-click the thumbnail and choose Open With to open the picture in whatever program you like, or choose a program name from the Preview toolbar button.

- To show or hide the ribbon bar, click the Minimize the Ribbon or Expand the Ribbon arrow on the right side of the menu bar. You also can press Ctrl + F1 (see Figure 17.11).

FIGURE 17.11

Layout options on the Organize menu.

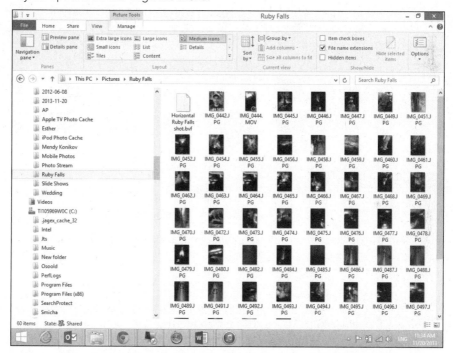

- To show or hide filename extensions, click Organize and choose Folder and Search Options. Select the View tab, select or clear the Hide Extensions for Known File Types check box, and click OK.

Why some pictures show icons

Not all file types show as pictures in your Pictures folder. Some, such as videos you import from a camera in MP4, MOV, or some other format, show only icons. For example, in Figure 17.12, the second icon is a video stored in MP4 format (.mp4 format).

FIGURE 17.12

The icon for a MP4 video.

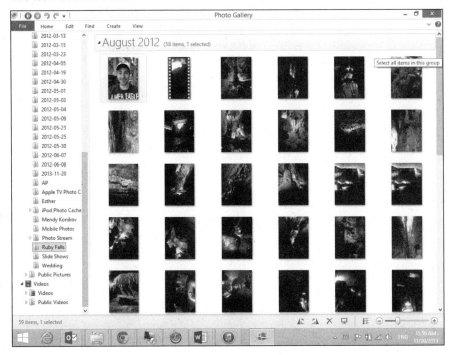

If you have an appropriate player for a file type, you can still open it by double-clicking. For example, if you have the Applian FlvPlayer program (available for free from `http://applian.com/flvplayer/download_flv_player_only)`, you can double-click any Flash video icon to watch it.

If it's important to be able to see the thumbnail of a picture or icon, you have to convert the image or video to a compatible format like JPEG (for a picture) or WMV (for a video). For a single picture, you can often achieve this just by opening the picture in a graphics program. If you don't have a favorite graphics program, you can use Paint (right-click any picture and choose Open With ➪ Paint). From the menu bar in your graphics program, choose File ➪ Save As. Use the Save as Type option in the Save dialog box to save the picture as a JPEG or some other compatible format and click Save.

Some graphics programs, like Corel's Paint Shop Pro, let you convert a whole group of pictures from one format to another instead of changing them one at a time. You can also go to any online shareware service such as `www.tucows.com` or `http://download.cnet.com` and search for "convert picture" to find programs that specifically offer batch conversions. Search for "convert video" for programs that can convert videos.

> **TIP**
>
> If you want to put videos on your mobile devices, such as an iPod, iPad, Android, or other mobile device, check out www.pqdvd.com for a converter.

Videos in your Pictures folder

If your digital camera lets you shoot video clips, those will be imported along with your still pictures. If the video is in a compatible format, its thumbnail shows the first frame of the video. It also shows a film-like border and the icon of the default program for playing that type of video.

When you select a video thumbnail, the Preview pane turns to a small video screen with controls that work like a DVD player. Figure 17.13 shows an example with a video selected. The video preview pane to the right shows the first frame of the video. To watch the video in that preview, click the Play button under the video.

FIGURE 17.13

A video thumbnail icon selected.

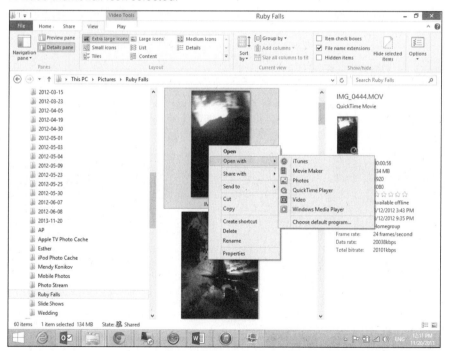

When the video starts playing, you can click the Full Screen button under the preview window to watch it full-screen. Click anywhere on that full-screen video to return to the desktop and your Pictures folder.

Renaming pictures and videos

Pictures and videos from cameras often have obscure meaningless filenames like `100_9630` or `DCM1234`. You can change the name of any file by right-clicking its thumbnail and choosing Rename. Or you can select multiple thumbnails, right-click any one of them, and choose Rename. The current filename is highlighted.

Type the new name. (Be careful not change the extension that comes after the period.) Then press Enter. If you renamed one file, only that file's name is changed. If you renamed several files, they'll all have the same name followed by a number; for example, `Swans (1)`, `Swans (2)`, `Swans (3)`, and so forth.

If you change your mind after renaming, press Undo (Ctrl + Z). But you have to do it right after pressing Enter. If you move on to other tasks, you may not be able to undo the rename.

There's much more to pictures and videos than looking at them in your Pictures folder. Next, we take a look at Photo Gallery, a handy tool that you can download from Microsoft to use with Windows 8.1.

Using Photo Gallery

Photo Gallery is a program that helps you bring together pictures and videos from all the subfolders in your Pictures folder. The program is not included with Windows 8.1, but you can download it from `http://explore.live.com/windows-live-photo-gallery`.

> **Tip**
> Photo Gallery is a great tool for managing a large photo collection.

Photo Gallery isn't a folder where you store files. Instead, it's a way of organizing and accessing files without having to navigate around multiple folders. For example, you can view all your photos at once, regardless of what folders they're in. Or better yet, you can locate and work with pictures that have certain things in common, such as all the pictures of your child (if you're a parent).

The only disadvantage of Photo Gallery is that it doesn't show icons for all pictures and videos. Anything that doesn't show a thumbnail in your Pictures folder doesn't show up at all in Photo Gallery! Photo Gallery shows thumbnails for BMP, JFIF, JPEG, PNG, TIFF, and WDP photos and WMV, AVI, ASF, and MPEG movies.

The easiest way to understand what Photo Gallery is all about is to fire it up and take a look for yourself. Use whichever method shown here is easiest for you:

- Click Photo Gallery on the Start screen.
- Press Windows, type **gal**, and click Photo Gallery.

Figure 17.14 shows how Photo Gallery might look when you first open it. Of course, the pictures you see will be your own (if you have any). Also, you might be prompted to associate various file types with Photo Gallery. If so, select the file format(s) you want associated with Photo Gallery.

Like any program window, you can minimize, maximize, move, and size Photo Gallery to your liking. (Although there is a limit to how small you can make it.) Photo Gallery has its own Help. Click the blue Help button at the right side of its toolbar to open Help (or press F1 if Photo Gallery is the active window).

FIGURE 17.14

Windows Photo Gallery.

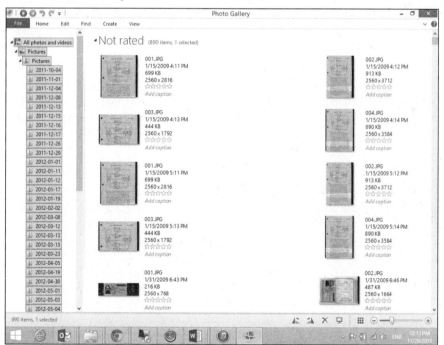

Choosing what to view and how

The Photo Gallery can show you all the photos and videos on your hard drive (or multiple hard drives), or it can show only certain ones. To get started, you'll want to see everything that's in the Photo Gallery right now. To do that, click All Photos and Videos at the top of the Navigation pane. If you just want to see pictures, click Pictures under the All Photos and Videos heading. If you just want to see Videos, click Videos under that same heading.

The gallery to the right of the Navigation pane shows a thumbnail for each photo and video currently in the gallery.

Use the slider at the bottom of the Photo Gallery window to change the size of the thumbnails. The button to the left of the slider lets you choose between Details view and regular thumbnail view. Details view shows the filename, date taken, file size, rating, and other details about each image.

To group or arrange pictures in the gallery, right-click in the right pane and choose View, Group By, or Sort By and whatever option best describes how you want things organized.

Also in the context menu when you right-click is a Table of Contents option. Clicking that opens a Table of Contents pane to the left of the Thumbnails. The Table of Contents works in conjunction with the current Group By option on the Thumbnail View button. For example, if you group by Month, the Table of Contents lets you jump to all pictures taken in a specific month and year. If you group by Image Size, the Table of Contents provides links to large, medium, and small pictures, and so forth.

Go ahead and play around with those buttons and options for a while. You can't do any harm. But some of the grouping and arranging options won't have any real effect until you've built up a sizable collection of pictures. Remember that anything you choose right now you can change at any time in the future. You're not making any long-term commitments here while experimenting with views and arrangements.

Photo Gallery quick tips

Following are some other good things to know:

- Rest the mouse pointer on any thumbnail to see a larger view of the picture.
- To rotate a picture, right-click it and choose a Rotate option.
- Select the View tab and then click the Tag and Caption pane. Next, click any picture to see its information in the Tag and Caption pane on the far right where you can add tags, captions, and geotags.
- Double-click any picture to preview it at a larger size and view options for adjusting the photo's image properties. Click Close File to leave the preview.
- Click View ➪ Slide Show to watch a slide show.
- To open a picture or video in a program, right-click its thumbnail, click the Open With option, and choose a program.

- Click the File button and choose Import Photos and Videos to import pictures from a digital camera or scanner.

- To print selected pictures, choose File ⇨ Print and then select a printing option. (See "Printing Pictures" later in this chapter for details and options.)

- To open the folder in which a picture is contained, right-click its thumbnail and choose Open File Location.

If any item listed doesn't work for you, see the section "Choosing Photo Gallery options," later in this chapter.

Selecting thumbnails in the Gallery

As in folders, you can select multiple thumbnails in Photo Gallery. This can be handy when you want to apply a similar rating, tag, or caption to pictures, or when you want to create a slide show from several pictures, print several pictures, and so forth. You can use the same techniques you use in folders to select thumbnails in the gallery.

In addition to the standard methods of selecting thumbnails (and icons), you can select multiple thumbnails just by clicking their check boxes. Any thumbnail that has a check mark is selected. Any thumbnail that doesn't have a check mark is unselected.

To select all the pictures in the gallery, click any single picture and press Ctrl + A, or right-click some empty space just outside the thumbnails and choose Select All. If you want to select most (but not all) of the pictures, select them all first. Then Ctrl + click the pictures you want to deselect, or clear their check boxes.

Dating, rating, tagging, and captioning

Tagging is one of the biggest advantages to having all your pictures in Photo Gallery. A *tag* is simply some keyword or phrase that you make up to identify pictures — for example, the location where the picture was shot, the subject of the picture, or the names of people in the picture. You can apply as many tags as you want to a picture, and you can add, change, or delete tags at any time.

Rating allows you to rate photos on a scale of one to five stars based on how much you like the picture. Captions allow you to title pictures with words of your own choosing. Use the Info pane to rate, tag, and caption pictures.

First, click the thumbnail picture that you want to rate. Or, if you want to apply the same rating, tags, or caption to multiple pictures, select all their icons. Then:

- To rate the selected picture(s), choose View ⇨ Rating, and click any star near the bottom of the picture (see Figure 17.15). To give a zero rating, click a star, and then click it again.

FIGURE 17.15

The Tag and caption pane.

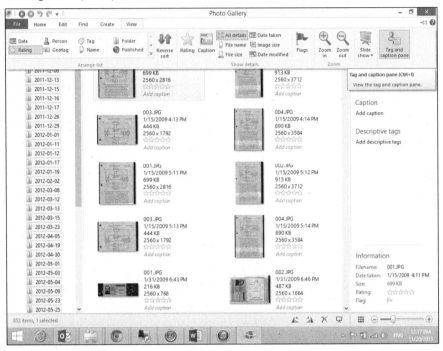

- To tag the selected picture(s), choose View ⇨ Tag and Caption Pane, click a picture, and then click Add Descriptive Tags under the Descriptive Tags item. Type one tag (preferably a single word or two) and press Enter. Optionally, type more tags in the same manner, pressing Enter after each tag.

> **TIP**
>
> If the picture contains people you know, consider typing each person's name as a separate tag. That way, you can later search for pictures of that person, or pictures that contain several specific people. Don't use commas or semicolons in an attempt to apply multiple tags to a picture. Always press Enter after typing a single tag.

- To caption, click Add Caption, type a caption in the Add a Caption box, or replace the text that already appears there with a caption of your own.

- Optionally, if you want to change the date or time that the picture was taken, click the current date and time shown above the Ratings stars.

Filtering pictures

The coolest thing about tagging pictures is that it makes specific pictures very easy to find in the future. This is especially useful after you've accumulated hundreds or thousands of pictures, and don't want to go digging through folders to find specific ones.

To see all pictures to which you've applied a tag, right-click in the Content pane, choose Group By and then click Tag. Figure 17.16 shows an example sorted by Ruby. The gallery at the top shows all photos tagged with the word *Ruby;* the photos below are not tagged.

To see pictures that contain multiple tags, use the Text Search tool. Choose Find ⇨ Text Search to open the Search By bar. For example, suppose you entered the word *nature* as tags for dozens of photos. But you also entered the term *vacation* for only three of those photos. In the Search By bar, if you type **nature vacation** and press Enter, you'll see only the three photos that match both tags.

To see all pictures to which you haven't yet applied any tags, click Find and then click the down arrow on the Tags button. Click Not Tagged near the bottom of the tag list. From there, you can start adding tags to any pictures that appear in the gallery.

To see all the pictures you took in a certain year, month, or day, select the Find tab and click Dates, Months, or Years. To see all the pictures to which you've applied a rating (or no rating), click an option under the Rated heading.

FIGURE 17.16

Viewing all pictures tagged "Ruby".

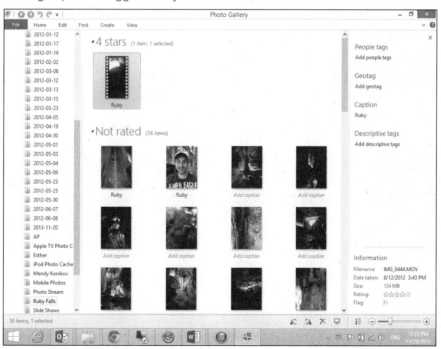

To search for pictures or videos by name, tag, or other keyword, first click All Photos and Videos at the top of the Navigation pane. Select the Find tab, and then click Text Search and type a word in the Search box. You can also narrow the search by first clicking Pictures, Videos, a tag, a year, or whatever to reduce the number of items in the gallery. Your next search will search only within items currently in the gallery.

Changing tags

Tags are flexible. You can add, rename, and change them at will. To change the spelling of a tag, just right-click it in the Navigation pane and choose Rename. Type in the corrected name and press Enter. The spelling will automatically be corrected in every picture that contains that tag.

To delete a tag from a single picture, without removing the tag from any other pictures, first select the picture's thumbnail. Or if you want to delete the tag from a few pictures, select their thumbnails. Then right-click the tag you want to remove and choose Delete. Note that deleting a tag does not delete any pictures. It simply removes the tag from any pictures to which you previously applied the tag.

Use a picture as your desktop background

If you have a favorite photo you'd like to use as a desktop background, right-click its thumbnail and choose Set as Desktop Background.

If you can't see the desktop, click the Show Desktop button at the far right of the taskbar. Then click the Windows Photo Gallery taskbar button to bring Photo Gallery back onto the desktop.

Adding pictures to Photo Gallery

Photo Gallery doesn't scan your entire hard disk for photos. By default it includes only pictures from the Pictures folder in your user account. If you have pictures in other folders, you can add them to Photo Gallery in several ways. If the pictures are in some arbitrary location where they just happened to end up, consider moving them to your Pictures folder. Use any technique described in Chapter 21 to move and copy files.

If the pictures are in some other folder for good reason, you can add that folder to Photo Gallery. This has no effect on the pictures or the folder, so you won't mess up your existing organization. To add a folder to the Photo Gallery:

1. Select the File tab and choose Include Folder.

2. Navigate to any folder that contains pictures and videos you'd like to include in your gallery and click OK.

Repeat Steps 1 and 2 for each folder you want to add. As you add new pictures to those folders in the future, they'll show up automatically in Photo Gallery.

Use your Photo Gallery as a screen saver

To use photos in your Photo Gallery as a screen saver, select the File tab and choose Screen Saver Settings. Set the Screen Saver name to Photo Gallery. Then click the Settings button. You can choose to show all photos and videos or narrow the selection to a specific folder. If you like, you can also narrow things down to only pictures that have a certain tag or rating, and exclude files with specific tags. You can also set the general speed of the screen saver slide show. Select Shuffle Contents to randomize the photo and video selection. Click Save after making your selections. Click Preview for a preview of how the screen saver will look. Click OK when you're happy with your selections to return to Photo Gallery.

Fixing photos

Photo Gallery comes complete with a simple graphics editor specifically designed to work with photos. The editing tools are located on the Edit tab (see Figure 17.17), and you can get to it simply by clicking a thumbnail and then clicking the Edit tab.

> **TIP**
>
> The Fix pane makes it easy to touch up your photos. It's a far cry from a "real" graphics editor such as Photoshop or Paint Shop Pro, but it can fix the most common photo problems.

FIGURE 17.17

The Edit tab.

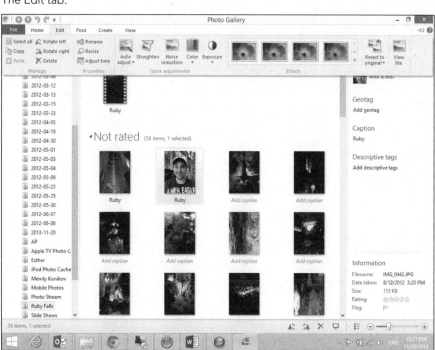

Before you try anything, notice the Undo button at the top of the Photo Gallery window. If you don't like the results of a change, click this button to undo the change. If you change your mind after Undo, click Redo to bring the change back. When you point to Undo and Redo after making changes to a picture, you'll see a little arrow on the button that you can click to undo only one change or all changes. The buttons are disabled (dimmed) when there's nothing to undo or redo. You also can use the Revert to Original button on the Edit tab if you want to remove all edits and return to the original photo.

The sections that follow describe several of the main tools on the Edit tab.

Auto Adjust

Click Auto Adjust to let Photo Gallery take a shot at cleaning up the brightness, contrast, and such. Don't expect miracles, however. Sometimes Auto Adjust might make things worse. If so, just click Undo.

Exposure

Click this option to adjust the brightness and contrast of the picture. The Exposure Adjustment settings are especially useful for pictures that are poorly lit. Click one of the nine predefined exposures to improve your photo. For a description of the exposure, hover the mouse pointer over an exposure to see the brightness, shadow, and highlight settings.

Color

Click Color to change the color temperature and tint. Click one of the nine predefined color adjustments to improve your photo. Temperature and tint can be defined as follows:

- **Color temperature:** The overall tone of your picture from low temperature to high.
- **Tint:** Changes the color cast in a picture by adding or removing green from your picture.

To fine-tune a photo's color, double-click the photo and then choose the Fine Tune tool on the Edit tab. In the right pane, click Adjust Color and move the Color Temperature, Tint, and Saturation sliders left or right until you get the desired color you want.

Straighten

This option straightens your photo. If you took a photo with the camera at a slight angle, use this option to straighten the photo.

Crop

Cropping a picture lets you get rid of any unnecessary background. This is useful when the main subject of the photo looks too small or far away. Figure 17.18 shows an example. The photo on the left is a crop of the entire original photo shown on the right. The cropped photo on the left brings attention to a few features by eliminating much of the foreground.

TIP

Figure 17.18 is also a good example of why you might want to make a duplicate of the original before cropping. The photo on the right is a good photo and is worth keeping. The cropped copy on the left is good for showing one of the main subjects of the photo.

FIGURE 17.18

Original photo (right) and cropped photo (left).

To crop a photo, first double-click the photo you want to crop. Next click Crop on the Edit tab. A white box with sizing handles (little squares) appears on the picture. The idea is to get exactly what you want the finished photo to look like inside that box. Anything you want to crop out of the picture should be outside the box.

If you plan on printing the finished photo on pre-sized photographic paper, click the down arrow on the Crop button and click Proportion. Choose your print size. Doing so keeps the proportions of the cropping box at the proper aspect ratio for the print size.

NOTE

The aspect ratio is the ratio of the width of the photo to its height. Different print sizes have slightly different aspect ratios.

Here's how you use the cropping box that's on the picture:

- To make the box larger or smaller, drag any sizing handle (little square) around the box border.
- To recenter the box around the main subject of the photo, put the mouse pointer inside the box and drag it to a better location on the picture.
- To zoom in and out while cropping, spin the mouse wheel or use the Zoom slider.

When the inside of the box looks the way you want your photo to look, click the Crop button. The picture is cropped. (If you change your mind, click Undo.)

Fix red eye

Red eye is a common problem caused by the retina at the back of the eye reflecting the flash back to the camera. Fixing it isn't too tough. First, if the eyes are very small in the photo, spin the mouse wheel or use the Zoom button to zoom in on the eyes. You may need to zoom a little, pan a little, zoom a little. The idea is to make the eyes as large as possible in the viewing area. Next, click Red Eye on the Edit tab and follow the instructions that appear there. Drag a rectangle around the pupil of the eyeball, not the entire eye. Figure 17.19 shows an example where we've dragged a rectangle around an eye.

FIGURE 17.19

Fixing red eye.

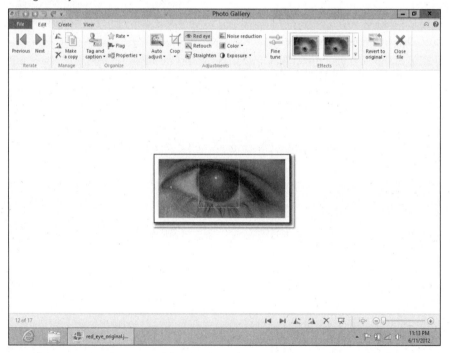

If dragging a rectangle around the eye once doesn't fix the red eye, drag another rectangle around the same eye. Keep doing so until all the red is gone. Then pan over to the other eye, if necessary, and drag a square around that eye. If you don't like the results, click Undo. Then try again.

Effects

You can use the black-and-white Effects options on the Edit tab to turn your photo into a black-and-white image with no filter or a choice of orange, yellow, or red filter. Each filter gives a different result. You can also create a sepia tone or cyan tone image.

Saving changes

When you've finished touching up your photo in the Fix pane, click Close File. Your changes are saved automatically.

If you made a mess of things in the editing window, click Revert to Original to undo your previous changes.

TIP

You can recover previous versions of many different kinds of files, not just photos. If you're interested in that sort of thing, see Chapter 24 for the whole story.

Using people tags

Photo Gallery includes a feature called *people tags* that you can use to identify people in your photos. People tags work in conjunction with Photo Gallery's face detection capability, enabling you to assign a tag to a person's face, rather than just to the photo. So, instead of just adding Edna as a general tag to a photo with 20 people in it, you can assign the people tag to Great Aunt Edna's face, so you can remember who she is in that family reunion photo.

Photo Gallery's face detection capability does not equal *facial recognition.* Photo Gallery won't tag all the photos that contain Aunt Edna automatically. Instead, face detection simply enables Photo Gallery to identify faces in a picture. You can then assign tags to each face.

Assigning a people tag is easy. First, just click a photo. If Photo Gallery is able to detect faces in the photo, you'll see a People Found link in the Info pane. Click Identify, and then type the name of the person whose face is highlighted. Repeat the process for other faces in the photo.

If Photo Gallery can't detect faces in the photo, you can add the people tags manually. Double-click the photo to preview it. Then, on the Edit tab, click Tag and Caption. Photo Gallery will draw a rectangle around a face that it finds in the photo (see Figure 17.20).

In the information pane on the right, click Who Is This under the Tag Someone label or in the dialog that appears next to the rectangle. Enter the name of the person or select a name from the list of previously entered names.

FIGURE 17.20

Adding a people tag.

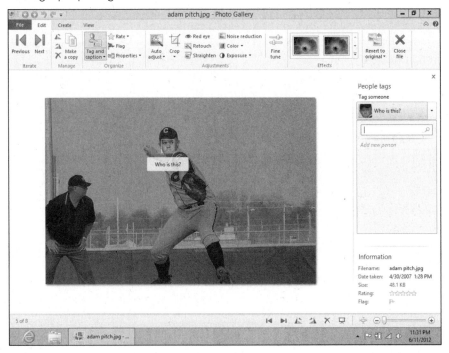

If Photo Gallery does not automatically detect a face, click the arrow on the Tag and Caption button, click People Tag ⇨ Tag a Person. Drag a box around the person's face and then fill out the Tag Someone box.

Choosing Photo Gallery options

Like most programs, Photo Gallery has an Options dialog box that lets you tweak certain program features to your own work style. To open Photo Gallery's Options dialog box, click the File toolbar button and choose Options. Figure 17.21 shows the Photo Gallery Options dialog box, which contains six tabs: General, Import, Publish, Originals, Edit, and Trust Center.

FIGURE 17.21

Photo Gallery options.

Selecting the first option, Show Photo and Video Previews in Tooltips, ensures that when you point to a thumbnail in Photo Gallery, you see a larger version of the thumbnail or video. Clearing that check box prevents the tooltips from showing.

The Find People in Your Photos option on the General tab turns on or off face detection, described previously.

The Navigation pane options let you set to show date taken information and descriptive tags of your photos.

The Import tab lets you customize how pictures that you import to Photo Gallery are handled. You can import pictures into Photo Gallery by clicking File in its toolbar and choosing Import from Camera or Scanner.

- **Settings For:** Specify the device or medium for which you want to define settings.
- **Import To:** Choose the folder to which pictures and videos will be imported. The default is the Pictures folder for your user account.

- **Folder Name:** Imported pictures are automatically placed in a folder. Use this option to specify how you want that folder named. You can choose from various combinations of the following:

  - **Date Imported:** Today's date (the date on which you're performing the import).

  - **Name:** Photo or video name.

  - **Date Taken:** The date in the first picture's Date Taken property.

  - **Date Taken Range:** The Date Taken property of the first and last pictures being imported.

- **File Name:** Each imported picture is automatically assigned a filename. To use the original filename as assigned by the camera, choose Original File Name. Some digital cameras organize photos into folders. To preserve both the camera folder and filenames, choose Original File Name (Preserve Folders).

- **Open Photo Gallery after Importing Files:** When selected, this option ensures that Photo Gallery opens automatically as soon as you've finished importing pictures.

- **Delete Files from Device after Importing:** If selected, pictures and videos will be erased from the camera automatically after importing.

- **Rotate Photos during Import:** Some digital cameras can sense when you're holding the camera vertically and mark each such picture accordingly. Choosing this option causes those pictures to be rotated to the correct upright position automatically when imported.

- **Restore Defaults:** Sets options back to the original factory settings.

Click OK after making your selections. Your choices on the Import tab will be applied only to pictures you import in the future. They have no effect on pictures you've already imported. Of course, you can rename, rotate, tag, and move pictures at any time, regardless of settings in the Options dialog box.

The Publish tab provides options for setting file details (called *metadata*) that you want to include with your files. For example, you can include all file details, none, or select details that you don't want to show (such as camera information, location information, and the like).

The Originals tab has to do with the Revert button in Fix. By default, previous versions of photos stay on the hard disk permanently, even though you don't see them. After a few years, or even months, the storage space they require could be significant. Choosing Move Original Files to Recycle Bin After lets you put a time on those saved originals. You can choose from several time frames, ranging from One Day to Never.

 The Recycle Bin is much like a wastepaper basket. It holds your trash (deleted files) until you empty it. See Chapter 21 for more information.

Keep in mind that you can't revert a modified picture to its original form, or find a previous version of a file after the time limit expires. If you consistently work with duplicates of pictures rather than originals, this isn't a big deal because you always have the original in plain sight in its folder.

Use the Edit tab to select Auto Adjust settings, including Straighten, Noise Reduction, Color, and Exposure. By selecting these items, you can tell Photo Gallery which auto adjust options to use when you click Auto Adjust on the Edit tab when editing a photo.

Microsoft includes the Trust Center tab so that you can opt to provide Microsoft with information that helps them make better products. If you select the Help Improve Windows Live option, Microsoft collects system information and data about the way in which you use their Live products. That data is then uploaded to Microsoft.

Click OK when you finish changing options.

Making movies from Photo Gallery

The Movie option on the Create toolbar button in Photo Gallery is really just a shortcut to Movie Maker. The idea is to get all the pictures and videos you want to put in a movie into the gallery, perhaps by giving all those items a tag and then clicking the tag name in Photo Gallery's Navigation pane. Then you select all those items and choose Create ⇨ Movie. Movie Maker opens with all the selected items, ready to insert into a new movie.

Printing Pictures

You can print pictures to almost any printer, although photo printers produce much better results. However, you'll need to refer to the instructions that came with that printer for specifics on connecting the printer. You might also need to install or download a special driver from the printer manufacturer. If in doubt, refer to the manual that came with the photo printer or to the manufacturer's website.

Most modern inkjet and laser printers let you print on either plain paper or photographic paper. Photographic paper is considerably more expensive, so you might want to stick with plain paper for drafts and informal prints. Use photographic paper for more formal prints of your best photos.

Printing from Photo Gallery

If the pictures you want to print are in Photo Gallery, you can print from there. Use the Navigation pane to display the pictures you want to print. Then select (check) the picture (or pictures) you want to print. If you want to print all the pictures showing in the gallery, you can click the group heading to select all the icons, or click any one picture in the gallery and press Ctrl + A. If you want to print only some pictures, select their icons. You can do so by pointing to any image and clicking its check box. Or you can use the universal techniques for selecting icons discussed in Chapter 21.

After you've selected the pictures you want to print, choose File ⇨ Print ⇨ Print. The Print Pictures window shown in Figure 17.22 opens.

> **NOTE**
>
> Don't worry about sideways pictures in the Print Pictures window. You don't need to rotate them. The printed pictures will look fine even if they're sideways in the Print Pictures window.

FIGURE 17.22

The Print Pictures window.

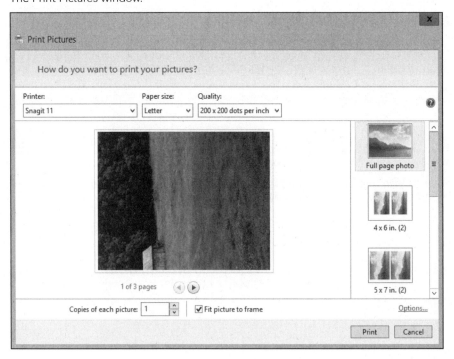

Now you get to make a whole bunch of choices as to how you want to print your picture(s). The choices available to you depend on what kind of printer you're using. If you have multiple printers attached to your computer, the first step is to select the printer you want to use from the Printer drop-down list.

If your printer supports multiple paper sizes, click the Paper Size drop-down and choose the size paper you want to print to. Depending on your printer, you might also be able to click the Quality drop-down and choose the output resolution. The higher the DPI, the better the quality of the print, and the longer it takes to print.

If your selected printer supports multiple paper types, click Paper Type and choose the paper you're using.

If you're printing multiple pictures on large paper, choose a layout from the right column. Use the scroll bar at the right side of the window to view all your options. Typically, you can choose any size from a full-page photo down to tiny wallet-size prints. After you scroll, be sure to click the layout you want to use. The preview area shows you how things will look on each printed page.

> **NOTE**
> If you change your mind about the pictures you selected to print, click Cancel to return to Photo Gallery.

To print more than one copy of each picture, specify how many you want to print in the Copies of Each Picture. Choose Fit Picture to Frame to ensure that any small pictures are expanded to fill the page on which they're printed.

With all the choices made, just click Print and wait. Don't expect the printer to start right away. It takes some time for the computer to get everything together before sending it to the printer. Be patient. When your pictures are finished printing, click Finish in the window that appears.

Printing pictures from a folder

If you have pictures that don't show in Photo Gallery, you can print them straight from the folder in which they're stored. Open the folder that contains the pictures. Then select the icons of the pictures you want to print. Be careful you don't select any icons for non-picture files, or this technique won't work.

Once you've selected the picture icons, choose Share ⇨ Print from the toolbar. If the Print button isn't visible, first click > > at the end of the toolbar to see if it's just off the edge. If you still don't see a Print option, chances are, one or more of your selected icons isn't a picture. When you do see the Print button, click it. You'll be taken to the Print Pictures window. Choose your settings, as described in the previous section, and click Print.

Pixels and Megapixels

Every picture you see on your screen is actually a bunch of little lighted dots on the screen called *pixels*. You don't see the individual pixels because they're too small, but if you take a small original picture and zoom way in, each pixel reveals itself as a small colored square. Figure 17.23 shows an example. The picture on the left is the original. The picture on the right is an extreme zoom in. There you can see how the picture is actually lots of pixels — little colored squares.

FIGURE 17.23

Zoomed in to see pixels.

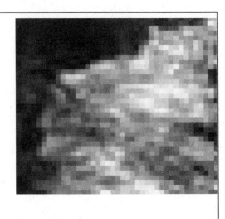

When shopping for digital cameras, *megapixels* are a key pricing factor. A megapixel isn't one humongous pixel. It's a million regular-size pixels. The basic rule of thumb is, the more pixels, the better the quality of the pictures. The term *quality* in this context really means how big you can make it (or print it) without the picture looking *pixelated*. A pixelated picture looks, at best, blotchy; at worst, it looks like a bunch of pixels rather than a coherent picture.

Table 17.1 provides some general guidelines on how the number of megapixels translates to print quality. You can always print any picture at any size, of course, but you start to lose quality if you go above the recommended maximum size shown in the second column. All numbers are approximate, of course, because many other factors come into play in determining overall print quality.

TABLE 17.1   Megapixels and Print Size

Megapixels	Recommended Maximum Print Size
1–2	3 x 5
2–3	5 x 7
3–4	8 x 10
4–5	11 x 14
5+	18 x 24

File extension, size, and dimensions

Every picture has a type, indicated by its filename extension. It also has a size measured in kilobytes (KB) or megabytes (MB). And it has dimensions. You see that information when you point to a picture's thumbnail in a folder. The Details view in a folder can show the Dimension, Size, and Type of every picture in the folder (see Figure 17.24). Right-click any column heading and choose the name of the column you want to see.

FIGURE 17.24

Viewing photo file details in File Explorer.

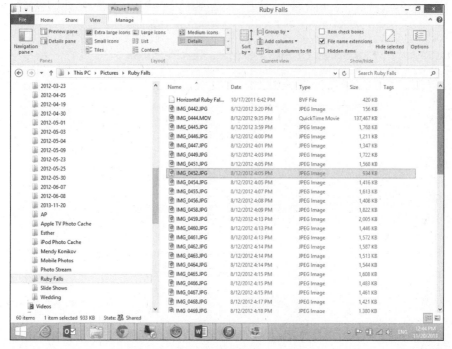

In Photo Gallery, the file extension, size, and dimensions of a photo show when you point to a thumbnail or use the Details view.

A picture's dimensions are its width and height measured in pixels. As a rule, the bigger the dimensions, the better, because it means you can print the picture at a very large size with no loss of quality. You can also zoom in quite far, and crop out quite a bit, and still end up with a picture that has significant detail.

Recall that the term *megapixels* refers to the number of pixels in a picture, where 1 megapixel equals a million pixels. A 5-megapixel camera will create pictures with dimensions of around 2,576 x 1,932. Multiplying those two numbers gives you the total number of pixels in the picture: 4,976,832. That's just about 5 million pixels — hence, the 5-megapixel rating.

The file size is the amount of disk space required to store the picture. Bigger is better in terms of picture quality because a large file size indicates that there's lots of information in the file, which means you can print it at large sizes and zoom in on any portion of the picture without losing much clarity.

The filename extension is the picture's file type. Many types of picture files exist. Table 17.2 lists some examples. Some file types are so old or so rare you may never see one. The most commonly used picture types are TIFF, JPEG, PNG, BMP, and GIF, described next.

TABLE 17.2   Examples of File Formats for Pictures

Filename Extension	Format
.art	AOL Art file
.bmp	Windows Bitmap
.cdr	CorelDraw Drawing
.cgm	Computer Graphics Metafile
.clp	Windows Clipboard
.cmx	Corel Clipart
.cut	Dr. Halo
.dcx	Zsoft Multipage Paintbrush
.dib	Windows Device Independent Bitmap
.drw	Micrografx Draw
.dxf	Autodesk Drawing Interchange
.emf	Windows Enhanced Metafile
.tif, .ai, .ps	Encapsulated PostScript
.fpx	FlashPix
.gem	Ventura/GEM Drawing
.gif	CompuServe Graphics Interchange
.hgl	HP Graphics Language
.iff	Amiga
.img	GEM Paint
.jpg, .jif, .jpeg	Joint Photographic Experts Group
.kdc	Kodak Digital Camera
.lbm	Deluxe Paint

Filename Extension	Format
.mac	MacPaint
.msp	Microsoft Paint
.pbm	Portable Bitmap
.pcd	Kodak Photo CD
.pct	Macintosh PICT
.pcx	Zsoft Paintbrush
.pgm	Portable Greymap
.pic	Lotus PIC
.pic	PC Paint
.png	Portable Network Graphics
.ppm	Portable Pixelmap
.psd	Photoshop
.psp	Paint Shop Pro
.ras	Sun RasterImage
.raw	Raw File Format
.rle	Windows or CompuServe RLE
.sct, .ct	SciTex Continuous Tone
.tga	Truevision Targa
.tif, .tiff	Tagged Image File Format
.wdp	Windows Digital Photo
.wmf	Windows Meta File
.wpg	WordPerfect Bitmap or Vector

17

TIFF pictures

TIFF (Tagging Information File Format) is the preferred method of storing high-quality photos for printing. In fact, TIFF is widely used by the publishing industry for that very reason. TIFF files tend to be large, because they contain a lot of detailed information and generally use little or no compression to reduce file size.

JPEG pictures

Joint Photographic Experts Group (JPEG) is the most widely used photo format for photos displayed on web pages. JPEG uses compression to reduce file size while maintaining large dimensions. The compression results in some small loss of picture quality. That loss usually isn't noticeable until you zoom in very tightly on some small area within the picture.

The amount of compression applied to a JPEG can vary. In fact, many high-end graphics programs allow you to choose exactly how much compression you want when saving a picture as a JPEG. Many digital cameras save pictures as JPEGs with minimal compression to preserve picture quality while at the same time conserving some storage space on memory cards.

GIF pictures

Graphics Interchange Format (GIF) is commonly used in web pages for illustrations and animations. It's limited to 256 colors, which makes it unsuitable for photos. Photos need millions of colors and tend to look blotchy when saved in GIF format. GIF also allows for transparency and simple animations.

PNG pictures

Portable Network Graphics (PNG) format is a compressed format that's gaining popularity as a format for web pictures. Like JPEG, it supports millions of colors and is, therefore, suitable for photos. Like GIF, it allows for transparency and is, therefore, useful for creating images with a transparent background.

BMP pictures

Windows Bitmap (BMP) is an older, uncompressed format that conserves picture quality at the cost of a large file size. Though once widely used in Windows, BMP is quickly becoming obsolete in favor of the more widely used TIFF and JPEG formats.

Changing a picture type or size

Sometimes you'll need to change a picture's type, perhaps so you can edit it in Photo Gallery or publish it on a website. There may also be times when you want to reduce the file size and/or dimensions of a picture to send it by e-mail or, again, to post it on a website.

You can manually create a smaller image for e-mailing without losing your original picture. This also works if you want to post a picture on a website. Just about any graphics program on the market allows you to resize a picture and save it in a different format. If you don't have a graphics program, you can use the Paint program that comes with Windows 8.1.

1. Right-click the icon or thumbnail of the picture you want to reduce and choose Open With ➪ Paint. Don't be alarmed if you see only a small portion of a large picture. Paint doesn't automatically scale the picture to fit in the program window.

2. Choose File ➪ Save As and type a new name for this copy of the picture. For example, use the existing filename followed by TIFF if you're just changing the file type, or the word *Small* if you're also reducing the picture's dimensions.

3. If the picture isn't already a TIFF, JPEG, or PNG, click the current file type next to Save as Type and choose JPEG or PNG.

4. Click Save.

NOTE

TIFF is best for pictures you intend to refine and then print but don't intend to e-mail or post on a website. JPEG and PNG are best for pictures you do intend to e-mail or post on a website for editing and printing purposes.

5. If your goal is simply to change the picture's type (such as from BMP to another format), skip to Step 10. Otherwise, continue with the following steps.

6. To reduce the picture's size, click the Resize button on the Home tab.

7. Under Resize in the Resize and Skew dialog box, enter a percent value for both Horizontal and Vertical. Make sure to use equal numbers so as not to skew or stretch the pictures. For example, to resize a 2,576 x 1,932 picture down to near 644 x 483, enter **25%** for both Horizontal and Vertical.

8. To see the picture as it will appear on a web page or to an e-mail recipient, select the Edit tab and then click 100%. (If Paint's program window is small, double-click its title bar to maximize it to full-screen.)

9. If the picture it too large or too small, press Ctrl + Z to undo your changes, and repeat Steps 6 and 7 until you find a size you like.

10. Close Paint (click its Close button or choose File ⇨ Exit from its menu bar). If asked about saving your changes, choose Yes.

If you started from Photo Gallery, the new copy of the picture may not show up right away. You might have to close Photo Gallery and reopen it. Also, the new picture may not contain the tags that the original picture had, so you might find it in the Not Tagged category in Photo Gallery.

Pictures, Tags, and Virtual Folders

You can use the Search box in Photo Gallery to find pictures based on rating, tags, name, and other properties. Outside of Photo Gallery, you can do much more with tags and other photo properties when searching, enabling you to find and organize pictures in ways that transcend tags.

NOTE

Photos Gallery's tagging capabilities are just the tip of the proverbial iceberg in Windows 8.1. Tagging applies to many file types and is a key component in Windows 8.1's search capabilities.

For starters, you can display the Charms Bar, click Search, type in a tag name, click Files, and see icons for all pictures that contain that tag. You can right-click the picture's icon and choose Open File Location or right-click it and choose Open With, Preview, Send To, or whatever it is you want to do with that item. That's pretty cool. If you prefer, you can open your Pictures folder and use the Search box in its upper-right corner to search for a tag. That will limit the search to pictures in your Pictures folder and its subfolders.

When you search from the Search box, you can opt to search for all files or just pictures. Be sure to click the Files item under the Search box to look for pictures.

If you want to find pictures that contain two tags, separate the tags with a space. For example, a search for

```
Ashley Alec
```

searches for pictures that contain both Ashley and Alec. Use OR to broaden the search to find pictures that contain either Ashley or Alec, as you can see here:

```
Ashley OR Alec
```

If you need to specify your search condition more stringently, use the Search box in the upper-right corner of the Search window. For example, here's a search that finds only TIFF files that contain either Ashley or Alec:

```
type:tiff AND tag:(ashley OR alec)
```

Here's a search that finds all JPEG images that have Hawaii as a tag:

```
type:jpeg AND tag:Hawaii
```

You can still use DOS and Windows wildcard characters to search for filenames. For example, you could type

```
haw*
```

into the Filename box and click Search, or type

```
filename:haw*
```

into the Search box to find all pictures whose filenames start with haw.

You can save the results of any search as a virtual folder. When you open that folder, it shows all pictures that currently meet the search condition. For people who have a lot of pictures to deal with, these kinds of searches can be an extremely valuable tool. For more information on searching and virtual folders, see Chapters 22 and 23.

Wrap-Up

You can do lots of things with pictures and photos in Windows 8.1. You don't get the kind of power and flexibility you would with a dedicated graphics program such as Adobe Photoshop or Corel Paint Shop Pro. But nonetheless, you can perform the most basic operations such as cropping, red-eye removal, and some file type conversions with just the built-in Windows 8.1 tools and programs.

The following are the primary points covered in this chapter:

- To get pictures from a digital camera, connect the camera to the computer, turn it on, and choose Import.

- To get pictures from a CD or memory card, insert the card or disk and choose Import. Or open the disk or card and copy files using standard methods.

- To copy and paste a picture, right-click the picture and choose Copy. Then right-click at the destination and choose Paste.

- Your Pictures folder is the best place to store pictures.

- Photo Gallery lets you organize and find photos as though they were all stored in a single folder.

- Use the Fix button in Photo Gallery to crop and improve pictures.

- Use the Print button in your Pictures folder or Photo Gallery to print pictures.

- Large photos are good for printing and editing. Smaller, compressed photos are best for e-mail and web publishing.

17

Making Music with Media Player

U sing your computer to collect, manage, and play music is a lot of fun. You can build up a collection of all your favorite songs, make custom CDs from those songs, or copy them to a portable MP3 player. You can use your computer as a stereo to play any songs you like in any order you like. If your computer is part of a network, you can share songs and play them on any computer that's in the network.

Windows 8.1 comes with two programs and one Windows 8.1 app for collecting and playing music. One program is Windows Media Player, which we discuss in this chapter. The other program is Media Center (not included with all editions of Windows 8.1), which may not work with all editions. The app is simply called Music and it can be found on the Apps screen. Music is more suited to Windows tablets and other devices, like Xbox, and its raison d'etre is more for playing music and creating playlists. It also has an online radio component.

Controlling Sound Volume

Before we get into Windows Media Player, you need to know a few things upfront about music and video. In particular, you want to get your sound working and under control, so you can listen to whatever you like, without blasting your eardrums out!

Before you get started, make sure that you can control the volume of your speakers. At any given time, you're likely to have at least three volume controls available to you. Whichever control is set the lowest wins, in the sense that it puts an upper limit on the other volume controls.

If you have powered speakers, you need to make sure that the speakers are plugged in and turned on and connected to the Speaker output jack on your computer. If the speakers have a Mute button, make sure that it's turned off. If the speakers have a volume control button, that needs to be turned up.

You can control the volume of sound coming from your computer's speakers using the Volume Control icon in the notification area. It looks like a little speaker with sound waves coming out. Pointing to that icon shows the current volume setting as in the left side of Figure 18.1. Clicking that icon displays a volume control slider and a Mute button, as in the right side of Figure 18.1.

FIGURE 18.1

Volume control icon and slider.

Unhiding the Speaker Icon

If you don't see a speaker icon in your notification area, chances are, it's just hidden. Follow these steps to bring it out of hiding:

1. Right-click the clock or any blank area in the notification area and choose Customize Notification Icons.

2. Locate Volume in the Icons list, and choose Show Icon and Notifications from the drop-down list.

3. Click OK.

Now you should have a speaker icon in your notification area. Click it to see the volume control slider and Mute button. To ensure that you can hear any music you play, make sure the sound isn't muted and that the volume isn't turned down too low to hear.

To adjust the volume, just drag the slider handle up or down the bar. To mute the sound, click the Mute button at the bottom of the slider. When the sound is muted, the icon shows a little red international No symbol (circle and slash) and no sound comes from your computer. To get the sound back, click the Mute button a second time.

With your speakers and volume control slider under control, you're ready to start using Media Player for Music.

TIP

If you have multiple sound cards and can't get any sound, make sure the default sound card is the one that's connected to the speakers. Open the Sound applet from the Control Panel. On the Playback tab, click the icon of the sound card you're using and click Set Default. If both sound cards have speakers attached, you can configure each to act as the default for different types of audio using the down arrow next to the Set Default button.

Starting Windows Media Player

To start Windows Media Player, use whichever method is easiest for you:

- Display the Charms Bar, click Search, type **med**, and choose Windows Media Player.

- Open any music file for which Windows Media Player is the default program.

The first time you open Windows Media Player, it takes you through a series of steps asking for your preferences. Don't worry if you don't know how to answer some questions. You can change your answer at any time. So, if you see a window titled "Welcome to

Windows Media Player" and don't know what to do, just click Recommended Settings and then click Finish. You can change settings at any time, so you're not making any settings permanent by accepting the suggested defaults.

Media Player program window

Like most programs, Windows Media Player opens in its own program window and has a taskbar button. The player can have many different appearances. Exactly how it looks at any time is up to you. You'll see different ways to display things in a moment. For now, we need to cover the names of things so you know what we're talking about in the sections that follow.

Figure 18.2 points out the major components of Media Player's Player Library program window.

FIGURE 18.2

Major Media Player components.

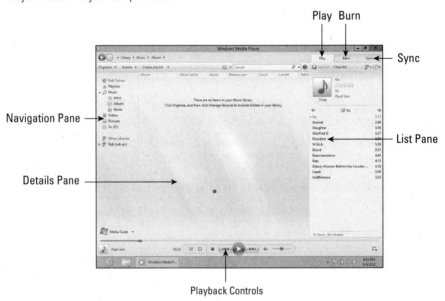

The Features taskbar across the top of the program window represents different areas of Media Player, each of which helps you perform a specific task. In Figure 18.2, the Play tab is selected. Here's a quick summary of the program components and what each tab offers:

- **Navigation pane:** Takes you to your collection of songs and other media files.

- **Details pane:** Shows details for the currently selected library, album, genre, video, and so on.

- **List pane:** Shows information about the current playlist and item.

- **Playback controls:** Provides controls for playing the currently selected media, and for switching to Now Playing mode.

- **Play:** Shows the movie or video you're currently watching or song that is currently playing (if any). You can also rip (copy) CDs to your computer.

- **Burn:** Lets you create custom CDs from songs in your media library.

- **Sync:** Allows you to copy songs and other media files to a portable media player.

The toolbar

The Media Player toolbar gives you quick access to frequently used commands and options. The buttons in the toolbar change depending on what you have selected at the moment. The following list summarizes the available buttons:

- **Organize:** Manage your media libraries, sort media, customize the Navigation pane, change the Player Library layout, and access Media Player options.

- **Stream:** Enable Internet access to your home media and turn on media streaming, which allows you to send your media to other computers on the local network or the Internet.

- **Create Playlist:** Create a playback list (playlist) of media so you can play the selected items as a group. For example, you might create a playlist called My Top 100 that contains 100 of your favorite songs.

- **Rip CD:** Copy music from a CD to your media library on your computer so you can play it from your computer and optionally share it.

- **Rip Settings:** Specify settings to control the way Media Player rips music from CDs to your computer.

- **View Options:** Choose between Icon, title, and Details views for the List pane.

- **Search:** Search for media in your library.

- **Help:** Open Media Player's Help content.

> **TIP**
> Rip CD and Rip Settings only appear in the toolbar if an audio CD is inserted in the drive.

Media Player menus

Media Player has lots of menus. They're hidden from view most of the time, but they're also easy to get to. Many of the toolbar buttons have their own menus. You'll see a little down-pointing triangle at the right of the button if it offers commands. Get the tip of the mouse pointer right on that little triangle and click the left mouse button to see the menu for that taskbar button. In Figure 18.3, for example, you can see the menu for the Organize button.

FIGURE 18.3

Organize menu.

To see the main menu, right-click an empty area near the play controls, as at the bottom of Figure 18.4. Optionally, you can right-click an empty spot on the left or right side of the features taskbar to get to the same menu. To make those same options visible in a menu bar, choose Show Menu Bar from the bottom of that main menu.

FIGURE 18.4

Media Player play controls.

Play controls

The play controls (also called the *playback controls*) are at the bottom of Media Player's program window (refer to Figure 18.4). They work only when you're playing a song or video or you've selected something to play. They work much like the controls on a stereo or DVD player. The exact role of each button varies slightly with the type of content you're viewing. Here's what each of the play controls offers:

- **Seek bar:** When content is playing, a green indicator moves along the seek bar. You can click anywhere along the seek bar to jump forward or backward in the playing item. When you point to the end of the green indicator, a button appears. You can drag that button left or right to move back or forward within the item that's playing.

- **Shuffle:** When selected, multiple songs from the current playlist are played in random order. When turned off, songs from the playlist are played in the same order as in the playlist.

- **Repeat:** When turned on, the same song or playlist plays repeatedly. When turned off, the song or playlist plays only once.

- **Stop:** Stops whatever is playing and rewinds to the beginning.

- **Previous:** Skips back to the previous song in the playlist or DVD chapter. Or if you point to the button and hold down the left mouse button, plays the current item backward in fast motion.

- **Play/Pause:** When content is playing, you can click this button to pause playback. Click again to resume playback.

- **Next:** Skips to the next song in the playlist or next chapter on a DVD. Point to this button and hold down the left mouse button to fast-forward through the content that's playing.

- **Mute:** Click to mute the playback sound. Click a second time to hear the sound again.

- **Volume:** Drag the handle left or right to increase or decrease the volume.

- **Now Playing:** Switches to Now Playing mode, a simplified version of the Media Player window. Also useful when you want to see a video or DVD played at full-screen size. Once in the full-screen mode, right-click anywhere on the screen and choose Exit Full Screen to return to the Player Library window. Or click Switch To Library to return to the Player Library window.

Other items in the Features taskbar are discussed later in this chapter. For now, let's stick with some of the basics of using Media Player's program window.

Closing/minimizing Windows Media Player

You can close Windows Media Player as you would any other program:

- Click the Close (X) button in the upper-right corner of Media Player's program window.

- Right-click the toolbar at the top of the window, choose File ⇨ Exit from Media Player's menu.

- Right-click Media Player's taskbar button and choose Close.

- If Media Player is in the active window, press Alt + F4.

When you close Media Player, it stops playing.

If you want to continue to listen to music, but you want Media Player off the screen, minimize Media Player's program window. Use any of the following techniques to minimize Media Player's program window:

- Click the Minimize button in Media Player's title bar.

- Right-click Media Player's title bar and choose Minimize.

- Right-click Media Player's taskbar button and choose Minimize.

In Windows 7, the Media Player icon appeared on the Windows taskbar by default, even if the program was not running. For Windows 8.1, however, you have to launch the program from the Search tool or by finding it on the Apps window, in the Windows Accessories group. To do this, show the Charms Bar, click Search, and type **Media**. Click Windows Media Player to launch it.

If Media Player is running, pointing to it on the taskbar displays a preview window as shown in Figure 18.5. You can click the controls at the bottom of the preview to play, stop, or skip forward or back in the playlist. Click the small preview window or the taskbar icon to open Media Player.

FIGURE 18.5

Media Player on the Windows taskbar.

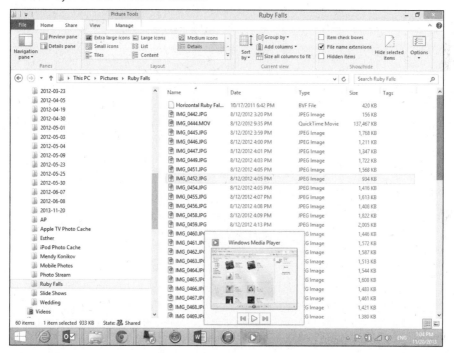

That should be enough to get you started using Media Player. Next, we look at various ways in which you can use Media Player to listen to music or watch videos.

Listening to a CD

A *music CD* (also called an *audio CD*) is the kind of CD you normally play in a stereo or CD player. Typically, you buy these at a music store. As you learn later in this chapter, you can also create your own custom music CDs.

To listen to a music CD, just put it in your CD drive, label side up, and close the drive door. Then wait a few seconds. Windows Media Player might open and start playing the CD automatically. However, other things could happen:

- **A Windows message asks what you want to do.** If you see a dialog box like the example in Figure 18.6, click Play Audio CD Windows Media Player. You also have the option of clicking Take No Action if you don't want Windows Media Player to play your CD.

FIGURE 18.6

A dialog box asking about a music CD.

- **Nothing happens.** If absolutely nothing happens after you insert an audio CD, or if some other program opened and you closed it, start Windows Media Player. From Windows Media Player's Play menu (right-click the Media Player toolbar), choose Play VCD or CD Audio.
- **Windows Media Player opens:** If Windows Media Player opens and starts playing the song, you don't have to do anything else.

After the CD starts playing, you should be able to hear it (assuming your speakers are properly connected and not turned down too far). Use the volume slider in the play controls to adjust the volume of the music.

Now Playing, Visualizations, and Enhancements

When music is playing, Media Player by default shows the album art, if available, in the Now Playing window. However, you can instead watch a *visualization* of the music. The visualization is a pattern of colors and shapes that change in rhythm to the music. Media Player offers many visualizations from which to choose.

To try a different visualization, first make sure that you're viewing the Now Playing window (press Alt and choose View ➪ Now Playing). Then right-click in the Now Playing window, choose Visualizations, and then choose an option from the resulting cascading menu (see Figure 18.7).

FIGURE 18.7

Choosing a visualization.

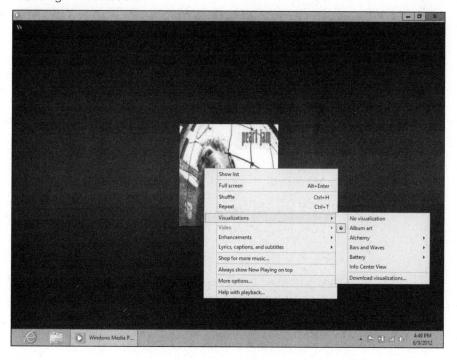

Regardless of which method you use, you'll see a menu of visualization names. Clicking a name displays a submenu of still more visualizations. Just pick any one to see how it looks. Go ahead and try a bunch while a song is playing to find one you like.

TIP

You can download plenty of visualizations for free. Right-click in the Now Playing window and choose Visualizations ⇨ Download Visualizations.

Using the playlist in Now Playing view

When you're playing a music CD in Now Playing view, the Playlist pane to the right of the visualization (see Figure 18.8) shows songs from the CD. That pane is optional. To show or hide that pane, right-click in the Now Playing window and choose Show List.

FIGURE 18.8

The Playlist pane on the right side of the window.

In the Playlist pane, you might see the song titles, as in Figure 18.8. Or you might just see more generic names such as Track1, Track2, and so forth. Many CDs don't have song titles stored on CD, so the song titles have to be downloaded from the Internet. You'll see song titles only if they're available on the CD or they've been downloaded from the Internet.

NOTE

Song titles are a form of media information. We discuss how all that works in the section "Options for ripping CDs," later in this chapter.

If you want to listen to a specific song on the CD, just double-click its title in the Playlist pane, or use the Previous and Next buttons in the play controls to highlight the song you want to listen to.

To change the width of the Playlist pane, get the tip of the mouse pointer right on the left border of the pane, so the mouse pointer turns to a two-headed arrow. Then drag left or right.

Using Enhancements

While you're listening to music and you're in the Now Playing area, you can also use Enhancements to adjust the sound and perform other tasks. The many Enhancements windows are invisible until you open them.

To show or hide Enhancements, right-click in the Now Playing window and choose Enhancements. Or press Alt to open the menu bar, and then choose View ➪ Enhancements from Media Player's menu. When the Enhancements menu is open, you can choose which type of enhancement you want to see. Your options are summarized here:

- **Crossfading and Auto Volume Leveling:** When Crossfading is turned on, one song gradually fades out while the next song fades in. Auto Volume Leveling keeps songs at roughly equal volumes.

- **Graphic Equalizer:** Adjust the relative strengths of low, middle, and high tones. Optionally, click Default and choose a music type such as Rock or Classical. Click Reset to return to the default settings.

- **Play Speed Settings:** Use this to adjust the play speed of content. This option only works when playing .wma, .wmv, .wm, .mpe, and .asf files. Careful with this one. You don't want all your albums sounding like The Chipmunks!

- **Quiet Mode:** Adjusts the audio dynamic range of music (the difference between the loudest and softest sounds). You'd most likely use this option when listening to headphones or watching a movie in Media Player.

- **SRS WOW Effects:** When activated, SRS WOW effects add depth to your music. This one is definitely worth turning on and trying out if you have good speakers attached to your system.

- **Video Settings:** Adjust the brightness, contrast, hue, saturation, and size of video when viewing a movie or video in Media Player.

The selected Enhancements appear in a separate window. You can cycle through the various Enhancements options by clicking the Next or Previous buttons in the upper-left corner of the Enhancements window.

18

> **TIP**
>
> You can resize the Enhancements window as needed. Click the red X icon to close the window.

Stopping a CD

When you've finished listening to a CD, click the Stop button in the play controls. To eject the CD, choose Play ➪ Eject from Media Player's menu, press Ctrl + J, or push the Eject button on your CD drive.

Play CDs automatically with Media Player

If you want to ensure that Media Player opens and plays music CDs automatically, you need to make Media Player the default player for CDs. Here's how:

1. Press Windows + X and choose the Control Panel.
2. Click Hardware and Sound.
3. Click AutoPlay.
4. Next to Audio CD, choose Play Audio CD (Windows Media Player).
5. Click the Save button.
6. Close the Control Panel.

From that point on, whenever you put a music CD in your CD drive, Windows Media Player should open and play the CD automatically.

> **TIP**
>
> Here's a shortcut to the AutoPlay options: Show the Charms Bar, click Search, and type auto. Click Settings and choose AutoPlay from the Settings window.

Ripping (Copying) Music CDs

Media Player isn't just about playing CDs. The real idea is to build up a library of digital media on your hard drive, from which you can create custom playlists and music CDs. If you already own some music CDs, *ripping* a few CDs will be a great way to start creating your personal media library. Though the term *rip* might sound like something bad, it's not. It simply means to "copy," and no harm will come to the CD when you rip songs from it to your media library.

When you rip a CD, you store a copy of each song from the CD on your hard drive. That song is in a format that's more suitable for computers than the song that's on the CD. You can put the original CD back in its case, and leave it there so it doesn't get scratched up. Play the songs straight from your PC, or make your own CDs to play the songs in a stereo. Keep the original CD as a backup in case you accidentally delete some songs you've copied.

Ripping CDs is easy, as you'll see. But you need to make a few decisions upfront, such as where you want to put the songs, how you want them titled, what format you want them stored in, and so forth. The sections that follow look at all your options.

Options for ripping CDs

To choose options for how you want to copy CDs to your hard disk, use the Rip Music tab in Media Player's Options dialog box. To get to those options:

1. Open Windows Media Player (if it isn't already open).

2. Insert an audio CD in the drive and click the drive in the Library pane so that the Rip and Rip Settings buttons are available in the toolbar. Then choose More Options to open the Rip Music tab of Media Player's Options dialog box.

You're taken to the Rip Music tab in Media Player's Options dialog box, as shown in Figure 18.9.

FIGURE 18.9

The Rip Music tab in Media Player's Options dialog box.

The following sections describe what each option offers. Note that you don't need to make selections from the dialog box for every CD you copy. Instead, you choose your options once. All CDs that you copy from that point forward will use whatever settings you chose.

Choosing where to put songs

By default, all songs you copy from a CD are placed in your Music folder. That's a perfectly fine place to put them, but there's no rule that says you have to put them there. You can store them in any folder you want. For example, you might put them in the Public Music folder if you want everyone who uses the PC to access the songs. Or, if you have multiple hard drives, you can put them in a folder on some drive other than C:.

> **NOTE**
>
> If you're not very familiar with the concepts of drives and folders, don't worry about it. Just leave the Rip Music to This Location setting alone. Your songs end up in your personal Music folder. Note that whatever folder you choose is referred to as the *rip music folder* in Media Player options.

To choose a drive and folder for storing CDs, click the Change button in the dialog box. Then navigate to the drive and folder in which you want to store the songs. For example, if you want to put the songs in your Public Music folder, expand the This PC, Local Disk (C:), Users, and Public folders, and click Public Music. Then click OK.

The path in the dialog box shows where the songs will be stored. For example, in Figure 18.9 the path C:\Users\Rob\Music tells you that the songs will be stored in the personal Music folder for the user account named Rob. (C: is the hard disk and Users is the name of the folder in which all user accounts are stored.)

Choosing how to name files

Each song you copy from a CD is stored as a file. Like all files, each song will have a filename. Windows Media Player names the files automatically, based on the track number, song title, and other media information.

How you name the songs is entirely up to you and won't affect how they play. The default filename is the CD track number followed by the song name. You might prefer to have the song name first. To make your selections, click the File Name button on the Rip Music tab of the dialog box. The File Name Options dialog box, shown in Figure 18.10, opens.

FIGURE 18.10

The File Name Options dialog box.

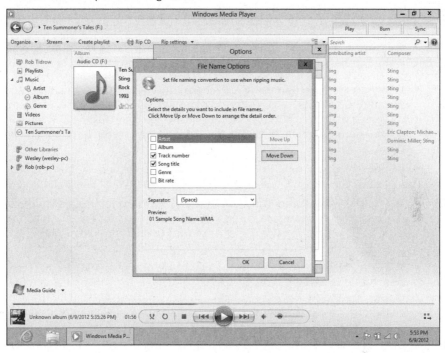

Choose the elements you want to use in each song's filename. At the very least, you should choose Song Title, because that's certainly a key piece of information. Use the Separator drop-down list to choose which character will separate each portion of the name.

To change the order of items in the filename, click any selected item and use the Move Up or Move Down button to change its position in the filename. As you choose components and change their order, the generic filename under Preview gives you a sense of how each song title will look with your current settings.

Click OK after you decide how you want your filenames to look.

Choosing a file format and quality

Under Rip Settings on the Rip Music tab, the Format drop-down list lets you choose a format and quality in which to store songs you copy. Basically, this all boils down to a trade-off between file size and music quality. File size has to do with how much hard disk space each song consumes. Quality has to do with the depth, clarity, and richness of the music when you listen to it. Music quality is measured in kilobits per second, abbreviated Kbps. The higher the Kbps number, the better the music quality, but the more disk space each song consumes.

Options for choosing are under the Rip Settings heading in the Options dialog box. First, use the Format drop-down list to choose one of the following formats:

- **Windows Media Audio:** Songs are copied to Windows Media Audio (.wma) format files and compressed to conserve disk space. You can choose the amount of compression using the Audio Quality slider in the same dialog box. This is a good general-purpose format that plays on all Windows computers and many portable media devices.

- **Windows Media Audio Pro:** Similar to the preceding format, but includes features that make the music sound better on high-end multi-channel sound systems.

- **Windows Media Audio (Variable Bit Rate):** Same as the preceding format, but the amount of compression varies with the complexity of the information being stored. As a rule, you get better quality with smaller file sizes using a variable bit rate. This format is not compatible with all portable music players.

- **Windows Media Audio Lossless:** Same as the preceding format, but files are not compressed at all. (*Lossless* means that no data is lost when the audio file is being made.) The sound quality is excellent, but the files are huge. Still, if you're a true audiophile, or you're interested in creating HighMAT (High-Performance Media Access Technology) CDs, this is an excellent choice.

- **MP3:** MP3 is the most widely used format for digital music. It's been around the longest. You can play MP3 songs on any MP3-compatible player.

- **WAV (Lossless):** Stores each song as a WAV file, which offers high quality but creates enormous files. So, you probably want to stay away from this format unless you have some good reason to use it.

If you're new to all this, and at a complete loss as to what to choose, go with WMA or MP3. Those are common formats that almost any device can play.

If you choose anything but a lossless format, you can then use the Audio Quality slider to choose a quality setting. Again, the basic rule of better quality creating larger files applies. Hard disk space is cheap and plentiful, so there's no need to settle for the lowest-quality setting. If in doubt, don't go below 128 Kbps or your music may all end up sounding shallow or kind of "tinny."

As you move the Audio Quality slider to different settings, text beneath the slider tells you roughly how much disk space an entire CD will consume at that setting. To better illustrate how format and audio quality relate to disk space consumption, we ripped a three-minute song at various sound qualities and put their sizes in Table 18.1. The last column, "Songs per GB," gives you a sense of how many songs you can get into a single gigabyte of hard disk space at various quality settings.

TABLE 18.1   A Three-Minute Song in Various Formats and Bit Rates

Format/Quality	Bit Rate	Size	Songs per GB
Windows Media Audio	192 Kbps	4.17MB	246
Windows Media Audio Pro	192 Kbps	4.18MB	245
WMA Variable Bit Rate	103 Kbps	2.22MB	461
Window Media Audio Lossless	480 Kbps	14.20MB	72
MP3	192 Kbps	4.12MB	249
WAV (Lossless)	320 Kbps	30.30MB	34

 See Chapter 20 for more information on disk drives, capacities, and discovering how much space you have. You might want to take a peek at your available space each time you copy a CD, so you can get a sense of how much free space each copied CD consumes.

After you've chosen a format and audio quality, you have a few more options on the Rip Music tab to choose from.

Copy Protect Music

The Copy Protect Music option on the Rip Music tab lets you decide whether to put copyright protection on the songs you copy. We suspect that a lot of people choose that option thinking it will somehow protect them from messing up the songs. But that's not how it works. The protection that the option offers is for the copyright holder, not for you.

If you choose the Copy Protect option, the songs you copy play only on the computer you're using. This option also puts other restrictions on the songs. For example, you won't be able to import them into Movie Maker or other programs that normally let you edit music. If you want to keep things simple and make sure you can use your copied songs freely, we suggest you leave the Copy Protect Music check box empty.

Rip CD Automatically

If selected, this option tells Windows Media Player to copy all the songs from a CD as soon as you insert the audio CD. Choosing this option, along with the Eject CD option described next, makes it easy to rip a whole collection of CDs in assembly-line fashion. For example, if you have a few dozen CDs you want to rip, you can just insert a CD, wait for it to be copied and ejected, and then insert the next CD.

When you've finished ripping your CD collection, you can then clear this option so that you have more flexibility in deciding what you want to do with each CD you insert into your hard drive.

Eject CD after Ripping

If selected, this option just tells Media Player to eject the CD from the drive when it's finished copying the CD. As mentioned, choosing this option along with the Rip CD Automatically option is a great way to copy multiple CDs in a quick, assembly-line manner.

Still more rip options

Media Player's Options dialog box contains some additional options that affect what happens when you rip CDs. While you still have the Options dialog box open, select the Privacy tab. Then choose among the options summarized next. But remember that not all CDs have media information posted on the Internet. Therefore, even if you do select options as indicated, you may need to manually update media information for a song or album.

- **Display Media Information from the Internet:** Choose (check) this option to have media information, such as song titles, appear automatically when you play or copy a CD.

- **Update Music Files by Retrieving Media Info from the Internet:** Choose this option to have Media Player automatically fill in information from songs you've already copied to your computer.

When you've finished making all your selections, click OK in the Options dialog box. Now you're ready to start ripping CDs. Remember that you don't need to change the preceding settings every time you copy a CD. The settings you choose apply to all CDs that you copy.

Copying songs

With all the details of choosing how you want to copy CDs out of the way, you're ready to start copying. Follow these steps:

1. If your Internet account requires logging in, get online so that you're connected to the Internet and Media Player can download media information (song titles).

2. Insert the music CD you want to rip (copy) into your CD drive and close the drive door.

3. If Windows Media Player doesn't open automatically, open it yourself. (If some other program opened when you inserted the CD, close that program, and then open Media Player.)

4. If you chose the Rip CD Automatically option described earlier in this chapter, skip to Step 10.

5. If the CD starts playing, click the Stop button down in the play controls.

6. Wait for song titles to appear. If song titles don't appear within 30 seconds or so, the CD might not be in the Compact Disk Database (CDDB), an online database that contains song titles for most (but not all) commercially sold CDs. In that case, you can go ahead and rip the CD and then fill in the details later in your media library.

7. Optionally, clear the check box to the left of any songs that you don't want to copy. Media Player will only copy songs that have a check mark.

8. Click the Rip CD button in the toolbar. Figure 18.11 shows Media Player ripping a Sting CD to disk.

FIGURE 18.11

Media Player ripping a CD to disk.

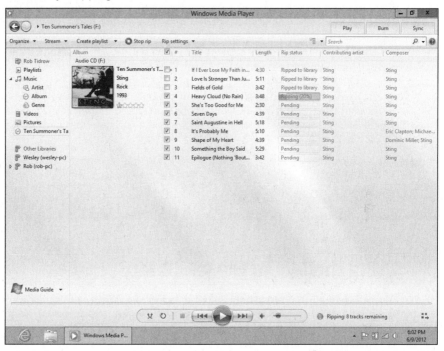

9. Wait until the Rip Status column shows Ripped To Library for all songs you've opted to copy. If the CD doesn't eject automatically, go ahead and eject it.

10. Put the CD back to wherever you normally keep your CDs. You won't need it any more to play songs from your computer or to copy files to custom audio CDs or an MP3 player.

That's it for ripping one CD. To rip more CDs, just repeat Steps 4 through 10 for each CD. If, at any time, you want to check your available hard disk space, open your Computer folder. If you don't see any indication of available disk space for your hard disk (typically Local Disk c:), choose Tiles from the Views menu in that folder.

Copying songs from CDs you already own is one way to build up your Media Player music library. Any songs you don't already own, but would like to, you can purchase online and download to your Media Player library. We discuss how that works in the next section.

Getting Music Online

In addition to ripping CDs you already own, you can download music from online stores. The exact procedure varies from one online store to the next. Some are membership sites. Some let you purchase and download songs without joining or paying a membership fee. New stores and services come online all the time, so there's little that we can tell you specifically that applies to all the available vendors, other than that you should shop around and not necessarily sign up with the first vendor to pop up on your screen. In the bottom left of the Navigation pane, click the arrow beside the Media Guide button and choose Browse All Online Stores to see other options. The button changes to Online Stores. Click the arrow and choose Media Guide if you want to view the Media Guide.

> **NOTE**
>
> Windows 8.1 includes the Music App available on the Windows 8.1 Start screen. It provides access to the Windows Store for downloading and managing online music resources.

Using the Media Player Library

The whole point of a program like Windows Media Player is to build and manage a library of digital media. That includes music, pictures, video, and recorded TV (even though we're focusing on music in this chapter).

To see and manage your Media Player library, open Media Player in Library mode. If Media Player is currently running in Now Playing mode, click the Switch to Library button.

Navigating the library

There is almost no limit to the ways in which you can view, organize, and change things in the library. You can view media by artist, album, genre, playlist, and other ways. If you want to add other properties to your Navigation pane, choose Organize ⇨ Customize Navigation Pane to show the Customize Navigation Pane dialog box shown in Figure 18.12.

If your Media Player library doesn't show songs, but instead shows pictures or other kinds of media, click an option under Music in the Navigation pane.

FIGURE 18.12

The Customize Navigation Pane dialog box.

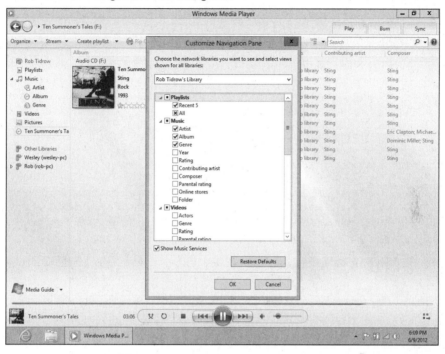

In the Navigation pane, you can click the triangle button (if any) next to an item to view different categories such as Artist, Album, Genre, and so on. The following list covers the views you can add to the Navigation pane for music:

- **Artist:** Shows artist names in alphabetical order.
- **Album:** Shows album titles in alphabetical order.
- **Genre:** Shows names of music genres (such as Classical, Rock, Jazz).
- **Year:** Shows albums organized by publication year.
- **Rating:** Shows songs organized by rating (one to five stars). The songs are separated into those you've rated and those that are rated automatically based on your listening habits. Songs that are unrated appear under the Unrated category.
- **Contributing Artist:** Shows songs organized by contributing artists, if any.

- **Composer:** Shows songs organized by composer.
- **Parental Rating:** Shows songs organized by parental rating.
- **Online Stores:** Shows songs based on the store from which it was obtained.
- **Folder:** Shows songs organized by the folder in which they're stored.

You'll be better able to appreciate the library if you have at least 30 or 40 songs — or better yet, several hundred songs — in your library before reading this section. As you explore your library, keep in mind that you can right-click any icon, stack, category name, or whatever to view, edit, or play items.

Use the View Options button to choose how you want to view things. Depending on where you are at the moment, some View options will be disabled (dimmed) because they're not applicable to the current way of looking at things.

Of course, there's no right way or wrong way to view icons. Just choose whichever view works best for you. Feel free to try things out. You can't do any harm by checking out different ways to view things. And nothing you choose is set in stone. You can change your view at any time.

How you use a view depends on what you're viewing. For example, if you're viewing genres, you'll see an icon or stack for each genre in your library. Double-clicking an icon or stack shows you all the songs in that genre. Double-clicking an icon that represents a single album displays songs on that album. To play all the items that an icon represents, right-click the icon and choose Play. Again, doing some exploring on your own is your best bet. You're not permanently changing anything as you explore, so there's no need to be worried.

Choosing columns for Media Library

In addition to choosing how you want media information to look, you can choose exactly which information you do and don't want to see. The exact options available to you depend on what you're viewing and how you're viewing it at the moment. To see the full set of options, click Music in the Navigation pane, and then choose Details from the View Options menu. You'll see detailed information about each song organized into rows and columns.

To choose which columns you want to view, right-click a column heading, such as Title or Length, and click Choose Columns on the menu. The Choose Columns dialog box shown in Figure 18.13 opens. The number of columns depends on what you have open in the navigation tree.

In the Choose Columns dialog box, select (check) the columns you want to see. Clear (uncheck) columns you don't want to see. You can also control the order of columns, either in the dialog box, or after you exit the dialog box. To control the order of columns while you're in the dialog box, click any selected column name, and then click the Move Up or Move Down button to move it up or down. The higher a column name is in the dialog box, the farther to the left it is in the Details view.

After you've chosen the columns you want to view, click OK. Most likely you won't be able to see all the columns at the same time. But you can use the horizontal scroll bar under the columns to scroll left and right through columns.

FIGURE 18.13

The Choose Columns dialog box.

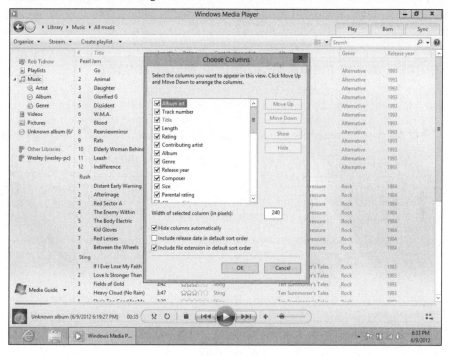

Sizing columns

To adjust the width of any column, get the mouse pointer to the right side of the column heading. You'll know the mouse pointer is in the right place when it turns to a two-headed arrow. Then just drag the column to the width you want.

Moving columns

To move a column left or right, first put the mouse pointer right on the column heading — for example, the heading Title, Length, Album, or Album Artist. Then hold down the left mouse button and drag the column left or right. Release the mouse pointer when the column is where you want it to be.

Sorting songs

When you're in a Details view, you can also sort items by any column. For example, you can sort them by Title, Length, Album, Album Artist, or any other column heading. The first time you click, items will be sorted into ascending order (alphabetically, or smallest to largest). The second time you click, items will be sorted into descending order (reverse alphabetical, or largest to smallest).

> **TIP**
> The techniques for sizing, moving, and sorting by columns apply to most columnar views of data in most programs. This feature is not unique to Media Player.

Getting missing media information automatically

Recall that media information refers to things such as song titles, artist name, and so forth. That information might be missing from some of your songs for a couple of reasons. One reason might be that the information isn't available from the Internet. In that case, you may have to fill in the missing information manually, using techniques described later in this chapter.

A second reason why you might be missing media information is that you weren't online when you copied some CDs. If that's the case, it's not too late to retrieve that information. It's quicker and easier to retrieve the information automatically. So, before you start manually changing media information, use the technique described in this section to see how much of that information you can get automatically.

First, you need to check your options for updating media information automatically. Click the Organize button and choose Options. The Library tab in Media Player's Options dialog box appears, as shown in Figure 18.14.

FIGURE 18.14

The Library tab in the Options dialog box.

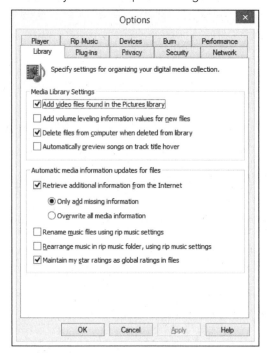

Under the Automatic Media Information Updates for Files heading, choose (check) Retrieve Additional Information from the Internet.

- If you've already added some media information manually and you don't want the new information to replace that, choose Only Add Missing Information.

- Otherwise, choose Overwrite All Media Information if you want information you've added yourself to be replaced with information from the Internet.

When you've finished making your selection, click OK in the dialog box. Then click the Organize button and choose Apply Media Information Changes. After the changes are applied, click the Close button to exit the Apply Changes dialog box.

There's no guarantee that all missing information will be filled in. You may have songs for which there is no online media information. You'll still have to edit those manually. To change the title of a single song, right-click the current title (Track1, Track2, or whatever), choose Edit, and type the correct song title.

Information other than the title is likely to be the same for all the songs on a given album. It's not necessary to change that information one song at a time. You can select multiple songs to which you want to make a change. The change you make is then applied to all the selected songs. We'll get to that in a moment. First, let's look at how you can add songs that you have elsewhere on your computer to your Media Player library.

Choosing what files to include in your library

If you set up multiple user accounts on your computer, each user gets to have his or her own media library. Parents don't have to dig through the kids' songs, and vice versa. But you're not stuck with only those songs. Each user also has the option to share songs, and each user has the option to choose or reject songs shared by others. To choose which songs display in your own media library:

1. Click Organize in the taskbar and choose Manage Libraries ➪ Music to open the Music Library Locations dialog box (see Figure 18.15).

2. Click the Add button. The Include Folder in Music dialog box opens.

> **NOTE**
>
> Even though we're focusing on music here, Media Player can also display pictures, videos, and recorded TV. You can add folders for those types of files using the same process for those libraries.

3. Browse to the drive and folder that you want to include and click Include Folder. You can repeat this step to monitor as many folders as you wish.

4. To prevent songs from a folder from being added to your library, click the folder (while in the Music Library Locations dialog box) you want to exclude and click the Remove button.

5. Click OK after making your selections to have Media Player search any newly added folders.

Media Player updated your library according to the selections you made.

FIGURE 18.15

The Music Library Locations dialog box.

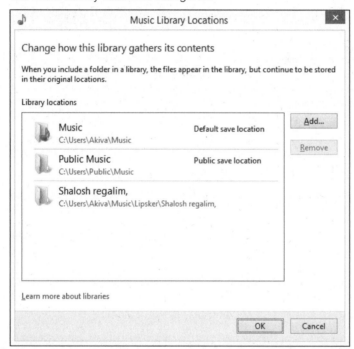

Sharing (streaming) your media library

Each user can opt to share all songs or some songs with other user accounts on the same computer. Likewise, if your computer is part of a private network, each user can choose to share songs with other Windows Vista, Windows 7, Windows 8, and Windows 8.1

computers. In addition, you can share with Windows 8.1–compatible devices, such as the Microsoft Xbox 360 gaming device. A great feature in Windows Media Player 12 is the capability to share and stream music to the Internet. So, you can enjoy the music library stored on your home computer when you're at work.

The first step in sharing your music is to enable streaming. To do so, click the Stream button in the toolbar and choose the More Streaming Options menu. Choose the media streaming options (see Figure 18.16) you want for this device and click Next to see the HomeGroup dialog box. Make sure the Shared option next to Music is selected and click Next. A dialog box (see Figure 18.17) with a password displays; it will enable you to add other computers to the homegroup to access your music. Write down this password. Click Finish.

FIGURE 18.16

Media streaming options.

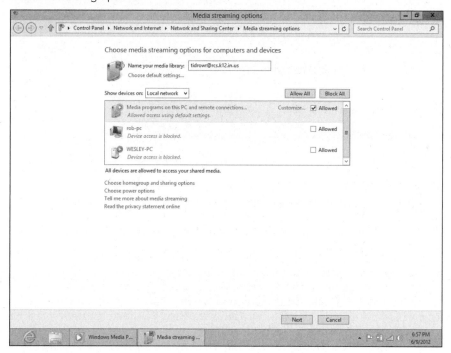

FIGURE 18.17

The password option to add other computers to access your music.

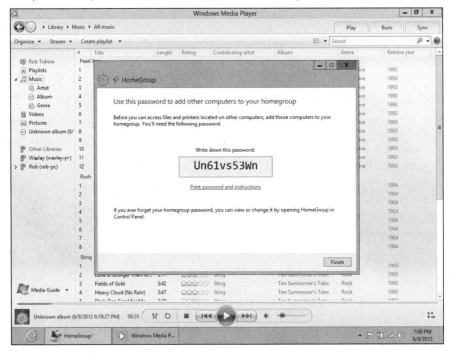

Allowing Internet streaming

As mentioned previously in this chapter, you can use Media Player to stream media to other devices on the Internet. For example, you might listen to your home music library while you're at work. Whatever the case, you must first set up that capability because it is not enabled by default.

Open Media Player and click Stream ⇨ Allow Internet Access to Home Media. In the resulting Internet Home Media Access dialog box, click Allow Internet Access to Home Media. If prompted for an administrative password, enter it, or if prompted with a User Account Control dialog box, click Yes. Click OK when Windows 8.1 indicates it has successfully enabled sharing (see Figure 18.18).

FIGURE 18.18

Remote libraries are set up for Internet access.

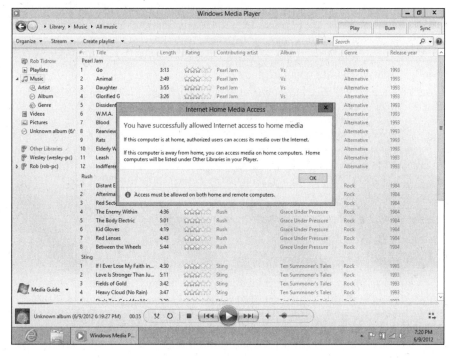

Using a remote stream

After you configure streaming on a computer, you can then access that stream from another computer, whether on the local network or on the Internet. To play a stream from another computer, first open Media Player. Then, in the Library view, look under the Other Libraries branch in the Navigation pane. You should see the other computer(s) listed there. Click the server from which you want to play, and then play items from the List pane just as you would for a local library.

TIP

If you don't see devices listed in the Other Libraries branch in the Navigation pane, choose Organize ➪ Customize Navigation Pane. Choose Other Libraries from the drop-down list, and then place a check mark beside each device you want to see listed in the Navigation pane. Click OK.

Allow Remote Control

If you want to let other computers and devices push music, video, and photos to Media Player on your computer, you need to enable remote control of Media Player on your computer. To do so, open Media Player and choose Stream ➪ Allow Remote Control of My Player. In the resulting Allow Remote Control dialog box, click Allow Remote Control on This Network.

Pushing media to another computer

If you have a media player at home, such as an Xbox 360, Roku SoundBridge, D-Link MediaLounge, or other device, you can stream music from your computer to that device using Media Player. For example, let's say you have a MediaLounge in your living room hooked up to your entertainment center. Your music collection is on your home PC. No problem, just push the music from your PC to the MediaLounge. Open Media Player, and then create the playlist that you want to stream to the remote device. At the top of the List pane, click the Play To button and choose the device from the list.

 See Part IX for more information on private networks and sharing.

Automatically renaming songs

Earlier in this chapter, you learned how you could control filenames of songs you rip (copy) from CDs. Those filenames don't have a big impact on how information shows up in your library. The media information from each song actually comes from properties in the file rather than the filename. Nonetheless, it never hurts to have some consistency in your filenames.

For example, suppose you ripped a bunch of CDs before you realized you could control how the filenames of those songs are formatted. You change the rip settings to something you like better. That change won't affect songs you've already ripped; it will only affect songs that you rip after changing the setting. You can, however, get Media Player to rename previously named songs according to your new settings. Here's how:

1. Click Organize and choose Options.
2. On the Library tab, choose Rename Music Files Using Rip Music Settings.
3. Optionally, if you also want to have the songs rearranged in your rip music folder (typically the Music folder in your user account), choose Rearrange Music in Rip Music Folder Using Rip Music Settings.
4. Click OK after making your selections.
5. To apply changes, click Organize and choose Apply Media Information Changes.

It may take a while to update and rearrange all the songs in your rip music folder. When the change is complete, click the Close button that appears in the progress indicator. You may not notice any changes in Media Player's library, but you likely will notice changes when you open your rip music folder outside of Media Player.

Most of the options and settings discussed so far have to do with groups of songs and things the Media Player does on its own. No matter what settings you choose, there may be times when you need to manually edit (or remove) items in your library.

In some cases, you may need to change a single song title. For example, suppose you have songs named Track1, Track2, Track3, and so forth. You've already tried updating that information through techniques described earlier, but the song titles still don't appear because the song titles aren't available online. When that happens, you'll need to manually change the media information.

When changing a song title, you'll want to work with one song at a time. In other cases, such as when changing a genre or artist name, you may want to make the same change to several songs at once. To make the same change to multiple songs in your library, you first have to select the songs you want to change. So, before talking about manually editing songs, let's look at techniques for selecting the songs you want to change.

Selecting in Media Library

Your media library isn't set in stone. You can change the information you see at any time. Typically, you just right-click the thing you want to change and choose Edit to change it or Delete to remove it. We'll get to the specifics in a moment, but first, let's talk about *selecting* items in the library. Selecting two or more items allows you to make the same change to all those selected items in one fell swoop.

Selecting items in media library is much like selecting icons in folders, so if you already know how to do that, you're ahead of the game. You can select items in any view, but you might find it easiest to work in the Details view. For example, click Music in the Navigation pane at the left side of the window. Then choose Details from the View Options drop-down list. Finally, click whatever column heading arranges the songs in a way that groups them in whatever way is easiest for you to work with at the moment.

One way to select all the items in a group is to click the heading that precedes the group. For example, in Figure 18.19, we clicked the artist name Yes to select all the songs under that category. The selected songs are highlighted. Any change you make to one of the selected songs is applied to all the selected songs.

Another way to select multiple adjacent songs is to click the first one you want to select. Then hold down the Shift key and click the last one you want to select. The two songs you clicked and all the songs in between are selected.

To select multiple songs that aren't adjacent to one another, click the first one that you want to select. Then hold down the Ctrl key while clicking other songs you want to select. That same technique lets you deselect one selected song without deselecting any other songs.

You can also use the keyboard to select songs, as follows:

- To select every song in the library, click Songs in the Navigation pane, click a song title, and press Ctrl + A.
- To select all the songs from the current song to the bottom of the list, click the first song you want to select and press Shift + End.
- To select all the songs to the top of the list, click the first song and press Shift + Home.

FIGURE 18.19

Selected songs under the Yes heading.

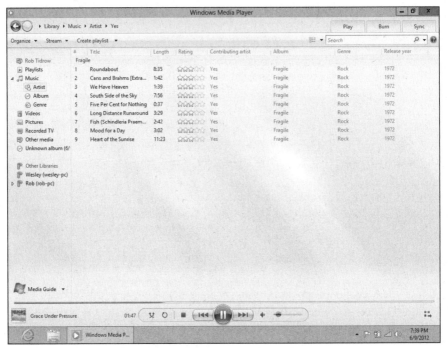

To deselect songs, click a neutral area in the program window, such as the empty space to the left of the play controls.

Selecting songs doesn't have any effect on them, other than to highlight them. However, any action you take while the songs are selected is applied to all the selected songs. The following sections look at things you can do with any one song or any number of selected songs.

Changing a song title

Every song on a CD is likely to have its own unique title, so you generally have to change titles one at a time. To change just one song title, first make sure you don't have multiple songs selected. (Click the song you want to change so that only that song is selected.) Then right-click the title you want to change and choose Edit. Type the new title and press Enter.

Changing genre, artist, and so on

You can change the genre, artist, album title, or any other media information for a song by right-clicking in a specific column and choosing Edit. But because all the songs on a CD may have that same artist, or belong to the same genre, you might want to make the change to several songs. First, select all the songs to which you want to apply the change. Then click the word or name you want to change in any one of the selected songs and choose Edit. Type in the new name or word and press Enter. The change will occur in all the selected songs.

Changing incorrect media information

Sometimes Media Player will get media information from the Internet, but it's the wrong information. This is especially true when working with multiple CD sets. Instead of manually typing all the information for the CD, you can take a shot at finding the correct information online. To do so, click Album in the Navigation pane. Then scroll to the album that has the incorrect icon, right-click its icon, and choose Update Album Info. Then double-click the album's icon to see whether the situation has improved at all.

If updating the album info didn't help, you can try right-clicking the album title just above its song titles and choosing Find Album Info. Most likely, you'll get the same faulty information you got the first time. But you can click the Search button in the lower-left corner of the Album Info window that opens and try searching by the artist's name or album title. You may get lucky and find the exact album you're looking for. The Album Info window acts like a wizard, so you can just follow the instructions on the screen and use the buttons along the bottom of the window to aid in your search.

If you do find the exact album you're looking for, click the Finish button in the Album Info window and Media Player copies the media information to the album in your media library. If you don't have any such luck, you can still manually enter the correct information for each song on the album using the techniques described in the previous sections.

Rating songs

You've probably noticed the star ratings that Media Player adds to each song. By default, the ratings are all the same (three stars) because the idea is for you to rate each song according to your own likes and dislikes. Give five stars to your favorite songs, one star to songs you don't like, and something in between for all the rest.

To change the rating of a single song, right-click the title of the song you want to rate, choose Rate, and enter the number of stars you want to give it. To rate multiple songs, first decide what rating you want to apply (such as five stars). Then select all the songs to which you want to apply that rating. (You can use the Ctrl + click method to select multiple nonadjacent songs.) After you've selected all the songs to which you want to apply a rating, right-click any selected song, choose Rate, and choose the desired rating.

Any time you want to view all the songs to which you've applied a rating, choose Organize ⇨ Sort By ⇨ Rating. The Contents pane in the center of the program window will show rating categories: one category for ratings you've applied and another for songs you haven't rated yet but were given ratings automatically, like the example in Figure 18.20.

To play all the songs to which you've given a certain rating, right-click the rating icon and choose Play. To see all the songs to which you've applied a given rating, double-click the rating icon.

18

FIGURE 18.20

Stars representing ratings.

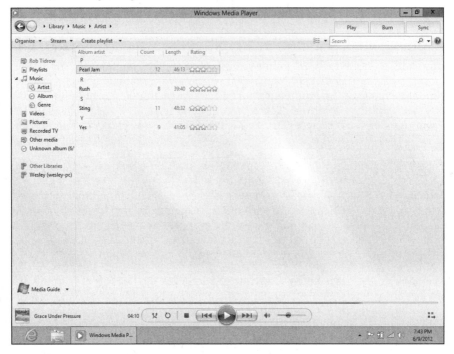

Making Custom Playlists

A *playlist* is a group of songs, photos, video, or other Media Player items. In Media Player's library, every icon, stack, and Navigation pane category is a playlist in its own right, which you can play by right-clicking and choosing Play. So, every time you open Windows Media Player and click the Library button in the features taskbar, you have many playlists from which to choose.

A custom playlist is one you create yourself. A custom playlist can contain any songs you like, in any order you like. For example, you can create a Party playlist of songs to play during a party. You can create a Favorites playlist of just your favorite songs. You can also create custom playlists of songs you want to copy to your own custom CDs, DVDs, or portable music player.

To get started on creating a custom playlist, follow these steps:

1. If you haven't already done so, open Windows Media Player.

2. Open the Library view if currently in Now Playing view.

3. If you don't see the Playlist pane at the right side of the program window, do either of the following to make it visible:

   - Select the Play tab.
   - Click the Organize button and choose Layout ⇨ Show List.

To create your own custom playlist, you'll need to start with an empty one, like the example at the right side of Figure 18.21. If your List pane isn't empty, click the Clear List button at the top of the Playlist pane.

FIGURE 18.21

The Empty List pane.

To create your custom playlist, drag any song titles you want from the Contents pane to the left of the playlist into the playlist. As an alternative to dragging one song title at a time, you can select multiple songs and drag them all at once. As an alternative to dragging, you can right-click any song title and choose Add to Playlist. Or select multiple songs, right-click any selected song, and choose Add to Playlist.

> **NOTE**
>
> If you skipped the earlier section, "Using the Media Player Library," you'll need to go back and learn some basic library navigation skills before you can find songs to add to your playlist.

To add all the songs from an album to the playlist, right-click the album's icon and choose Add to Playlist. Likewise, you can right-click any icon or stack that represents a category of songs — such as a genre, artist name, or rating — and choose Add to Playlist. All the songs within that category are added to the playlist.

Don't worry about adding too much stuff to the playlist. There's almost no limit to how large a playlist can be. And you can also remove any song from the playlist at any time.

Managing songs in a playlist

After you have some songs in a playlist, you can arrange them as you see fit. Use any of the following techniques to do so:

- Drag any song title up or down to change its position in the list.
- Right-click any song title and choose Move Up or Move Down.
- Click the List Options button above the list, and choose whichever option best describes how you want them sorted (see Figure 18.22).
- To put the songs in random order, choose Shuffle List from the List Options menu.

FIGURE 18.22

Sorting songs in a playlist.

TIP

To widen or narrow the List pane, drag its inner border left or right.

Figure 18.23 shows a completed playlist.

FIGURE 18.23

A playlist.

To remove a song from the playlist, right-click the song title and choose Remove from List. Optionally, you can select multiple songs using the Ctrl + click or Shift + click method. Then press Delete (Del) or right-click any selected item and choose Remove from List.

Saving a playlist

To save a playlist, name the list by clicking Unsaved List and entering a name. To rename a list, simply click the name and type a new one; then press Enter.

Viewing, playing, and changing playlists

To play all the songs in a playlist, or change a playlist, first select the Play tab. If the Navigation pane isn't open, use the Layout Options button to open it. The playlists appear under the Playlists branch in the Navigation pane. If you click Playlists in the Navigation pane, you'll see all your saved playlists in the Contents pane as icons. Recent playlists will be listed first, followed by all playlists, as in Figure 18.27. In the example, we chose Tile from the View Options to show the playlists.

To use a playlist, right-click its icon or name and choose an option, depending on what you want to do:

- **Open:** Shows the contents of the playlist in the Contents pane
- **Play:** Plays all the songs in the playlist
- **Add To:** Adds the songs from the playlist to whatever playlist is currently in the List pane
- **Rename:** Enables you to change the name of the playlist
- **Delete:** Deletes the playlist
- **Open File Location:** Opens the folder in which the playlist is stored

Using and creating Auto Playlists

An Auto Playlist is one that gets its content automatically. You can also create your own Auto Playlists based on any criteria you like. To create an Auto Playlist, click the arrow beside the Create Playlist button in the toolbar and choose Create Auto Playlist. The New Auto Playlist dialog box opens, as shown in Figure 18.24.

To specify a criterion for the Auto Playlist, click the plus sign under Music in My Library and choose an option from the resulting drop-down list. Then specify criteria by clicking options that appear next to the funnel icon. For example, if you wanted to create an Auto Playlist for songs in which Carlos Santana is a contributing artist, choose Contributing Artist from the list, and then click the Click to Set link and either choose an artist's name or type the artist's name.

You could create an Auto Playlist, perhaps named "Today's Tunes," by choosing Date Added from the drop-down list and then choosing a date specification (such as Last 7 Days) from the links that appear beside the new criteria item.

Suppose you have many different types of files in your library and you want to be able to quickly view just the MP3 files. You could create an Auto Playlist named "MP3s" (or whatever) and use the criteria File Type and MP3.

You can specify multiple criteria if you like. Multiple criteria are always treated as "and" logic, which means each new criterion narrows, rather than expands, the Auto Playlist's contents. For example, if you specify the criteria Contributing Artist Contains Santana and Date Added to Library Is After Last 30 Days, you'll see all songs added to the library in the last 30 days where a contributing artist is Santana.

FIGURE 18.24

The New Auto Playlist dialog box.

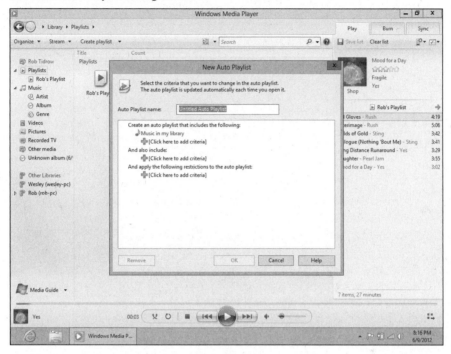

To include pictures, video, or TV shows in the Auto Playlist, choose an option under the And Also Include heading. Or to place additional restrictions on the content, choose options under And Apply the Following Restrictions to the Auto Playlist.

When you've finished specifying criteria for your Auto Playlist, click OK. The Auto Playlist will be listed in the Navigation pane along with all others. To play the Auto Playlist and see its current contents, double-click its name or icon. To change the criteria that define the Auto Playlist's contents, right-click its icon, and choose Edit.

Creating Your Own Music CDs

Although CD players are becoming less and less popular (because of smartphones, MP3 players, iPhones, and the like), many people still have CD players in their vehicles. For that reason, you may want to opt for a custom CD of your favorite music. Creating your own custom music CDs is a lot of fun. It's also a great way to protect any new CDs you purchase from getting scratched and ruined. When you buy a new CD, rip it to your Media Library, and then put it back in its case for safekeeping. Burn a copy of the CD (or just your favorite songs from the CD along with some other favorite songs), and use the copy in your home or car stereo. In some cases, you can also copy songs you purchased online to CDs.

If you buy blank CDs in spindles of 50 or more, they're typically very inexpensive. You won't get the little plastic jewel case, but you can buy paper sleeves or jewel cases separately. Or you can keep all the CDs in a CD binder.

Types of music CDs

Before we get into the specifics of burning CDs, it's important to understand that you can create two different types of music CDs:

- **Audio CD:** This type of CD plays in any home stereo, car stereo, portable CD player, or computer. You must burn songs to a CD-R disk (preferably an Audio CD-R) to create this type of CD because most non-computer players can't play CD-RW disks or DVD disks.

- **Data CD:** This type of music CD plays in computers, or in any stereo that's capable of playing this type of CD. You can use CD-R or CD-RW disks. However, you must choose a disk type that is compatible with both your computer's CD/DVD burner and the device on which you want to play the disk.

> **TIP**
>
> CDs and DVDs are examples of *optical media*, so named because they use a laser rather than magnetism to read and write data. All the different types of disks (CD-R, CD-RW, DVD-R, DVD+R, DVD-RW, DVD+RW, and so forth) make things woefully confusing.

If you don't know what type of disks your stereo can play, refer to the instructions that came with that device. Optionally, create an RW (Read/Write) disk and try it out. There's no loss if the disk doesn't play because you can always erase the disk and use it for something else. Once burned, R (Recordable) disks cannot be erased or changed.

Choosing music disk options

The first step in creating a music CD is to specify which type of disk you want to create, and perhaps some other options. In Media Player, select the Burn tab, and then click Burn Options to see the menu shown in Figure 18.25. Choose options as summarized in the following list:

- **Hide List:** Hide the burn list.
- **Eject Disc after Burning:** Have the CD ejected automatically when it's ready for use. This is especially useful when burning multiple CDs from a single Burn list.
- **Data CD or DVD:** Choose this option if you want to create a music CD or DVD that plays only on computers and devices that are capable of playing nontraditional music CDs.
- **Audio CD:** Create the type of CD that all stereos and players can play. For best results, use an 80-minute Audio CD-R disk.
- **Name Disc:** Specify a name for the disk.

FIGURE 18.25

Burn options.

- **More Burn Options:** Choosing More Burn Options takes you to the Burn tab of Media Player's Options dialog box, shown in Figure 18.26. Most of the options duplicate options on the menu. Here are the ones that are unique:

  - **Burn Speed:** The default setting is Fastest. But if you have problems burning disks, or the sound quality isn't up to par on the disks you burn, consider reducing this to a slower speed.

  - **Automatically Eject the Disc after Burning:** Instruct Windows to open the disk tray after the CD burning completes.

  - **Apply Volume Leveling across Tracks:** Ensure that the volume of each song is the same when listening to the finished CD.

  - **Burn CD without Gaps:** Omit the two-second gap normally inserted between audio tracks.

  - **Add a List of All Burned Files to the Disc in This Format:** Choose WPL if your player can read Windows playlists. Choose M3U if your player can only read MP3-style playlists.

  - **Use Media Information to Arrange Files in Folders on the Disc:** If selected, items on the CD will be organized into folders. If you're unsure about whether your player can handle folders, clear the check box for this option.

FIGURE 18.26

The Burn tab of the Options dialog box.

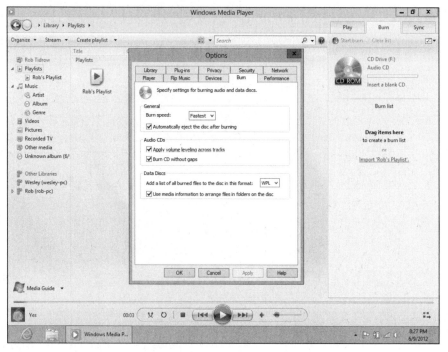

Click OK in the Options dialog box to save any settings you changed. With your options selected and squared away, you're ready to choose which songs you want to copy to your custom CD.

- **Help with Burning:** Choose this option for help with burning music CDs.

Choosing songs to put on the CD

The skills needed to choose songs to put on a CD are the same as those for creating a custom playlist. You can drag songs individually, or you can drag an entire album or other category. But you have to make sure you're dragging to the Burn list, not just any playlist. Here's the basic process:

1. Select the Burn tab to make sure you're viewing the Burn list.

2. If your Burn list contains songs from a previously burned CD and you want to create a new one, click Clear List at the top of the Burn list. Click the Burn Options button and choose Audio CD if you're burning a music CD for stereos. Otherwise, you can choose Data CD or DVD if you're creating a music disk for computers and appropriate players.

3. Use a felt-tip pen or disk labeler to write the name of your custom CD on a blank CD. Then put that CD in your CD drive.

Your Media Player window should look something like Figure 18.27. The songs that appear in the center Contents pane will, of course, be songs you have in your own library. How your icons look depends on what category you're viewing and what option you've selected from the View Options drop-down list.

FIGURE 18.27

Ready to copy songs to a Burn list.

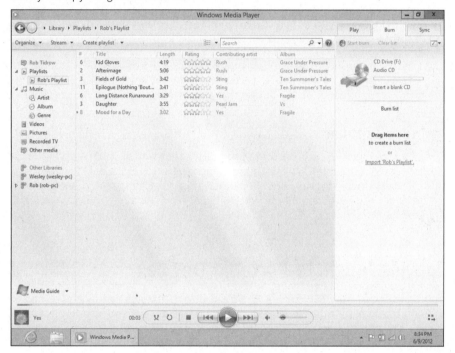

At this point, just drag the songs you want to burn to your custom CD to the Burn list, or right-click any song title and choose Add to Burn List. As you add songs, the indicator at the top of the Burn list keeps you informed of how much space will be used on the CD. You can keep adding songs until the disk capacity is exhausted. Any additional songs you add at that point are added to a new disk. Media Player numbers the disk sequentially in the list.

TIP

Clicking the Length column heading sorts songs from longest to shortest, or vice versa. When you have little time left on a CD, that order can make it easy to find a song that will fit.

Options that apply to custom playlists also apply to the Burn list. For example, to remove a song from the Burn list, right-click its title and choose Remove from List. To change the order of songs, click Burn Options, choose Sort List By, and choose a sort option. Or drag any song title up or down within the list.

When you're happy with the songs you've selected and their order, you're ready to burn the CD.

Creating the disk

When the Burn list contains all the songs you want to copy to the CD, click the Start Burn button at the top of the Burn list. Then wait. How long it takes depends on the type of CD you're creating, the speed of your drive, and other factors. The status column in the Contents pane and an indicator below the Burn list keep you apprised of the progress.

When the CD is finished, remove it from the CD drive. If you created a standard audio disk, you can insert and play it in a stereo as you would any other disk. If you created a data disk, you can play it in any device that supports the type of disk you created.

Saving a Burn list

It's a good idea to save each Burn list you create. That way, if you ever want to create another copy of the same CD, you can just open the saved Burn list. To save a Burn list, click the Burn Options button and choose Save List As. Change the name to something that describes the Burn list and click Save. Then, to create a new Burn list, click the Clear List Pane button.

Copying Music to Portable Devices

A portable device is an MP3 player or similar device that lets you take your music with you. To put songs (or other media) on your portable device, you *sync* songs from Media Player's library to the device. You can put any songs you wish onto your player. The only limit is the storage capacity of the device.

Windows Media Player works with many MP3 players. However, it does not work with the Apple iPhone, iPod, or iPad (you use iTunes to sync to those). Nor does it work with some older devices.

> **TIP**
> See "Converting file types," later in this chapter, for tips on using iTunes files with Windows Media Player.

If you don't already have a portable device but you're thinking of getting one, visit `http://windows.microsoft.com/en-US/windows/products/windows-media-player`.

Different devices work a little differently. So, if you already have a device, the first step is to learn the basics of using it and connecting it to your computer. That information you can get only from the instructions that came with the device. Despite the differences among devices, we can tell you generally how synchronization works with Media Player.

The first step is to open Windows Media Player and select the Sync tab. Then connect your device to the computer and turn it on. If a dialog box opens asking you to name the device, type in a name of your own choosing and click Finish. What happens next depends on the storage capacity of the device:

- If the device capacity is 4GB or greater, and your media library can fit within that capacity, Media Player automatically copies your entire library to the device. Each time you connect the device in the future, Media Player copies any new songs you've acquired since the last connection so that the device stays in sync with your library.

- If the device capacity is less than 4GB, or your library is too large to fit in the device, nothing is copied automatically. But you can manually copy any songs you like to the device.

You can change what happens when you connect your device. We'll get to that in a moment. First, let's look at how you manually choose songs to put on your device.

Manual syncing

When your device is connected to your computer and you want to choose songs to copy to the device, select the Sync tab. The List pane at the right side of the program window shows the storage capacity of the device, and the amount of space that's currently on the device. Beneath that is an empty playlist, called the Sync list.

To add songs to the device, you need to drag them from the contents pane to the Sync list, just as you would when burning a CD or creating a custom playlist. As always, you can select multiple songs and drag them all at once. You can also right-click any song, album, icon, or category name and choose Add to Sync List.

As you add songs, an indicator near the top of the Sync list shows you how much space you have remaining. If the indicator turns red and shows "Filled," you've gone over the limit. To remove a song from the Sync list, right-click its title and choose Remove from List. Do so until the indicator turns green again. Figure 18.28 shows an example with many songs already chosen and about 26.5GB of space left on a portable player.

As always, you can arrange songs in the Sync list by dragging them up or down. Optionally, click Sync List, choose Sort, and choose a sort order. When you're happy with the songs you've selected and their order, click the Start Sync button at the bottom of the Sync list.

The Contents pane of Media Player shows the synchronization progress as songs are copied to the device. When the Status column shows "Synchronized to Device" for every song, you're done. You can disconnect the device from the computer, plug in your headphones, and take your music with you.

18

FIGURE 18.28

Songs added to the Sync list.

Managing songs on a device

Portable media players are much more flexible than CDs. For example, you can delete individual songs from a portable device and replace them with other songs. When your device is connected, it shows up as its own set of categories in the Navigation pane. When you click a category name under the device name, the Contents pane to the right shows the contents of the device only, not the contents of your entire library.

Figure 18.29 shows an example. In the Navigation pane at left, we've clicked the Transformer TF101 device and clicked the All Music category name. The Contents pane to the right is showing songs that are currently on the synced device. When viewing songs in that manner with your own device, you can right-click any song title and choose Delete to remove it from the device.

Manual syncing is easy (once you've played around with it a bit). Most people like to choose exactly what's on their portable player so manual syncing is also the most commonly used method. To use auto syncing, you need to enable automatic syncing and specify what syncs automatically. Let's look at that next.

FIGURE 18.29

Music on an MP3 player.

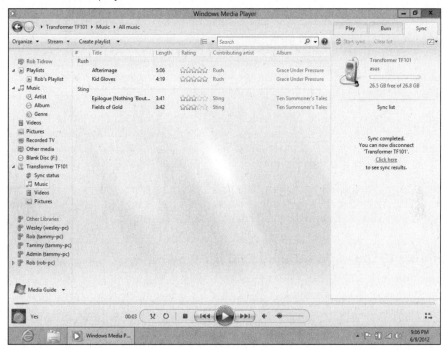

Auto syncing devices

Auto sync is a method of keeping a portable player up to date with whatever content is currently available in your Media Player library. If your device doesn't have enough capacity to store your entire library, exactly what you end up with can be somewhat arbitrary. The first step is to connect the device to the computer and make sure it's turned on.

Next, select the Sync tab and then click Sync Options, point to your device name, and choose Set Up Sync. If you have not set up the device previously, you'll see the Windows Media Player – Device Setup dialog box, which asks if you want to sync temporarily (this session only) or permanently. If you choose the latter, you'll have additional options available for syncing, including the capability to specify which playlists are synced.

The Device Setup dialog box opens. The left column shows available playlists. The right column shows playlists that are currently used to sync songs to the device. To remove a playlist from the right column, click its name and choose Remove.

To add a playlist to the right column, click its name in the left column and click Add. To see Auto Playlists specifically designed for syncing, click the My Playlists button under Available Playlists and choose Sync Playlists.

If no playlist defines the kinds of songs you want to sync automatically, you can create your own. Click New Auto Playlist and give your playlist a name. For example, to make an Auto Playlist that copies new songs added to your library in the last week, create a criterion that specifies Date Added to Library Is after Last 7 Days.

Give the new playlist a name, perhaps New This Week, and save it. Then click the Add button to copy it from Available Playlists to Playlists To Sync. If that's the only playlist you put in the right column, then each time you connect your device, Media Player copies only songs that you've added to your library within the last week.

Optionally, choose Shuffle What Syncs. If you do, each time you connect the device, files that are currently on the device are removed automatically and replaced with songs that match the criteria of your selected Auto Playlists. So, each time you connect the device, you automatically get however many songs your playlist provides added to the device.

Click Finish when you're done, and Media Player syncs based on your selections. Remove the device when the syncing is finished. Any time you want to change the contents of your player, just connect it to the PC and click the Finish button.

Choosing between manual and auto sync

You can choose whether you want to use manual sync or auto sync at any time. Just connect your device, click the arrow under Sync, click the device name, and choose Set Up Sync. To use manual syncing, clear the check mark next to Sync This Device Automatically. To enable auto syncing, select (check) that same check box. Then click Finish.

Setting player options

To see other options that your player supports, connect the player, right-click its name in the Navigation pane, and choose Properties. A Properties dialog box for the device opens. The options available to you will depend on the capabilities of your player. If you're not sure what an option in the dialog box means, check the manual that came with your device or click the Help button in the dialog box for more information.

> **NOTE**
>
> Most portable players are USB mass storage devices. Once connected, these show up as a disk drive in your This PC folder. You can see the current contents of your device by opening its icon in your This PC folder. You can also erase any songs from the device using the same techniques you use to erase files from folders and drives.

Fun with Skins

Whenever you're using a program, the part that you see on the screen is just one snowflake on the tip of the proverbial iceberg. The real "guts" are in memory and invisible. The part you see on the screen is called the *user interface,* abbreviated UI, and often referred to as simply the *interface* or *skin.* Some programs, including Windows Media Player, allow you to change the interface without changing the functionality of the program.

Windows Media Player comes with several skins for you to try out. These skins are for Now Playing mode, not for Library mode. To see them if Media Player is in Now Playing mode, press Alt to open the menu, and choose View ⇨ Skin Chooser. If Media Player is in Library mode, right-click the area to the right of the breadcrumb trail, and then choose View ⇨ Skin Chooser.

Click each skin name in the left pane to get a preview of how Media Player will look if you apply the skin. To download additional free skins, click the More Skins button above the left column. When you find a skin you like, click the Apply Skin button.

Figure 18.30 shows an example using the Blue Crush skin. Once you're in a skin, point to various symbols and buttons on it to figure out what's up. You'll see the name of the control in a tooltip.

FIGURE 18.30

Media Player in the Blue Crush skin.

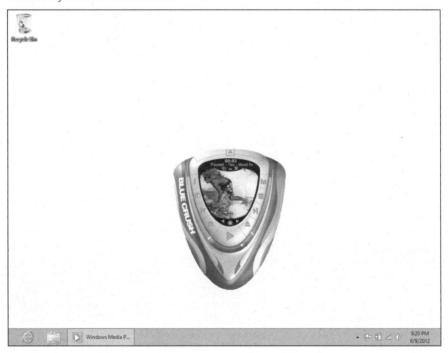

When you're in the normal Full mode, you can click the Switch to Skin Mode button in the lower-left corner of Media Player's program window to switch to a skin. From the keyboard, press Ctrl + 2 to switch to Skin mode. Press Ctrl + 1 to switch back to Full mode. To get out of the Skin Chooser in Full mode, click the Back button.

Extending Media Player with Plug-ins

Plug-ins are optional add-on capabilities that you can purchase or, in some cases, download for free. A plug-in might be as simple as a new visualization or skin. Or it could be an audio or DVD driver or enhancer that extends the capabilities of Media Player. Some plug-ins add capabilities to Media Player. It all depends on what you download and install. To see your options, press Alt and then choose Tools ➪ Download Plug-Ins.

Some plug-ins are free; others aren't. Once you're at the site for downloading plug-ins, you'll need to review what's available and decide for yourself what's of value to you.

To manage any plug-ins you acquire, choose Tools ➪ Plug-ins and then choose Options.

Converting File Types

Suppose you've ripped a bunch of CDs to WMA format and then acquire a portable media device that only plays MP3s. Do you need to rip all those same CDs again? The answer is no. Media Player 12 can automatically convert files as it syncs them to your portable device. For example, it can convert WMA files to MP3 format. It can also convert video files.

To configure file conversion options, press Alt and then click Tools ➪ Options and select the Devices tab. Then click the Advanced button to open the File Conversion Options dialog box (see Figure 18.31).

In the File Conversion Options dialog box, you can specify whether video or audio file conversion happens in the background. Conversion in the background can speed up syncing. By default, background conversion is on for video and off for audio. You can also specify a better quality for video by choosing the Choose Quality over Speed When Converting Video option. If you need more space for temporary files created during conversion, click the Change button and choose a different location. You can also specify the amount of disk space to allocate for the temporary files and delete any temporary files currently in the temporary location. For other types of conversion options, consider searching any download site for the type of conversion you need to perform. For example, you might go to www.tucows.com or http://download.cnet.com. Or you could use a more generic search engine such as Bing or Google. Type in the words that best define the type of conversion you need to perform, such as **Convert WMA MP4**. We're also partial to Pocket DVD Studio at www.pqdvd.com. It has versions to convert DVDs for various devices, including PSP, iPad, iPod, and others.

FIGURE 18.31

The File Conversion Options dialog box.

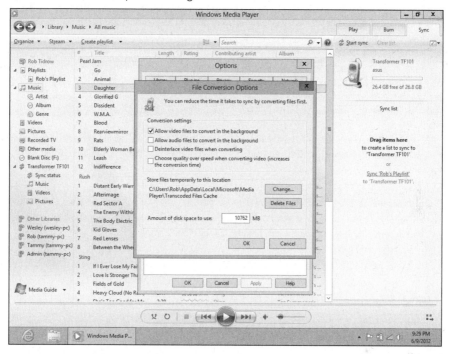

Music, Metadata, and Searches

Earlier in this chapter you discovered how you can store media information such as artist, album title, genre, and so forth with songs. That media information is a form of *metadata.* Metadata, in turn, is information *about* a file, and it doesn't apply only to music. Pictures, videos, Microsoft Office documents, and many other file types support metadata.

> **TIP**
>
> Whether or not you're in Windows Media Player, you can search for and group things based on metadata in any file.

You don't have to be in Windows Media Player to take advantage of metadata. The Search features in Windows 8.1 allow you to search and group things based on metadata in any file. For example, if you select Search from the Charms Bar and type an artist's name into the Search box, songs by that artist show up in the Files window (click Files under the search box).

You're also not limited to searching for one thing. You can specify multiple criteria separated by the words *AND* or *OR* (uppercase letters). For example, here's a search that finds all tracks in which the composer is either Beethoven or Mozart: **composer:beethoven OR composer:mozart**.

> **TIP**
>
> You might think that it should be **composer:Beethoven AND composer:Mozart**. But it doesn't work that way. A song can't have both Beethoven *and* Mozart as the composer. You're looking for tracks that have either Beethoven *or* Mozart as the composer.

If you want to locate all MP3 songs that have Nickelback as an artist and a year greater than 2010, the following search would do the trick: **type:mp3 AND artist:nickelback AND year: > 2010**.

 For experienced users, this is a far cry from the old days of searching for filenames. But it's not the kind of thing you master in a minute. Searches are successful only when you know how to construct them correctly. See Chapter 22 and Chapter 23 for the full story.

Wrap-Up

This chapter looked at the Windows Media Player main music capabilities, but all its capabilities haven't been covered yet. In the next chapter, you learn about using Windows 8.1 with DVDs and videos. If you have an edition of Windows 8.1 that includes Media Center, you can also use Media Center to play songs from your media library. The following points were covered in this chapter:

- Controlling sound volume on your computer is a necessary first step to playing music.
- The Features taskbar along the top of Media Player's program window provides easy access to all of Media Player's main components.
- The Now Playing mode can show a visualization of music that's playing or the visual content of the playing video or DVD.
- The Navigation pane gives you access to all songs and other media you've downloaded or copied from CDs.
- You can rip (copy) songs from music CDs to your media library.
- You can burn your own custom music CDs.
- You can sync (copy) music to portable media devices.

Working with Videos and Photos

IN THIS CHAPTER

Watching video files with the Video app

Watching video files with Media Player

Managing photos with Media Player

Windows 8.1 provides two tools to help you play back video files stored on your computer: the Windows 8.1 Video app and Windows Media Player. The Video app provides basic playback features, while Windows Media Player includes ways to create playlists and more. You can even use Media Player to manage photos and copy them to portable devices.

If you have Media Center working on your version of Windows 8.1, you can use Media Center or Media Player to manage and watch recorded TV.

Watching Video Files

A video file is a file on a hard disk that contains video and audio. These files include videos you capture from video cameras, smartphones, digital cameras, recorded TV shows, and videos you download from the web. Video files come in many formats, and thanks to the Windows 8.1 Video app and Media Player 12's support for additional formats, Windows can now play almost any type of video. The following sections will help you understand how to manage and play videos in the Video app and Media Player.

> **NOTE**
> Unlike previous versions of Media Player, Windows 8.1's Media Player 12 application does not support playback of DVD movies.

Using your Videos library

TIP

You can store video files in any folder you want. But to stay organized, you may want to put video files that are private in your user account's Videos folder. Video files that you want to share with all users should go into the Public Videos folder. Both folders offer similar features. So, before we get to playing videos, take a moment to look at your Videos folder.

To open your Videos folder, start File Explorer. Then click Videos in the Navigation pane. Figure 19.1 shows an example where there are already some videos and other items in the Videos folder. Only the icons that look like thumbnails are actual videos. When you click one of those, it shows in the Preview pane (if the Preview pane is open).

TIP

To open and close optional panes, click the Organize button and choose Layout. See Chapter 22 for the full story on folders and panes.

FIGURE 19.1

Videos folder example.

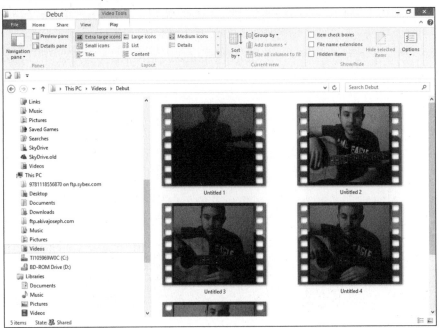

If you want to see filename extensions of video files but they're not currently visible, select the View tab and then click Options. In the Folder Options dialog box, select the View tab, clear the check mark next to Hide Extensions for Known File Types, and click OK.

Recorded TV

Recorded TV shows are video files stored in the .dvr-ms (Digital Video Recording — Microsoft) format. You use Media Center (which you may have to install) to define times and channels to record, as on a VCR or DVD recorder. You can also decide where you want to store recorded TV shows in Media Center. And of course, you can watch recorded TV shows in Media Center.

You can also watch recorded TV shows in Windows Media Player. To view your recorded TV shows in Media Player, click the Recorded TV branch in the Navigation pane.

If some of your recorded TV shows don't show up, Media Player may not be monitoring their folders. Launch Media Player while on the Windows Start screen by typing **media**. Click Windows Media Player on the results. In Media Player, choose Organize ⇨ Manage Libraries ⇨ Recorded TV. In the resulting Recorded TV Library Locations dialog box, click the Add button to add folders that contain recorded TV to the list of the monitored folders.

Playing videos using the Video App

To watch a video using the Windows 8.1 Video app, open File Explorer and right-click a video you want to play. Choose Open With and select Video. Or, if Video is the default video player, you simply have to double-click that video from File Explorer, and Windows automatically launches the Video app with your video playing. Figure 19.2 shows the Video app playing back a selected video.

Notice in Figure 19.2 that the video controls display to help you control the video playback. These controls include the following:

- **Rewind:** Enables you to skip back to a previously played section of the video.
- **Pause/Play:** During playback, the Pause button appears so you can halt the playback. While paused, the Play button appears so you can restart the playback of the video.
- **Fast Forward:** Enables you to skip forward in the video.
- **Now Playing Bar:** Shows a progress timeline of the video. Slide the Now Playing controller (usually a green circle) forward and backward to move the video to a specific place on the timeline.

19

If you don't click on any of these playback controls, after a few moments they'll disappear from view. Bring them back into view by moving the mouse or tapping the screen on a touchscreen monitor.

While playing a video, you can display additional tools by right-clicking. Figure 19.2 also shows playback and Video app tools at the bottom of the screen. You can click the Open File button to display the Files app to see a list of videos you can play. You also have buttons to repeat, rewind, play, and fast forward.

FIGURE 19.2

The Video app playing a video.

Playing videos using Media Player

To watch a video file in the Media Player, open Media Player (show the Charms Bar, click Search, type **media**, and click Windows Media Player on the Start screen). If the video is stored in a format supported by Media Player, it should open in Media Player (see Figure 19.3). If it opens in some other program, close that program. Then follow these steps to watch it in Media Player:

1. Right-click the video icon in File Explorer and choose Open With ⇨ Choose Default Program.

2. To ensure that files of that type open in Media Player by default, choose Use This App for All of the Chosen File Types (such as .mp4, .avi, and so on).

3. Click Windows Media Player (or whatever program you want to set as the default).

FIGURE 19.3

Using Media Player to play a video.

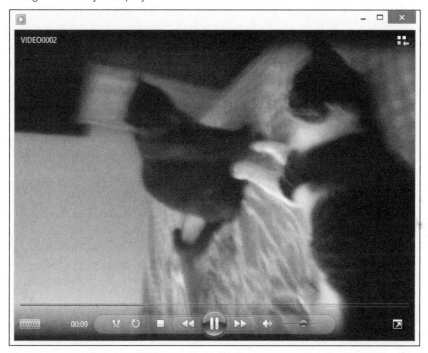

Adding videos to your Media Library

You can store information about your video files in Media Player's library. Depending on how Media Player is configured, video files from your Videos folder, and perhaps Public Videos folders, should already appear in Media Player. To find out, click Videos in the Navigation pane.

To add video files to your media library, monitor the folders in which they're stored by following these steps:

1. If you're not already in Windows Media Player, open it now.

2. Choose Organize ⇨ Manage Libraries ⇨ Videos. Videos appear in the Video Library Locations dialog box by default (shown in Figure 19.4).

FIGURE 19.4

Using the Video Library Locations dialog box.

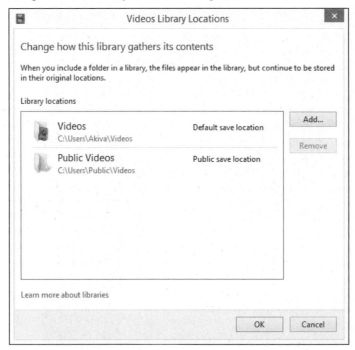

3. Click the Add button and navigate to the drive and folder that contains other videos you want to include. Then click Include Folder. Repeat this step for each folder you want to add.

4. Click OK in each open dialog box to save all your changes.

Media files from the folders you specified are added to your library. You can use the View Options button on the toolbar to display icons in Icon, Tile, or Details view. You also can add your own media information to better organize your videos by genre, director, actor, or whatever. To add a genre to a video, choose the Details view, and then click in the Genre column and type a tag, such as SciFi, Sports, Nature, and so on.

By default, the Navigation pane doesn't show Genre as an option under the Videos branch. To add Genre, choose Organize ➪ Customize Navigation Pane to open the Customize Navigation Pane dialog box. Under the Videos branch, place a check beside Genre and any other items you want to show, and click OK.

Figure 19.5 shows an example where we've already categorized video files by Genre. We clicked the Genre icon in the Navigation pane at the left to see video files stacked by categories.

FIGURE 19.5

Video files organized by genre.

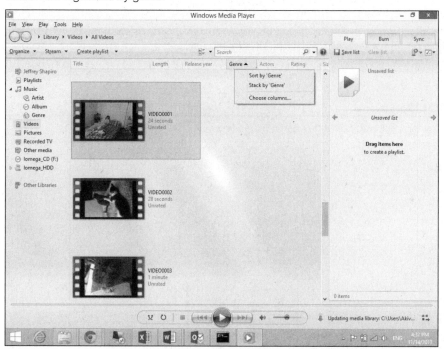

Playing videos from your library

Playing videos in Media Player is no different from playing songs. In the library, just double-click the video's title or icon. Or right-click an icon, stack, or category name, and choose Play.

Managing Photos with Media Player

In Chapter 17, you discovered ways to acquire and manage photos with Photo Gallery. There's no need to bring that information into Media Player, but you can if you want to. For example, if you have a portable media device that displays pictures, you might want to bring the photos into Media Player so you can sync music and video files.

To view photos in Media Player, the photos need to be in a folder that's monitored by Media Player. Or you'll need to add that folder to your list of monitored folders. By default, the Pictures library appears in Media Player's Navigation pane but without any options such as Tags or Date Taken. You can add those options by clicking the Organize button in Windows Media Player and choosing Customize Navigation Pane. Scroll down to find Pictures in the list and select the desired options.

To view photos in Media Player, click Pictures in the Navigation pane. Figure 19.6 shows an example where we're viewing photos by date taken. Each stack represents a group of photos.

FIGURE 19.6

Viewing photos by date taken in Media Player.

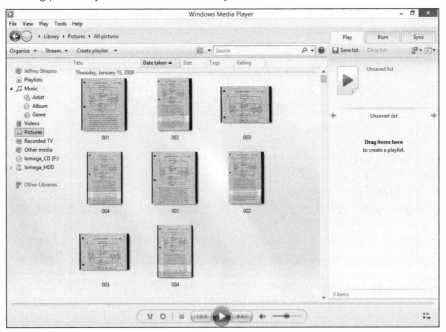

More on Playlists

In Media Player, you can include videos and photos in any music playlists you create. This is mostly useful for creating Auto Playlists for syncing to devices that support music, photos, and video. (When you play the playlist in Media Player, the videos and photos play in sequence, not simultaneously, so you'll still see only a visualization or album art when music is playing.)

> **TIP**
>
> If you want to create a movie that contains videos, photos, and music, use Windows Live Movie Maker. If you want to copy Media Player content to a DVD as a data disk, use the Burn tab in Media Player. Read Windows online Help for details on burning files to DVD. Chapter 6 of this book details how to access and search the Windows 8.1 help system.

To create an Auto Playlist that includes music, photos, and/or videos, click the arrow beside the Create Playlist button in the toolbar and choose Create Auto Playlist. Or right-click the name of an existing Auto Playlist and choose Edit. In the New Auto Playlist dialog box (shown in Figure 19.7), name the playlist however you like. Under Music in My Library, add your criteria for music. Then, under And Also Include, set criteria for Pictures, TV, and Video as you see fit.

FIGURE 19.7

Creating an Auto Playlist in Windows Media Player.

19

You can use that Auto Playlist to keep your portable media player up to date with media content on your computer on a daily basis. To update manually, connect your device and select the Sync tab. Drag the playlist name from the Navigation pane into the List pane. Then click the Start Sync button.

To use the daily Auto Playlist for automatic syncing, first connect your device. Then right-click the device in the Navigation pane and choose Set Up Sync. Choose Sync This Device Automatically. Then add the Auto Playlist to the Playlists to Sync column. Remove any other playlists that are in that Playlists to Sync column.

> **TIP**
>
> If you want to copy music (only) daily to your portable player, edit the playlist and remove the And Also Include criteria for photos, recorded TV, and video. Just click whichever criterion you want to remove, and then click the Remove button.

Limiting playlist size

If you discover that your Auto Playlists are too large, containing more content than you can fit on your portable player, you can limit the amount of content the playlist contains. Open the playlist for editing, and at the bottom of the Auto Playlist, click the + sign under And Apply the Following Restrictions to the Auto Playlist. You'll see the options shown in Figure 19.8 and described here:

- **Limit Number of Items:** Choose this option to limit the number of items the playlist may contain. For example, if you choose 10, the Auto Playlist will list only the first ten items that meet the criterion.

- **Limit Total Duration To:** Choose this option to set a maximum time limit to match the time duration of the disk to which you'll be copying items. For example, if you'll be copying playlist items to an Audio CD, the time limit is 80 minutes.

- **Limit Total Size To:** When syncing to portable devices, choose this option to limit the playlist items to the storage capacity of your device in kilobytes (KB), megabytes (MB), or gigabytes (GB).

Click OK when you've finished setting criteria. To see which items the Auto Playlist includes, click its name under Playlists in the Navigation pane. Or click Playlists in the Navigation pane, and then double-click the playlist name in the Details pane. To use your new playlist for auto syncing, connect your portable device to the computer. Then right-click the device in the Navigation pane and click Set Up Sync. Choose the Sync This Device Automatically check box and remove any items listed in the Playlists To Sync column. Then add your new playlist to that same column.

FIGURE 19.8

Options for restricting an Auto Playlist.

Limiting playlists to favorite items

When you manually create playlists by dragging items to the List pane, criteria you set in an Auto Playlist have no effect. But you can limit manual playlists to favorite items, providing you rate your items before dragging them over.

First, before you drag an album or category to the List pane, open the album or group and rate the songs. To rate a song, right-click its title in the contents pane and choose Rate. Or select several songs to which you want to apply the same rating, right-click any one selected song, and choose Rate. Give a four- or five-star rating to any songs you do want copied to playlists. Give a three-star or lower rating to songs you don't want copied.

To copy only favorites from the category to the playlist, right-click the album's icon or category name and choose " < *playlist name* > (Favorites Only)." Only the four- and five-star rated items appear in the List pane.

Skipping playlist items

When you're playing items in a playlist, you can skip over any item by clicking the Next button in the play controls. Media Player can remember which items you skipped and then skip them automatically the next time you play the list. It can also automatically omit skipped items when you save the playlist.

To choose how Media Player treats skipped items, click the List Options button above the list (shows an icon with a check mark on it) and choose Skipped Items, as in Figure 19.9. A selected option is active; an unselected option is inactive. You can click the option to activate or deactivate it. The following section describes how those options work.

FIGURE 19.9

Options for skipping items.

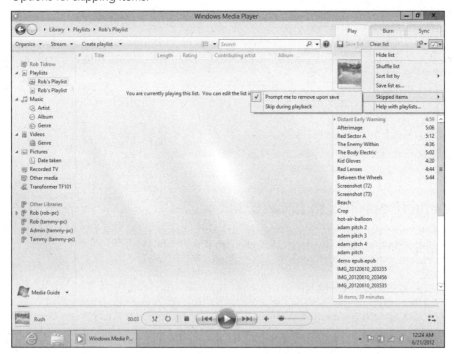

Prompt Me to Remove Upon Save

Activating the Prompt Me to Remove Upon Save option causes a message to appear whenever you save a playlist that contains skipped items. You can choose whether you want to leave the skipped items in the saved playlist or omit them. If you choose to keep the items in the playlist, you can choose Skip During Playback to have the songs skipped over the next time you play the playlist.

If you choose the Don't Show This Message Again option, Media Player automatically saves the playlist, and skipped songs will be skipped over on playback. Clear this option if you want to be prompted about these skipped items again.

Wrap-Up

Windows 8.1 includes two tools to play back videos — the Video app and Windows Media Player 12. Here's a quick summary of key points made in this chapter about using the Video app and Media Player to watch videos and view photos:

- To view a video using the new Windows 8.1 Videos app, open File Explorer and double-click a video file or right-click the video and choose Open With ⇨ Video.

- To open your Videos folder, open File Explorer and open the Videos folder.

- To view video files you've imported to Media Player, click Videos in the Navigation pane.

- For help, troubleshooting, and more information, click the Help button on the toolbar.

19

Part V

Managing Your Content

IN THIS PART

Understanding Drives, Folders, and Files

IN THIS CHAPTER

Disk drives, disks, and memory cards

Navigating through folders with File Explorer

Clicking, viewing, and arranging icons your way

Stop losing saved files

Beginners and casual users are often thrown by terms like *drive, folder, file, icon, kilobyte, megabyte, gigabyte, terabyte,* and so forth. Virtually every resource you turn to assumes that you already know what these things mean. Nobody ever bothers to explain them. That's because these terms and concepts have remained unchanged for the past 25 years or so.

Of course, just because those terms have been around for a long time doesn't mean everyone understands them. In fact, for every person who knows what those terms mean, you can be sure many thousands don't. So in this chapter, we're going to break from tradition and explain those terms.

Understanding Disks and Drives

Computers work with information. That information has to be stored on some type of *medium.* These days, that medium is most likely to be in the form of a disk or a card. You can also store information on tape, but tape is used primarily for backup.

Your computer's hard disk

All the programs and information that are in your computer are actually stored on a disk. In most cases, you will never see that disk because it's inside a sealed case. That disk goes by many names including *hard disk, hard drive,* and *fixed disk.* You may even hear it referred to as a *solid-state drive.*

Essentially, all the data you work with, with the exception of information you browse to on the Internet, is stored on one or more hard disks in your computer. This includes Windows itself, your programs, and all your documents, photos, videos, music, and other data.

NOTE

Don't confuse your hard disk with *memory* (also called RAM, short for *random access memory*). Your hard disk stores everything that's in your computer. Memory stores data temporarily while you're using it.

You can also add extra hard drives to your system, either internally or externally. Each shows up as an icon in your Computer folder, as discussed later in this chapter.

Your main hard disk, drive c:, is called *a non-removable* disk because you can't just pop it out of the computer by pressing some button. Other types of disks are called *removable* media because you can pop them in and out of the computer quite easily. Flash drives, CDs, and DVDs are examples of removable media.

Hard drives come in two primary types for the PC. The standard hard drive comprises multiple platters of disks that rotate around a spindle. Data is written and read on the platters by way of a magnetic head. These types of drives are available in large sizes and are relatively cheap when compared to the second type of drives, *solid-state drives.* Solid-state drives use integrated circuits to create memory to store data. You can find solid-state drives on many of the newer slim and lightweight laptops and netbooks. Solid-state drives are not as vulnerable to mechanical or physical errors (such as physical damage to the drive) but are more expensive than standard hard drives. Solid-state drives also provide greater speeds than traditional hard drives, providing users with improved access speeds to data, files, and other disk-related functions.

Removable media

Removable media are disks and devices you can pop into and out of the computer at will. Most removable media require a specific disk drive, or *drive* for short. The drive is a device into which you can place the disk. The drive then spins the disk. A drive head can then read data from, or write data to, the disk as it is spinning. The following sections are about removable media.

CDs and DVDs

CDs and DVDs are very popular storage media. The record companies use CDs to sell albums. The movie industry sells movies on DVDs. The computer industry uses both CDs and DVDs to distribute software. Figure 20.1 shows a DVD, but it could just as easily be a CD. The two look exactly alike.

When putting a CD or DVD disk into its drive, push the eject button to open the drive or to eject the disk from the system. Make sure to insert the disk in the tray or disk slot with the label facing up. For systems with disk trays, you then need to push the eject button on the drive to close the drive.

FIGURE 20.1

CD or DVD.

To listen to music on a CD, you usually just stick the CD into your CD drive, wait a few seconds, and the CD starts playing in your default music program, usually Windows Media Player. The same is true for most movie DVDs, but only if your computer has the appropriate hardware and software.

For more information on listening to, copying from, or creating your own music CDs, turn to Chapter 18. For more on watching DVD movies, turn to Chapter 19.

The most common mistake people make with CDs and DVDs is assuming they're the same. After all, they *look* the same. But they're not the same at all. Nor do you treat them like other kinds of disks. That's why we've dedicated an entire chapter (Chapter 19) just to CDs and DVDs.

Portable devices

Technically, portable devices aren't disks or disk drives. But some can store files. For example, digital cameras store pictures. Portable MP3 players store songs. When you connect such a device to your computer, Windows 8.1 provides access to the device as if it's a disk drive. The contents of the device, such as photos or videos, show up in your Computer folder.

20

You can copy things to and from portable devices using many different techniques. For example, you can use Windows Photo Gallery (see Chapter 17) to get pictures from a digital camera. Windows Photo Gallery is included with the Live Essentials programs, both of which are available for free from Microsoft. Use Windows Media Player to copy songs to and from a portable MP3 player. You can also use more general techniques, described in Chapter 21, to copy files to and from some portable devices.

Flash cards and memory sticks

Flash cards (also called *memory cards* and *memory sticks*) are a solid-state medium, which just means there's no spinning disk or drive head involved in getting information to and from the card. Memory cards come in many shapes and sizes. Figure 20.2 shows some examples.

Most digital cameras and portable MP3 players use memory cards to store songs and pictures. When you connect the device to the computer, you get access to that memory card so you can copy files from it or to it.

FIGURE 20.2

Memory cards.

If your computer has memory card slots, you also have the option of putting the card right into a slot. Each slot into which you can insert a card shows up as an icon in your

Computer folder. When you insert a card into a slot, you can copy files from it (or to it) using techniques described in Chapter 22.

Flash drives

A flash drive (or *thumb drive*) isn't a disk at all. It's more like a little gizmo you hang from a keychain, although you can also hide them in pens and pocket knives. Furthermore, you don't need any special kind of drive for this storage medium because it *is* a drive. You just plug it into a USB port on your computer. Figure 20.3 shows examples of flash drives.

> **TIP**
> A flash drive is basically a memory card with a USB plug connected to it.

Once the flash drive is plugged in, it looks and acts just like a disk drive to Windows. You can move or copy files to it and from it using any technique described in Chapter 21. Flash drives come in all shapes and sizes. To see examples, go to any online retailer that sells computer accessories (www.newegg.com, www.cdw.com, www.amazon.com, or wherever) and search for "thumb drive" or "flash drive."

FIGURE 20.3

Flash drives.

Viewing your computer's drives

Every disk drive in your computer is represented by an icon in your Computer folder. To open that folder, use whichever of the following techniques works for you:

- Click the Desktop icon on the Windows 8.1 interface and click the File Explorer button. On the left pane choose Computer.

- Click the File Explorer icon on the Windows 8.1 interface and click Computer on the left pane of File Explorer.

- Show the Charms Bar and choose Search. Type **computer** and choose the Computer option that displays.

- From the Windows desktop, click File Explorer and choose Computer from the left pane of File Explorer.

- Press Windows + X, click File Explorer, and choose This PC from the left pane of File Explorer.

Exactly what you see depends on what's available in your PC. Figure 20.4 shows an example of a PC with a single hard drive.

FIGURE 20.4

File Explorer open over a single drive.

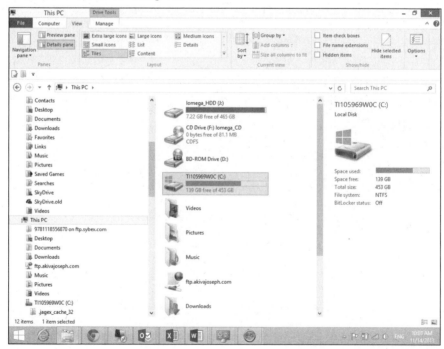

Don't expect your Computer folder to look like the one in Figure 20.4. All computers are different and have different drives, slots, and portable devices that can connect. But you should see at least two categories of drives.

NOTE

Your Computer folder is unique in that it contains an icon for each disk drive in your computer, as well as for devices that can store files. Most other folders contain subfolders and files.

The first category is Hard Disk Drives. Your computer will have at least one of these traditionally named C:. That's the drive where everything in your computer is stored. One hard drive is sufficient for most users.

Under Devices with Removable Storage, you'll see icons for other media. For computers that are older than five years old, you may have a floppy disk drive (A:). You probably have a CD or DVD drive. Its letter could be D: or something else. In the figure, the DVD drive is D:. The computer in that picture also has a removable disk connected to it (E:).

Another category you might see, Portable Devices, shows icons only for devices that are currently connected to your computer. If you don't have a camera or similar device connected when you open your Computer folder, you might not see a Portable Devices category. In the figure, a digital camera is connected to the computer and turned on, so it shows up under Portable Devices.

Finally, your Computer folder might also list other computers in your homegroup or local area network. This category is called Network Location. These devices are computers and shared drives that appear on networked computers.

You can leave your Computer folder open as you insert and remove disks. The names of icons that represent removable drives change to reflect the content of the disk that's currently in the drive. When you remove the disk, the name reverts to the generic name for the drive. That's a good thing to know if you're new to all this and don't know what the icons in your own computer represent on your system.

Sizes and capacities

Every disk is like a container in which you store things. There's a limit to how much data you can put on a disk. This is no different from any other container. For example, you can store water in a drinking glass, bucket, bathtub, or swimming pool. They're all containers for water. They just vary greatly in their *capacity* (how much water each can hold).

If you liken different computer media to water containers, a floppy disk or Zip disk is like a drinking glass. A CD is like a bucket, a DVD like a bathtub, and your hard disk like a swimming pool. Memory cards and flash drives vary in capacity, so it's tough to liken any one to a water container, but they're basically in the bucket-to-bathtub range.

With water, you measure things in ounces, liters, gallons, and such. In the computer world, the basic unit of measure is the *byte*. One byte equals roughly the amount of space required to store one character, like the letter *a*. For example, the word *cat* requires 3 bytes.

20

> **NOTE**
> The smallest unit of measure is the *bit* (binary digit), which can contain either 0 or 1. A byte is 8 bits.

Most disks can hold thousands, millions, billions, even trillions of bytes. Most often the capacities are rounded to the nearest thousand, million, or billion bytes. That's because disk storage is cheap and plentiful and there's no point in fussing over a few thousand bytes here or there. Also, computer folks don't even use the words *thousand, million,* or *billion.* They have shorter terms as follows:

- **Kilo:** Thousand
- **Mega:** Million
- **Giga:** Billion
- **Tera:** Trillion

That's all you really need to know about those terms. For those who like their numbers more exact, Table 20.1 shows the facts in detail.

TABLE 20.1   Buzzwords for Disk Capacities and File Sizes

Word	Abbreviation	Approximate Size (Number of Bytes)	Approximate (Word)	Actual Bytes
Kilo	K or KB	1,000	Thousand	2^{10} or 1,024
Mega	M or MB	1,000,000	Million	2^{20} or 1,048,576
Giga	G or GB	1,000,000,000	Billion	2^{30} or 1,073,741,824
Tera	T or TB	1,000,000,000,000	Trillion	2^{40} or 1,099,511,627,776
Peta	P or PB	1,000,000,000,000,000	Quadrillion	2^{50} or 1,125,899,906,842,624
Exa	E or EB	1,000,000,000,000,000,0000	Quintillion	2^{60} or 1,152,921,504,606,846,976

Let's return to our analogy of water containers. Here are approximate capacities of common disk types:

- **Floppy:** 1.44MB
- **CD:** 650–700MB
- **DVD:** 4.7GB
- **Flash drive:** 4GB or more
- **Hard disk:** 230GB or more

Note that hard disks are available in many different capacities from about 230GB to 2TB or more. (Some computer systems still come with smaller hard drives, as little as 120GB.) Zip disks, memory cards, flash drives, and portable devices also vary greatly in capacity. The hard disk reigns supreme in its ability to store large amounts of information.

How much room is there?

Everything you store on a disk takes up some space. So, once you start putting things on a disk, you have some used space and some free space. It's easy to see how much space you have on a disk.

When you open your Computer folder, each hard disk has a little meter beside it (in Tile view) that shows how much space is used (blue) and how much free space is still available for storing data (white). For example, in Figure 20.4, Removable Disk E: has 790MB of free space left. Its total capacity is 995MB (or about 1GB). Disk F:, on the other hand, has 2.28GB free of a total of 3.80GB.

> **TIP**
>
> If your Computer folder doesn't show the disk-size meters, click Views in its toolbar and choose Tiles. If yours aren't grouped, choose Group By and select the Type column heading.

To see how much space is left on a flash drive, memory card, or other device, first insert the disk or card. Right-click the icon for that drive and choose Properties. You see a dialog box like the example shown in Figure 20.5. There you can see how much space is used, how much is still available, and the total capacity of the disk or card.

If you see 0 bytes capacity, that means you right-clicked the icon for a drive or slot that's empty. An empty drive has no capacity because there's no disk in it. The drive or slot doesn't have a capacity. The disk or card in it has a capacity. No disk or card in a drive means no capacity (0 bytes).

If you check the capacity of a CD-ROM or DVD-ROM that's already been burned, you might see 0 bytes free, even if the used space doesn't match the total capacity of that drive. That's because optical media (CDs and DVDs) don't work quite like other types.

If you right-click the icon for a portable device, you might not see used space, free space, or capacity. Again, that's just because the properties sheet for a portable device tends to show information about the device as a whole, not just its storage. It's no big deal, however, because typically you copy files *from* portable devices, not to them. Also, you tend to use programs such as Photo Gallery and Windows Media Player to work with portable devices, not your Computer folder.

20

FIGURE 20.5

Used space, free space, and capacity.

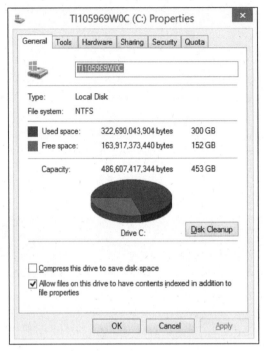

Viewing disk contents

Disks exist for one reason only — to store information. That information is stored in files, often organized into folders. To view the contents of a disk or memory card, insert it into its drive or slot and then open (double-click) its icon in your Computer folder. Make sure you insert the disk or card first because it makes no sense to open the icon for an empty drive.

For example, if there is no DVD in your DVD drive, it makes no sense to open that icon. There has to be a disk in the drive whose contents you want to view.

Like your hard disk, external disks store data in folders and files. Each folder and file on the disk is represented by an icon. Double-click a folder's icon to view its contents. Double-click a file's icon to open the file and see its contents. Use the Back button to back out of a folder to wherever you were before.

Formatting disks

Just about everyone has heard about *formatting* a disk. But not many people really understand what that's about. So, let's start with some basic rules of thumb:

- Not all disks need to be formatted. Only blank, unformatted disks and a few other types need to be formatted. But only once, not each time you use the disk.

- Never presume that you have to format a disk. If a disk needs to be formatted, you'll see a message telling you so and an option to format it right on the spot. If you don't see such a message, don't format the disk or even think about formatting the disk.

- Formatting a disk permanently erases the contents of that disk. Never format a disk unless you're 100 percent certain you'll never need anything on that disk again for the rest of your life.

Don't even *think* about formatting your computer's primary hard disk. You won't be able to anyway. But formatting your hard disk would erase Windows 8.1, all your installed programs, contacts, saved e-mails, and saved files — everything. You don't want to do that unless you really know what you're doing and you're certain that you can easily get back everything you lost in the process.

About Folders

Information stored on a disk is organized into files. For example, a photograph is stored as a file. A song is stored as a file. The files may be organized into *folders*. Folders on a disk play exactly the same role as *folders* in a filing cabinet — to organize things so they're easier to find when you need them.

If you're confused as to why folders exist at all, look at it this way: Suppose you went to your filing cabinet (the real one with paper in it) and dumped the contents of every single folder onto your desk. You end up with a big messy pile of paper on your desk. Finding anything in that pile would not be easy. That's why you put things into folders in filing cabinets in the first place — to make it easy to find things when you need them.

Disks can store millions of files. If every time you opened a disk's icon you were faced with millions of filenames, you'd have the same basic problem as the mountain of papers on your desk. You'd spend all your time looking through icons and filenames rather than getting stuff done.

20

In short, folders on disks exist for exactly the same reason manila file folders in filing cabinets exist — to organize information. When you're looking at a disk's contents, it's fairly easy to tell which icons represent folders:

- The icon for a folder usually looks like a manila file folder.
- Folders are usually listed first.

Figure 20.6 shows some examples of icons that represent folders.

FIGURE 20.6

Icons that represent folders.

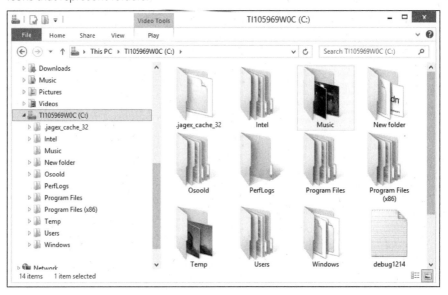

Viewing the contents of a folder

To open a folder and see what's inside, you just double-click the folder's icon. The name of the folder whose contents you're currently viewing always appears at the end of the file path near the top of the window. The contents of the folder appear in the main pane at the center of the window. Figure 20.7 shows an example where we're viewing the contents of a library named Music.

It might seem odd that the folder named Music contains icons for still more folders (in the case of Figure 20.7, the Music folder contains folders named Sample Music and Syriana). But that's the way it often works. Any folder can contain still more folders, files, or both. That's different from the way folders in a filing cabinet work, so let's take a look at that.

FIGURE 20.7

Viewing the contents of a folder.

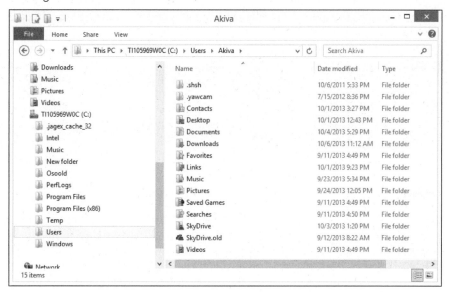

Folders within folders (subfolders)

In a filing cabinet, a folder usually contains documents, not other folders. But any computer folder can contain still more folders. We call the folders within a folder *subfolders*, but they're still just folders. For example, Figure 20.7 shows the contents of a folder named Music. All the folder icons that appear in the main pane are subfolders of that Music folder (but they're still just folders).

Subfolders allow you to organize information hierarchically so things are easier to find when you need them. For example, let's say you copy thousands of songs from your audio CDs into your Music folder with Windows Media Player or a music app. If you opened your Music folder and saw an icon for every single song, that could be a pain if you were looking for a specific song. You'd have to read through lots of filenames until you found the one you wanted.

To better organize things, Media Player organizes your songs by artist and album. So when you open your Music folder, you see a folder icon for each artist. When you open an artist's folder, you see an icon for each album by that artist. And when you open the folder for an album, you see all the songs by that artist.

So, once again, the important thing to remember about folders and subfolders is that they're really just a means of organizing files into groups — the same as folders in a filing cabinet. Of course, you need to know how to *navigate* through folders for any of this to be useful, because all your files are stored in folders.

20

Parent folders

The folder in which a subfolder is contained is called the *parent* to that folder. For example, if you open File Explorer and then click the Documents folder, the main document folder for your user account opens. That folder you opened is the parent to all the subfolders you see in the main pane.

TIP

When you're navigating through folders, it's easy to get to the current folder's parent. Just click its name in the Address bar. That name is the second-to-last one in the breadcrumb trail. (See "File Explorer components," later in this chapter, for more on the breadcrumb trail.)

About Files

Every file has a filename and an icon. A file can be just about anything — a photograph, a song, a video clip, a typed report, a spreadsheet, a contact, whatever. In the preceding section, we likened a computer folder to a manila file folder in a filing cabinet. If we use the same analogy here, a file is roughly equivalent to one thing you'd put inside a manila file folder. In fact, that's the whole idea. You organize your computer files into folders just as you organize your paper files into manila file folders.

In the preceding section, you also saw how the icon that represents a folder often looks like a manila file folder. Icons that represent files don't have a manila file folder in their icon because that would just confuse things. Icons that represent files tend to look more like little dog-eared sheets of paper. On top of that sheet of paper, you might see the logo of the program that opens or plays the file. More on that topic in a moment.

Figure 20.8 shows examples of some icons that represent files. But you have to bear in mind that there are thousands of different kinds of files and thousands of different programs. So, don't expect to find those exact examples anywhere on your system. The key is that the icons for files don't look like manila file folders.

Pictures and videos are also files. But their icons don't always sport the dog-eared sheet of paper look. Instead, their icons usually look like the actual picture that's in the file, or a frame from the video in the file. Windows 8.1 shows them that way so that you don't have to open the file to see what picture it contains (see Figure 20.9).

FIGURE 20.8

Sample icons that represent files.

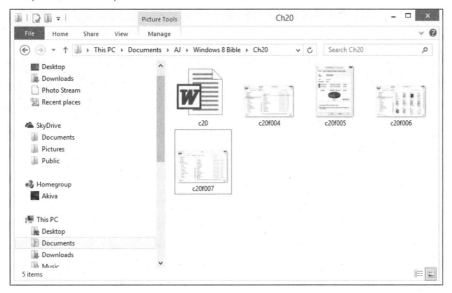

FIGURE 20.9

Sample icons for pictures.

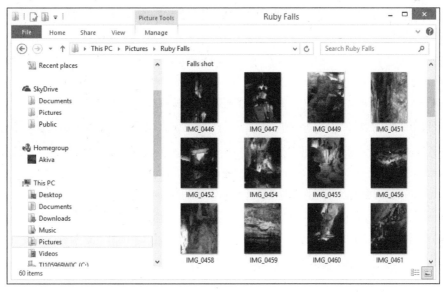

Opening and closing files

To see, change, or print what's in a file, you *open* that file. You do that in the same way that you open a folder or the icon that represents a disk drive: by double-clicking the file's icon.

TIP

You might be able to open a drive, folder, or file by single-clicking its icon. It all depends on a setting in the Folder Options dialog box, described later in this chapter.

Document files never open by themselves. A file has to open within some program. There are thousands of different kinds of files and thousands of different programs so we can't tell you offhand what program that will be. But if you can open the file at all, it will open and appear within a program.

Showing/hiding filename extensions

Windows uses a file's *extension* to determine what program to use to open a file. The extension is a short abbreviation, preceded by a period, at the end of the filename, as in the example shown in Figure 20.10.

If you want to see the filename extension for a single file, right-click the file's icon and choose Properties. In the Properties dialog box that opens, you'll see the file's type (in words) followed by the extension in parentheses. For example, if you right-click the icon for a video file, you might see something like the following (the .wmv in parentheses is the filename extension that's hidden in Explorer's main contents pane):

```
Type of file: WMV File (.wmv)
```

To see filename extensions for all files in Explorer, select the View tab in File Explorer and choose Options. In the dialog box that opens, select the View tab and clear the check mark next to Hide Extensions for Known File Types. Then click OK.

NOTE

Folders typically don't have extensions on their names, so you'll seldom see an extension in either its properties sheet or Explorer.

If you opt to make filename extensions visible in Explorer, you have to be careful not to change the extension when renaming a file. Changing a file's extension doesn't change the file's type. It just assigns the wrong type to the file, which could make it impossible to open the file. You'll need to rename the file back to its original extension before you can open the file again.

FIGURE 20.10

Filename and extension.

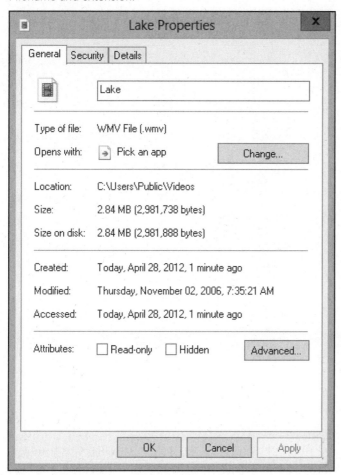

Choosing a program or app to open a file

The program or app that opens automatically when you open a file icon is called the *default program* for that file type. But you're not stuck with that. If you have two or more programs capable of opening a file type, you can right-click the file's icon, choose Open With, and then click the name of the program you want to open the file with (see Figure 20.11). The file will open in the specified program this one time.

FIGURE 20.11

Choosing Open With.

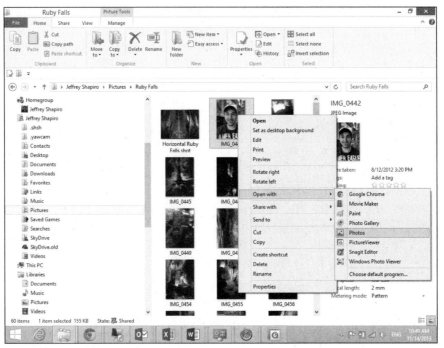

Changing the default program or app

If you want to permanently change the default program or app that opens when you open a particular type of file, right-click the file's icon and choose Open With as just described. But don't click a program name. Instead, click Choose Default Program. A list appears like the one shown in Figure 20.12. This shows programs and apps that Windows 8.1 recognizes that will support the file type you want to open. The programs and apps that appear in your dialog box depend on the type of file you right-clicked and the programs or apps installed on your computer.

FIGURE 20.12

The Open With list.

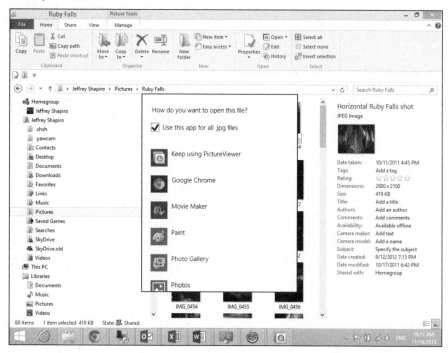

You can click any program or app name to make it the default for opening files of the same type as the one you right-clicked. If the program or app you want to use doesn't show in the Open With list, you can use the More Options link at the bottom of the list to see additional programs Windows 8.1 finds on your computer.

Windows 8.1 also includes the following links to help you find a program or app to open your selected file:

- Look for an App in the Store connects you to the Windows Store online where you can search for an app that supports your selected file type.

- Look for an App on This PC displays the Open With dialog box, which you can use to navigate your computer to locate a program that will open the selected file type.

When choosing a program or app to open the file, make sure you choose a program that *can* open that file type. Otherwise, you'll end up with an error message or gobbledygook when the file tries to open in that program.

To make the change permanent, select (check) the Use This App for All < *file type* > Files check box. By default, Windows 8.1 selects this option.

Upon selection of the program, Windows opens the program or app you specified with the selected file open. If you chose a program or app that cannot open that file type, you'll end up with an error message or a bunch of meaningless gobbledygook. If that happens, you need to get back to the Open With list and choose a recommended program or app, or any program or app that you know for sure can handle that type of file.

Windows cannot open this file

It's possible that Windows won't be able to open a file at all. For example, suppose someone sends you an Adobe Photoshop file (.psd) attached to an e-mail message. If you don't have Adobe Photoshop installed on your computer, Windows won't be able to open the file. Instead, it will display the Open With list, as in the example in Figure 20.13.

FIGURE 20.13

When Windows can't open a file.

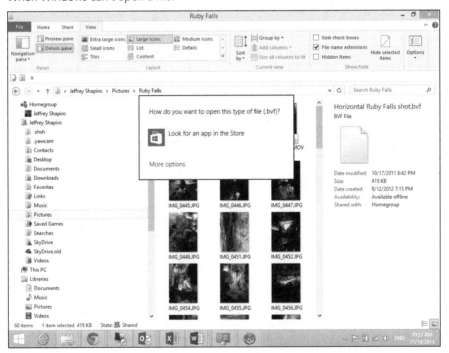

If you're new to all of this, there's no easy way to guess what program might work to open the file. As we said, there are thousands of file types and thousands of programs out there. Your best bet might be to ask the person who sent you the file what program you need to open the file. Or ask the sender to send you the file in some other format that you can open.

File paths

Every file on your system is in a specific location defined as the *path* to the file. The *path* starts with the drive letter (for example, C: for your primary hard disk), then the folder in which the file is stored, and then all the higher-level folders leading up to that folder. Each part of the path is separated by a backslash (\).

For example, let's say you're in your user account (Tech_Sup) and you save a file named MyMovie.wmv to your Videos folder. The path to that folder would be:

    C:\Users\Tech_Sup\Videos\MyMovie.wmv

Figure 20.14 shows why this is so. Your hard disk has, at its highest level, at least three folders. One is named Program Files, and it contains subfolders and files for all the programs that are installed on your system. A second folder named Users contains a subfolder for each user account. A third folder, named Windows, contains all the folders and files that make up the Windows 8.1 operating system.

FIGURE 20.14

C:\Users\Akiva\Videos.

CAUTION

The Program Files and Windows folders contain files used by the system. Your best bet is to stay out of those folders. Never save your own files to those folders. Whatever you do, never delete, move, or rename a file in any of those folders. Doing so could render your computer useless until a professional can figure out how to fix your mistake!

Each user account folder in the Users folder contains the built-in folders people can use to store their documents. These include the Music, Pictures, and Videos folders, among others.

The path `C:\Users\Tech_Sup\Videos\MyMovie.wmv` tells Windows exactly how to get to the file. It has to start by going to the hard drive (`C:`), drilling down through the folders named Users and Tech_Sup until it gets to the folder named Videos. There it will find the file named `MyMovie.wmv`. Figure 20.14 shows the basic idea, using a few sample folders from the folder hierarchy.

It isn't often that you need to know or type the path to a file. We mention it only because you'll see paths like that from time to time. The program you'll use to navigate through folders, File Explorer, makes it very easy for you to get around without worrying about paths.

TIP

If you ever need to see the actual path to the folder you're currently viewing, there's an easy way to do it. Just click the folder icon at the left side of the Address bar. The breadcrumb trail in the Address bar changes to the actual path of the folder. The path is also selected so you can press Ctrl+C to copy it to the Clipboard and paste wherever appropriate.

Using File Explorer

Knowing about drives, folders, and files is certainly important. In fact, you really can't do much with a computer until you've mastered those concepts. To review:

- All computer information is stored on some medium, usually disks.
- All the stuff that's in your computer right now is stored on a hard disk that you never see or remove from the computer.
- Information is stored in files.
- Files are organized into folders just like files in a filing cabinet are organized into folders.

Once you understand the concepts, the next step is to learn how to use the tool that gives you access to drives, folders, and files. That tool is a program named *File Explorer* (or just *Explorer* for short).

File Explorer is the main program for getting around your computer to access all the disks, folders, and files available to you. Notice that we didn't say Internet Explorer. Despite the name similarity, the two programs serve two entirely different purposes:

- **File Explorer (or Explorer):** Enables you to explore and access stuff that's *inside* your computer or on your local area network (LAN)
- **Internet Explorer:** Enables you to explore and access stuff that's *outside* your computer on the Internet

That's a huge difference. For one thing, you have to be online (connected to the Internet) to use Internet Explorer to access resources currently online because the Internet exists outside your personal computer. You don't have to be online to use File Explorer because all the stuff you're exploring is inside your computer.

There's also a big size difference. The Internet consists of billions of computers all over the world. A lifetime isn't nearly enough time to explore the entire Internet. Your own computer is just one computer. It doesn't take anywhere near a lifetime to explore your own computer! But you do have to invest some time in learning how to use Explorer if you want to be able to use everything your computer has to offer.

Opening File Explorer

You start most programs on your computer by going through the Windows 8.1 interface or from pinned items on the taskbar of the desktop. You *can* start File Explorer that way if you want to. Show the Charms Bar, choose Start, navigate to and click File Explorer. You also can show the desktop and click the File Explorer icon on the Windows taskbar. Finally, you can press Windows + X and click File Explorer.

File Explorer components

File Explorer has many optional panes and other gizmos. Figure 20.15 points out the names of the main ones. Some may not be visible when you first open a folder, but they're easy to show or hide, so don't worry about that.

20

FIGURE 20.15

Explorer panes and tools showing tooltip.

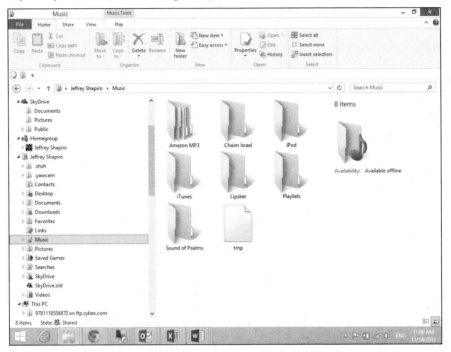

Here's a quick overview of the main components:

- **Quick Access toolbar:** Provides commonly used tools while you're in File Explorer. For example, the Properties button and New Folder buttons are available on the Quick Access toolbar by default. You can add other tools, including Undo, Redo, Delete, and Rename by clicking the down arrow to the right of the New Folder button.

- **Title bar:** Use this to move the whole window. Use the Minimize, Maximize, and Close buttons to size the window as you would in any other program.

- **Ribbon bar:** Displays the File Explorer ribbon bar. The ribbon bar includes tabs that provide quick access to toolbar options you can perform with files and folders. Buttons in the toolbar enable you to do things with files and folders in the contents pane. Ribbon bars change depending on the types of icons you select in the folder.

- **Address bar:** Displays a *breadcrumb trail* (also called an eyebrow menu) of drives and folders leading up to the folder you're viewing. The name of the folder you're currently viewing appears at the end.

- **Search box:** Enables you to search by name for an item within the current folder.

- **Search pane:** Enables you to conduct a more thorough and exact search than the Search box. This topic is covered in Chapter 22.
- **Navigation pane:** Makes it easy to get to any drive or folder in your computer.
- **Contents:** The contents of the folder you're currently viewing.
- **Preview pane:** When you select an icon, this pane provides a sneak peek into the file's contents, when possible. Otherwise it just shows an enlarged version of the icon.
- **Details pane:** Shows some detailed information about the icon(s) currently selected in the contents pane.

Show or hide ribbon bar

New to Windows 8.1 is the ribbon bar on File Explorer. To show or hide the ribbon bar, click the Minimize the Ribbon or Expand the Ribbon arrow on the top right of the File Explorer window. It appears directly below the Close button (X) and to the left of the Help question mark (?). To quickly show or hide the ribbon bar, press Ctrl + F1 on the keyboard. Figure 20.16 shows a tooltip displayed when you hover over the ribbon bar on/off arrow.

FIGURE 20.16

Show or hide the ribbon bar.

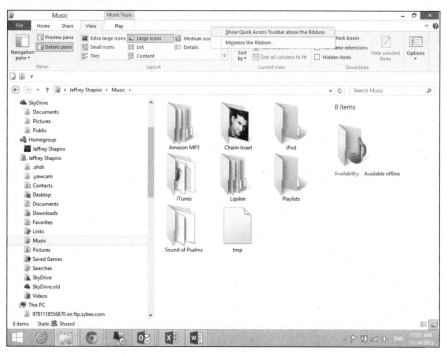

Navigating with the Address bar

No matter how you open File Explorer, it's easy to get just about anywhere from the Address bar. Don't assume that only the names in the Address bar matter. You can click the left or right triangle symbols (if any) or any triangle between names to see nearby places to which you can navigate just by clicking the item's name.

If you see the name of the folder you want to open, click that name. Otherwise, click the triangle to the left of any name to see its subfolders, as in Figure 20.17, and then click the folder you want to open. Or click the up arrow at the left side of the trail to get to higher-level places. Or click the Previous Locations button (the down triangle at the right side of the Address bar) or the Recent Pages button (the triangle to the right of the Forward button) to return to any recently visited folder.

> **NOTE**
>
> The button with the two curvy arrows is a Refresh button. That one doesn't take you to a different location. It just ensures that the contents of the folder you're currently viewing are up to date.

FIGURE 20.17

Show or hide Explorer components.

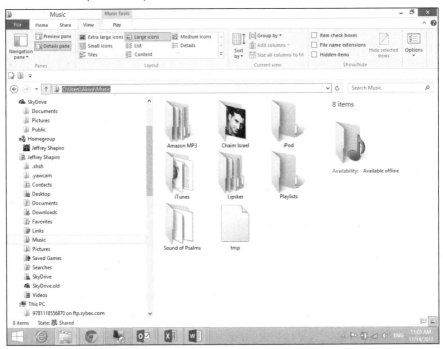

You can also type the name of the folder that you want to navigate to right into the Address bar. But that works only with certain built-in folders. First, click the icon that appears at the left side of the Address bar. Then, type the first few letters of the place you want to go. A drop-down menu will display matching locations as you type. When you see the name of the folder to which you want to navigate, click that name. Or type the entire name and press Enter.

> **TIP**
>
> You can type the URL (address) of an Internet location into the Address bar. When you press Enter, Internet Explorer will open to show the page at that URL. To return to File Explorer, close Internet Explorer or click the taskbar button on the folder you were in.

Of course, you can also use the Back and Forward buttons to the left of the Address bar to navigate. At first, both buttons may be disabled (dimmed) because there's no place to go back or forward to. But when you go from one folder to another, the Back button is enabled, so you can click that to return to the place you just left. After you click the Back button, the Forward button is enabled. Click the Forward button to return to the folder you just backed out of.

Navigating with the Navigation pane

You can get anywhere from the Address bar. But at times, you may find it more convenient to use the Navigation pane. When open, the Navigation pane offers two ways to get around:

- You can use the Favorites group at the top of the pane, which shows links for commonly used folders, or any locations you want. Click any link to open it in the current window.

- You can right-click a link and choose Open In New Window to open it in a new window. This is handy when you want to move or copy files to the new location by dragging.

> **TIP**
>
> Choosing Open Folder Location opens a folder's parent folder. For example, right-clicking the Downloads folder in the Favorites box and choosing Open Folder Location opens your user folder (where Contacts, Favorites, Documents, and other folders are located, along with Downloads).

In the middle of the Navigation pane is the Libraries group, which gives you quick access to your user libraries. By default, these include Documents, Music, Pictures, and Video.

Below this group is the Homegroup group, which shows shared files, printers, devices, and other resources available on your home network. If you don't have any homegroups established, see Chapter 39 for more information on setting up home networks.

Below this group in the Navigation pane, you'll find the Computer group, which includes items for your local and removable disks. You can expand each of these to access the

20

folders they contain. Under the Computer group is the Network group, which gives you quick access to devices and shared resources on your local network.

To widen or narrow the Navigation pane, get the tip of the mouse pointer on its right border so the mouse pointer turns to a two-headed arrow. Then drag left or right.

You can expand and collapse libraries, drives, and folders in the Folders list to see more, or fewer, details. Click the white triangle next to any name to expand. Click the black triangle next to any name to collapse. Figure 20.18 shows where all these things are located.

FIGURE 20.18

Working with the Navigation pane.

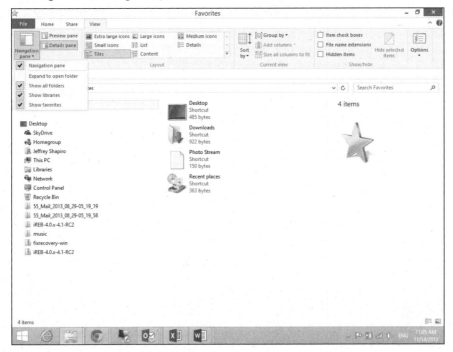

When you click a folder name or drive in the Navigation pane, it opens in the current window. If you want to open the folder or drive in a separate window, right-click and choose Open in New Window.

Adding places to Favorites

The Favorites group can provide easy one-click access to any drive or folder on your system. Initially, you'll see a few shortcuts in it. But you can replace those with any you like. Just drag the icon for any item to which you want easy access into the Favorites group. Figure 20.19 shows an example where we're in the process of dragging the Contacts icon from the user account folder into the Favorite Links pane. Release the mouse button to create the link.

Managing favorites

Managing favorites is easy, too. Here are the basics of managing shortcuts in your Favorites:

- To rename a shortcut, right-click the shortcut, choose Rename, type the new name or edit the existing name, and press Enter.

- To alphabetize shortcuts, right-click Favorites and choose Sort by Name.

- To remove a shortcut you don't use, right-click it and choose Remove. Then choose Yes when asked for confirmation.

FIGURE 20.19

Create your own favorite link.

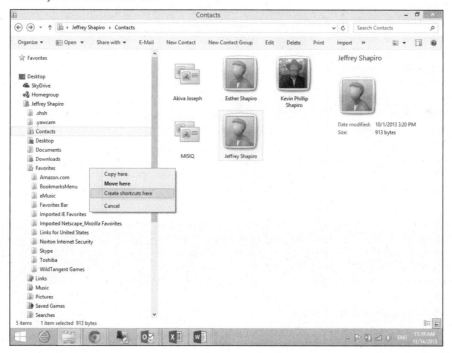

> **NOTE**
>
> Removing a favorite does not delete the associated folder. So, don't worry about losing anything when you right-click and choose Remove.

Navigating from the contents pane

The main contents pane at the center of Explorer's program window shows you the contents of whatever folder you're viewing at the moment. If the folder you've opened contains subfolders, you can open a subfolder by double-clicking its icon, or by single-clicking, if you've configured Folder Options for single clicking. After you've opened a subfolder, you can click the Back button to return to the parent folder.

If you want to open a subfolder in a separate window, right-click the folder's icon and choose Open in New Window. You can size and position the two open folder windows so you can see the contents of both. Then you can move files from one folder to the other just by dragging their icons.

Regardless of how you navigate, you can get to any folder on any drive on your system. Some people want to use buttons in the Address bar. Others want to use the more traditional Folders list in the Navigation pane. It doesn't matter which you use or how you get to the folder you need. All that matters is that you're able to get there when you need to go.

Navigating to a disk drive

You can open any disk drive right from the Navigation pane. If you see a white triangle next to This PC in the Folders list, click the triangle to see all your available drives. Click the name of the drive you want to open. Or right-click the drive and choose Open in New Window to open it in a new window. If the drive name shows a white triangle in the Folders list, you can click that triangle to see folders and files on the disk in the drive without opening the drive.

> **TIP**
>
> Here are a couple tricks you can use with USB drives in the Folders list: Right-click and choose Open as Portable Device to see how much space is available. Right-click and choose Eject to close the drive before pulling it from the USB slot.

Choosing an icon view

Once you've opened a folder, you can view its contents in several different ways. As usual, there's no right or wrong way, or good or bad way. There are just different ways, and you should use whichever one is most convenient at the moment. To choose how you want to view icons, select the View tab on the File Explorer ribbon bar to see the Layout options shown in Figure 20.20.

FIGURE 20.20

Choosing a view.

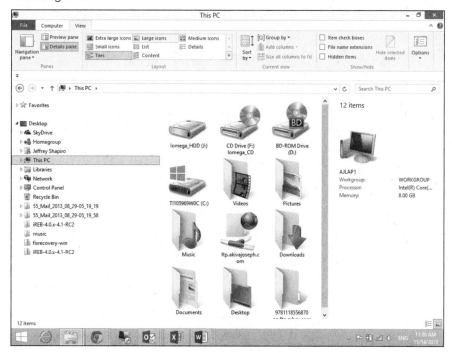

To choose how you want to view icons, hover over any option in the Layout box on the View tab. As you move from one view to the next, such as Extra Large Icons to Details, views of your folders and files change to match the layout.

Most of the options show each item as an icon and filename. The Tiles view shows the type and size of each file. For folders, it just shows File Folder.

Using columns in the Details view

The Details view of a folder shows icons for folders and files in a tabular view like the example in Figure 20.21. You can use this view to show a lot of information about each folder and file. The column headings you see across the top of the display (Name, Date Modified, Type, and so forth) don't tell the whole story. You can choose columns to view as you see fit. Just right-click any column heading to reveal more column names, as in Figure 20.22.

20

FIGURE 20.21

Showing drive contents in Details view.

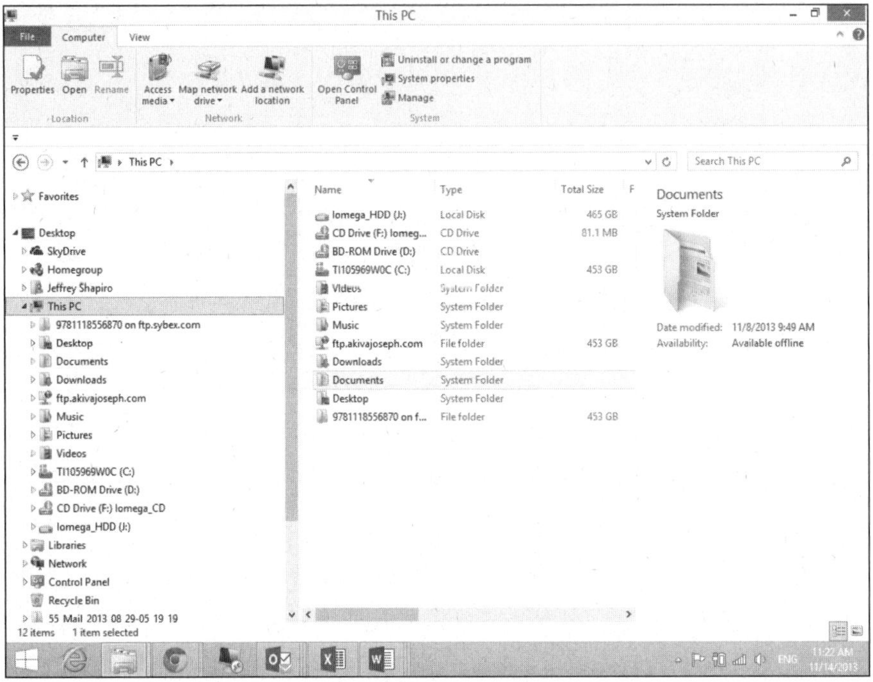

What about E-mail Messages?

Computer files are like files in your filing cabinet. There's a basic assumption that you intend to keep them forever. E-mail messages aren't files, per se. They're *messages,* and they have roughly the same status as messages left on your telephone answering machine. There is a basic assumption that you don't intend to keep them. As such, messages are usually stored in folders that exist only in your *e-mail client* (the program you use to send and receive e-mail).

Attachments to e-mail messages are files. But they don't automatically go into the kinds of folders we're discussing in this chapter. An attachment stays in your e-mail client unless you specifically save the attachment to a regular folder such as Pictures or Documents. Exactly how you save an attachment depends on your e-mail client, but typically you right-click the attachment's icon and choose Save or Save As.

If you happen to use Windows Mail as your e-mail client, your messages *are* actually stored in folders on your computer's hard disk. Each message in Windows Mail is stored as an .eml file in a hidden folder under your main user folder.

FIGURE 20.22

Right-click any column heading.

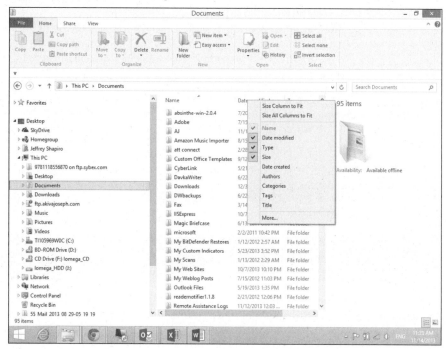

To add a column to the display, click its name on the menu. To remove a column, click its name on the menu to clear its check mark. To see other columns to display, click More at the bottom of the menu. Then select (check) the columns you want to see. Clear the check marks of columns you don't want to see. Then click OK.

If you choose more columns than can fit within the window, you'll see a horizontal scroll bar at the bottom of the contents pane. Use that to scroll left and right through the columns you've selected.

To size a column, put the tip of the mouse pointer on the right border of the column heading so the mouse pointer turns into a two-headed arrow. Then drag left or right. To move a column left or right, put the tip of the mouse pointer right on the column name, and then drag left or right.

TIP

The techniques for moving and sizing columns aren't unique to the Details view. They work in just about any tabular view in any program.

20

Sorting icons

The View tab lets you choose different ways of viewing icons. The column headings under the toolbar enable you to choose different ways of *arranging* the icons in a folder. Those column headings aren't only visible in the Details view. They're visible in all views. It might seem weird to have column headings showing when the icons aren't arranged into columns. But they're there for a good reason — you can click any one of them to sort and alphabetize icons on an as-needed basis.

To sort icons, you just click the column heading that you want to sort by. The first click usually puts the headings in ascending order (A to Z, smallest to largest, or oldest to newest). When icons are sorted into ascending order, the column heading shows an up triangle.

For example, when you click the Name column heading and see an up triangle in that column heading, you know the icons are in ascending alphanumeric order. Folders are typically listed before files. So, the folders will be listed first in alphanumeric order, followed by files in alphanumeric order.

TIP

Alphanumeric order sorts by letters and numbers, not just letters (as with alphabetical order).

When you click the Date Modified column heading, you sort icons by the date they were last modified. The first click puts them in *ascending order* (newest to oldest). The second click puts them in *descending order* (oldest to newest).

You can sort icons by any column heading, in any view. Click the Choose Columns item from the Sort By drop-down menu to sort by some other column. If the column on which you want to base the sort isn't available, you can add that column heading as described in the previous section.

Filtering a folder

When you point to a column heading in Details view, a triangle appears to the right of the column name. Clicking that triangle displays options for filtering icons in the folder. These options work best in folders or search results that contain lots of icons. The exact options you see vary from one column heading to the next because different columns offer different ways of arranging things. Depending on the age of the files you are viewing, Figure 20.23 shows options that can appear when you click the arrow next to Date Modified.

FIGURE 20.23

Click the arrow next to Date Modified.

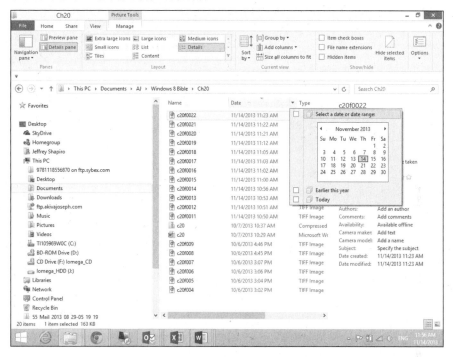

Depending on the selection you make in a column's header, you can end up with a filtered view of the folder's contents. For example, if you click the arrow beside Name and place a check in the A–H box, you see only folders or files whose names begin with any letter from *A* through *H*. The column header then shows a check mark at the right edge of the column to indicate that a filter is applied. Click the check mark and clear the check box for any selection to clear the filter view and show all items. The following section offers more detail.

TIP

To select only files of a certain type in a folder, group by the Type column. Then click the heading of the group whose icons you want to select.

Filtering is a means of temporarily hiding things when they're just in the way. For example, let's say you're viewing a folder that contains dozens, or even hundreds, of icons. You want to focus on just the files and folders you modified today or yesterday. You don't want to delete the other icons. You just want to put them into hiding temporarily so you can focus on the more recently edited icons.

20

To view just the icons of files you modified today, you would select (check) the Today check box shown previously in Figure 20.23. Then click outside the menu. Icons for files that were modified today remain visible while all other icons disappear. The Date Modified column heading shows a check mark to serve as a visual reminder that you're not viewing all icons — only icons that meet certain Date Modified criteria, as in Figure 20.24.

FIGURE 20.24

The check mark next to Date Modified tells you some icons are hidden.

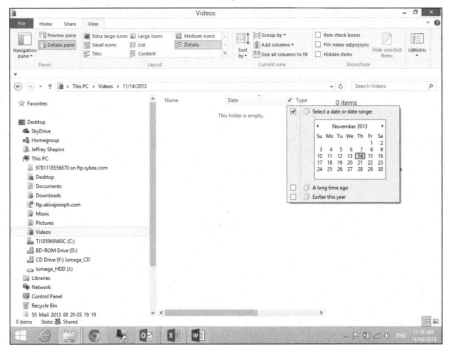

The Search box in the upper-right corner of a folder also plays a filtering role (see Figure 20.25). As you type in the Search box, only files from the current folder and its sub-folders that match those characters remain visible. Icons that don't match what you've typed are temporarily hidden from view. This makes it easy to quickly locate icons in a large folder based on their names. When you search from the Search box, the Address bar shows the words "Search Results" rather than the folder name. To undo the search and bring all icons from the folder back into view, click the X button beside the Search box.

Chapters 21 and 22 discuss searching in detail.

FIGURE 20.25

Filter a view with the Search box.

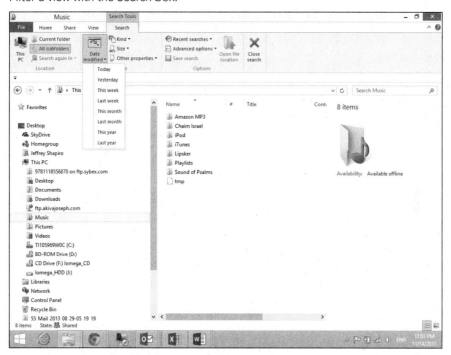

Using the Preview pane

The optional Preview pane at the right side of Explorer tries to show the contents of whatever icon is selected in Explorer. If no icon is selected, the Preview pane shows only the words "Select a file to preview." If the Preview pane isn't open, select the View tab and choose Preview Pane in the Panes area (at the far left).

The window has to be wide enough to accommodate the contents of the pane and whatever else is showing. If the window is too narrow, the Preview pane disappears. You have to widen the window or close the Navigation pane to make room for the Preview pane.

See Chapter 21 for the many different ways you can select icons.

What shows in the Preview pane depends on the type of icon you select, as follows:

- If you select a picture's icon, the pane shows that picture.
- If you select a music or video file, the pane shows options for playing that file.

20

- If you select an icon whose contents can be read directly by Windows 8.1, you see a portion of the file's contents in the pane.

- If you select a folder icon or any file that can't be previewed, the pane just shows No Preview Available.

As with any pane, you can widen and narrow the Preview pane by dragging its inner border. Just make sure you get the tip of the mouse pointer right on the bar, so you see the two-headed arrow before you hold down the left mouse button and start dragging. The wider you make the Preview pane, the larger the preview image.

Figure 20.26 shows an example of a video file icon selected in a folder. Note the two-headed mouse pointer you need to see in order to widen or narrow the pane.

FIGURE 20.26

The Preview pane, a selected icon, and the sizing mouse pointer.

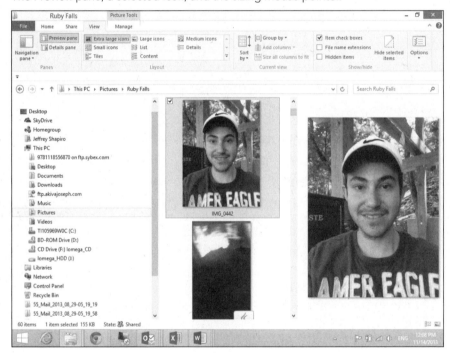

Using the Details pane

The optional Details pane at the right of Explorer's window also shows information about the currently selected icon(s). To show or hide that pane, click Details Pane on the View toolbar. The icon(s) you select and how tall you make the pane determine how much information is displayed. Drag the left border of the pane to make it shorter or taller.

In Figure 20.27, we've selected three icons that represent files containing pictures. Depending on the type of file(s) selected, you might be able to change the Authors, Tags, Comments, Categories, Status, Content Type, or Subject of the selected items right in the Details pane. That information becomes *metadata* used by the search index to quickly find and arrange icons in a way that transcends their physical locations in folders. Chapter 23 describes metadata and searching in detail.

FIGURE 20.27

The Details pane and three icons selected.

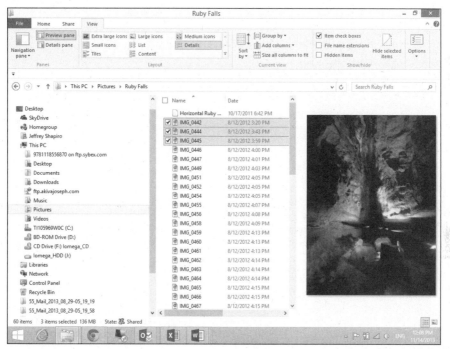

To Click or Double-Click?

As mentioned throughout this book, you may have to double-click icons to open them. Or you may have to click only once on an icon to open it. Whether you have to double-click or single-click is entirely up to you. The default is usually to double-click because that method allows you to select icons by clicking, which is easier for people who haven't fully mastered the mouse.

20

You use the Folder Options dialog box to choose between the double-click and single-click methods. Here's how:

1. Open any folder so you're in File Explorer.
2. Click the Options button on the View tab. The Folder Options dialog box opens, as in Figure 20.28.

FIGURE 20.28

The General tab of Folder Options.

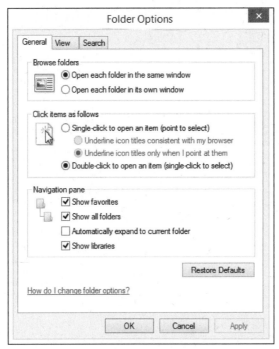

3. Under Click Items as Follows, choose how you want to handle icons:
   - **Single-Click to Open an Item (Point to Select):** Choose this option if you want to be able to open icons by clicking once. If you choose this option, also choose one of the following:
     - **Underline Icon Titles Consistent with My Browser:** Choosing this option will usually make all icon names look like hyperlinks (blue and underlined).
     - **Underline Icon Titles Only When I Point At Them:** Choosing this option leaves icon names alone so they look normal. The name only looks like a hyperlink when you touch it with your mouse pointer.

- **Double-Click to Open an Item (Single-Click to Select):** This is the more classical approach where you have to double-click icons to open them. If you're new to computers or have difficulty using a mouse, this might be your best bet.

4. Click OK.

TIP

Here are a couple of other ways to get to Folder Options: Show the Charms Bar, choose Search, type **fol**, click Settings, and click Folder Options in the search results area. You also can open the Control Panel and choose Appearance And Personalization and then click Folder Options.

Personalizing folder behavior

The Folder Options dialog box offers many options in addition to double-click and single-click preferences. On the General tab, you can choose from the following options:

- **Open Each Folder in the Same Window:** This is the default behavior; each time you open a folder, the current instance of Explorer shows the contents of that folder.

- **Open Each Folder in Its Own Window:** Choosing this option causes each folder to open in a separate instance of Explorer so you end up with an instance of Explorer for each open folder.

- **Show Favorites:** This option turns on or off the Favorites folder in the File Explorer Navigation pane. By default, it's turned on.

- **Show All Folders:** This option in the Navigation pane group, when enabled, causes File Explorer to show additional icons in the Navigation pane, such as Control Panel and the Recycle Bin.

- **Automatically Expand to Current Folder:** This option, if enabled, causes File Explorer to automatically expand the Navigation pane to show the currently opened folder.

When two or more folders are open, you can right-click the clock and choose the options Cascade Windows, Show Windows Stacked, or Show Windows Side by Side to arrange them in different ways on the desktop. Use taskbar buttons or Alt + Tab to switch among them.

By default, the taskbar buttons for folder windows will collapse into a single taskbar File Explorer button. You can close them all in one fell swoop by right-clicking that taskbar button and choosing Close All Windows. You can also hover the mouse over the icon to see a preview of all windows in the group.

Options on the View tab

Selecting the View tab in the Folder Options dialog box takes you to a whole bunch of options for controlling folder behavior (see Figure 20.29). Most of the options are self-explanatory. If you open a folder that shows icons for pictures and a Navigation pane, you'll be able to try out many on the fly. Just fill or clear a check box and click Apply to see how it affects that open folder.

20

FIGURE 20.29

The View tab of Folder Options.

> **CAUTION**
>
> The settings you choose in Folder Options apply to all folders, not just the folder you have open at the moment. The one oddball exception is the first one on the tab. See "Personalizing your folder" later in this chapter for ways to customize a single folder.

Some options aren't quite so obvious. In the interest of being complete, we'll run through them all in the following list:

- **Always Show Icons, Never Thumbnails:** If you choose this option, icons for pictures and videos will be generic icons rather than mini-pictures of the file's contents. It might help speed things along on an extremely slow computer. But to see the picture in a file, you'll need to open that picture. You won't be able to see the picture in Explorer.

- **Always Show Menus:** Choose this option if you want the classic menu bar to open automatically with Explorer. If you don't choose this option, the menu bar is hidden when you first open Explorer.

- **Display File Icon on Thumbnails:** If you choose this option, thumbnails will show the logo of the default program for opening the file. If you clear the option, thumbnails show without the logo.

- **Display File Size Information in Folder Tips:** This option is about the size of files and folders in terms of how much disk space they use, not the visual size of the icon on the screen. When you choose this option, you're telling Explorer to show a folder's size when you point to (rest the mouse pointer on) a folder's icon. That size is the sum of the sizes of all the files in the folder. For example, all the songs in the Music folder shown in Figure 20.30 are taking up 84.2MB of disk space. You can see that in the tooltip that appears under the mouse pointer.

If you clear this option, the tooltip shows only the Date Created for the folder.

FIGURE 20.30

Size of folder (84.2MB) in the folder's tooltip.

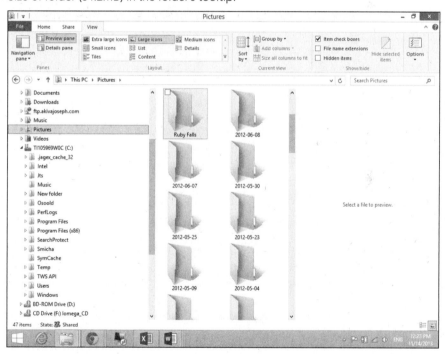

- **Display the Full Path in the Title Bar:** The title bar normally displays only the name of the folder you're currently viewing, such as `Music`. If you choose this option, the title bar shows the complete path to the file, such as `C:\Users\YourUserAccountName\My Music`.

- **Show Hidden Files and Folders:** Hidden files are those that have the Hidden attribute checked on the properties sheet. If you choose Don't Show Hidden Files, Folders, and Drives, then files and folders that have the Hidden attribute checked won't appear at all in Explorer. If you choose Show Hidden Files, Folders, and Drives, you'll see those folders and files. But their icons are dimmed to distinguish them from items that aren't marked as hidden.

> **TIP**
>
> To get to the properties sheet for a file or folder, right-click its icon and choose Properties.

- **Hide Empty Drives:** Choose this option to have Windows 8.1 hide drives that don't contain media. For example, if the CD drive is empty, that drive will not appear under the This PC branch of the File Explorer Navigation pane.

- **Hide Extensions for Known File Types:** As mentioned earlier in this chapter, most files have a filename extension that indicates the file type. That extension also determines which program will open when you open the file. A *known file* is one for which you already have a default program installed and defined.

  Choosing Hide Extensions for Known File Types hides filename extensions for known file types so you see only the filename without the extension for those kinds of files. Clearing that option displays filename extensions for all files.

  As always, choosing one option or the other is strictly a matter of personal preference. Sometimes it's convenient to see filename extensions. Other times they might just seem to be adding unnecessary clutter. Of course, it only takes a few mouse clicks to turn them on or off, so you can easily change from one setting to the other just as conveniently.

  There's a slight security risk to hiding filename extensions. Malware files delivered by e-mail sometimes have a dot in the filename, as in `MyDocument.txt.exe`. If filename extensions are hidden, you see only `MyDocument.txt` because the extension is the part that comes after the last dot in the name. Text (`.txt`) files are harmless, so you might open the file. Executable (`.exe`) files can contain malware. Of course, millions of `.exe` files are perfectly safe, but one where someone is trying to hide the `.exe` extension is certainly suspicious, and probably not safe. Then again, opening e-mail attachments from people you don't know, in general, isn't safe either!

- **Hide Protected Operating System Files (Recommended):** Protected operating system files are files that Windows 8.1 needs to do its job. These files are for the computer's use. Choosing this option keeps those files hidden so you don't see their icons. This is the recommended choice based on the "out of sight, out of mind" theory. If you can't see files you shouldn't be concerned with, you don't have to wonder what they are. Nor can you do bad things, like delete or rename them, which could cause a lot of problems with your computer.

  If you clear this option, those protected operating system files will be visible in Explorer. Do this at your own risk. If you mess with one of those files, you could render your computer inoperable.

- **Launch Folder Windows in a Separate Process:** This oddly named option really has nothing to do with processes listed in Task Manager. Typically, File Explorer sets aside a little bit of memory to store the contents of the currently selected folder. As you go from one folder to the next, it overwrites that portion of memory with the current folder's contents.

  If you choose this option, each folder's contents are stored in a separate area in memory. This won't change how things look on your screen. But if your computer crashes frequently while exploring folders, this setting might solve the problem.

- **Restore Previous Folder Windows at Logon:** This option launches File Explorer and opens the last folder that was open.

- **Show Drive Letters:** By default, whenever you open your Computer folder, each drive's icon displays both a friendly name and a drive letter (such as c:). Choose this option if you want to hide the drive letters and see only the friendly name.

- **Show Encrypted or Compressed NTFS Files in Color:** The NTFS file system used in Windows 8.1 lets you encrypt and/or compress folders. Choose this option if you want the names of those folders to appear in color, to distinguish them from regular unencrypted, uncompressed folders. Names of encrypted folders will be green. Names of compressed folders will be blue.

> **NOTE**
>
> To compress or encrypt a file, right-click its icon and choose Properties. Then click the Advanced button in the Properties dialog box that opens. You can compress the folder (to reduce its size) or encrypt it to secure its contents. But you can't do both.

- **Show Pop-up Description for Folder and Desktop Items:** Selecting this option ensures that when you point to a file, folder, or desktop icon you see a tooltip. If you clear this option, you won't see a tooltip when pointing to such an icon (or anything else).

- **Show Preview Handlers in Preview Pane:** When you select a file icon in Explorer, the Preview pane (if open) will attempt to show some content from that file. It doesn't work with all file types, so often you'll just see "No preview available."

  If you clear this option, the Preview pane will never attempt to show the contents of any file icon you select. If it takes too long to show the contents of a file, and that's slowing you down, clearing this option will help speed things along. But you won't see the contents of any file you select.

- **Use Check Boxes to Select Items:** Chapter 21 describes different ways you can select icons in a folder. If you find it difficult to use those techniques, choose this option to have each icon show a check box. Then you can select multiple icons by clicking their check boxes. You'll also see a check box next to the Name column heading. Select (check) that one if you want to select all icons in the folder.

- **Use Sharing Wizard (Recommended):** To share a folder or file with other users, you typically right-click the icon and choose Share, or select icons and click Share in Explorer's toolbar. When you choose this option, the Sharing Wizard opens to help you through the sharing process.

20

If you clear this option, the Sharing Wizard won't open when you click the Share button. Instead you're taken to the folder's Properties dialog box. There, you share the folder by choosing specific options rather than using the simpler wizard.

- **When Typing into List View:** The options in this group determine what happens when you start typing in a list view. The default behavior is to select the item that matches what you're typing. You can choose to have the text you type appear in the Search box instead.

- **Restore Defaults:** Click this button if you've experimented with settings and you want to get things back the way they were originally set in Windows 8.1.

As always, be sure to click OK after changing options in the Folder Options dialog box.

Saving Things in Folders

The most common complaint among casual computer users is the inability to find things they're certain they've saved. This occurs because users don't choose *where* they want to save an item, or *what* they want to name it. They just click the Save button. This is roughly the same as handing an important paper document to a colleague and saying, "Stick this in the filing cabinet somewhere, but don't tell me where you put it." Finding that document later isn't going to be easy.

Another common mistake is to save things on external media such as flash drives, DVDs, CDs, and such. That's a bad idea. You only use external media to save *copies* of files that you've previously saved on your hard disk. The copy might be for backup or to give to a friend. But either way, it should be a copy of the file, not the one and only original file.

> **TIP**
>
> If the goal of storing a file on an external disk is to conserve hard disk space, ask yourself this: "How much hard disk space do I have available right now, and how much will I have after I save this file to my hard disk?" If the answer is "I don't know," you may be wasting your time, energy, and a ton of available hard disk space!

What folder should I use?

Windows 8.1 comes with several folders already created for you to store your files in. When you're saving a file, first ask yourself, "What is this thing I'm saving?" Then based on your answer, use the folder whose name matches the type of thing you're saving:

- If it's a picture or photograph, save it in your Pictures folder.
- If it's a video, save it in your Videos folder.
- If it's a song or sound clip, save it in your Music folder.
- If it's any other kind of typed document or worksheet, save it in your Documents folder.

There's no rule that states you *must* save a file in a specific folder. Remember, folders exist mainly to help you organize files so they're easy to find later when you need them. Also, saving to a folder is no big commitment. You can easily move any file from any folder to another folder whenever you want.

How to save in folders

There are basically two times when you have to choose where to save a folder:

- After you've created a new document from scratch in some program and chosen File ⇨ Save from that program's menu, or closed the program and answered Yes when asked if you want to save it
- When you've opted to download a file from the Internet and chosen Save

In either case, a dialog box titled Save (perhaps Save As, Save Picture, or Save Webpage, or something like that) appears. It's in that dialog box where most people make their mistake. They click the Save button without first thinking about and specifying where to put the file and what to name it.

> **TIP**
>
> Why do the Save and Save As dialog boxes look the same for many different programs? The answer is: They *are* the same. Windows 8.1 includes a "stock" set of dialog boxes that any program can invoke when opening or saving files. Other programs provide their own custom dialog boxes to add capabilities, but most use the standard Windows dialog boxes.

Saving in Windows 8.1–style dialog boxes

The name at the end of the Address bar is the name of the folder where the file will be saved unless you specify otherwise. The file will be saved in the Documents folder for the current user. At the very least, you should look at that name so you know where the file is going, and where you can find it in the future.

If you don't want to save the file to the folder that's suggested in the Address bar, navigate to the folder in which you want to save the file. A simple way to do this is to navigate folders and drives in the Navigation pane (left-side pane). Then click the folder into which you want to save the document.

> **CAUTION**
>
> Another common mistake is to save the file in an inappropriate place such as the desktop or a subfolder under `C:\Program Files` or `C:\Windows`. Those places aren't for storing documents so don't save things there.

Depending on the type of document you're saving, you may be given an option to enter *metadata,* such as an author's name, tags, or other information. Metadata is information *about* the file that is stored in the file's properties or Windows 8.1's search index. At first,

20

you might see only a couple of metadata options. If you enlarge the Save As dialog box by dragging any corner or edge, you might see many more. Figure 20.31 shows an example from Microsoft Word, which lets you add tags to the file.

FIGURE 20.31

Sample metadata tags entered.

Fill in whatever metadata seems appropriate for your way of organizing and searching for things. If you're not up on Windows 8.1–style searching yet, don't worry about it. You can still add any information that seems reasonable. But the main thing to keep in mind when filling in the blanks is the question "If I lost this thing, what word(s) might I type into the Search box to find it?" Whatever words come to mind are the words you should put into metadata. Also keep in mind that Windows 8.1 can search within documents to find words or phrases in the document.

After you've chosen where you want to save the file (and filled in some metadata, if available), you can name the file.

Tips on Naming Things

Whenever you save a file or create a folder, you need to give it a name. Before you do, ask yourself "If I needed this thing a year from now, and forgot its name, what would I look for?" Whatever word pops into your head is probably the best name to give to the item. You're not limited to a single word, but you want to keep the name short. There's not always room to show the entire name of a file or folder. So. put the most important word first so that if the name is cut off, you can at least see the most recognizable part of the name.

In some situations, it makes sense to name files by number. When using numbers to name files, it's best to use the same amount of digits in each number. Otherwise, when you sort by name, files won't be in the order you expect. For example, for this book, we know there will never be more than 99 pictures in a chapter. So, we use two-digit numbers for each figure. The 20 is the chapter number. The last two digits are the figure number. So, the first figure is 2001 and the highest possible figure number is 2099. You can use hyphens in a name if you prefer, such as 20-04.

If you name things by date, consider using the yyyymmdd format. This provides for the best results when sorting by name. But again, you need to be consistent about it, always using four digits for the year, two for the month, and two for the day — for instance, 19990101 or 20121231. It's okay to use hyphens if you like.

Naming the file

After you've chosen *where* you want to save the file, the next step is to choose *what* to name it. Again, think to yourself "If I were to look for this thing six months from now, what name would I look for?" Then name the file accordingly. Keep the name short and specific. You can use spaces and some basic punctuation such as apostrophes. The characters \, /, ?, :, *, ", ", >, <, and | are not allowed in a filename because they have special meanings and will be rejected.

Choosing a Save As type

It's usually best to ignore the Save As Type drop-down at the bottom of a Save dialog box. The suggested type is the "normal" type for the type of file you're saving. If you have a good and specific reason for choosing a different type, then go ahead and choose it. But otherwise you might just create unnecessary headaches for yourself!

Click Save

The last step in the process of saving a file is to click the Save button in the dialog box. Before you do, you might want to take a quick look at the last folder name in the Address bar again or the name in the Save In box so you know where you're about to save the file. Take another quick look at the name in the File Name box so you know its name. Then click Save. The file is saved to the folder you specified with the name you specified.

Opening the saved file

To open the file in the future, use File Explorer to navigate to the folder in which you placed the file, as described earlier in this chapter. Then double-click the file's icon.

20

Nothing Happens When I Save!

The *first* time you save a new document, the Save As dialog box opens so you can tell Windows where you want to put the file and what you want to name it. When you click Save, the document is saved.

Every time you save after that, the program saves only changes you made since your last save to that same file. It doesn't ask where to put the file or what to name it again. It just brings the currently saved copy up to date with what's on your screen. That's important, and not doing that often enough is yet another common beginner mistake.

It's important to save your work often because that's what keeps the permanent copy on your disk up-to-date with the copy you see on the screen. While creating or editing a document, you should save every two minutes or so, even if your application autosaves for you. That way, if a power outage or other mishap wipes the document off your screen, the most you can lose is two minutes of work!

If the file you saved is a document, you may be able to re-open it by opening the program you used to create the document, and then opening its File menu and clicking the filename on the recently used list (this name varies according to the program or app). But keep in mind that those places only include recently used files. Your file won't stay in either list forever!

After you open the file, keep in mind that changes you make are not *saved* automatically by most programs. Changes you make to an open file are stored in RAM, not on the hard disk. If you want to save changes you've made, you must choose Save from the File menu while the document is open. Or remember to choose Yes when asked about saving your changes when you close the document.

Creating Your Own Folders

You can create your own folders at any time. For example, if you have many files in your Documents folder or some other folder, you might want to start organizing into subfolders within your Documents folder. You can create as many folders as you wish and name them anything you wish. You can move or save any files you wish into any folder you create.

The main trick when creating your own folders is to put them where they make the most sense. Any folder you create will be a subfolder of some other folder. So, the first thing you want to do is get to that *parent folder* — the folder in which your own custom folder will be stored. If you're new to all this and you aren't sure what we're talking about, here are some suggestions:

- If you're creating a subfolder to organize pictures, use your Pictures folder as the parent folder.
- If you're creating a subfolder to organize songs, use your Music folder as the parent folder.

- If you're creating a subfolder to organize videos, use your Videos folder as the parent folder.

- If you're creating a subfolder to organize some other type of files, use your Documents folder as the parent folder.

You can create a folder anywhere you like. The preceding items are just suggestions. For example, you can create a folder on a flash drive, memory card, or external hard drive. In those cases, whichever disk is currently in the drive would be like the parent folder. Make sure you put a disk in the drive before you perform the following steps:

CAUTION

You can create folders on CDs and DVDs, too, but not necessarily by following the steps here. You must create the folders first in File Explorer, and then when you copy those files to the CD or DVD, Windows 8.1 duplicates your file and folder structure on the disk.

1. In File Explorer, open the parent folder for the folder you're about to create. Or open your This PC folder and then open the icon for the disk drive on which you want to create a folder.

2. Do whichever of the following is easiest for you:

   a. Select the Home tab and click New Folder.

   b. Right-click some empty space below or to the right of icons in the current folder and choose New ➪ Folder.

3. Type in a name of your own choosing and press Enter.

The new folder appears with the name you specified. When you double-click its icon to open it, you'll find it's empty. That's because it's brand new and you haven't put anything in it yet. (Click the Back button or press Backspace to leave the folder.)

TIP

If you're not happy with the name you gave to a folder, right-click its icon and choose Rename. Then type the new name or edit the existing name and press Enter.

You can move existing files into the folder using techniques described in Chapter 21. You can save new files to the folder just by opening the folder from the Save dialog box.

Creating folders on the fly while saving

There may be times when you're in the middle of saving a file and suddenly think, "I should have created a new folder for this file and others like it." You don't have to cancel out of the current save operation to create a folder. Instead, navigate to the folder that will act as the parent to the new folder you want to create.

If you're using a Windows 8.1–style Save dialog box, right-click in the file list area of the dialog box and choose New ➪ Folder. Or click the New Folder button on the Save As dialog box. If you're using an older-style Save dialog box, point to each toolbar button until

20

you find the one that lets you create a new folder at the bottom of that same figure, and click it. A new empty folder appears in the main pane at the center of the dialog box. Type in a new name of your own choosing and press Enter.

Double-click the new folder's icon in the main pane of the Save As dialog box so that the name appears at the end of the Address bar or in the Save In box. Then click the Save button in the dialog box. Your file is saved in that new folder.

Personalizing your folder

You can customize a folder in several ways. Unlike the Folder Options described earlier, which apply to all folders, these settings apply to only one folder — the one whose icon you right-click to specify your settings. To get started on customization, first right-click the icon you want to customize and choose Properties. In the Properties dialog box that opens, select the Customize tab to see the options shown in Figure 20.32.

FIGURE 20.32

The Customize tab for a folder's properties.

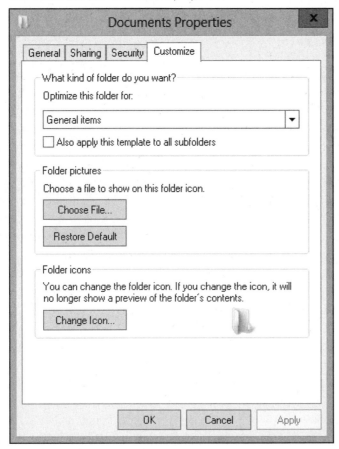

TIP

You can't access the Customize tab when working from a Windows 8.1 library. For example, if you create a folder in your Documents folder and then open its properties, the Customize tab will be missing. However, you can open `C:\Users\YourAccount\My Documents`, where `YourAccount` is your Windows account name, and then right-click the folder you want to customize and choose Properties.

Specify a folder type

All folders have a default view that defines what tools appear in the toolbar and how icons look when you first open the folder. To define a default view, click the button under "What kind of folder do you want?" and choose from the menu. There isn't any rule that says you must choose a specific kind. But in general, you want to choose an option that reflects the type of items that the folder contains, or will contain:

- **General Items:** Use this option if the folder will contain multiple file types and subfolders.
- **Documents:** Use this type if the folder will contain mostly non-media document files (text, spreadsheets, database data, and such).
- **Pictures:** Use this if the folder will contain pictures.
- **Music:** Use this if the folder will contain mostly albums or other subfolders that contain songs.
- **Videos:** Use this if the folder will contain mostly video files.

If you want your selection to be applied to subfolders within the folder, choose Also Apply This Template to All Subfolders.

NOTE

If you chose Remember Each Folder's View Settings in the Folder Options dialog box, the view you were using when you left the folder will override the default view.

Folder pictures

Folder icons always look like partially opened manila file folders because, like real-world manila file folders, computer folders are containers in which you store files (written documents, pictures, songs, videos, and such). Items listed in the folder represent files that are actually in the folder. For example, folders that contain albums show the covers of albums that are in the folder, as in Figure 20.33.

20

FIGURE 20.33

Folder icons showing album covers.

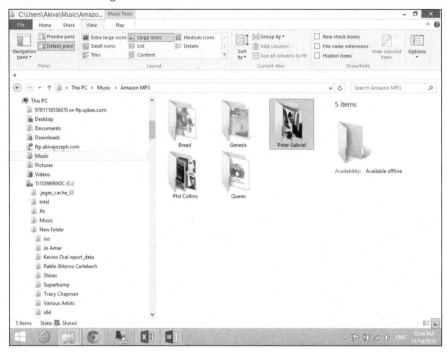

If you don't like the file that a folder icon shows, you can change it to a picture. Just click the Choose File button on the Customize tab and click the file you want the folder icon to show.

> **TIP**
>
> If you can't use a file because it's not the right type, you can take a screenshot of the open file you want to use. Save the screenshot as a JPEG file. Then use the JPEG as the folder's picture.

If you ever change your mind and want to go back to the original, click the Restore Default button in the properties sheet.

Changing a folder's icon

You can choose an entirely different icon for a folder. You'll likely lose the open folder effect you normally see in folder icons, so you might consider changing the folder's picture rather than its icon. But if you really want to change the folder's icon to something else, just click the Change Icon button. Click the icon you want to use, or use the Browse button to browse to any location that contains icon (.ico) files, and choose an icon there.

If you change the icon and then change your mind, click the Change Icon button again and click Restore Default. Don't forget to click OK or Apply after changing any settings in any dialog boxes. Your changes won't take effect until you do.

If your changes don't take effect immediately, refresh the folder. (Right-click some empty space in the folder and choose Refresh or press F5.)

Read-Only, Hidden, and Advanced attributes

When you right-click a folder icon (or file icon) and choose Properties, the General tab of the Properties dialog box shows the options shown in Figure 20.34. The Read-Only and Hidden options often confuse folks, so let's take a moment to discuss what those are about.

FIGURE 20.34

The General tab of a folder's Properties.

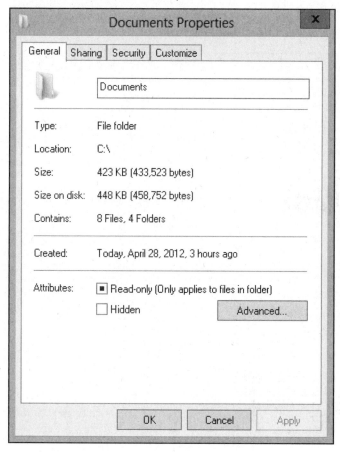

The Read-Only attribute can be

- **Empty:** The contents of the folder can be read (viewed and opened) by everyone who has access to the folder.
- **Black Square:** The contents can be read and written to (changed) by the owner of the folder (the person who created the folder). Other users with whom the folder is shared can view the contents of the folder but not change its contents.
- **Checked:** Everyone can view the contents of the folder, but nobody (not even the owner) can change the folder's contents.

The Hidden attribute, if checked, makes the folder's icon invisible in the folder if the Do Not Show Hidden Files and Folders option in Folder Options is selected. The folder's icon is dimmed if Show Hidden Files and Folders is selected in Folder Options.

Clicking the Advanced button on the General tab reveals the options shown in Figure 20.35.

FIGURE 20.35

Advanced folder or file attributes.

The Folder Is Ready for Archiving check box is handled automatically by Windows File History (the backup feature of Windows 8.1), so it's unlikely you'd ever need to change that yourself. The check box is selected if you've never backed up the folder (or file) or if its contents have changed since the last backup; that tells Windows File History to back it up again the next time you do a backup. The check box is empty if its contents haven't changed since the last backup; that tells Windows File History that there's no need to back it up again.

The Allow Files in This Folder to Have Contents Indexed in Addition to File Properties check box, if selected, allows Windows to index the contents of files in the folder, as well as the file properties. For example, if the folder contains Microsoft Word documents, Windows will index the contents of those documents, enabling you to search for and locate files based on words or phrases inside the documents.

The other two options in the dialog box deserve some special attention and are described next.

Compress Contents to Save Disk Space

Choosing this option tells Windows to compress everything in the folder to reduce its disk space consumption. (This works only on hard disks that use the NTFS file system.) When you open a file from the folder, it's automatically decompressed for you. So, the compression is transparent, in the sense that you don't have to constantly compress and decompress files yourself.

> **CAUTION**
>
> This option has nothing to do with Zip files (also called compressed folders). If your goal is to e-mail someone a Zip file, this option won't help at all. Right-click a file (or selection of files) and choose Send To – Compressed (Zipped) Folder to create a compressed file of your selected files.

Folder and file compression is a good way to conserve disk space. But before you jump in and start compressing all your folders, there are some costs to consider. For one, there is a time cost. It takes a little time to automatically compress every file you save and automatically decompress every file you open. Furthermore, many file types already have a degree of compression built into them. Putting such files into a compressed folder may have little or no effect on the amount of disk space they consume.

With today's computers, the amount of time it takes to compress and decompress a file on the fly is negligible. So, you can generally compress folders without worrying about a performance impact. However, you should generally not compress all of drive c:. Instead, just compress those folders where you store lots of documents that are taking up a lot of space. If you want to turn off compression for a folder, just clear the check box beside the Compress Contents to Save Disk Space option.

Encrypt Contents to Secure Data

This check box enables you to apply Encrypting File System (EFS) to the folder. EFS encrypts the contents of the folder (or a single file) to make it almost impossible to open without logging in to the computer using the account that encrypted it. EFS is not the most complete form of encryption available for PCs, but it is nevertheless a very effective tool for securing data.

20

> **NOTE**
>
> Companies that are concerned about data being compromised when computers are stolen often use *whole-disk encryption* to encrypt the computer's entire disk drive. This encryption is applied even below the operating system level, making it nearly impossible to decrypt the contents of the computer. EFS in Windows does not provide this type of whole-disk encryption, although you can encrypt an entire disk if you want to. In reality, whole-disk encryption should really be called whole-*system* encryption when the system is encrypted below the operating system.

First, understand that anyone who has access to your user account also has access to files in your encrypted folders. Therefore, there is no point in using EFS if your user account isn't password protected.

If you forget the password to your user account, you'll lose access to all files in the encrypted folders. To play it safe, you must make a backup copy of your encryption key, preferably on a CD-R or other disk where it can't be erased. You need to store that disk in a safe place, preferably in a fireproof safe.

The act of encrypting a folder is easy. Just select (check) the Encrypt Contents to Secure Data check box. Then follow the steps in the wizard that appears to make a backup copy of your encryption key (see Figure 20.36). If you save that file to your hard disk, copy it to a CD-R or other medium, and delete the copy that's on your hard disk.

> **NOTE**
>
> An encryption key applies to all encrypted folders in your user account so you'll only be prompted to back up your key the first time you encrypt a folder.

Once you've encrypted a folder, you really don't have to do anything else to secure its contents. When you save a file to that folder, or move a file into that folder, its contents are encrypted automatically. When you open a file, the contents are decrypted. So, working with the files in the encrypted folder is like working with any other files in any other folder.

If someone tries to open a file in the encrypted folder from another user account, he'll be denied access to the file. There is no way he can access anything in the folder unless he can get a copy of your encryption key.

> **NOTE**
>
> For more information on encryption and backing up keys, search Windows Help for "EFS" or "certificate backup."

After all this talk of creating folders, you may be wondering how to get some of your existing files into one. That's a topic for the next chapter.

FIGURE 20.36

Make a backup copy of your encryption key.

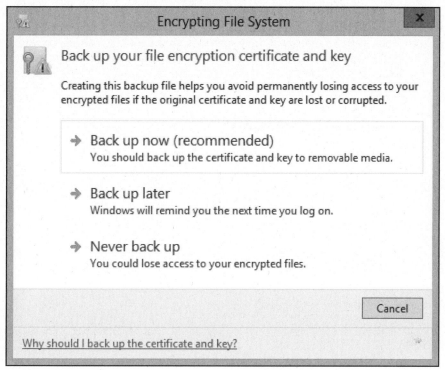

Wrap-Up

This chapter covered some basic facts about how computers store information. It also covered some basic (and some not-so-basic) skills for navigating through your system to find things. Here's a quick review:

- Everything that's in your computer is stored on your hard disk, typically drive C:.
- The This PC folder shows icons for all the disk drives in your system. To open that folder, click the Quick Access and choose This PC.
- A folder is a container in which files (and perhaps subfolders) are stored.
- Icons that represent folders usually look like little manila file folders. Double-click a folder's icon to open the folder and see what's inside.

20

- File Explorer (also called Explorer) is the program you use to navigate through and explore the contents of all the drives and folders in your system.

- Explorer's ribbon bar, Address bar, Navigation pane, and main contents window are all tools for navigating through drives and folders in your system.

- When saving a file, always navigate to an appropriate folder and provide a meaningful filename before you click Save. Otherwise, it may be difficult to find the file later when you need it.

- You can create your own folders from the Organize button in Explorer or from the Save dialog box.

- To customize a folder, right-click its icon and choose Properties.

Managing Files and Folders

Your computer's hard disk has enough space on it to store thousands of pictures, songs, and other files. Having lots of stuff on your computer can be a good thing, but only if you can find what you're looking for when you need it. Therefore, keeping things organized so they're easy to find is an important basic skill that every computer user needs to learn.

Chapter 20 discusses drives, folders, and files in terms of what they are and why you need them. It also tells you how to use Explorer to navigate your system and get to things you need. The chapter covers strategies for saving things in such a way that prevents you from losing them.

This chapter picks up where that one left off. Here, we assume you've read and understood most of that chapter. Now you're ready to start reorganizing what you already have. That requires that you know how to select, move, and copy files. You'll also discover other important techniques in this chapter, such as how to rename, delete, and un-delete files. These basic skills are important to acquire if you ever intend to use your computer for anything beyond basic e-mail and web browsing.

Selecting Icons

You'll often find that you want to perform some operation on many files. For example, let's say you want to copy a couple dozen files to an external disk. You could do them one at a time, but that would take a lot of time and effort. It would be better and easier to *select* all the icons you want to copy, and copy them all in one fell swoop.

As you'll see, you can select icons in many ways. As always, there is no right way or wrong way, no good way or bad way. It's usually a matter of choosing the method that is easiest for you, or is best for whatever you're trying to accomplish.

 How you select icons depends largely on whether you're using the double-click or single-click method to open icons. If you don't know what that's about, see Chapter 20.

Thumbnails for pictures and videos are icons, too. So all the techniques described in this chapter apply to thumbnails.

Selecting one icon

Selecting a single icon is easy. If you're using the double-click method to open documents or programs, you click (once) on the icon you want to select. If you're using the single-click method to open icons, you just point to the icon (rest the tip of the mouse pointer right on the icon you want to select). The selected icon will be highlighted to stand out from the others. The toolbar will likely change to reflect things you can do with that selected icon. If the Details pane is open, it will show information about the selected icon, as illustrated in Figure 21.1.

> **TIP**
>
> If you're new to selecting multiple icons, you might find it easiest in Windows 8.1 to use the check box feature to select icons.

FIGURE 21.1

A selected icon.

If you turned on the option to select icons using check boxes in Folder Options, you have to point to the icon first and then click its check box. The only thing that's unique about this method is that the selected icon's check box has a check mark, as in Figure 21.2.

FIGURE 21.2

A selected icon shows a check mark.

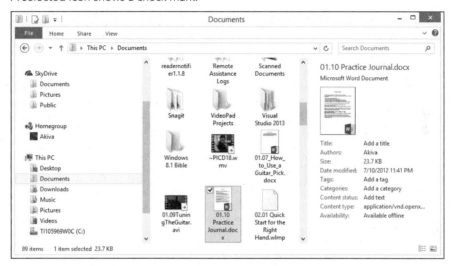

To turn on the option to use check boxes, select the View tab and choose Options. Select the View tab in the dialog box that opens. Then scroll down to and check Use Check Boxes to Select Items. Click OK. The check box won't show on an icon until you point to or click the icon.

 See Chapter 20 for more information on folder options.

> **TIP**
>
> If you unintentionally keep opening files when you only intended to select their icons, consider using the double-click method to open icons.

Selecting all icons

If you want to select all the icons in a folder, use whichever of the following techniques is easiest for you:

- Select the Home tab and click Select All.
- Press Ctrl+A.

All the icons are selected.

Selecting a range of icons

You can easily select a range of icons using the mouse and keyboard. If there are many icons in the folder, you might consider using the Layout buttons on the View tab (or the Ctrl key and your mouse wheel) to make the icons small enough so you can see all the icons you want to select. If the items you want to select have something in common, consider sorting the icons so the ones you want to select are adjacent to one another.

To select multiple icons:

1. Select the first one by pointing or clicking.
2. Hold down the Shift key and click the last one.

Both icons and all the icons in between are selected. The toolbar changes to show things you can do with all those icons. If the Details pane is open, it shows some information about the selected icons. The Size detail tells the combined size of all the selected icons. Figure 21.3 shows an example when you don't have any folders selected.

FIGURE 21.3

A range of icons selected.

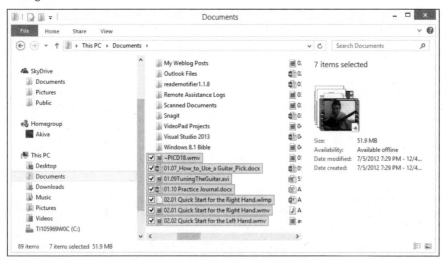

Selecting and unselecting one at a time

To select a single icon without unselecting others, Ctrl+click the icons you want to select (or unselect). Ctrl+click means hold down the Ctrl key as you click. For example, if you wanted to unselect only the highlighted icon in Figure 21.3, you'd Ctrl+click its icon. All the other icons would remain selected.

If you're using the single-click method to open icons, you can Ctrl+click or Ctrl+point to select or unselect a single icon. It doesn't matter which — the result is the same.

Here's another way to look at it. When you select an icon by pointing or clicking, only that one icon is selected. Any other selected icons are instantly deselected. But if you hold down the Ctrl key as you go, other selected icons remain unchanged, as shown in Figure 21.4. So, you can hold down the Ctrl key to select or unselect without disturbing other selected icons.

Of course, you can use the Ctrl key to select multiple non-adjacent icons.

FIGURE 21.4

Select multiple icons.

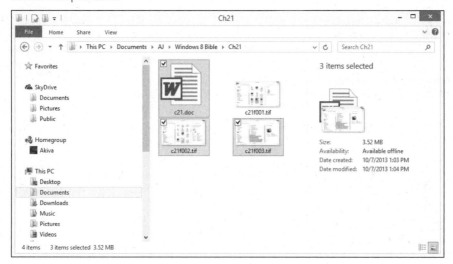

Selecting with a touchscreen

Windows 8.1 is designed for mobile devices such as mobile phones and tablets. Another way to select onscreen files is to touch the files using your finger (as long as your screen is a touchscreen). To select multiple files with touch, touch each file you want to select. To unselect a file in a group of selected ones, simply re-touch that file.

There are a handful of touch-based gestures you'll use with Windows 8.1, along with mouse-based alternatives for use on non-touch devices (or for when you have a mouse connected to a touch device). Chapter 2 discusses these gestures in more detail. In addition, see Appendix D for a list of common touch gestures.

Selecting with the keyboard

You can select icons without using the mouse at all. First, you have to make sure the keyboard focus is in Explorer's main contents pane. If you're not sure, press the arrow keys on the keyboard until you notice the selection box moving from icon to icon within the main content pane. Then move the focus to the first icon you want to select using the navigation keys ($\leftarrow$, $\rightarrow$, $\uparrow$, $\downarrow$, Home, End, PgUp, and PgDn).

To select multiple adjacent icons, hold down the Shift key as you move through icons using the navigation keys. All icons through which you pass are selected. To select multiple non-adjacent icons, hold down the Ctrl key as you move from icon to icon with the navigation keys. When you get to an icon you want to select, tap the Spacebar (but don't let go of the Ctrl key). To unselect all selected icons with the keyboard, press any navigation key alone, without holding down Shift or Ctrl.

Selecting by filtering

Yet another way to select icons that have something in common is to filter out (hide) the icons you don't want to select. For example, let's say you want to select only files that were created or edited today. On the View tab, choose the Details Layout option. Click the arrow next to the Date Modified column heading and choose the Today option. Or, perhaps you want to select only TIFF files, as in Figure 21.5. In that case, use the Type column to filter the view.

FIGURE 21.5

Hide all except TIFF files.

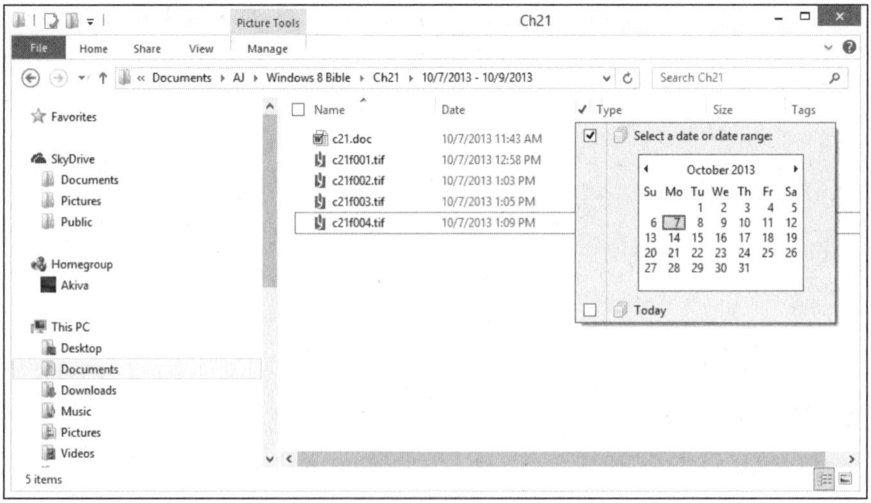

TIP

Don't forget that if you don't see a column heading you need, you can click the >> symbol at the end of the column headings to see other open columns. Or right-click any column heading to see other columns you can choose. Note that the >> symbol only appears when the window is not wide enough to show all columns.

You also can filter by using the Search box at the top of the folder. Just be aware that the search results might include files from subfolders. It all depends on your selection choice in Folder and Search Options, as discussed in Chapter 20. But for the sake of example, let's say you want to select all PNG and GIF images in a folder. You could type the following into the Search box for the folder:

type:gif OR type:png

Or the following:

*.gif OR *.png

Just make sure you use an uppercase **OR** to separate the two types. The search results include only files with `.gif` and `.png` extensions.

CAUTION

Using **AND** in the preceding examples wouldn't work because no file can have both a `.gif` extension *and* a `.png` extension. Be sure to read Chapters 22 and 23 for a full understanding of how index searches work, because it's not always intuitive.

When only the icons you want to select remain visible, select them all using any technique described earlier (for example, press Ctrl+A). None of the hidden icons will be selected, so you can move, copy, delete, or rename the selected icons without affecting anything else.

Selecting by lassoing

You can also select multiple icons by dragging the mouse pointer or your finger (on a touchscreen device) through them. But this is more difficult to do in Windows 8.1 than in older versions of Windows. The problem is that if you want to select by lassoing, you have to get the mouse pointer to some empty spot near the first icon you want to select, without selecting any icons. That's difficult in Windows 8.1 because there is little or no empty space between icons. What appears to be empty space isn't empty at all.

You can see this if you use the single-click method to open icons. Once you get the mouse pointer anywhere near an icon, you select the icon. Once you've selected an icon, if you start dragging, you only move the icon; you don't select multiple icons. The mouse pointer has to be in neutral territory (not on an icon) *before* you start dragging.

To see where the empty space is in the current view, press Ctrl+A to select icons. If there's any empty space at all, it will be white. To select by dragging, you have to get the tip of the mouse pointer into a white area near the first icon you want to select. Then hold down the left mouse button and drag through all the icons you want to select.

Selecting most icons in a folder

The old "invert selection" technique from previous versions of Windows still works, too. But the option is available only from the Home tab. As the name implies, the Invert Selection option unselects all selected icons and selects the ones that weren't selected. Say, for example, you want to select most, but not all, of the icons in a folder. You could start by selecting the few icons you *don't* want to select. Then choose the Home tab and click the Invert Selection option.

Selecting from multiple folders

To select icons from multiple folders, perform a search that finds all the icons you want to select. In the search results, you can select all icons, or just specific icons using any of the preceding methods.

 For more information on performing searches, see Chapters 23 and 24.

Unselecting all icons

If you have one or more icons selected and want to unselect them all, click some neutral area to the right of, below, or between icons (if you can find such an area). Or click the Refresh button (the two arrows to the right of the Address bar).

Moving and Copying Files

Many reasons exist for moving and copying files. If you've been saving files in a willy-nilly manner, you may want to move them around into folders that make more sense so they're easier to find. Or, if you end up with hundreds or thousands of files in a folder and you get sick of looking through all their names, you might want to create some subfolders and then move some of those files into subfolders.

If you have a bunch of files on external disks, you may want to copy them to your hard disk where they're easier to get to and work with. Or, if you need to send files to someone whose e-mail account has file-size limits, you might want to copy some files to an external disk to put in the mail. Then again, you may want to copy some files to an external disk as a backup, just in case some mishap damages the copy on your hard disk.

Whatever your reason for moving or copying files, the techniques are the same. First, understand that there is a difference between moving and copying. The words mean the same things they do in English. When you move a file from one place to another, you still have only one instance of the file. It's just in the new location rather than the old location. When you copy a file, you end up with two instances: the original in the original location and an exact copy in the new location.

Moving and copying usually involves two locations. These locations may be two different folders in the same drive, or two entirely different drives. But that doesn't really matter because one location is always the *source*. The other location is the *target* or *destination*. Here's the difference:

- **Source:** The drive and/or folder that contains the files you want to move or copy (the "from" drive and/or folder).

- **Destination or target:** The drive and/or folder to which you want to move or copy files (the "to" drive and/or folder).

The source can be any folder on your network, hard disk, a flash drive, a memory card, an external device (such as a digital video camera), or a DVD. The same is true for the destination in most cases, although copying files to CDs and DVDs requires methods that are different from those described in this chapter.

Moving files to a subfolder

One of the most common reasons to move files is that you've created a new, empty subfolder within some existing folder and want to move some files into that new subfolder. To do so, do one of the following:

- Drag any item onto the subfolder's icon, and release the mouse button.

- Select the items you want to move and drag any one of the selected items to the subfolder's icon; then release the mouse button.

- For touchscreens, press and hold down on the file's icon and drag the file to its new location. Lift your finger off the screen when the file reaches the new destination.

The main trick is to make sure that you get the mouse pointer or your finger on the subfolder's icon. When the mouse pointer is right on the subfolder's icon, you'll see the words `Move to foldername` at the mouse pointer (where `foldername` is the name of the folder into which you're moving the file). For example, in Figure 21.6 we're about to drop a selected icon into a subfolder named Tomorrow. To drop the files into the folder, release the mouse button without moving the mouse pointer away from that folder.

FIGURE 21.6

About to drop selected icons onto a subfolder's icon.

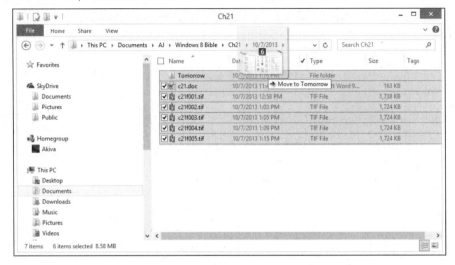

If you change your mind partway through the drag-and-drop operation, just tap the Esc key and then release the mouse button. If it's too late for that because you've already dropped the items, press Ctrl+Z to undo the move.

If you want to copy, rather than move, the files to a subfolder, drag with the right mouse button. After you drop the file, click Copy Here on the menu that appears. Optionally, you can drag with the left mouse button, but you have to press and hold down the Ctrl key before you release the mouse button.

> **CAUTION**
>
> Make sure you don't select the subfolder into which you want to move or copy the items. It won't work if you do it that way. Select only the items you want to move or copy into the subfolder.

Copying to/from external disks

You can copy things to external disks in many ways. But don't forget that size is limited on those. And the rules for copying to CDs and DVDs are different from those described here. You'll want to refer to Windows Help if you plan on copying files to a CD or DVD.

Anyway, you first have to know how much space you have on the external disk, which means you have to put the disc into its drive and open your This PC folder. When you view icons in the This PC folder as Tiles, each drive's available space shows with its icon.

Or if you can see the drive's icon in the Folders list, right-click that and choose Properties. In the properties sheet that opens, the Free Space number tells you how much room you have.

Then you need to know how much space the file(s) you're about to copy will require. For that, you can select the icons you intend to copy. If the Details pane is open, you'll see their combined size next to the Size option. But that size isn't entirely accurate because it doesn't take into account the small amount of additional overhead involved in storing files on disk. For a more accurate size, right-click any selected icon and choose Properties. The Size On Disk number in the properties sheet more accurately describes how much disk space you'll need to store all the selected files. If there isn't enough space on the external disk, you'll need to select and copy fewer files.

Once you know the files will fit, you can use any of the techniques in the sections that follow to copy files to the external disk, or for that matter, to copy files from an external disk or portable device (camera or music player) to your hard disk.

Moving and copying by dragging

You can move or copy any file (or selected files) to any location whose name you can see in the Navigation pane. You can also create a shortcut to the file. As usual, if you want to move or copy multiple items, first select their icons. Then just drag any one of them to the appropriate location in the Navigation pane, as illustrated in Figure 21.7. That location can be any folder or any drive.

FIGURE 21.7

Drag icons to any drive or folder in the Navigation pane.

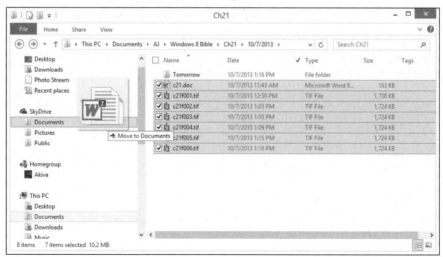

When dragging, make sure you get the tip of the mouse pointer right on the name of the drive or folder to which you want to copy. If you drag with the left mouse button, you'll see Move To or Copy To when the mouse pointer is in position. The rules are

- If you drag to a different drive, including an external drive or a network drive, Windows assumes you want to copy.

- If you drag to another folder on the same drive, Windows assumes you want to move.

There's rarely any need to move a file to an external disk. External disks are mainly used for copies of files on your hard disk. Likewise, there's rarely any need to have two copies of the same file on your hard drive. But you're not stuck letting Windows 8.1 decide whether to move or copy. Just press and hold down Alt, Shift, or Ctrl before you release the mouse button to drop the files. When you press

- **Ctrl:** Files will be copied to the location.

- **Shift:** Files will be moved to the location.

- **Alt:** A shortcut to the file will be created.

As an alternative to relying on the keys, you can drag with the right mouse button instead of the left. When you release the mouse button to drop, you'll see a menu like the one in Figure 21.8. Click Move or Copy depending on what you want to do. Click Cancel if you change your mind and decide to do neither.

FIGURE 21.8

The menu when you right-drag and then drop.

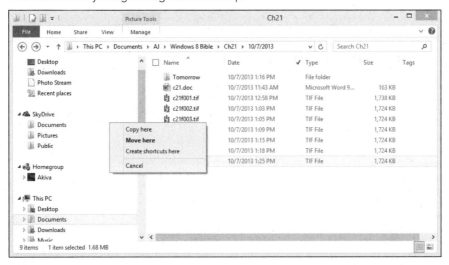

Moving or copying by using two open folders

It's not always easy getting the tip of the mouse pointer right on the destination drive or folder in the Navigation pane. You might find it easier to open both the source and destination locations at the same time. Then just drag from one open window to the other.

The trick here is to open two instances of Explorer: one for the source and one for the destination. Then size and position so you can see at least some portion of both. For example, in Figure 21.9, the left window is a folder on the hard drive. The right window is a jump drive.

1. Open the source folder or drive (from which you want to move/copy files).

2. Right-click the File Explorer icon on the taskbar and choose File Explorer. This starts a second instance of a File Explorer window.

3. In the second Explorer window, navigate to the destination drive or folder.

4. Right-click the clock in the lower-right corner of the screen and choose Show Windows Side by Side, or simply size and position the windows to suit your needs, as shown in Figure 21.9.

FIGURE 21.9

Drag icons from one folder to the other.

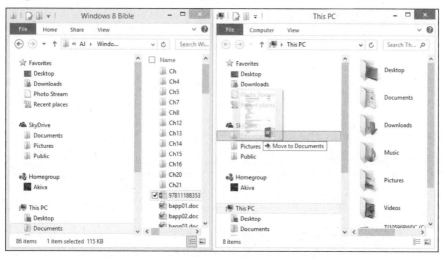

TIP

File Explorer is the program that displays folders. You can use all the techniques described in Chapter 4 to move and size the File Explorer window.

That gets you to the point where you can see both open folders. Now you just have to select the items you want to move or copy. Then drag them into the main center pane of the destination folder and drop them there. Or, right-drag the items so you can choose Move or Copy after you release the mouse button.

> **CAUTION**
>
> Don't drag to the Navigation pane in the destination window. Either close the Navigation pane in the destination location's window, or make sure you drag past it into the main center pane of that window.

Using cut-and-paste to move or copy files

You can also copy and paste files to copy them, or cut and paste to move files. The procedure goes like this:

1. Navigate to the drive or folder that contains the items you want to move or copy.

2. To move or copy multiple items, select their icons. Then:

   - To move the items, right-click its icon or any selected item and choose Cut or press Ctrl+X.

   - To copy the items, right-click its icon or any selected icon and choose Copy or press Ctrl+C.

3. Navigate to the destination drive or folder.

4. Paste using any of the following methods:

   - Click the Home button and choose Paste.

   - Press Ctrl+V.

   - Right-click some empty space in the main, center pane of the destination window and choose Paste.

Making a copy in the same folder

You may want to make a copy of a file within the same folder. For example, maybe you have a large photo from your digital camera. You want to make a smaller version for e-mail or for use in documents. Of course, you don't want to shrink down your original because that's the best one to use for editing and printing. Here's the quick and easy way to make copies:

1. Select the icon (or icons) you want to copy.

2. Press Ctrl+C and then press Ctrl+V (to copy, then paste).

The copied files have the same name as the originals followed by – Copy, as in Figure 21.10. You can rename the copies if you like, but that isn't necessary. You can make any changes you want to the copies. Those changes will have no effect on the originals.

FIGURE 21.10

Original files and copies.

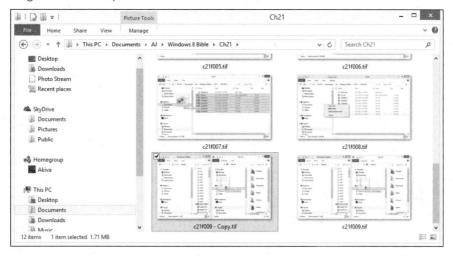

TIP

Click the Name column heading once or twice to get the files back into alphanumeric order, if needed.

Undoing a move or copy

If you complete a move or copy operation and then change your mind, you can undo the action. But you have to do it soon because you can only undo your most recent action. For example, you can't move or copy, then do a bunch of other things, and then come back and undo the move or copy. Use whichever technique is easiest for you to undo a move/copy:

- Press Ctrl+Z.
- Click the down arrow on the Quick Access toolbar (which is on the File Explorer title bar) and choose Undo.
- Right-click some empty white space in the main pane of either folder and choose Undo Move or Undo Copy.

This location already contains ...

A folder cannot contain two files that have the same name. If you move or copy a file into a folder (or onto a drive) and that destination already has a file with the same name as the one you're bringing in, you'll see a message similar to the one in Figure 21.11. In this example, we're copying a file. Notice that the message simply explains what's going on and gives you some choices as to what you can do about it.

FIGURE 21.11

The destination already has a file with that name.

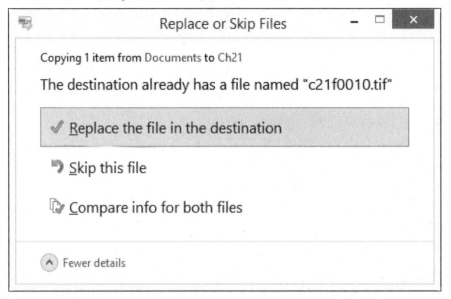

Before you make a decision, take a look at the source you're copying from and the destination to which you're copying. That information appears at the top of the Replace or Skip Files dialog. If that isn't where you intended to copy from and to, click the Close button to cancel the whole operation. Then rethink where you want to move/copy from and to, and start over. But this time, make sure you get both locations right.

If the source and destination are correct, then think what you want to do about the copy that's already in the destination. The following options are available in the Windows 8.1 Replace or Skip Files dialog box:

- If you want to replace the file at the destination with the one you're moving or copying, click the first option, Replace the File in the Destination Folder.

- If you want to keep the file that's already at the destination and leave well enough alone, click Skip This File. The move/copy operation will be canceled and it will be just as though you never even tried to move or copy.

- If you want to compare file information for both files, click the third option — Choose Compare Info for Both Files. This displays the File Conflicts dialog box, which is shown in Figure 21.12. This dialog box is new to Windows 8 and 8.1. You select one or both of the files. If you select both, the file will be moved or copied. Its name will be the same as the original name followed by a number, like Landscape-EastWing-(2), for example.

FIGURE 21.12

The File Conflicts dialog box displays when a folder already includes the same file as the one you want to copy or move there.

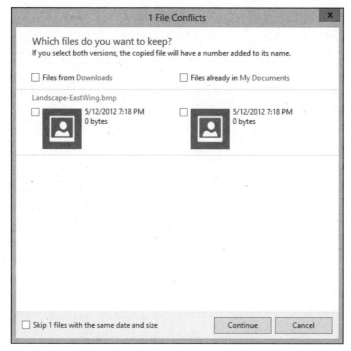

Click Continue when you're ready to complete the copy procedure.

The bottom line here is that you can move or copy any file anywhere at any time. There are no restrictions. It's simply a matter of first knowing why you want to move or copy, because there is no point in doing such things purely for the heck of it. Then you need to know where the item is now and where you want to move or copy it to. Once all that is squared away, use either a dragging method or a copy-and-paste method described earlier to do the move or copy.

In addition to the techniques already described, you can get stuff into your computer using methods listed here:

- To get pictures from a digital camera into your computer, use the Photos app (see Chapter 17).

- To get music from a CD or portable music player into your computer, use Windows Media Player (see Chapter 18).

Renaming Files

Renaming a file or folder is simple. Just right-click the item you want to rename and choose Rename. The existing name will become highlighted in a new color (the default is blue). You can type a new name, or edit the current name, and then press Enter.

If you've taken filename extensions out of hiding, that part of the name won't be highlighted. For example, the .jpg extension on the highlighted photo shown in Figure 21.13 isn't highlighted. That's because you don't want to change the extension unless you *really* know what you're doing. Guessing is unlikely to work. At the very least, make sure you know the extension you're about to change. That way, if you ruin the file, you can rename the file back to the original extension (in case you miss the opportunity to undo the rename).

FIGURE 21.13

The filename extension is not highlighted.

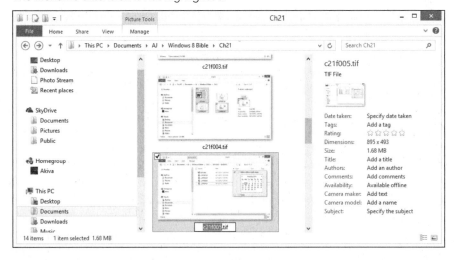

> **TIP**
>
> Click once to select a file, pause briefly, and then click the filename again to highlight the name and rename it.

Undoing a rename

You can undo a rename as you can undo just about anything else. But as always, you have to do so fairly soon after the rename. Just press Ctrl+Z. If it's too late for that, you have to manually rename the file back to its original name and extension.

How to Change a File's Type

You can't simply change a file's extension to change the file's type. If you can open the file, and it's not a music or video file, you may be able to just choose File ⇨ Save As from the opening program's menu. Then set the Save As Type option to the file type you want before you click the Save button.

If it's a music or video file, you'll likely need a conversion program. Search the web or a download site such as www.download.com or www.tucows.com for "convert ext1 to ext2" (where ext1 is the extension of the file type from which you want to copy, and ext2 is the extension of the file type to which you want to copy) and see what programs you can find.

In some cases, you simply need the right program, app, or reader to open the file without converting it. Some common examples include PDFs, which require Adobe Reader (www.adobe.com) or the new Windows Reader app, QuickTime movies and iTunes (players are available from www.apple.com), and Office documents and snapshots. Viewers for many such files are available from the Windows Store and http://download.microsoft.com.

Renaming multiple files

To rename multiple files, select all their icons using any methods described near the start of the chapter. Then right-click any one of them and choose Rename. Type the new name (again, don't change the extension if it shows up) and press Enter. The files will all be given the name you specified. All but the first will have numbers. For example, if you renamed to River, the files will be named River, River (2), River (3), River (4), and so forth.

> **TIP**
>
> If the lack of a number on the first renamed file bugs you, right-click its icon and choose Rename. Then add the (1) to the name yourself.

If you have a relatively large number of files and want to rename just a part of the filename for each one, you can turn to the Command Prompt to rename the files. For example, assume that you have a set of files named img-old-01.jpg, img-old-02.jpg, img-old-03.jpg, and so on in sequence. You want to replace the word old with the word new. Here's how to do it:

1. Press Windows+X and choose Command Prompt to open a command console.

2. Type **CD \\(path)** where *(path)* is the path to the folder where the files reside that you want to rename. For example, assuming the files are located in your Documents folder and your username is rtidrow, type **CD \Users\rtidrow\My Documents.**

3. Type the command **rename img-old-??.jpg img-new-??.jpg** and press Enter.

The question marks in the command essentially tell Windows to leave those characters alone. In this example, the sequential image numbers remain the same and only the word in the middle of the filename is changed.

Before you try renaming multiple files using the command console in this way, we suggest you make a backup copy of the files in a different folder. That way, if you really mess up the filenames by typing an incorrect command, you can simply copy the files back to the original folder to restore the old filenames.

Deleting Files

In computers, the term *delete* is synonymous with "throw in the trash." That's important to know because you wouldn't want to throw important paper documents from your filing cabinet into the trash. Likewise, you don't want to delete anything important that's on your computer.

It's easy to delete files and folders. Perhaps it's too easy, because it's a leading cause of headaches and disasters, especially among beginners and casual computer users who try to learn by guessing and figuring things out. Deleting and "moving to the Recycle Bin" are basically the same thing. So, let's start with a couple of good rules of thumb. Before you delete an item or move it to the Recycle Bin, ask yourself two questions:

- Do I know exactly what this file (or folder) is?
- Am I 100 percent certain that neither I nor my computer will need it in the future, ever?

If the answer to both questions is "Yes," go ahead and delete the file. If the answer to either question is "No," don't delete the file or move it to the Recycle Bin.

> **CAUTION**
> When you delete a folder, you delete all the files and subfolders inside that folder! That means one small delete can lead to many lost files. Never delete a folder unless you're absolutely sure that the folder and its subfolders contain only files that you'll never need again.

Deleting is a simple process. If you want to delete a single file or folder, first select its icon. Optionally, if you want to delete multiple items in one fell swoop, select their icons. Then do whichever of the following is most convenient for you:

- Right-click the icon (or any selected icon) and choose Delete.
- Press the Delete (Del) key.
- Select the Home tab and click Delete.
- Drag the selected item(s) to the Recycle Bin.

By default, with Windows 8.1, you aren't prompted to confirm before the item(s) are deleted. In previous Windows versions, a confirmation appeared as a question asking if you were sure, and gave you a choice as to whether you wanted to proceed. This is no longer the default behavior option. Once you delete the file, it's sent to the Recycle Bin.

However, you can set up Windows 8.1 to display the confirmation if you want. To do so, right-click the Recycle Bin and choose Properties. In the Recycle Bin Properties dialog box, choose Display Delete Confirmation Dialog, and then click OK.

Now when you delete a file using the preceding methods, the Delete File dialog box appears. Figure 21.14 shows an example of the confirmation message.

FIGURE 21.14

Asking for confirmation before deleting.

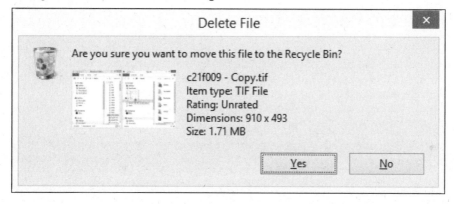

The idea is to read the message, and then click Yes only if you're sure. If you're not so sure, you should click No. Clicking Yes deletes the files. Clicking No keeps the files right where they are.

When you send something to the Recycle Bin, you still get one last chance to change your mind. It's kind of like fishing something out of the wastepaper basket before you empty it for good. That doesn't mean you should put things you intend to keep in the Recycle Bin. You wouldn't put important papers in your trash can. Never put important files or folders in your Recycle Bin.

CAUTION

Despite its environmentally friendly name, the Recycle Bin *is* a trash can and should be treated as such. Neither the Recycle Bin nor your trash can are good places to put things you intend to keep!

When you permanently delete a file or folder, there's no turning back. Whatever you permanently deleted is gone for good and there's no changing your mind and getting it back. Permanently deleting a file is akin to putting something down the garbage disposal. Or dousing the thing with gasoline and burning it to ashes. There is no "undo" for such actions.

> **TIP**
>
> In some cases, it might be possible to use the Previous Versions feature described in Chapter 24 to recover a permanently deleted file. But to play it safe, you should treat all deletions as though they were permanent. There are also third-party programs that can recover deleted files, as well as data recovery services that can recover deleted data. However, the likelihood of recovering the deleted data decreases if any data is written to the disk before recovery is attempted.

Using the Recycle Bin

The Recycle Bin stores copies of files you've deleted from your hard disk. You can quickly see if one or more files are in the Recycle Bin by looking at its icon on the desktop. If the icon shows that the trash can is empty, then no files or folders are currently in the Recycle Bin. If the icon appears to have "trash" in it, then you know that one or more files or folders have been sent to the Recycle Bin and it has not been emptied since the last file was sent there.

> **NOTE**
>
> Pressing the Shift key and then the delete button on a file will permanently delete the file with no option to recover the file in the Recycle Bin. However, with Shift+Delete you will be prompted before you delete the file.

To open your Recycle Bin, use whichever method is easiest for you:

- Open the Recycle Bin on the desktop.
- Click Recycle Bin in the Folder list in Explorer's Navigation pane.
- Click the leftmost arrow in Explorer's Address bar and choose Recycle Bin.
- Type **Recycle Bin** in Explorer's Address bar and press Enter.

When the Recycle Bin opens, it looks like any other folder. Figure 21.15 shows an example.

FIGURE 21.15

An open Recycle Bin.

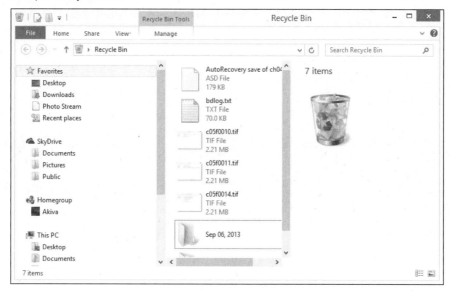

Each icon in the Recycle Bin represents an item that's in your computer trash can, so to speak. You have basically two ways to use the Recycle Bin:

- Restore files that you've accidentally deleted, so they go back to their original folders. (Same as fishing something out of your real trash can.)
- Empty the Recycle Bin, thereby permanently deleting the files within it to reclaim the disk space they were using. (Same as emptying your real trash can into a dumpster or incinerator.)

The sections that follow look at each option.

Recovering accidentally deleted files

If you accidentally deleted some files or folders from your hard disk, and if they were sent to the Recycle Bin, you can get them back, provided that you don't empty the Recycle Bin first. You have three ways to do that:

- To put all items back where they were, click Restore All Items on the Manage tab.
- To put a single item back where it was, right-click its icon and choose Restore. You can also click the Manage menu to access the Restore option.
- Select multiple icons, right-click any selected icon, and choose Restore to put all those selected items back where they were.

Each file and folder you restore will be returned to its original location.

Permanently deleting Recycle Bin files

When you feel confident that the Recycle Bin contains only folders and files that you'll never need again, click Empty the Recycle Bin in the toolbar. The icons in the Recycle Bin disappear. The files and folders that those icons represented are permanently deleted from your hard disk. The space they occupied is freed up for anything you might want to save in the future.

If you want to remove only one or a selection of files from the Recycle Bin, select those files, right-click, and choose Delete. Windows asks if you want to permanently delete the files, removing them from the Recycle Bin. Click Yes to delete them, or No to leave them in the Recycle Bin.

> **TIP**
>
> You can empty the Recycle Bin without opening it first. Right-click the Recycle Bin's icon and choose Empty Recycle Bin. Just keep in mind that in doing so, you're presuming there's nothing in the Recycle Bin you intended to keep.

When you've finished with the Recycle Bin, you can close it as you would any other window — by clicking the Close (X) button in its upper-right corner.

For all intents and purposes, you should consider the files that were in the Recycle Bin as permanently gone. But if you messed up and emptied too early, you *might* be able to get some of the files that were in there back using the Previous Versions feature discussed in Chapter 24.

Creating and Deleting Shortcuts

Shortcuts provide an easy way to get to a file or folder without having to navigate through a bunch of folders. For example, let's say you have an external disk drive X. On that drive, you have a folder named My Big Project inside another folder named Xternal Docs. To view the contents of your My Big Project folder, you have to open your Computer folder, open the icon for drive X, open the Xternal Docs folder, and then open the My Big Project folder. Doing that repeatedly gets tiresome.

If you create a shortcut to My Big Project, you won't have to go through all those steps. You just have to open the My Big Project shortcut icon. That shortcut icon can be anywhere you like — on the desktop, in your Documents folder, in the Favorites pane — or any combination thereof.

You can create a desktop shortcut to virtually any program, folder or file just by right-clicking that item's icon and choosing Send To ➪ Desktop (create shortcut). You can also use any of the following methods to create a shortcut to a file or folder:

- Hold down the Alt key as you drag an icon to the folder in which you want to place the shortcut.
- Drag, using the right mouse button, the selected icon(s) to where you want to put the shortcuts. After you release the right mouse button, click Create Shortcuts Here.

- Copy the selected icon(s) to the Clipboard (press Ctrl+C or right-click and choose Copy). Then right-click some empty space at the location where you want to place the shortcuts and choose Paste Shortcut.

Once you have a shortcut, you can double-click (or click) its icon to open the item to which the shortcut refers.

It's important to understand that when you delete a shortcut to a resource, you delete only the shortcut. You don't delete the folder or file to which the shortcut refers. That means you can easily create a bunch of shortcuts to a folder you're working with right now.

Later, when you move on to another project in another folder, you can delete all those shortcuts and replace them with new shortcuts to whatever folder you're working in currently. But you have to make sure you delete the shortcuts only, not the real folder because when you delete the real folder, you also delete everything that's in that folder. You also render the shortcuts useless because the location to which they refer no longer exists. When you try to open a shortcut that points to a nonexistent file or folder, you see a message like the one in Figure 21.16.

FIGURE 21.16

Opening a shortcut that leads nowhere.

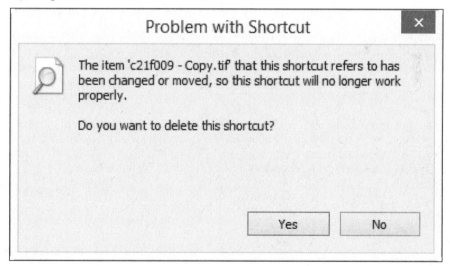

521

If you deleted the item recently and it's still in the Recycle Bin, click the Restore button. The original item will be taken out of the trash and put back where it belongs, and the shortcut will work. Otherwise, if there's no way to recover the item to which the shortcut refers, all you can do is delete the now-useless shortcut by clicking the Yes button.

> **NOTE**
>
> If the shortcut refers to an item on external media (such as a flash drive, external USB drive, or DVD), that disk has to be in its drive for the shortcut to work.

If you're thinking about deleting an icon, but you aren't sure if it's a shortcut or the real thing, there are ways to find out. For one thing, all links in the Favorites portion of Explorer's Navigation bar are shortcuts. Desktop icons you control from the Desktop Icon Settings dialog box are also shortcuts. We're not suggesting you delete any of those unless you have a very good reason, but if you do delete one, be aware that you're deleting only the shortcut and not the actual item.

 Chapters 10 and 20 provide more detailed information about the items described in the preceding paragraph.

Shortcut icons of your own making have many characteristics that make it easy to distinguish them from the items to which they refer. The most obvious is the curved arrow that appears right on the icon. The name of the icon usually has - shortcut at the end (if you don't rename the shortcut). The filename extension for a shortcut icon is always .lnk (for link). The size of a shortcut will always be tiny (1KB or less). When you right-click the icon and choose Properties, the General tab shows the Type of File as Shortcut (.lnk). The Shortcut tab shows information about the icon and its target, as in Figure 21.17.

When you delete a shortcut, you delete only the shortcut, not the item to which it refers. So, you can create and delete shortcuts on-the-fly without losing any important files or folders. But the number-one rule of deleting still applies: Know exactly what you're deleting and why you're deleting it *before* you delete. It's as simple as that.

FIGURE 21.17

Anatomy of a custom shortcut icon.

Managing Files with DOS Commands

This section is for people who were around in the DOS days and remember commands such as CD (change directory), Copy (to copy files), and so forth. All those old DOS commands still work. Using DOS commands is useful in some instances, such as when you want to print a list of filenames or paste them into a file. So, in this section, we'll look at how all that works.

Getting to a command prompt

The first step to using DOS commands is to get to the Command Prompt window (also called a *console* window). To do so, press Windows+X and then choose Command Prompt. A window reminiscent of ye olde DOS days opens, complete with the standard prompt that displays the folder (*directory* in DOS terms) that you're currently in. Figure 21.18 shows an example. Note that we've changed the size of the default window from 80 x 25 pixels to 120 x 60. Also we've changed colors for the console to be black text on a white background. The default is white text on a black background.

FIGURE 21.18

The Command Prompt window.

The Command Prompt window has a title bar and taskbar button. You can drag the window around by its title bar. To a limited extent, you can size the Command Prompt window by dragging any corner or edge, but the height is limited to the number of lines currently displayed within the window.

To get full control over the size of the Command Prompt window, you need to use its Properties dialog box. That Properties dialog box also lets you choose a cursor size, a Full Screen View, a font, text and background colors, and so forth.

You can get to the Command Prompt window's Properties dialog box in two ways: If you want to change properties for the current session only, right-click the Command Prompt title bar and choose Properties. If you want to change the defaults for future sessions as well, right-click the title bar and choose Defaults. The dialog box that opens is self-explanatory and is a normal Windows dialog box.

You can scroll up and down through the Command Prompt window using the vertical scroll bar at its right. The navigation keys don't work unless you right-click within the window and choose Scroll. You can't type normal characters in the scroll mode; you can just navigate up and down. To get out of scroll mode and back to normal typing, press Enter.

To exit a command prompt session, type **exit** and press Enter. Or close the Command Prompt program window by clicking its Close (X) button or by right-clicking its taskbar button and choosing Close.

Using the command prompt

The Command Prompt window works just like the screen did in DOS. You type a command and press Enter (assuming that you're not in the aforementioned "scroll mode," wherein typing normal characters just triggers a beep). After you press Enter, you see the results of the command and another command prompt appears. For example, if you enter **Help** (that is, type the word *Help* and press Enter), you see a list of all the supported DOS commands.

To get help with a command, type its name followed by a forward slash and question mark. For example, entering the command **dir /?** shows help for the Dir command. The Doskey feature is enabled automatically (again assuming that you're not in the bizarre scroll mode). So, you can use the up and down arrow keys (↑ and ↓) to retrieve previous commands from the current session. Press the left and right arrow keys (← and →) to bring back and remove the previous command one character at a time.

> **NOTE**
> If the characters you type result only in a beep and nothing on the screen, right-click in the Command Prompt window and choose Scroll to get back to normal typing.

The mouse doesn't do much in the Command Prompt window. As mentioned, you can right-click the title bar (or its taskbar button) to get to the properties sheet. You can right-click and choose Scroll to enter the (disturbing) scroll mode where navigation keys move through the window and normal characters do nothing but beep at you (although pressing Enter terminates the scroll mode).

Copy and paste in the Command Prompt window

Right-clicking in the Command Prompt window provides some options that allow you to use copy-and-paste. It's a bit tricky, but handy when you want to copy a lengthy list of filenames into a Word, WordPad, or Notepad document. If you'll be using the keyboard to select only a portion of the text, you first want to use the scroll bar to navigate to the text that you want to select. If you'll be using the mouse to select a portion of text, or you'll be selecting all the text in the window, it's not so important where you start.

To select the entire window, right-click within the window and choose Select All. To select only a portion of the window's contents, right-click within the Command Prompt window and choose Mark. You'll see a square cursor. To select with the keyboard, hold down the Shift key and use the arrow keys, PgUp, and PgDn keys to extend the selection through the text you want to select. With the mouse, move the mouse pointer to the far-right edge of the window, hold down the left mouse button, and then drag diagonally through the text you want to select.

Once you've selected some text, press Enter to copy the selected text and also clear the selection. From there, you can paste the copied text into any document that accepts pasted text.

You can paste a command into the window, but it has to be a valid DOS command. Just right-click near the command prompt and choose Paste.

Navigating from the command prompt

Navigating to a particular drive at the command prompt is easy. Type the drive letter followed by a colon and press Enter. For example, entering **d:** takes you to drive D:. Entering **c:** takes you to drive C:.

Use the cd (Change Directory) command, just as you did in DOS, to go to a folder on the current drive. You can use the following three cd commands:

- cd\ takes you to the root folder of the current drive.
- cd.. takes you to the parent of the current folder.
- cd folder takes you to the subfolder specified by folder.

Using wildcards

When specifying filenames in most DOS commands, you can use wildcard characters to represent characters in the filename. Use the ? character to represent a single character and the * character to represent multiple characters. For example, a?c.txt would match abc.txt, a2c.txt, aqc.txt, and so on. By comparison, a*c.txt would match abc.txt, a12345c.txt, anotherc.txt, and so on.

A common use for the wildcard is to find all files of the same type, such as *.jpg, which would match all JPG files. So, the following command would list all JPG files in the current folder:

```
dir *.jpg
```

The following section explains how to use the dir command.

Printing a list of filenames

Perhaps the one thing that the DOS command offers that Explorer doesn't is the ability to easily print a list of filenames from any folder, or even a parent folder and all its subfolders. Although you can print directly by following any command with `>prn`, we're sure most people would prefer to get that list into a Word or WordPad document. From there, you can edit and sort the filename list to your liking, and then print it.

You use the `dir` command to list the filenames. You may find some of the following optional switches useful for controlling how `dir` displays its output:

- `/s`: Include filenames from subfolders.
- `/b`: Display filenames in bare format (no headings or summary).
- `/w`: Show in wide format.
- `/d`: Same as wide, but sorted by columns.
- `/n`: Use long list format with filenames to the far right.
- `/l`: Use lowercase letters.
- `/o`: Sort output by column as follows: n (by name), s (by size), e (by extension), d (by date), - (prefix for descending sort), g (group folder names first).

As an example of using the `/o` switch, the command `dir /on` lists filenames in ascending alphabetical order. The command `dir /o-s` lists filenames by size, in descending order.

Let's look at a practical example. Suppose that you've downloaded music to your Music folder. The songs are organized into folders by artist and album. But you want a list of all song filenames, from all the subfolders.

Step 1 is to get to the parent folder of all the files you want to list. The DOS command would be `cd` followed by the full path to that folder: for example, `cd C:\Users\yourUser-Name\Music` where `yourUserName` is the name of your user account.

Next, you need to enter a `dir` command with the `/s` switch to list the filenames from all the subfolders. You can use any other switches in combination with `/s`. For example, here's a `dir` command that lists all the filenames in bare format:

```
dir /b /s
```

Here's one that lists files in the columnar wide format with filenames listed alphabetically by name:

```
dir /d /on /s
```

You can try out various DOS commands to see which presents the most reasonable list of filenames. Then, when you get a decent list, enter that command again, but follow it with `>filename.txt` where `filename` is any name of your choosing. The file will be stored in whatever folder you're currently in. For this example, we'll use `SongList.txt` as the filename. So, you might enter a command like this at the command prompt:

```
dir /d /on /s >SongList.txt
```

You won't get any feedback on the screen after you redirect the output to a file. You can just exit the Command Prompt window. Then use File Explorer to navigate to the folder from which you ran the `dir` command. You'll find your `SongList.txt` file there. Right-click it and choose Open With ➪ Microsoft Word (or whatever program you want to use to edit the file).

> **TIP**
>
> To open a text from a DOS prompt, type the command **notepad file.txt**, where **file.txt** is the name of the text file you want to open.

The list will look exactly like DOS output, which might not be ideal. But if you know how to use the program, it shouldn't be too tough to select and delete anything you don't want in the document. Then, save it, print it, and keep it for future reference.

> **TIP**
>
> If you're a Microsoft Office guru, you could create a macro to clean up the output from a DOS command, maybe even convert it to a list of comma-separated values. Then you could save *that* file as a text file, and import it into an Access table or Excel spreadsheet.

Whether this example of exporting filenames is of any value to you, we can't say. But it's just an example. If you know DOS, you may be able to come up with more useful applications of your own. You can do anything at the Command Prompt window that you could do in DOS — even copy and delete files. Remember that for a quick overview of all the DOS commands available in the Command Prompt window, just type **help** at the command prompt and press Enter.

Wrap-Up

Managing files and folders in Windows 8.1 is a lot like it was in earlier versions of Windows. You just have more ways of doing things. Here's a quick wrap-up of the main topics covered in this chapter:

- To select a single icon to work with, click it (if you're using double-click to open files) or point to it (if you're using single-click to open files).

- To select multiple icons, use Ctrl+click or Shift+click, or select it with your finger (if you have a touchscreen device) or the drag-through method, whichever is appropriate to your goal and easiest for you to use.

- To move or copy selected files and folders, drag them to some new location, or use copy-and-paste, or use the Copy or Move options under File and Folder Tasks in the Explorer bar.

- To rename a file or selected files, right-click and choose Rename.

- To delete a file or selected files, right-click and choose Delete.

- Small items you delete from your hard drive are just moved to the Recycle Bin.
- Large files, and files you delete from removable media, are not sent to the Recycle Bin.
- To recover a file from the Recycle Bin, right-click its icon and choose Restore.
- To permanently delete all the files in the Recycle Bin and reclaim the disk space they're using, empty the Recycle Bin.
- When you delete a shortcut to a resource, you delete only the shortcut — not the resource itself.
- If you're a DOS guru, you can still use DOS commands to manage files. Press Windows+X and choose Command Prompt to get to the Command Prompt window.

Searching for Files and Messages on Your Computer

IN THIS CHAPTER

Searching from the Charms Bar

Searching from folders

Searching your computer and network

Specifying search criteria

Saving and reusing searches

H ard disk storage in the 21st century is reliable, fast, and cheap. Just about every computer sold in the past few years has lots of it. The result is that people now store many thousands of files on their computers. To organize their folders, people use lots of folders and subfolders. Although having lots of well-organized files on your hard disk is certainly good, it has a couple of downsides. For one, drilling down through a ton of folders to get to a specific file gets tedious. For another, it's easy to forget where you put things and what you named them.

In earlier versions of Windows, you could use shortcuts and searches to help with these problems, but too many shortcuts just add that much more clutter to the screen. The old style of searching is slow and tedious. Searching in Windows 8.1 is a lot like searching on the Internet. You don't have to search for specific filenames. You can search by content and meaning. And in most cases the search results are instantaneous. You don't have to wait for the system to slog through the whole file system looking at every file.

Basics of Searching

Like filing cabinets, computers just store information. The information in your filing cabinet has no "meaning" to your filing cabinet. Likewise, the information in your computer has no meaning to the computer. Searching a computer is much like searching through a filing cabinet or the index at the back of a book.

In the next sections, we try to clear up some common misconceptions about searching. Along the way, we offer some tips and techniques that should make it easier to find what you're looking for.

You're not asking it questions

The most basic thing you need to understand about searching is that you're not asking the computer a question. Computers don't understand human languages the way people do. As mentioned, searching a computer (or the Internet) is much like searching the index at the back of a book. You need to zero in on a specific word or phrase. The more specific that word or phrase, the more specific the search results.

Let's use the Internet as an example. You certainly can search for something like

> What is the capital of Kansas?

You will likely get your answer from any Internet search engine. However, you'd probably get the same or similar results if you searched for

> capital Kansas

The keywords in the search are **capital** and **Kansas**. The other words don't help to narrow the search much because you're searching for words, not meaning. Virtually every page on the Internet contains the words **what**, **is**, **the**, and **of**, even if the page has nothing to do with Kansas or capital.

We're not saying you *can't* conduct a search for **What is the capital of Kansas?** You certainly can if you want to, and you will get results. However, the results won't be much different than if you left out the *noise words* (words that appear in virtually all written documents and don't help describe what the page is about). Examples of noise words include the following:

a	it	the	want	who
about	me	then	was	will
an	my	there	we	with
are	of	these	were	would
but	should	they	what	you
did	so	this	when	your
how	than	to	where	
is	that	too	which	

Some search programs will actually remove all the noise words before conducting the search. Others will include them. But sometimes that works against you because you find things in your search results that have nothing to do with what you were really searching for.

The bottom line is this: When you search for something, don't try to word it as a question. Instead, search for an exact word or phrase that has a specific meaning.

Be specific

The key to successful searches, whether on the Internet or on your computer, is to be specific. The more specific you are about what you're searching for, the better the results.

Here's an Internet search as an example. Suppose you're looking for quotes by Benjamin Franklin on health. If you search Google for **health**, you get links to about 4.3 billion pages. That doesn't help much because a lifetime isn't enough time to look through all those. If you search Google for **Benjamin Franklin**, you get links to 28.7 million web pages. That's still too many.

If you search Google for **Benjamin Franklin health**, you get links to 39.7 million pages. If you search for **Benjamin Franklin quotation health**, you get links to 3.7 million pages. Now, if you add the word **wise** to the search (because the quote contains that word), you get about 625,000 hits. Notice how the more specific words there are in the search, the smaller (and also better targeted) the search results. In fact, one of the first pages listed will probably contain exactly what you're looking for. The moral of the story being: The more specific the search, the more specific the search results.

TIP

After you've clicked a link to a page, you can search that specific page for a word by choosing Edit ⇨ Find on this page (or pressing Ctrl+F) in Microsoft Internet Explorer. If you use some other web browser, check its Edit menu or Help for a similar feature.

Of course, searching the Internet and searching your own computer are two entirely different things, for the simple reason that the Internet exists *outside* your computer, and its searches don't include things that are inside your computer. But the general rule of specificity applies to all searches.

Spelling counts

When you write text for a human to read, you can get away with a ton of spelling errors. For example, the following sentence is loaded with spelling errors, but you can probably still figure out what the sentence says:

Th kwik brwn dogg jmpt ovr teh lzy mune.

You can figure it out because you have a brain, and brains have many strategies for figuring things out based on context, the sounds the letters make when read aloud, and so forth. Computers don't have brains and can't figure things out.

Plenty of computer programs (including tools built directly into Windows 8.1) are available that can correct your spelling, suggest alternate spellings, and such, but those programs aren't as good as a human brain. Spelling is one of those traits that some people are good at, and other people aren't. But knowing how to spell the words you're searching for is a good thing.

If you're not sure how to spell something, try typing it into a word-processing system that has spell checking. Or, if that's not an option for you, try an online service such as www.spellcheck.net or www.dictionary.reference.com. If it's a tech term, try www.webopedia.com.

Where you start the search matters

You can search in many different places and for many different kinds of things. Where you start your search and what you search for matters a lot. For example, there's the World Wide Web, which consists of several billion pages of text that exist outside your computer. It makes no sense to search the Internet when you're looking for something that's in your own computer.

Inside your own computer are basically two types of searches to consider. One is a search for *help*. There, you're typically looking for instructions on how to perform some task. Chapter 7 provides strategies for getting help with Windows 8.1. You also can rely on app- or application-specific help for assistance while using an app or program. This chapter has nothing to do with searching for help.

This chapter is mostly about searching for programs, folders, files, and messages that are inside, or directly connected to, your computer — the kinds of things you can use even when you're *offline* (not connected to the Internet).

How Searching Works

Understanding how searches work in Windows 8.1 is critical to performing quick, successful searches. Most searches are performed on an *index*. The index is like the index at the back of this or any other book. It's basically a list of keywords. Of course, Windows 8.1's index doesn't contain page numbers. In place of page numbers, it contains filenames and locations. You never see the index with your own eyes. The index is built, maintained, and searched behind the scenes without any intervention on your part.

Some searches you perform search the entire index. Others search only for programs, files, e-mail messages, or contacts. Still others ignore the index and search through every single folder on one or more drives. It all depends on where you start the search and how you perform the search. Let's start with common, everyday searches that are fast and easy to do.

> **TIP**
>
> The Quick Link menu Search box (press Windows+X) uses the Windows 8.1 Interface search tool and provides a quick and easy way to open programs, folders, files, and messages.

Quick Charms Bar Searches

The quick-and-easy way to find a program, Windows 8.1 app, favorite website, file, contact, or e-mail message is to search right from the Charms menu. Display the Charms Bar and choose Search. The Search box displays at the top right of the Search page (see Figure 22.1). This is the same search box you see even if you choose to search from the Windows desktop. The cursor is already in the Search box, so you can just start typing.

FIGURE 22.1

The Search box at the top right of the Search page

Windows 8.1 breaks down the type of searches into the following categories. The default is "Everywhere," but here's a list of some of the popular locations into which search reaches:

- **Apps:** Searches apps and programs that are currently installed on your computer and ready to use.

- **Settings:** Searches Windows configuration settings, such as those that can change the display resolution on your computer.

- **Files:** Searches documents and other files on your hard drive. Search also drills into SkyDrive, which is integrated into Windows 8.1.

- **People:** Searches contacts stored on your computer.

- **Finance:** Searches current financial information about a company.

- **Internet Explorer:** Displays the Bing search engine and searches on the word or term you enter.

- **Mail:** Searches your local e-mail account for messages containing the search criteria.

- **Maps:** Displays the Maps app and searches for the location you specify.

- **Music:** Searches the Music app for music stored on your computer and available through the Music Marketplace. Through the Marketplace, you can preview and purchase songs.

- **Photos:** Searches the Photos app for photos matching your search criteria.
- **Store:** Displays the Windows Store and returns apps that meet your search criteria. You can click an app to learn more about it. If you like it, you can download it to your computer.
- **Video:** Displays the Video app and returns videos based on the search criteria you enter.
- **Weather:** Displays the Weather app and returns weather information and forecasts about the location you specify.
- **Xbox Companion:** Displays the Microsoft Xbox Companion app to search using an Xbox 360 console.
- **Xbox LIVE Games:** Displays the Microsoft Xbox LIVE Games marketplace to enable you to search Xbox LIVE content.

As soon as you type one character, the search results appear on the Search screen to the left of the Search box. Each character you type reduces the search results to include only items that contain those letters. You get instant feedback as you type, so you can just keep typing as many characters as necessary until you see the item you want. To search within a category, such as Music, click that category after you type in a few letters. An example of a search result for apps matching the word *productivity* is shown in Figure 22.2. The Windows Store appears with apps that match your search criteria.

FIGURE 22.2

Results of searching for productivity apps in the Windows Store

When conducting searches in Windows 8.1, the searches do not look exclusively at file and folder names — they look at the contents of files, tags, and properties as well. (And with Windows 8.1, Search can even scan inside images for hidden text.) We talk about what those things are in Chapter 23. We mention it here in case you're wondering why some of your recent search results include search criteria not necessarily found in the names of files or folders. For example, you might search on the term **money** and the files and folder that display as a result do not have the word *money* in them. It's because the word *money* appears within the message or contact's information.

You can do many things with the search results:

- To open an item, click it.
- To see other things you can do with an item, right-click it.
- If an item you were expecting to find doesn't show up, or if you want to improve the search, redo the search with other criteria.
- To discard the search results, press Esc or choose something else from the Charms Bar.

You can do wildcard searches from the Quick Link menu, where * stands for any characters and **?** stands for a single character. But do keep in mind that when you search from the Search box, you're only searching the index, not the entire hard disk. So, don't be too surprised if some files don't show up.

You can also do **AND** and **OR** searches from the Start menu. For example, a search for *.jpg OR *.jpeg finds files that have either a `.jpg` or `.jpeg` extension. We talk about these kinds of searches in more detail later in this chapter and in the next chapter.

Customizing Windows Search

You can customize Windows Search to store a history of your searches, show the most popular searched apps at the top of the search list, and include or exclude certain apps to search.

To set these options, you open the PC Settings window by choosing the Settings item from the Charms Bar and then choosing the PC Settings link. Once on the PC Settings window, click Search and Apps. You have the following options, as shown in Figure 22.3:

- **Clear Search History:** Click the Clear button to remove previous search results.
- **Use Bing to Search Online:** Specifies that Windows should use Bing for search suggestions and web results.
- **Your Search Experience:** Specifies personalization options for Bing searches.
- **Safe Search:** Specifies safe search options to filter out adult results from your searches.
- **Metered Connections:** Specifies getting search results over metered connections.

FIGURE 22.3

Search setting options

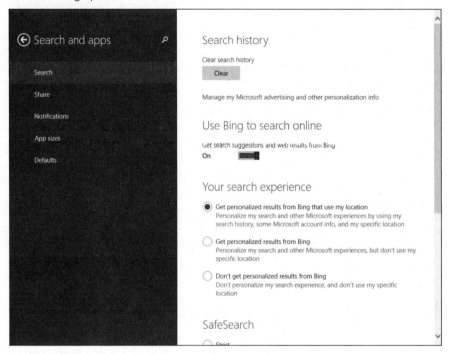

Extending a Start menu search

If the thing you're looking for doesn't show up in your search, first check your spelling. Make sure the word you're searching for matches something on your computer. For example, if you're looking for photos of your dog named Spot, a search for **Spot** won't find them unless the photos have Spot in the filename, tags, or properties.

Search box searches are ideal for finding the kinds of things most people use most often — apps, music, programs, folders, Control Panel dialog boxes, favorite websites, messages, and documents (text, worksheets, pictures, music, and videos). If you're a quick typist, using the Search box can save you a lot of time you'd otherwise spend clicking and opening things through the traditional methods. But Search box searches aren't the end of the story. Not by a long shot. There's much more, as you'll see.

> **TIP**
>
> The Search box in File Explorer's upper-right corner provides a quick-and-easy way to search the current folder and its subfolders.

Searching Folders and Views

By now you may have noticed File Explorer has a Search box in its upper-right corner. The Search box, by default, includes text that describes the search context, such as Search Libraries, as in Figure 22.4.

FIGURE 22.4

The Search box in Explorer (all folders)

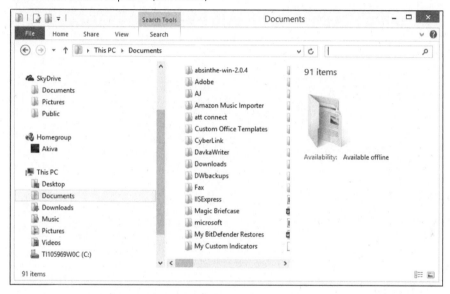

22

Like the Search box on the Charms Bar, the one in File Explorer gives you instant keystroke-by-keystroke search results. With Windows 8.1, you can search for different kinds of items from the Explorer window. You aren't limited to just files and folders. You can, for example, search for music playlists, programs, recorded TV programs, tasks, and other kinds of items. The view consists of all files and subfolders you see in the main content pane, but it also can be expanded to search for all subfolders. The Search box in Explorer doesn't look strictly at file and folder names either. It looks at the contents of files that contain text, tags, and other metadata. So, once again, you use it in much the same way you use an Internet search engine: not just to search for a specific filename, but to search for keywords or phrases.

The Search box in Explorer works best when you have some idea where the item you're looking for is located. For example, let's say you have thousands of songs in your Music folder and its subfolders. You want to see all songs in the Jazz genre. Step 1 is to open your Music folder. Step 2 is to type **Jazz** into the Search box. Instantly, you see all songs in the jazz genre. To ensure that you're searching all the subfolders, click the All Subfolders option on the Search Tool tab of File Explorer.

You certainly aren't limited to searching a genre. You can type an artist's name to see all songs by that artist. You can type a few characters from a song title. Basically, you can type anything you want to find, whatever it is you're looking for. Just keep in mind that you're searching only the current folder or its subfolders.

When you're first learning to use the Search box in Explorer, there will be times when you don't find a file you might have been expecting to find. This might happen for several reasons:

- The file isn't in the folder you're searching (or one of its subfolders).
- The way you spelled the search term in the Search box doesn't match how it's spelled in the file(s).
- The file you were expecting to find isn't one of the file types selected from the Kind drop-down list (shown in Figure 22.5).

FIGURE 22.5

You can specify the kind of file you're searching for.

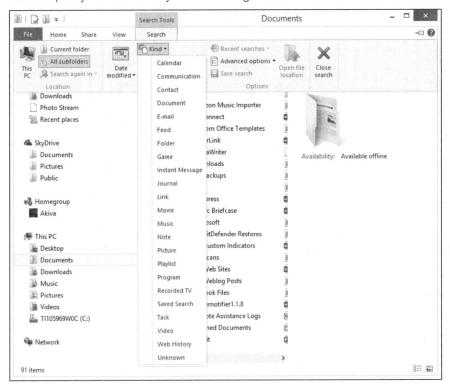

If you get more results than you were expecting, keep in mind that the search isn't looking only at the filenames, or only at the columns you see in the results. It's searching properties that might not even be visible in the Details view and the contents of files that contain text.

Specifying search criteria

Anything you type into a Search box is a *search criterion.* As soon as you click in the search box, the Search ribbon appears at the top of File Manager under Search Tools. The ribbon gives you access to the most advanced search options yet to be included in Windows. Basically, the search criterion is telling Windows 8.1, "Show me all items that have these characteristics." The "items" are things such as files, folders, music, contacts, messages, contacts, and Internet Explorer favorites.

The search criterion can be as simple as a few characters of text. For example, you can click in the Search box, type a person's name, and find whatever files and messages on your computer that contain that person's name. You can also use multiple search criteria to locate items. First, let's take a look at how to perform a search using different types of search criteria.

Search by date

You can narrow your search to specific kinds of dates by adding a date filter to your search. For example, you can search by using the following Date Modified options (the last time you opened, changed, and saved the file):

- Today
- Yesterday
- This Week
- Last Week
- This Month
- Last Month
- This Year
- Last Year

To select a date option, click the Date Modified button on the Search tab. Figure 22.6 shows these options.

22

FIGURE 22.6

You can specify the modify date of files you're searching.

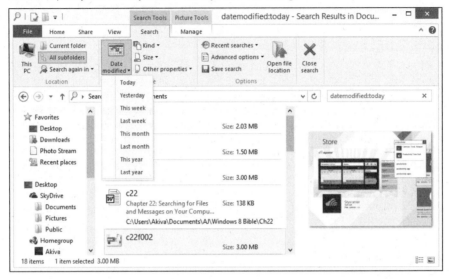

If you're working in the Pictures folder, you can choose Date Taken from the File Explorer search box to find pictures taken (created) on a particular day or in a particular date range.

Here's an example: Click the File Explorer icon on the desktop or from the Windows 8.1 interface to open File Explorer. Click in the Search box and then click Date Modified from the drop-down menu that appears. You can then click a date from the date picker or click an option like Yesterday or This Month. Windows 8.1 searches in your libraries for the files that meet those criteria.

Although Date Modified is the only date option available when you search at the Libraries level, it isn't the only date criteria you can use to search. For example, you can search by date created, date modified, and last accessed. If you don't see the search option you need, you can type it.

Let's say today is October 8, 2013, and you've just created or downloaded a file. The problem is, you clicked the Save button without choosing where to put the file, and you didn't notice the name of the file. So, now you don't know where it is. Open the parent folder where you downloaded the file, click in the Search box, and type **datecreated:today** to see all files created today. That might help you find the file. When you do this, Windows 8.1 displays a helpful calendar tool and the set of Date Modified options in case you want to select a different date or date range. Figure 22.7 shows an example of how this works.

FIGURE 22.7

Searching a date range

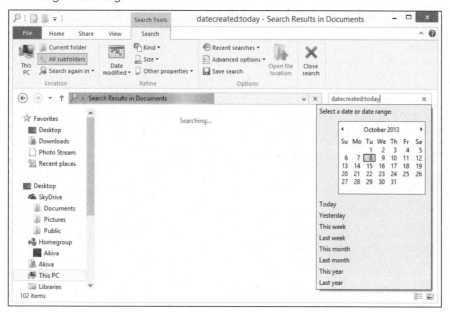

To search for files within a range of dates, choose one of the date criteria (like Date Modified). In the calendar that drops down, click the start or end date. Then hold down the Shift key and click the other date. Or simply click and drag across the date range with the mouse. Both dates, and all the dates in between, are highlighted. Windows 8.1 displays the files that fill the criteria within that date range.

Search by size

The Size option lets you search for files that are an exact size, or files that are larger or smaller than some size. For example, let's say you bought a second hard drive and want to move some large video files to it. You could search for Size and choose the Gigantic option, which finds files larger than 128MB. Or, you can specify a particular size, such as 500MB or 1GB. To search by a specific size, click the Size option in the Search box and then type a size after the colon. Use the modifiers K for kilobyte, M for megabyte, and G for gigabyte.

> **NOTE**
>
> A megabyte (MB) is about 1,000KB (exactly 1,024KB). A gigabyte (GB) is about 1,000,000KB (exactly 1,048,576KB).

Search by filename or subject

In the Search box, you can type a specific filename or part of a filename. For example, a search for **sunset** finds all files that have the word *sunset* in the filename. You can use wildcard characters as in earlier versions of Windows (and DOS). Use **?** to stand for a single character, and * to stand for any group of characters. For example, let's say you have files named Sunset (1), Sunset (2), Sunset (3), and so forth. A search for **sunset*** finds them all.

You can include filename extensions to narrow down the search. For example, a search for **.jpg** finds all files that have a .jpg extension. A search for **sunset*.jpg** finds all files that start with sunset and end with a .jpg filename extension.

You can use the word **OR** (in uppercase letters, with a space before and after the word) to extend the search to multiple criteria. For example, consider the following typed into the Filename box:

*.jpg OR *.jpeg

When you click the Search button, you get all files that have either a .jpg extension or a .jpeg extension. Similarly, you could search for

sunset*.jpg OR sunset*.jpeg

to find all files that start with *sunset* and end with either .jpg or .jpeg.

You're not limited to just one **OR**. For example, placing the following in the Filename box

*.avi OR *.wmv OR *.mpg OR *.mpeg

finds all files that end with .avi, .wmv, .mpg, or .mpeg.

CAUTION

Make sure you use OR, not AND. It's a common misunderstanding that we discuss in Chapter 30.

If you're searching a folder that contains e-mail messages, you can search using e-mail–specific criteria. For example, you can search for e-mail messages that have a certain word or phrase in the Subject line. There's no need to use wildcards or filename extensions because the Subject line is just text, not a filename. To search by subject, click in the Search box and type **subject:(subject text)**, where *subject text* is the text for which you're searching. You can also simply type the text in the Search box without the **subject:** modifier, but you'll return results from matches other than in the subject of the e-mail messages. You can use other criteria such as From and To when searching for e-mail messages, as well as enter text that appears in the body of the message.

Search by kind

Windows 8.1 enables you to search by the type of object you want to find. For example, you can search for contacts, documents, e-mail, feeds, folders, games, and more. On the Search tab, Windows 8.1 displays the Kind tool (refer to Figure 22.5). This tool enables you to choose the kind(s) of objects to search for.

> **TIP**
>
> To search for multiple kinds of objects, use the OR logical operator with multiple kind: specifications.

Search by tags, authors, title, and others

Depending on what type of folder you're searching in, you'll see other boxes such as Tags, Authors, or Title for specifying search criteria. These correspond to metadata stored in file properties. You can type in any word or phrase to search for files that have that word or phrase in the corresponding property.

 We talk more about those properties in Chapter 28.

Saving a search

Searches can be used in two ways. In some cases, you might just be looking for a file you've lost track of. In that case, once you've found the file, there's probably no need to repeat the search in the future. You can just double-click the found file to open it. Then close the Search by clicking the Close Search button on the Search tab in File Explorer.

There may be other times when you put some time into constructing a search to pull together files from multiple folders. For example, a search for ***.avi OR *.wmv OR *.mpg OR *.mpeg** shows all video files with those extensions. If you think you'll want to check up on your current video files often, you don't need to re-create the search from scratch each time. You can save the search. Any time you want to check up on your current video files, open the saved search. It will show you all *current* files that meet those criteria.

Saving a search is easy. After you've performed the search, you'll see a Save Search button on the Search tab. Just click that button and a Save As dialog box opens. The name of the search will reflect the search criteria you specified. But you don't need to keep that name. Type in any name that will be easy to recognize in the future. For example, Figure 22.8 shows a named search about to be saved as Graphics Files. Windows 8.1 suggests putting it in the Searches folder for your user account. That's as good a place as any to keep it, so don't change that unless you have some good reason.

FIGURE 22.8

Saving a search for video files

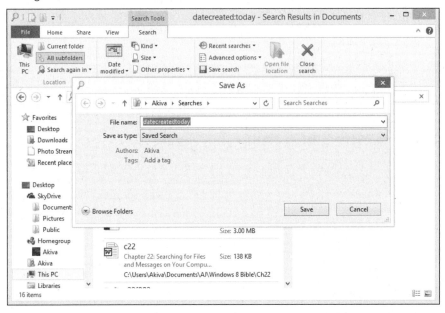

TIP

Windows stores these saved searches using the Saved Search format, which is `.search-ms`. This is good to know if you ever need to look for saved searches on your system.

At the bottom of the Save As dialog box, your username is saved as the default author, but you can click that name and change it to another name or add author names. To add a tag to the saved search file, click the Add a Tag item if you like. Then click the Save button.

Using saved searches

Unless you specify otherwise, your saved searches are stored in the Searches folder for your user account. Your searches are also added to the Favorites folder. You can open the Searches folder using the following methods:

- Choose Search from the Charms Bar and type **searches** in the Search box. In the Results area, click the Searches folder.

- Open File Explorer from the Windows 8.1 interface or from the desktop, click your user account name, and open the Searches folder.

- If you're in a folder and the Navigation pane is open, click the saved search under Favorites.

- Choose Windows + X from the desktop, click Search, and type **searches** in the Search box. Click the Searches folder to open it.

Unless you opened a specific search, the Searches folder opens. You'll see searches you've saved yourself. Figure 22.9 shows an example.

FIGURE 22.9

Saved searches

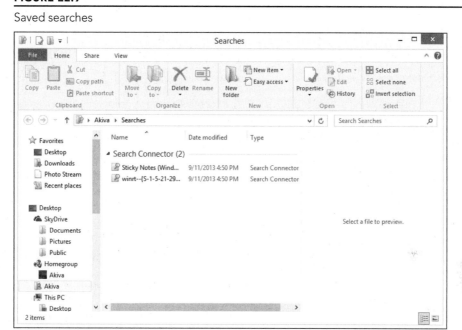

To perform a saved search, just open it by double-clicking its icon. The opened search looks just like any real folder. In fact, you can treat it just as you would any folder. The only difference between a saved search and another folder is that the saved search doesn't actually contain files. The saved search is a *virtual folder* that looks and acts like a real folder. But the files you see in the saved search are still in the folder where you originally saved them. The virtual folder lets you see all the files that match the search criteria *as though* they were all in one folder. This allows you to work with the files as a unit, regardless of their actual physical location in folders.

A search in Windows 8.1 is similar to an Internet search. When you search in Windows 8.1, or open a saved search, you're really just looking at links to files that match the search criteria. But do be aware that when you do something to a file in the search results, you perform that action on the actual file. For example, when you delete a file from a saved search, you delete it from its actual location. Likewise, if you restore that file from the Recycle Bin, you restore it back to its original location.

Wrap-Up

You have many ways to find things in Windows 8.1. The primary method includes typing a word in the Search box on the Search page to find items that contain that word, or searching in File Explorer using a wide range of criteria.

Each box is similar to a mini search engine for finding documents and messages based on content, properties, tags, or name. By default, only items in your user account are searched.

 If you want to include more items in those searches, see Chapter 30.

Here's a quick review of the main points covered in this chapter:

- Windows 8.1 has a built-in index of programs, files, folders, and messages in your user account. When you search the index, you get keystroke-by-keystroke results.
- To search from the Windows 8.1 interface or the Windows desktop, choose Search from the Charms Bar. Then start typing your search text.
- To search for a file when you know its general location, open the folder or a parent folder of the item. Then use the Search box in Explorer's upper-right corner to search.
- You can specify multiple criteria in both the Search box and in File Explorer by entering search keywords such as date modified, subject, size, and others, followed by a colon and the search parameter. You can combine multiple criteria in a single search.
- To save a search for future use, click Save Search on the Search tab of File Explorer.
- To reuse saved searches, click Search from the Charms Bar, type **searches** in the Search box, and click the Searches folder. Or click Searches under Favorites (if available) in the Navigation pane of any folder.

 If you frequently use files that are outside your user account folders, see Chapter 30 for info on adding those folders to your search index.

Metadata and Power Searches

IN THIS CHAPTER

Working with file properties

Adding and changing properties

Adding locations to your search index

Customizing the search index

Implementing power searches

C hapter 22 covers different ways you can search your computer. When you search for files, you actually search an index of filenames and properties. The index isn't something you see on the screen. Nor do you have to do anything to create or update the index. Windows 8.1 takes care of all the details automatically and behind the scenes. The beauty of the index is that it allows Windows 8.1 to find things much more quickly than it could without the index.

The information about files that's in the index comes from each file's properties. Those properties are sometimes referred to as *metadata* because they're different from the file's content. The file's content is what you see on the screen when you open the file. The file's properties are stored in the file and are visible from the file's properties sheet.

Properties provide a way of organizing files that goes beyond their physical location in folders. This is a great help to people who have many files to manage — sometimes a simple folder name and filename just aren't enough. Sometimes you want to see all files based on authorship, date created, tags, subject, or even comments you've jotted down about the file. In other words, you want to pull together and work with files in a way that transcends their physical locations in folders. Metadata in Windows 8.1's indexed searches allows you to do that quickly and easily.

> **TIP**
> You can view file metadata in File Explorer's Details pane.

Working with File Properties

Taking a wild guess, we'd say you can put several thousand different types of files on a PC. No one person needs them all or uses them all. Some file types are so esoteric that you might never come across one.

In File Explorer, you can view and edit a file's properties in many ways. One way is to open the folder in which the file is contained and then select the file's icon. The Details pane, if open, displays the file's properties. If the Details pane isn't open, select the View tab and click the Details Pane button.

Initially, the Details pane might be too short to show all the file's properties, but you can drag its top border upward to see more properties. Figure 23.1 shows an example displaying the properties for a Microsoft Word 2010 document. Other file types will have other properties.

FIGURE 23.1

A file's properties in the Details pane

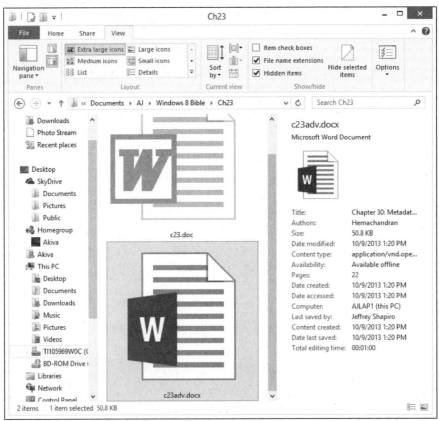

Viewing properties sheets

Here's another way to view a file's properties: Right-click the file's icon and choose Properties. A dialog box opens. If that dialog box has a Details tab, that's where you're most likely to find the kinds of properties you can create and edit. You'll often hear the term *properties sheet* used to describe that set of properties because it's kind of like a sheet of paper on which properties are written.

Figure 23.2 shows a couple of sample properties sheets. On the left is the properties sheet for the Word document shown in Figure 23.1. On the right is the properties sheet for a JPG image. When there are more properties than fit in the box, use the scroll bar at the right side of the box to see others.

FIGURE 23.2

Examples of properties sheets for two different files

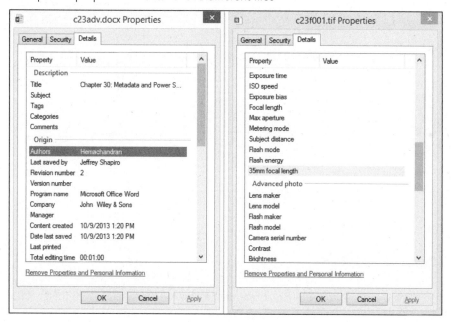

Every property has a name and a *value* (some text, date, or number that's assigned to the property). In the properties sheets, the property names are listed down the left column. The value assigned to each property (if any) appears to the right of the property name.

Viewing properties in columns

Yet a third way to view properties is through the Details view in File Explorer. In any folder (including the results of a search), select the Views tab and choose Details. You'll see a few columns across the top of the contents pane. But what you see isn't necessarily all there is. The horizontal scroll bar across the bottom of the pane lets you scroll to other columns. You can also add columns to the view (or remove columns) by right-clicking any column heading, as in Figure 23.3. The menu that appears shows a few other columns from which you can choose. Click More at the bottom of that menu to see others.

 See Chapter 27 for information on choosing, moving, and sizing columns in the Details view.

FIGURE 23.3

Choosing columns in Details view

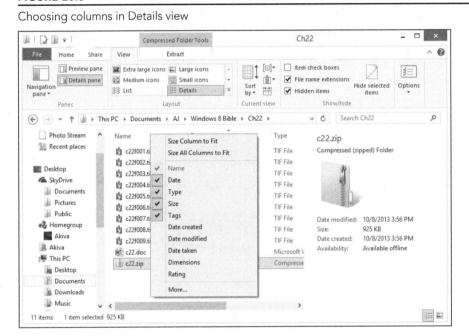

Editing properties

To change a file's properties, select its icon and make your changes in the Details pane. Or right-click the file's icon, choose Properties, select the Details tab, and make your changes there.

You can change properties for multiple files using the same basic method. You just have to select the icons for the files first. But there is a catch: You'll be limited to changing properties that all the selected files have in common. This can be a real pain when you're working with multiple file types. For example, many different types of files for storing pictures exist — JPEG, TIFF, PNG, BMP, and GIF to name a few. The newer file types — JPEG, TIFF, and PNG — offer many properties. The older file types — BMP and GIF — offer relatively few.

Figure 23.4 shows an example of what can happen when you select multiple file types. We selected all the icons in the folder, each of which is a picture. Then we right-clicked one of them, chose Properties, and selected the Details tab. Hardly any properties are showing because all those different file types have few properties in common.

FIGURE 23.4

Properties for multiple files

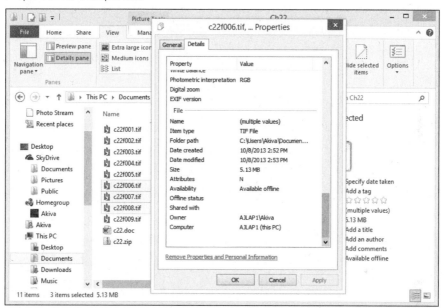

With old file types that support few properties, about the only thing you can do is convert them to newer file types. For example, you might have a lot of GIF images on your system when you installed Windows 8.1. That file type doesn't offer any really usable properties. To resolve this, you can use the batch conversion feature of your graphics program (PaintShop Pro) to convert them all to PNG files. We suggest PNG because it supports transparency like GIF does.

> **NOTE**
> PNG does not support animation, so you may not want to convert animated GIFs to PNG.

If you have many files that you want to assign new properties to, you might consider creating a search that brings similar files together all under one roof, so to speak. Open the Libraries folder (or other folder that is a parent of the one you want to search) and click in the Search box to specify the types of files you want to work with. In Figure 23.5, we typed the following into the Filename box:

```
*.jpg OR *.jpeg OR *.tif OR *.tiff OR *.png NOT *.lnk
```

FIGURE 23.5

Specify the types of files in the Search box

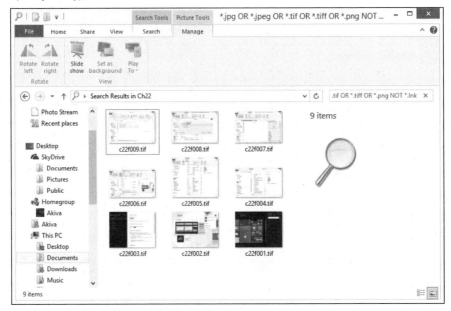

That brings together all the TIFF, JPEG, and PNG files in the search scope, and omits any shortcuts (.lnk files). (The .lnk files won't have many editable properties either.) Perform the search and then use column headings to sort items based on their current folder location. You can also add columns that allow you to see the properties you intend to work with. Of course, that's just an example. You can set up searches to find and organize things as you see fit.

Save the search when you're done so you can open and use it whenever you have time to work with properties. To change properties for any single file, click its name. To assign the same property value to multiple files, select their icons. Then use the Details pane or properties sheet to make your changes. It will take some time if you have a number of files to work with. But having all the files together in one place, and the properties of interest in plain view, can make the job less daunting.

TIP

Windows 8.1's Save As dialog box offers tools for entering metadata (such as tags) when you save a file.

Setting Properties When You Save

Search indexes are nothing new. Database administrators have been using them for decades. Every time you do an Internet search, you're actually searching an index of websites somewhere. Windows XP and other operating systems allow for some limited, indexed searching through add-on programs. But Windows Vista was the first Windows version to have indexed searching — its own built-in search engine — built in from the ground up. Windows 7 expanded upon and improved the search capabilities introduced in Vista. Windows 8.1 continues the search capabilities with the capabilities to search Windows apps, the Windows Marketplace, Xbox LIVE, and Xbox Companion areas from within Windows. Other software developers understand the value of that. As the years roll by, new versions of old programs will include the ability to tag files and set properties at the moment you first save the program. In addition, the relationship of the desktop environment to the online environment is much tighter and more seamless with Windows 8.1.

When you save a new file, be sure to look around for any options in the Save As dialog box that allow you to add tags or properties. Figure 23.6 shows an example of the Save As dialog box for a Microsoft PowerPoint 2013 presentation. As you can see, the dialog box allows you to add tags and authors right on the spot.

FIGURE 23.6

Save As dialog box for PowerPoint 2013

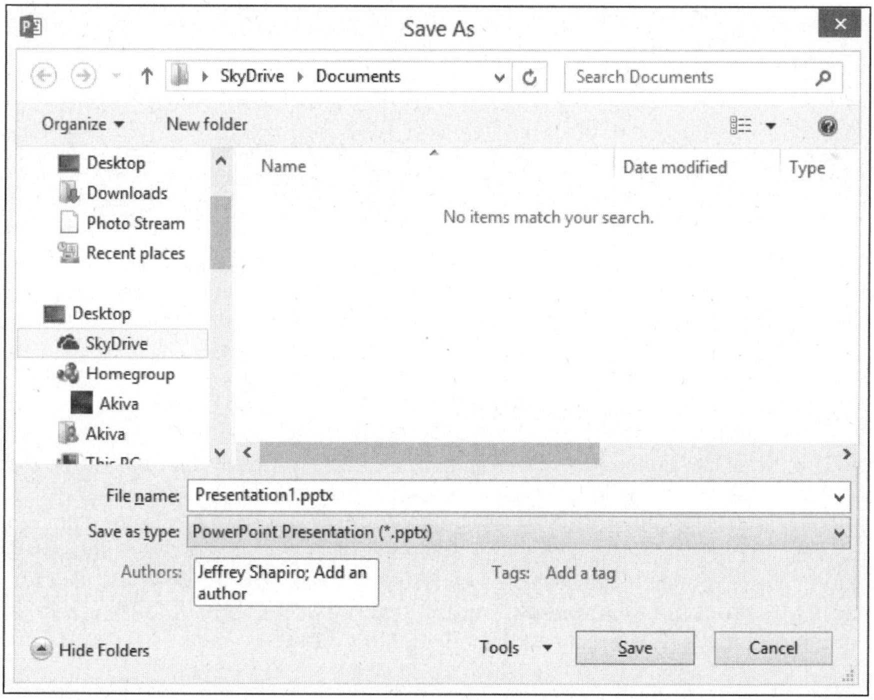

When you're faced with such options, think about words you might want to type into a Search box to find the file in the future. Ask yourself, "If I need this thing six months from now and forget its filename, what word might I use to search for it?" or "How should

I categorize this file in relation to other similar kinds of documents?" As your collection of files grows, and your searching skills grow, the few moments you spend thinking up keywords for tags and properties will pay off in spades.

> **TIP**
>
> You have many options for personalizing and configuring Windows 8.1's Search tools.

Personalizing Searches

Getting the most from Windows 8.1's searches includes knowing how to tweak its settings to work in ways that support the kinds of things you do. You can tweak some aspects of indexed searches through the Folder and Search Options dialog box. To get to the search options, do any of the following:

- If you're in a folder, select the View tab and click the Options button.
- Choose Search from Charms, type **fol** in the Search box, click the Settings category, and then click Folder Options in the Search Results area.

The Folder Options dialog box opens. Select the Search tab to see the options shown in Figure 23.7.

> **TIP**
>
> If some files aren't showing up in your searches because they're not in your user account folders, these options really won't help. Better to extend the index to include those files. We talk about how you do that in the next section.

The Find Partial Matches option, when selected, lets you type a few characters into the Search box and still get a match. For example, let's say you have numerous files with the name Sarah in the filename, artist name, or other property. When you type **sar** into the Search box, you see those items that contain "Sarah." But if you clear the Find Partial Matches check box, it won't work that way. You wouldn't see items that contain Sarah until you type all five characters, **sarah**.

The Don't Use the Index When Searching in File Folders for System Files (Searches Might Take Longer) option applies when you search non-indexed locations. When you select that option, searches outside the index work like non-indexed searches from older Windows versions. The search looks at every file in every folder and doesn't even look at the search option. When you leave that option unselected, the search still uses the index for files in indexed locations. So, that part of the search goes quickly. Then it falls back to the old non-indexed method, but only for files that aren't indexed.

The last three options apply only when you're searching non-indexed locations. Choose Include System Directories if you want non-indexed searches to include Windows and other program files that are essential to proper functioning of your PC. These are not files you normally open or modify yourself. So, it would make sense to choose this option only if you're a power user or administrator who needs frequent access to files in those locations. Otherwise, you're just slowing down your searches for no good reason.

FIGURE 23.7

Search options

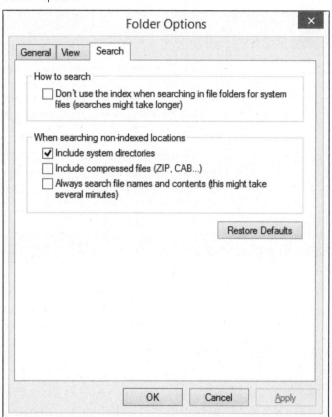

Choosing the Include Compressed Files (ZIP, CAB...) option extends the search into compressed Zip folders and the like. (CAB files are "cabinet" files, and they're compressed as well.) Typically, people only use compressed files for archived files that they don't use often because the compression and decompression add some time overhead to opening and closing the files. Including their contents in searches can also slow down searches. But if you want to include those files' contents in your non-indexed searches, just select the check box.

The option Always Search File Names and Contents (This Might Take Several Minutes) — forces searches to look at the contents of non-indexed files, which can really slow things down. Better to index the non-indexed document files to get the speedier index searches.

As always, clicking Restore Defaults sets all options back to their original defaults. Those are the options that provide the best performance for indexed searches and cover the things most people would typically want included in their searches.

Managing the Search Index

To get the best performance and value from the search index, you want to make sure it includes all the files you regularly use in your work. But you don't want to go overboard and also include files you never, or rarely, use. If you do, you're forcing Windows to search through thousands of filenames and properties for no good reason. By default, Windows 8.1 maximizes the search index by including messages and documents from a limited number of folders.

> **TIP**
>
> Some indexing settings can be changed by regular users. Advanced settings can only be changed by a user with administrative rights. Of course, many people use multiple hard disks to store their files. If you want to include files from other drives and folders, you'll need to add them to your search index. But do exercise some discretion. The larger the index, the more overhead involved in maintaining the index and the slower things go. Don't add a folder to the index if it contains a bunch of non-document files or files you don't open and use regularly.

Adding indexed locations

Windows 8.1 indexes certain folders by default. You can add or remove locations through the Indexing Options dialog box (see Figure 23.8) with the following steps:

1. Open the Indexing Options item from the Control Panel to open the Indexing Options dialog box.

2. Click Modify.

3. Expand drives and folders, as necessary, to get to the folder(s) you want to add. Use white triangles to expand, black triangles to collapse.

> **CAUTION**
>
> Items with check marks are already indexed. Don't clear any check marks unless you specifically want to remove that folder from your index. If you goof and lose track, click Cancel to leave the dialog box without saving any changes.

4. Select (check) the folder(s) you want to add. Choosing a folder automatically chooses all subfolders, so there's no need to select those individually. But you could clear the check mark on one if you wanted to exclude it from the index. Those excluded folders will show up in the Excluded column in Indexing Options.

5. Click OK.

What's with the Offline Files?

Offline files are files that primarily exist on some other computer. You use Sync Center to copy them to and from a portable notebook in a way that prevents the copies on your computer from becoming out of sync with copies on the main computer. The files are included in the search index, by default, because they're usually documents. And the search index is all about finding and opening documents quickly.

You can exclude offline files from the search index just by clearing the check box in the Indexed Locations dialog box. Any user can do that; administrative privileges aren't required. If you don't use offline files, there's no overhead to leaving that option selected. After all, if you don't use offline files, the folder is empty. It takes no time at all to index an empty folder.

FIGURE 23.8

Indexing options

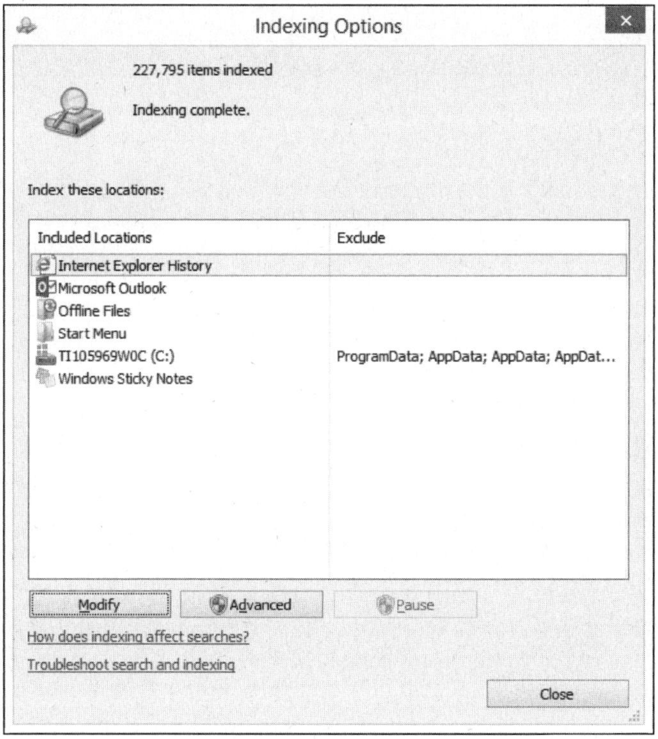

The folder is added to the index without any fanfare. About the only change you'll see is that the folder name appears in the Index These Locations list in Indexing Options.

Use the scroll bar to the right of that list if the folder name isn't immediately visible. Also, if you look at the text near the top of Indexing Options, you'll see the number of items indexed.

If you're actively using the computer, you see a message indicating that indexing speed is reduced due to user activity. Not to worry — it just means that the index-building process is giving priority to things you want to do. This message is replaced by others when the index is being built at full speed, and when indexing is compete.

You can add as many folders as you wish, from as many drives as you wish, using those same methods. But again, prudence is a virtue. *Remember:* Don't add folders just for the heck of it or because you don't know what's in a given folder. The more you can keep your index focused on files you want to find in searches and access through virtual folders, the better performance you'll get from the index.

> **TIP**
>
> With administrative rights, you can click Show All Locations in the Indexed Locations dialog box to show additional folders that are not shown by default. These include Offline Files folders for all users, rather than just the current user. You can also view user folders for users other than yourself when you click Show All Locations.

Remove a location from the index

Removing a folder from the index is the opposite of adding one. Repeat the preceding steps to get to the Indexed Locations dialog box shown in Figure 23.9. Expand drives and folders, as necessary, so you can see the items you've selected (checked). If you want to exclude some subfolders from one of your indexed folders, expand that folder first. Then clear the check marks from the subfolders you don't want in the index. Those subfolders show up in the Exclude column in the lower pane of the dialog box. Click OK after making your changes.

Choosing file types to index

The index intentionally excludes unknown file types, certain kinds of executable files, and libraries because they're not normally the kinds of things you want to locate in a quick file search or virtual folder. You can add any file type you wish to your index, and you can remove any file type you don't want to see.

Filenames and properties of selected file types are always indexed. For files that contain text, such as word-processing documents and spreadsheets, you can choose whether to index file contents. The advantage of indexing file contents is that when you search for files, the file shows up even if the search term isn't in the filename or properties. The slight disadvantage is that it adds some size to the index. But in this case, the advantage of including file contents probably outweighs the cost, unless you're using older, slower hardware and your searches are very slow.

FIGURE 23.9

The Indexed Locations dialog box

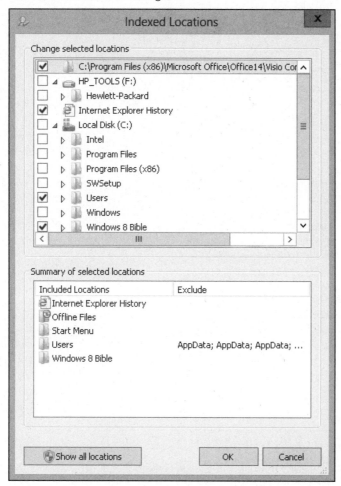

To change options for file types, open the Indexing Options dialog box and follow these steps:

1. Click the Advanced button (enter an administrative password if prompted).

2. In the dialog box that opens, select the File Types tab. You see a list of all file extensions, as in Figure 23.10:

   - To include a file type, select its check box.
   - To exclude a file type, clear its check box.
   - If you opted to include a file type, choose whether you want to index properties only or properties and file contents.

FIGURE 23.10

Choosing file types to index

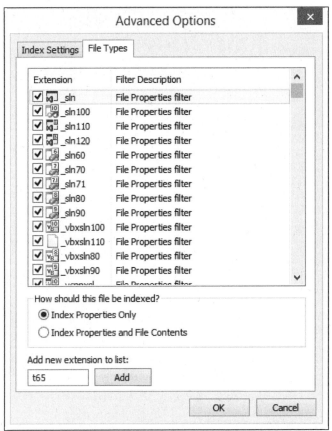

3. To add a file extension that isn't in the list, type the extension next to the Add button and click the Add button.

4. Click OK after making your changes.

More advanced options

You can make some more advanced tweaks to the index to change how it operates. You'll see them when you first click the Advanced button in Indexing Options. Figure 23.11 shows those advanced options on the Index Settings tab.

FIGURE 23.11

The Index Settings tab

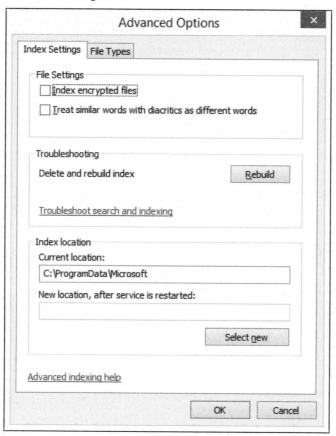

Choosing Index Encrypted Files ensures that encrypted files are included in searches and virtual indexes. People encrypt files to keep out prying eyes. Keeping those same files out of the index adds another layer of security by making them invisible to basic file searches. But if that's not a problem for you and you want your encrypted files to show up in searches, just choose the option to index encrypted files.

A *diacritic* (or diacritical mark) is an accent mark added to a letter to change a word's pronunciation. Some examples include the acute accent (á), circumflex (â), and umlaut (ä). When used in filenames and properties, Windows 8.1 usually treats characters with diacritics as being identical to the character without the mark. Choosing Treat Similar Words with Diacritics as Different Words changes the search behavior so that the diacritics are no longer lumped together as though they were a single character.

The Index Location option lets you specify where you want to store the search index. The default is the `C:\ProgramData\Microsoft` folder. If you have a separate hard drive that runs faster than your `C:` drive, you could relocate the index to that drive for better performance. Just make sure you choose a drive that's always attached to the computer, not a removable drive. Click the Select New button and use the Browse for Folder dialog box that appears to navigate the drive and folder in which you want to store the index.

If you see error messages about a corrupt index, or the system is crashing when you try to perform a search, the problem might be a corrupted index. You can rebuild the index to see if that helps, but the process could take several hours. So, if at all possible, you might consider doing this job as an overnighter. The process is simple: Just click the Rebuild button on the Index Settings tab of the Advanced Options dialog box (refer to Figure 23.11).

You can continue to use the computer while the index is being rebuilt. Any searches you perform while the index is being rebuilt will likely be incomplete.

Power Searches

The ability to display the Search box, type a few characters, and see all items that contain those characters is really a great thing. For most people, it saves a lot of time otherwise spent opening programs or navigating through folders to open a program, document, contact, or message. It's so useful that you might not even need to bother with more complex searches.

When you do need a more complex search, you can just use the Search box in File Explorer to search for particular types of files, and limit the search by date, filename, size, or whatever. You can create complex searches and save them. When you want to do the same search again in the future, that's handy, too. For folks who want still more, there's the query language.

You may have noticed that after you fill in the blanks in an Advanced Search and click the Search button, you see some text in the Search box. Take a look at Figure 23.12 for an example. There the date criterion is set to Date Modified 10/7/2013. This puts the following into the Search box:

```
datemodified:10/7/2013
```

That little line of text in the Search box, called a *query,* is what's actually returning the search results. When you perform the search, Windows 8.1 looks through the whole index. But the query acts as a filter of sorts. Only items that meet the conditions set forth by the query show in the search results. In this example, only files whose Date Modified date is 10/7/2013 appear in the search results. Items that don't match the criterion don't appear in the search results. Those items aren't deleted or changed in any way. They're simply "filtered out" so as not to show up in the search results.

FIGURE 23.12

Sample search

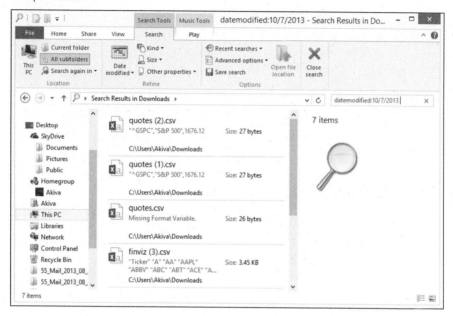

You can type your own queries into the Search box to perform complex searches. But, it's not as simple as "asking a question" or typing a bunch of words at random. You have to follow some rules and write the query in such a way that it can be interpreted properly. Otherwise, the search returns the wrong items, or no items at all. The following sections look at some ways you can type your own complex queries.

Searching specific properties

When you type a word into the search box, the results show files that contain that word in their filename, contents, and properties. For example, a search for jazz finds songs in the jazz music genre, any folder or file that has the word *jazz* in its filename or contents, and any file that has the word *jazz* in any property. In other words, you could end up with a whole lot of files in the search results.

You can always narrow a search by specifying a property name followed by a colon and the text for which you're searching. For example, a search for genre:jazz finds only music files in the jazz genre.

Similarly, a search for susan finds all files that have *susan* somewhere in the file, name, or a property, whereas a search for from:susan finds only e-mail messages that have the name *susan* in the From address (for a local e-mail client, not a web e-mail client).

You can assign ratings to pictures and music files, and use ratings as a search word. For example, `rating:5 stars` finds files with 5-star ratings.

Greater than and less than

When you're searching for a property that contains a date or a number, you can use comparison operators shown in Table 23-1.

TABLE 23.1   Comparison Operators Available with Search

Operator	Meaning
=	Equal to (this is assumed if you don't specify an operator below)
>	Greater than
>=	Greater than or equal to
<	Less than
<=	Less than or equal to
<>	Does not equal

A search for `rating:>=4` stars finds pictures and music with 4- or 5-star ratings. A search for `width:<600` finds pictures with widths less than 600 pixels. The query `modified:<2007` finds files last modified in 2006 or earlier. A search for `kind:video size:<300KB` finds video files less than 300KB in size.

AND, OR, and NOT searches

You can use the keywords AND, OR, and NOT in searches. You must type the word in upper-case letters. Be sure to include a space before and after the word.

Not using any word is the same as using AND. For example, consider the following search:

```
Datemodified:5/9/2012 name:koala
```

That means the same thing as this:

```
Datemodified:5/9/2012 AND name:koala
```

Any time you create an AND query, you *narrow* the search results. Intuitively, you might think it would have the opposite effect. But that's not the way it works. The query is a filter. To show up in the search results, a file must meet *all* criteria posed by the filter. For example, files that don't have *koala* in the Filename property won't show up at all, no matter what's in their Date Modified property. And files that were modified on dates other than 5/9/2012 won't show up either, even if they do have *koala* in the Filename field.

Here's a common mistake that might help to better illustrate this:

```
filename:(*.jpg AND *.jpeg)
```

Intuitively, you might expect this search to identify files with `.jpg` and `.jpeg` extensions. But it doesn't. The result of this search is nothing! Why? Because the criterion is a filter, not a question. To get through the filter, a file needs to have a `.jpg` extension *and* a `.jpeg` extension. But a file can't have two extensions. Every file has only one filename extension. Therefore, no single file could get past this filter.

When you want to *broaden*, not narrow, a search, you use OR. For example, take a look at this:

```
filename:(*.jpg OR *.jpeg)
```

To get past this filter, a file needs to have either a `.jpg` or a `.jpeg` extension. So, the result of the search displays all files that have either a `.jpg` or `.jpeg` filename extension.

> **TIP**
>
> If you don't see filename extensions in search results, select the View tab and click the Options button. Then select the View tab, clear the check mark next to Hide Extensions for Known File Types, and click OK.

By the way, you don't have to use the * and dot if you use `extension:`, `ext:`, or `type:` as the property name. For example, this search criterion also shows all files that have `.jpg` or `.jpeg` extensions:

```
ext:(jpg OR jpeg)
```

You're not limited to a single OR. Here's a search that shows all files that have `.avi`, `.wmv`, `.mpg`, and `.mpeg` extensions:

```
ext:(avi OR wmv OR mpg OR mpeg)
```

When you use `type:` you can use whatever appears in the Type column (in Details view) rather than the extension. For example, this search finds Microsoft Word documents:

```
type:word
```

This one finds Word documents that have *john* in the filename or inside the document text:

```
john AND type:word
```

Because the keyword AND is assumed if omitted, the following search works the same as the preceding one:

```
john type:word
```

23

If you want to look only at the filename and not the contents, use the `name:` property. For example, here's a query that looks for Excel spreadsheets that have the word *festival* in the filename:

```
name:festival type:excel
```

In addition to searching for extensions, you can use `kind:` to find certain kinds of files. For example, `kind:music` finds music files; `kind:picture` finds pictures; `kind:contact` finds contacts; `kind:e-mail` finds e-mail messages; and `kind:communication` finds messages and contacts.

The `NOT` keyword narrows a search by excluding items that match the criterion that follows. For example, when you use the `kind:` keyword, you get both the file type, as well as shortcuts that open the file type. To hide the shortcut files, use `NOT shortcut`. For example, here's a search criterion that shows all communications files excluding any shortcuts to those files:

```
kind:(communication NOT shortcut)
```

A search for `kind:video` shows all video files. This search shows all video files except the ones that have a `.mov` filename extension:

```
kind:video NOT extension:mov
```

It's not always necessary to specify the kind or type of file. For example, consider this query:

```
homecity:Cucamonga
```

That one finds all contacts whose Home City is Cucamonga. Because Contacts are the only type of file that have a Home City property, you'd probably only get contacts in the search results even without specifying `kind:contact`.

You can use `tag:` as a search property, too. For example, the query `tag:(alec OR ashley)` finds files that have either *alec* or *ashley* in the Tags property. The query `tag:(alec AND ashley)` finds files that have both *alec* and *ashley* in the Tags property.

If you use the Comments and Categories properties in files, use `comment:` and `category:` to search just those properties. Similarly, you can use `title:` to search the Title property and `subject:` to search the Subject property.

Date and number searches

When searching for files based on a date, you can use the following property names for specific dates:

- `modified`: Date the file was last modified
- `accessed`: Date the file was last opened

- `created`: Date the file was created
- `sent`: Date that a message was sent
- `received`: Date that a message was received
- `taken`: Date that a picture was taken

To search a range of dates, use the keywords followed by a start date, two dots (. .), and an end date. For example, to find all pictures taken between June 1, 2012, and September 1, 2012, use the criterion:

```
taken:6/1/2012..9/1/2012
```

You can also use comparison operators with date searches. For example, to see all files modified on or after January 1, 2012, use:

```
modified:>=1/1/2012
```

You can also use the following keywords with dates:

- `today`
- `tomorrow`
- `yesterday`
- `this week`
- `last week`
- `this month`
- `last month`
- `next month`
- `this year`
- `last year`
- `next year`

For example, this search finds all files modified today:

```
modified: today
```

This search shows all files that were created this week:

```
created:this week
```

Here's a query that lists all picture files that were taken this month:

```
taken:this month
```

To see all files modified between some date (say 1/1/2012) and today, use this query:

```
modified:>=1/1/2012 AND modified:<=today
```

If you're interested in a certain month and year, use the month name and year like this:

```
modified:july 2012
```

For a day of the week, use the weekday name like this:

```
modified:monday
```

The comparison operators work with numbers, too. When searching sizes, you can use KB, MB, and GB abbreviations. For example, here's a search criterion that finds all files that are 1MB or greater in size:

```
size:>=1MB
```

Here is one that finds files larger than 2GB in size:

```
size:>2GB
```

Here's one that finds files between 500KB and 1,000KB in size:

```
size:>=500KB AND size:<=1000KB
```

If you save music in various bit rates, here's a query that will find all files with bit rates greater than 300 Kbps:

```
bitrate:>=300kbps
```

If you wanted only MP3 files with those large bit rates, use

```
bitrate:>=300kbps AND type:mp3
```

Here's a query that finds all pictures whose height is 800 pixels or less:

```
kind:picture height:<=800
```

Searching for phrases

When searching for two or more words, you'll likely end up with documents that contain the words you specified, but not necessarily in the order you typed them. To prevent that problem, you can enclose the phrase is quotation marks. For example, typing the following into a Search box displays all files that contain the words *dear* and *wanda* regardless of their relative positions to one another:

```
dear wanda
```

But typing the following into a Search box displays files where the words *dear* and *wanda* appear right next to each other in the document:

```
"dear wanda"
```

Message searching

For Windows Live Mail messages (both e-mail and newsgroup), key properties include `to:`, `from:`, `about:`, `subject:`, `sent:`, and `received:`. Both `to:` and `from:` can contain any word that appears in the To: and From: columns in the message. The `about:` keyword looks at the contents of the messages, not just the subject line. For example, the following is a query that you could enter in the Search box on the Start menu, which finds all messages from someone named Kay that contain the word *lunch:*

```
from:kay about:lunch
```

Here's a query that shows all messages addressed to Alan that arrived today:

```
to:alan received:today
```

Here's a search that shows all messages addressed to Susan, sent by Alan, that have *contract* in the Subject line:

```
to:susan from:alan subject:contract
```

Here's a query for e-mail messages sent this week from Alan to Wanda that contain the words *chow mein:*

```
to:wanda about:"chow mein" from:alan sent:this week
```

Natural language queries

Earlier in this chapter, you saw the option Use Natural Language Search in the Folder and Search Options dialog box. If you choose that, you can omit the colons after property names and use uppercase or lowercase letters in search queries. This really does make it easier to type most queries. For example, with natural language, the following query finds all messages from Susan that contain the word *dinner:*

```
from susan about dinner
```

This search finds all video files excluding ones with a `.avi` filename extension:

```
kind video not avi
```

Here's the natural language version of the query about "chow mein" e-mail messages:

```
to wanda about chow mein from alan sent this week
```

Here's a query that finds all files whose size is greater than 5MB:

```
size > 5MB
```

Here's a natural language query that finds all songs by Led Zeppelin:

```
music by zeppelin
```

This natural language query finds all pictures that have the word *flower* in the filename:

```
flower pictures
```

Here's a natural language query that finds all files that contain the word *peas,* the word *carrots,* or both words:

```
peas or carrots
```

Here's a natural language search that finds files that contain the words *peas* and *carrots* (although not necessarily together):

```
peas and carrots
```

Here's one that finds files that contain all three words, *peas and carrots,* together:

```
"peas and carrots"
```

Looking for a file you just downloaded or saved today? Try this natural language search in the Search box on the Start menu:

```
created today
```

Here's a natural language search that lists all files modified yesterday:

```
modified yesterday
```

Here are some other natural language searches you can probably figure out without our telling you what they mean:

- `e-mail received today`
- `e-mail from alec received yesterday`
- `contact message`
- `pictures alec`
- `genre rock`
- `artists Santana`
- `rating 5 stars`

Using natural language syntax doesn't mean you can ignore all the other things described in this chapter. The folder from which you start the search still matters. And all the other options in the Folder and Search Options and Indexing Options dialog boxes still apply. But in most cases you can type a useful search query with minimal fuss. If you can't get a search to work, try turning off natural language searches and use the stricter syntax with colons after property names.

Wrap-Up

Windows 8.1's searching and indexing features pick up where Windows 7 and Windows 8 left off. Search is now a vast improvement over earlier versions of Windows and the add-on Search Companion used in Windows XP. Windows 8.1 searching isn't really about finding lost files, although you can certainly use it for that. But if you use it only for that, you're missing out on the big picture and some key features of Windows 8.1.

Windows 8.1 searches use an index of filenames, properties, and file contents to make searches quick and nimble. It also looks only at files in the search index because that's a lot faster than slogging through the entire file system to look at every file in every folder. But it only works right if your index includes all the locations where you keep your frequently used document files.

One thing is for sure. If you've been managing thousands of files in hundred of folders, and you're sick of opening programs and folders to get to things, you're sure to love the new search index. Maybe not at first, because you really have to understand what it is and how it works. And you may have to spend some time tweaking settings in a couple of dialog boxes. But once you're past that small bump in the road, you'll spend a lot less time *getting to* things, and a lot more time *doing* things!

This chapter introduced the following points:

- The search index includes information about files stored in the file's properties sheets.

- When you select a file in a folder, the Details pane shows the properties currently assigned to the file.

- You can also view a file's properties by right-clicking its icon and choosing Properties. Most editable properties are on the Details tab.

- File properties are also visible in any folder's Details view. That includes virtual folders (saved searches).

- The search index generally covers all files in your user account, people in your Contacts folder, and Windows Live Mail messages.

- The Folder and Search Options dialog box provides some options for personalizing searches.

- The Indexing Options dialog box provides a means of customizing the index to better suit how you organize your files.

23

Protecting Your Files

S ome things on your hard drive are valuable. Pictures and videos from digital cameras are irreplaceable. Documents you spent hours creating required an investment of your time. You wouldn't want to lose those things because of some technical problem or mistake you made, so it's a good idea to keep backups. That way, if you do lose the originals on your hard drive, you can just restore them from your backup copy.

In addition to the files you create and use yourself, many *system files* reside on your hard drive. These are files that Windows 8.1 needs to function properly. If those files get messed up, your computer may not work correctly. So, you need some means of backing up those system files as well.

This chapter explains how to back up both your personal files and your system files. (We'll also cover the ability to save your system settings and configuration to your SkyDrive.) Of course, the backups won't do you any good if you can't use them when you need them. So, of course, we discuss how to use those backups should the need ever arise to get your system back in shape. We also discuss System Protection, which creates restore points to keep copies of some files around temporarily, to help you fix minor mishaps on the spot without having to fumble around with external disks.

Simple File Backups

A simple way to back up items from your user account is to copy files to an external disk. You can use any of the methods described in Chapter 21 for copying files to accomplish this sort of backup. You just need to make sure that the disk to which you're copying has enough space to store what you're copying.

This chapter focuses on using hard drives, flash drives, and similar local disks to make backups. For ways to back up to the "cloud," read Chapter 16, which covers Microsoft SkyDrive. That chapter shows you how to store files online to give you the ability to back up files to an offsite location, and use those files from anyplace you have Internet access.

To see how much stuff is in a folder in your user account, open File Explorer and then point to the folder you're considering backing up, or right-click that folder and choose Properties. When you point, the size of the folder shows in a tooltip. When you right-click and choose Properties, the size of the folder shows up next to Size on Disk in the Properties dialog box (see Figure 24.1).

FIGURE 24.1

A folder's size shown in the Properties dialog box

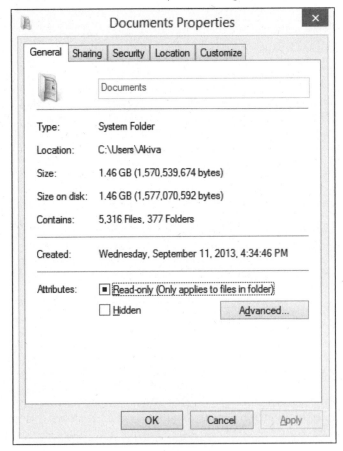

> **NOTE**
>
> Folder sizes show in tooltips only if you selected Show Pop-Up Description for Folder and Desktop Items in the Folder Options dialog box. For more information on that and other terms and concepts used in this chapter, see Chapter 21.

To see how much space is available on a removable disk, such as a flash drive, connect it to a USB port and then open your Computer folder. With some kinds of drives, you'll see the amount of available space right on the icon. For example, drive c: in Figure 24.2 has 149GB free.

FIGURE 24.2

A disk's available space

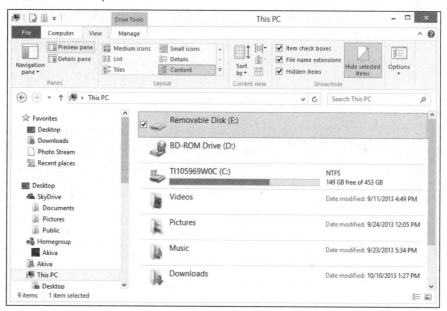

The layout for Windows 8.1 is very different from previous versions of File Explorer or Windows Explorer. As you can see there are no longer libraries.

> **TIP**
>
> 1KB is 1,024 bytes, 1MB is a little more than a million ($1,024^2$) bytes, and 1GB is about a billion ($1,024^3$) bytes.

If there's enough space on the disk for the item you want to copy, just go ahead and copy it using any method described in Chapter 21. If you ever lose or damage a file on your hard drive, you can get it back from the copy that's on the external disk.

> **NOTE**
>
> It's difficult for us to tell you how to back up your e-mail messages because dozens, if not hundreds, of different e-mail services and multiple e-mail clients exist, and they don't all work the same. In fact, e-mail really has nothing to do with Windows 8.1 at all. It's a service provided by your ISP or mail service provider. Your only real resource for information on that is the tech support provided by your ISP or mail service (or someone who happens to use and know that same service).

That's the quick-and-easy way to make backups of important files. More elaborate methods exist. The next two sections discuss ways of backing up all your files, and even your entire hard drive.

Using File History

Windows 8.1's File History feature is an alternative to the simple method for backing up files described earlier and is an upgrade to the Windows Backup feature released with Windows 7. File History can back up individual folders, all files for all user accounts, or even your entire hard drive. It works with an external hard drive, USB drive, or a shared network drive. File History makes recovering files very easy as it allows you to access backed-up files from File Explorer.

> **NOTE**
>
> File History will not use SkyDrive as an external drive. You must supply one of the following: a physical hard disk that is attached to your local computer, a drive on a server somewhere in your office, or a drive on a server in the cloud. Drives on servers can be found by configuring network connections to these resources.

Starting File History

File History is a tool for backing up files in all user accounts so you need administrative privileges to run it. If you're logged in to a standard account, log off. Then log back in to an administrative account.

To launch File History, display the Charms Bar, click Search, and type **File History**. Click Settings and then click File History from the Settings screen, as shown in Figure 24.3.

By default, File History is turned off under Windows 8.1. A message on the main File History page indicates such. Also, File History recommends that you use an external drive for your backup storage device, or use a network location for backups. In fact, notice that the Turn On button is grayed out. You cannot even turn on File History until it recognizes a supported drive. In the example shown, File History has accepted an external USB hard drive.

To turn on File History, connect an external drive to your computer. Press F5 on your keyboard or click the Refresh button on the Address bar to refresh the page. If you would rather use a network drive than an external drive, click the Use Network Location link and follow the instructions in the next section, "Backing up to a network location."

FIGURE 24.3

The File History main page

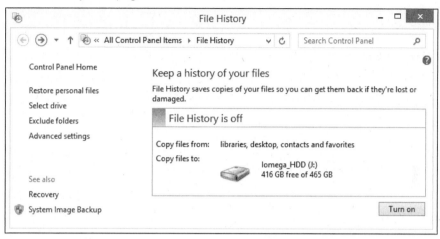

The example here uses an external USB drive to back up files. Figure 24.4 shows what the File History page looks like after plugging in the USB drive and refreshing the page.

FIGURE 24.4

The File History page after connecting our USB drive

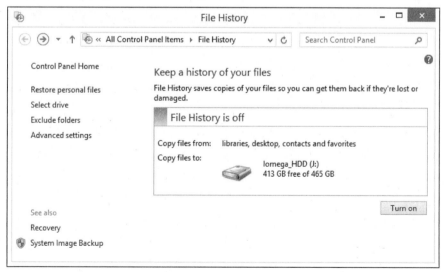

Before turning on File History, note that File History will back up files from the following locations by default:

- Libraries
- Desktop
- Contacts
- Favorites

Its main purpose is to make sure that you can recover documents like pictures, music, videos, and so on, in case you lose the originals on your hard drive.

Click the Turn On button to activate File History. The Recommend a Drive for File History dialog box appears, asking if you want to allow others in your network homegroup to use this drive as their backup drive as well. (You learn about Windows 8.1 homegroups in Chapter 38.) If you want to allow this, click Yes; otherwise, click No.

After you activate File History, the File History page changes to show that it's turned on and that File History is making a copy of your files for the first time (see Figure 24.5). This initial backup may take several minutes or even hours, depending on the number of files you have in the folders being backed up. You'll know the backup is done when you see a Run Now link below the Removable Disk icon, as shown in Figure 24.6.

FIGURE 24.5

File History is now activated.

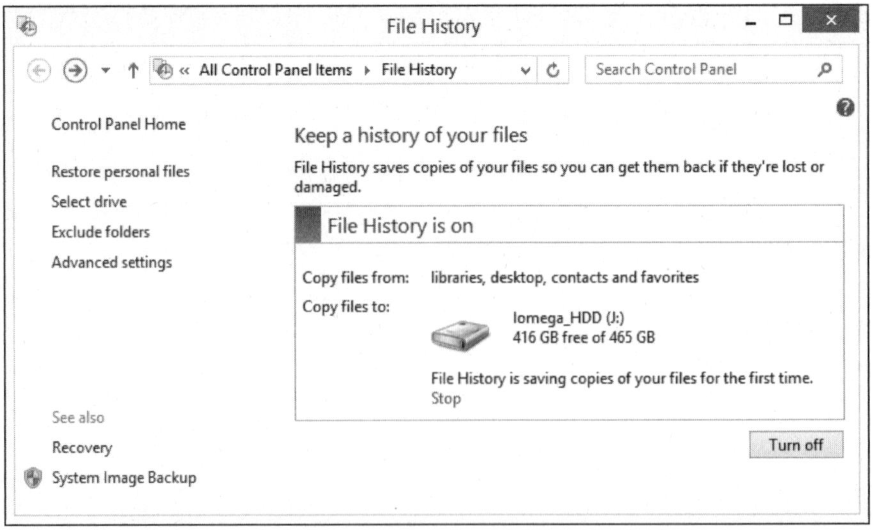

FIGURE 24.6

The Run Now link indicates that your files are backed up.

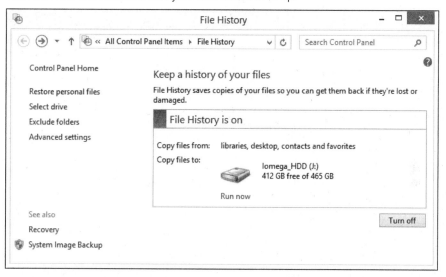

> **TIP**
>
> The first file backup you perform might take several hours. It will run in the background, so you can continue to use your computer during the backup. But the backup will consume some computer resources, slowing things down, so you may want to run the first backup overnight, starting it at a time when you can leave the computer on and running.

As mentioned, the first backup may take a while. But subsequent backups will copy only files that have changed since the last backup, so they'll go more quickly.

Backing up to a network location

You can use a network location to back up files. This is handy if you have multiple computers in a location and want to use it as a shared backup location. Another benefit to using a network location is access to hard drives that may have large amounts of unused space. Typically, networked computers have larger hard drives than dedicated external drives. In many cases, you can use these larger hard drives to back up files.

To use a network location, click the Use Network Location link when you initially access the File History page. Or click the Select Drive link on the left side of the File History window. This opens the Select Drive window, as shown in Figure 24.7.

FIGURE 24.7

The Select Drive window for choosing different drives to back up files to

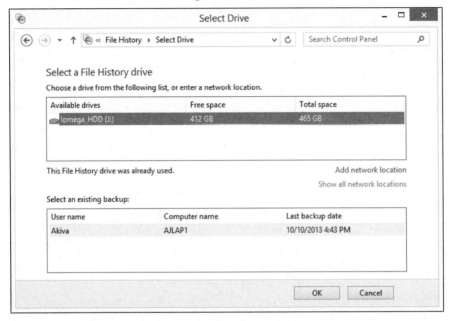

Click the Add Network Location button to display the Select Folder window (shown in Figure 24.8). Find the computer and folder to back up your files to. You must have network access privileges to access a computer and folder on your network. (Chapter 39 discusses sharing resources on a network.) Click Select Folder after you find the location on the network to back up your files.

The Select Drive window reappears, listing the network drive you just selected (see Figure 24.9). If it's not selected, select it and then click OK to save your selection.

For systems on which you've already backed up files to a drive (such as to a USB drive), File History prompts you with a message asking if you want to move your currently backed-up files to the network location. Click Yes to ensure all your backed-up files are available on the new network location. This move may take several minutes or even hours depending on the number of files on your backup drive.

If you use the Select Drive feature again and select a drive that you've previously used for backups (in the example, if you reselect the USB drive), you'll be presented with a listing that shows at least one existing backup exists (see Figure 24.10). To ensure all your backed-up files are on the most recent drive selection, select an existing backup, choose OK, and then click Yes when prompted to reselect a drive you've previously used.

FIGURE 24.8

Selecting a network location for backups

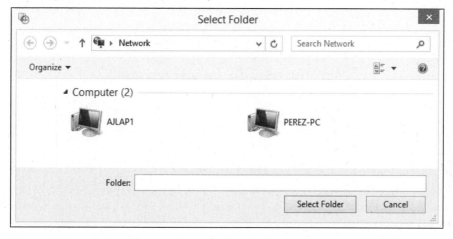

FIGURE 24.9

The Select Drive window showing the network drive we just selected.

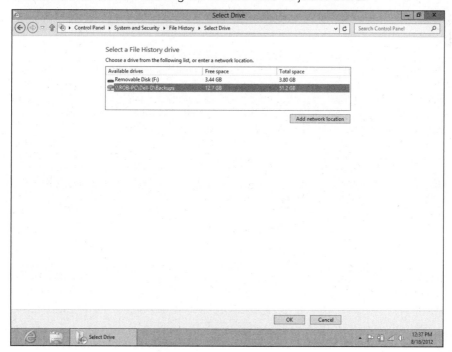

FIGURE 24.10

Reselecting a previously used drive shows existing backups on that drive.

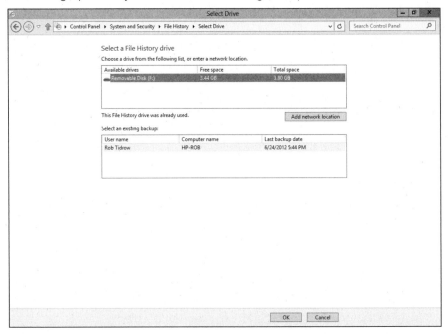

Excluding folders during backups

There may be some folders on your computer that you do not need to back up. For example, you may find that all your music is backed up using a different backup utility or music program. In this case, you don't need to use File History resources (backup time and drive space, for example) to back up your music.

To specify folders that you don't want to back up, click the Exclude Folders link on the left side of the File History window. The Exclude Folders window appears, as shown in Figure 24.11. By default, folders are not excluded so your Excluded Folders and Libraries list will simply say No Excluded Items.

FIGURE 24.11

The Excluded Folders window

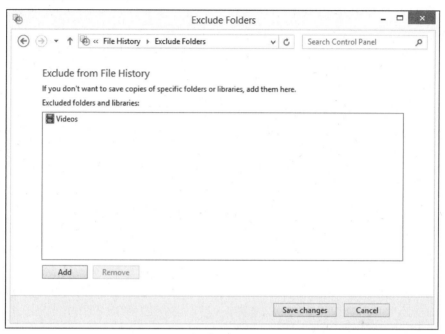

Click the Add button to display the Select Folder window (see Figure 24.12). Select a folder to exclude and then click Select Folder. File History adds that selected folder to the list of excluded folders. Continue this process until all the folders you want to exclude from back-ups are selected. In Figure 24.13, for example, we've added the Videos folders to exclude in our backups. Click Save Changes to save your changes.

FIGURE 24.12

The Select Folder window

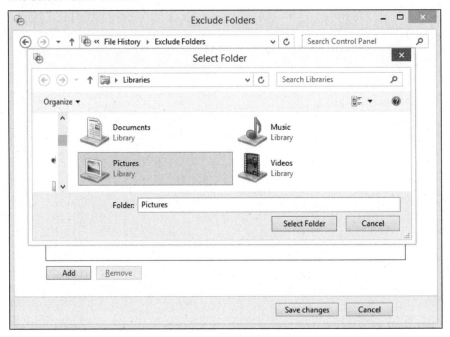

FIGURE 24.13

The Excluded Folders window showing what folders to exclude during backups

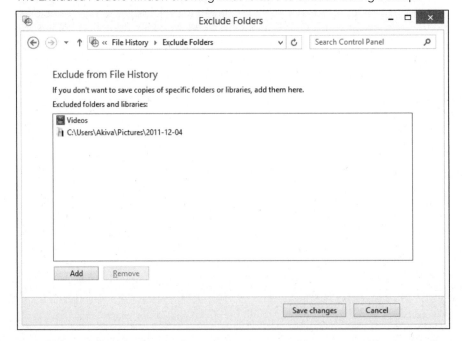

TIP

If you want to remove folders or libraries from the Exclude Folders list, select the item and then click Remove. This enables File History to back up files in that folder once again.

Setting the File History advanced option

To change File History advanced settings, click the Advanced Settings link on the File History window. Figure 24.14 shows what the Advanced Settings window looks like. The following paragraphs describe the settings you can modify on this window.

FIGURE 24.14

The Advanced Settings window

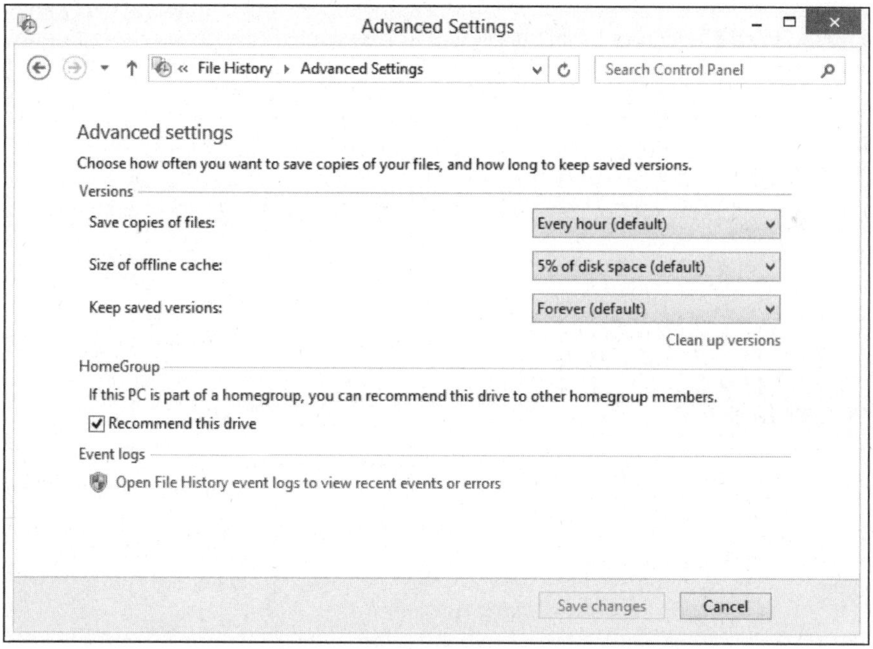

By default, File History looks to see if you've made changes to already backed-up files every hour. If changes have been made, File History saves the most current file to your backup location. If hourly is not an appropriate length of time — too short of a time or too long of a time — change it by choosing a new time from the Save Copies of Files drop-down list. You have the following options:

- Every 10 Minutes
- Every 15 Minutes

- Every 20 Minutes
- Every 30 Minutes
- Every Hour (Default)
- Every 3 Hours
- Every 6 Hours
- Every 12 Hours
- Daily

The Size of Offline Cache setting pertains to the amount of offline file cache to use when backing up. By default, you can use 5 percent of disk space for offline files. Other settings include 2%, 10%, and 20%.

One setting you might want to change is the Keep Saved Versions option. This instructs File History on how long to keep backup copies of your files. File History keeps multiple copies of your files so that you can restore a file to a previous date and time. This feature is great when you accidentally delete a file and want to return to a previous version of that file. The downside comes in the amount of space needed to store all these multiple copies.

By default, File History saves all copies forever, as long as there is sufficient storage space. You may want to change this to a shorter period of time, such as 1 month or 3 months if you know that you won't need to return to all those multiple versions of the same file. File History keeps the last copies within the time frame you choose, so you do have the option of returning to more recent copies. But you may not ever return to a version that is two years old, for example.

Your options for saved versions include

- Until Space Is Needed
- 1 Month
- 3 Months
- 6 Months
- 9 Months
- 1 Year
- 2 Years
- Forever (Default)

> **TIP**
> The Clean Up Versions link is used when you want to get back some space on your backup drive. Click that link, and File History removes old versions of the same file so that only the most recent copy is on the backup drive.

You can choose the Recommend This Drive option. This option is used only if your computer belongs to a homegroup and you want others on the network to be able to use your drive to back up their files.

Finally, you view File History event logs by clicking the Open File History Event Logs to View Recent Events or Errors option. Event Viewer, which is shown in Figure 24.15, provides helpful information in case you encounter problems with File History. (Chapter 11 includes information on using Event Viewer to read about warnings, errors, and other Windows 8.1 event information.)

FIGURE 24.15

View File History event logs using the Windows 8.1 Event Viewer.

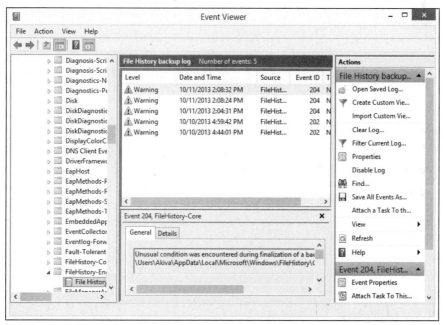

When you finish modifying the advanced settings for File History, click Save Changes.

Restoring files from a backup

If there ever comes a time when you've lost or destroyed some important files, you can restore them from your File History backup. But understand that this method is only needed if the files or folders are not in the Windows 8.1 Recycle Bin. Before you bother with the method described here, open the Recycle Bin and look for the missing file or folder. If you find what you're looking for, right-click it and choose Restore. The deleted item is right back where it was, and there's no need to proceed with the procedure described here.

If this method does not help you recover the lost items, you can restore from your backup. First, log in to the user account from which you lost the files. Open the File History application (type **File History** in the Search field, for example), and then click the Restore Personal Files link on the left side of the File History window. You can see the Restore Personal Files link in Figure 24.4, which appears earlier in this chapter.

The File History window appears, as shown in Figure 24.16. This window shows all your saved folders.

FIGURE 24.16

Restore a file using the File History window.

TIP

You also can access files to restore by opening File Explorer to the folder or library that you want to restore files to. On the Home tab, click the History button. This opens the Home – File History window.

Find the file you want to restore by opening an appropriate folder. If you know the file is in a previous version, for example, you want to return to a version of a file that is several days old, and if you know it's not the most recent version backed up, use the Previous Version button at the bottom of the window to navigate back in time to see previous versions.

Right-click the file to restore and choose Restore (see Figure 24.17).

FIGURE 24.17

Right-click a file to choose restore options.

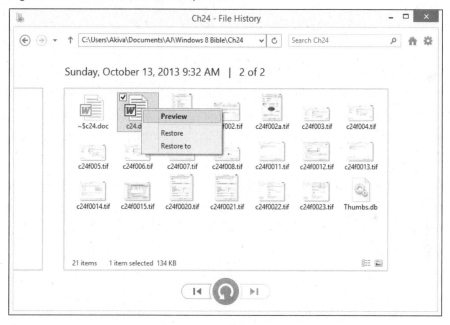

The Replace or Skip Files dialog box appears (see Figure 24.18). This dialog box gives you the following options:

- **Replace the File in the Destination:** This option replaces the current file on your hard disk with the backed-up version you just selected.

- **Skip This File:** This option instructs File History to ignore this file during the restore phase. The option makes sense only if you're choosing multiple files to restore or you suddenly want to cancel the current restore.

- **Compare Info for Both Files:** Use this option when you want to see file details about the file you selected to restore and the file currently on your hard drive. Figure 24.19 shows an example of the dialog box that appears. From this dialog box, you can select the file you want to keep or keep both copies. (A sequential number will be added to the filename of the restored file. Click Continue to complete the restoration process.)

FIGURE 24.18

The Replace or Skip Files dialog box

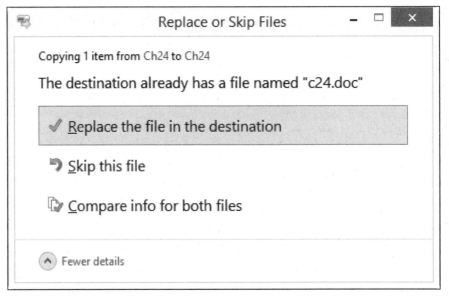

FIGURE 24.19

If you aren't sure which version of a file to keep or restore, you can keep both.

When restoring a file, you can click Preview to preview the file first. If you want to restore the file but restore it to a different location — which makes a copy of that file somewhere other than its original location — click Restore To and specify a location for it to be restored to. Click Select Folder after you select a folder and to complete the restoration of the file.

Not only can you restore individual or multiple files, but you can use the preceding instructions for restoring complete folders as well.

The following sections do not use File History, so you can close its window by clicking the red Close button (X).

Using System Protection

System Protection enables you to create a restore point, which is a way to back up important Windows system files. Unlike File History, System Protection doesn't require or use any external disks. Also, it does not back up any installed programs or all of Windows 8.1. Instead, System Protection creates System restore points that maintain copies of the most important system files needed for Windows 8.1 to operate properly, as well as hidden *shadow copies* of some of your own personal files.

The idea behind System Protection isn't to protect you from rare catastrophic hard drive disasters; it's to protect you from smaller and much more common mishaps. For example, you install some program or device that wasn't really designed for Windows 8.1, on the grounds that "It worked fine in another version of Windows, so it should work fine here," only to discover that it doesn't work as well as you assumed it would (because it wasn't designed for Windows 8.1). Even after uninstalling the program, you find that some Windows 8.1 features don't work as they did before you got the notion to give the old program or device a try.

Another common mishap occurs when you make some changes to an important file, but they're not particularly good changes. But you save the changes anyway out of habit, thereby losing the original good copy of the file you started with. Sometimes System Protection can even help you recover a file that you deleted and removed from the Recycle Bin.

Turning System Protection on or off

System Protection is turned on by default for the drive on which Windows 8.1 is installed. That means it's protecting your Windows 8.1 operating system and also documents you keep in your user account folders such as Documents, Pictures, Music, and so forth.

If you have documents on other hard drives, you can extend System Protection to protect documents on those drives, too. However, it would be best not to try to use System Protection to protect a hard drive that has another operating system installed on it.

24

System Protection is an optional feature. You can turn it on and off at will (providing you have administrative privileges, because it affects all user accounts). And you can choose for yourself which *volumes* it monitors. (A volume is any hard drive or hard drive partition that looks like a hard drive in your Computer folder.) To get to the options for controlling System Protection, first open your System folder using any of the following techniques:

- Display the Charms Bar, choose Search, type **System Protection**, and click Settings. Click Create a Restore Point on the Settings page.

- Display the Charms Bar, choose Search, type **Restore**, and click Settings. Click Create a Restore Point on the Settings page.

The System Properties dialog box appears, with the System Protection tab selected (see Figure 24.20).

FIGURE 24.20

The System Protection tab in System Properties

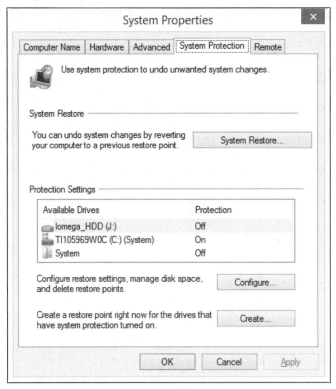

To ensure that system protection for Windows 8.1 and user account files are turned on, first look in the Protection Settings box to verify that the Protection column shows "On" for your system disk (typically drive c:). If the Protection column indicates that protection is off, click the Configure button to open the System Protection dialog box. Then choose one of the first two settings in the Restore Settings group. You can also specify how much disk space to allocate to system protection with the Max Usage slider.

> **CAUTION**
>
> Note that if you turn off System Protection, all existing restore points are deleted.

If your computer contains other volumes, whether you apply System Protection to them depends on what's on the volumes and whether you find it worthwhile to enable System Protection on them.

After you've made your selections, click OK. You're done. Nothing happens immediately, but Windows 8.1 creates restore points every 24 hours. Each restore point contains copies of your important system files and shadow copies of files on the volumes you specified.

System Protection needs a minimum of 300MB of space on each protected volume for restore points. If necessary, it will use from 3 percent to 5 percent of the total drive capacity. It won't grow indefinitely or consume a significant amount of disk space. Instead, it deletes old restore points before creating new ones. (Old restore points are of dubious value anyway.)

Creating a restore point

System Restore is the component of System Protection that protects your important system files — the ones Windows 8.1 needs to work correctly. System Restore automatically creates a restore point daily. It also creates a restore point when it detects that you're about to do something that changes system files. But you can also create your own restore points. This might be a good idea when you're about to install some older hardware or software that wasn't specifically designed for Windows 8.1. It's certainly not required, but it's a smart and safe thing to do.

To create a restore point, get to the System Protection tab shown back in Figure 24.20 and click the Create button. When prompted, you can type a brief explanation as to why you manually created the restore point: perhaps "Before Acme widget install" if you're about to install an Acme widget. Then click Create. Windows creates a restore point, after which you can click Close. Click OK to close the System Properties dialog box.

Next, you install your Acme widget or whatever. Take it for a spin, and make sure it works. If it works fine and you don't notice any adverse effects, great. You can forget about the restore point and go on your merry way.

If it turns out that change you made wasn't such a great idea after all, first you have to uninstall it. That's true whether it's hardware or software.

After you've uninstalled the bad device or program, you can make sure no remnants of it lag behind by returning to the restore point you specifically set up for that program or device.

24

If you install other programs or devices after the bad one, don't skip over other restore points to the one you created for the new item. If you do, you'll also undo the good changes made by the good programs and devices, which will likely make those stop working! You have to be methodical about these things. Set the restore point, install the program or device, and test the program or device. If (and only if) you encounter problems, uninstall the device or program and return to the last restore point you set.

Returning to a previous restore point

Say you installed something that didn't work out, uninstalled it, and now you want to make sure your system files are exactly as they were before. Open the System Properties dialog box and select the System Protection tab. Click System Restore (see Figure 24.21).

The System Restore starts. Click the Recommended Restore option and click Next. This will launch the System Restore Wizard. Click Finish to undo the most recent update, driver installation, or software install (for example, our Acme Widget installation). Windows 8.1 makes those changes and then restarts your computer. Upon restart, you see a confirmation about restoring your system files.

FIGURE 24.21

Using a restore point can fix issues with the way Windows runs.

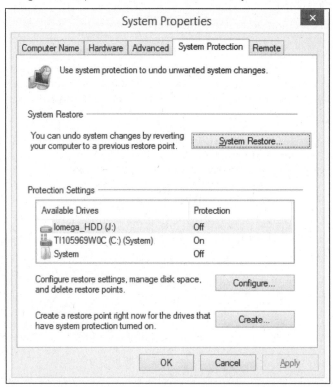

NOTE

For technical readers, we should mention that you can run System Restore from a command prompt. This is good to know if you can only start the computer in Safe Mode with the command prompt. Type **rstrui.exe** at the command prompt, and press Enter.

Undoing a System Restore

If you use System Restore and restore points exactly as described in the preceding sections, things will go smoothly. If you try to use it in other ways, things probably will not go smoothly. In fact, returning your system to an earlier restore point might cause more problems than it solves. When that happens, you can undo that last restore. Here's how:

1. Open System Restore.

2. Click Choose a Different Restore Point and click Next.

3. Choose the restore point labeled Undo and click Next.

4. Click Finish and follow the onscreen instructions.

Your computer restarts, and you see a confirmation message about undoing the restore point.

System Restore and the restore points you've just learned about have absolutely nothing to do with your document files. System Restore does not change, delete, undelete, or affect document files in any way, shape, or form. You should only use System Restore and restore points exactly as described.

Using BitLocker Drive Encryption

File History and System Protection ensure the *availability* of your files, in that they allow you to restore lost or damaged files by restoring from a backup copy. BitLocker drive encryption isn't about availability — it's about *confidentiality.* If your notebook computer is lost or stolen, that's certainly a bad thing. But if it contains confidential personal, client, or patient information, that's even worse. BitLocker drive encryption ensures that lost or stolen data can't be read by prying eyes.

24

TIP

BitLocker differs from the Encrypting File System (EFS) in that EFS encrypts individual folders and files, whereas BitLocker encrypts the whole disk.

BitLocker drive encryption works by encrypting all the data on a hard drive. With BitLocker drive encryption active, you can still use the computer normally. All the necessary encryption and decryption takes place automatically behind the scenes. But a thief would be unable to access data, passwords, or confidential information on the drive.

> **TIP**
> BitLocker drive encryption ensures the confidentiality of data stored in portable computers.

BitLocker hardware requirements

BitLocker drive encryption uses an encryption key to encrypt and decrypt data. That key must be stored in a Trusted Platform Module (TPM) Version 1.2 microchip and compatible BIOS. Only newer computers come with the appropriate hardware preinstalled. You'll also need a USB flash drive to store a copy of the password.

Caution, Caution, and More Caution

BitLocker drive encryption is primarily designed for organizations that have sensitive data stored on notebooks and PCs. Theft of that data could have a negative impact on the organization, its customers, or its shareholders. While transparent to the user, the act of setting up BitLocker would normally be entrusted to IT professionals within the organization.

If you're not an IT professional, you need to be aware of the risks involved, especially if you plan to set up BitLocker on a hard drive that already contains files. First, always back up your data before repartitioning a drive. Although many programs on the market allow you to repartition a disk without losing data, there's always a risk involved. A backup is your only real insurance. More important, you should understand that BitLocker is not for the technologically faint-of-heart. There is no way to undo any bad guesses or mistakes. If not handled with the utmost care, BitLocker can render your computer useless and your data unrecoverable. If you're not technologically inclined, but you have a serious need for drive encryption, consider getting professional support in setting up BitLocker for your system.

> **NOTE**
> The first time you open the BitLocker task page, you'll see a message indicating whether you have a TPM Version 1.2 chip installed. If you're certain that you have such a chip, but Windows 8.1 fails to recognize it, check with your computer manufacturer for instructions on making it available to Windows 8.1.

In addition to a TPM chip, your hard drive must contain at least two volumes (also called *partitions*). One volume, called the *system volume*, must be at least 1.5GB in size. That one contains some startup files and cannot be encrypted. The other volume, called the *operating system volume*, will contain Windows 8.1, your installed programs, and user account folders. Both volumes must be formatted with NTFS.

Encrypting the volume

When all the necessary hardware is in place, setting up BitLocker drive encryption is a relatively easy task:

1. Display the Charms Bar, choose Search, and type **BitLocker**. Click Settings and then click Manage BitLocker on the Settings window.

   If your hardware setup doesn't support BitLocker, you'll see messages to that effect. You cannot continue without appropriate hardware and disk partitions.

2. If all systems are go, the BitLocker Drive Encryption window appears (see Figure 24.22).

FIGURE 24.22

The BitLocker Drive Encryption window

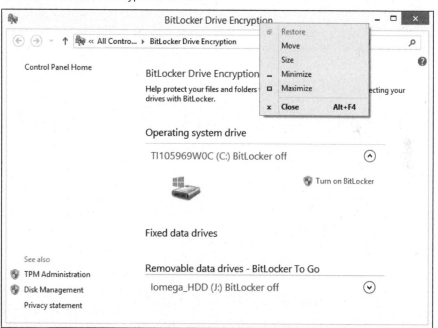

3. Click Turn On BitLocker. If your TPM isn't initialized, a wizard takes you through the steps to initialize it. Follow the onscreen instructions to complete the initialization.

4. When prompted, choose your preferred password storage method, store the password, and click Next.

5. On the encryption page, select Run BitLocker System Check and click Continue.

6. Insert the password recovery USB flash drive (or whatever medium you used for password recovery) and click Restart Now.

7. Follow the onscreen instructions.

The wizard will ensure that all systems are working and it's safe to encrypt the drive. Just follow the instructions to the end to complete the procedure.

Make sure you password-protect all user accounts to prevent unauthorized access to the system. Otherwise a thief can get at the encrypted data just by logging in to a user account that requires no password!

When the computer won't start

Once BitLocker is enabled, you should be able to start the computer and log in to it normally. BitLocker will only prevent normal startup if it detects changes that could indicate tampering. For example, putting the drive in a different computer, or even making BIOS changes that look like tampering, will cause BitLocker to prevent bootup. To get past the block, you'll need to supply the appropriate password.

Turning off BitLocker

If you ever change your mind about using BitLocker, repeat the steps in the section "Encrypting the volume" and choose the option to turn off BitLocker drive encryption.

More info on BitLocker

The setup wizard for BitLocker drive encryption is designed to simplify the process as much as possible for people using computers with TPM 1.2. Other scenarios are possible, but they go beyond the scope of this book. For more information, search Windows Help for "BitLocker." Or better yet, browse to www.technet.com and search for "BitLocker."

Performing a System Backup

Performing a system image backup lets you capture your system's image and save it to a remote device. The system image is a copy of the drive on which Windows is installed. If some of the files get destroyed or the drive gets damaged, you may have to restore your system image as a last resort to getting back up and running. (The system image can be saved to any remote media, such as a DVD, or the same external drive used by File History.)

System Image Backup combined with File History is an excellent and reliable (and free) alternative to a costly local or online backup service or software.

To capture your system image, click the System Image Backup link on the bottom-left corner of the File History screen (refer to Figure 24.6). A dialog box will now open to allow you to select a remote device or location for the system backup. This is shown in Figure 24.23.

FIGURE 24.23

The image location for System Backup

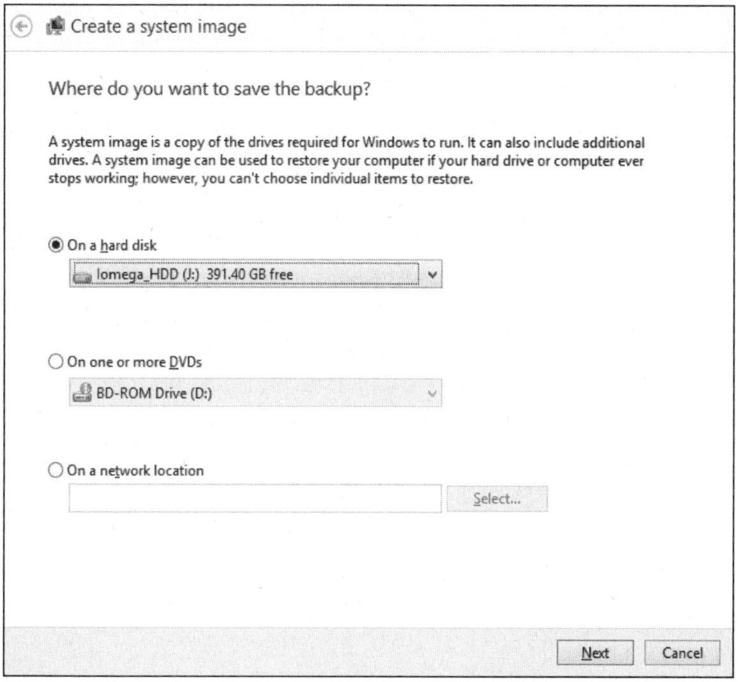

The next screen will prompt you to confirm your choices and start the backup.

Wrap-Up

Any way you slice it, having two or more copies of important files is better than having only one copy. The reason is simple and obvious: If you have two or more copies, you can afford to lose one. This is about different ways to make backup copies of important files. Here's a summary:

- To make simple backups of files on the fly, copy them to external disks as convenient.

- To restore an accidentally deleted file, first try to restore it from the Recycle Bin.

- To back up files in the Libraries, Desktop, Contacts, and Favorites folders, use File History.

- To recover deleted files, use the Restore Personal Files link on the File History window.

- Use System Protection to make automatic daily backups of important system files and documents. These won't protect you from a hard drive disaster because they're on the same disk as the system files and documents. But they provide a relatively easy means of recovering from minor mishaps without messing with external disks.

- To use System Restore properly, create a restore point just before installing new hardware or software. If the new product creates a problem, uninstall it. Then return to your restore point to ensure all traces of the installation are wiped away.

- For data confidentiality on portable computers, Windows 8.1 offers BitLocker drive encryption.

- Windows 8.1 includes features to let you take a system image of your computer. This image can be used to restore a "broken" system. Combined with File History, you can get a computer that refuses to reboot or restore back up and running within an hour.

Part VI

Printing and Managing Printers

Installing and Managing Printers

Installing a printer is usually an easy job. There's one rule that applies to installing any hardware, and it certainly applies to printers: *Read the instructions that came with the printer first.* Trying to save time by ignoring the instructions and winging it is likely to cost you more time in getting the thing to work.

In many cases, you'll have the option to connect the printer to a USB port or a printer port. If your computer is a member of a network, you might want to install a shared printer that's physically connected to some other computer or a printer that is directly connected to the network. This chapter looks at different ways of installing printers, including using the new Windows 8.1 Devices tool, as well as techniques for managing installed printers.

Windows 8.1 also packs new support for wireless printing (WI-FI Direct) and far easier and more efficient support for ad-hoc connection to printers. Windows 8.1 also supports NFC (Near Field Communications) tap-to-pair technology.

There is nothing special you have to do to connect to printers using these technologies. Both WI-FI Direct and NFC tap-to-pair implementation depends on the printers. Newer printers support WI-FI Direct, while older printers can use NFC tap-to-pair if you attach NFC tags to them. On the client side, you don't have to do anything extra to connect to printers using this technology with Windows 8.1. NFC tap-to-pair is a boon for users on tablets, phones, and other handheld devices. (Tap-to-pair is not practical from your desktop computer.)

Printer Properties Versus Printing Properties

Two types of properties are covered in this chapter: *printer properties* and *printing preferences*. The distinction isn't obvious from the terminology, so here's a general description to help you understand the difference:

- **Printer properties:** These properties apply to the printer itself, such as the way it's connected to the computer, whether and how it's shared on the network, the way the computer sends information to the printer, when the printer is available, and more.

- **Printing preferences:** These properties apply to how the printer creates a printed document, including such features as paper source, paper size, duplex printing, paper quality settings, print scaling, watermarks, and other document output properties.

In a way, you can think of printer properties as related to how the printer prints *all* documents, and printing preferences as related to how the printer prints *specific* documents. That's not 100 percent accurate, but it should begin to help you understand the distinction between the two.

If you're a typical Windows user, you'll be more likely to spend time configuring printing properties than printer properties. If you're a power user or administrator, however, you'll no doubt spend some time configuring printer properties to control how the printer operates.

Before diving into printer and printing preferences, you need to get your printer installed. That's covered in the following section.

> **NEW FEATURE**
>
> Windows 8.1 has two ways to view and manage your printers. First, the new Windows 8.1 Devices tool lets you view, add, and remove hardware devices, including printers. The Devices and Printers folder, which was introduced in Windows 7, is still around. It is the place to go to manage hardware devices such as displays, keyboards, input devices, wireless network adapters, and printers.

Add a Printer with the Devices Tool

Windows 8.1 includes a new Devices tool in the PC Settings area. The Devices tool provides a way to add, remove, and view your hardware devices, such as a printer. What we have found is that once Windows 8.1 recognizes a new printer connected to your computer, regardless of whether you're actively using the Devices tool, Windows 8.1 automatically installs device drivers for it (as long as those device drivers are part of the Windows 8.1 installation).

To get to the Devices tool, do the following:

1. Show the Charms Bar.

2. Choose Settings.

3. Click Change PC Settings.

4. Click PC and devices on the PC Settings list. An example of the Devices tool is shown in Figure 25.1.

In this example, a printer named MFC-J835DW has been added to the Devices list. If your printer is not showing up in this list, make sure the printer is connected to an active USB port (or other printer port) and ensure the printer is turned on. If, after doing these checks, the printer does not start installing, click the Add a Device button on the Devices page. Windows 8.1 will look for the new device (your printer in this case) and upon locating it will install the necessary drivers or prompt you for a location to find the drivers. In some cases, those drivers can be located online from the printer manufacturer's website. In other cases, the drivers are located on a distribution disk that was bundled with your printer.

FIGURE 25.1

The new Windows 8.1 Devices tool.

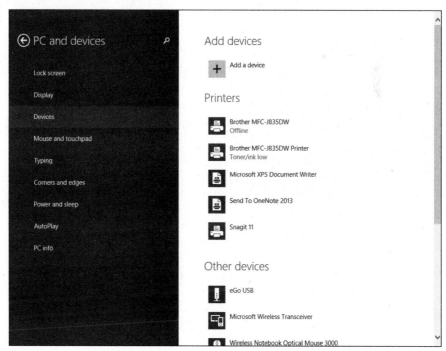

You can learn more about installing printers in the "Installing a New Printer" section, later in this chapter.

Once you have a printer installed, you really can do only two other things in the Devices tool. You can view the name of the printer, such as HP DeskJet 970Cse, and you can remove a device from your computer. To remove a device, select it and click the Remove Device button that appears to the right of the device name (see Figure 25.2). A message pops up asking if you're sure you want to uninstall the device. Click Yes. (If you aren't sure and you want to keep the device installed as is, press Esc on your computer's keyboard.)

FIGURE 25.2

Removing a printer using the new Windows 8.1 Devices tool.

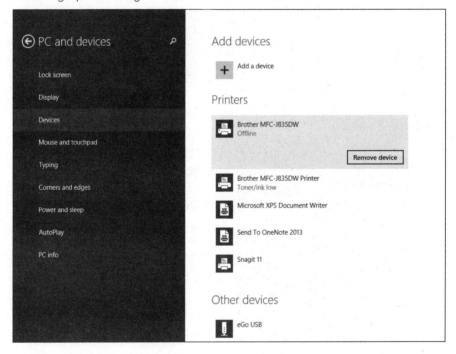

Opening the Devices and Printers Folder

Another tool to use for setting up and managing printers is the Devices and Printers folder. This folder includes the same features of the new Windows 8.1 Devices tool (see the preceding section), but it also adds management of properties and printer options to the list of tasks available to you.

In the past, aside from actually printing documents, just about everything you did with printers took place in the Devices and Printers folder. As you read already, some tasks can be done using the new Devices tool.

As with everything else in Windows 8.1, you can get to the Devices and Printers folder in several ways. Use whichever works for you and is most convenient at the moment:

- Show the Charms Bar, choose Search, and type **dev** and click the Settings link. On the Settings Results page, click the Devices and Printers item.

- On the Windows desktop, press Windows+X, choose Control Panel⇨View Devices and Printers under Hardware and Sound.

When you're in your Devices and Printers folder, you'll see an icon for each printer (or similar device) that you can print to. Figure 25.3 shows an example; your folder will, of course, look different.

Setting the default printer

If your Devices and Printers folder contains more than one printer icon, only one of them will be the *default* device for printing. By "default," we mean the printer that's used automatically if you don't specify something else. For example, many programs allow you to print a document to the default printer by pressing Ctrl+P. The program may not ask what printer you want to use. Instead, it just sends the document to the default printer.

FIGURE 25.3

A sample Devices and Printers folder.

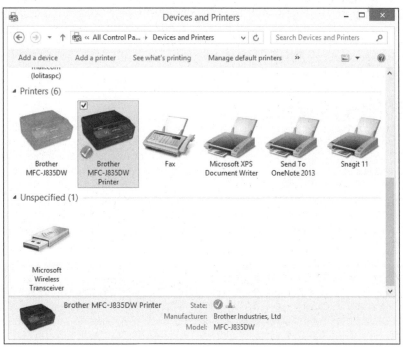

In the Devices and Printers folder, the default printer is indicated by a check mark. If you want to change the default printer, right-click the printer's icon and choose Set As Default Printer. The printer or device you specified will now sport the green check mark, and will be used for printing when you don't specify some other printer or device.

Testing a printer

If you've just installed a printer and you want to test it out, follow these steps (here, we're assuming that you're already in the Devices and Printers folder):

1. Right-click the printer's icon and choose Printer Properties. (Be careful not to click Printing Preferences or the Printer Properties items.)

2. Select the General tab.

3. At the bottom of the Properties dialog box that opens, click the Print Test Page button.

4. Wait a few seconds (few printers start immediately). The printer should print a sample page.

   - If the page prints and doesn't look garbled, click OK in each open box.
   - If nothing prints within 15 or 30 seconds, click Get Help with Printing for some tips on solving the problem.

If you had to click Get Help with Printing, follow the advice in the Help documentation first to resolve the problem. You can click the Click to Open the Print Troubleshooter link to launch the printing troubleshooter from the Control Panel. Also, keep in mind that hundreds of different makes and models of printers are on the market, and no single rule applies to all. So, don't overlook the documentation that came with your printer or the printer manufacturer's website, which may provide troubleshooting advice.

Installing a New Printer

Before you can use a new printer, you need to connect it to the computer and install it. Earlier in this chapter, you learned how to set up a printer using the new Windows 8.1 Devices tool. Let's look at adding a printer using the Devices and Printers folder. Many printers give you the choice of using the USB port to connect the printer or a parallel printer port. In most cases, USB will work just fine for printing. In fact, most of today's standard computer configurations don't even have a parallel printer port, so USB might be your only option. Likewise, most new printers don't have parallel or serial port connections.

> **TIP**
>
> If your printer offers only a parallel port, and your computer doesn't have one, you can either buy an add-on adapter card to add the parallel port or buy a new printer that supports USB.

As mentioned at the beginning of this chapter, the main rule on installing a printer is to follow the instructions that came with it. Sometimes you need to install drivers first; sometimes you don't. There is no "one rule fits all" when it comes to installing printers, or any other hardware device for that matter. But in a pinch, when there are no instructions, the techniques in the following sections will be your best first guess.

Installing printers with USB and infrared connections

If you have the option to connect the printer through a USB port, or by infrared, the installation procedure should go like this:

1. Close all open programs on your Windows desktop so that you're at the Windows desktop with nothing else showing.

2. Check the documentation that came with the printer, and if directed to install the drivers before connecting the printer to the computer, do so.

3. Plug the printer into the power outlet; connect the printer to the computer with its USB connection, or configure the infrared connection as instructed by the printer manufacturer.

4. Turn on the printer, and wait a few seconds.

You should see a message in the notification area that tells you the device is connected and ready to use. You're done. The printer is installed and ready to go.

Regardless of which of these methods you use, you'll want to test the printer, and perhaps make it the default printer, as discussed later in this chapter.

> **TIP**
>
> If the printer documentation tells you to install the software before you attach the printer to the computer for the first time, don't skip that step. If you connect the printer before installing the drivers, Windows might have problems detecting the printer.

Installing printers with parallel and serial port connections

If your printer is an older model (for example, an older HP LaserJet that you refuse to get rid of) that is not a typical plug-and-play USB printer, it probably connects to the computer via an LPT port or COM port. The following is the best approach to installing it on Windows 8.1:

1. Save any unsaved work, close all open programs, shut down Windows, and shut down your computer.

2. Plug the printer into the power outlet, connect the printer to the computer's LPT or serial port, turn on the printer, and turn on the computer.

3. When Windows restarts, look for the Found New Hardware notification message to appear.

25

It's tough to say what will happen next. You might be prompted for a disk if Windows can't find the driver for the printer. If you see a notification message indicating that the printer is installed and ready to use, you're probably done.

If your printer is not located automatically, you might want to use Google or Bing to locate instructions on the web for setting up your printer in Windows 8.1. Because so many different printers are available, this book cannot even begin to show how to install your particular printer. Often, the manufacturer's website includes updated device drivers and/or updated instructions on how to get legacy printers (those that are several years old) working with the latest operating systems such as Windows 8.1.

You might also try installing the printer using the Program Compatibility feature of Windows 8.1.

Installing a network, wireless, or Bluetooth printer

If your computer is a member of a home or small business network, and you know of a shared printer on another computer in that network, you can use the technique described here to install that printer on your own computer. The same is true of many wireless and Bluetooth printers. But again, this procedure may not be necessary because Windows 8.1 often detects network printers and makes them available automatically. Be sure to check the manual that came with a wireless or Bluetooth printer for an alternative procedure before trying the method described here. Also, be sure to turn on the printer before you try to install it.

If you're trying to install a printer that's attached to another computer in your private network, make sure that both the printer and the computer to which the printer is physically connected are turned on. Make sure your network is set up and you've enabled discovery and sharing as discussed in Part IX of this book. Then go to the computer that needs to access the network printer and perform the steps to follow on that computer. You install a network, wireless, or Bluetooth printer in much the same way you install a local printer. First, open the Devices and Printers folder using any technique described at the start of this chapter.

If the printer's name appears in the new Devices tool of the Settings area or in the Devices and Printers folder, you don't need to install it. If you want to make it the default printer, right-click its icon and choose Set As Default Printer (only available while in the Devices and Printers folder). Then close the Devices and Printers folder and Control Panel. You'll be able to use the printer as described in Chapter 26.

If there's no sign of the printer in the Devices tool or in your Devices and Printers folder, open the Devices and Printers folder and follow these steps to install it:

1. Click Add a Printer in the toolbar. The Add Printer Wizard opens.
2. If the printer is located automatically, select it and click Next to work through the wizard to install it. If the printer is not located, click The Printer That I Want Isn't Listed. The Find a Printer by Other Options window opens, as shown Figure 25.4.

FIGURE 25.4

Setting up a network shared printer.

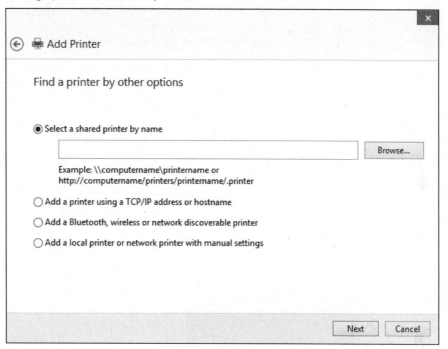

3. If you know the UNC name or IP address of the printer to which you want to connect, fill in the appropriate information. Otherwise, click Browse, and navigate to the computer and printer to which you want to connect. Click the printer's name and click Select. Then click Next.

4. After the printer is successfully installed, click Next. On the next wizard page, you can opt to print a test page and make the shared printer your default printer. Make your choices and click Finish.

An icon for the shared printer will appear in your Devices and Printers folder. If you made it the default printer, it will also show a check mark.

Managing Printer Drivers

Virtually all hardware devices, including printers, come with a special program called a *device driver,* or just *driver* for short. The driver provides the interface between the device and a specific operating system, such as Windows 8 and Windows 8.1, Windows 7, Windows Vista, or Windows XP. You need to have the correct and current printer driver installed on your computer to get your printer to work correctly.

25

TIP

In most cases, the Windows 7 version of a printer driver will work just fine for Windows 8.1. However, you should always use the Windows 8.1 version of a printer driver if one is available to ensure you have access to all your printer's features. Also, keep in mind that if you have Windows 8.1 64-bit installed, you'll need 64-bit printer drivers as well.

Many printers come with the drivers on a CD. How you install a driver from the disk depends on the printer you're using, but an older printer may not even have a Windows 8.1 driver to offer. In that case, you'll need to look for a current driver online. Try Windows Update first by following these steps:

1. Display the Charms Bar and choose Settings.
2. Click Change PC Settings.
3. Click the Update and Recover link in the PC Settings list. You may have to scroll down to view the Windows Update item.
4. Click Check for Updates, which you can see in Figure 25.5.

FIGURE 25.5

Checking Windows Update for updated printer device drivers.

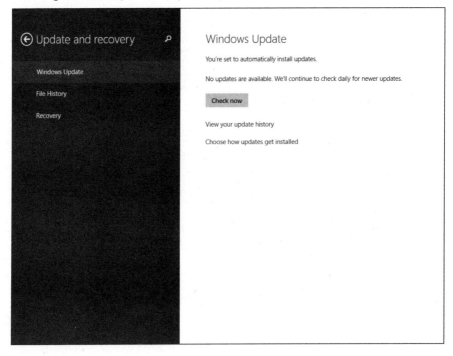

5. When the update search is complete, click the link for available updates (if any).

6. If the driver for your printer appears, go ahead and install it per the onscreen instructions.

If Windows Update doesn't find an updated driver, it might mean your printer manufacturer hasn't posted the driver on their site yet. Browse to the printer manufacturer's website and look around for a Drivers link or Support page with downloads. Or go to the Support page and send an e-mail asking if there's an updated driver for your printer model.

Setting Default Printing Preferences

Remember the discussion early in this chapter about printing preferences versus printer properties? This section explains how to configure the default printing properties that a printer will use to print documents.

Like objects on your screen, many devices have properties that you can customize. Most printers have such properties. You can make selections from those properties to define defaults for the printer. Those default settings for properties won't be set in stone. You can override the defaults any time you print a document.

As with other objects, a printer's properties are accessible from its icons. To view the properties for an installed printer, first open the Devices and Printers folder if you haven't already done so. Then right-click the printer's icon and choose Printing Preferences. The options available to you depend on your printer. The options shown in Figure 25.6 are for an MFC-J835DW printer.

The Printing Preferences dialog box varies from one printer to the next and often offers multiple tabs, each with several options. The following sections cover some of the more common settings that you might want to set for your printer.

Portrait versus landscape printing

Unless your printing needs are very unusual, you'll probably want to print most of your documents in a portrait orientation. That's the orientation that normal letters and other documents use, so you'll almost always want to choose Portrait as your default orientation, as in Figure 25.6.

You can always override that default and print the occasional document in Landscape orientation (sideways, so the page is wider than it is tall).

25

FIGURE 25.6

Sample printing preferences.

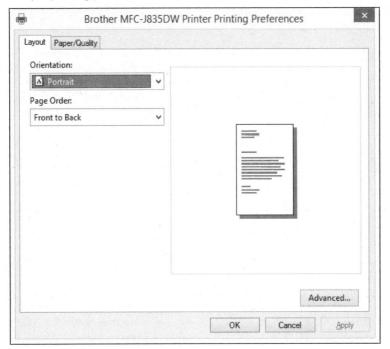

Printing on both sides

On some printers, you have the option of printing a multi-page document on both sides of a piece of paper. For our example, this option is located in the Print on Both Sides drop-down list. You can choose None, which prints on a single side of a piece of paper. The Flip on Long Edge option results in a multi-page document being printed front to back, also called *duplexing.* The Flip on Short Edge option prints on both sides, but is usually used for documents printed in landscape mode.

Making pages print in the correct order

When you print a multi-page document, you don't want to have to shuffle the pages around to get them in the correct order. You want the pages to come out of the printer in the correct order. The Page Order property is the option that determines whether the pages are printed in the correct order. The rules are as follows:

- If the pages come out of the printer face down, use Front to Back order.
- If the pages come out of the printer face up, use Back to Front order.

Said another way, if you have to reshuffle printed pages, choose whichever of those options currently *isn't* selected.

Saving time and money

Printers, as a rule, are just plain slow. That's because they're clunky mechanical devices, and it takes time to move a page through a printer and get the ink or toner onto the paper. Faster printers are typically more expensive than slower ones. But no matter what the cost or general speed of your printer, one general rule will apply: The higher the print quality of the document you're printing at the moment, the longer it will take to print.

Here's another fact about printers in general. Many printers are cheap, but ink cartridges typically are not. In some cases, buying a new printer is actually cheaper than buying replacement cartridges for your printer. Also, some manufacturers ship new printers with starter cartridges, which typically contain less than a full-size replacement cartridge.

The printer property that most determines how quickly your documents print and how much ink or laser toner you use per document is called *print quality*. The higher the print quality, the longer it takes to print a document, and the more ink or laser toner you use in the process. You can save time and money by doing all your day-to-day printing in Draft quality, perhaps even without color if you want to conserve color ink or laser toner.

On the Brother printer shown in Figure 25.7, quality settings are on the Paper/Quality tab. The Draft quality setting for the Brother, for example, causes the printer to use less ink when it prints, but the quality of the finished document is naturally lower. Your printer might have similar options.

As with other printer properties, setting the printer defaults to low-quality and black-and-white settings won't prevent you from printing the occasional color document. You can override those defaults any time you print a document. When you want to print a professional-looking report or a fine photo, just increase the print quality and activate color for that one print job.

Beyond these features, the properties vary greatly from one printer to the next. The only resource for learning all the details of your particular make and model of printer is the documentation that came with that printer, or the printer manufacturer's website.

25

FIGURE 25.7

Paper/Quality settings.

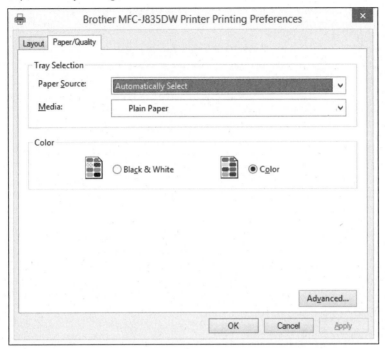

Setting Printer Properties

If you're an average Windows user, you might never need to configure printer properties for a printer. In most cases, you'll be more concerned with printing preferences that control how the printed documents look. If you're an advanced user or administrator, however, you'll likely need to understand how to configure printer properties.

To configure properties for a printer, start by opening the Devices and Printers folder, as described earlier in this chapter (you should find it on the Control Panel). Then right-click the printer and choose Printing Properties to open a Properties dialog box similar to the one shown in Figure 25.8.

The tabs shown in the Properties dialog box for a printer can vary from one type of printer to another, but you'll see some common settings between them. The following sections use the HP DeskJet 970Cse as an example to illustrate common concepts such as port configuration, printer pooling, spooling options, and more.

FIGURE 25.8

A sample Properties dialog box.

TIP

Use the Print Test Page button on the General tab of a printer's Properties dialog box to test the printer.

Configuring shared printers

The Sharing tab (see Figure 25.9) enables you to set up your printer so that you can share it with others on your home or work network. By clicking the Share This Printer option, you enable sharing and then must provide a share name for the printer. You can use the default, which is the name of the printer, or name it something more descriptive. For example, you might name it something like "Rob's Printer" or "Laser Printer in Room 100" so others in your network know which printer it is by looking at the name.

25

FIGURE 25.9

The Sharing tab.

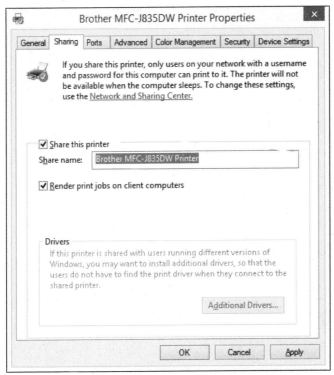

The Additional Drivers button contains a way for you to install additional drivers to support multiple versions of Windows. For example, you might be running Windows 8.1 on your computer, but the person down the hallway or in another part of the house may be on Windows Vista or Windows XP still. By installing those drivers now, you can be assured that users of those other versions of Windows will have an easier time setting up to use your shared printer.

After you set up these options, click Apply. You may be prompted to shut down and restart Windows before your sharing takes effect.

Configuring printer ports

The Ports tab (see Figure 25.10) lets you view and configure the printer's ports, which define the way the printer is connected to the computer. Typically, a printer will have only one port, but it's possible to have multiple ports.

FIGURE 25.10

The Ports tab.

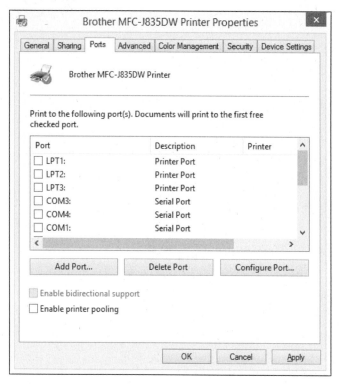

Users visit the Ports tab for two primary reasons: to configure a printer for a different network port, or to switch from one LPT port to another. You can also configure the printer to print by default to a file by selecting the File port.

Some port types offer settings that you can configure. LPT ports, for example, enable you to specify the Transmission Retry setting, which determines how long the computer will wait for a response from the printer before timing out. For serial printers on a COM port, you can specify several settings that control the speed of the port and how data flows from the computer to the printer. To configure a port, select the port from the list and click Configure Port. Use the settings in the resulting dialog box to specify settings for the port.

If you need to add a new port for a printer, click the Add Port button. Windows displays the Printer Ports dialog box shown in Figure 25.11. Select the type of port you want to create and click New Port. If the selected port type supports creating new ports, Windows displays a dialog box or a wizard (depending on the port type) that you use to specify the settings for the new port.

FIGURE 25.11

Printer Ports dialog box.

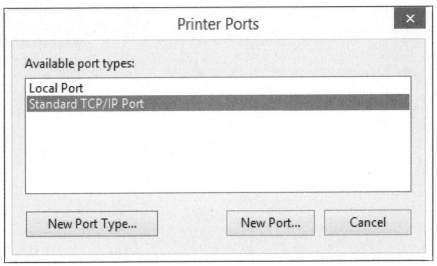

Setting up printer pooling

A *printer pool* is a group of identical printers that Windows treats as a single printer instance. You can then print to the printer pool as if it were a single printer, and Windows handles sending the document to an appropriate printer in the pool. Before we explain pooling in more detail, take a look at how a *printer driver instance* differs from a *printer*.

A printer that you see listed in the Devices and Printers folder is really not a printer per se. Instead, it's an instance of a printer driver. The printer driver is the middleware between Windows and the printer hardware (the real *printer* in this discussion) that enables Windows to communicate with the printer. The phrase *instance of a printer driver* refers to a named copy of the printer driver that has its own set of properties. You can have two instances of the same printer driver with different settings, both of which control the same printer. Or you can have one instance of a printer driver that controls more than one printer, and that's a *printer pool*.

For example, assume your office has three identical network printers. You can create a printer pool using those three printers, assigning three ports to the single instance of the printer driver in your Devices and Printers folder. So, you might have one HP LaserJet 1250N network printer in your Devices and Printers folder, for example, but that instance of the driver could actually print to any of the three printers.

Why would you want to do that? First, you need to manage only one instance of the printer driver in your computer, which can simplify printer and document management, particularly if you typically use the same settings for each one. Second, you don't have to worry about selecting a printer when you print. Instead, assuming you've assigned the printer driver instance for the pool as your default printer, you just click Print and send the document on its way. Windows decides which printer to send the document to.

To set up a printer pool, first install the printer driver for the printers in the pool. Then open the properties for the printer from the Devices and Printers folder and select the Enable Printer Pooling option on the Ports tab. When that option is selected, you can select multiple ports from the ports list. Add ports as needed (such as additional TCP/IP ports for network printers), and select the ports for all the printers in the pool. Then click OK.

Configuring printer availability

You can specify when a printer is available. For example, you might want to restrict access to a printer to business hours to keep people from using it when no one is around. Whatever the reason, you configure printer availability from the Advanced tab of the Printer Properties dialog box (see Figure 25.12).

FIGURE 25.12

The Advanced tab.

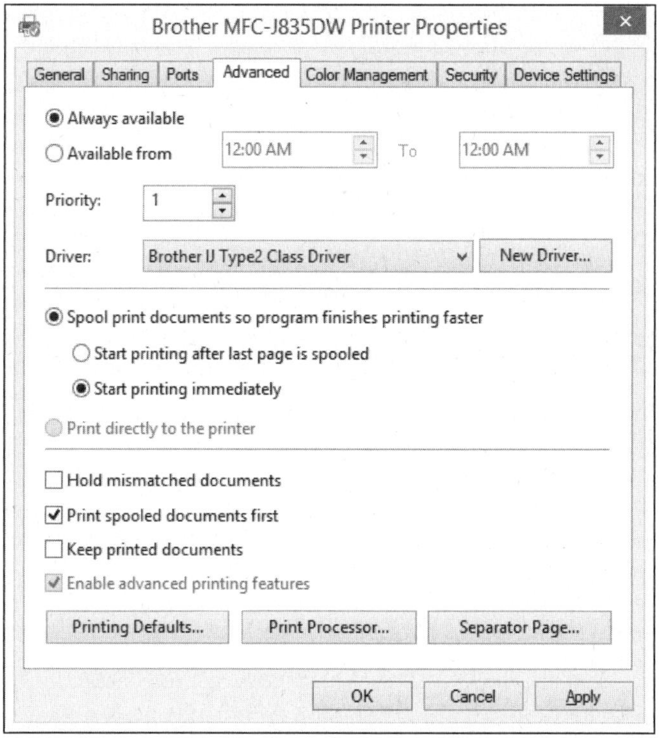

By default, a printer is configured to be always available. To limit its availability, click the Available From option; then use the spin controls to set the start and end times for the time range when the printer will be available. If you or a network user of a shared printer sends a document to a printer when it isn't available, the document is held in the printer queue on the sending computer until the printer becomes available.

Setting other advanced options

As Figure 25.12 illustrates, Windows offers several other advanced options for configuring a printer. For example, the spooling options determine how the printer driver sends data to the printer. The option Spool Print Documents So Program Finishes Printing Faster causes documents to be spooled to an on-disk queue, where it waits until the printer driver can send it to the printer. To the printing application, printing is complete as soon as the last page of the document is sent to the queue and you can then continue using the program.

Alternatively, you can configure the printer driver to print directly to the printer, bypassing the on-disk document queue. The downside to this option is that you can't use the program until it finishes printing, which can potentially take much longer than sending the document to a queue if the document is complex or very large.

In most cases, today's computers are fast enough and have enough disk capacity that you will never need to print directly to the printer. If you're trying to print a huge document and you have very little free space on your disk, however, sending the document directly to the printer could enable the document to print when it might not otherwise.

Following are some additional settings on the Advanced tab:

- **Hold Mismatched Documents:** The spooler checks the configuration of the printer against the document setup before sending the document to the printer. If the document setup doesn't match the printer, the document is held in the queue and not sent to the printer. You can then address the configuration mismatch, and restart the document from the queue to send it to the printer.

- **Print Spooled Documents First:** Documents that have completed spooling to the queue are printed before documents that are still spooling, even if they have a lower priority.

- **Keep Printed Documents:** Documents remain in the queue even after they're printed, enabling you to restart the document from the queue if needed to reprint them.

These aren't the only properties available for a printer. We cover other properties, such as the sharing properties, in other chapters.

Wrap-Up

That about wraps it up for installing and managing printers. In the next chapter, you learn how to print documents, choose color and quality settings on the fly, and so forth. The main points from this chapter are as follows:

- Many makes and models of printers exist. Your best resource for your specific printer is the documentation that came with that printer.

- Installed printers, and options for installing printers, are in the new Windows 8.1 Devices tool, or in your Devices and Printers folder.

- If you have access to multiple printers, right-click the icon for the printer you want to use on a day-to-day basis and choose Set As Default Printer.

- To test a printer, right-click its icon and choose Printer Properties. Then click the Print Test Page button.

- To connect a printer by USB, don't shut down the computer. Instead, leave the computer on, connect the printer to the computer, and then turn on the printer. Check the printer documentation to see whether you need to install the drivers before connecting the printer.

- The typical scenario for installing a printer that connects to a printer port (LPT port) is to shut down the computer, connect the printer and turn it on, and then restart the computer.

- To ensure that your printer driver is appropriate for your operating system, check the Windows Update site and the printer manufacturer's website.

- To set default properties for day-to-day printing, right-click the printer's icon and choose Printing Preferences.

2 5

Managing Print Jobs

W hen you print a document, there's more going on than you might expect. The printer doesn't immediately start printing. Instead, the computer needs to convert your document to a set of instructions that tells the printer what to do. Then those printer instructions have to be sent to the printer in small chunks because the printer is a slow mechanical device compared to a computer, which is much faster.

Each document you print becomes a *print job* that has to wait its turn in line if other documents are already printing, or waiting to be printed. Most of this activity takes place in the background, meaning that you don't have to do anything to make it happen. In fact, you can just go about using your computer normally. There's no need to wait for the document to finish printing.

How Printing Works

When you print a document, quite a bit of work takes place invisibly in the background before the printer even "knows" there's a document to print. First, a program called a *print spooler* (or *spooler* for short) makes a special copy of the document that contains instructions that tell the printer exactly what to do. Those instructions don't look anything like the document you're printing. They're just codes that tell the printer what to do so that the document it spits out ends up looking like the document that you printed.

After the spooler creates the special printer file, it can't just hand the whole thing off to the printer as one giant set of instructions. Most printers are slow mechanical devices that can hold only a small amount of information at a time in a *buffer*. The buffer is a storage area within the printer that holds the data to be printed until it's printed. The amount of data that can reside in the buffer depends on the size of the buffer. In some cases, the buffer will hold a large number of pages.

In others, it might hold only a single page, or in the case of a complex document such as a photo, and a relatively small buffer, only part of the page might fit in the buffer at one time.

Furthermore, when the spooler has finished creating the special printer file, another document may already be printing. There may even be several documents waiting to be printed. So, the spooler has to put all the print jobs into a *queue* (line). All this activity takes the computer time (not *your* time, per se). And because each document has to be fed to the printer in small chunks, there's often time for you to do things such as cancel documents you've told Windows to print but that haven't yet been fully printed.

To manage those print jobs, you use the *print queue.* If a document is already printing, or waiting to print, you'll see a tiny printer icon in the notification area. When you point to that icon, the number of documents waiting to be printed appears in a tooltip, as in the example shown in Figure 26.1. Double-click that small icon to open the print queue.

FIGURE 26.1

The printer icon in the notification area.

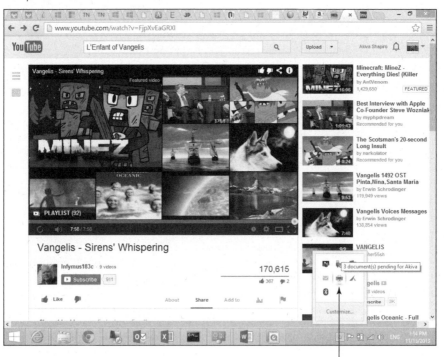

Printer icon

As an alternative to using the notification area, you can get to the print queue from the Devices and Printers folder. To open your Devices and Printers folder, press Windows + X, click Control Panel, and click View Devices and Printers.

Once you're in the Devices and Printers folder, double-click the printer's icon to open its print queue.

TIP

To make a desktop shortcut to a specific printer, right-click the printer's icon in the Devices and Printers folder and choose Create Shortcut. Any time you need to open the printer's queue, just double-click (or click) that shortcut icon on the desktop.

26

Managing Print Jobs

The print queue for a printer contains all the documents that are currently printing or waiting to print. Figure 26.2 shows an example where we've already told Windows to print two documents. The first document we sent (which happens to be the document listed on the bottom of the list in this example) is currently printing. The other is waiting in line for its turn.

FIGURE 26.2

Sample documents in a print queue.

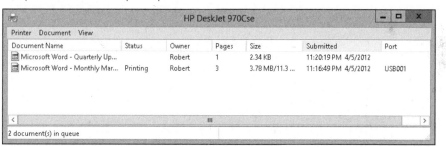

Managing a single document

To pause or cancel a specific print job, right-click its line in the print queue and choose one of the following options from the shortcut menu that appears:

- **Pause:** Stops printing the document until you restart it.
- **Restart:** Restarts the paused print job.
- **Cancel:** Cancels the print job so that it doesn't print and removes the job from the print queue.
- **Properties:** Provides detailed information about the print job. You can also set the document's priority. The higher the priority, the more likely the print job is to cut in line ahead of other documents waiting to be printed.

Managing several documents

To pause, restart, or cancel several documents in the queue, select their icons. For example, click the first job you want to change. Then hold down the Shift key and select the last one. Optionally, you can select (or deselect) icons by holding down the Ctrl key as you click. Then right-click any selected item, or choose Document from the menu bar, and choose an action. The action will be applied to all selected icons.

Managing all documents

You can use commands on the print queue's Printer menu, shown in Figure 26.3, to manage all the documents in the queue without selecting any items first. The following options apply to all documents:

- **Pause Printing:** Pause the current print job and all those waiting in line. See the section "Printing Offline," later in this chapter, for an example of when this would be useful.

- **Cancel All Documents:** You guessed it — this cancels the current print job and all those waiting to be printed.

FIGURE 26.3

The Printer menu in the print queue.

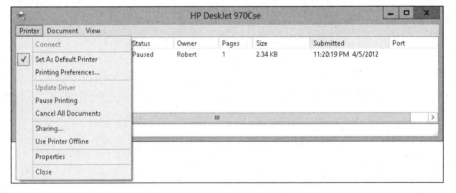

How Do I Stop This Thing?

Don't expect a paused or canceled print job to stop right away. Several more pages may print, even after you've canceled a print job. That's because the print queue sends chunks of a document to the printer's buffer. That buffer, in turn, holds information waiting to be printed. Canceling a print job prevents any more data from being sent to the buffer, but the printer won't stop printing until its buffer is empty (unless, of course, you just turn off the printer).

Changing the print queue order

In the print queue, you can change the order in which documents in the queue will print. For example, if you need a particular printout right now, and there's a long line of documents waiting ahead of it, you can give your document a higher priority so it prints sooner. In other words, your print job gets to cut in line ahead of others.

To change an item in the print queue's priority, right-click the item in the queue and choose Properties. On the General tab of the dialog box that opens, drag the Priority slider, shown in Figure 26.4, to the right. The farther you drag, the higher your document's priority. Click OK. Your document won't stop the document that's currently printing, but it may well be the next one to print.

FIGURE 26.4

The Priority slider in a print queue item's Properties dialog box.

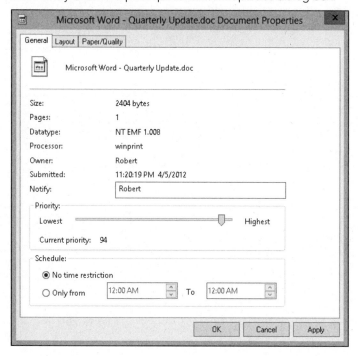

You can close the print queue as you would any other window — by clicking the Close button in the upper-right corner or by choosing Printer ⇨ Close from the menu bar. To get help with the print queue while it's open, choose Help from the menu bar.

Solving Common Printer Problems

If you experience a problem printing a document, the problem could well be something to do with the printer. Before you assume the worst and delve into any major troubleshooting, check for some of the more common problems that cause such errors:

- Is the printer turned on and set online?
- Are both ends of the printer cable plugged in securely?
- Is there paper in the printer, and is it inserted properly?
- Is there a paper jam in the printer?
- Does the printer still have ink or toner?

More often than not, you'll find that the printer problem is something as simple as the printer being out of paper or ink.

If there seem to be no issues with the printer itself, you can do some troubleshooting in Windows. Open the Devices and Printers folder, right-click the printer, and choose Troubleshoot, as shown in Figure 26.5. Windows 8.1 then runs through several troubleshooting steps to attempt to identify and fix the problem.

FIGURE 26.5

Troubleshoot a printer from Devices and Printers.

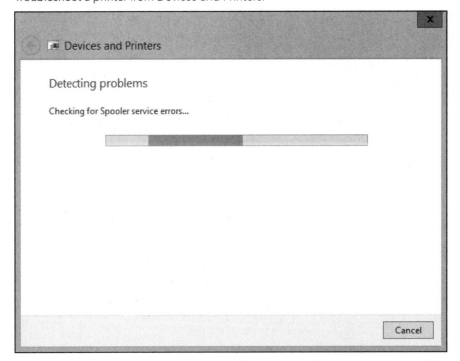

In some situations, Windows 8.1 will be able to identify the problem and fix it for you. In others, it will suggest a fix, as shown in Figure 26.6.

FIGURE 26.6

Suggested troubleshooting action.

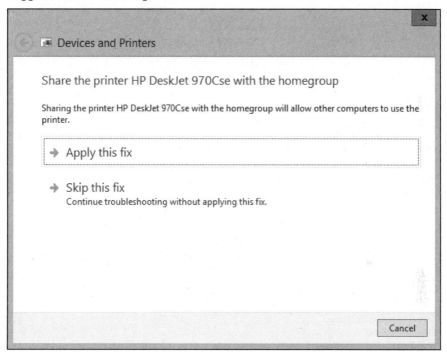

Printing Offline

Printing offline is a means of going through the process of creating the spool file for the printer without actually printing the document. There are times when this is useful, such as when you're working on a notebook computer with no printer attached but you intend to print later when you can attach the computer to a printer or connect to a network.

To make this work, open the printer's queue and choose Use Printer Offline from the Printer menu, as shown in Figure 26.7. The printer's icon will dim and show the word *offline.* You can disconnect the printer from the computer.

FIGURE 26.7

Use Printer Offline.

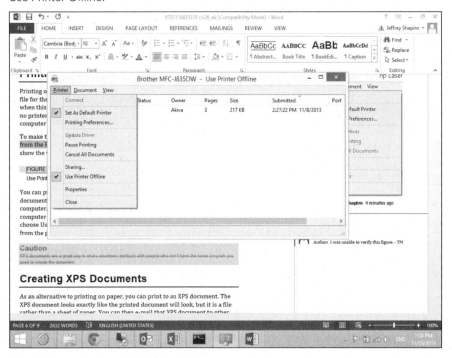

You can print any document while the printer is offline. Of course, the document won't actually print because the printer isn't connected to the computer. When you get back to the printer, connect the printer to the computer again. Open the Printers folder, right-click the printer's icon, and choose Use Printer Online. Any documents you "printed" while disconnected from the printer will start printing.

Creating XPS Documents

As an alternative to printing on paper, you can print to an XPS document. The XPS document looks exactly like the printed document will look, but it is a file rather than a sheet of paper. You can then e-mail that XPS document to other people. Or, if you have a website, let people download it from your site.

> **TIP**
> You can also use this technique to print other people's web pages to files on your own hard disk. You can view that file at any time — you don't need to be online.

To print to an XPS document, start printing as you normally would. For example, choose File ⇨ Print from the program's menu bar. Or if you're in Internet Explorer, click the Print toolbar button. When the Print dialog box opens, choose Microsoft XPS Document Writer instead of your usual printer, as shown in Figure 26.8. Then click OK or Print.

FIGURE 26.8

Print to an XPS document.

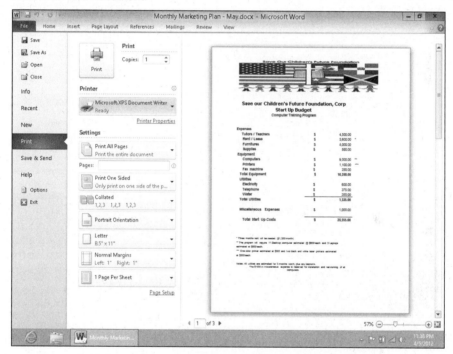

Because you're printing to a file, a Save As dialog box will open. There you can choose the folder in which you want to place the file and give the file a name. Figure 26.9 shows a file named `crimemap.xps` located in the Documents folder about to be printed. Click Save.

The Save As dialog box closes. To verify that the document was printed to a file, open the folder you printed to. The file is closed so it will look like an icon (see Figure 26.10), but you can treat it as any other document. For example, double-click the icon to open it into the new Windows 8.1 Windows Reader app, as shown in Figure 26.11. Or, if you want to e-mail it to someone using an installed e-mail program, such as Windows Live Mail or Microsoft Outlook, right-click the icon and choose Send To ⇨ Mail Recipient.

FIGURE 26.9

Printing `crimemap.xps` in the Documents folder.

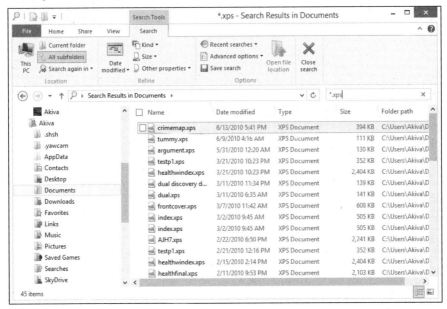

FIGURE 26.10

The icon for an XPS document.

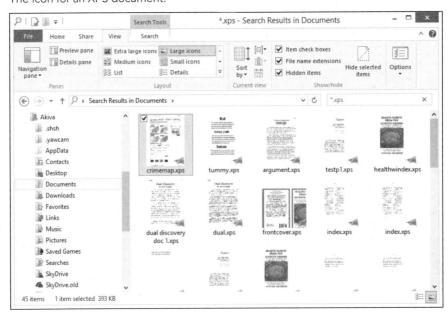

FIGURE 26.11

Reading an XPS document in the Windows Reader app.

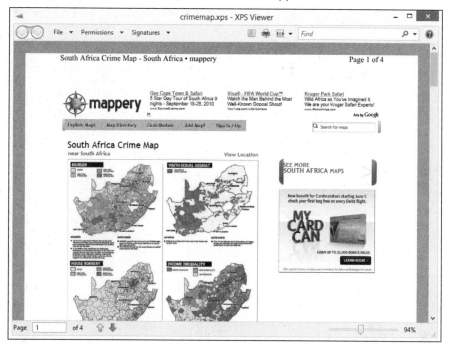

Printing from Windows 8.1 Apps

Printing from Windows 8.1 apps isn't as straightforward as printing from standard (non–Windows 8.1) applications. Windows 8.1 apps don't have standard menu bars, or menu tabs from which to choose the Print command. For Windows 8.1 apps, you use the Devices interface from the Charms Bar to select a printer.

To print from a Windows 8.1 app, follow these steps:

1. Open a Windows 8.1 app, such as Maps.

2. Open the Charms Bar.

3. Click Devices. A list of printers and other printer-related options displays, as shown in Figure 26.12. These other options vary depending on the devices and applications installed on your computer. For example, Figure 26.12 shows three devices.

FIGURE 26.12

Displaying the Devices list when printing from a Windows 8.1 app.

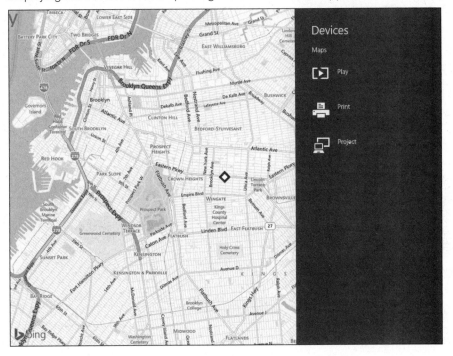

4. For the example here, we want to choose to print to a printer, so click the name of a printer installed on your computer. A screen similar to the one shown in Figure 26.13 appears. This screen varies depending on the printer options available.

5. Click Print to print the document. As the document prints, the Devices screen is removed from the screen, and you return to the Windows 8.1 app that you're printing from.

FIGURE 26.13

Selecting options when printing to a printer.

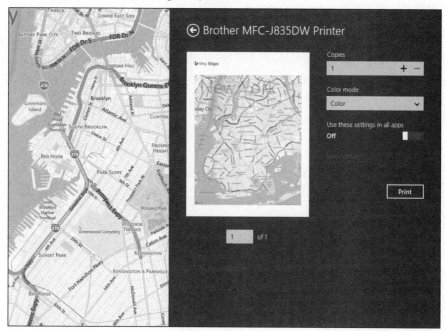

Wrap-Up

The typical printing scenario is that you choose File ⇨ Print from a program's menu bar, or press Ctrl + P, to print whatever document you're viewing at the moment. But as you've seen in this chapter, there's more going on behind the scenes, and there are things you can do to manage your print jobs.

- Every document you print is a print job, temporarily stored in a print queue.
- To open the print queue, double-click the printer icon in the notification area, or the printer's icon in the Printers folder.
- To manage print jobs in the queue, right-click any job and choose an option from the shortcut menu.

- To cancel all documents that are waiting to be printed, choose Printer ⇨ Cancel All Documents from the print queue's menu bar.

- To print to an XPS document rather than paper, start printing and get to the Print dialog box as you normally would, but choose Microsoft XPS Document Writer as the printer.

- To read an XPS document, open it in the new Windows Reader app.

- To print from a Windows 8.1 app, choose the Devices item from the Charms Bar, and then select the printer to print to.

Part VII

Installing and Removing Programs

IN THIS PART

Adding and Managing Windows 8.1 Applications

T he Windows Store is an online location where you can find and install Windows 8.1 apps. Once you find an app you like, you must install it on your computer before you can start using it. This chapter explores how to access the Windows Store, how to navigate it, how to install apps, how to look for and install app updates, and how to remove apps.

Using the Windows Store

The Windows Store (shown in Figure 27.1) is a new feature of Windows 8 and Windows 8.1. It provides an online area where you can download Windows 8.1 apps for your computer, tablet, or Windows phone. Windows 8.1 apps are typically single-functioning applications (for example, reading and responding to Twitter feeds) designed for the Windows 8.1 interface and must adhere to strict application development guidelines before they're approved for the Windows Store. Users can browse the Windows Store for apps. (Future Windows Store offerings might include full-featured applications, such as Microsoft Office.)

FIGURE 27.1

The new Windows Store available with Windows 8.1.

As you read in Chapter 2, the Windows 8.1 interface represents a shift toward touch-based interaction with the operating system and applications, driven in large part by the growth of the tablet and handheld device markets. But Windows 8.1 is not just about touch; it's also about simplification and putting applications within easy reach. The Windows Store makes acquiring apps easy and quick. The Windows Store is available online and requires that your computer meet the following requirements:

- High-speed Internet connection.
- Screen resolution of at least 1024 x 768.
- For the Snap feature to work, your screen resolution must be set to a minimum of 1366 x 768.

To use the Windows Store, show the Start screen and click the Store app tile (shown in Figure 27.2). The Windows Store page appears (refer to Figure 27.1).

FIGURE 27.2

The Windows Store tile pinned to the Start screen.

Reviewing Windows 8.1 apps

Using the Windows Store is pretty straightforward. When you enter the site, the Spotlight area highlights some of the most popular apps. To see the apps and your account, right-click your mouse on any part of the store. The Store menu drops down giving you access to your apps, app categories, and your account. The Store menu is shown in Figure 27.3.

FIGURE 27.3

The Windows Store menu.

> **NOTE**
>
> Microsoft releases guidelines for programmers who want to create Windows 8.1 apps. Besides programming requirements, the guidelines also list general requirements for all apps: For example, apps cannot contain adult material, cannot include defamatory or obscene material, and cannot include content that encourages irresponsible use of alcohol, tobacco, drugs, or weapons.

To learn more about an app, click its tile. A page appears that includes information about the app, such as cost (many apps are free), ratings, description, and features.

Figure 27.4 shows an example of the app page for a free calculator.

To learn what other users have to say about the app, scroll or swipe to the right of the Description to the Review area, or click the Ratings and Reviews link (see Figure 27.5). This shows any reviews that have been added for the app. You can add a review as well by clicking the Write a Review link on the left side of the screen and filling out the resulting form. You may have to scroll to the right to see the Ratings and Review section.

FIGURE 27.4

The details page of a free calculator app.

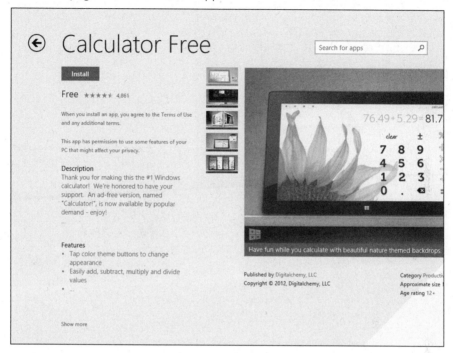

Navigating the Windows Store

Navigating the Windows Store is like navigating a full-screen web page. All the information for a page is displayed on a single page so you don't have to scroll down very much. Instead, additional Windows Store pages are accessed by scrolling to the right using one of the following methods:

- If you have a scroll wheel on your mouse, scroll toward you to scroll to pages to the right. Scroll away from you to return to previous pages on the left.

- Drag the scroll bar at the bottom of the page to the right to see additional pages to the right. Scroll to the left to return to previous pages on the left.

- On touch devices, swipe from right to left to see pages on the right. Swipe from left to right to return to previous pages on the left.

You can navigate back to the main Windows Store page by using the following methods:

- **Clicking the Back button on the top left of the window:** You may have to do this several times if you've viewed several pages already.

- **Using the three methods listed previously to return to previous pages to the left until you arrive at the main Windows Store page.**

FIGURE 27.5

The review page of a free calculator app.

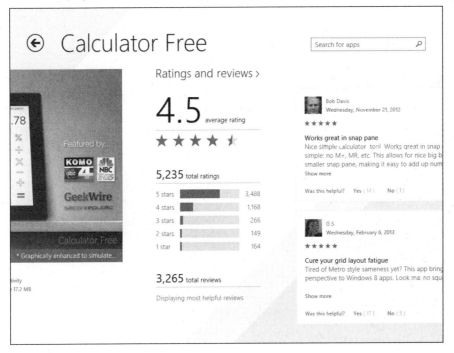

- **Right-clicking the top of a page or swipe down from the top edge of the page to show the app menu:** From this menu (refer to Figure 27.3) click Home to return immediately to the Windows Store home page.

Windows Store categories

The Windows Store displays apps in categories to help you locate them. Apps are available within the following main categories:

- **Games:** Provides game apps, such as Fruit Ninja, Cut the Rope, Mahjong Deluxe, and more.
- **Social:** Provides apps for accessing social media sites, such as Rowi and Tweetro for Twitter, WordPress.com for WordPress sites, FlipToast for Facebook and Twitter, and more.
- **Entertainment:** Shows apps that provide entertainment value, such as the Naturespace Holographic Audio app, Kids Song Machine apps, and the CW TV network app.
- **Photo:** Lists digital photography apps, such as Camera, Photo Monkey, and Composite.
- **Music & Video:** Shows apps for sharing and storing videos, accessing podcasts, listening to Internet radio, and working with music. Apps you can find in this category include Givit, SlapDash Podcasts, and Slacker Radio.

- **Sports:** Provides sports-related apps, such as Major League Soccer, Basketball Coach's Clipboard, and New Zealand Cricket.

- **Books & Reference:** Shows apps relating to books, e-books, references, the Bible, and online magazines.

- **News & Weather:** Provides apps for news and weather resources, such as the *Los Angeles Times, USA Today*, and AccuWeather.com.

- **Health & Fitness:** Lists apps for helping you stay healthy, get in shape, and lose weight, including Fit Ball and Medicine Cabinet.

- **Food & Dining:** Provides recipe and food- and drink-related apps, such as Fine Cooking, Cocktail Flow, Matias Winery, and AllRecipes.

- **Lifestyle:** Lists apps that fall into general lifestyle areas, such as AutoTrader, PRINZ Cityguide, and AuctionKing.

- **Shopping:** Shows apps for shopping, such as Yellow Pages, Amazon Windows 8.1 for Windows, and CBAZAAR.

- **Travel:** Lists travel-related apps, such as Kayak Hotels, INRIX Traffic, and Navitime.

- **Finance:** Provides apps for helping you manage finances, including the Finance app and the Ameriprise Financial app.

- **Productivity:** Includes apps for computer and tablet productivity, including EverNote, Skitch, and Quick Note.

- **Tools:** Shows computer tools, such as WinZip 16.5, Maps, and Dr.eye.

- **Security:** Lists computer security-related apps.

- **Business:** Shows apps that help you in the business world, such as MyStarJob, Captain Dash, and Presenter.

- **Education:** Provides educational apps, such as SATMax, My Baby Piano, Star Chart, and ICT Break.

- **Government:** Lists government-related apps.

Within each category, individual apps are showcased. Some categories also show an All Stars category for apps that have been rated the highest for a category, a New Releases category for just released apps, and a Top Free category that lists top-rated free apps.

Costs of apps

The costs of apps vary. Typically, the costs fall into one of three payment structures:

- **Free:** Many free apps are free because they also include built-in advertisements to offset the cost of development, support, and upgrades. In some cases, you have the option of upgrading from a free version to a full-featured version that includes additional features and no ads.

- **Trial:** Gives you many of the features available in a full paid version, but for a limited time period.

- **Paid:** Gives you access to a full version of the app. Costs vary from 99¢ to several hundred dollars.

Searching for apps

Because the Windows Store is itself a Windows 8.1 app, you can use the Windows Search tool to locate apps in the Windows Store. To do this, display the Charms Bar and click Search. In the Search field, type an app name or a keyword for an app and press Enter. The Windows Store returns a listing of apps that meet your search criteria. Figure 27.6, for example, shows a screen with the Search tool visible with a keyword called **calculator apps** and a search results screen from the Windows Store.

FIGURE 27.6

Use the Windows Search tool to locate Windows Store apps.

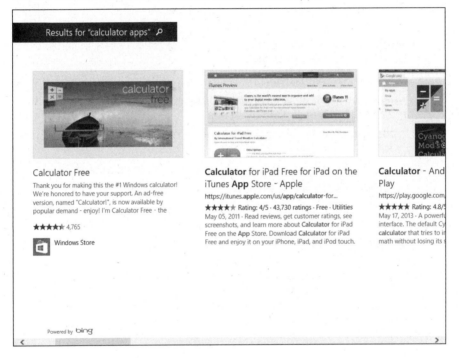

Installing Windows 8.1 apps

When you find an app you like, you must first install it before you can use it on your computer or tablet. Apps are very easy to install. Click an app tile to show the app's description page. Next, click the Install button on the left side of the page. The Windows Store shows a message at the top of the page that your app is installing. Once it's installed, Windows displays a message notifying you of the installation.

After the app is installed on your computer, the install button is no longer available when you go to the app's page in the Windows Store. Instead, it shows that you own this app. An example of this is shown in Figure 27.7.

To start using the app, display the Start screen and click the app's tile.

FIGURE 27.7

Your app's page showing that the page is installed.

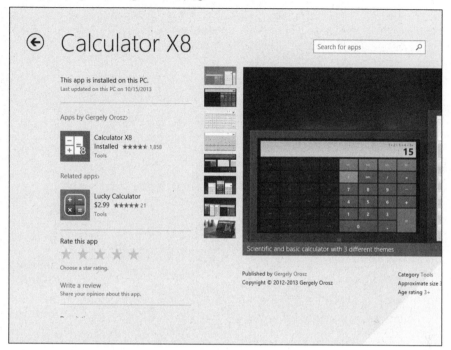

Updating Apps

Periodically, app developers enhance an app by adding features or improving its performance by providing an update. If updates are available, the Store tile on the Windows Start screen shows a number corresponding to the number of updates available.

Click that tile to open the Windows Store. At the top right of the Windows Store, click Update. Windows displays the App Updates page and begins the process of downloading updates available for your installed apps. These updates run in the background and display a message when the updates are installed on your computer.

Removing Apps

If you no longer want an app installed on your computer, you can remove it by uninstalling it. To do this, use the following steps:

1. Display the Start screen.
2. Right-click the app that you want to remove. Windows puts a check mark on the app's tile and displays a menu at the bottom of the screen (see Figure 27.8).

FIGURE 27.8

Use the Uninstall feature to remove an app from your computer.

3. Click Uninstall from the menu. A message appears telling you that the app will be removed and any information related to that app will also be removed.

4. Click the Uninstall button to remove the selected app.

Wrap-Up

The Windows Store provides access to many different types of apps, including productivity apps, games, news apps, and more.

Here's a quick summary of the main points presented in this chapter:

- You use the Windows Store to install apps to your computer.
- Apps are divided into categories in the Windows Store, such as Social, Entertainment, Business, and Productivity.
- Many apps are free.
- You use the Windows Store to install updates to your installed apps.
- To remove an app from Windows, right-click it and click Uninstall. Click Uninstall to confirm that you want to remove that app.

Installing and Upgrading Legacy Programs

IN THIS CHAPTER

Playing it safe with program installations

Updating versus upgrading

Installing programs from disks

U nlike documents, which you can freely copy to your hard disk and use on the spot, most new programs you acquire need to be installed before you can use them. The installation process configures the software to work with your particular hardware and software. The process also creates an icon or program group on the Windows 8.1 Start screen so that you can start the new program as you would any other.

> **NOTE**
>
> If you're upgrading from Windows 7 or earlier, don't take it for granted that upgrading to Windows 8.1 will preserve all your legacy applications (even Microsoft Office 2010 applications are at risk). Before you upgrade, make sure that you have your installation media and registration or license keys handy, and be prepared to reinstall.

You need to install a program only once, not each time you intend to use it. Once you've installed a program from a disk, you can put the disk away for safekeeping. You'll need the original installation disk to reinstall the program only if you accidentally delete it from your hard disk or if some sort of hard disk crash damages the program.

This chapter explores the common methods and issues you'll likely experience when installing programs for Windows 8.1. Keep in mind that the installation process, although similar across different programs, can still vary from one program to the next. So, the examples in this chapter are general, rather than specific.

> **NOTE**
>
> There is one rare exception to requiring installation; self-contained program files simply copy to your computer and require you to double-click them to run.

Playing It Safe with Program Installations

Programs you buy in a store aren't likely to contain any malicious code such as viruses, worms, or spyware. Those things tend to be spread by e-mail attachments and free downloads from the web. However, there's always an outside chance that the new program is incompatible with Windows 8.1 or a hardware device on your computer. So, there may be times when you need to uninstall a program and then get all your system files back into shape to undo any changes made to your system by the new program.

> **NOTE**
> This chapter covers installing legacy applications on Windows 8.1.

 The Windows 8.1 System Protection greatly simplifies the task of getting things back in shape should a program installation or upgrade cause problems. But it helps only if it's turned on and you know how to use it. For details, see Chapter 24.

Updates Versus Upgrades

Non-technical people often assume that updates and upgrades are the same thing. They aren't. An *update* is usually something you do online. There is nothing to buy at a store, no disk to insert in a disk drive. Updates are generally free, and often automatic (many programs scan for updates and offer them to you automatically). You don't have to make an effort to seek those out and install them.

Updates for some programs may not be quite so automatic. But you can often find out if any updates are available right from the program's Help menu. For example, in Microsoft Office 2010 programs, select the File tab and choose Help. On the right pane, click Check for Updates to search the web for any Microsoft Office–related updates.

> **TIP**
> You can also use Windows Update to check for Microsoft product updates. See Chapter 8 to learn about Windows Update.

Unlike updates, upgrades are usually not free. You have to purchase them and install them. For example, let's say you have Microsoft Office 2010 installed on a computer. You want to get Office 2013 on that computer. In that case, you'd seek out an Office 2013 Upgrade Edition (which is cheaper than the regular edition). Then you'd install that upgrade right over your existing version. In other words, you wouldn't uninstall (remove) your existing version first.

Installing and Upgrading from a Disk

Before you get started here, you must have administrative privileges to install a program. In other words, you need to know the password for an administrative account on your computer. If you have a limited user account and don't know the administrative password, you'll need to get an administrator to install the program for you.

Most programs that you purchase will be delivered on a CD or DVD, or via an Internet download. You should always follow the installation instructions that come with such a program. But just so that you know what to expect, here's how the process usually works, once you have the installation files or CD/DVD in hand:

1. Although not required, it's a good idea to run the installation with no other programs running to make sure you have plenty of system resources available and that no files that need to be updated by the installation are in use. Close all open program windows on your desktop by clicking their Close buttons or by right-clicking their taskbar buttons and choosing Close.

> **NOTE**
> You don't need to close programs whose icons are in the notification area, unless specifically instructed to by the installation instructions for the program you're installing.

2. For programs released on a disk, insert the CD or DVD into your computer's CD or DVD drive and wait a few seconds. Wait for the installation program to appear on your screen. If it doesn't appear within 30 seconds, see the section "Using the installed program" later in this chapter. Skip to Step 4.

3. For programs released on a download from the Internet, find the installation or setup file, which will usually have an .exe file extension. Double-click that file to launch it.

4. Follow the onscreen instructions to perform the installation.

That's really all there is to it. You'll be presented with some questions and options along the way. Exactly what you see varies from one program to the next, but some common items include the End User License Agreement (EULA), and the option to choose a folder in which to store the program, which we discuss in a moment.

For programs on a CD/DVD, sometimes your Windows setup may not launch the installation program automatically. If nothing happens within half a minute or so after you have inserted a program's installation CD/DVD into your computer's CD/DVD drive, you may need to start the installation program manually. Here's how:

1. Open your Computer folder by clicking the File Explorer icon on the desktop taskbar and choosing Computer.

2. Open the icon that represents the drive into which you placed the disk.

3. If the installation program doesn't start automatically in a few seconds, click (or double-click) the icon named Setup or Setup.exe.

That should be enough to get the installation program started. From there you can follow the onscreen instructions to complete the installation.

The onscreen instructions and prompts you see during the installation vary from one program to the next. The next section discusses some common things you're likely to come across when installing just about any program.

Common Installation Prompts

Even though every program is unique in some ways, you're likely to come across some common elements during a program installation. When you install a program, you probably won't see all the prompts described in the sections that follow, so don't be alarmed if your installation procedure is much simpler. (Be thankful instead.)

The initial CD or DVD prompt

Shortly after you insert the installation disk for a program, you may see a prompt like the one in Figure 28.1. This is a new setup feature. Click this message to display the actions you can take with the installation disk. Figure 28.2 shows examples of setup options Windows 8.1 provides. In this case, you want to choose the Run ShelExec.Exe option. The most common option is Run SETUP.EXE, which is what you would click.

FIGURE 28.1

The first prompt after inserting an installation disk.

FIGURE 28.2

Windows 8.1 displays a message when it recognizes a disk with a setup program on it.

Entering an administrator password

Only people with administrative privileges can install programs in Windows 8.1. If you're signed into a limited account, you'll see a dialog box asking you to enter an administrative password. If you're already logged on with an administrative account, Windows 8.1 asks you if you want to allow the program to make changes to the computer. Click Yes to continue with Setup.

The product key or serial number

Many programs (including ones published by Microsoft, Adobe, Apple, and others) require that you enter a product key or serial number to install the program. That number is usually on a sticker on the case or sleeve in which the program was delivered.

TIP

You may want to keep track of all your product keys in a word processing or spreadsheet document in case you ever need to reinstall everything. Print a copy of the document and keep it safe in case your hard disk crashes. Belarc (www.belarc.com) offers a free program called Belarc Adviser that lists the product keys for all your installed programs, as well as a good deal more useful information about your systems. It's one of those free programs that's worth its proverbial weight in gold! Also check out Magical Jelly Bean Finder, at www.magicaljellybean.com/keyfinder.

If you do need to enter a product key or serial number, you'll see a prompt similar to the example shown in Figure 28.3. Type the product key exactly as it is provided by the software developer, and click Continue (or whatever button the installation program offers to continue the installation process).

FIGURE 28.3

Enter a product key.

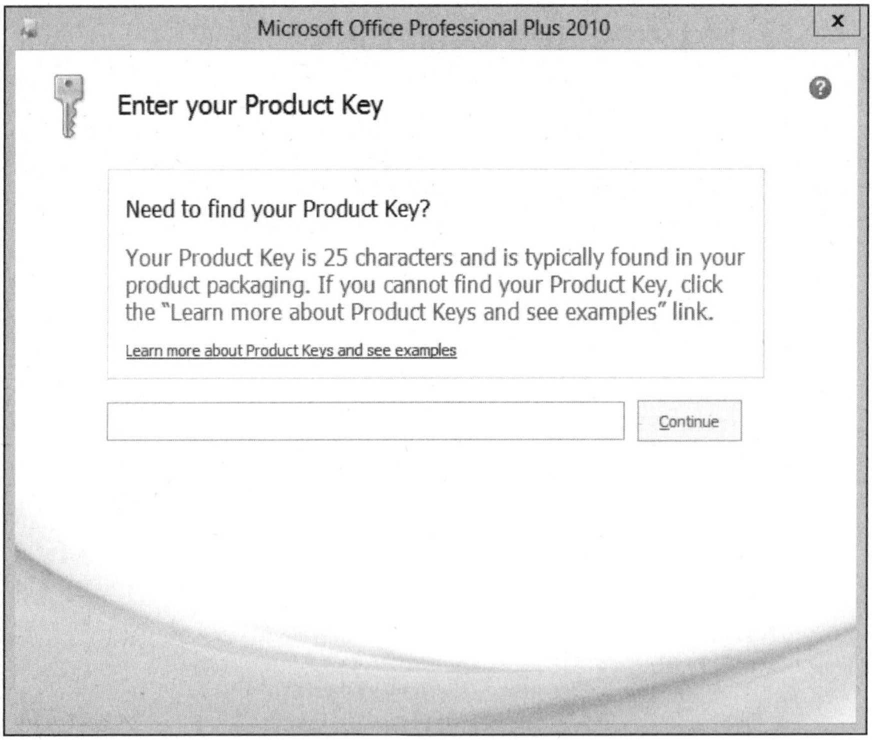

Microsoft Office Professional Plus 2010

Enter your Product Key

Need to find your Product Key?

Your Product Key is 25 characters and is typically found in your product packaging. If you cannot find your Product Key, click the "Learn more about Product Keys and see examples" link.

Learn more about Product Keys and see examples

Continue

Compliance check

If you're installing an upgrade of a new program and you already have the older version installed on your computer, the installation program likely will detect the existing product and move through the upgrade. In other situations, particularly where you don't already have a previous edition of the program installed, you might be prompted to insert the CD/DVD for the old version and/or enter the product key for the old version. This depends entirely on the requirements of the application's upgrade program. Follow the prompts displayed by the upgrade program to provide the requested information.

> **NOTE**
> You might see a message asking what you want to do with the CD/DVD you just inserted. You do *not* want to install the program on the CD/DVD. The goal here is to simply prove you have the older version, not to install the older version. So, if you do see a dialog box asking what you want to do with the CD/DVD, click the Close (X) button in the upper-right corner of that dialog box.

User information prompt

Some programs offer prompts that ask for your username or initials. These are optional but useful. The username will automatically be entered as the author name in any documents you create with the program. The initials will be used in settings where multiple people edit documents to identify changes you made to the document.

The End User License Agreement

Just about every commercial program and most freeware and open-source programs require that you accept the End User License Agreement (EULA) as part of the installation process. Figure 28.4 shows an example. The agreement is a legal document that defines your rights to the program, as well as the developer's retained rights.

The EULA differs from one program to the next. In most cases, the EULA gives you the right to install a program on one computer. However, that is not always the case. The EULA for Microsoft Office 2010 applications, for example, allows you to install the software on a licensed device (such as your desktop computer) and one portable device (such as your notebook PC). The intent of this clause is that you'll use the software on only one computer at a time. What's more, you can access and use the software on the device remotely from any other device. For example, this means you can connect to your office PC from home and run the Office application remotely on your office PC (or vice versa).

Although many people never read the EULA when installing a program, you should take the time to do so. You'll discover interesting bits of information (such as the fact that you can install Office on more than one computer) and also potential problems. For example, we've seen EULAs for shareware and commercial programs that explain that the Setup

FIGURE 28.4

A sample End User License Agreement.

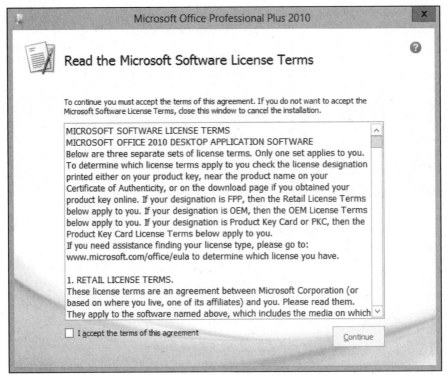

program will install other, third-party applications along with the program, and that by accepting the EULA you're indicating your acceptance of those other programs. These programs might have nothing to do with the program you're installing, such as weather monitors, Internet Explorer add-ons, toolbars, and so on. Often, the installation program gives you the option of not installing these additional programs, but that's not always the case. So, my best advice is to always read the EULA.

You can't install the program if you don't accept the terms of the agreement, so assuming you're happy with (or at least resigned to) the terms of the EULA, check the I Accept option and click Next, Continue, or whatever button continues the installation process.

Type of installation

Sometimes you'll be given some choices as to how and where you want to install the program. Figure 28.5 shows an example from Microsoft Office Professional 2010. Unless your computer is low on disk space, it's generally a good idea to install the program with all features. Otherwise, months later you may go to use some advanced feature of the program only to get an error message saying it's not installed. A nice compromise in Microsoft Office Setup is to choose the Installed On First Use option for a feature, which causes Setup to run when you try to use a feature that is not yet installed. Then you just pop in the CD or DVD, let Setup install the feature, and continue working.

FIGURE 28.5

Type of installation.

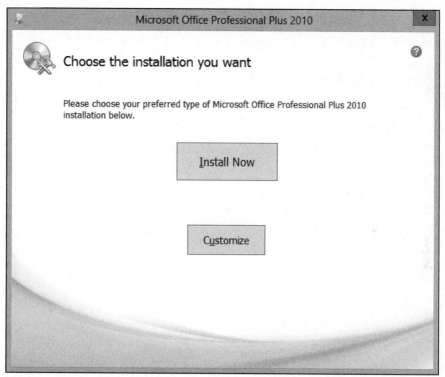

As to the *where* to install the program, there is rarely any reason to change the suggested location, which is typically some folder in C:\Program Files. Don't change that unless you really have some good reason for doing it. Whatever you do, don't make the common newbie mistake of installing it in your Documents folder or someplace like that. You're not installing a document. You're installing a program. And it's best to keep all your programs in subfolders under C:\Program Files.

Installation summary

The installation procedure might give you a summary of the options you chose along the way. Typically, you'll have a Back button or some other means to back up and make changes if needed.

Setup completed

The last page of the installation options might offer a couple of final options, as in the example shown in Figure 28.6. Whether you choose these options is relatively unimportant. You can check the web for updates and additional downloads at any time, whether through the program itself or by visiting the software company's website (or the Microsoft Update site).

FIGURE 28.6

Setup complete.

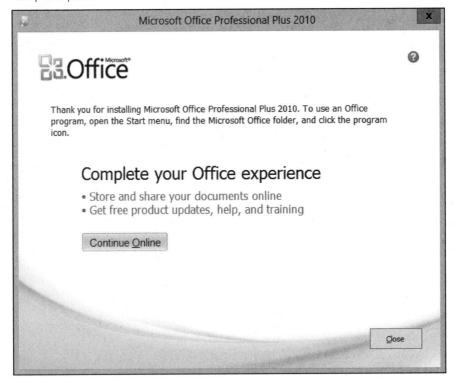

Some applications give you the option of keeping installation files on the computer rather than deleting them. Keeping the installation files can make it easier to change program settings or install missing components in the future. They usually don't take up any significant amount of disk space. Click Finish, remove the CD/DVD from the drive, and put it someplace safe in case you ever need to reinstall in the future.

You may also be prompted to shut down and restart Windows after the program is installed. If prompted, you can click Yes to restart now or click No to restart later. In any event, you must restart at least once before running the program for the first time.

> **NOTE**
>
> Most insurance policies don't cover computer software. So, if at all possible, consider keeping your original program DVD/CDs in a fireproof safe.

Using the installed program

Once the program is installed, you can run it from the Windows 8.1 Start screen. The preceding steps installed Microsoft Office Professional 2010. So, to run it, you'd show the Windows 8.1 Start screen, scroll over to the application you want to start and click its tile.

Wrap-Up

Installing programs from files, CDs, or DVDs is easy to do. It's basically a matter of running the executable file, or putting the program installation disk into your CD or DVD drive and following the onscreen instructions. Here's a quick summary of the main points presented in this chapter:

- Consider creating a system restore point (see Chapter 31) before installing any program. That way, if the new program creates problems, use that restore point and return to the protection point to undo every change made during the program installation. Note that Windows 8.1 will create a restore point for you automatically in most situations.

- You need to install a program only once, not each time you want to use it. Once installed, you run the program from the new Windows 8.1 Start screen, without the program CD or DVD in the drive. In a few cases, the program requires the CD or DVD in the drive to validate that you have a licensed copy of the program (because possession of the CD or DVD implies that you haven't installed it by using someone else's media).

- If you're upgrading a program that's already installed, do not remove the existing version unless the installation instructions tell you to do so.

- The typical procedure for installing a new program is to insert the program's installation CD or DVD and follow the onscreen instructions. For a program that you download from the Internet, you simply need to double-click its setup filename.

- If nothing happens within a minute of inserting the installation disk, open your Computer folder, open the icon for the CD drive, and double-click the Setup or Setup.exe icon on the CD.

- When the installation is complete, store the installation disk in a safe place. In most cases you won't need it to run the program. But you may need it to reinstall the program should some mishap cause you to lose the program.

Getting Older Programs to Run

Y ou can run almost any program that's installed on your computer just by clicking its tile on the Windows 8.1 Start screen. But there are always exceptions to the rule. Chief among the list of exceptions are old programs that were originally written to work with earlier versions of Windows. Or, even worse, programs that were written to run on DOS.

That's not to say Windows *can't* run old programs. Most of the time, it can run an older program as is, without any changes at all on your part. This is especially true if the program was written for Windows XP or later versions of Windows. So, before you assume that you have to do something to try to get an older program to run, try running the program normally. If it runs, you're done. If it won't run, then this is the chapter you need to (hopefully) get the program to run.

Understanding Program Types

A couple types of programs could be considered old in the context of this chapter:

- **DOS programs:** These programs were developed to run under various versions of the Disk Operating System (DOS) that was the precursor to Windows.
- **16-bit Windows programs:** These Windows applications were written for Windows 98 and earlier versions of Windows.

What does "16-bit" mean? Three classes of Windows applications exist: 16-bit, 32-bit, and 64-bit. The number of bits indicates the maximum amount of addressable memory supported by the program. Table 29.1 indicates the differences.

TABLE 29.1   Processor Technology and Directly Addressable Memory

Technology	Meaning	Memory Addresses
16-bit	2^{16}	65,536
32-bit	2^{32}	4,294,967,296
64-bit	2^{64}	18,446,744,073,709,600,000

Windows NT, Windows 2000, and Windows XP were all originally 32-bit operating systems. Windows XP was also offered in a 64-bit edition. Windows 98 and earlier were 16-bit operating systems. Windows Vista and Windows 7 were offered in two versions, 32-bit and 64-bit. Likewise, Windows 8/8.1 is available in 32-bit and 64-bit versions. Suffice it to say, the higher the bits, the more capable the operating system. For the purposes of this chapter, the key point is that you can run a program on the OS it was designed for or (possibly) on a later version, but you can't go backward. For example, you can run a 32-bit application on a 64-bit OS, but you can't run a 64-bit program on a 32-bit OS.

DOS programs

Let's make a distinction between DOS programs and DOS commands that you can run in Windows 8.1. *DOS programs* are programs that were written specifically to run on a DOS without (and prior to) Windows. It's so unlikely that you would want to run an old DOS program on Windows 8.1 that we don't even cover the topic in this chapter (although we do have a copy of Zork lying around somewhere that would be fun to play again . . .). That doesn't mean you *can't* run that DOS program under Windows 8.1 — many of them will run without any major problems.

DOS commands are developed by Microsoft and included as part of the Windows package, instead of being developed and marketed by third parties. We do cover DOS commands to some degree later in this chapter.

Old programs to avoid altogether

Windows 8.1 is a revision of the Windows 7 operating system, so almost all Windows 7 programs should have no problems running on Windows 8.1. Likewise, many of your basic Windows Vista and Windows XP application programs will work. But you should validate compatibility for other kinds of programs before attempting to run them under Windows 8.1. These include

- **Old disk utility programs:** Older disk utility programs such as Norton Utilities (later it went by Symantec Norton Utilities) and various disk compression and partitioning tools should never be run on Windows 8.1. Many older DVD- or CD-burning programs are likely to cause problems, too. If you have such a program, you should really upgrade to the Windows 8.1 version of that program or find a similar product that's designed to work with Windows 8.1.

- **Old backup programs:** If you have an older backup program, using it in compatibility mode could prove disastrous. Even if you're able to perform the backup, there's an outside chance you won't be able to restore from the backup if and when you need to. Consider using Windows File History, which comes with your copy of Windows 8.1.

- **Old cleanup programs:** Older programs that purport to keep your computer running in tip-top shape, clean up your registry, and so forth should not be used at all in Windows 8.1. If you like the program, look into getting a version that's specifically written for or certified by the developer as compatible with Windows 8.1.

- **Old optimizing programs:** Programs designed to make your computer run at maximum performance won't necessarily make Windows 8.1 run that way. In fact, they may do a lot more harm than good. If you use such programs, check to see if there's a Windows 8.1 version available before you install the old version.

- **Old antivirus programs:** Virus detection and removal is dicey business and needs to be handled with great care. Antivirus programs written for pre–Windows 8.1 versions of Windows should *never* be installed or run on a Windows 8.1 computer unless certified by the developer as compatible. The same goes for anti-spyware and other anti-malware programs. Better to seek out a Windows 8.1 version of the program than to presume the older version will work. Better yet, use Windows Defender, which comes pre-installed on your computer.

 Read Chapter 6 on how to deal with malicious software that attacks your computer.

Installing Incompatible Programs

To install an older program, first try installing it normally. For example, if it's on a CD, insert the CD and wait for the installation program to appear automatically. If nothing starts automatically, open your root folder (open File Explorer and choose the root folder or This PC). Then click the icon to open the drive that contains the installation disc and double-click the setup launcher program (typically setup.exe, setup, install.exe, or install). If Windows 8.1 determines that the program is older, you'll see the Program Compatibility Assistant.

29

If you believe that the program installed normally, just click the option that indicates that the program installed properly. Otherwise, click the option that specifies compatibility mode. Windows 8.1 assigns some compatibility mode attributes to the program and tries the installation again. With any luck, the second try will do the trick.

If you still have problems, here are some things to consider:

- If you're installing from a standard user account, log out and log in to an administrative account; then try to install from that account.

- If you have to create any file or folder names, use old 8.3 conventions (keep filenames to eight characters maximum with no blank spaces and provide a three- character extension).

- If you get stuck in an installation program, use the Applications tab in Task Manager to end the stuck program.

 See Chapter 32 for details on Task Manager.

If all else fails, contact the program publisher (if it's still in business) or look for information about that program online. Only the program publisher really knows if the program will even run in Windows 8.1 and what's required to get it to run.

To check out your installed applications and devices before upgrading to Windows 8.1 visit the program compatibility web page at Microsoft at `http://windows.microsoft.com/en-us/windows-8/get-apps-devices-working`.

Using the Program Compatibility Troubleshooter

Installing a program is one thing; getting it to run after it's installed is another. If an installed program won't start or isn't working right, try using the Program Compatibility Troubleshooter on it.

The Program Compatibility Troubleshooter provides a step-by-step means of configuring and testing an older program so that it will run in Windows 8.1. Before you bother to use it, try running the installed program without it. You could discover that the program runs just fine without any compatibility settings and save yourself quite a bit of trouble.

If you're sure an installed program isn't running, or is not running correctly, follow these steps to start the Program Compatibility Troubleshooter:

TIP

You can right-click a program's icon on the Start screen, choose File Location, right-click the file, and then choose Troubleshoot Compatibility to launch the Program Compatibility Wizard.

1. Open Control Panel and click the Troubleshooting icon.
2. When the Troubleshooting applet opens click the Programs option and then click on the Program Compatibility Troubleshooter.
3. On the first page of the troubleshooter click Next. The troubleshooter will now gather a list of applications for troubleshooting (see Figure 29.1).
4. If you want Windows 8.1 to try to determine the right settings on its own, click Try Recommended Settings. To specify your own settings, click Troubleshoot Program. The following steps assume you've selected the second option.

FIGURE 29.1

Program Compatibility Troubleshooter.

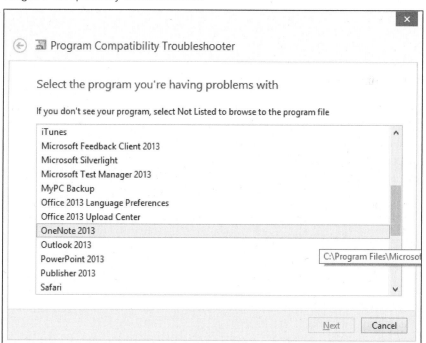

29

5. Next, the wizard prompts you to answer questions about the program (see Figure 29.2). Selecting any of the first three options causes the wizard to prompt you with related questions. For example, if you choose the option The Program Worked in Earlier Versions of Windows But Won't Install or Run Now, the wizard asks you to specify on which version of the OS it worked previously. Likewise, choosing the option The Program Opens But Doesn't Display Correctly results in a list of questions similar to that shown in Figure 29.3.

6. Complete the wizard by selecting options that relate to the problems you're having with the program.

FIGURE 29.2

Program Compatibility questions.

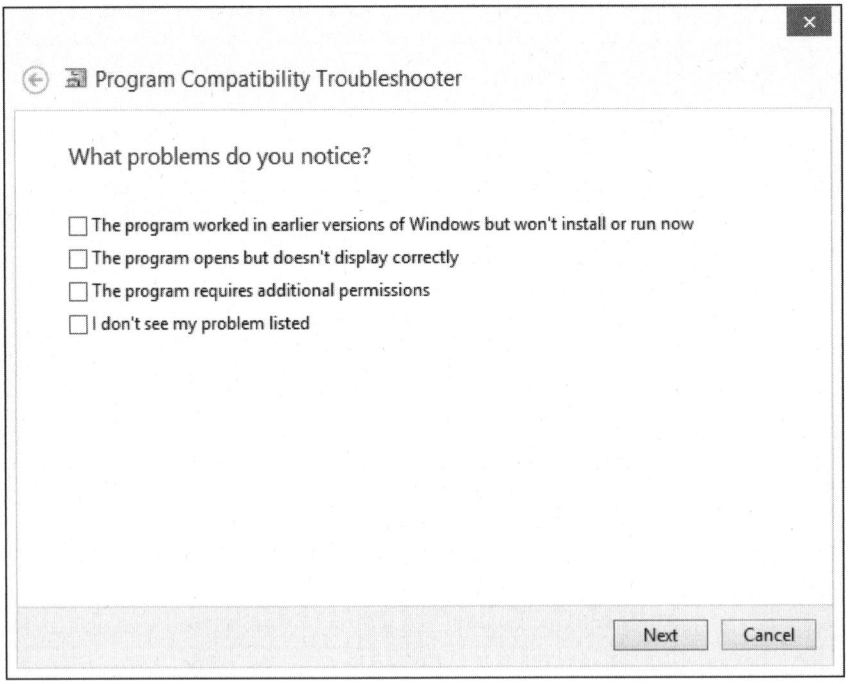

FIGURE 29.3

Display options for compatibility.

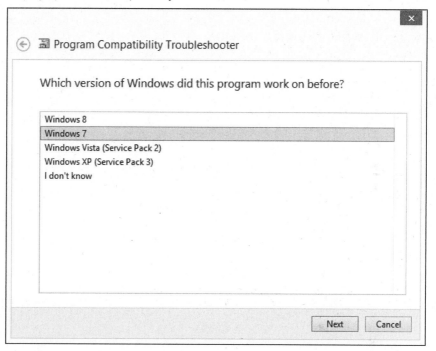

The process is mostly trial and error. If the program runs when you finish the wizard, great. Otherwise you can run it again to try some different settings until you can get the program to work right.

Here are some general guidelines to help you get your programs running:

- If the program won't install or won't run, run the wizard, choose the option The Program Worked in Earlier Versions of Windows But Won't Install or Run Now and specify the operating system for which the program was written. For example, if it is a Windows XP game, choose that OS from the OS list provided by the wizard.

- If you have problems with the program's display, choose the option The Program Opens But Doesn't Display Correctly and click Next. Choose the symptoms the program is exhibiting and click Next to let the wizard set display options as needed.

- If you think the program is having permissions issues (for example, the program says it can't write a file), choose the option The Program Requires Additional Permissions. The wizard configures the program to run as an administrator, which should resolve the issue.

29

There's no guarantee that the Program Compatibility Troubleshooter will make the program run. Some programs are so old and so far removed from modern computing capabilities that there's just no way to force them to run. In those cases, the only hope is to contact the program publisher or search online to see if they have any solutions or a compatible version of the program.

Quick-and-Dirty Program Compatibility

The Program Compatibility Wizard provides an easy way to choose and test settings for program compatibility. Those settings are stored on the Compatibility tab of the program file's properties sheet. You can use the wizard to change compatibility settings, or you change settings manually right in the properties sheet by following these steps:

1. On the Start screen, right-click the program you want to examine. Choose Open File Location at the bottom of the screen (see Figure 29.4).

FIGURE 29.4

Display program options.

2. Right-click the program's icon and choose Properties.

3. In the Properties dialog box that opens, select the Compatibility tab. You'll see the options shown in Figure 29.5.

FIGURE 29.5

Compatibility settings.

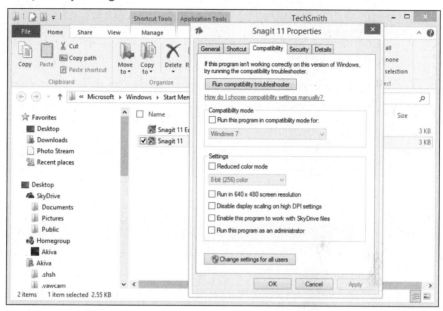

4. Select the Run This Program in Compatibility Mode For check box, and then choose the operating system for which the program was written. If the program installs and runs, but exhibits other symptoms (such as display problems), leave this option unselected.

5. If you're having problems with the program's display, choose appropriate display settings in the Settings group.

6. If the program seems to have permission problems, select Run This Program as an Administrator.

7. If you want to apply the settings for everyone who uses the program, click the Change Settings for All Users button to open a similar Properties dialog box and set properties there as needed.

8. Click OK.

The compatibility settings stick to the program so you can just start the program normally, from the All Programs menu, at any time. Just keep in mind that there's no guarantee you'll be able to force all programs to run in Windows 8.1.

Using DOS Commands in Windows 8.1

If you've used personal computers since the DOS days, you might still want to enter the occasional DOS command. DOS commands will let you do things you can't really do in Windows. For example, in those rare instances where you can't delete a file in Windows, using a DOS `erase` or `del` command with the `/F` switch will often do the trick. You can use the DOS `dir` command to print filenames from a folder to paper or a text file.

There is one big catch to using commands in Windows 8.1. User Account Control (UAC) may prevent you from doing things you'd otherwise take for granted. You can get around many of those by using the Run as Administrator option to open the command prompt. Here are two different ways to open the Command Prompt window:

- From the desktop, press Windows + X and click Command Prompt.
- Display the Charms Bar, click Search, and type **cmd**. Choose cmd.exe or right-click cmd.exe and choose Run as Administrator (see Figure 29.6).

FIGURE 29.6

Open Command Prompt.

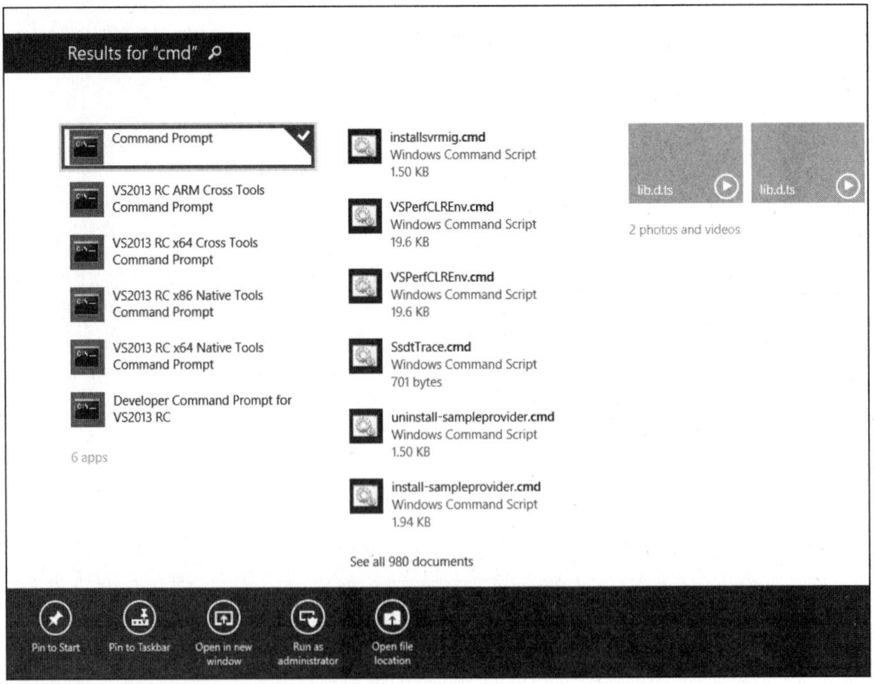

The Command Prompt window that opens is much like DOS. By default, you're taken to the home directory for your user account. But you can navigate around using the DOS `cd` command. For example, enter **cd..** to go to the parent directory, or **cd "program files"** to go to the Program Files folders.

To see a list of all supported commands, enter **help** at the command prompt. For the syntax of a command, type the command followed by **/?**. For example, entering **dir /?** displays the Help for the `dir` command.

> **NOTE**
> You can change the height and width of the Command Prompt window. To do so, click its control menu in the upper-left corner and choose Properties.

You can copy and paste a lengthy pathname to a `cd` command to simplify opening that folder in a DOS window. In Windows, open the folder in File Explorer, highlight the path in the address bar as in Figure 29.7, and press Ctrl + C to copy it.

FIGURE 29.7

Select a directory path.

29

TIP

To see the name you need to type to launch any program, right-click the program's icon on the All Programs menu and choose Properties. The filename at the end of the Target path is the name you type in the Search or Run box.

In the Command Prompt window, type cd and a space. Then right-click the Command Prompt window and choose Paste. Press Enter, and you'll be in that folder.

Use the `dir` command with various switches to view, or optionally print, all the filenames in a folder and also its subfolders if you like. For example, let's say you navigate to the Music folder for your account (`C:\Users\yourUserName\Music`). From that folder, entering **dir /s** lists all file and folder names for all artists, albums, and songs in your Music folder.

You can use the /b, /n, and /w switches to choose how you want the information displayed. For example, entering **dir /s /w.** shows filenames in the wide format.

To send `dir` output directly to the printer, try `dir /s /w > prn`. You're probably better off sending the output to a text file rather than straight to the printer. That way you can open and edit the text file before you print or even import it into Excel or Access to make it more like tabular data. To send output to a file, end the command with a filename (or path and filename). For example, entering the following from the Music folder puts the output listing in a file named MyMusic.txt in the Music folder.

```
dir /s /w >MyMusic.txt
```

You can then open that MyMusic.txt file with any text editor or word processor to clean it up. If you have database management skills, you can import the data to Access or a similar program and treat it like any other tabular data.

CAUTION

This section is just a side topic for people who are already familiar with DOS. Don't experiment with DOS commands carelessly. You could lose a lot of files and have no means of getting them back!

To exit the Command Prompt window, enter the `exit` command or just close the window.

Wrap-Up

This chapter has focused on techniques for getting older programs to work in Windows 8.1. Windows 8.1 offers several tools to help with compatibility issues. Whether you have any luck with them depends on how old and how incompatible the program is. Most of your programs will run fine under Windows 8.1. A few won't, until you upgrade to the Windows 8.1 version, but those should be few and far between. The main points are as follows:

- Most programs written for Windows Vista and Windows 7 are already compatible with Windows 8.1 and require no special handling.

- When you attempt to install an older program, the Program Compatibility Assistant kicks in automatically to help out.

- The Program Compatibility Wizard helps you with installed programs that won't start or run correctly.

- Compatibility settings are stored in the program file's properties sheet on the Compatibility tab.

- To use DOS commands in Windows 8.1 with minimal flack from UAC, choose Run as Administrator to open the Command Prompt window.

29

Repairing and Removing Programs

IN THIS CHAPTER

Installing missing program features

Repairing damaged programs

Removing programs you don't want

Most of the time, your applications will operate smoothly and without incident. Occasionally, however, you might need to repair a program that is having problems. Or, you might want to remove a program or a Windows feature that you aren't using.

In this chapter, you learn techniques for managing installed programs. You learn how to change or repair programs, as well as how to remove programs you no longer need or want. You'll do most of these tasks in the Control Panel's Programs and Features applet or from the Windows Start screen.

Changing and Repairing Programs

Some large programs let you choose how you want to install the program. For example, you may be given options to do a Minimum Install, Typical Install, or Complete Install. You might do a Minimum or Typical installation to conserve disk space but later discover you need a feature that only the Complete Install would have provided.

Sometimes a program might become corrupted and not work properly anymore. That can happen when you inadvertently delete a file that the program needed. Or it might be caused by some minor glitch that compromised a file that the program uses.

The first step to changing or repairing a program is to get to the Programs and Features applet in the Control Panel. Here's how:

1. Press Windows+Xon the desktop and click Control Panel.
2. In the category view, click Programs.
3. Click Programs and Features.

You can also get to Programs and Features from the Search screen. Simply start typing **fea**, or display the Charms Bar and choose Search. Type **fea**, click Settings, and choose Programs and Features from the Settings screen.

The page that opens lists all your installed application programs. (It doesn't include programs that come with Windows 8.1.)

Not all programs offer change or repair options. To see what options an installed program offers, right-click the program name. Or, click the program name and take a look at the buttons above the list of program names. Things you can do with that program will be listed in a toolbar above the list. For example, in Figure 30.1, we clicked Bonjour, which offers options to Uninstall, Change, and Repair.

In most cases, you'll need the CD or DVD that you originally used to install the program to change or repair the program. If you have the CD handy, go ahead and put it in the CD drive. If Windows asks what you want to do with the disk, choose Take No Action. If the installation program opens automatically, just cancel or close that program.

FIGURE 30.1

A list of installed programs.

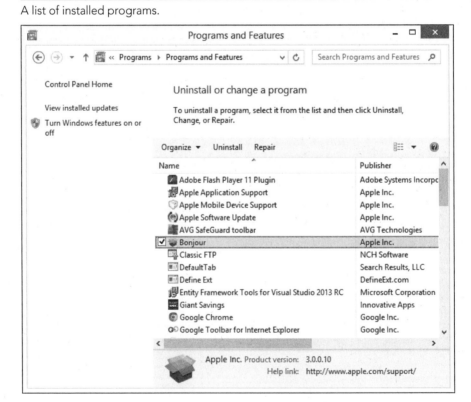

NOTE

Changes you make to a program affect all users. Therefore, you must know the password for an Administrator account on your computer to change or repair programs.

Exactly how things play out from here will vary from one program to the next, so we can only provide some general guidelines and examples. But all you really have to do is make your selections and follow the instructions on the screen. For example, to repair a corrupted program, click the Repair button and do whatever the resulting instructions tell you to do.

The Change option for a program is generally for adding components you didn't install the first time around, although you can also remove any components you don't need. The exact process will vary from one program to the next, but a typical approach is to list all program features in a tree, like the example in Figure 30.2.

FIGURE 30.2

Click an optional component.

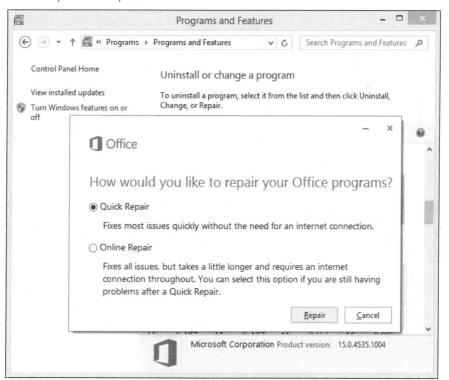

681

> **NOTE**
>
> Don't use Programs and Features to change settings within a program. Instead, use the program's Options or Preferences dialog box. Open the program as you normally would and look through its menus for a Tools or Preferences option. Or search that program's help for the word *preferences* or *options*.

In the tree, click a program feature to choose an action. For example, choose Run from My Computer to install a feature. To remove an optional feature, choose Not Available. That feature will be removed and its icon will display a red X. When you're finished making your selections, click OK or Next and follow the onscreen instructions.

Uninstalling Programs

Unlike documents and other files, copying a program to your hard disk isn't enough to make it usable. You have to *install* programs before you can use them. Likewise, simply deleting the startup icon for a program isn't enough to remove the program from your system. You have to *uninstall* the program. These steps are necessary because a program often consists of many files. For example, Microsoft Office comprises hundreds of files! Furthermore, installing a program makes other changes to the system. Uninstalling is necessary to undo those changes.

> **NOTE**
>
> You must be logged in to an administrative account, or know the administrator password for your PC, to remove a program.

Before you remove (uninstall) any program, make sure you know what you're removing and why. Just because you don't know what a program is or what purpose it serves doesn't mean you should remove it. Removing programs isn't likely to solve any computer problems.

> **CAUTION**
>
> There is no Undo or Recycle Bin for reinstating removed programs. The only way to get a removed program back is to reinstall it from its original installation CD or DVD, or to download it again from the original website.

With all those cautions out of the way, removing a program is quite simple. Windows 8.1 provides two methods for uninstalling programs. From the Start screen, right-click a program icon and choose Uninstall. Or you can use the Programs and Features Control Panel applet. Assuming you're already in the applet, right-click the name of the program you want to remove and choose Uninstall. Or select that program's icon or name and click the Uninstall button in the toolbar. If prompted, enter an administrative password. Follow any additional instructions that appear on the screen.

Unpinning from the Start screen

If you don't find a program that you want to remove in Programs and Features, you might still be able to remove its icon from the Start screen. When a program is on the Start screen, it's pinned to the screen. To unpin it, right-click the icon you want to remove and click Unpin from Start, like the example in Figure 30.3. If you find such an option, you can click it to remove the program from your system.

FIGURE 30.3

Unpinning from the Start screen.

Dealing with stuck programs

Occasionally, you might come across a situation where removing a program generates an error message before the program is completely removed. The first thing to do, of course, is to read the error message and see what options it offers. You may be able to finish the removal just by choosing options that the error message provides.

If you can't get rid of a program through the normal means or error message, your next best bet is to install the program again. That might seem counterproductive, but the problem might be that the program only partially installed in the first place. A partially installed program may not have enough stuff installed to do a thorough removal. Once you've completed the initial installation, you should be able to remove the program without any problems.

Turning Windows Features On and Off

Windows 8.1 comes with many programs and features built right in. How many depends on which edition of Windows 8.1 you purchased. Regardless of the edition you bought, there may be some features you want to use and some you don't.

> **TIP**
>
> Unlike Add/Remove Programs in Windows XP, program features in Windows Vista, Windows 7, and Windows 8/8.1 allow you to turn features on and off without the hassles of installing and uninstalling.

To turn Windows Features on or off, open the Programs and Features Control Panel applet discussed earlier in this chapter. Then click Turn Windows Features On or Off in the left pane. A list of available Windows Features opens, as in Figure 30.4. Items that are selected are currently installed and working. Unselected features are not active. A filled check box represents a feature that's active but that also has additional subfeatures. Click the plus sign next to a feature to see what subfeatures it offers.

FIGURE 30.4

Windows features.

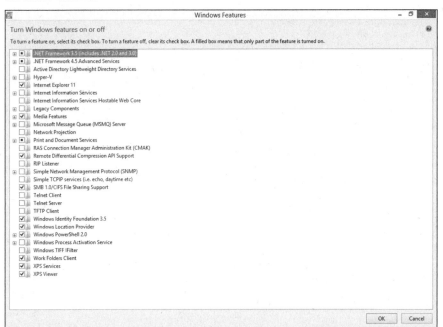

CAUTION

Turn off only those program features that you're certain you don't need. If you don't know what a feature is or does, better to err in favor of keeping it active than to find out, the hard way, that you shouldn't have disabled it!

The rest is easy. To disable a feature or subfeature, clear its check box. To enable a disabled feature, click its empty check box to select it. Click OK after making your changes.

Wrap-Up

Managing installed programs in Windows 8.1 is easy enough. It all takes place through the Programs and Features page. Here's a quick review of what's involved:

- You need administrative privileges to change, repair, or remove programs.
- Use Programs and Features to change, repair, or remove installed programs (open Control Panel click Programs).
- To see what options an installed program offers, click its name in Programs and Features and look at the buttons in the toolbar.
- Repairing a program generally involves reinstalling it from the original CD.
- Changing a program refers to installing features you didn't choose initially or removing features you don't use.
- Uninstalling a program removes it from your computer and from all user accounts.
- The Programs and Features window also provides an option to turn Windows features on and off.

30

Setting Default Programs

IN THIS CHAPTER

Setting default programs for documents

Setting defaults for your user account

Setting default actions for disks and devices

Setting defaults for all users

A s everyone knows, there are many different brands of toothpaste, shampoo, cars, and just about every other kind of product you can buy. The same is true of software. Everyone uses a web browser to browse the Internet, and you have many different brands of web browsers to choose from. There's Internet Explorer, which comes with Windows 8.1. There's also Safari, Firefox, and Google Chrome, to name a few.

For media players, Windows 8.1 comes with Media Player, Media Center, or both depending on which edition of Windows 8.1 you have. In addition to those, there's QuickTime, Musicmatch, and many others. When you have two or more programs capable of handling the same type of document, you might want to make one the *default program* that opens automatically when you open a document. Setting such defaults is what this chapter is all about.

Setting Default Programs for Files

Typed text, pictures, music files, and video clips are all examples of documents and other types of files that you can create or download to your computer. There are thousands of different file types. Each type is indicated by its filename extension. For example, a picture might be a JPEG (.jpeg or .jpg), BMP (.bmp), GIF (.gif), TIFF (.tif or .tiff), PNG (.png), or any of a couple dozen other formats.

When you click (or double-click) a file icon while in File Explorer, the file opens in whatever is the default program for its type. If you have more than one program that can open the file type, you can override the default and open the file with some other program. Right-click the file's icon and choose Open With, as shown in Figure 31.1. The Open With option is available only if you have two or more programs installed that can open that type of file.

If you want to keep the current default program for this type of file, and override that just this time, click the name of the program you want to use to open the file.

FIGURE 31.1

Using the Open With option.

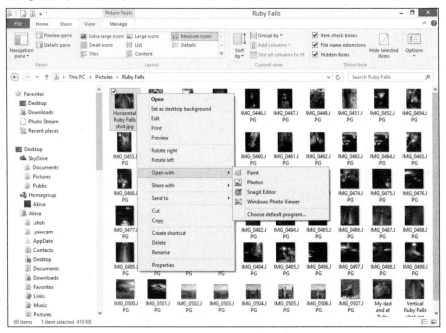

If you want to change the default program that Windows always uses to open that type of file, click Choose Default Program at the bottom of the Open With menu. The Open With dialog box shown in Figure 31.2 opens.

I Don't See Any Filename Extensions

If Windows is configured to hide known filename extensions, you won't see them in your Pictures folder or other folders. But you can point to a file icon and see the filename extension in the tooltip that appears at the mouse pointer. Optionally, you can make filename extensions visible by clicking the File Name Extensions item on the View tab in Explorer.

Click whatever program you want to use for opening that type of document. Also, make sure the Use This App for All < *filetype* > Files option is selected (checked). Otherwise your new choice won't be saved.

If you can't find the program you want to use as the default, you can click the More Options link to look for it. Just make sure that the program you want to use is capable of opening that type of document.

FIGURE 31.2

The Open With dialog box.

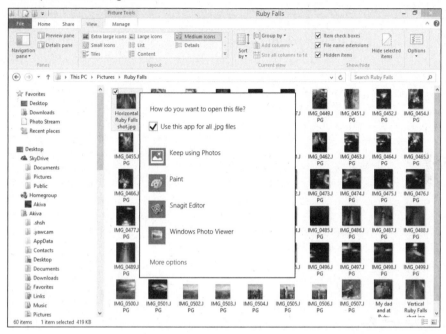

Setting default programs using the Open With dialog box is just one way to do it. Many programs have options within them that enable you to choose which file types you want to associate with the program. The settings within the program might even override the settings you specify in Windows. So sometimes you have to go into the program that's acting as the default for a file type and make a change there.

Unfortunately, there's no one-rule-fits-all for the hundreds of programs that allow you to change associations within a program. Typically you start by opening the program and choosing Tools ⇨ Options or Edit ⇨ Preferences, or something like that, to get to the program's main options. To illustrate, we'll use QuickTime (Version 7) as an example because many people have that program.

In QuickTime, you first open the QuickTime Player from the Windows 8.1 Start screen. Then choose Edit ⇨ Preferences ⇨ QuickTime Preferences from its menu bar. Select the Browser tab, click File Types, and you're taken to a dialog box where you can specify file types that should open automatically in QuickTime. Select the file types you do want to open in QuickTime automatically. Clear the check marks for those file types for which QuickTime should not act as the default program. Figure 31.3 shows an example.

When you associate a program with a given file type, you just have to make sure to always specify a program that *can* open files of a given type. For example, it wouldn't make sense to associate video or audio files with Word or Excel because those programs don't play multimedia files.

FIGURE 31.3

Select QuickTime as the default program for audio and video file type.

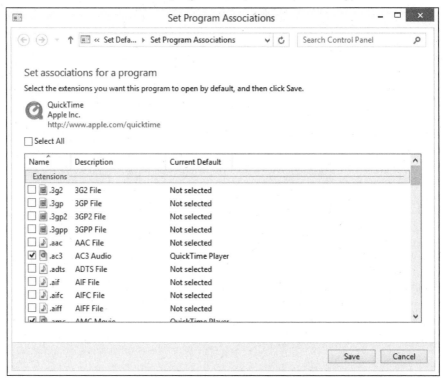

If the program you're setting up does not have a preferences option, open Control Panel, select All Control Panel Options, Default Programs, Set Default Programs, and then choose Set Program Associations from the dialog box that loads.

Using the Default Programs Page

Right-clicking a document's icon and choosing Open With is the quick and easy way to set a default program on the fly, but it's not the only method, and you're not limited to setting defaults based on file types. You can also set defaults for protocols. A *protocol* is a standardized way of doing things. Different Internet services use different protocols. For example, the web uses HTTP, which stands for Hypertext Transfer Protocol.

You can also set default actions for CDs, DVDs, and devices you connect to your computer. Use the Default Programs page in the Control Panel to set all these different kinds of defaults. To get there, use whichever method is easiest for you:

- Press Windows + X and choose Control Panel ⇨ Programs ⇨ Default Programs.
- From the Windows 8.1 Start screen, display the Charms and click Search. On the Apps screen, choose Default Programs.

You'll see the options shown in Figure 31.4 and summarized here.

31

- **Set Your Default Programs:** Use this option to choose default programs for your user account only.
- **Associate a File Type or Protocol with a Program:** Like the preceding item, except you start by choosing a file type or protocol rather than a program.
- **Change AutoPlay Settings:** Use this option to change what happens when you insert a CD or DVD or connect a camera to your computer.
- **Set Program Access and Computer Defaults:** This one is strictly for administrators. It sets defaults for Internet access and media players for all user accounts.

The following sections describe each option.

FIGURE 31.4

Setting programs in the Default Programs tool.

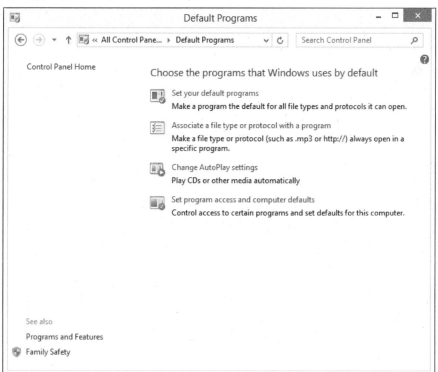

691

Setting your default programs

The first item in Default Programs lets you pick and choose which file types and protocols you want to associate with programs. When you click Set Your Default Programs, you're taken to a page like the one in Figure 31.5.

Click a program name in the left column to see a description of that program in the right column. Then you can choose one of the following options below that description:

- **Set This Program as Default:** Choose this option to make the selected program the default for all file types and protocols it can handle.

- **Choose Defaults for This Program:** Limit the program to act as the default for only certain file types and protocols.

FIGURE 31.5

Setting programs as defaults for file types and protocols.

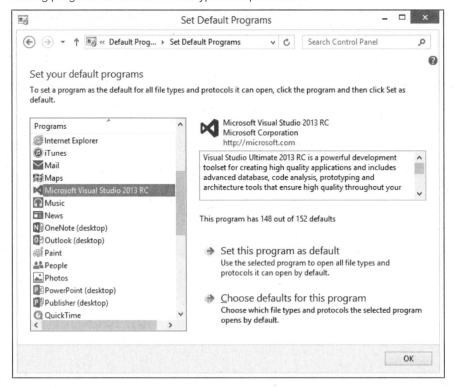

Choosing the second option takes you to a list of all the file types and protocols that the program supports, as in Figure 31.6. You can scroll through the list and select the file types and protocols for which the program should act as default. Clear the check box of any file type or protocol for which you want some other program to act as the default. Then click Save to return to the previous page.

When you've finished choosing defaults for programs, click OK to return to the main Default Programs page.

You can also choose default app from PC Settings on your handheld or mobile device. Open the Settings charm and select the Settings link at the bottom of the bar. When the PC Settings page opens, choose Search and Apps and then select Defaults. The screen shown in Figure 31.7 loads.

FIGURE 31.6

Setting file type associations for a program.

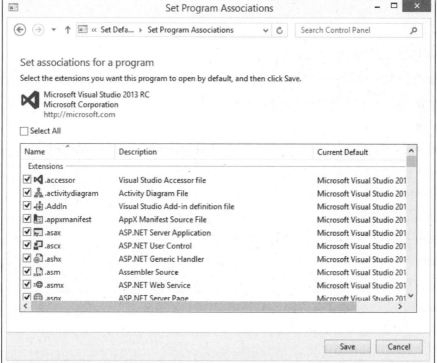

FIGURE 31.7

The Defaults screen for setting defaults for apps.

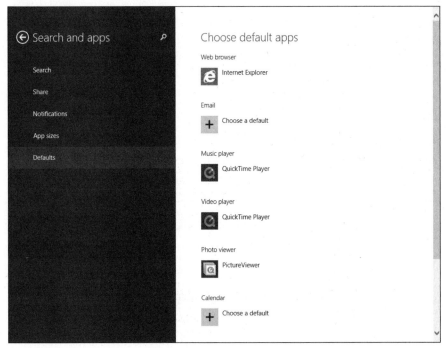

In Figure 31.7, we haven't chosen a default program for mail. To select a default program click the Choose a Default link, as shown in Figure 31.7, next to the program that has no default. The menu shown in Figure 31.8 loads. Continue to select the program you want to use.

Associating a file type or protocol with a specific program

The second option in Default Programs is similar to the first. But instead of starting with a program, you start with a file type or protocol. When you click Associate a File Type or Protocol with a Specific Program, you see options similar to those in Figure 31.9.

FIGURE 31.8

The options presented for setting defaults for apps.

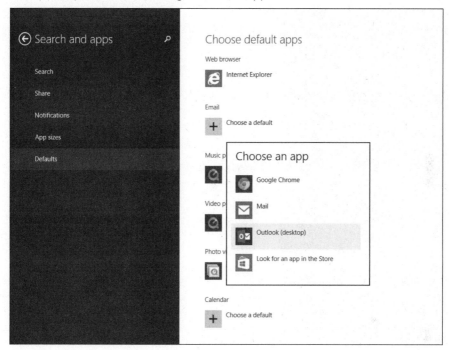

File types are listed first, in alphabetical order. Protocols are separate at the bottom of the list. Use the scroll bar to scroll through the list. To assign a default program to a file type or protocol, first click the item you want to change and click the Change Program button. Then use the Open With dialog box that opens to choose a program.

Choosing default apps by file types and/or protocol is also possible from PC Settings. Click on the respective link at the bottom of the Search and Apps page as shown in Figure 31.9.

> **NOTE**
> Don't worry about items marked as Unknown Application. Most of those aren't documents anyway and don't need to have a default program. You don't have to assign a default program to every item in the list.

FIGURE 31.9

Setting file types with specific programs.

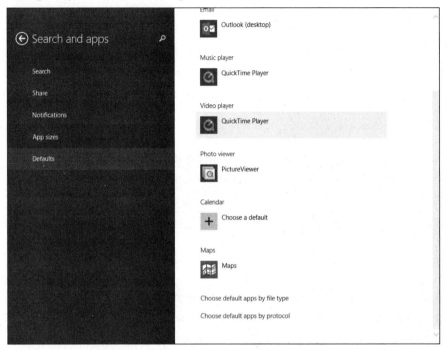

Changing AutoPlay settings

AutoPlay is a Windows feature that lets you choose what program you want to use to play content on CDs, DVDs, and devices (such as MP3 devices). Chances are you've already seen the AutoPlay screen at least once, after you inserted a CD or DVD, or connected a camera, mobile phone, or disk drive. Figure 31.10 shows an example.

Click the AutoPlay screen to see a list of actions to take. The AutoPlay dialog box lets you choose the action you want to take with the selected media. For a removable device that always has pictures on it, you might choose one of the Import Pictures and Videos options. Or, as the example in Figure 31.11 shows, the actions for the iPhone that we inserted include using the drive for backup purposes or showing the contents of the drive. Until you set a default AutoPlay option, however, Windows continues to ask you what you want to do when you attach the device.

When you click View More AutoPlay Options in the Control Panel, you get to see all your current AutoPlay default settings, as in Figure 31.12. You can also get there by clicking Change AutoPlay Settings in the Default Programs item in the Control Panel. Scroll to the bottom of the list to find icons for devices you connect to your computer, such as digital cameras.

FIGURE 31.10

The Windows 8.1 AutoPlay screen appears at the top of the window.

FIGURE 31.11

Selecting an action to take when inserting a device.

The Shift Key Doesn't Work Like It Used To

In previous versions of Windows, you could hold down the Shift key while inserting a disc or connecting a device to override the default action for the device. You can still do that in Windows 8.1. But the AutoPlay dialog box still opens. (The default program doesn't open.) To prevent the AutoPlay dialog box from opening when using the Shift key, you need to deselect the Use AutoPlay for All Media and Devices check box at the top of the AutoPlay page shown in Figure 31.13.

FIGURE 31.12

Setting AutoPlay options for each type of media or device you attach to your PC.

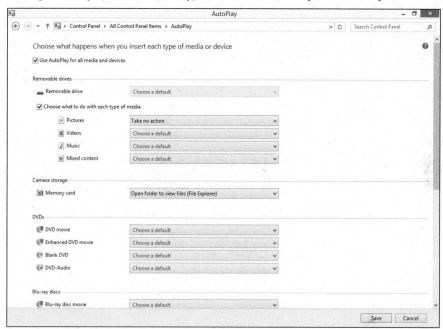

To change the default action for any item, click the current action and choose the action you want from the menu that drops down. Click Save after making your changes to return to Program Defaults.

FIGURE 31.13

Setting program access and computer defaults.

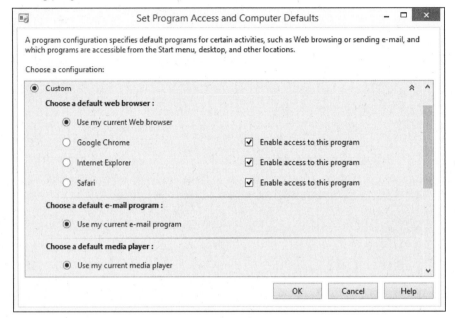

Setting program access and computer defaults

Anybody who has a user account can choose defaults using any of the methods described in this chapter. The Set Program Access and Computer Defaults option is strictly for computer administrators. It sets defaults that apply to all user accounts, and can even be used to limit programs that they can use. This is most often used in corporate settings when administrators want very tight control over how staff members use their computers. But anyone with an administrative user account on a home computer can use it to control family members' program use as well.

Because the Set Program Access and Computer Defaults option can so severely limit what all users can do, you need administrative privileges just to start it. If you're in a standard user account, you'll need to log out. Then log in to an administrative account to open that option. When you first open it, you'll see three options:

- **Microsoft Windows:** Choose this option if you want to set the Internet programs that came with Windows 8.1 as the default programs.

- **Non-Microsoft:** Choose this option if you don't want to use any Microsoft Internet programs.

- **Custom:** Choose this option if you want to use a combination of Microsoft and non-Microsoft Internet programs.

After you choose one of these options, you'll see more options under that category. The exact options vary depending on what you choose. But they work in a similar manner. We'll use the Custom category, shown in Figure 31.13, as an example, because it offers the most options.

What's a Java Virtual Machine?

Java is a programming language often used with Internet programs and *applets* (small programs embedded in web pages). The virtual machine (also called a runtime environment) allows those programs to run on your computer. It's not a mandatory item unless you use programs that require it or visit websites that require it.

Typically, if you needed the Java Virtual Machine, you'd be prompted to download it automatically when it's required. You can also download and install it at any time from www.java.com/download.

As you can see in Figure 31.13, the first options let you choose the default web browser, e-mail client, and media player for online music and video. Scrolling down enables you to choose a default instant messaging program and Java virtual machine. The options available to you depend on what programs you have installed on your computer at the moment. For each program, you have the following options:

- **Use My Current:** Choose this option to keep whatever program you're currently using as the default program. This will be the only option when you don't have multiple programs to choose from.

- **< *Program Name* > :** To specify a program as the default, click the option button to the left of its name.

- **Enable Access to This Program:** Choosing this option allows users to run the program. Clearing the check box hides the program's icon on the Start menu and elsewhere, preventing users from running the program.

There will be times when you can't choose exactly the option you want. Or when you choose an option, the selected program doesn't comply. That's because the programmers who create these programs aren't required to make them work with the Program Defaults selections. If that's a problem, your only recourse is to contact the program publisher. They may have a newer version that's compatible with setting program defaults in Windows 8.1.

Click OK when you've finished making your selections. You might see a message stating that your choices might not work because of current file associations. If you click Yes, Windows 8.1 will try to change the file associations to go with the new default program automatically. If it doesn't work, you can change file associations manually.

Wrap-Up

Default programs are programs that start automatically when you open a document or use an Internet protocol such as e-mail or the web. When you have two or more programs that can open a document or use an Internet protocol, you can choose which one acts as the default. Choosing a default doesn't preclude you from using other programs. The default just determines which program is used when you don't specify otherwise. Windows 8.1 offers several methods of choosing default programs:

- To set the default for a file type on the fly, right-click a file's icon and choose Open With ⇨ Choose Default Program.

- To use some program other than the default for a document, right-click the icon, and choose Open With and the name of the program you want to use.

- The Program Defaults page in the Control Panel provides ways of setting multiple default programs from a single page.

- The Set Your Default Programs option enables you to choose a program and specify the documents and protocols for which it should act as the default.

- The Associate a File Type or Protocol with a Program option enables you to first choose a filename extension or protocol, and then choose the program that will be the default.

- The Change AutoPlay Settings option enables you to choose what happens when you insert a disc or connect a device.

- The Set Program Access and Computer Defaults option allows an administrator to control defaults and programs for all user accounts.

Managing Programs and Processes

IN THIS CHAPTER

Starting and using Task Manager

What to do when your system freezes up

Viewing running processes

Monitoring performance and resource use

You are no doubt familiar with the terms *application* and *program*. These two terms describe program code that, whether one component or several components, serve a specific function. For example, a word processor is an application. Some applications, however, comprise multiple *processes* running at the same time. In addition, a process can comprise multiple threads of execution, each performing a specific task. Although you typically concern yourself with programs, you sometimes need to think about the processes that make up a program, particularly if one of those processes fails. That's where Task Manager comes into play.

Task Manager is a program included with Windows 8.1 for viewing and managing running programs and processes. You can use it to seek out performance bottlenecks, close hung programs and processes without restarting the system, and more.

Getting to Know Task Manager

Task Manager is a program that lets you view and manage running programs and processes, as well as view performance data for your computer and network. In Windows 8.1, Task Manager has changed from releases prior to Windows 8. If you're familiar with Task Manager in Windows 7, for example, you're in for quite a change with the new (and, in our opinion, improved) Task Manager.

You can start Task Manager in several ways:

- Press Ctrl + Alt + Del and click Start Task Manager.
- Right-click the clock or an empty spot on the taskbar and choose Start Task Manager.
- Display the Charms Bar, click Search, and type **task**. Click Task Manager on the Apps screen.

> **TIP**
>
> If a program is hung (frozen), right-clicking the taskbar might not work. But pressing Ctrl+Alt+Del might still work. If Ctrl+Alt+Del doesn't work to bring up Task Manager and the computer is unresponsive, turning the computer off and back on is generally the only way to get it going again.

Figure 32.1 shows the new Task Manager and a number of apps and programs running. Task Manager behaves much like any program window. It has a button on the Windows taskbar when open. You can drag the program window around by its title bar and size it by dragging any corner or edge. You can also configure it so it stays on the top of the stack of open windows so you can always see it. You can change that by right-clicking a blank area on the window or on the bottom of the window and choosing Always On Top.

FIGURE 32.1

Task Manager in its normal view.

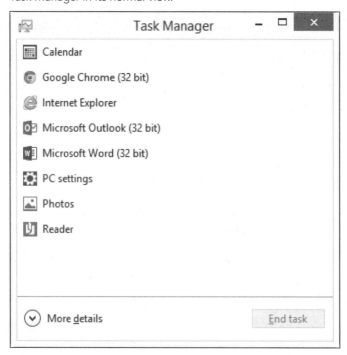

Viewing more and less detail

With Windows 8.1 Task Manager, you have the choice of showing a list of just the running applications, as shown in Figure 32.1, or a display with multiple tabs filled with system and application data (as shown in Figure 32.2). The former view shows fewer details while the latter shows more details. When showing less detail, you have fewer options for controlling and viewing application information, but you can still stop an app or application.

FIGURE 32.2

Task Manager in its detailed view.

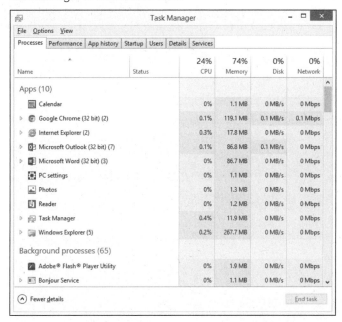

To switch between detail views, click the More Details button on the bottom of Task Manager. When viewing the More Details view, you can click the Fewer Details button to display the less details view.

Choosing Task Manager views

While viewing Task Manager in the More Details view, you can view and use Task Manager in several ways. On the Options menu in the menu bar, you have the following options:

- **Always On Top:** Choosing this option ensures that Task Manager is always on the top of the stack when it's open, so no other program windows can cover it.

- **Minimize On Use:** If selected, this option minimizes Task Manager whenever you choose the Switch To option to switch to another running program.

- **Hide When Minimized:** Normally when you minimize Task Manager, only its taskbar button remains visible. Choosing this option also hides the taskbar button when you minimize Task Manager.

- **Show Full Account Name:** When viewing information on the Users tab, you show the full user account name in the User column.

- **Show History for All Processes:** This option activates when you select the App History tab. It shows your resource usage history for the past month.

Whenever Task Manager is open, you'll see a small greenish blue square in the notification area unless Task Manager is configured to show notifications only. Pointing to that icon displays the current CPU (central processing unit) usage, as shown in Figure 32.3. When Task Manager is minimized, you can double-click that little square to bring Task Manager back onto the desktop.

FIGURE 32.3

The Task Manager notification icon.

If you prefer to have Task Manager show only notifications and not appear in the tray, click the Show Hidden Icons button on the tray and choose Customize. In the notification area Icons applet, find Task Manager in the Icons list, choose Only Show Notifications from the drop-down list, and click OK.

On the View menu in Task Manager, you have the following choices, as shown in Figure 32.4:

- **Refresh Now:** Causes Task Manager to refresh all its data immediately, regardless of the Update Speed setting.

- **Update Speed:** Task Manager needs to use some computer resources to keep itself up to date with what's happening in the system at the moment. The Update Speed option lets you choose how often Task Manager updates itself, as follows:

  - **High:** Updates Task Manager twice per second.

  - **Normal:** Updates Task Manager every two seconds.

  - **Low:** Updates Task Manager every four seconds.

  - **Paused:** Updates Task Manager only when you choose View ➪ Refresh Now.

- **Group by Type:** Shows apps, Windows process, and background processes in groups.

- **Expand All:** Expands the lists of apps and processes to show any open documents, open websites (if you're running Internet Explorer or another browser), and subprocesses.

- **Collapse All:** Collapses the list of running apps and processes.

- **Status Values:** Displays on the Processes tab only and shows the status of suspended processes.

FIGURE 32.4

Task Manager's View menu.

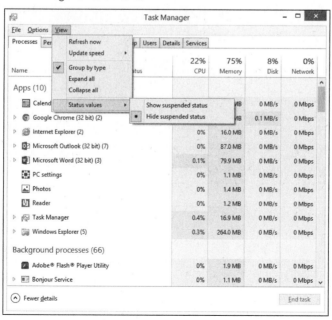

Not Responding? Task Manager to the Rescue

One of Task Manager's most useful roles is that of dealing with problems that cause programs, or your whole computer, to *hang* (freeze up, so that the mouse and keyboard don't work normally). Even when you can't get the mouse or keyboard to work, pressing Ctrl + Alt + Del and choosing Start Task Manager may get Task Manager open for you.

Closing frozen programs

Once Task Manager is open, select the Details tab, as shown in Figure 32.5. If a particular program is hung, its Status column usually reads Not Responding rather than Running. To close the hung program, click its name in the Name column, and then click the End Task button, which appears at the bottom right of the window. Task Manager tries to close the program normally, so that if you were working on a document at the time, you may be able to save any changes. (So, don't expect the program to close immediately.)

FIGURE 32.5

Task Manager's Details tab.

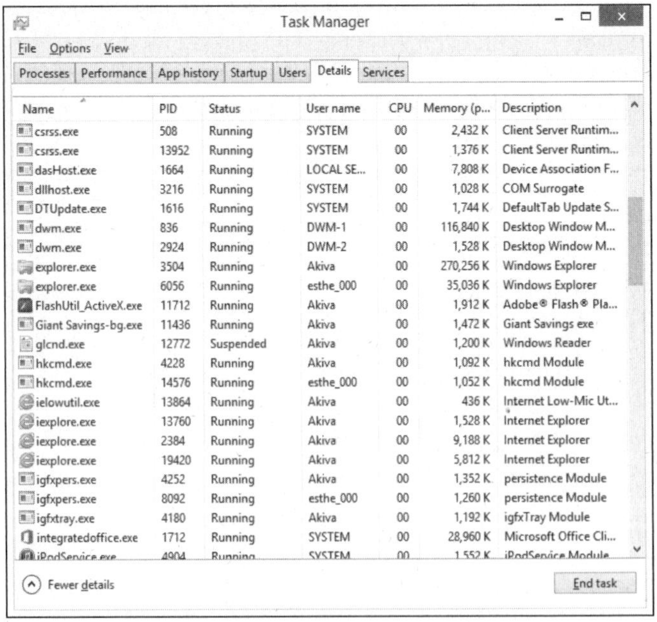

Name	PID	Status	User name	CPU	Memory (p...	Description
csrss.exe	508	Running	SYSTEM	00	2,432 K	Client Server Runtim...
csrss.exe	13952	Running	SYSTEM	00	1,376 K	Client Server Runtim...
dasHost.exe	1664	Running	LOCAL SE...	00	7,808 K	Device Association F...
dllhost.exe	3216	Running	SYSTEM	00	1,028 K	COM Surrogate
DTUpdate.exe	1616	Running	SYSTEM	00	1,744 K	DefaultTab Update S...
dwm.exe	836	Running	DWM-1	00	116,840 K	Desktop Window M...
dwm.exe	2924	Running	DWM-2	00	1,528 K	Desktop Window M...
explorer.exe	3504	Running	Akiva	00	270,256 K	Windows Explorer
explorer.exe	6056	Running	esthe_000	00	35,036 K	Windows Explorer
FlashUtil_ActiveX.exe	11712	Running	Akiva	00	1,912 K	Adobe® Flash® Pla...
Giant Savings-bg.exe	11436	Running	Akiva	00	1,472 K	Giant Savings exe
glcnd.exe	12772	Suspended	Akiva	00	1,200 K	Windows Reader
hkcmd.exe	4228	Running	Akiva	00	1,092 K	hkcmd Module
hkcmd.exe	14576	Running	esthe_000	00	1,052 K	hkcmd Module
ielowutil.exe	13864	Running	Akiva	00	436 K	Internet Low-Mic Ut...
iexplore.exe	13760	Running	Akiva	00	1,528 K	Internet Explorer
iexplore.exe	2384	Running	Akiva	00	9,188 K	Internet Explorer
iexplore.exe	19420	Running	Akiva	00	5,812 K	Internet Explorer
igfxpers.exe	4252	Running	Akiva	00	1,352 K	persistence Module
igfxpers.exe	8092	Running	esthe_000	00	1,260 K	persistence Module
igfxtray.exe	4180	Running	Akiva	00	1,192 K	igfxTray Module
integratedoffice.exe	1712	Running	SYSTEM	00	28,960 K	Microsoft Office Cli...
iPodService.exe	4904	Running	SYSTEM	00	1,552 K	iPodService Module

If the program won't close, you'll see a warning that moving ahead will close the program and leave unsaved work behind. To forge ahead, click End Process. The program may try to restart itself, depending on how it's designed.

Most likely, a process of reporting the problem and finding a solution will start after you end a program in this way. If you choose to allow Windows to send information about the program error, Windows sends information to a database of problems and searches that database for known problems and their solutions. You won't always get a solution to the problem, but you may receive information about an incompatible device driver or other issue by allowing Windows to report the problem.

If you don't have time to wait through that whole reporting process, you can cancel out of each dialog box by clicking its Cancel button.

Switching and starting tasks

If the system is hung in such a way that you can't use the taskbar normally, and you want to work with open program windows individually, Task Manager provides some ways to accomplish that.

To bring a running program to the top of the stack of windows on the screen and make it the active window, click its name in the list of running tasks on Task Manager's Fewer Details screen, and then click the Switch To button. If you were working on a document in that program, you can save your work, and then exit the program normally (assuming that program is running normally).

If you need to bring up a diagnostic program or debugger, or simply need to start some other program, and you know the startup command for that program, right-click and choose Run New Task. The Create New Task dialog box, shown in Figure 32.6, opens. Type the startup command for the program (or the complete path to the program, if necessary), and click OK. You can also access this dialog box when in the More Details view. Choose File ➪ Run New Task.

FIGURE 32.6

The Create New Task dialog box.

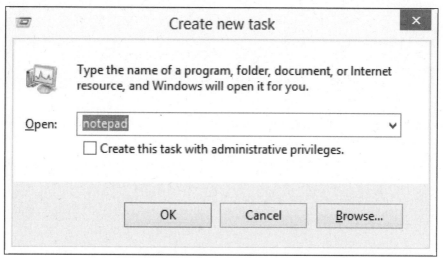

709

Restarting a hung computer

If your computer is so locked up that you can't get to Task Manager, or stop the offending program, you can try other things. If pressing Ctrl + Alt + Del works, you are taken to a Windows 8.1 screen with four options: Lock, Switch User, Sign Out, and Task Manager. You also have the Shut Down option at the lower right of the screen. Logging off or restarting will likely be your best bet. If at all possible, Windows attempts to give you a chance to save any unsaved work.

If the program that's hung is also the one that contains the unsaved work, there may be no way to save that work. You may have to restart without saving. For this reason, you should save your work often.

> **Tip**
>
> You can configure some programs to save automatically after a given period of time that you determine. Check the program's options to see if this capability is available in the programs you use most often.

Monitoring Performance with Task Manager

In addition to helping you deal with hung programs, Task Manager lets you see which processes in your system are using computer resources. On the Performance tab, as shown in Figure 32.7, you can see these key resources. The Performance tab in Task Manager provides both graphical and numeric summaries of CPU, memory, disk, and network hardware resource usage. To watch resource usage, leave Task Manager open and always on top as you run programs and use your computer in the usual ways. If you have multiple processors or a multi-core processor, each may be represented in a separate pane in the CPU history, as shown at the top of the figure.

> **Tip**
>
> Double-click any chart or a blank area inside the window to show just the Graph Summary view. This shows only the graph, which you can leave onscreen as you analyze your system performance. Double-click it again to return to the normal Task Manager window. You can right-click on the graph on the Performance tab to choose Graph Summary view, which is the same as double-clicking it.

The Performance charts are useful for identifying major *performance bottlenecks*. For example, if the CPU charts run high, your CPU is working very hard. An errant application can consume inordinate amounts of CPU capacity. Also, reducing the number of running programs reduces CPU load.

A common performance bottleneck is limited physical memory. Running lots of programs when memory is limited forces the system to use lots of virtual memory, which in turn slows down performance because of the added overhead of swapping pages in and out. Increasing the amount of virtual memory (as discussed in Chapter 36) can help, but the best solution is to add more RAM (physical memory) to the system.

FIGURE 32.7

The Performance tab shows performance data.

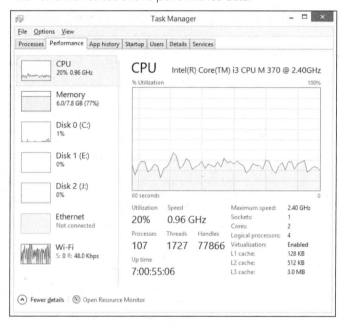

TIP

Microsoft's published minimum requirement is 1GB of RAM for 32-bit Windows 8.1 and 2GB for the 64-bit edition, although Windows 8.1 will run with less. Naturally, having more than the specified minimums provides better performance. With the relatively low cost of memory today, it's not unreasonable to have 2GB to 4GB of physical memory.

Some of the resources you may see include the following:

- **CPU:** Shows information about your computer's central processing unit. Data includes utilization, speed, processes, threads, handles, and up time. The bar graph shows a 60-second view of the CPU usage. Refer back to Figure 32.7 for an example of the CPU data.

- **Memory:** Provides data about the RAM on your computer, including the amount of RAM in use, how much is available on your computer, the committed memory (RAM plus virtual memory), cached memory, the Windows page pool, and the non-page pool (shown in Figure 32.8).

FIGURE 32.8

The Performance tab shows memory data.

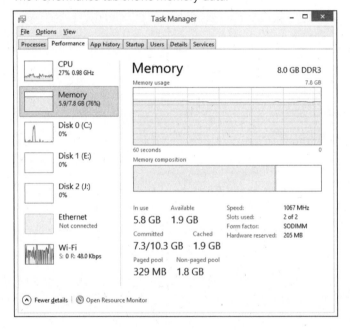

- **Disk:** Provides data about your installed hard disks, including disk transfer rate, active time in percentage, average response time, disk read speed, and disk write speed (shown in Figure 32.9).

- **Bluetooth:** Provides performance data about your Bluetooth devices.

- **Wi-Fi:** Displays data about wireless network devices installed on your computer. You can see send and receive data (see Figure 32.10).

FIGURE 32.9

The Performance tab shows disk data.

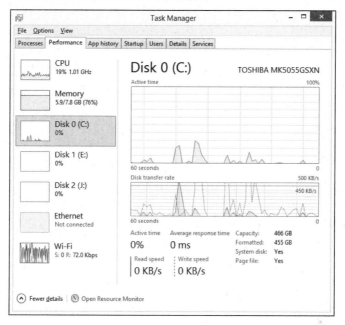

FIGURE 32.10

The Performance tab shows Wi-Fi data.

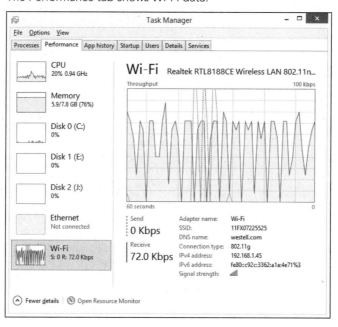

Physical Memory versus Virtual Memory

The term *physical memory* refers to the actual amount of RAM, on computer chips, installed in your computer. When you press Windows+X and choose System, the number to the right of the words *Installed Memory (RAM)* indicates the amount of physical memory installed on the motherboard inside your computer.

When things are busy in RAM, Windows moves some lesser-used items out to a special section of the hard disk called a *paging file*. The paging file looks and acts like RAM (to the CPU), even though it's actually space on your hard disk. Although Windows can be configured to not use a paging file, Windows, by default, sets aside some hard disk space for this paging file. (More on that topic in Chapter 36.)

A *page fault* is when the CPU "expects" to find something in RAM but has to fetch it from virtual memory instead. The term *fault* is a bit harsh here, because a certain amount of memory paging is normal and to be expected. Other terms used in this context include *nonpaged memory* for physical memory and *paged memory* for virtual memory.

Exactly how fast your computer runs at any given moment depends on the resources available to it at that moment. For example, if you have half a dozen programs running, all doing intensive tasks, they're eating up CPU resources. If you start another program, that program may run slower than usual, because the other running programs are consuming CPU resources.

Likewise, everything you open stores something in RAM. If RAM is nearly full, and you start another program that needs more memory than what's currently left in RAM, Windows has to start sloughing some of what's currently in RAM off to the hard disk (called *virtual memory*) to make room. It takes time to do that, so everything slows down.

Managing Processes with Task Manager

Whereas applications usually run in windows and are listed on the Processes tab in Task Manager, processes have no program window. We say that processes run in the background because they don't show anything in particular on the screen.

Your running applications are actually one or more processes. To see all currently running processes, select the Processes tab in Task Manager. Each process is shown under the Windows Process category heading, as in the example shown in Figure 32.11.

The Processes tab shows its information in columns. To help you differentiate between data values (that is, for data points that are low, medium, or high), Windows 8.1 uses a "heat map" paradigm. This type of display lets you look across columns and rows and data that represent different types of data (CPU, memory, disk, and network usages) and get a quick view of the data and see any hot spots in the values. For example, if memory usage for a process or application is high compared to other running processes or applications, the heat map shows a brighter orange color. Lower values are in lighter shades, such as light tan or light yellow. Microsoft designed these heat maps to allow users to visualize and digest the information quickly.

FIGURE 32.11

The Processes tab in Task Manager.

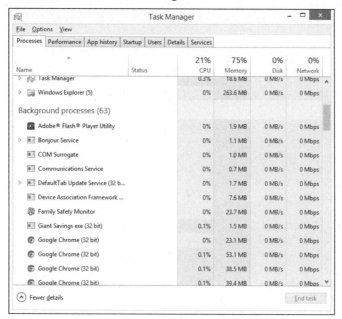

You can sort items by clicking any column heading. For example, you can click the Memory column to sort processes by the amount of memory each one takes up, in ascending order (smallest to largest) or descending order (largest to smallest). Seeing those in largest-to-smallest order lets you know which processes are using up the most memory.

Here's what each column shows:

- **CPU:** The percent of CPU resources that the process is currently using
- **Memory:** The amount of memory the process is currently using
- **Disks:** The amount of disk resources the process is currently using
- **Network:** The amount of network resources the process is currently using

Memory usage is probably the main cause of slow-running computers. The more stuff you cram into RAM, the more Windows has to use the paging file, and hence the slower everything goes. You can see which processes are hogging up the most RAM just by clicking the Memory column heading until the largest numbers are at the top of the list.

Showing other columns

Windows 8.1 Task Manager provides additional columns of data that you can view on the Process tab. To see these columns, right-click on the column area. A menu appears with the names of the available columns, including the following ones that are not shown by default:

- **Type:** Displays the same information at the group type, such as App, Background Process, or Windows Process
- **Publisher:** Name of the company that produces the application
- **PID:** Process ID number, which is a unique number created by Windows for each process that is running.
- **Process Name:** Shows the executable name of the process
- **Command Line:** Shows the path to the source file of the process

Figure 32.12 shows what Task Manager looks like when you turn on all the columns. The information shown in the default columns (CPU, Memory, Disks, and Network) appears on the far right of Task Manager, and in this example the window is too wide to fit in this screen shot.

FIGURE 32.12

The Processes tab with additional columns showing.

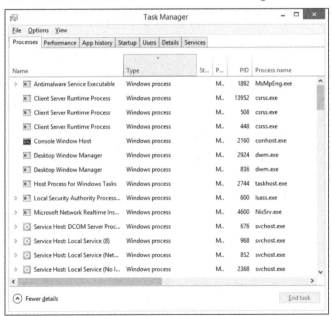

You can resize columns by dragging the separator line between the columns.

Common processes

You can end any running process by right-clicking its name and choosing End Task (or by clicking its name and clicking the End Task button). But doing so isn't a good idea unless you know exactly what service you're terminating. If a process represents a running program with unsaved work, ending the process will close the program without saving the work.

Some processes are required for normal operation of the computer. For example, Desktop Window Manager and Runtime Broker are important parts of Windows 8.1 so you definitely don't want to mess with those.

> **NOTE**
>
> Just because a process is near the top of the list when you sort things in largest-to-smallest order doesn't mean the biggest items are hogs or outrageously large. Even seemingly large numbers such as 50,000K and 60,000K are trivial when you consider how much RAM most systems have and how cheap it is to add more.

32

If you're unsure about a process, you can search for it by name on Google, Bing, or any other search engine. Just be sure to check out multiple sources and read carefully. Virtually every resource you find will tell you that perfectly legitimate and necessary processes such as dwm.exe and explorer.exe could be a Trojan, spyware, or other malicious item. But *could* is not synonymous with *is*. So, read carefully and don't assume the worst.

Choosing columns on the Details tab

The Details tab on Task Manager provides additional ways to analyze performance issues with running processes. The columns that display by default are Name, User Name, CPU, Memory, Status, and Description.

You can choose to display other columns here in case you need to capture different types of data about a particular problem you're having with a program or Windows in general. To choose other columns to view, right-click the column area and choose Select Columns. The Select Columns dialog box appears (as shown in Figure 32.13). Each column shows some detail of the process, mostly related to resource consumption. A programmer might use this information to fine-tune a program she's writing. Beyond that, it's hard to think of anything terribly practical to be gained from this information. But here's a quick summary of what the other, optional columns show:

- **Base Priority:** The priority assigned to the process. When the CPU is busy, low-priority processes have to wait for normal and high-priority processes to be completed. To change a process's priority, right-click its name and choose Set Priority.
- **Command Line:** The command, with parameters, that was used to initiate the process.

- **CPU Time:** Total number of seconds of CPU time this process has used since starting. The number will be doubled for dual-processor systems, quadrupled for systems with four processors.

- **CPU:** The amount of processor time, as a percent of the whole, this process has used since first started (the CPU column).

- **Cycle:** Current percent of CPU cycle time consumption time by the process.

- **Data Execution Prevention (DEP):** Specifies whether DEP is enabled or disabled for the specified process. DEP is a set of hardware and software technologies that help prevent malicious code from running by marking some areas of memory as non-executable.

- **Description:** A description of the process.

- **Elevated:** Specifies whether the process is being elevated or not.

- **GDI Objects:** The number of Graphics Device Interface (GDI) objects used by this process, since starting, to display content on the screen.

- **Handles:** The number of objects to which the process currently has handles.

FIGURE 32.13

Picking additional columns for the Details tab.

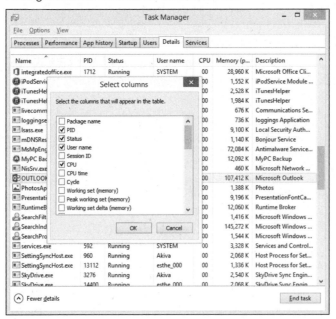

- **I/O Other:** Non-disk input/output calls made by the object since it started. Excludes file, network, and device operations.

- **I/O Other Bytes:** The number of bytes transferred to devices since the process started. Excludes file, network, and device operations.

- **I/O Reads:** The number of file, network, and device Read input/output operations since the process started.

- **I/O Read Bytes:** The number of bytes transferred by Read file, network, and device input/output operations.

- **I/O Writes:** The number of file, network, and device Write input/output operations since the process started.

- **I/O Write Bytes:** The number of bytes transferred by Write file, network, and device input/output operations.

- **Image Path Name:** The path to the executable specified in the Image Name column.

- **Working Set Delta (Memory):** The amount of memory used by the process (also called the process's *working set*) since starting.

- **Peak Working Set (Memory):** The largest amount of physical memory used by the process since it started.

- **Working Set Delta (Memory):** The change in memory usage since the last Task Manager update.

- **Memory (Private Working Set):** The amount of memory allocated to the process's private data.

- **Memory (Shared Working Set):** The amount of memory allocated to the process's shared data.

- **Commit Size:** The amount of virtual memory currently committed to the process.

- **Operating System Context:** Specifies the operating system context in which the process is operating.

- **Paged Pool:** The amount of system-allocated virtual memory that's been committed to the process by the operating system.

- **NP Pool:** The amount of physical RAM used by the process since starting.

- **Page Faults:** The number of times the process has read data from virtual memory since starting.

- **PF Delta:** The change in the number of page faults since the last Task Manager update.

- **PID:** A number assigned to the process at startup. The operating system accesses all processes by their numbers, not their names.

- **Platform:** Specifies whether the process is running on a 32-bit or 64-bit platform.

- **Session ID:** The Terminal Session ID that owns the process. Always zero unless Terminal Services are in use on the network.

- **Status:** Shows if the process is running or suspended.

- **Threads:** The number of threads running in a process.

32

> **TIP**
>
> A *thread* is a tiny sequence of instructions that the CPU must carry out to perform some tasks. Some programs divide tasks into separate threads that can be executed in parallel (simultaneously), to speed execution. This is called *multi-threaded execution.*

- **UAC Virtualization:** Specifies whether User Account Control (UAC) is virtualized for the specified process. When enabled, data is written to a user area rather than to a system area.
- **User Name:** The user, user account, or service that started the process.
- **User Objects:** The number of objects from Window Manager used by the object, including program windows, cursors, icons, and other objects.

App History tab

The new Windows 8.1 Task Manager includes the App History tab shown in Figure 32.14. This tab lists all the apps that you've used on this computer since a given time. By default, you can see history since the time you installed Windows 8.1. In actuality, you may want to click the Delete Usage History link periodically to remove all old app history. This will limit the amount of data Windows keeps stored in a log file somewhere on your hard drive.

FIGURE 32.14

The App History tab in Task Manager.

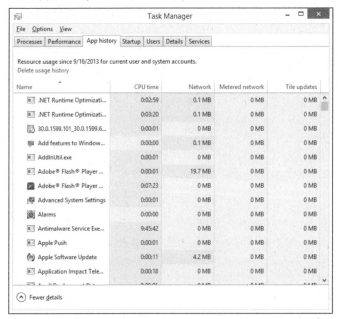

The columns available on the App History tab include the following:

- **Name:** The name of the app that has been used
- **CPU Time:** The amount of CPU time consumed by an app
- **Network:** The amount of network data utilized by an app
- **Metered Network:** The amount of metered network resources consumed by an app
- **Tile Updates:** The amount of resources used for updating Windows 8.1 app tile information
- **Non-Metered Network:** The amount of network data consumed by an app that is not considered metered data
- **Downloads:** The amount of data an app downloads from the Internet or other network resource
- **Uploads:** The amount of data an app uploads to a network resource

To launch an app or see related apps under a category of apps (look for an arrow to the left of a name), double-click the app name.

Startup tab

The Startup tab shows a list of the apps that start when you start Windows 8.1. Figure 32.15 shows an example of the Startup tab and the application that will start at boot up time. In this example, only one application will start when Windows starts.

FIGURE 32.15

The Startup tab of Task Manager.

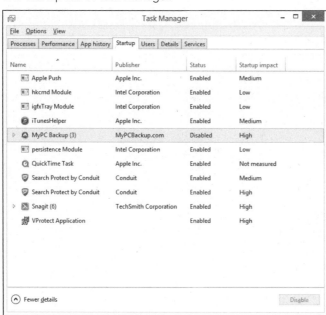

The columns on this tab include the following:

- **Name:** The name of the app that will start at boot time
- **Publisher:** The company that distributes the app
- **Status:** Lists either Enabled or Disabled depending on whether the app will (Enabled) or will not (Disabled) start at boot time
- **Startup Impact:** Shows a relative rating of the impact the app will have during boot time
- **Startup Type:** Shows the type of app that starts, such as one that is hidden (such as running from a Registry key), or one that launches from the interface
- **Disk I/O at Startup:** Displays the amount of memory used at startup by the app
- **CPU at Startup:** Displays the amount of CPU resources used at startup by the app
- **Running Now:** Lists only those apps currently running under Windows
- **Disabled Time:** Lists the amount of time the app is disabled
- **Command Line:** Shows the hard drive path of the listed app

If you don't want the app to start at boot time, select it and then click the Disable button.

Users tab

The Users tab in Task Manager displays information about your user accounts. The Users tab (shown in Figure 32.16) shows the names of people currently logged in to the computer. Most users will see only themselves, even if other users are logged in.

FIGURE 32.16

The Users tab of Task Manager.

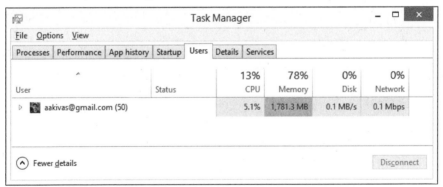

If your system is running slowly because users are not logging out of their accounts, you can send a message to those users asking them to log off when done using the computer. Click a username and click Disconnect to disconnect that user. Any unsaved data will be lost. In general, this is a bad idea, so try to get the user to log off normally before taking this action.

To see the apps and processes that a user uses, double-click the username. Figure 32.16, for example, shows the apps listed under the aakivas user.

The Users tab includes the following columns:

- **ID:** A unique integer for each user signed on to the computer
- **Session:** The type of session, including console or remote
- **Client name:** The name of a computer ("client") connected to your computer
- **Users:** The name of the user logged into the computer
- **Status:** Whether an app is suspended or disabled
- **CPU:** The amount of CPU a user is using
- **Memory:** The amount of RAM a user is using
- **Disk:** The amount of disk resources a user is using
- **Network:** The amount of network resources a user is using

Services tab

The Services tab provides a view of the services running under Windows. This tab is discussed in more detail in Chapter 11.

Wrap-Up

A new Task Manager is available in Windows 8.1. Task Manager is a handy tool for terminating hung programs (programs that are not responding) and for monitoring computer resource usage. Task Manager also provides detailed information that's of interest only to programmers and network administrators. The following are the main things to remember about Task Manager:

- To open Task Manager, press Ctrl + Alt + Del and click Start Task Manager, or right-click the time and choose Start Task Manager.
- The Processes tab shows the names of all running applications. To end a program that's not responding, right-click its name and choose End Task.
- To see which process an application relates to, right-click the application name and choose Go to Details.
- The Processes tab shows all running processes, including application programs, background programs such as antivirus software, and operating system processes.
- The Performance tab presents a bird's-eye view of overall CPU and memory usage.
- The Users tab shows which users are currently logged in.

Troubleshooting Software Problems

IN THIS CHAPTER

Troubleshooting installations

Troubleshooting programs

Researching application errors

Editing the Windows Registry

Most programs designed for Windows 7 (and possibly Windows Vista) will work with Windows 8.1. However, not all programs that were designed for Windows XP (or earlier versions of Windows) will work with Windows 8.1. This chapter helps you troubleshoot problems with programs running on Windows 8.1.

> **NOTE**
> Microsoft support for the Windows XP operating system ends on April 8, 2014.

Troubleshooting Installations

Avoid installing utility and security programs unless they're specifically written for Windows 8.1. (Most basic application programs will run fine.) If you can't get an older program to install, or it doesn't work after you install it, check the program manufacturer's website to see if a Windows 8.1 version is available. Or, use the methods discussed in Chapter 29 to configure settings that might enable the older program to run on Windows 8.1. Or, consider installing and using Windows XP Mode with Windows Virtual PC to run the application. If these steps fail, you can take some general troubleshooting steps to get the program working properly.

Troubleshooting Programs

Because so many programs are available for Windows, no troubleshooting magic bullets exist that will solve all problems. Every program and every problem is unique, but pinpointing what's causing the problem is often easy.

One of the most common mistakes users make is that they don't invest the necessary time in learning how to use a program. They guess and hack their way through it, and when things don't work the way they hoped, they think there's something wrong with the program, when in fact, the problem is that the person using the program has no clue how to use it correctly. Troubleshooting can't fix ignorance; only learning can fix that.

Every program has its own built-in Help feature for a reason — because every program is unique. The only ways to get information about a specific program are from the Help that came with that program, or from the support website for that program. The Help feature, which is usually the last item on a menu bar or tab, provides all the Help options available to you.

The whole concept of troubleshooting applies only when you *do* know how to do something, but things aren't working the way the documentation says they should.

The trick is to explore a number of different avenues for help. There is no book, web page, person, place, or thing that has all the answers to all questions, nor the solutions to all problems. Sometimes you really have to dig around for a solution. Start with the narrowest, simplest solution and work your way out from there, as follows:

- Try the Help that's available from the program's menu bar or tab.

- Try the program manufacturer's website. You may want to try searching `www.bing.com`, `http://support.microsoft.com`, or `http://office.microsoft.com` for Microsoft Office products. At the program manufacturer's website, look around for other support options such as Frequently Asked Questions (FAQs), troubleshooting information, and discussion groups or newsgroups.

- For Microsoft products, you'll also want to go to `http://support.microsoft.com` and click a product link for links to support for specific products. A great resource for Microsoft products is the Microsoft Community "Answers" website (as shown in Figure 33.1) at `http://answers.microsoft.com`. This page takes you to areas for specific products where you can post questions and get answers.

Don't forget, too, that you can search the entire planet using a search engine like Google or Bing. However, when you're searching the entire planet, you want to use as many exact, descriptive words as possible in your search. Otherwise, you'll get links to more pages than you could visit in a lifetime. Include the product name, version number, and specific words that describe what you're looking for.

FIGURE 33.1

The Microsoft Community website.

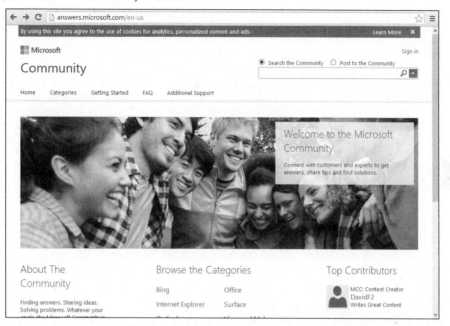

33

TIP

To find out what version of a program you're using, choose the program's Help ⇨ About command. On newer programs, the About information sometimes can be located by selecting the File tab and then clicking Help. Or you can also check the version in the Control Panel: Open the Control Panel, click Programs, and click Programs and Features. The Version column shows the program version.

When searching the web, use specific keywords and skip the noise words like *how*. For example, if you're looking for help with Mail backups, get all the appropriate words into your search, as in "Backup Mail." To find specific phrases, enclose the phrase in quotes. Be as specific as you can possibly be. The more specific you are when typing your search words, the better your results will be.

NOTE

We would be lost without Google. When our team experiences a problem with a server for which we don't have a ready fix, invariably the first place we turn is Google. We're not alone in that. Even some auto repair shops search Google to find the probable cause for engine lights that come on.

Researching Application Errors

Many software errors provide hexadecimal memory locations in their error messages. Sometimes, searching for the number won't do any good. The title bar may provide some clues as to exactly what caused the problem. Look through the error messages for some unique keywords that you can enter into different support search engines.

Searching for a combination of the program name and keywords from the error message text can sometimes provide clues. You may want to start with a narrow search, such as http://support.microsoft.com, to avoid getting too many hits. If that doesn't work, you can broaden the search to all of Microsoft.com (www.bing.com). If all else fails, you can search all five billion (or so) pages in Google's index at www.google.com.

But the key thing, in all searches, is to get the most unique words from the message into your search string. For example, if searching for the hexadecimal memory addresses from the error message doesn't return useful results, you could try a combination of other words. If you keep getting results that are clearly not germane, such as pages about UNIX system problems when you're searching for a Windows issue, preface the keyword you want to exclude with a minus sign. For example, searching Google using "Windows 8.1 backup restore –UNIX –Linux" returns a list of pages that contain the words *Windows, 8.1, backup,* and *restore,* but not pages that also include the words *UNIX* or *Linux.*

Ideally, you'll want to try to dig up as much information about the error as you can via the web. Search the company's website; because they're the ones who created that application, they may be able to provide additional information.

Editing the Registry

After researching a software problem, you might find that the solution involves a "Registry hack," also known as "editing the Windows Registry." This is serious business with little margin for error. Never attempt to fix a problem by guessing at a Registry hack. When you do get specific instructions on making a Registry change, make sure you make *exactly* the change indicated in the message. Even the slightest typographical error can cause a world of problems. If you're not a technical person and don't want to risk creating a really big mess you can't rectify, consider hiring a professional to resolve the problem. In any event, if you're going to make a Registry change, backup your Registry by doing a System Image backup as described in Chapter 24. File History also keeps a copy of your Registry (see also "Backing up the Registry," later in this chapter).

Before you launch into Registry hacking, you need to understand what you're doing. First, be aware that the Registry is a database where Windows and other programs store data that they need to operate properly on your computer. The average computer user typically doesn't need to know that the Registry exists. In fact, we're sure most do not. There is absolutely nothing that's user friendly about the Registry. In fact, it's probably just about as user hostile as you can get. Microsoft provides the Registry Editor described in this chapter because programmers and other IT professionals occasionally need to view or modify Registry entries.

> **CAUTION**
> The Windows Registry is not a safe place to mess around. Pay attention to all cautions in this chapter!

How Registry data is organized

The Windows Registry comprises several *hives,* each of which holds specific types of data. Within each hive, the registry uses *keys* and *subkeys* to organize data. Just as a folder can contain subfolders, a key can contain subkeys.

The Registry doesn't store files or documents, however. Instead, it stores *values.* Some of these values make sense to the average user, but some do not. For example, if you have Microsoft Office 2010 installed, there is a value in the Registry that stores the path to the Office installation folder, and the value is typically `C:\Program Files\Microsoft Office\Office14\`. That's easy to understand. However, you'll also find a lot of values in the Registry that look something like `{89820200-ECBD-11cf-8B85-00AA005B4383}` `!8,0,7100,0`, and it's highly unlikely that this value will mean anything to you. But whether the value of a given Registry entry makes sense to you, it makes sense to the application that is using the value, and that value must be entered exactly as required.

33

Hives, keys, and subkeys

We get into the specifics of editing the Registry in a moment. But first, Figure 33.2 shows an example of the Registry Editor as it might look when you first open it. The names listed down the left column are hives. As defined by Microsoft, a *hive* is a logical group of keys, subkeys, and values in the Registry that has a set of supporting files containing backups of its data. So, each hive contains keys, subkeys, and data. Each hive stores a particular type of information, as summarized in Table 33.1. Note that most keys have a standard abbreviation, such as HKCU for HKEY_CURRENT_USER.

FIGURE 33.2

Standard hives at left in the Registry Editor.

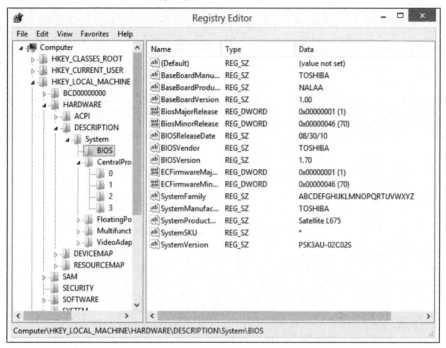

TABLE 33.1 Standard Root Keys

Name	Abbreviation	Description
HKEY_CLASSES_ROOT	HKCR	Stores information about document types and extensions, registered programs that can open each file type, the default program for each file type, and options that appear when you right-click an icon.
HKEY_CURRENT_USER	HKCU	Stores information about the person who is currently using the computer, based on which user account that person is logged in to, and settings that particular user chose within his or her account.
HKEY_LOCAL_ MACHINE	HKLM	Stores information about all the hardware that's available to the computer, including devices that might not be plugged in at the moment.
HKEY_USERS	HKU	Stores information about all users, based on user accounts you've defined via the Control Panel.
HKEY_CURRENT_ CONFIG	N/A	Similar to HKEY_LOCAL_MACHINE, this key stores information about hardware available to the computer. However, this key limits its storage to hardware that's connected and functioning currently.

TIP

To open Registry Editor, press Windows+X, click Run, type regedit, and press Enter. You also can display the Charms Bar, choose Search, and type regedit. Click `Regedit.exe` on the Apps screen.

When you click the white triangle next to a hive, it expands to display its keys. Most of the keys have subkeys, and those subkeys might also have subkeys of their own. In that case, the subkey itself has a white triangle, too, which you can click to see another level of subkeys. For example, in Figure 33.3, the HKEY_CLASSES_ROOT key is expanded to reveal its subkeys. Each subkey represents a particular file type in that case. A few subkeys are also expanded in this example.

FIGURE 33.3

The HKEY_CLASSES_ROOT and some subkeys expanded.

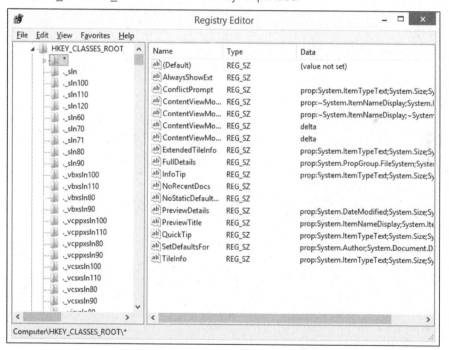

Often, a reference to a specific subkey is expressed as a path, in much the same way that a file's location and name are expressed as a path. For example, the path to a file might be expressed as C:\Users\rtidrow\Pictures\Summit01.jpg. The path tells Windows exactly where to find the file Summit01.jpg in my Pictures folder.

A registry path is the same idea, and even uses backslashes to separate the key and subkey names. For example, the highlighted subkey in Figure 33.3 is at `Computer\HKEY_CLASSES_ROOT\*`.

Sometimes you'll see instructions telling you the path to a key or subkey, as in `HKEY_CURRENT_USER\Control Panel\Appearance\Schemes`. You have to manually expand each folder down the path to get to the subkey. Figure 33.4 shows the result of following that sample path. The values in the Data column for that key are mostly binary numbers — a good example of just how user *unfriendly* the Registry can be!

FIGURE 33.4

The `HKEY_CURRENT_USER\Control Panel\Appearance\Schemes` subkey selected.

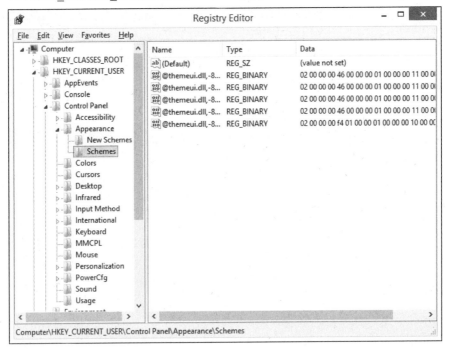

Key values

The data stored in a subkey is called a *value*. The value is a specific piece of information that can be stored as a string (text) or a number. However, the terms *string* and *number* don't tell the whole story because those types can be further broken down into the specific *data types* listed in Table 33.2.

TABLE 33.2 Registry Value Data Types

Name	Data Type	Description
Binary value	REG_BINARY	Raw binary data used mostly by hardware components. Often displayed in hexadecimal format.
DWORD value	REG_DWORD	An integer often used to store parameters for device drivers and services. Subtypes include related types such as DWORD_LITTLE_ENDIAN and REG_DWORD_BIG_ENDIAN with the least significant bit at the lowest/highest address, respectively.
Expandable string value	REG_EXPAND_SZ	A variable-length string often used to store data for application programs and services.
Multistring value	REG_MULTI_SZ	A string that actually consists of multiple substrings separated by spaces, commas, or other special characters.
String value	REG_SZ	A simple fixed-length text string.
Binary value	REG_RESOURCE_LIST	A series of nested arrays (lists) often used by hardware and device drivers. Usually displayed in hexadecimal.
Binary value	REG_RESOURCE_REQUIREMENTS_LIST	A series of nested arrays (lists) containing a device driver's hardware resources, displayed in hexadecimal.
Binary value	REG_FULL_RESOURCE_DESCRIPTOR	A series of nested lists of actual hardware device capabilities, usually displayed in hexadecimal.
None	REG_NONE	Data with no particular type that's displayed as a binary value in hexadecimal.
Link	REG_LINK	A string naming a symbolic link.
QWORD value	REG_QWORD	A 64-bit number displayed as a binary value.

33

In the vast majority of situations, you'll be working with strings, DWORDs, or QWORDs when you create or modify Registry entries. Entering a string in the Registry is just like entering characters in a text box. When you enter DWORD and QWORD values, however, you enter those either as a decimal or a hexadecimal value. We won't go into detail about the differences here, and if you want a clearer understanding of hexadecimal numbering, a quick search on the web will turn up lots of explanations and examples. Just keep in mind that when you edit a DWORD or QWORD value, you need to choose the option that matches the value you're entering. Figure 33.5 shows an example of a value entered as a decimal number.

FIGURE 33.5

The Edit DWORD (32-bit) Value dialog box.

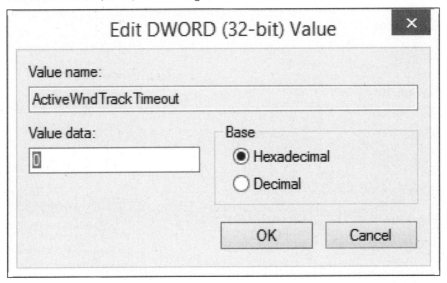

If the troubleshooting steps that you're using direct you to enter a decimal value, click the Decimal option and then type the value specified. If you need to enter a hexadecimal value, click the Hexadecimal option before you type the value.

Backing up the Registry

Every time you start your computer, Windows automatically creates the Registry based on the hardware and software available to it. Then it makes a backup copy of that Registry. When you plan to manually change the Registry, you should also make a backup copy of the Registry just before you make your change. When it comes to editing the Registry, there is no margin for error and even a tiny typographical error can have far-reaching, unpleasant consequences.

TIP

The System Restore feature described in Chapter 31 also makes periodic backup copies of the Registry.

You need administrative privileges to edit the Registry. The program you use is named regedit. You can start it using either of these methods:

- Show the Charms Bar, click Search, type **regedit**, and click `regedit.exe` on the Apps screen.
- Press Windows + X, choose Run, type **regedit**, and press Enter.

The Registry Editor opens. You *always* want to make a backup of the Registry before you change anything. It's easy to do:

1. Choose File ⇨ Export from the menu bar in the Registry Editor.
2. Choose a folder and enter a filename of your own choosing.
3. To export the entire Registry, choose All under the Export Range heading.
4. Click the Save button.

That's it. In the event of a disaster, you can choose File ⇨ Import from the Registry Editor's menu bar to restore all the entries you copied in the preceding steps.

Making the Registry change

You can change any value in the Registry. First, you need to get to the appropriate subkey. For example, let's say that you've found the solution to some problem via Microsoft's website. Part of that solution involves changing a value in the following subkey:

```
HKEY_LOCAL_MACHINE\SOFTWARE\Microsoft\Windows\CurrentVersion\Run
```

The first step is to get to the subkey by expanding the `HKEY_LOCAL_MACHINE\SOFTWARE\Microsoft\Windows\CurrentVersion` node. Then click Run. The pane to the right shows values in the subkey. The status bar shows the complete path name, as in Figure 33.6.

To change a subkey's value, double-click that value. A dialog box opens, allowing you to make a change. The appearance of the dialog box depends on the type of value you're editing. Figure 33.7 shows a general example.

33

FIGURE 33.6

HKEY_LOCAL_MACHINE\SOFTWARE\Microsoft\Windows\CurrentVersion\Run selected.

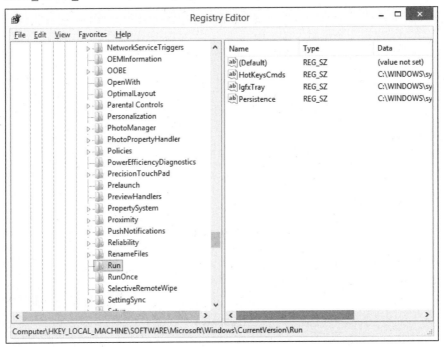

FIGURE 33.7

The dialog box to edit a string value.

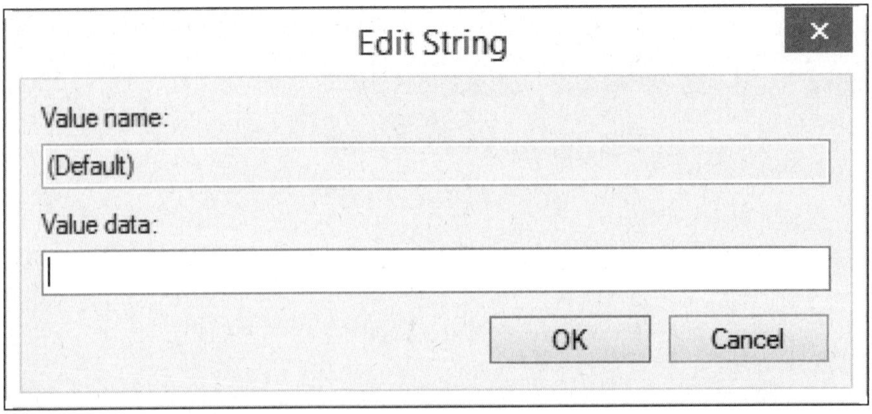

CAUTION

Make sure you get to the correct key, and make *exactly* the change your instructions tell you to. Even the slightest mistake here could cause big problems down the road.

The Value Data box contains the value you can edit. Make your change there and click OK. Then close the Registry Editor. You've finished making your Registry change.

Whether you see any change on the screen depends on the value you changed. Many Registry hacks have no effect until you restart the computer.

If it turns out that you created more problems than you solved, you can restore your Registry from the backup you made. Open the Registry Editor and choose File ⇨ Import to import the backed-up Registry file. Otherwise, if all seems well, you can delete the backed-up Registry file.

Troubleshooting Tips

One important approach will help ensure your troubleshooting success: You *must* be methodical.

Don't start changing program settings, Windows settings, or Registry settings; deleting files; and taking other actions without an understanding of what you're doing. Just as important, don't make lots of changes at once. Instead, make a single change, see if it fixes the problem, and then try the next change if needed.

Here are some key pieces of advice:

- When searching the web for answers, be as precise as possible. Include as many keywords as possible that are related to the issue. If you're receiving an error message, enclose the exact error message in quotes in your search.

- Ask yourself what has changed. Did you add something new? Did you change a setting? Knowing when the problem started occurring and what changes happened right before it began could give you a great head start on finding the solution.

- Make one change at a time, testing the problem after each change to see if it's resolved.

- Keep notes. As you make a change or test something, make a note of it so you'll know what you changed and when.

- Don't be surprised to find that what appears to be a single problem is actually multiple problems.

- Use restore points to restore your system to the state it was in just prior to when the problem started occurring.

33

- Make backups of your critical data before you make any drastic changes.
- Make backup copies of the Registry key in which you're about to make changes before you make those changes.

TIP

For more help with troubleshooting programs, search Windows Help and Support or post a question in the appropriate area online at Microsoft Communities.

Wrap Up

As you work in Windows 8.1, you'll notice that some older programs run better than others. Generally speaking, programs designed for Windows 7 will work with Windows 8.1. You may find, however, that not all programs that were designed for Windows XP or earlier versions of Windows will work with Windows 8.1. This chapter discussed how to troubleshoot software problems in Windows 8.1.

Specifically, this chapter discussed

- How to troubleshoot problems that may occur during software installations
- How to troubleshoot problems with programs running under Windows 8.1
- How to research application errors that occur under Windows 8.1
- How to edit the Windows Registry

Part VIII

Hardware and Performance Tuning

Installing and Removing Hardware

IN THIS CHAPTER

Using hot-pluggable devices

Disconnecting hot-pluggable devices

Installing not-so-hot-pluggable devices

Removing hardware devices

A typical computer consists of hardware, firmware, and software. These three components work together to make the computer both usable and useful. This chapter will help you understand each of these with a focus on installing and removing hardware in Windows 8.1.

Before jumping into hardware-related tasks, take a quick look at just what hardware, firmware, and software really are.

Hardware, Firmware, and Software Demystified

Hardware is any physical device used by the computer, whether internal to the computer (such as the CPU on the computer's motherboard) or attached externally to the computer. A discrete hardware component that performs a given function is generally referred to as a *hardware device* or just *device* for short. You can use numerous types of hardware devices with a computer. Printers, scanners, mice, keyboards, monitors, disk drives, digital cameras, iPods, MP3 players, modems, and routers are all examples of hardware devices.

Before we describe firmware, it helps to get a better understanding of *software*. Software is program code that is written to perform a given function. For example, all the program code that makes up WordPad is software. Likewise, all the program code that constitutes Windows 8.1 is software.

Device drivers are also software. A device driver is a program that serves as an intermediary between a piece of hardware and an application or the operating system. For example, a display driver enables Windows 8.1 to communicate with and control your computer's display. Likewise, a printer driver enables Windows 8.1 to communicate with and control a printer.

Firmware is also software, in the context that it is program code. The difference is in how the program code is stored. *Firmware* is program code stored in a hardware device, typically in read-only memory. For example, the program code that makes your Apple iPad or your digital camera work is firmware.

Generally, as a typical Windows 8.1 user, you deal with firmware only when updating firmware on your removable devices, such as MP3 players. You'll be adding device drivers and working with Windows updates much more so than you will with firmware.

A Few Words About Device Drivers

As indicated in the previous section, device drivers enable the Windows operating system to communicate with and control devices. Although Windows 8.1 comes with a very large number of device drivers for a wide range of devices, most device drivers are written and distributed by the manufacturers of a given device. For example, your video adapter's device driver was written by the company that designed and manufactured the adapter.

Device drivers are very much device-specific. That is, a device driver written for one device won't work for a different type of device. For that reason, make sure you have the necessary device driver(s) for a device before you install it. If you've just purchased a new device that requires a device driver not included with Windows, that driver will be included with the new device, typically on a CD or available for download on the manufacturer's website. Because the version of the device driver was developed specifically for the device, you don't have to obtain an updated driver before installing the new device. However, you can certainly visit the manufacturer's website to see if an updated driver is available that adds features or fixes issues with the version you have. We recommend installing the device with the driver you have, and then checking later for an updated driver as needed.

Support for 3D Printers?

Windows 8.1 now supports 3D printers, which are devices that use laser and lathe-like technology to "print" three-dimensional objects from solids, such as certain prototyping plastics and metals. By providing 3D printer manufacturers with a 3D printing API, Windows 8.1 users will find installing and supporting these new devices as simple as connecting standard printers.

Using Hot-Pluggable Devices

Many modern hardware devices are *hot-pluggable,* which means you just connect them to your computer and start using them. There's no need to shut down the computer before connecting the device. Nor is there any need to go through a formal installation process after you connect the device. However, you should always read the instructions that came with a device before you connect it for the first time because sometimes you need to install some software before you connect the device. When that's the case, as mentioned earlier, the software is usually on a CD that comes with the device.

> **TIP**
>
> Because Windows 8.1 includes a large library of device drivers, you can just connect a device and begin using it without going through the process of installing a device driver yourself. For example, you can connect a USB flash drive or one of many USB external hard drives and begin using them right away. Because most digital cameras look and act to Windows 8.1 as flash drives, you can do the same with cameras.

Hot-pluggable devices generally connect to the computer through USB, IEEE 1392 (FireWire), or PC Card (different versions called PCMCIA, Cardbus, and ExpressCard). The latter two types of connections are not as popular now as they were several years ago. USB has become the predominant hot-pluggable connection on most desktop computers, laptops, and some tablets.

We look at USB in the sections that follow.

Connecting USB devices

Universal Serial Bus (USB) is the most common type of hot-pluggable device. USB is used by flash drives, smartphones, digital cameras, some types of microphones and headphones, external disk drives, and many other types of devices. Like most technologies, USB has evolved over the years, and several versions of USB are currently on the market.

The main differences among USB standard versions have to do with speed. USB 1.0 and 1.1 have two speeds: Low Speed (1.5 Mbps) used by mice and keyboards, and Full Speed (12 Mbps), more often used by digital cameras and disk drives. USB 2.0 added a third, High Speed, data rate, which can transfer data at the much faster rate of 480 Mbps. USB 3.0 and USB 3.1 now transfer data 5 Gbps and higher.

USB 2.0 is downwardly compatible with USB 1.1 and 1.0, which means that you can use a USB 2.0 device in a computer with USB 1.*x* ports. However, the device will transfer at the 12 Mbps speed rather than the 480 Mbps speed available only in USB 2.0. So, you don't really need to know exactly which type of USB your computer has. If you plug a USB 2.0 device into a USB 1.0 or 1.1 port, Windows displays a message telling you that you'd get better performance from a USB 2.0 port. The device will still work; it'll just be a lot slower than if you'd plugged it into a USB 2.0 port.

Released in 2008, USB 3.0 is the latest specification for USB. It has a speed that is ten times faster than USB 2.0, with a transfer speed of 5 Gbit/s (625MB per second). USB 3.0 is backward compatible with USB 2.0.

34

There are three different USB plug shapes: Type A, Type B, and Mini-USB or On-the-Go (OTG). The computer has female Type A ports, into which you plug the male Type A plug on the cable. The device might have Type A, B, or a mini-port. Figure 34.1 shows the symbol for USB and the general shape of USB ports on the computer. An example of the Type A plug is on the far right of that figure. USB plugs are all keyed so that they fit only one way. Try pushing the plug gently into the port, and if it won't fit, flip the plug over and try again.

FIGURE 34.1

USB symbol, ports, and plug types.

Connecting a USB device should be easy, provided you've done any preliminary installations required by your specific device. The steps are as follows:

1. If the device has an on/off switch, turn it off.
2. Connect the device to the computer using the appropriate USB cable.
3. If the device has an on/off switch, turn it on.

The very first time you connect a device, you might get some feedback on the screen indicating that Windows is loading drivers for the device. That message is followed by one indicating that the device is ready for use.

In many cases, you get a Windows 8.1 message instructing you to tap it to see options after you've connected a device. After you tap (or click) that message, a list appears with options so you can choose what you want to do with the device. In the case of a hard drive, that would most likely be the Open Folder to View Files option, unless you were using that hard drive to store one specific type of file.

What's "Speed Up My System" and ReadyBoost?

Some USB devices can be used to speed up your system with ReadyBoost. When you plug a flash drive into a USB port, AutoPlay options might include an option to speed up your system using ReadyBoost, which is a Windows 8.1 feature designed to speed up some operations by using flash memory as intermediary storage between the processor and the hard drive. It works only with USB devices that actually can play that role. Flash memory has fast random I/O capabilities, and therefore isn't supported by all USB devices. See Chapter 36 for more information on ReadyBoost.

Connecting IEEE 1394 devices

IEEE 1394 (often called 1394 for short) is a high-speed (800 Mbps) standard typically used to connect digital video cameras and high-speed disk drives to computers. The symbol and plug shape for an IEEE 1394 port are shown in Figure 34.2. IEEE 1394 also goes by the names FireWire and iLink.

FIGURE 34.2

The FireWire symbol and plug shape.

> **TIP**
> 1394a supports speeds up to 400 Mbps, and 1394b supports speeds up to 800 Mbps.

Connecting a 1394 device is much the same as connecting a USB device:

1. Leave the computer running, and turn the device off (if it has an on/off switch).
2. Connect one end of the 1394 cable to the computer and the other end to the device.
3. Turn on the device and wait.

As always, what happens next depends on the device.

34

PC cards

PC Cards, Cardbus, and ExpressCard cards were once commonly used on laptop computers. It's almost impossible to find newer laptops with PC card capabilities, because of the availability and pervasiveness of USB devices. However, you may still have a computer that includes a PC card slot and those devices can still operate with Windows 8.1. You may need to hunt around for a device driver that supports Windows 8.1 (or even Windows Vista or Windows 7) for that device to work.

A PC card device is usually a little larger and thicker than a credit card. Figure 34.3 shows an example of a PC ExpressCard wireless network adapter.

FIGURE 34.3

A PC card.

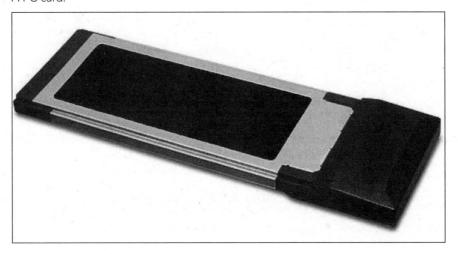

Connecting a PC card to a notebook computer is simple: Just slide the card into the slot, right side up, and push until it's firmly seated. As with USB and FireWire devices, you should get some feedback on the screen indicating when the device is connected and ready for use. How you use the device depends on the type of device you inserted.

Using memory cards

Memory cards are hot-pluggable storage devices. Figure 34.4 shows examples of some memory cards. Most memory cards are used in digital cameras, tablet computers, and jump drives. You just connect the camera or jump drive to a USB port to access the content on the memory card. However, if your computer has slots for memory cards, you can also insert the card directly into the appropriate slot.

FIGURE 34.4

Examples of memory cards.

After you insert a memory card into a slot, you should get some feedback on the screen indicating that the card is ready for use. That may be in the form of the Windows 8.1 auto play dialog box, or an Explorer window may open to show you the contents of the card. Either way, the card will be treated as a USB mass storage device, as discussed next.

Memory cards and USB mass storage

Memory cards and USB devices that store data act like disk drives when you connect them to a computer. As such, each will have an icon in your Computer folder when it's connected. Figure 34.5 shows an example where we have connected a flash drive named ATTACHE (drive G:), and an external Hard Disk (made by Iomega) through USB ports.

34

FIGURE 34.5

External devices in the Computer folder.

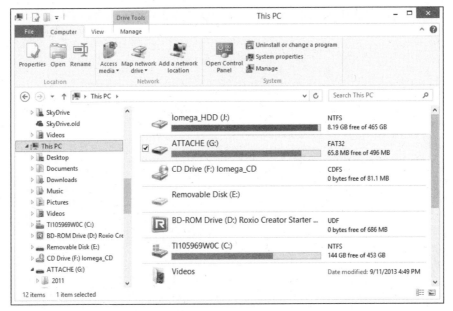

Using such a device is no different from using any other disk drive. To see the contents of the device, open its icon. Use the standard techniques to navigate through folders, to delete files and folders, and to move and copy files and folders. See Chapters 20 and 21 for the necessary buzzwords and basic skills.

Disconnecting hot-pluggable devices

Before you disconnect a hot-pluggable device from a computer, you might want to make sure it's not in the middle of a file transfer or holding a file that you have open in some program. To do that, look in the notification area and see if there's one that looks like the one shown in Figure 34.6. (That icon shows only when you have a storage device attached.) Note that the icon displays a tooltip called Safely Remove Hardware and Eject Media.

FIGURE 34.6

The Safely Remove Hardware and Eject Media icon.

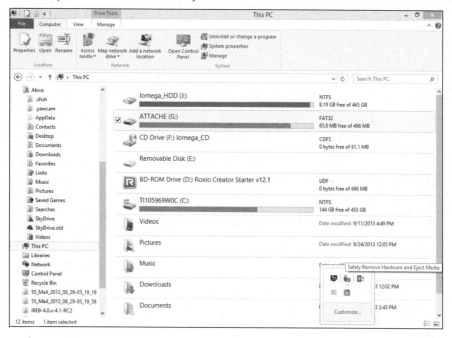

To safely remove a device, click the Safely Remove Hardware and Eject Media icon. The menu shown in Figure 34.7 opens, listing each connected mass storage device. Click the action you want to take from the menu.

> **TIP**
>
> If it's difficult to reach around to the back of the computer to connect a USB or FireWire device, just leave that end of the cable plugged into the computer. Disconnect the cable from the device, and leave that end of the cable within easy reach for future connections. Or get an external USB or FireWire hub, connect the hub to the back of the computer by its cable, and leave the hub on your desk within easy reach.

3 4

FIGURE 34.7

Safely Remove Hardware menu.

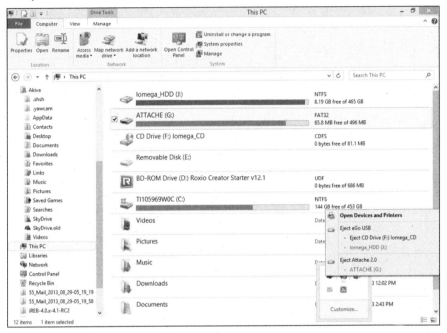

Simply click the Eject command for the drive you want to disconnect. The media will not physically eject from the computer, but Windows closes it and displays a message that the device can safely be disconnected from the computer. You can then safely remove it from the computer.

Not all devices are hot-pluggable. Some require a more elaborate connection and installation procedures. Those kinds of devices are discussed in the next section.

Not-So-Hot-Pluggable Devices

Hardware devices that aren't hot-pluggable require a bit more effort than hot-pluggable devices. Most require that you turn off the computer, connect the device, turn the device on, and then turn the computer back on. You might also need to install some software to get the device to work. It all depends on the device you're connecting. As always, you have to read the instructions that came with the device for specifics. We can only provide general guidelines and examples here that give you an idea of what to expect.

Most computers have the ports pointed out in Figure 34.8. Your computer may have more or fewer such ports, and your ports probably won't be arranged exactly like that. On a notebook computer, some of the ports are likely to be on the side of the computer, perhaps hidden under a sliding or hinged door. But the basic shape of each port will be as shown in the figure.

FIGURE 34.8

Ports on the back of a computer.

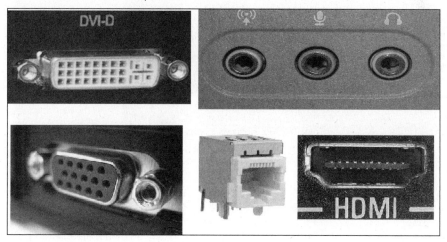

You can install some devices inside the computer case. These connect to sockets inside the computer case on the *motherboard* (also called the *mainboard*). The motherboard is a circuit board that provides the wiring between all the hardware devices that make up the system, including the CPU, memory (RAM), internal disk drives, and everything else. The sockets that accept these devices are called *expansion slots,* and the devices that go in them are typically called *adapter cards.*

Figure 34.9 provides a general idea of what different types of internal slots and ports look like.

34

FIGURE 34.9

Slots on a computer motherboard.

Installing expansion cards

Many internal hardware devices are PCI cards, which slide into a PCI slot. The slots are positioned so that one end of the card lines up perfectly with the back of the computer, exposing one or more external connectors. Figure 34.10 shows a general example of what such a card looks like.

Many motherboards may have PCI Express (PCIe) and PCI Express 16. These provide faster communication between the motherboard, which in turn allows for more powerful expansion cards. The PCI Express 16 slot is ideal for high-powered graphics cards designed to work with advanced graphics and large high-definition TV screens. The Accelerated Graphics Port (AGP) is designed specifically for a graphics card.

FIGURE 34.10

A sample expansion card.

Before you buy an expansion card, you need to know what slots are available on your motherboard. Before you install a card, you need to read the instructions that came with the card. There is no one-size-fits-all rule that applies to all the thousands of hardware devices you can add to a PC. You should install the device exactly as instructed in the instructions provided by the manufacturer of the device. Winging it is likely to lead to many hours of hair-pulling frustration. It's also very important that you turn off the computer before opening the case to install a card. Remove the power cord, too. Ideally, you should wear an antistatic wrist strap so that you don't generate any static electricity that could damage any of the components in the computer, potentially rendering it unusable and voiding your warranty.

34

> **TIP**
>
> You can buy an antistatic wrist strap at computer hardware stores, including online stores such as TigerDirect.com (www.tigerdirect.com), CDW (www.cdw.com), and Cyberguys (www.cyberguys.com).

Many AGP and PCIe 16 slots have a locking mechanism to hold the card steady in the slot. You have to make sure that it's in the unlocked position before you try to insert the card into the slot. When installing the card, push firmly on the card to make sure you really get it in there. Don't force it and break it, but push it in well enough to ensure that it's firmly and evenly seated within its slot. If the slot has a locking mechanism, push it into the locked position. Put the case cover back together again, plug in the power cord, and then turn on the PC.

> **CAUTION**
>
> When removing a card that has a locking device, don't forget to slide it into the unlocked position. Trying to force the card out of the locked slot would likely cause a lot of damage!

If the device is plug-and-play (as many modern devices are), the rest should be easy. The computer should boot up normally, but you won't necessarily get to the desktop right away. Instead, Windows should detect the new device and go through an installation procedure to get the device working. You'll get some feedback on the screen as that's happening in the form of notification area messages. When the notification messages stop and the desktop looks normal, the device should be ready to use.

Installing more memory (RAM)

Installing more RAM isn't exactly like installing other devices because you're not likely to get any feedback at all on the Windows desktop when you're done. RAM is such an integral part of the computer that it doesn't really get "installed." The processor just detects it as soon as you turn on the power. One of the few places you'd even see that you have more RAM is on the System screen of the Control Panel applets.

The key consideration to adding more RAM is finding the right type of memory. You need to match the type and speed of your existing RAM chip, and you need an available DIMM slot on the motherboard. Also, every motherboard has a limit as to the maximum speed and type of memory it can handle. When you build a PC, you know exactly what's involved. But when you buy a prebuilt PC, it's not always easy to find out what you need to know.

Your best bet is to go to the computer manufacturer's website and find the main web page for your exact model of computer. You can often find out exactly what type and speed of RAM chip is currently installed using that method. PNY (a company that sells RAM chips) has memory information on its website (www.pny.com) to help you understand terms and product offerings.

> **TIP**
>
> The PNY site also has installation guides, which might help you get a feel for what you'll be doing when you purchase more RAM. Remember that you have to look inside the computer and see if you even have an available slot for adding more RAM first.

Even so, installing more RAM isn't really something for the technologically timid to undertake. Even the slightest mistake could prevent the computer from starting at all. If the speed of the new chip doesn't exactly match the speed of the existing chip, the computer will start but you're likely to end up with endless error messages when you try to do just about anything.

Upgrading the CPU

Every motherboard has a certain maximum CPU speed it can handle. You won't know what that is unless you can get the specs on your exact motherboard. Rather than try to upgrade just the CPU, you'd probably be better off upgrading the motherboard, CPU, and RAM while you're at it. That way you can speed up everything but still use your existing hard drive, DVD drive, mouse, keyboard, monitor, and everything else. Or, for a little extra, you can probably purchase a new PC almost as inexpensively as upgrading your old one.

A barebones kit might be the best way to go. With a barebones kit you can get a motherboard, CPU, RAM, and power supply already assembled in a new case. You then transfer your existing hard drive, CD drive, mouse, keyboard, monitor, and everything else to that new case. You get the benefits of a newer, faster computer without the expense of buying an entirely new PC. A word of caution: Windows may require you to reenter the product key after a hardware upgrade.

Installing a second hard drive

If you need more hard disk space, installing a second hard drive is a good option. Hard disk space is cheap, and it's a lot easier to just add another drive than it is to try to pinch a few more megabytes out of a single drive by compressing files and moving things out to removable disks.

Most internal drives are relatively easy to install. What's more, with today's computers, the computer will automatically detect the drive type on boot. If you don't feel up to the task of installing a new internal drive, however, consider an external drive.

> **TIP**
>
> If the computer doesn't recognize the new disk, enter the computer's BIOS Setup program and make sure the BIOS is configured to auto-detect drives on the new drive's interface.

External hard drives are relatively simple to install. Basically you just connect the drive to a USB or FireWire port. If you already bought an internal hard drive but you haven't connected it yet, you can convert it to an external drive just by putting it in an external drive enclosure. Just make sure you get an enclosure that has the right internal connectors (IDE or SATA) for your drive.

> **TIP**
>
> To see examples of hard drive enclosures, search an online retailer such as www.newegg.com, www.tigerdirect.com, or even http://froogle.google.com for "external drive enclosure." Drives that connect via USB 2.0 can move data at 480 Mbps, which is plenty fast for a hard drive and won't be a performance bottleneck. USB 3.0/3.1-compatible drives can move data at 5 Gbps, but many standard desktop and laptops don't yet support USB 3.0.

34

Hard drives for most non-server PCs fall into two main categories, Serial ATA (SATA) and Parallel ATA (PATA), more commonly referred to as Integrated Drive Electronics (IDE) drives. (The ATA stands for Advanced Technology Attachment.) SATA III is the newer, faster, and easier technology.

> **NOTE**
>
> Servers and some workstations use Small Computer System Interface (SCSI) drives. However, SATA drives provide faster data rates than SCSI drives.

The original SATA drives moved data at a good 150 Mbps (150 million bits per second). The newer SATA II drives move data at 300 Mbps, and third-generation SATA drives support 600 Mbps. Before adding a second SATA drive, you need to make sure your motherboard has SATA connectors, and whether they're the appropriate connectors for the type of SATA device you want to install.

IDE drives come in multiple speeds, too, ranging from 33 Mbps to 133 Mbps. The maximum speed your PC can use depends on the speed of the IDE connectors on the motherboard.

IDE drives have an unusual configuration where you can connect two drives to a single IDE port. One drive is called the *master drive;* the other, the *slave drive.* You have to physically set a jumper on the drive to make the drive either master or slave. Then you have to connect the drive to the right place on the cable. The master goes at the end of the cable. The slave goes on the plug in the center of the cable.

Again, your best bet before installing any hardware device is to follow the instructions that came with the device — to the letter — before you even turn the computer back on and use Windows to configure the device. If in doubt, have a pro install the hardware for you. But, assuming you've installed the drive, either internally or externally, you can then use Windows 8.1 to partition and format the drive.

Primary and extended partitions

You can divide a basic disk into multiple *partitions.* Each partition looks like a separate item in your Computer folder. The drive can be divided into a maximum of four *primary* partitions, or three primary partitions and one *extended* partition. The difference is that a primary partition can be used as a *system partition,* meaning you can install an operating system on it and boot the computer from it. An extended partition can't be a boot disk and can't contain an operating system. However, you can divide an extended partition into multiple logical drives, where each logical drive has its own drive letter and icon in the This PC folder, and looks like a separate drive.

In Windows XP and previous versions of Windows, you could explicitly create extended partitions using the Disk Management console. Microsoft changed that in Windows Vista, and that change carries over to Windows 8.1. Now, instead of giving you the option to create either a primary partition or an extended partition, Disk Management gives you the option of creating a new simple volume. The type of volume created when you use this command depends on the number of partitions already on the disk. The first three partitions you create are created as primary partitions. The fourth is created as an extended partition.

> **TIP**
>
> If you do need an extended partition, you can use the DiskPart command in a command console to create it. To learn more about DiskPart, open a command console and enter **diskpart**. At the DiskPart command prompt, enter **Help** to see a list of commands.

You can use two types of disks in Windows 8.1:

- **Basic:** This is the type of disk supported by DOS and all previous versions of Windows.
- **Dynamic:** This type of disk was introduced in Windows 2000. Dynamic disks support the following types of volumes:
  - **Simple:** These volumes make up space for a single dynamic disk and can use a single region on the disk or multiple regions on the disk.
  - **Spanned:** These volumes make up space on more than one physical disk (they span multiple physical drives — hence, the name).
  - **Striped:** These volumes stripe the data for a single logical volume across multiple physical disks, providing improved performance by distributing the read/write load across multiple disks.
  - **GPT:** This stands for Globally Unique Identifier Partition Table. GPT supports theoretical volume sizes up to 18 EB. The primary advantages to using GPT are the very large volume size and the large number of partitions you can create on a GPT disk. Disk structure is also optimized for performance and reliability.

> **TIP**
>
> EB stands for exabyte, which is equal to about a million terabytes. A terabyte (TB) is about a trillion bytes or 1,024GB.

Which disk type you choose really depends on the type of disk and your needs. If you're re-installing a very high-capacity disk in a Windows 8.1 computer, we recommend using GPT. If you need to create a spanned or striped volume, use a dynamic disk. For general-purpose disks, a basic disk is fine.

Partitioning and formatting the disk

After you have a new hard drive installed, you can start Windows 8.1 and use the Disk Management tool to partition and format the drive. Log in to an account with administrative privileges for this task. If the Computer Management tool doesn't start automatically after you've logged in, you can get to it by following these steps:

1. On the desktop, press Windows + X.
2. Click Disk Management from the Quick Link menu.

34

> **CAUTION**
>
> Repartitioning and/or reformatting a disk that already contains files will result in the permanent loss of all files on that disk. You should not attempt to repartition or reformat an existing disk unless you fully understand the consequences and are fully prepared to recover any lost files. Again, if you don't have any formal training and experience in technical matters, it's best to leave this sort of thing to the pros. An in-depth treatment of these more technical hardware matters is beyond the scope of this book.

The new drive appears at the bottom of the display, most likely as Disk 1 (assuming the system has one other disk drive, which will show as Disk 0), as shown in Figure 34.11. The drive's space is indicated by a dark bar showing Unallocated in the lower-left corner.

FIGURE 34.11

The Disk Management tool.

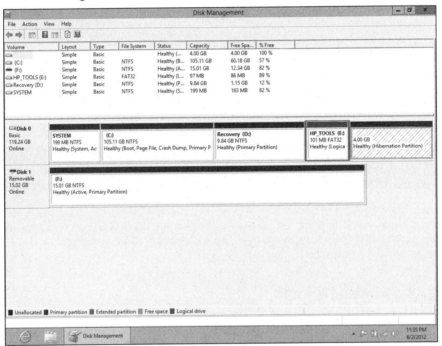

To partition the drive as a basic disk with a simple volume:

1. Right-click within the unallocated space of the new drive and choose New Simple Volume.

2. On the first page of the New Simple Volume Wizard that opens, click Next.

3. The next wizard page asks what size you want to make the partition and suggests the full capacity of the disk. You can choose a smaller size if you intend to divide the disk into multiple partitions. After you make your selection, click Next.

4. The next wizard page asks you to assign a drive letter to the drive. It suggests the next available drive letter, which is a good choice. Click Next.

5. The next wizard page asks how you want to format and label the disk. Your options are as follows:

   - **Do Not Format This Volume:** If you choose this option, you'll have to format the partition later. We don't suggest choosing this option.

   - **File System:** Your choices here depend on the disk type. For volumes on basic and dynamic disks, you can choose between exFAT and NTFS. On a GPT disk, you can choose only NTFS.

   - **Allocation Unit Size:** This defines the cluster size. The Default option automatically chooses the best allocation unit size given the type and capacity of the disk, so that would be your best choice.

   - **Volume Label:** This is the name that appears with the drive's icon in This PC. You can also change that name at any time in the future.

   - **Perform a Quick Format:** If you choose this option, formatting will go quickly, but the drive won't be checked for errors. Better to leave this option unselected.

   - **Enable File and Folder Compression:** Only available if you chose NTFS as the file system, this option automatically compresses all files and folders on the drive. This conserves disk space, but there is a minimal performance overhead for the compression/decompression as the drive is used. You can still compress individual files and folders if you leave this option unselected.

6. Click Next after making your selections.

7. The last wizard page summarizes your selections. Click Finish.

Now you get to wait for the disk to be formatted. This could take some time, depending on the size of the volume and if you chose the quick format option. You can continue to use your computer while the drive is being formatted or you can wait until it finishes.

If you set up the drive as one large partition, you're done when the Formatting indicator reaches 100 percent. You can close the Disk Management tool.

If you're partitioning the disk into smaller units, you can repeat the steps outlined previously for each partition. Just make sure that you right-click an unpartitioned portion of the disk in Step 1. If you create an extended partition with the DiskPart command, you need to add one or more physical volumes to the disk through the Disk Management console. Just right-click the extended partition and choose New Simple Volume; then follow the steps described previously to create the new volume. Repeat the process for any other volumes you want to create in the extended partition.

When the partitioning and formatting are complete, exit the Disk Management tool. Access the drive as you would any other — through the This PC folder. Figure 34.11 shows an example. Notice how each Hard Disk Drive icon represents a drive (or partition) defined in the Disk Management tool.

34

Other hard drive operations

This section covers some general issues concerning hard disks. All these operations pose some risk of data loss and should be attempted only by people who understand the risks and are confident they have backups of all important data.

Converting a disk to NTFS

Windows 8.1 offers three different file systems for formatting a hard drive. FAT32 was introduced with Windows 95. New Technology File System (NTFS) was introduced in Windows NT 4.0, largely to support user access control required in domain networking. Extended FAT (exFAT) is a new file system that removes several limitations of the older FAT file systems while providing compatibility with other operating systems and devices.

When you divide a hard drive into multiple volumes, you can format each independently of the other. (A *volume* is any partition or logical drive that has its own drive letter and icon in File Explorer's Computer view.) NTFS is the preferred file system for Windows 8.1 because of its better performance and stronger security. There's no reason to use FAT32 or exFAT file systems unless you have multiple operating systems installed and can choose one or the other at startup. For example, if you can boot to Windows 8.1 and Linux, the Linux operating system will not be able to access files on a local NTFS volume (without adding third-party Linux tools).

Each file system imposes minimum and maximum volume sizes, and a maximum file size. Keep in mind that these file systems apply only to the hard drives, not to media such as USB flash drives, CDs, or DVDs. Table 34.1 summarizes the differences among the file systems.

TABLE 34.1 Differences among NTFS, exFAT, and FAT32 File Systems for Hard Drives

Description	NTFS	exFAT	FAT32
Locally accessible to	Windows 8.1, Windows 7, 2008 Server, Windows Vista, 2003, XP, and 2000	Windows XP, Vista, and 7; Linux	Windows 95 and later
Minimum volume size	10MB		512MB
Maximum volume size	More than 2TB	64ZB*	32GB
Maximum file size	Entire volume	64ZB	4GB
Access Control Lists (ACLs)	Yes	No	No

* Zettabyte, a sextillion bytes or 1 billion terabytes

> **TIP**
>
> See the section, "The exFAT file system," later in this chapter to learn more about the exFAT file system.

> **CAUTION**
>
> Changing the file system on a drive poses some risk of data loss and should be attempted only by people who understand the risks and are prepared to recover from any loss of data.

You can convert a FAT32 file system to NTFS, but it's not possible to go in the other direction. That is, you can always upgrade to NTFS, but you can't downgrade. Be sure to close all open documents and program windows prior to starting the conversion. To convert a FAT32 volume to NTFS, use the following syntax with the command console `convert` command:

```
convert volume: /fs:ntfs
```

where *volume* is the letter of the hard drive you want to convert. Advanced users can enter **convert /?** at the command prompt or search Windows Help and Support for more advanced options. To enter the command:

1. Close all open documents and program windows.

2. Press Windows + X and choose Command Prompt (Admin).

3. Type the command using the syntax shown. For example, to convert hard disk drive `D:` from FAT32 to NTFS, type **convert d: /fs:ntfs**.

4. Press Enter and follow the instructions on the screen.

If you're converting your system drive (`C:`), you'll need to restart the computer to start the conversion. Don't use the computer during the conversion process.

Shrinking and extending partitions

> **TIP**
>
> You can shrink and extend partitions without reformatting, either from the Disk Management tool or by using the `DISKPART` command.

34

You can shrink existing partitions to free up unallocated space. And if you have any unallocated space, you can extend existing partitions into that space. As always, there is some risk in doing this. Therefore, you should back up everything before even attempting to shrink or extend a partition.

> **CAUTION**
>
> The techniques described in this section will not increase the amount of hard disk space you have. The techniques described in this section are best left to professionals and highly knowledgeable computer users. The slightest error could cost you everything on your hard drive! Not recommended for casual computer users.

You can shrink a basic volume that's either raw (unformatted) or formatted with NTFS quite easily right in the Disk Management tool. You can shrink to the current used space size or to the first unmovable files (such as a paging file) on the volume. To shrink a volume, just right-click it at the bottom of the Disk Management screen and choose Shrink Volume. A dialog box opens to show how far you can shrink the selected volume. Just make your selection and click OK.

Likewise, if you have some unallocated space on the drive, you can extend an existing partition into that space. A wizard opens to take you step-by-step through the process.

For more information on extending and shrinking volumes, including spanned volumes, search the Help in the Disk Management tool.

Changing a volume label

A *volume label* is the name of a volume as it appears in your This PC folder. By default, each volume is labeled Local Disk. To change a drive's volume label, right-click its icon in your This PC folder and choose Properties. On the General tab of the properties sheet, type the new name into the first text box, where you see New Volume in Figure 34.12.

FIGURE 34.12

Changing a volume label.

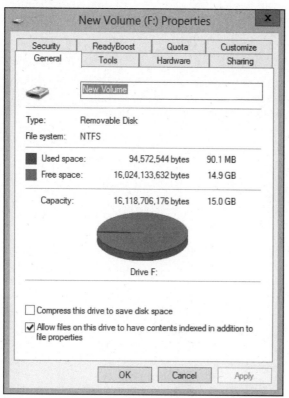

Changing a drive letter

Drive letters A, B, and C are reserved for floppy disk drives and your hard drive, and cannot be changed. Beyond those first three letters, you can assign drive letters as you see fit. Just be aware that when you do, Windows will *not* update your settings and programs to reflect those changes. All settings you've made concerning locations of files in all programs will be invalid. Virtual folders and items in Media Player and Live Photo Gallery need to be updated to reflect the new drive locations. If you're not sure how to deal with these things, you're better off not changing any drive letters.

CAUTION

Changing drive letters is an operation that's best left to experienced users who understand the consequences and can solve, on their own, the problems that are likely to follow.

No two drives can have the same drive letter. If you need to swap two drive letters (for example, change drive E: to drive F: and change drive F: to drive E:), you'll need to temporarily leave one of the drives without a letter or assign it an unused drive letter. The Disk Management tool, which you need to make this change, will allow you to do that. Here's how it works:

1. Navigate to the Disk Management tool described at the start of this section.

2. Right-click the graphical representation of the drive whose letter you want to change. Or, to change a removable drive, right-click its drive letter as in Figure 34.13. Choose Change Drive Letter and Paths.

FIGURE 34.13

Changing a drive letter.

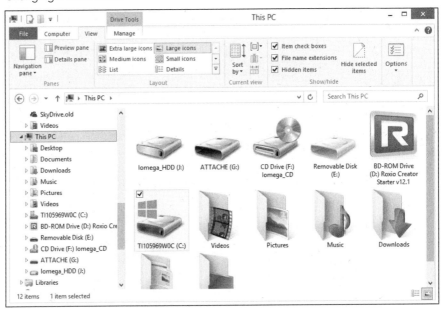

The new drive letter shows up the next time you open your This PC folder.

3. If the new letter to which you want to assign the drive is available, click Change, choose the new drive letter, and click OK. Otherwise, if you want to assign the current drive's letter to a different drive, click Remove and click Yes.

4. Repeat steps 2 and 3 until all drives have the letters you want them to have. Then close the Disk Management tool.

The exFAT file system

Microsoft developed a file system called exFAT, for Extended FAT. exFAT is also sometimes referred to as FAT 64 (for 64-bit).

exFAT is not intended as a replacement for NTFS. Instead, exFAT is geared primarily toward mobile personal storage, as used in MP3 players and other mobile devices. exFAT offers several advantages:

- Theoretical volume size of 64ZB (recommended size 512TB)
- Theoretical maximum file size of 64ZB (recommended size 512TB)
- Supports more than 1,000 files per directory
- Provides cluster bitmap for fast storage allocation
- Better contiguous on-disk layout, useful for recording movies
- Is extensible

exFAT is supported natively by Windows 8.1, Windows 8, Windows 7, and Windows Vista. Windows Vista does not support the use of exFAT with ReadyBoost, but Windows 7, Windows 8 and Windows 8.1 do support it. exFAT is also supported under Linux through kernel update.

If you want to optimize performance for removable media such as flash drives, consider formatting the drive with exFAT. However, keep in mind that the device will only be usable in a computer that supports exFAT.

Removing Hardware

Hot-pluggable devices don't follow the type of removal discussed in this section. To remove a USB or FireWire device, or a PC card or memory card, see the section "Disconnecting hot-pluggable devices," earlier in this chapter. This section is about removing more complex devices such as internal components. Before you follow the procedures described in this section, make sure you understand what you're removing and why you're removing it. Do not attempt to fix a problem by removing devices based on sheer guesswork.

You'll need administrative privileges to perform the tasks described here. It might be best to sign into a user account before you get started so you don't have to rely on privilege escalation along the way.

Before you physically remove a device from the system, first uninstall its driver through Device Manager by following these steps:

1. Open File Explorer and right-click This PC.
2. Choose Manage and then click Device Manager in the left pane to open Device Manager.

3. Expand the category in which the device is listed. Then, right-click the name of the device you intend to remove and choose Uninstall, as shown in Figure 34.14.

FIGURE 34.14

Uninstall a hardware device.

4. Click OK.

Now you need to shut down the computer, unplug the power cord, and physically remove the device from the system. Then plug the machine back in, start it up, and everything should be back to the way it was before you ever installed the device. If you set a protection point just before installing the hardware, you can return to that protection point just to make sure.

Updating Drivers

At the start of this chapter, we discussed the importance of using Windows 8.1 drivers with your hardware. The quickest and easiest way to get an updated driver for a device is usually to search for it online by following these steps:

1. Open Device Manager (press Windows + X and choose Device Manager).

2. Right-click the device that needs an updated driver and choose Update Driver Software, as shown in Figure 34.15.

FIGURE 34.15

Update a device driver.

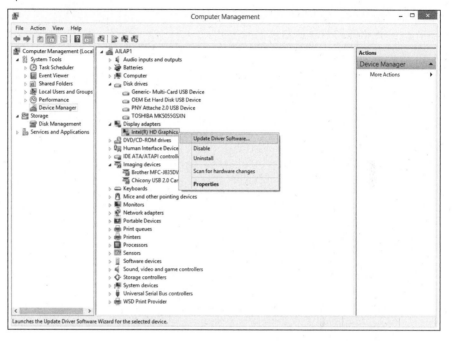

3. Click Search Automatically for Updated Driver Software and follow the onscreen instructions.

Often, that's all it takes. You might need to restart the computer after the driver installation is complete.

If that method doesn't work, you may have to go to the product manufacturer's website and search for a Windows 8.1 driver there. If you find the driver, make sure to follow the manufacturer's instructions carefully to download and install the updated driver. If you can't find a driver specifically for Windows 8.1 and Windows 8, but you do find one for Windows 7 or Vista, that driver should work.

Dealing with Devices That Prevent Windows 8.1 from Starting

There may be times when a newly installed hardware device prevents Windows 8.1 from starting properly. In most cases, such devices will be disabled automatically so that Windows 8.1 can start. If it works that way, you can typically follow the steps described in the preceding section to try to get the updated driver online.

If Windows 8.1 cannot disable or work with the new device, you may be able to start in Safe Mode with Networking and either get updated drivers there or disable the device manually. You also need to log in with the Administrator account.

 Windows 8.1 has a new way to start in Safe Mode. To learn how to boot your computer in Safe Mode, see Chapter 6 of this book.

When you're at the desktop, follow the procedure described in the preceding section to search for updated drivers. If you can't find updated drivers, your best bet might be to disable the device by right-clicking its name and choosing Disable from the shortcut menu. Close Device Manager and restart the computer again normally.

If you had to disable the device, it won't work when you restart the computer normally. But at least you can get Windows 8.1 started and try to find an updated driver through the product manufacturer's website.

Wrap-Up

This chapter has been about connecting, installing, and removing hardware. Some of this material is intended for more advanced users who are familiar with computer hardware. If some of the content is beyond your technical capabilities or comfort level and you need to install or remove some hardware, consider having the job done professionally. The following are the main points to take away from this chapter:

- Most modern devices are hot-pluggable, which means you just connect them to the computer as needed.
- Always read and follow the instructions that come with a device before connecting it to your computer. Winging it will likely result in frustration.
- Hot-pluggable devices that act as storage devices have icons in your This PC folder while connected. You can transfer files to and from such a device using basic techniques described in Chapter 20.
- More-advanced hardware devices generally require shutting down the computer, connecting the device, turning on the device, and then starting the computer again.
- Use the Disk Management tool to partition and format a new drive.
- To remove a hot-pluggable storage device, click the Safely Remove Hardware icon in the notification area and stop the device before physically removing it.
- To remove other devices, first uninstall them in Device Manager. Then shut down the computer and physically remove the device from the system.

Using Wireless Bluetooth Devices

IN THIS CHAPTER

What Bluetooth is all about

Connecting and configuring a Bluetooth adapter

Associating with different Bluetooth devices

Connecting to a Bluetooth-enabled personal area network

Transferring files between two systems using the personal area network

I n a nutshell, Bluetooth is a wireless technology that provides wireless communications among computers, printers, mobile phones, tablets, digital cameras, and other electronic devices. You can connect as many as eight devices together with Bluetooth, with one device acting as the master device and up to seven slave devices. (This labyrinth of connected devices is called a *piconet;* you can have up to two piconets.) For example, you could have a desktop PC, a laptop, a smartphone, digital camera, MP3 player, digital video camera, and headphones all linked wirelessly. They could all share a high-speed Internet connection, share data, and use a single printer.

The World of Bluetooth

Bluetooth is a wireless specification intended to replace the need to use physical cables between devices. Bluetooth, for example, enables you to wirelessly connect keyboards, mice, and printers to your laptop or computer. You also can use Bluetooth to wirelessly connect a mobile phone to your computer or laptop to sync settings, transfer photos or videos, or share contacts. Many other types of Bluetooth devices are available as well, including ones that don't even connect to computers or laptops such as devices used inside automobiles, exercise equipment, and games.

Bluetooth uses radio waves to transmit signals, much like many other types of technologies such as FM radio, television, and Wi-Fi. One primary difference between Bluetooth and other radio wave technologies is the distance between devices. Bluetooth is designed for very small distances; the idea is that Bluetooth is personal. You set up connections between your devices in a personal area network (called a PAN). Bluetooth is good within about 164 feet (50 meters), whereas other radio wave technologies can reach miles or hundreds of miles.

At the time of this writing, the current Bluetooth version is 4.0. Bluetooth 4.0 introduced low-energy wireless transfers to allow small, low-powered devices to use Bluetooth. Transfer rates allow data to be sent at up to 25 Mbps (megabytes per second, which is quite fast. If you're thinking of setting up a permanent wireless network between computers, however, you may want to stick with the 802.11 standards described in Chapter 38. But when it comes to connecting non-computer Bluetooth devices, wirelessly connecting a printer, or occasionally transferring files between computers, Bluetooth can't be beat.

The following are some Bluetooth buzzwords and concepts that you'll encounter in this section, as well as in the instructions that come with Bluetooth devices:

- **Discovery:** A Bluetooth device finds other Bluetooth devices to which it can connect through a process called *discovery*. To prevent Bluetooth devices from connecting at random, discovery is usually turned off by default on a Bluetooth device. You manually turn on discovery when you're ready for that device to be discovered. After a device has been discovered, you can turn discovery off.

- **Discoverable:** A *discoverable* (or visible) Bluetooth device is one that has discovery turned on, so other Bluetooth devices within range can see and connect to the device.

- **Pairing:** Once two or more Bluetooth devices have discovered one another and have been *paired* (connected), you can turn off their discovery features. The devices will forever be able to connect to one another, and unauthorized foreign devices will not be able to discover and hack into the paired devices.

- **Encryption:** A process by which transferred data is encoded to make it unreadable to any unauthorized device that picks up a signal from the device. Bluetooth offers powerful 128-bit data encryption to secure the content of all transferred data.

- **Passkey:** Similar to a password, only devices that share a passkey can communicate with one another. This is yet another means of preventing unauthorized access to data transmitted across Bluetooth radio waves.

- **Bluejacking:** A process by which one user sends a picture or message to an unsuspecting person's Bluetooth device.

A non-computer gadget such as a smartphone, MP3 player, or electronic pedometer that supports Bluetooth is called a *Bluetooth device*. A standard desktop PC or laptop computer usually isn't a Bluetooth device, although many laptops do include built-in Bluetooth capabilities. As a rule, it's easy to turn your PC or laptop into a Bluetooth device. You just plug a Bluetooth USB adapter — a tiny device about the size of your thumb — into any available USB port, and presto, your computer is a Bluetooth device. Making your computer into a Bluetooth device doesn't limit it in any way. It just extends the capabilities of your computer so that you can do things such as:

- Connect a Bluetooth mouse, keyboard, or other pointing device

- Use the Devices tool in the PC Settings area to add a Bluetooth device

- Use the Add Printer Wizard to use a Bluetooth printer wirelessly

- Use a Bluetooth-enabled phone or dial-up device as a modem

- Transfer files between Bluetooth-ready computers or devices by using Bluetooth

- Join an ad hoc PAN of Bluetooth-connected devices (an ad hoc network is an informal network, where devices connect and disconnect on an as-needed basis, without the need for a central hub or base station)

When you install a Bluetooth adapter on your PC or laptop, you also install *radio drivers*. Windows 8.1 comes with many radio drivers preinstalled.

> **NOTE**
>
> If a built-in radio driver doesn't work with your device, install the drivers that came with the device per the device manufacturer's instructions.

Configuring Your Bluetooth Adapter

If you plan to share a single Internet account among several computers or Bluetooth devices, you should install your first Bluetooth USB adapter in the computer that connects directly to the router. That will give other Bluetooth devices that you add later easy access to the Internet through that computer's Internet connection.

After you've installed a Bluetooth adapter, you'll find a new icon named Bluetooth 2.0 USB Device (or similar) in the PC Settings Devices list. You also can view Bluetooth information in the Device Manager.

To view the Devices list, show the Charms Bar, choose Settings, click Change PC Settings at the bottom of the PC Settings pane, and click PC and Devices. Figure 35.1 shows the

FIGURE 35.1

Bluetooth showing on the PC Settings page.

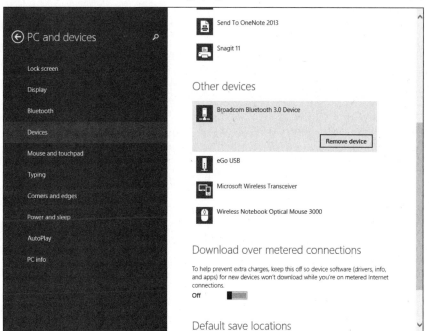

35

Bluetooth menu option that appears in PC Settings when a Bluetooth device is attached or built-in to the computer.

To see how the same device looks in Device Manager, show the desktop and press Windows + X. Choose Device Manager and expand the Bluetooth list, as shown in Figure 35.2. Your list may be different from the one shown here, but the important thing to note is that you can view and manage the Bluetooth device here as well.

FIGURE 35.2

Bluetooth USB device showing on the Devices list.

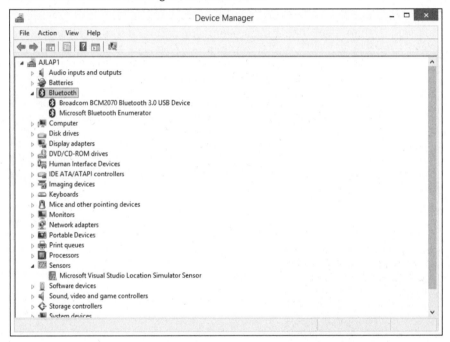

You also will have a Bluetooth icon (which looks very similar to the letter *B*) in the notification area of the Windows desktop taskbar. The Bluetooth Settings screen will be your central point for installing Bluetooth. To open that screen, use the earlier procedure from the Charms Bar, or double-click the Bluetooth Devices notification area icon (see Figure 35.3). Initially, the Devices list will be empty. If you don't see a Bluetooth Devices icon in your notification area, make sure to select the Show the Bluetooth Icon in the Notification Area check box.

As you install devices and join devices to a Bluetooth PAN, you'll see the names of those devices listed on that screen.

FIGURE 35.3

Bluetooth icon shown in the notification area.

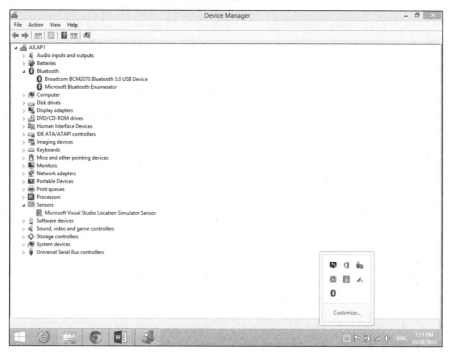

The shortcut icon that appears when you right-click the notification area provides options for adding a Bluetooth device, sending and receiving files, and joining a PAN.

Adding Bluetooth-Enabled Devices

Many different types of Bluetooth devices are available on the market. Most have some means of making the device discoverable (visible) to other devices. Whether you have to make your PC discoverable to install a device depends on the type of installation you're about to perform. As always, you need to read the documentation that came with your device for specifics.

35

On the shortcut menu for the Bluetooth Devices notification icon, clicking the Add a Bluetooth Device option opens the PC Settings window with the Devices option showing. Windows attempts to locate any devices available. The sections that follow show you how easy it is to connect Bluetooth devices to your laptop or computer. This example shows you how to set up a smartphone to your computer. We then walk you through the process of transferring files to and from that device.

Connecting a smartphone

To add a smartphone to your computer using Bluetooth, you must have a device that supports Bluetooth. Also, your computer or laptop must have built-in Bluetooth or a Bluetooth adapter plugged into it.

Use the following steps to connect the device to your Windows computer:

1. On the Windows 8.1 desktop, click the Bluetooth icon on the notification bar.

2. Click Add a Bluetooth Device, as shown in Figure 35.4. The Devices screen appears.

FIGURE 35.4

Choose to add a Bluetooth device.

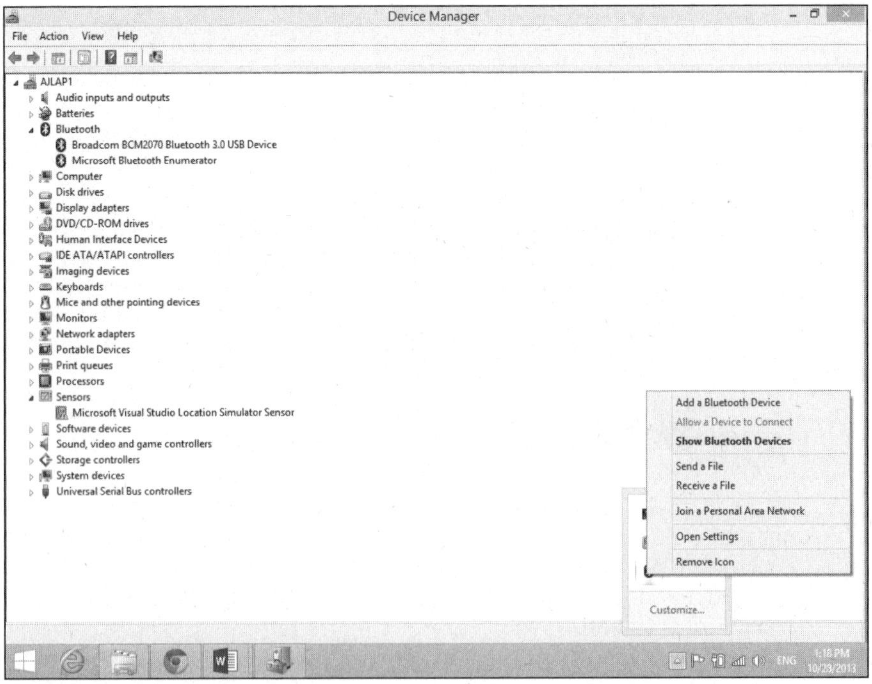

3. Turn on the Bluetooth feature on the device. In the example shown, we're going to add an iPhone. How you do that depends on your version of device and the model of phone. The device listed uses the Settings menu in the iPhone. From here, you can turn on the Bluetooth feature and then use the Bluetooth settings item to make the phone discoverable. Windows searches for all Bluetooth devices that are nearby, including the phone.

4. When the computer and phone find each other, a window similar to the one shown in Figure 35.5 appears. Click the item you want to connect with in Windows.

FIGURE 35.5

Windows finds the phone device.

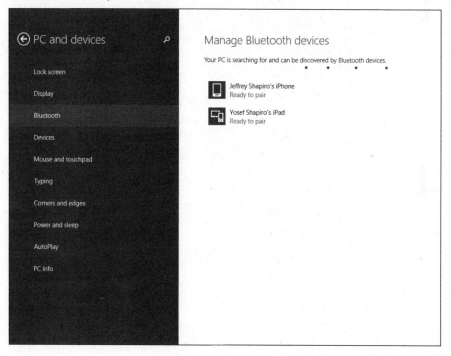

5. A message appears on both your phone and in Windows. A passcode should appear that is identical on both devices. If they are, click Yes on your phone and in Windows to set up the Bluetooth connection. Figure 35.6 shows an example of a passcode that appears during this transaction.

FIGURE 35.6

Windows and your phone display a passcode.

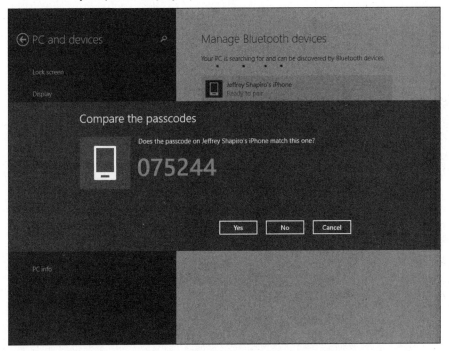

Windows sets up a connection between the two devices.

> **NOTE**
>
> On some devices, you may need to type in the passcode that appears on the Windows screen. If so, be aware that you have only a short amount of time to enter the code (approximately 60 seconds) before Windows and your device decide that a connection is not desired at this time. If the passcode screen disappears, you have to restart the connection process to get the two devices to "see" each other again.

Joining a personal area network

Once your two devices are connected, you can join them as a PAN so you can transfer files between them using the Bluetooth connection. To do so, follow these steps:

1. Click the Bluetooth icon on the desktop notification bar.
2. Click the Join a Personal Area Network option, as shown in Figure 35.7. The Devices and Printers window appears (see Figure 35.8).

FIGURE 35.7

Setting up a PAN.

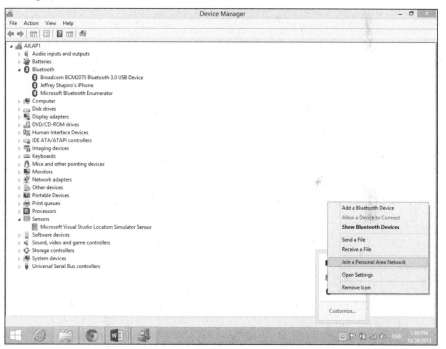

FIGURE 35.8

Selecting a device to connect to the PAN.

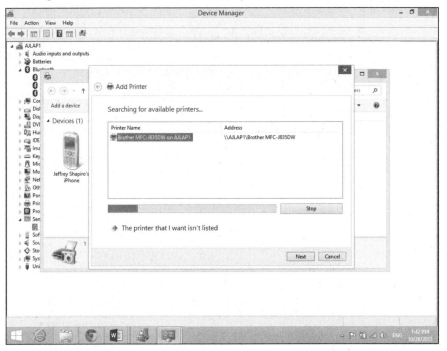

3. Click the device you want to join to the PAN, which in our case is a printer.

4. Click Connect Using – Access Point. Once connected to the PAN, the command choices change to Disconnect from Device Network. Your device will say something like Connected to PAN or similar.

Now that your devices are joined to a PAN, you can transfer files between the two, print to a Bluetooth printer and so on. Read the following two sections to find out how to do this.

Receiving files from a Bluetooth device

There's not much you can do when you connect a smartphone to a computer via Bluetooth. One feature that is handy, however, is the feature to send files from your phone to Windows. You can, for example, send picture or video files from your phone to your computer. To do this, follow these steps:

1. Click the Bluetooth icon on the desktop notification bar.

2. Click Receive a File, as shown in Figure 35.9. The Bluetooth File Transfer window appears (see Figure 35.10). Windows 8.1 now waits until files from your phone begin transmitting to your computer.

FIGURE 35.9

Receive a file from a smartphone.

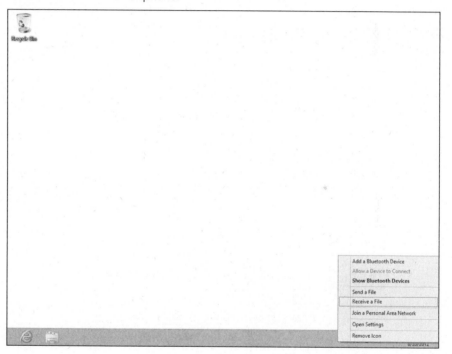

FIGURE 35.10

The Bluetooth File Transfer window.

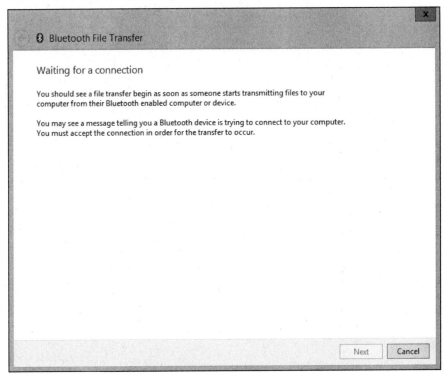

3. On your phone, locate the feature that enables you to send files to a remote location or a media-sharing app. Some Android-based phones include an app called Media Share. With this app, you can share media files (pictures, videos, and audio) with devices on a Bluetooth connection.

4. On your phone, select the file you want to transfer to Windows and transfer it.

5. In Windows, the Bluetooth File Transfer window shows device information, file information, and progress of the file transfer. Figure 35.11 shows an example. In Figure 35.12, the transfer is finished and you can see the filename and size of file, and browse to the location to which it was saved.

FIGURE 35.11

Receiving a file from a smartphone.

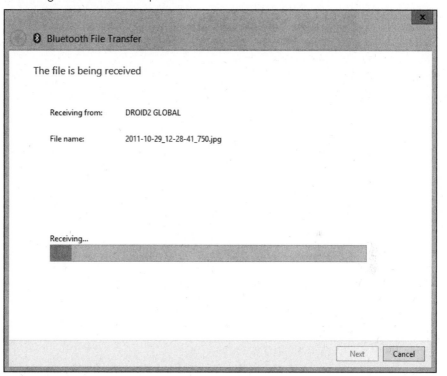

FIGURE 35.12

After Windows receives the transferred file.

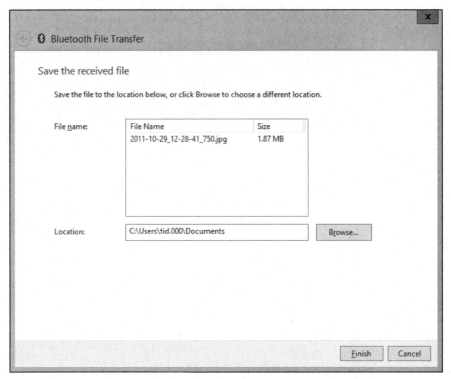

6. Click Finish when you're finished sharing files from the phone.

Sending files to a Bluetooth device

Not only does Windows 8.1 make it easy to receive files from a Bluetooth device, such as an Android-based smartphone, but it also makes it easy to send files to a device:

1. Click the Bluetooth icon on the desktop notification bar.

2. Click Send a File. You can see this option in Figure 35.9 earlier in this chapter.

3. Select the Bluetooth device to which you want to send the file. In the example shown in Figure 35.13, our choice is the DROID2 GLOBAL device. In some cases, you may have multiple devices showing, so be sure to choose the correct one.

FIGURE 35.13

Select a device to send a file to.

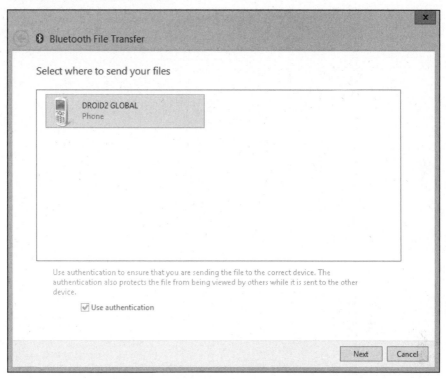

4. Click Next.

5. Specify the path and name of the file you want to share, as shown in Figure 35.14. Use the Browse button to locate the file(s) to send. If you choose multiple files, they're separated by a semicolon.

FIGURE 35.14

Select files to send.

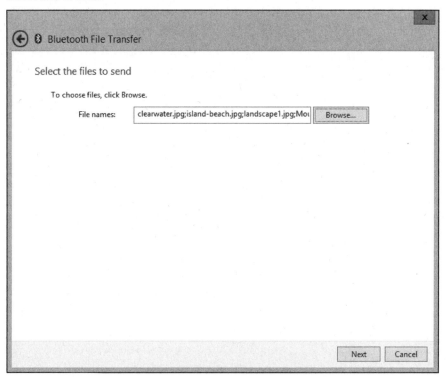

6. Click Next. The Bluetooth File Transfer window appears showing the progress of the file being sent (see Figure 35.15). Make sure your phone is turned on. You may need to confirm the file transfer on your phone.

Windows sends the file(s) from your computer to your phone. Depending on the size of the files, the transfer process may take several minutes.

FIGURE 35.15

Sending files from Windows to a smartphone.

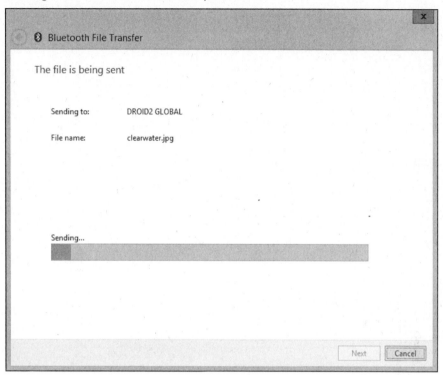

Creating a Bluetooth personal area network

You've seen how to create a PAN to allow a smartphone to connect to your computer. You also can create a Bluetooth PAN as a short-range wireless network to connect other types of devices together wirelessly. A PAN is commonly used to connect a laptop to a desktop PC, although it can be used to connect other types of Bluetooth devices. As a rule, there's not much to joining Bluetooth devices to a Bluetooth network. Most of the action takes place automatically behind the scenes.

To explain the basic procedure, let's assume you already have a desktop computer with a functional Internet connection. You've already installed a Bluetooth USB adapter on that computer, so it's now a Bluetooth device. On that desktop computer, click the Bluetooth adapter icon in the notification area of the Windows desktop. Click Open Settings and make sure Allow Bluetooth Devices to Find This Computer is selected, as shown in Figure 35.16.

35

FIGURE 35.16

Make sure Bluetooth is set up on both computers.

On a laptop computer (or second computer), activate Bluetooth or, if necessary, plug in a second Bluetooth USB adapter. You want to connect the laptop to the desktop in a PAN. To do so, starting from the laptop computer, follow these steps:

1. Right-click the Bluetooth Devices notification area icon and choose Join a Personal Area Network. A list of Bluetooth devices should appear. If at least one device does *not* appear, click the Add a Bluetooth Device button and follow the steps to locate a Bluetooth-enabled computer. When the search completes, you should see a list of all of the available devices.

2. Click the name of the computer to which you want to connect, and click the Next button.

3. Choose a passkey method from the next wizard screen (the Choose a Passkey for Me option is sufficient), and then click Next.

4. You'll be given a passkey. On the other computer, you'll be asked to type in that same passkey. Type in the passkey exactly as shown in the first computer and click Next.

5. Follow any remaining instructions in the wizards on both computers until you get to the final page, and then click the Close button in each wizard.

Once the connection is established, you should have Internet access on both computers. You can share printers and folders, and move and copy files between computers using the techniques described in Chapter 21 and Chapter 25.

Note, however, that if you made the Bluetooth connection to only one computer in an existing local area network (LAN), you'll have access only to the shared resources on the Bluetooth-enabled computer, not all the computers in the LAN.

Troubleshooting a Bluetooth network connection

If you can't get any connectivity at all using Bluetooth, try the following remedy:

1. Go to the computer that's having trouble connecting to the PAN.

2. Open the Network and Sharing Center by pressing Windows+X and choosing Control Panel ➪ Network and Internet ➪ Network and Sharing Center.

3. Scroll down to the Bluetooth Network Connection group. If you're unable to locate the Bluetooth Network Connection group, you'll need to follow the steps outlined earlier, including entering a passkey from the other system in the PAN.

By the time you complete the wizards on both screens, you should have a connection. The Network and Sharing Center folders on each PC should have similar Bluetooth network entries.

Sharing an Internet connection

If you're unable to get Internet connectivity from the computer you're connecting to the PAN that already has Internet connectivity, go to the computer that's connected to the cable modem or router. Open the Network and Sharing Center and click the network item next to the Connections label. In the Activity area, click Properties and select the Sharing tab. Choose Allow Other Network Users to Connect through This Computer's Internet Connection and click OK twice to save your settings.

If you still have problems connecting to the Internet, check the settings for the Windows Firewall. Display the Charms Bar, choose Search, type **fire**, and then click Windows Firewall in the results area. Double-click a rule from the inbound or outbound rules list to adjust the settings.

With these settings, you should now be able to connect to the Internet from the other computers in the PAN.

Remember that many different Bluetooth devices are available on the market. If none of the techniques described here help you make the connection between two computers in a PAN, be sure to refer to the instructions that came with your Bluetooth device.

35

Wrap-Up

This chapter has been about installing and configuring Bluetooth devices and Bluetooth networks. Bluetooth devices provide an excellent alternative to many commonly wired devices. Also, they're usually fast and easy to set up and can provide a great way for users to communicate between computers without having to rely on more complex networking. Here's a recap of the technologies covered in this chapter:

- Bluetooth is currently at version 4.0 and allows you to connect smartphones, mice, keyboards, exercise equipment, and other Bluetooth devices.

- To turn a computer into a Bluetooth device, simply connect a Bluetooth USB adapter to a USB port on the computer.

- To connect a Bluetooth device to a computer, activate discovery on the device, bring it within range of the computer, click the Bluetooth Devices icon in the notification area, and choose Add a Device.

- To create a PAN between two or more computers, add a Bluetooth USB adapter to each computer, or use the built-in Bluetooth if applicable. Then click the Bluetooth Devices notification area icon and choose Join a Personal Area Network.

- Regardless of what type of device you intend to connect to your computer, always read the instructions that came with the device first.

Performance-Tuning Your System

Compared to most machines, a computer requires virtually no maintenance. That's because it has fewer moving parts compared to other machines. And the new mobile and handheld devices that Windows 8.1 runs on have practically no moving parts. However, there are things you can do to keep your computer running at its optimum.

For example, the more the hard drive is used to store data, the more fragmented the data on the drive becomes. That doesn't pose any problems for reading the data, but it does slow down the process. To speed it up again, you can defragment the drive. This topic, and others that will help you optimize your computer's performance, are covered in this chapter.

Getting to Know Your System

A computer system is made up of many different components. The two main components that make up the actual "computer" are the CPU and RAM. The overall speed of your system is largely determined by the speed of your CPU and the amount of RAM in your system. The speed of a CPU is measured in gigahertz (GHz), billions of instructions per second, or for older (and slower) systems in megahertz (MHz), millions of instructions per second.

The amount of RAM determines how much data the CPU can work with at any one time without accessing the much slower hard drive. RAM chips do come in various speeds. But the amount of RAM you have, more so than its speed, really determines the overall speed of your system. RAM is measured in megabytes (MB) or gigabytes (GB). A megabyte is roughly a million bytes. (A byte is the amount of memory required to store approximately a single character, such as the letter *A*.). A gigabyte (GB) is 1,024 megabytes. In short, the faster your CPU and the more RAM the computer has, the better its performance.

Knowing your CPU and RAM

To see the brand name and speed of your processor and the amount of RAM you have, right-click your This PC icon from File Explorer and choose Properties. Or, show the Charms Bar, type **sys**, click Settings, and click System in the Settings list. The System Control Panel applet that opens shows the basic computer information, as well as information about the version of Windows you're using, as you can see in Figure 36.1.

FIGURE 36.1

The System applet.

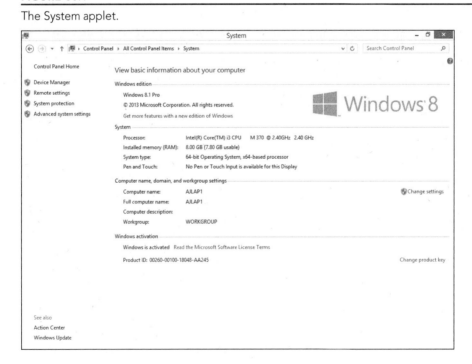

NOTE

The Windows Experience Index (WEI) that provided a quick snapshot of the major components that determined how you experience Windows 8 on your computer is no longer available. Microsoft pulled the WEI out of Windows 8.1. The Performance Information and Tools applet has also been removed.

For advanced performance analysis, Microsoft includes the Windows Performance Analyzer (WPA) and the Windows Performance Recorder (WPR) in Windows 8.1. Use WPR to collect performance data of your computer. This data is then saved to an XML file or kept in memory and then loaded into WPA for analysis.

To access WPA and WPR open to the Search Charm and search on "perf." These tools are extremely powerful and discussing them is beyond the scope of this book. Full documentation is, however, available from the Windows Performance Toolkit, which can be downloaded directly from Microsoft.

Getting more detailed information about your PC

You can get more detailed information about all the components that make up your computer system from the System Information program. To open System Information, display the desktop and press Windows + X. Click Run, type **msinfo32**, and press Enter. The System Information window shown in Figure.36.2 opens.

FIGURE 36.2

The System Information program window.

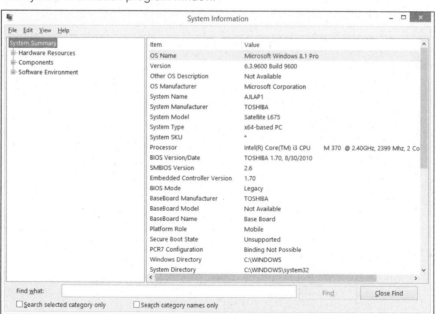

The left column of the System Information window organizes your system information into expandable and collapsible categories. For example, clicking the plus sign next to the Components category expands that category to display subcategories and the names of specific device types. When you click a specific type, such as Drives under the Storage category, the pane on the right shows information about the components installed in your computer system.

You don't actually do any work in the System Information program. Its job is to just present the facts about your particular computer's installed hardware and software. However, you can export a copy of the System Information data to a text file, which in turn you can open, format, or print using any word processing program or text editor. To export a copy of your system information to a file, just choose File ⇨ Export from System Information's menu bar.

You can also print your system information, either in whole or in part. To print all your system information, first click System Summary at the top of the left column. To print just a category, first click a category name, such as Components. Then choose File ⇨ Print from System Information's menu bar. In the Print dialog box that opens, choose All if you want to print everything, choose Selection to print just the text you may have selected, or choose Current Page to print the page you're viewing. To close System Information, click its Close (X) button or choose File ⇨ Exit.

Maximizing CPU and Memory Resources

Windows 8.1 takes care of managing the CPU and memory for you. Even so, you can do some things to improve performance as it relates to your system's memory and CPU. The following sections offer some tips.

Conserving memory

One of the best things you can do to improve your computer's performance is to ensure that it has plenty of memory. Initially, that means making sure the computer has a sufficient amount of physical memory installed. You should consider 2GB a minimum, although Windows can run with 1GB. If you use lots of programs at once, or use applications that require a lot of memory, consider using the 64-bit version of Windows and having at least 4GB of RAM in the computer, if not more.

Having a lot of memory is part of the solution, but managing the memory you do have is equally important. You can optimize your computer's RAM in these ways:

- **Reduce the number of programs you run concurrently.** If you aren't using a program, close it to reclaim the memory it's using. You can always open it again later if you need it.

- **Minimize the number of programs you install on your computer:** Do you really need a program on the tray that tells you what the weather is like outside? All the little add-on programs you install and run on your computer, even if they're running in the background, consume resources. The fewer, the better.

Reducing the number of programs running at one time not only improves performance from a memory perspective, but also reduces the load on the CPU, making processing cycles available to those programs that do need to be running.

Managing virtual memory

In the very early days of DOS, a computer could run only one program at a time. Programs had to be written to fit in the available (and minimal) memory in the computer. In today's Windows OS, you can run almost as many programs as you want at one time as a result of the design of today's CPUs and of the OS itself. The capability to manage memory effectively for all those programs is due, in part, to the use of *virtual memory.*

Modern computers can use two types of memory. The first type is *physical memory* (RAM), which consists of physical memory chips on memory modules (small circuit boards) that plug into the computer's motherboard.

TIP

The amount of RAM shown on the General tab of the System Properties dialog box (refer to Figure 36.1) is the amount of physical RAM in your system.

The second type of memory is *virtual memory,* and Windows 8.1 uses the computer's hard drive for that, using a file on the drive as a place to store data as an alternative to physical memory. The area on the hard drive that's used as virtual memory is called a *paging file* because data is swapped back and forth between physical and virtual memory in small chunks called *pages.* When you fill up both your physical memory and virtual memory, the computer doesn't just stop and display an error. Instead, it displays a message in advance, warning that the computer is running low on virtual memory and suggesting that you make room for more.

Because the virtual memory is just a paging file on the hard drive, you can easily add more just by increasing the size of the paging file. You don't have to buy or install anything. This is unlike physical memory in that the only way to increase physical memory is to buy and install more RAM. One downside to virtual memory is that it's much slower than physical memory because hard drives are slower than RAM chips.

To manage virtual memory in Windows 8.1, open the System applet from the Control Panel and click the Change Settings link to the right of the applet, as shown in Figure 36.3. In the resulting System Properties dialog box, click the Advanced System Settings item on the left side of the window, and click the Settings button in the Performance group. Then select the Advanced tab in the resulting Performance Options dialog box (see Figure 36.3). The Virtual Memory area on this dialog box shows the total paging file size for all drives. To adjust the settings, click the Change button to open the Virtual Memory dialog box shown in Figure 36.4.

FIGURE 36.3

The Advanced tab of the Performance Options dialog box.

In most cases, it makes sense to select the top check box, Automatically Manage Paging File Size for All Drives, to allow Windows to adjust the page file.

FIGURE 36.4

The Virtual Memory dialog box.

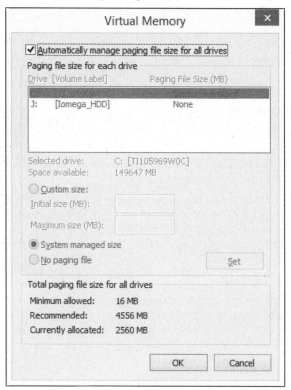

If you don't want Windows to manage the page file for you, your main options in the Paging File Size for Each Drive area of the Virtual Memory dialog box are as follows:

- **Custom Size:** You choose where you want to put your paging file(s), their initial size, and maximum size.

- **System Managed Size:** Tells Windows to create and size the paging file automatically for you.

- **No Paging File:** Eliminates the paging file from a drive. Not recommended unless you're moving the paging file from one drive to another.

If you have multiple hard drives, you can get the best performance by using the least busy drive for virtual memory. For example, if you have a D: drive on which you store documents, it may be better to use that, rather than the C: drive, because the C: drive is pretty busy with Windows and your installed programs.

If you have multiple *physical drives,* you can get a little performance boost by splitting the paging file across the two drives. A single drive that's partitioned into two or more partitions, to look like multiple drives, doesn't count. You don't want to divide the paging file across multiple partitions on a single drive because that will have the reverse effect and slow things down.

If you do opt for a custom size, you can work with any one hard drive at a time. The drives are listed by letter and labeled at the top of the dialog box. In the example shown, all the partitions actually reside on a single drive.

> **TIP**
>
> The Disk Management tool discussed in Chapter 34 lists hard drives by number. If you have a single physical hard drive, it will be Disk 0. If you have two physical hard drives, they'll be listed as Drive 0, Drive 1, and so forth.

If you don't select the check box at the top of the Virtual Memory dialog box, you'll need to set the paging file sizes individually. For example, to move the paging from drive C: to D:, first click drive C: at the top of the dialog box, choose No Paging File, and then click the Set button. Then click drive D:, choose Custom Size, set your sizes, and click Set.

The Total Paging File Size for All Drives section at the bottom of the dialog box shows the minimum allowable size, a recommended size, and the currently allocated size (the last measurement being the sum of all the Initial Size settings). The recommended size is usually about 1.5 times the amount of physical memory. The idea is to prevent you from loading up way more stuff than you have physical RAM to handle, which would definitely make your computer run more slowly.

If your computer keeps showing messages about running out of virtual memory, you'll definitely want to increase the initial and maximum size of the paging file. A gigabyte (1,024MB) is a nice round number. But if the computer runs slowly after you increase the amount of virtual memory, the best solution would be to add more physical RAM.

If you do change the Virtual Memory settings and click OK, you'll be asked if you want to restart your computer. If you have programs or documents open, you can choose No and close everything first. But because the paging file is only created when you first start your computer, you'll eventually need to restart the computer to take advantage of your new settings.

Priorities, foreground, and background

Your computer's CPU and RAM are very busy places, with potentially thousands of tasks occurring at one time. To try to optimize performance, Windows prioritizes those tasks. Your application programs typically run in the *foreground,* which means that when you click an item with your mouse or do something at the keyboard, fulfilling that request gets top priority in terms of being sent to the CPU for execution.

Most processes, by comparison, run in the *background.* This means that they get a lower priority and have to momentarily step aside when you tell Windows or an application to do something. For example, printing a document is treated as a low-priority background process, and for good reason. All printers are basically slow, mechanical devices anyway. So, by making printing a low-priority process, you can continue to use your computer at near normal speeds while the printer is slowly churning out its printed pages.

Controlling CPU priorities

36

By default, programs that you're using are given a higher priority than background processes. It's possible to reverse that by giving processes a higher priority than applications. If you have an intensive background task running and want to give it higher priority, you can reverse the order. Or if you want to make sure that your applications are getting top priority, as they should be, follow these steps:

1. Open the System window for your system.

> **TIP**
>
> The System icon in the Control Panel also opens the System window. If the Control Panel opens in Category view, click System and Security and click the System link.

2. Click the Advanced System Settings link on the left side of the screen to bring up the System Properties dialog box. Select the Advanced tab in the System Properties dialog box.

3. Under the Performance heading, click the Settings button. The Performance Options dialog box opens.

4. In the Performance Options dialog box, select the Advanced tab (refer to Figure 36.3).

The Processor Scheduling options determine whether your actions, or processes, get top priority when vying for CPU resources to do their jobs. If you choose Background Services, your computer may not be as responsive as you'd like, but background tasks will get higher priority. So, for example, if you're running a scan of your system in the background and you want it to finish faster, select Background Services in the Performance Options dialog box and click OK.

> **NOTE**
>
> Choosing Background Services won't make your printer print any faster. There's really nothing you can do to speed printing, other than use the printer's Draft mode (if it has one). But even so, printers are just inherently slow mechanical devices.

Monitoring and Adjusting Performance

Windows 8.1 includes a great selection of tools to help you monitor and tune your system's performance. You've already seen a couple of them, notably the Performance Information and Tools applet described earlier in this chapter. The following sections explore this tool in more detail, along with several others that will help you keep your system running at its best.

Performance Monitor

Performance Monitor, included in Windows 8.1, has also been available in previous versions of Windows. It provides an interface for viewing performance counters on your system. To open Performance Monitor, display the desktop and press Windows + X. Click Run, type **perfmon**, and press Enter. The Performance Monitor window shown in Figure 36.5 opens.

FIGURE 36.5

Performance Monitor.

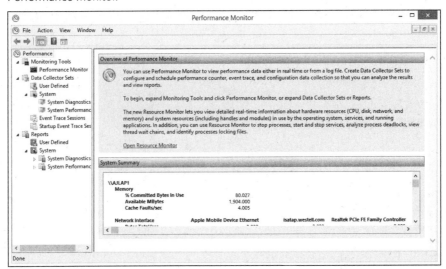

> **NOTE**
>
> Performance Monitor is a very complex application, and we could easily devote several chapters to it. For this reason, we're covering only some of the basic functions of the application. To get more information, search for Performance Monitor under Windows Help.

When Performance Monitor opens, the Performance branch in the left pane is selected and the Performance Monitor window displays general information about the program, a system summary, and some links to learn more using Performance Monitor. Although the System Summary area shows current performance data, you'll probably prefer to see a visual representation. To do so, click Performance Monitor under the Monitoring Tools branch in the left pane. Figure 36.6 shows an example.

FIGURE 36.6

Performance graphs in Performance Monitor.

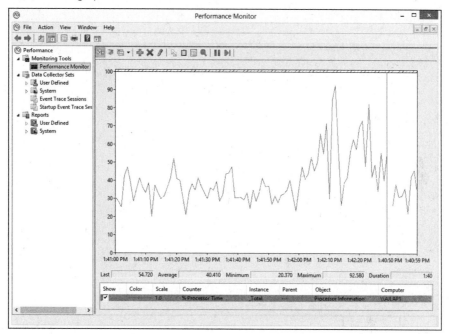

The line crossing the screen as you watch the Performance Monitor plots your system's CPU activity. The graph has a timeline along the bottom and a percentage on the side. Only tracking the CPU doesn't provide much more information than what Task Manager provides. By adding counters to the grid, you can track your system's performance. To add more counters to the graph, follow these steps:

1. Start by clicking the plus sign in the toolbar located just above the graph.

2. The Add Counters dialog box, shown in Figure 36.7, shows all the available performance objects for your system. In the left column, click the arrow to the right of the performance objects to expand and display the available counters for that object. We've selected Network Interface in Figure 36.7.

FIGURE 36.7

The Add Counters dialog box.

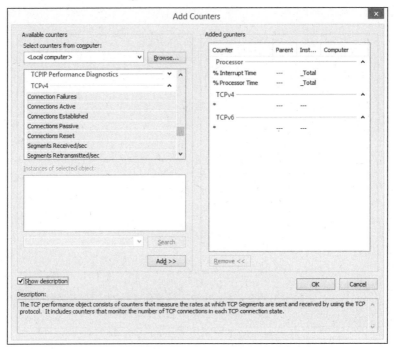

3. Depending on the counter you select, you may also have the option of selecting an instance of that counter. In the case of the Network Interface object, depending on your computer system, there might be multiple network interfaces, as shown in the Instances of Selected Object list box. This figure shows the Bytes Total/Sec selected as the counter and the wireless adapter for the instance.

4. Optionally, you can select the Show Description check box so you can view additional information about the counter.

5. Click the Add button to move the selection over to the Added Counters section of the window.

6. When you've selected all the counters you want to monitor, click OK to return to the graph.

7. As shown in Figure 36.8, the counter is added to the bottom of the window. If you select the counter in the list and click the highlighter icon in the toolbar, it highlights that specific counter. In this case, it has changed the color to a bold black. This is very helpful when you have several counters on the screen at the same time. When the highlighter is turned on, clicking any counter in the list causes that counter to be highlighted.

FIGURE 36.8

Network Interface object added to Performance Monitor.

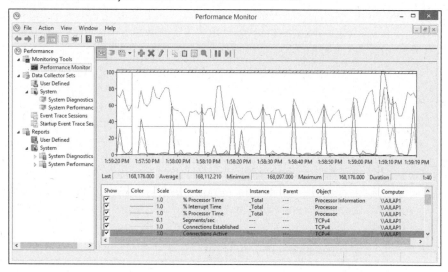

The scale of the graph is set automatically. In the case of the previous example, if the network utilization went off the screen, you'd able to adjust the scale for that specific counter so you'd have more meaningful information instead of a line running off the top of the graph.

Data collector sets and reports

The Performance Monitor interface provides a mechanism to log the information and events that occur on your system. Besides just logging the information, it also provides a way for you to use reports to look at the information.

> **NOTE**
>
> Data collector sets and reports are very involved topics. For this reason, we cover the basics in this section and suggest searching Help for "data collector sets" to get more details.

In the previous section, you learned about performance counters in Performance Monitor through the use of one example Bytes Total/Sec. A data collector set, as its name implies, is a set of objects that collect data about your computer. So, you might create a data collector set that gathers data about specific items. For example, you could create a data collector set to gather information about network performance through the use of a variety of network counters. Or you might create one to analyze drive performance by using multiple drive counters.

Within the Performance Monitor interface, you're able to create user-defined data collector sets, but let's start with the predefined data collector sets. To get started, follow these steps

1. Click the arrow to the left of Data Collector Sets to expand the tree beneath it. Then expand the System icon beneath Data Collector Sets and click System Performance.

2. Right-click System Performance and choose Start, or click the Start button in the toolbar. The system will start collecting data for the different components of the collector.

3. Let the system run for a while, and when you're ready, right-click System Performance again and choose Stop this time, or click the Stop button in the toolbar. Stopping the collector may take a few seconds.

4. Navigate to the Reports section within Performance Monitor and expand the System branch, as shown in Figure 36.9. In this figure, two performance reports are listed.

FIGURE 36.9

System Performance reports.

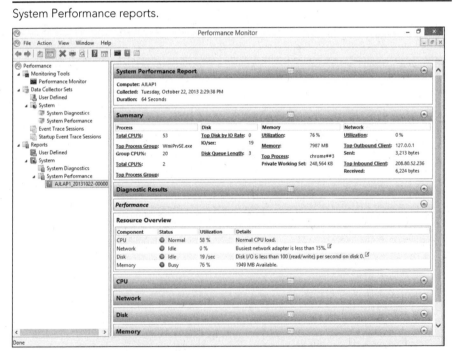

5. Expand or collapse different areas by clicking the arrows next to each group. Use the vertical scroll bar to see all the different report categories.

Generating system performance reports in Performance Monitor can help you understand where bottlenecks might exist in your system. For example, you can quickly identify an overtaxed CPU, problems with network saturation, or other issues.

In addition to creating performance reports with Performance Monitor, you can also create diagnostic reports. In the left pane, under Data Collector Sets, expand System and click System Diagnostics. Then click Start in the toolbar. Wait as Performance Monitor creates the report. While the report data is being gathered, the icon next to the System Diagnostics branch shows a small green arrow. This is replaced by an hourglass while Performance Monitor generates the report. When the icon returns to normal, the report is finished. You'll find a new report under the Reports ➪ System ➪ System Diagnostics branch in the left pane. Click the report to view its contents. Figure 36.10 shows an example of a diagnostics report.

FIGURE 36.10

A diagnostics report.

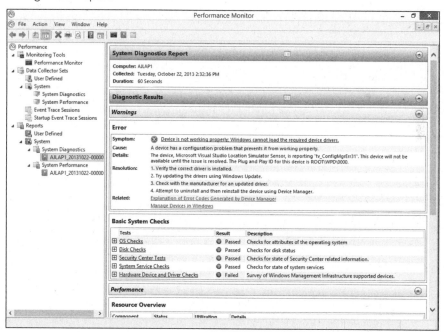

As with a performance report, expand and collapse different categories in the report to view the information in the report. The information in the report can help you pinpoint hardware errors and other problems.

Creating data collector sets

You're able to create your own user-defined data collector sets, which involves adding data from one of the four categories. From the properties window of the collector, you can set a variety of properties for each type, such as the sample interval maximum number of samples, Registry keys to monitor, and many more.

You can add the following four types of data collectors to your custom data collector sets:

- **Performance Counter Data:** This information is the same information that you're able to gather from Performance Monitor, discussed earlier in the chapter.

- **Event Trace data:** This data is gathered when different system events occur on your system.

- **Configuration data:** This data is gathered from changes that occur to the Registry of your system.

- **Performance Counter Alert:** This data is gathered when a performance counter you specify reaches a point either above or below a value that you define.

As explained previously, creating data collector sets assumes a certain level of technical capability and knowledge about how the computer and its components functions. Those topics are far outside the scope of this book. So, instead, we'll focus on the mechanics of creating the data collector set:

1. Open Performance Monitor and expand the Data Collector Sets branch.

2. Right-click User Defined and choose New ➪ Data Collector Set to start the Create New Data Collector Set Wizard (see Figure 36.11).

3. Enter a descriptive name in the Name text box.

4. Decide whether to create the data collector set from a template or from scratch (manually). If you choose the Create from a Template option, you can add data collectors to the ones already in the template. Click Next.

5. If you opted to start from a template, the wizard next prompts you to choose a template. Select one and click Next. Otherwise, the wizard prompts you to choose a type of data collector to add. In this example, let's assume you choose to start from a template, so choose Basic from the offered templates and then click Next.

6. Specify the directory where you want the data to be saved and click Next.

7. In the final page of the wizard, click Finish.

FIGURE 36.11

Create New Data Collector Set Wizard.

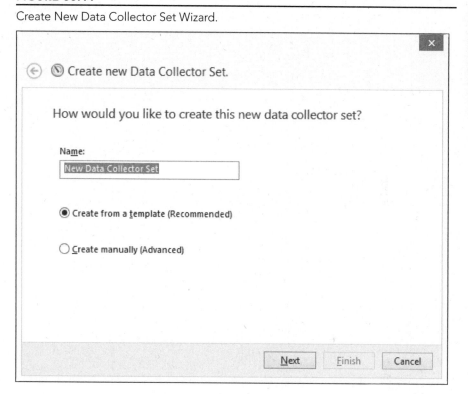

The new data collector set should now appear under the User Defined branch in the left pane. Let's assume that you now want to add some additional data collectors to the set. Right-click in the right pane (or on the new data collector set's name in the left pane) and choose New ⇨ Data Collector.

Performance Monitor opens the Create New Data Collector Wizard (see Figure 36.12). Specify a name for the collector and choose one of the four collector types, as described previously in this section. For example, to add a performance counter, choose Performance Counter Data Collector. Then click Next.

FIGURE 36.12

The Create New Data Collector Wizard.

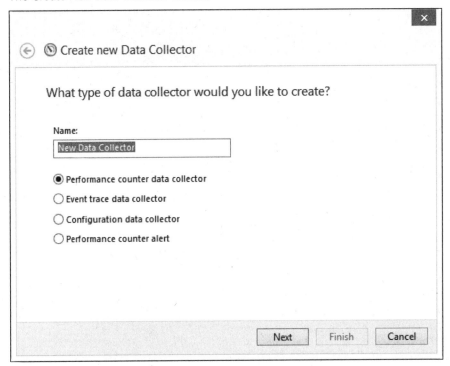

Depending on the type of collector you choose, the wizard prompts you for information about the collector. Specify the information needed to configure the collector to obtain the data you're looking for, and then click Finish.

After you create the data collector set, you can use it just as you can the predefined ones in the System branch.

Resource Monitor

Another handy tool for monitoring system performance is Resource Monitor, which collects and displays real-time information about the CPU, disk, network, and memory. To open Resource Monitor, select the root node in Performance Monitor and then click the Open Resource Monitor link. You can also open Resource Monitor by running resmon from Run as described for running perfmon (see "Performance Monitor," earlier in this chapter). Figure 36.13 shows Resource Monitor.

FIGURE 36.13

Resource Monitor.

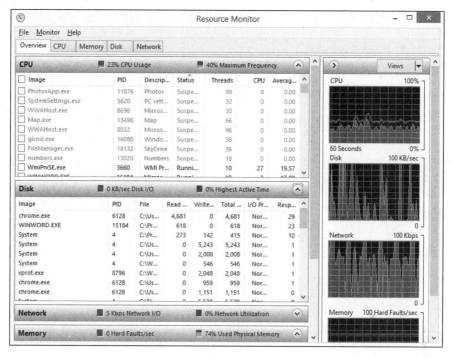

The Overview tab, shown in Figure.36.14, offers summary information about each of the four categories. To view activity for a specific process, select the check box next to the process's image name in the CPU list. Then click the category header for a category to view the data filtered by the selected process. For example, Figure 36.14 shows network activity filtered for Internet Explorer.

FIGURE 36.14

Network activity filtered for Internet Explorer.

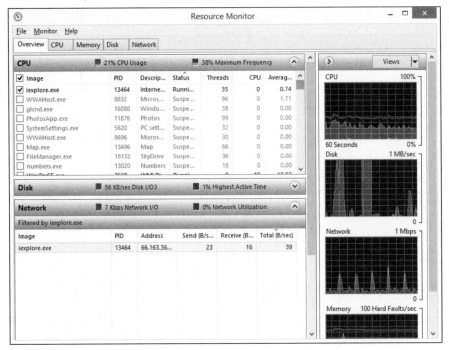

Each of the other tabs in Resource Monitor provides data specific to the specified category. For example, to see detailed information about memory utilization, select the Memory tab. The top area of each tab shows the running processes. You can filter by one or more processes by selecting them from the list. Deselect the Image check box to clear the filter.

Reliability Monitor

Reliability Monitor provides information regarding your system's overall stability. It tracks data and generates a report similar to the one shown in Figure 36.15, which indicates a relative reliability index from 1 to 10. Reliability Monitor uses five groups of information to determine the index, including application failures, Windows failures, miscellaneous failures, warnings, and informational events. To open Reliability Monitor, open Action Center, expand the Maintenance group, and click View Reliability History.

FIGURE 36.15

Reliability Monitor report of overall system stability.

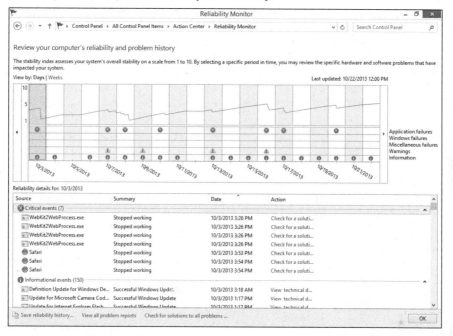

TIP

TIP

Reliability Monitor starts monitoring your system right after the operating system is installed and will keep one year's worth of data for analysis. Reliability Monitor requires 28 days of information before it will accurately determine a stability index. The line in the graph will also be dashed until Reliability Monitor has 28 days of information.

The icons on the chart in Reliability Monitor indicate the type of event that occurred on the specified date. The letter *i* inside a blue circle is an informational event, such as an update being applied successfully to the system. A yellow triangle with an exclamation point inside indicates a warning. An example would be a warning that a driver did not install successfully. Failures are indicated by a white X inside a red circle. Examples include an application hanging or Windows shutting down unexpectedly.

You can view the events for a particular day by clicking that day in the chart. Details for that day appear in the bottom Details pane. When viewing the graph in Weeks view, clicking a week in the graph shows all items for that week in the Details pane. Whichever view you use, double-clicking an item in the Details pane displays full information about the event. For example, Figure 36.16 shows the results of double-clicking an event related to an application hang event.

FIGURE 36.16

Details for an event in Reliability Monitor.

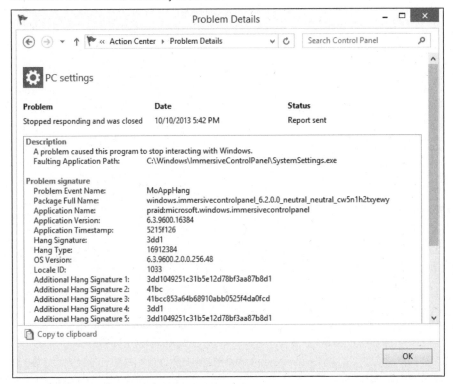

Reliability Monitor is a great tool for keeping track of the events that have occurred with your computer over a long period of time. It can be particularly useful in identifying repetitive problems or problems with specific items.

> **TIP**
>
> Windows ReadyBoost uses flash memory, rather than your hard drive, for the paging file. This allows programs to get drive data more quickly, providing a faster, more fluid computing experience.

Using Windows ReadyBoost

Historically, PCs had two ways to store data: memory and the hard drive. Memory (RAM) is very fast. But it's volatile, meaning everything in it gets erased the moment you shut down the computer. The hard drive isn't nearly as fast. But it has *persistence,* meaning that it retains information even when the computer is turned off.

RAM is also more expensive than hard drive storage. For example, a typical desktop computer might have 2GB of RAM. The hard drive, on the other hand, will likely hold hundreds or even thousands of gigabytes (called a terabyte) of data.

Windows 8.1 automatically uses the paging file (discussed earlier in this chapter) to store the data and conserve RAM.

The downside to using the paging file is that the processor can't move data to and from it as quickly as it can with RAM. The paging file becomes a little performance bottleneck. Prior to Windows Vista, there was no real solution to the problem. Windows Vista introduced a solution called ReadyBoost that lets Windows 8.1 use flash memory for the paging file. For paging file operations, flash memory is about ten times faster than a hard drive, which means ReadyBoost can get rid of many little short delays and offer a faster, smoother overall computing experience. Windows 7 and now Windows 8.1 support ReadyBoost.

> **NOTE**
>
> Contrary to popular belief, ReadyBoost doesn't add more RAM to your computer. It improves performance by using flash memory, rather than the hard drive, to store and access frequently used disk data.
>
> Windows 8.1 takes care of all the potential problems that using flash memory for disk data might impose. For example, it keeps the actual paging file on the drive in sync with the copy on the flash drive. So, if the flash memory suddenly disappears (as when you pull a flash drive out of its USB slot), there's no loss of data. Windows 8.1 even compresses and encrypts the data on the flash drive using high-strength AES encryption. If someone steals a ReadyBoost flash drive from your computer, he won't be able to read data from it to steal sensitive information.

There are basically three ways to get ReadyBoost capabilities in your system:

- Use a *hybrid* hard drive, which puts the flash memory right on the drive.
- Have ReadyBoost capability on the computer's motherboard.
- Use a USB flash drive (a small device, usually small enough to fit on a keychain, which you just plug into a USB 2.0 or 3.0 port on your computer) for ReadyBoost.

Not all flash drives are ReadyBoost-capable. They vary greatly in their capacity and speed. Windows 8.1 will only use a flash drive for ReadyBoost if it makes sense to do so. An 8GB flash drive with fast random I/O capability is a good choice for ReadyBoost.

If you already have a USB flash drive and want to see if it's ReadyBoost-capable, just plug the drive into a USB slot. After Windows 8.1 recognizes and analyzes the drive, you'll get some feedback on the screen letting you know that you can speed up your system by utilizing the available space on your device.

Some systems, such as newer laptops that use solid-state hard drives, will be fast enough that ReadyBoost won't provide any serious performance gains. Figure 36.17 shows an example of the ReadyBoost properties tab for a USB 2.0 flash drive. Notice that using

ReadyBoost would not provide additional performance benefit to laptops or handheld devices. Right-click the USB device in File Explorer and select properties. The ReadyBoost tab as shown in Figure 36.17 lets you know if the USB drive selected can be used for ReadyBoost.

FIGURE 36.17

Windows lets you know if the USB flash drive would not benefit from ReadyBoost.

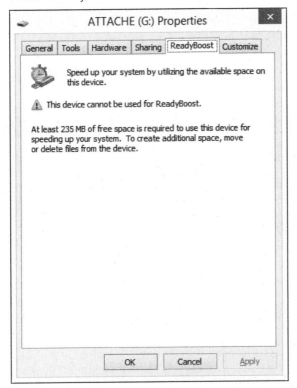

> **NOTE**
>
> ReadyBoost requires that you use a USB 2.0-compliant or higher flash drive. Anything preceding USB 2.0 is too slow to work as a ReadyBoost device.

If you want to use the device as virtual memory, select the Speed Up My System option. After you've selected that option, the properties for the removable disk will pop up. You can also bring up that dialog box by opening your Computer folder, right-clicking the drive's icon, and choosing Properties.

Select the Use This Device option and then you're able to set the amount of space for ReadyBoost. By default, Windows sets the value to the recommended amount and also lets you know that the space you allocate won't be available for general use. When you've set your value, click OK.

ReadyBoost works by copying as much of the information as possible from virtual memory to the USB thumb drive. There is still a copy of all the information within virtual memory; the system now knows to look at the ReadyBoost device first. If the system can't find the information there, it looks to the real virtual memory located on your hard drive. By keeping the original copy on your hard drive, you can remove your USB thumb drive without disrupting the computer.

Don't expect to see everything suddenly run faster with ReadyBoost. Its benefits might not be immediate. *Remember:* The main purpose of ReadyBoost is to eliminate the short delays you might experience when loading certain programs, switching among open programs, and performing other activities that usually involve a paging file. With time, you should experience quicker response times in those areas. You might even find your computer starts more quickly because it takes less time to load programs at startup.

Trading pretty for performance

All the visual effects you see on your screen while using Windows come with a price. It takes CPU resources to show drop-shadows beneath 3D objects, make objects fade into and out of view, and so forth. On an old system that has minimal CPU capabilities and memory, those little visual extras can bog down the system.

To change settings that control visual effects, open Control Panel, select the System link and then select Advanced system settings. The System Properties dialog box will load. Select the Advanced tab and then click the Performance Options Settings button. The Performance Options dialog box shown in Figure 36.18 loads.

FIGURE 36.18

The Visual Effects tab of the Performance Options dialog box.

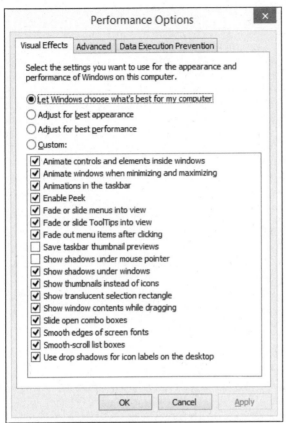

The Visual Effects tab of the Performance Options dialog box lets you choose how much performance you're willing to part with for a "pretty" interface. As shown in Figure 36.18, the Visual Effects tab gives you four main options:

- **Let Windows Choose What's Best for My Computer:** Use this option to enable Windows to automatically choose visual effects based on the capabilities of your computer.

- **Adjust for Best Appearance:** If selected, all visual effects are used, even at the cost of slowing down performance.

- **Adjust for Best Performance:** This option minimizes visual effects to preserve overall speed and responsiveness.

- **Custom:** With this option, you can pick and choose any or all of the visual effects listed beneath the Custom option.

How you choose options is entirely up to you. If you have a powerful system, the visual effects won't impact performance much, if at all. So, there's no need to turn off the visual effects. But if your computer isn't immediately responsive to operations that involve opening and closing menus, dragging, and other things you do on the screen, eliminating some visual effects should help make your computer more responsive.

Maintaining Your Hard Drive

The CPU and RAM are the most important factors for system performance, but your hard drive plays an important role in determining the overall speed of your computer. That's because the hard drive comes into play when you're opening programs or documents, when you're saving documents, or when you're moving and copying files. By moving less-used applications to your hard drive from RAM, it also comes into play when you're running low on RAM. So, keeping the hard drive running as near to peak performance as possible will have a positive impact on system performance.

Recovering wasted hard drive space

At any given time, some of the space on your hard drive is being eaten up by *temporary files.* As the name implies, temporary files are not like the programs you install or documents you save. Programs, apps, and documents are "forever," in the sense that Windows never deletes them at random. The only time a program is deleted, for example, is when you use Programs in the Control Panel to remove the program. Likewise, documents aren't deleted unless you intentionally delete them and also empty the Recycle Bin. Finally, Windows 8.1 apps can be removed from the Windows 8.1 interface.

The files in your *Internet cache,* also called your Temporary Internet Files folder, are good examples of temporary files. Every time you visit a web page, all the text and pictures that make up that page are stored in your Internet cache. When you use the Back or Forward button to revisit a page you've viewed recently, your browser just pulls a copy of the page out of the Internet cache. That saves a lot of time when compared to how long it would take to re-download a page each time you clicked the Back or Forward button to revisit a recently viewed page.

CAUTION

Before you click the Disk Cleanup tool, be forewarned that the process could take several minutes, maybe longer. It's never necessary to use Disk Cleanup to get rid of temporary files.

To recover some wasted disk space, click the Disk Cleanup button on the properties sheet for the hard drive. Open the This PC folder, right-click a drive, and choose Properties. In the Properties dialog box, click the Disk Cleanup button. Disk Cleanup then analyzes the drive for expendable files. Eventually, you'll get to the Disk Cleanup dialog box shown in Figure 36.19. The Files to Delete list shows categories of temporary files. When you click a category name, the Description below the names explains the types of files in that category. All the categories represent temporary files that you can definitely safely delete. There won't ever be any important programs or documents you saved on your own in the list of temporary files.

FIGURE 36.19

The Disk Cleanup dialog box.

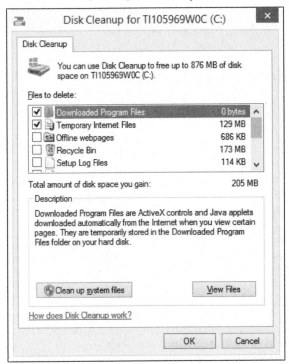

The number to the right of each category name indicates how much drive space the files in that category are using, and how much space you'll gain if you delete them. Choose which categories of files you want to delete by selecting (checking) their check boxes. If you don't want to delete a category of files, clear the check mark for that category. The amount of drive space you'll recover by deleting all the selected categories appears under the list. After you've selected the categories of files you want to delete, click OK. The files are deleted and the dialog box closes.

Deleting system restore files and unwanted features

If you click the Clean Up System Files button in Disk Cleanup, a More Options tab appears on the Disk Cleanup dialog box. Clicking that tab provides two more options for freeing up drive space:

- **Programs and Features:** Takes you to the Programs and Features window, where you can uninstall programs and Windows Features you don't use.

- **System Restore and Shadow Copies:** Deletes all restore points except the most recent one. This can be significant because system protection files are allowed to consume up to 15 percent of your available drive space.

 For more information on removing programs, see Chapter 30. For more information on restore points, see Chapter 24.

Defragmenting and optimizing your hard drive

When a drive is newly formatted, most of the free space on the drive is available in a contiguous chunk. This means the disk *clusters* (the smallest amount of storage space that can be allocated) are side-by-side in contiguous fashion. As Windows writes a file, it can do so in contiguous clusters, writing the entire file in one pass. When it reads the file back, it can also do so in one pass, making drive performance as good as possible.

However, the more a drive is used, the more fragmented the data becomes. Instead of writing data contiguously, Windows writes it here and there on the drive, splitting up the file into fragments (thus, the term *fragmentation*).

> **TIP**
>
> Data is not stored on solid-state hard drives the same way it's stored on traditional hard drives. Because of this, fragmentation of data does not exist, so defragmentation is not necessary for solid-state drives.

When that happens, the drive head has to move around a lot to read and write files. You might even be able to hear the drive chattering when things get really fragmented across the drive. This puts some extra stress on the mechanics of the drive and also slows things down a bit.

To really get things back together and running smoothly, you can *defragment* (or *defrag* for short) the drive. When you do, Windows takes most of the files that are split up into little chunks and brings them all together to make them contiguous again. It also moves most files to the beginning of the drive, where they're easiest to get to. The result is a drive that's no longer fragmented, doesn't chatter as much, and runs faster.

Defragmenting is one of those things you don't really have to do too often. Four or five times a year is probably sufficient. The process could take a few minutes or up to several hours, so it's another one of those tasks that you'll probably want to run overnight. However, note that Windows 8.1, by default, defragments the drive. You can view the current schedule, if any, in the Disk Defragmenter program.

> **TIP**
>
> You don't have to stop using the computer while Windows defragments the drive. You can continue to use it as you normally would. Doing so, however, continues to generate read/write operations on the drive, which ultimately slows down the defragmentation process. For that reason, it's best to run the defragmentation operation while you are not using the computer. See Step 5 in the following list to choose the best time to run optimization.

To defragment a hard drive, starting at the desktop:

1. Open the This PC folder in File Explorer.

2. Right-click the icon for your hard drive (c:), and choose Properties.

3. In the Properties dialog box that opens, select the Tools tab.

4. Click the Optimize button. The Optimize Drives program opens, as shown in Figure 36.20.

> **TIP**
>
> When you see a message that says you don't need to defragment, that doesn't mean that you can't or shouldn't. It just means the drive isn't badly fragmented. But you can still defragment it.

FIGURE 36.20

The Disk Defragmenter default settings.

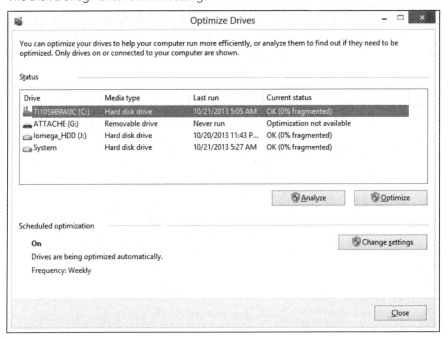

5. In the Optimize Drives dialog box, you're able to set up a schedule to run the optimizer. Click Change Settings to establish that schedule. You also can click the Analyze button to get the current status of the drive and to see if an optimization

process (defragmentation) would be beneficial. The program will start analyzing your drive and may take as little as a few minutes or up to a few hours.

6. When the defragmentation is complete, the Current Status column shows an OK (0% Fragmented) message for the drive you optimized.

When you optimize the drive, the Disk Defragmenter tool defragments all the fragmented files and moves some frequently used files to the beginning of the drive, where they can be accessed in the least time with the least effort. Some files won't be moved. That's normal. If Windows decides to leave them where they are, it's for good reason. You may hear a lot of drive chatter as Disk Defragmenter is working. That's because the drive head is moving things around to get everything into a better position.

When Disk Defragmenter is finished, you can just close any open dialog boxes and the Disk Defragmenter program window.

The Power Settings

The power settings under Power Options in the Control Panel provide features that enable you to adjust the performance of your system while conserving energy. To get to the power options for your system, open the Control Panel. If the Control Panel opens in Category view, click the System and Security link. Then click the Power Options icon. The Power Options applet will open, as shown in Figure 36.21. Click the down arrow beside Show Additional Plans to show the High Performance plan.

FIGURE 36.21

The different options for power settings for a laptop computer.

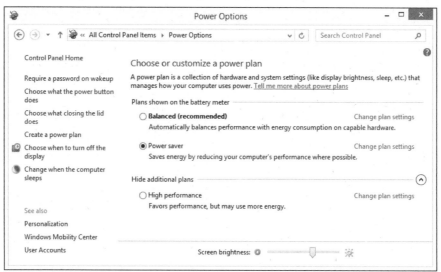

The Power Options applet provides the basic configuration for the power options on your system. The three plans listed — Balanced, Power Saver, and High Performance — are the default power plans for the system. You're able to alter the settings for the three default plans by either clicking the Change Plan Settings link beside the plan or, for the selected plan, clicking either Choose When to Turn Off the Display or Change When the Computer Sleeps from the left column. Clicking any of these links brings up the Edit Plan Settings dialog box shown in Figure 36.22.

FIGURE 36.22

The basic options for setting the power conservation features of Windows 8.1 running on a laptop computer.

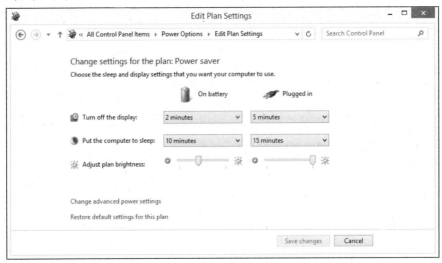

Adjusting either of these options alters the default plan you've selected. Clicking the Change Advanced Power Settings link brings up the Power Options dialog box, which includes the Advanced Settings tab shown in Figure 36.23.

With these options, you're able to drill down on individual options at a more granular level. If you change something that you think you shouldn't have, you can click the Restore Default Settings for This Plan link to get back to where you were. Note that notebook computers have additional power options not typically available on desktops.

FIGURE 36.23

The Advanced Settings tab.

Create a power plan

If none of the default options meets your needs and you'd like to build your own power plan, click the fourth link on the left side of the Power Options applet, Create a Power Plan. Clicking this link brings up the window shown in Figure 36.24.

FIGURE 36.24

The first step to creating your own power plan.

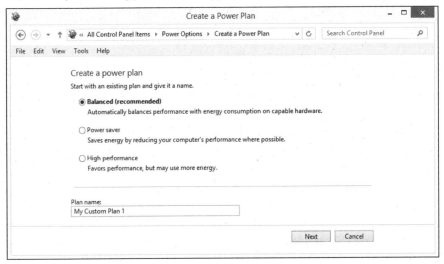

To make it easier, Windows lets you create your power plan from one of the three defaults. You're also able to name the plan on this page. After you've set the name of your plan, click Next. The next window allows you to set when you want to turn off the display and when you want to put the computer to sleep.

After you've configured these last two options, click the Create button. When you're back at the Power Options applet, your plan should be first on the list and selected. If you want to change some of the advanced options in your plans, click the Change Plan Settings link and then click Change Advanced Power Settings, as mentioned earlier in the chapter.

System settings

Clicking the first two links on the left side of the Power Options applet — either Require a Password on Wakeup or Choose What the Power Button Does — takes you to the System Settings page shown in Figure 36.25.

FIGURE 36.25

Options for power buttons and password protection on a laptop computer.

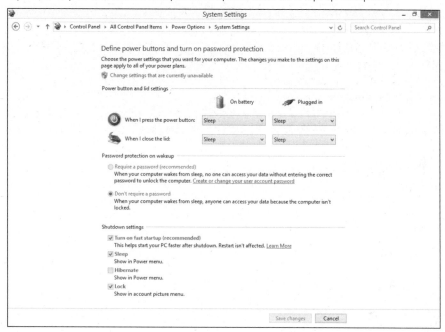

With older computers, when you pressed the power button, the system would power off. With current computers, the power buttons take on a different role. Under the first heading in this window, Power Button Settings, you determine what happens when the power button is pushed. You're given two options:

- **Sleep:** If you select this option, the data you're working on will be stored in memory and to the hard drive. The system will run using very little power until you press the keyboard or move the mouse. On a notebook computer, when Windows notices that the system is running low on battery power, Windows starts writing the information to the hard drive. Upon restarting, the system moves all the information from the hard drive to memory, just as the system was left originally. Usually, it takes two to three seconds to bring the computer back from Sleep. Sleep mode is not limited to notebooks. Most newer desktop computers also support it.

- **Shut Down:** This selection shuts down the computer without saving any of the data you have in memory. Windows prompts you to save your work before you shut down. This method does a graceful shutdown of Windows.

After you've determined which option you want, click the Save Changes button.

On the System Settings window, you're also able to set the password option for what happens when the computer wakes up. As indicated by the text next to each of the options, when your system wakes from Sleep, the user may be prompted for a password. Obviously, the more secure option is to use a password. However, if this is your home system and you're the only one with physical access to the system, the second option is good enough.

> **NOTE**
>
> The settings described in this section are the most common settings based on the hardware. For instance, if you're using a laptop, you may have two additional or different options on the left side of the Power Options window: Choose What Closing the Lid Does and Choose What Power Buttons Do. These options are specific to the system and offer additional options for power management.

With all the power options available in Windows 8.1, you should be able to conserve resources on your system while still making your system very responsive. The power options will probably benefit a portable user more than a desktop user.

Wrap-Up

The components of your computer system that most affect performance are its CPU and memory, but hard drive performance also affects overall system performance. (Internet access speed is determined primarily by the bandwidth of your Internet connection but can also be affected by slow system performance.) As an alternative to buying a faster computer, you can do some things to make your current computer run faster and keep it running at top speed. The main points in this chapter are as follows:

- The System Information program provides detailed information about all the components that make up your computer system.

- To ensure that your computer is responsive to your every mouse click and keyboard tap, Windows automatically prioritizes programs as foreground (high-priority) and background (low-priority) tasks.

- When your system runs out of physical memory (RAM), Windows automatically uses a portion of the hard drive as virtual memory to handle the overflow.

- ReadyBoost uses flash memory to store frequently accessed disk files to provide a faster, more fluid computing experience.

- If your computer is usually sluggish and unresponsive, consider turning off some of Windows 8.1's visual effects.

- The speed of your hard drive determines how long it takes to open and save files.

- To keep your hard drive running at top speed, consider deleting temporary files, scanning for and fixing bad sectors, and defragmenting the drive once or twice a month depending on how much time you spend at the computer.

- Power settings play a role in your system's overall performance and can also be adjusted to conserve power, especially when using a laptop.

Troubleshooting Hardware and Performance

IN THIS CHAPTER

Troubleshooting common hardware and device driver issues

Troubleshooting startup issues using System Recovery Options

Troubleshooting slow or unresponsive system performance

This chapter discusses the components of your computer and addresses some common problems and their solutions. Additionally, you'll find information for troubleshooting Bluetooth connectivity. Finally, we provide information for troubleshooting general performance issues.

First Aid for Troubleshooting Hardware

Whenever you have a hardware problem that's causing a device to misbehave or just not work at all, finding an updated driver is usually your best bet. But even before you do that, you might want to try Windows' built-in troubleshooting tools to see if they can resolve the problem.

To get help on programs, hardware, and drivers, open the Troubleshooting applet from the Control Panel (see Figure 37.1). Once you have the applet open, you can click on a number of categories. Each of the items in this Control Panel applet provides a troubleshooting wizard that can automatically search for, detect, and potentially fix problems. The applet offers the following groups:

FIGURE 37.1

The Troubleshooting applet provides options for troubleshooting hardware and driver issues.

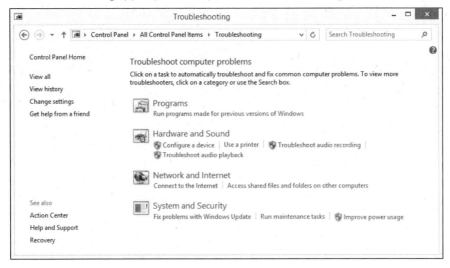

- **Programs:** Launch the Program Compatibility Troubleshooter, which enables you to apply settings to programs to make them run as if they were running in an earlier version of Windows. For example, you can potentially run a Windows XP program under Windows 8.1 by configuring its compatibility settings for Windows XP. This troubleshooting group also provides help for Internet Explorer issues, printer issues, and Media Player problems.

- **Hardware and Sound:** Use the Hardware and Sound item to scan for hardware changes and troubleshoot problems with general devices, printers, network adapters, and audio devices.

- **Network and Internet:** Troubleshoot problems connecting to the Internet or accessing shared files and folders on a local area network. Also troubleshoot Homegroup, incoming network connections, and DirectAccess.

- **System and Security:** Troubleshoot problems with Windows Update, modify power settings, check for computer performance issues, and run maintenance tasks, including cleaning up unused files and shortcuts. Also, check search and indexing problems, and adjust performance settings.

The Troubleshooting applet lists only some of the items for each category. Click the group name (such as Hardware and Sound or Network and Internet) to see all the troubleshooting tools for that category. Figure 37.2, for example, shows the System and Security category.

FIGURE 37.2

The System and Security category.

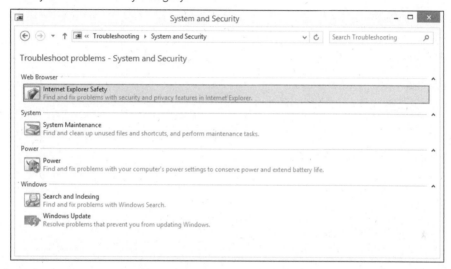

> **TIP**
>
> Make sure to leave enabled the option at the bottom of the Troubleshooting window, Get the Most Up-to-Date Troubleshooters from the Windows Online Troubleshooting Service, to allow Windows to update the troubleshooters as new or modified ones become available.

An alternative is to troubleshoot from the hardware device's Properties dialog box in Device Manager. To open Device Manager, press Windows + X and click Device Manager. If you're on the Start screen, simply start typing **dev**, click Settings, and then click Device Manager. You also can show the Charms Bar, type **dev**, click Settings, and click Device Manager. In Device Manager:

1. Right-click the name of the device that's causing problems and choose Properties.

2. If the device shows an error in the Device Manager (see Figure 37.3), use that information to begin troubleshooting. For example, if Device Manager indicates that there is no driver installed, try installing or reinstalling the device's driver.

FIGURE 37.3

Use Device Manager to help troubleshoot hardware problems.

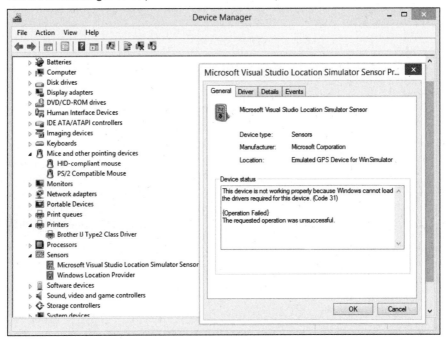

3. If needed, use the options on the Driver tab to reinstall the drivers for the device. You can also disable the device from this tab and eliminate potential conflicts with other devices.

4. On the Resources tab (see Figure 37.4), check for a conflict message under Conflicting Device List and resolve problems by reassigning resources to the conflicting devices, or by disabling one of them. Note that not all hardware devices will have a Resources tab.

FIGURE 37.4

The Resources tab.

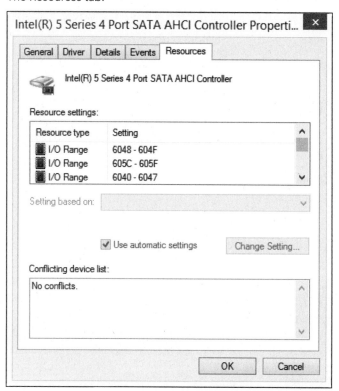

TIP

If you've made a hardware change but Windows hasn't noticed the change, open Device Manager and choose Action ⇨ Scan for Hardware Changes to have Windows rescan the system.

Dealing with Error Messages

Error messages come in all forms, from simple warnings to the *stop errors* and the blue screen of death, which causes the computer to stop dead in its tracks. If you were a user of Windows 7, you more than likely saw a decrease in the number of blue screen events. In Windows 8.1, that same pattern will more than likely follow — Windows 8.1 seems to be a stable operating system.

The more serious errors are often accompanied by one or more of the following pieces of information:

- **An error number:** An error number will often be a hexadecimal number in the format 0x00000*xxx* where the *xxx* could be any numbers in the message.

- **Symbolic error name:** Symbolic error names are usually shown in all uppercase with underlines between words, such as PAGE_FAULT_IN_NONPAGED_AREA.

- **Driver details:** If a device driver caused the problem, you might see a filename with a `.sys` extension in the error message.

- **Troubleshooting info:** Some errors will have their own built-in troubleshooting advice, or a Help button. Use that information to learn more about what went wrong.

Whenever you get an error message about a problem that you can't solve just by reading the advice presented on the screen, go to `http://support.microsoft.com` and search for the error number, or the symbolic error name, the driver name, or some combination of words in the text or troubleshooting of the error message.

If searching Microsoft's support site doesn't do the trick, consider searching the entire Internet using Google or Bing. You never know — someone out there may have had the same problem and posted the solution somewhere. When using a search engine, provide as much detail as possible to get the best results for your problem.

> **TIP**
>
> Odd as it might seem, a Google search will often turn up pages on Microsoft's own support site that can be difficult to find when searching at the Microsoft site. You can include "site:support.microsoft.com" in the search criteria in Google to help narrow down your search results to the Microsoft Support site.

Performing a Clean Boot

The biggest problem with hardware errors is that even a tiny error can have seemingly catastrophic results, such as suddenly shutting down the system and making it difficult to get the system started again. Clean booting can also help with software problems that prevent the computer from starting normally or cause frequent errors.

Not for the technologically challenged, this procedure is best left to more experienced users who can use it to diagnose the source of a problem that's preventing the computer from starting normally. The procedure for performing a clean boot is as follows:

> **NOTE**
>
> A clean boot is not the same as a clean install. During a clean boot, you may temporarily lose some normal functionality. But once you perform a normal startup, you should regain access to all your programs and documents, and full functionality.

1. Close all open programs and save any work in progress.

2. At the Windows desktop, press Windows +X, click Run, and enter **msconfig**.

3. The System Configuration tool opens, as shown in Figure 37.5.

FIGURE 37.5

System Configuration.

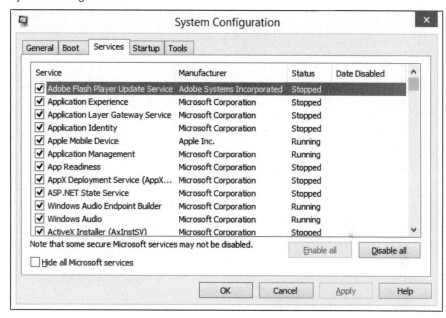

4. On the General tab, choose Selective Startup and make sure the Load Startup Items check box is cleared.

5. Click the Services tab.

6. Select Hide All Microsoft Services and click the Disable All button.

7. Click OK.

8. Click the Restart button.

To return to normal startup after diagnosis, open the System Configuration tool. On the Services tab, click Enable All. On the General tab, choose Normal Startup and click OK.

Using the System Recovery Options

For more severe problems that require repairing an existing Windows 8.1 installation, troubleshooting startup issues, performing system and complete PC restoration, using the Windows Memory Diagnostic Tool, or getting to a command prompt, you'll need to use the System Recovery Options. This method should only be used by experienced users who can perform such tasks from a command prompt.

To boot from the Windows disk, first make sure that the drive is enabled as a boot device in the BIOS with a higher priority than any hard drives. Insert the Windows disk into the drive. Restart the computer and follow these steps:

1. During the POST, watch for the Press Any Key to Boot From CD or DVD prompt, and tap a key.

2. After all files load from the disk, click the Next button on the page that is prompting for language, currency, and keyboard type.

3. On the next page, click the Repair Your Computer link near the bottom of the page.

4. Windows opens the System Recovery Options dialog box, which looks for an existing installation of Windows 8.1. If your system requires special hard drive controller drivers, you can click the Load Drivers button so your installation of Windows 8.1 can be located. If you see your version of Windows 8.1 in the list box, select it and click the Next button.

5. The next window shows all your options for recovery.

The System Recovery Options window provides different troubleshooting tools based on your set of circumstances:

- **Startup Repair:** Use this option if your system won't start up. This could be for any number of reasons, including a bad or misconfigured driver, an application that attempts to start at startup but causes the system to hang, or a faulty piece of hardware.

- **System Restore:** System Restore restores back to a designated restore point. By default, Windows is making restore points of your computer that store the state of your system. You'll be able to choose a restore point for your system from a previous day when you knew your system was performing correctly. The System Restore option doesn't alter any of your personal data or documents.

- **System Image Recovery:** For this feature to work, you need to have done a backup in the past. Windows searches hard drives and DVDs for valid backups to restore from. See Chapter 24 for information on backing up your system.

- **Windows Memory Diagnostic:** Some of the issues you may be experiencing may be the result of memory problems. Windows Memory Diagnostic Tool performs tests against the RAM in your system to see if there are any problems. For this tool to run, click the link, which will prompt you to restart your computer now and check for problems or to check for problems the next time you restart.

- **Command Prompt:** The Command Prompt option is for experienced users who need to access the file system and run commands specific to Windows 8.1. Choose this option only if you're sure you need it, and be careful when using the Command Prompt.

When you're finished using the System Recovery Options, you can click either Shut Down or Restart to exit. For additional information on System Recovery Options, use Help and Support and search on "System Recovery Options."

Troubleshooting Performance Problems

This section covers basic troubleshooting in terms of using Task Manager and Control Panel tools to monitor and troubleshoot performance. Keep in mind that hardware and software go hand in hand, so performance problems can be caused by either one. For example, if a device is malfunctioning or improperly configured, it can lead to performance problems. Likewise, having too many programs running at one time can eat up valuable memory and processor time, also foiling performance. So, don't assume that performance problems are always caused by hardware or software — the problem could well be one, the other, or both.

If your CPU Usage chart consistently runs at a high percentage in Task Manager, it may point to the running of two or more firewalls. Most likely, you'll need to disable and remove any third-party firewalls, or disable the built-in Windows Firewall.

Also, scan your system for viruses, adware, and other malware, and remove all that you can find to eliminate their resource consumption.

If neither of the previous suggestions fixes your problem, you may need to see if an individual process is keeping your system overly busy. To do this, use one of these methods to start Task Manager:

- With Windows running and while logged on to the computer, press Ctrl+Alt+Del and click Start Task Manager.
- Press Windows+X, click Run, and type **taskmgr** to locate and start Task Manager.
- Right-click the taskbar and click Start Task Manager.

Once you're in Task Manager, click More Details, and select the Processes tab. Next, sort the CPU column, as shown in Figure 37.6. Just click the CPU column to sort by CPU utilization.

> **TIP**
> If a task is spiking CPU utilization but not staying at a consistently high rate, first identify the processes by sorting by CPU. Then, when you've determined which processes are using the most CPU time, sort by process name to watch how those processes are using the CPU.

FIGURE 37.6

Task Manager sorting the processes based on CPU percentage

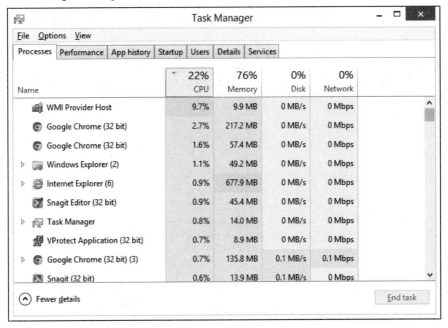

You should be able to identify the process that is using the majority of your CPU. You have a couple options at this point:

- Use the name of the process under the Name column to search the Internet to see if the process is a valid file or a potential virus. If it is a virus of some form, you'll need to update your virus definitions and rerun your virus scan. If it does not appear to be a virus, you'll need to contact the software vendor for help troubleshooting the problem.

- Short term, you can right-click the process and choose End Task. Sometimes applications run into problems or situations the developer never imagined and the process gets stuck in a loop, which taxes the CPU. Restarting the application resets the process, and with any luck, you'll avoid the circumstances that put the application in a loop.

Wrap-Up

Many thousands of hardware devices are available that you can use with Windows, and no single rule applies to troubleshooting all of them. So, you'll likely have to consider all your resources. Be sure to check the manual that came with the hardware device first. If that doesn't work, the device manufacturer's website will likely be your next best bet.

Part IX

Networking and Sharing

Creating a Home Network

IN THIS CHAPTER

Understanding why you create a network

Creating a traditional Ethernet network

Creating a wireless network

Setting up a wired network

Setting up a wireless network

I f you have two or more computers, you may already be using what's known as a *sneaker network*. For example, to get files from one computer to another, you copy files to a flash drive or CD. Then, you walk over to the other computer and copy the files from the disk to that computer. Wouldn't it be nice if you could just drag icons from one computer to the other without having to use a flash drive or CD?

What if you have several computers, but only one printer, one Internet connection, or one DVD burner? Wouldn't it be nice if all the computers could use that one printer, that one Internet connection, and that one DVD burner? All these things are possible if you connect the computers to one another in a *local area network* (LAN) or a private wireless network (WiFi).

After you've purchased and installed networking hardware, you're ready to set up your network. Windows 8.1 includes features that remove the complexities commonly associated with network configurations.

This chapter describes how to configure Windows for different types of hardware setups. Remember that you should always follow the instructions that came with your networking hardware first. After all, those instructions are written for the exact products you've purchased.

What Is a LAN?

A *local area network* (sometimes referred to as a LAN, a workgroup, a private network, or just a network) is a small group of computers within a relatively small geographic area such as a campus, single building, or household that can communicate with one another and share *resources*. A resource is anything useful to the computer. For example:

- All computers in the LAN can use a single printer.
- All computers in the LAN can connect to the Internet through a single Internet connection and Internet account.
- All computers in the LAN can access shared files and folders on any other computer in the LAN.

In addition, you can move and copy files and folders among computers using exactly the same techniques you use to move and copy files among folders on a single computer. However, it's not entirely necessary to move or copy a document that you want to work on, because if a document is in a shared folder, you can open and edit it from any computer in the network. This is good because you have only one copy of the document, and you don't have to worry about having multiple, slightly different copies of the same document all over the place to confuse matters.

Planning a LAN

To create a LAN, you need a plan and special hardware to make that plan work. For one thing, each computer will need a device known as a *network interface card* (NIC) or *Ethernet card*. You can purchase and install those yourself. Many PCs, however, come with an Ethernet card already installed for connecting to a wired network. In that case, you'll have an RJ-45 port on the back of the computer. It looks a lot like the plug for a telephone, just a little bigger. You just plug one end of an Ethernet cable into that port, and plug the other end of the cable into a network hub or wall jack. You can also connect computers without any cables at all by using wireless networking hardware. Exactly what you need, in terms of hardware, depends on what you want to do. The rest of this chapter describes your options.

Creating a Wired LAN

If you have two or more computers to connect, and they're all in the same room and close to one another, you can use a traditional Ethernet hub and Ethernet cables to connect the computers with cables. You'll need exactly one NIC and one Ethernet cable for each computer in the LAN. Figure 38.1 shows an example of four computers connected in a traditional LAN. Notice how each computer connects to the hub only — no cables run directly from one computer to another computer.

FIGURE 38.1

Four computers connected in a traditional Ethernet LAN.

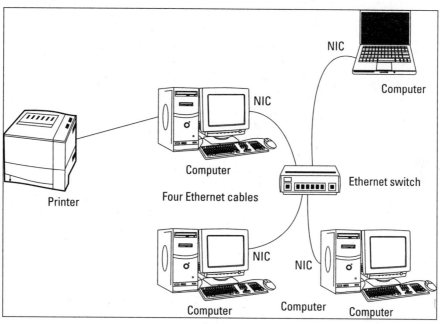

By the way, in Figure 38.1 a printer can be connected to any computer on the LAN. In fact, you could have several printers connected to several computers. All computers will be able to use all printers, no matter which computer that printer is (or those printers are) connected to. In addition, a printer with a network interface need not be connected to a computer at all, but rather can be connected directly to the network.

Traditional Ethernet speeds

When it comes time to purchase network interface cards, cables, and a hub, you'll need to decide on the speed you want. As with everything else in the computer industry, network speed costs money. However, in the case of networks, the cost differences are minor, whereas the speed differences are huge. The three possible speeds for Ethernet LANs are listed in Table 38.1.

TABLE 38.1   Common Ethernet Network Component Speeds

Name	Transfer Rate (speed)	Bits per Second	Cable
10Base-T	10 Mbps	10 million	Category 3 or better
100Base-T	100 Mbps	100 million	Category 5 or better
Gigabit Ethernet	1 Gbps	1,000 million (billion)	Category 6 or better

If it's difficult to relate the numbers to actual transfer rates, consider a dial-up modem, which tops out at about 50 Kbps. That's 51,000 bits per second. A 100Base-T network moves 100,000,000 bits per second. That's 2,000 times faster or, in other words, you only have to wait 1/2,000 as long for the same file to transfer across a 100Base-T connection. So, a file that takes 33 minutes (2,000 seconds) to transfer over a dial-up modem takes 1 second to transfer over a 100Base-T network.

> **TIP**
>
> It's possible to set up a 10 Gbps network that operates at ten times the speed of a 1 Gbps network. However, 10 Gbps network hardware is still generally much more expensive than 1 Gbps hardware, making it a less likely candidate for a home or small office network. For that reason, we don't cover 10 Gbps networks in this chapter.

The slowest component rules

When purchasing hardware, it's important to understand that the slowest component always rules. For example, if you get gigabit Ethernet cards, but connect them to a 100Base-T hub, the LAN will run at 100 Mbps. The faster gigabit NICs can't force the slower hub to move any faster.

It makes sense if you envision the electrons going through the wire as cars on a freeway. Let's say lots of cars are zooming down a ten-lane freeway, but there's some road construction where the freeway narrows to one lane. Cars are going to pile up behind that point because the one-lane portion is slowing things down. Where the one lane reopens back to ten lanes, cars will still be trickling out of the *bottleneck* — the single lane — one at a time. The ten lanes at the other side of the bottleneck can't "suck the cars through" the bottleneck any faster than one car at a time.

Likewise, if your computers are connected together with a gigabit LAN, but they all share a single 512 Kbps broadband connection to the Internet, your Internet connection is still 512 Kbps. Your fast LAN can't force the data from your ISP to get to your computer any faster than 512 Kbps. Furthermore, if two people are using the 512 Kbps broadband connection at the same time, they have to share the available bandwidth, meaning that each user might get only a portion of the available bandwidth. But if only one person is online, she gets the full 512 Kbps because she's not sharing bandwidth with anyone else.

> **NOTE**
>
> If you have only two computers to connect, and each has an Ethernet card, you don't really need a hub. Instead, you can connect the two computers directly using an Ethernet *crossover cable*. However, this won't enable the computers to connect to anything other than one another.

Creating a Wireless Network

Wireless networking reigns supreme when it comes to convenience and ease of use. As the name implies, with wireless networks you don't have to run any cables. Plus, no computer is tied down to any one cable. For example, you can use your notebook computer in any room in the house, or even out on the patio, and still have Internet access without being tied to a cable.

To set up a wireless network, you need a wireless NIC for each computer that you want to connect using wireless. To set up an ad-hoc wireless network, that's all you need. The computers can communicate with each other, so long as they're within range of one another. If you want Internet connectivity for all the computers in a wireless LAN, you'll need some kind of access point that acts as a central location for all the computers and also provides an Internet connection. Typically, that device would be a wireless broadband router, as illustrated in Figure 38.2.

FIGURE 38.2

Four computers connected in a wireless network.

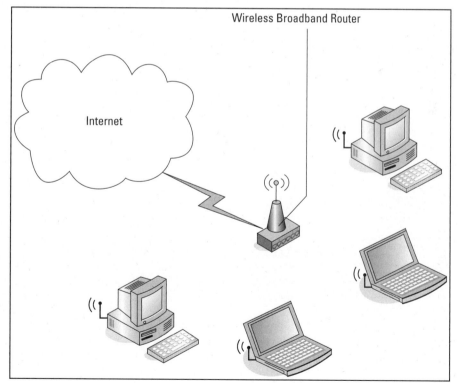

Wireless broadband router

The big advantage of wireless networking is, of course, the lack of cables. This is especially handy on a notebook computer or handheld device because the device isn't tethered to one location by a cable. Granted, you can't stray too far from the wireless access point (100 to 150 feet or so), but that will probably be sufficient in most cases.

Also, many universities and retail businesses offer public Internet access from any computer that has an 802 class (802.11b, 802.11g, 802.11n, and so on) wireless network interface. So, if you create your home wireless network using one of those standards, you'll also be able to use public Wi-Fi Internet access where it's available.

> **TIP**
>
> The only disadvantages to wireless networking, as compared to wired networks, are speed and reliability. 802.11g wireless networks run at a theoretical max of 54 Mbps. It's not as fast as the 100 Mbps or 1 Gbps speeds of traditional Ethernet cables, but it's still more than fast enough for typical networking tasks. Reliability isn't a problem with the technology, per se. Instead, it has to do with the rare "blind spot" here and there where the computer just won't connect to the network because the signal is blocked or it's out of range.

Wireless networks are built around four different standards. Table 38.2 summarizes the main differences between the four most common standards in use today. The Public Access column refers to Internet Wi-Fi hotspots such as those found at some airports, hotels, and other places.

TABLE 38.2 Wireless Networking Standards and Speeds

Standard	Speed	Range	Public Access
802.11b	11 Mbps	100–150 feet	Yes
802.11a	54 Mbps	25–75 feet	No
802.11g	54 Mbps	100–150 feet	Yes
802.11n	600 Mbps	150–300 feet	Yes

In most cases, when setting up your network you're really setting up two networks. The first network involves the computer-to-computer communication. This includes the wireless setup or a wired setup discussed earlier in the chapter. The second network is the Internet. Connecting to the Internet involves some form of an ISP. Today, two of the most popular methods are Digital Subscriber Line (DSL) modem connections and (more likely) broadband connections, which your cable TV company may be able to supply. If you're sharing an Internet connection, one device in your network will have physical access to the Internet, and the other computers will share the connection. The one device that actually sees the Internet can be a computer, or you can purchase an inexpensive device that connects to the Internet called a *broadband router*.

Other useful wireless goodies

If you already have a wired network with Internet connectivity and you just want to add some wireless computers to that network, you don't need a wireless broadband router. Instead, you need a *wireless access point* (WAP). First, you'll need to configure the WAP, as per the manufacturer's instructions, by connecting it directly to one of the computers in your wired network. Then you can disconnect the WAP from the computer and connect it directly to the switch for your wireless network. The wireless computer can use the same shared Internet connection that the wired network uses.

Getting a wireless network to cover a whole house can be a challenge, especially if you have two or more floors. If you want to extend Wi-Fi to the entire house, you may need to use one or more *wireless range expanders* to extend the reach of the network. Putting one near the staircase is a good idea when you need to reach upstairs or downstairs. You can also use multiple access points to achieve the same results.

A Wi-Fi finder can also be helpful. It's a small device (small enough to fit on a keychain) that measures the strength of a wireless network signal at wherever you're standing. It can help you determine where the edge of a signal is, which is a good place to put a range expander to get more coverage.

Acquiring and Installing Network Hardware

Almost all PCs manufactured in the last several years have networking capability built in. So, it's unlikely that you'll need to buy NICs for your devices. If you need one for a desktop PC and you aren't comfortable working inside the computer, just buy a USB network adapter. If you're not sure, check with your local PC dealer.

If you're new to all this and you just want to see what some of this stuff looks like, here are some websites you can visit. They're all network hardware manufacturers, not retailers:

- **D-Link:** www.d-link.com
- **GigaFast:** www.gigafast.com
- **Linksys:** http://www.linksys.com/en-us/home
- **Netgear:** www.netgear.com
- **SMC Networks:** www.smc.com
- **TRENDnet:** www.trendnet.com

In terms of actually purchasing the products, you can find these products at any store that sells computer supplies, including many of the large office supply chains such as Staples and OfficeMax. Of course, you can buy the devices online at any website that sells computer stuff. Shopping jaunts include websites such as www.amazon.com, www.cdw.com, www.cyberguys.com, www.officemax.com, www.staples.com, www.tigerdirect.com, and www.walmart.com, just to name a few.

After you've acquired the hardware, you need to install it. We can't help you much there either. You'll have to follow the manufacturer's instructions on that one because there is no one-rule-fits-all when it comes to installing hardware. As a general rule of thumb, you'll probably want to

- Get the hub or router (if any) set up first.
- Install the network interface cards second.
- Connect all the cables last.

Once all the hardware is connected and installed, you're ready to set up the network. That part isn't so complicated because Windows does a great job of searching out networks. You work through that next.

After the Hardware Setup

A couple steps are involved in actually setting up the networking hardware. First, make sure that the hardware you purchased is installed based on the manufacturer's instructions. This may include plugging in the device, then connecting the device to the Internet, and finally plugging in the other computers to the device. When this is complete, you can run the Set Up a New Connection or Network Wizard to let Windows finish the process.

> **CAUTION**
>
> Read and follow the network hardware manufacturer's instructions carefully before you configure your network. If there's any conflict between what they say and what's stated in this chapter, do as the manufacturer's instructions say. Failure to do so could lead to many hours of hair-pulling frustration!

Close any open programs and documents before you start configuring your network. The type of network hardware you have set up will determine what configuration you'll need to use. Here's where to look, depending on your network configuration:

- **If you have an Ethernet network, and you're using a modem inside of, or connected to, one computer in the network,** you can use Internet connection sharing (ICS) to share a single Internet account. Because this scenario isn't very common anymore, we don't cover it in this book. Search the web for "Internet connection sharing" for details.
- **If you have a router or residential gateway that all computers in your network connect to,** each computer will have its own direct access to the Internet via the router. See the section "Setting Up a Wired Network," later in this chapter.

- **If you have a wireless network,** see the section "Setting Up a Wireless Network," later in this chapter.

- **If you want to set up a Bluetooth personal area network,** see Chapter 35.

> **NOTE**
>
> In the past, the term *residential gateway* typically referred to networking devices that were relatively low cost networking devices that combined most or all of the devices needed to connect a LAN to a wide area network (WAN) such as the Internet. Today, the term is used to describe essentially the same type of device, but today's gateways offer much more capability than older devices. An example of a residential gateway is a cable modem that includes a hub and provides everything you need to connect your LAN to a cable-based Internet service. Another example is a wireless access point that includes a hub and integrated DSL modem. For the purposes of this chapter, we use the term *gateway* to refer to the device that connects your LAN to your Internet service. If you're not sure what you need to connect your LAN to the Internet, check with your local computer store.

Be sure to turn off all computers before you install the networking hardware (unless you're installing a USB adapter). Then install all the networking hardware and turn on all the computers. Chances are, Windows 8.1 will detect the hardware and start setting things up automatically. If you see any prompts asking what type of network you're installing, make sure you specify that it's a *private* network (not a public network). When asked about file sharing, make sure you make choices that allow for file and printer sharing among computers in the private network.

With those buzzwords and tips in mind, let's move on to the specifics of things to do after you get all the network hardware in place and all the computers turned on.

Setting Up a Wired Network

With a wired network, your first step after setting up the hardware and connecting the PCs to the hub (or gateway device that contains the hub) will usually be to get online from one computer. You'll need to refer to instructions that came with your router, as well as your ISP's instructions, to do that. In a typical scenario, however, you configure the router or gateway to automatically assign an IP address, default gateway address, and DNS addresses to your computers. Then you configure your devices for automatic address assignment. The computers should then receive their addresses (generally no need to reboot them) and have access to the network and the Internet.

> **TIP**
>
> While the computers on the network should have access to the Internet at this point, they won't necessarily have access to one another's resources such as files and printers. Instead, you need to configure sharing. See Chapter 39 to learn how to set up your computers to share resources.

38

After connecting and configuring your PCs, Windows attempts to find the network for you. To see where you stand, follow these steps:

1. Open the Control Panel.

2. If the Control Panel opens in Category view, click the Network and Internet icon.

3. Open the View Network Status and Tasks link below Network and Sharing Center.

   As shown in Figure 38.3, the system is connected to a local network and to the Internet.

4. If the connection doesn't show Internet as the access type, check your gateway configuration and make sure your settings are correct.

In Figure 38.3, Windows sees the local network and also sees the Internet connection from the local network. If your networking hardware is configured correctly, Windows sees the network and sets it up for you appropriately.

If you're working from the Start screen, you can also see your connection status, although with less detail. Open the Charms Bar and click Settings; then click Network. Figure 38.4 shows an example.

FIGURE 38.3

A computer connected to the network and also connected to the Internet.

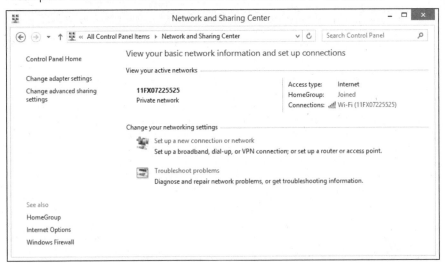

FIGURE 38.4

View the network status from the Charms Bar.

If your network is configured correctly for the first computer, try configuring your next system on the network using the steps outlined earlier.

If you have wireless devices that you want to connect to the network, follow the instructions in the next section.

Setting Up a Wireless Network

There's something about the term *wireless* that makes it seem as though it must be easier than *wired*. In truth, wireless networking is quite a bit more complicated terminology-wise. There are lots of buzzwords and acronyms everyone assumes that you already know. So, before we get into this topic, let's get all that out of the way.

The 802.11 standard

The Institute of Electrical and Electronics Engineers, Inc., abbreviated IEEE (pronounced eye-triple-E), is an organization of some 360,000 electrical engineers who develop many of the standards that PC products use to interact with one another. The IEEE isn't big on giving fancy names to things. They prefer numbers (which somehow seems fitting). Names often get tacked on later. For example, what is now called *Ethernet* is actually IEEE 802.3. What Apple calls FireWire and Sony calls iLink is actually IEEE 1394.

NOTE

The home page for IEEE is at `www.ieee.org`.

IEEE created the 802.11 standard for most wireless networking today. Several revisions to the original specification have been proposed, with 802.11a, 802.11b, 802.11g, and 802.11n are the most common (802.22 is the latest standard in use). Most likely, you'll be using 802.11g or 802.11n because they're the standard to which most of the recently released wireless networking products adhere.

Access point, SSID, WEP, and WPA

Wireless networking requires some kind of *wireless access point,* also called a *base station.* The base station is the central unit with which all computers in the network communicate. It's the same idea as a hub in Ethernet networking. It's just that there are no wires connecting computers to the access point. Instead, each computer has a wireless network interface card (NIC), as illustrated in Figure 38.5.

FIGURE 38.5

Wireless communications all go through an access point or base station.

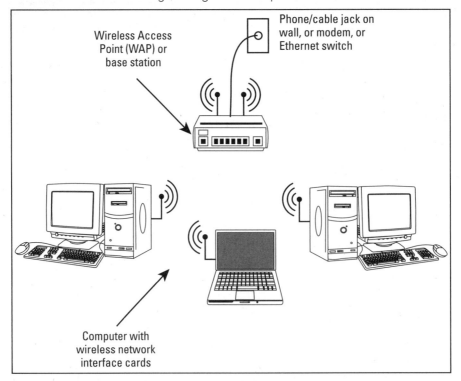

The access point in a wireless network plays the same role as the hub in a wired network in that all traffic goes to the access point first and is passed on to the appropriate destination from there. The problem is that, with wireless networks, you have radio waves, which aren't confined to the inside of a wire. Radio waves go all over the place, just as when you throw a rock in the water and make waves that spread out in a circle.

The radio waves can be a problem when you have multiple wireless networks that are close to each other. For example, let's say that a company has several departments, and each department has its own, separate wireless network.

To avoid that problem, you need some means of discriminating among multiple wireless access points. For example, you need some means of setting rules such as "these six computers in the marketing department communicate only with each other through access point X, while these 12 computers in the accounting department communicate with each other only through access point Z." The way you do that in today's wireless networking is through things such as network names, SSID, WEP, and WPA.

About SSIDs

Every wireless network has a unique name called a *service set identifier* (SSID), or just a *wireless network name* for simplicity. The access point in the network holds the SSID When you start a wireless network computer, it scans the airwaves for SSID. When you set up a wireless network access point (by reading the manufacturer's instructions, of course), you assign an SSID to your access point.

38

> **TIP**
>
> You can configure a WAP to not broadcast its SSID, which adds an extra measure of security for your wireless network. Rather than search for available wireless networks, you'll have to manually specify the network SSID when setting up the wireless connection on your device.

The name you assign doesn't have to be anything fancy, but it should be unique enough to avoid conflict with any close neighbors who also have wireless networks. The SSID doesn't provide any real network security. After all, the access point broadcasts the SSID out some distance from the access point. So, if some hackers happened to be driving by with a notebook computer, they might be able to pick up the name of your wireless LAN from the car. Then they could join your network and receive data being sent by computers in your network. WEP and WPA are encryption tools designed to avoid such intrusions.

About WEP and WPA

Wired Equivalent Privacy (WEP) is a wireless security protocol that protects wireless network data from falling into the wrong hands. Before any information leaves your computer, it's encrypted using a WEP key. The key is a simple string of characters that you can generate automatically, or have Windows generate for you.

Wi-Fi Protected Access (WPA) is a newer and stronger encryption system that supports modern EAP security devices such as smart cards, certificates, token cards, one-time passwords, and biometric devices. WPA2 adds support for the AES encryption algorithm, which provides better security than WPA. If your wireless devices support WPA2, you should use that rather than WPA.

Installing the wireless networking hardware

The most critical step in setting up a wireless network is installing the hardware devices. It's imperative that you follow the instructions that came with the device to the letter because guessing almost never works. In particular, it's important to note that even devices that plug into a hot-pluggable port such as USB devices or a PC Card need you to install drives *before* you install the hardware device. That's unusual for hot-pluggable devices, and most people just assume that they can plug in the device and go. But it just doesn't work that way with wireless networking devices.

Connecting to available networks

The main trick to wireless networking is setting up the access point. Typically, you do this by configuring one computer with a static IP address and connecting it to the access point with a wired connection. With both the computer and WAP on the same IP subnet, you can then open a browser and connect to the WAP's web-based configuration pages. Then you configure the access point from that computer. You give the network its name (SSID) and choose your encryption method. The access point then begins transmitting that name at regular intervals.

On any computer that's to join the wireless LAN, you install a wireless network adapter. On a notebook computer, it's likely that a card resides internal to the system. On a desktop computer, you can install an internal wireless network adapter, or connect one to a USB port.

Once you've installed the network adapter, you're ready to connect to the wireless network. If you're working from the Windows 8.1 interface, open the Charms Bar and click or tap Settings. Then click or tap the Change PC Settings link and select the Network link to view a list of available networks. Click or tap the connection you want to use and then click or tap Connect. If the connection requires that you enter a passphrase, type the passphrase and click or tap Next to connect to the network.

If you need to change network properties, press Windows + X and click Network Connections. Double-click the connection and then click the Wireless Properties button. The network's Network Properties dialog box opens as shown in Figure 38.6. Figure 38.7 shows the Connection tab for the connection.

FIGURE 38.6

Wireless Network Properties allow you to configure the connection.

FIGURE 38.7

The Connection tab for a wireless network connection.

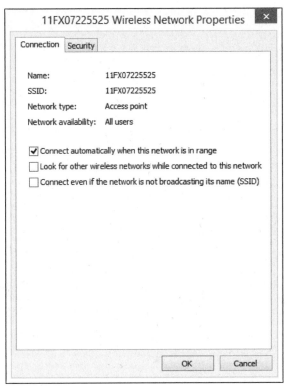

The Notification icon

Windows 8.1 can include your network connectivity information within the notification area. The icon for a wired connection is a computer with a network cable beside it. The icon for a wireless connection is a set of signal-strength bars. If you don't see an icon, check to make sure that it's not just hidden by clicking the < button at the left side of the notification area. If you still don't see the icon, click the up arrow at the left of the notification area and select Customize. Beside the Network item, click the drop-down list under the Behaviors column and choose Show Icon and Notifications. Then click OK.

When you've finished, you're ready to move on to Chapter 39 where you learn to share resources and use those shared resources from any computer in the network.

Wrap-Up

A LAN consists of two or more computers that can communicate with one another through networking hardware. Multiple computers in a network can share a single Internet account, printers, and files and folders. Moving and copying files among networked computers is a simple matter of dragging and dropping. No fumbling around with floppies, CDs, or other removable disks is required. The main points to remember when it comes to buying network hardware are as follows:

- The first step to creating a LAN is to purchase the computer networking hardware.
- Each computer in the network needs a NIC installed.
- Ethernet LANs provide the fastest speeds but require running special Ethernet cables.
- Wireless networking provides complete freedom from cables and wires.
- USB networking devices are easy to install and don't require opening the computer case.
- On a notebook computer, you can use a PC Card NIC (not to be confused with PCI card), USB NIC, or an integrated wireless network card to connect to the network.
- After you acquire your network hardware, you have to set it all up per the manufacturer's instructions. When you've finished that step, you can use the Network and Sharing Center to help configure the hardware.

38

Sharing Resources on a Network

A local area network (LAN) consists of two or more computers connected through some sort of networking hardware. In a LAN, you can use *shared resources* from other computers in much the same way as you use local resources on your own computer. In fact, the way you do things in a LAN is almost identical to the way you do things on a single computer.

For example, everything you learned about printing documents on your own computer earlier in this book works just as well for printing on a network printer. Opening a document on some other computer in a network is no different from opening a document on your own computer.

Before you can access shared resources, however, you need to share them. You have more than one method for sharing resources, and this chapter covers those methods. Before getting into the particulars of resource sharing, the following section takes a quick look at some terminology.

Some Networking Buzzwords

Networking has its own set of buzzwords. All the buzzwords you learned in earlier chapters still apply, but you have some new words to learn, as defined here:

- **Resource:** Items you use on the network, including a folder, shared media, a printer, or other device.
- **Shared resource:** A resource accessible to other users within a network. A shared folder is often referred to as a *share* or a *network share*.

- **Local computer:** The computer you're currently using.

- **Local resource:** A folder, printer, or other useful thing on the local computer or directly connected to the local computer by a cable. For example, if a printer is connected to your computer by a cable, it's a local resource (or more specifically, a *local printer*).

- **Remote computer:** Any computer in the network other than the one you're currently using.

- **Remote resource:** A folder, printer, or other useful thing on some computer other than the local computer. For example, a printer connected to someone else's computer on the network is a remote resource (or more specifically, a *remote printer*).

Figure 39.1 shows an example of how the terms *local* and *remote* are always used in reference to the computer you're currently using.

FIGURE 39.1

Examples of local and remote resources, from your perspective.

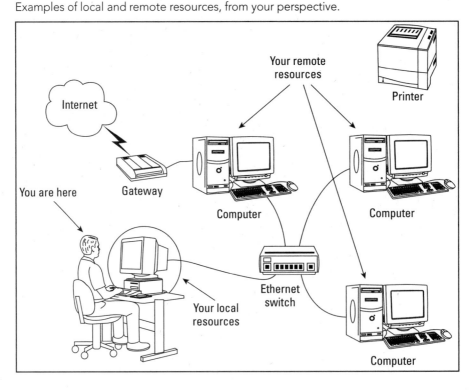

Methods for Sharing in Windows 8.1

Windows 8.1 includes three methods for sharing resources, each of which has its own advantages. The following sections explain these different methods.

Homegroups

Homegroups were first introduced as a feature in Windows 7 designed to simplify resource sharing and access for home networks. Homegroups are also available with Windows 8.1. The first Windows 7, Windows 8, or Windows 8.1 computer added to a network creates the homegroup, and then other Windows 7 or Windows 8.1 computers on that same network can join the homegroup. Once your computer is part of the homegroup, you have access to the resources shared by the other computers in the homegroup. (See "Windows 8.1 Homegroups," later in this chapter, to learn how to create and join a homegroup.)

When you use a homegroup for sharing, you specify which folders you want to share. You can share those folders with either read or read/write permissions with the rest of the homegroup. You can also set permissions on a per-user basis to allow one person to access a folder or file but not others.

Only Windows 7, Windows 8, and Windows 8.1 computers can participate in a homegroup. A computer running any edition of Windows 7 or Windows 8.1 can join a homegroup, but computers running Windows 7 Home Basic and Windows 7 Starter can only join a homegroup, not create one.

> **NOTE**
> Computers in a homegroup do not have to belong to the same workgroup.

Workgroup

Although homegroups are a great new way to share resources in a network, only the Windows 7 or Windows 8.1 computers on the network can participate. Computers running other versions of Windows cannot participate in the homegroup. In these situations, you can use workgroups to share resources on the network.

A Windows PC, regardless of the version of Windows it's running, must be a member of either a workgroup or a domain (covered in the next section). A workgroup isn't a boundary that controls security. Instead, workgroups provide a means for organizing and discovering resources on the network.

The default workgroup name in Windows is, not surprisingly, Workgroup. Computers that share the same workgroup name and reside on the same network segment appear grouped together when you browse the network. Figure 39.2 shows a workgroup.

39

FIGURE 39.2

Browsing a workgroup for shared resources.

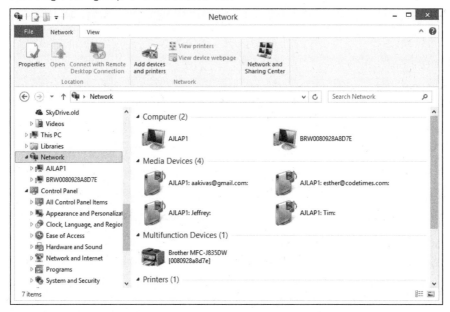

To access shared resources in a workgroup, you must have an account on the computer that is sharing the resource. Assuming a small home network of three computers and the desire to access resources on each one, this means you either need to have your own account on each computer or you create a common account on each computer that everyone uses for sharing resources.

Domain

In a domain environment, one or more domain controllers running Windows Server host all user accounts in a centralized directory called Active Directory (AD). Typically, instead of belonging to a workgroup, your computer would be joined to the domain. When you log on, you log on with a domain account (stored in AD) rather than a local account (stored on your local computer).

In a domain, AD handles authentication services. So, if you share a folder on your computer, you can specify which other domain users or groups can access that shared resource, and what permissions they have in it. The advantage of this type of resource sharing is that every user needs only a single user account in AD, and that account can be used to access resources anywhere on the network.

How to choose

If you're setting up a home network and all your computers are running Windows 7, Windows 8, or Windows 8.1, a homegroup probably makes the most sense. If your home network includes Windows Vista or Windows XP computers, using a common workgroup to share resources is a good option. Or you can use a hybrid model where your Windows 7, Windows 8, and Windows 8.1 computers share their resources through a homegroup and other computers use the workgroup.

In a business network, the number of computers generally dictates whether you choose a workgroup or a domain model for sharing. You can set up a Windows workstation as a file server, create an account for each person on the network on that computer, and use it to share resources. Whether you choose that route or use a domain and Windows Server for sharing really depends on how you'll be using the network. In most cases, when you have about five to ten computers, a domain and server make the most sense.

> **TIP**
>
> Windows client computers running Windows Vista and earlier are limited to a maximum of ten concurrent connections, making them useful for centralized sharing in small networks but not in larger ones. Windows 7, Windows 8, and Windows 8.1 all support up to 20 concurrent connections.

> **NOTE**
>
> Using a domain for sharing implies that you have one or more centralized file and print servers on the network, so sharing from your client computer is unlikely (although possible). For that reason, we don't cover domain sharing in detail in this chapter.

Turn on Sharing and Discovery

Before you start sharing resources on your network, you need to make sure you configure Windows 8.1 to enable it to share and access shared resources. By default, Windows does not make network resources available to everyone. Instead, Windows 8.1 requires users to explicitly share resources before others can access them.

A first step on each computer is to make sure sharing and discovery is enabled and all computers belong to the same workgroup. When you first connect to a new network, Windows asks if you want to enable sharing (see Figure 39.3). If the connection is a private one, such as your own wireless network at home, choose the option to turn on sharing by opening the Network and Sharing applet from the Control Panel and then clicking the Change Advanced Sharing Settings link. If you're connecting to a public network, you should *not* turn on sharing. The sharing options screen is shown in Figure 39.3.

39

FIGURE 39.3

Choose whether to turn on sharing.

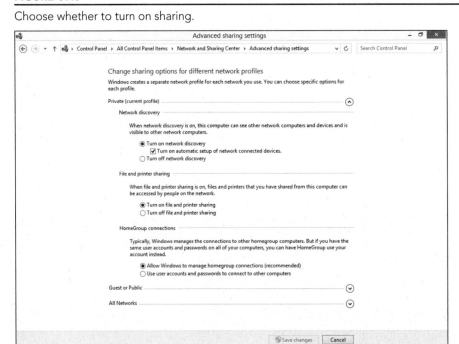

All computers must belong to the same workgroup if you're going to use workgroup sharing rather than a homegroup. So, on each computer you also want to make sure Network Discovery is turned on and all computers have the same workgroup name.

In the Network and Sharing Center section of the Control Panel, click Change Advanced Sharing Settings in the left pane to open the Advanced Sharing Settings dialog box (see Figure 39.3). Click the arrow beside Private to access the settings for private networks. If it isn't already on, enable the options for network discovery and file and printer sharing.

If you want to use public folders for sharing, expand the options for All Networks and choose the option to turn on public folder sharing (refer to Figure 39.3). If you want to enable people to access shared resources without a user account, choose the option Turn Off Password Protected Sharing. Otherwise, turn on this option.

If your network is small and you won't be using a domain for sharing, make sure all computers are in the same workgroup. On a Windows 7, Windows 8, or Windows 8.1 computer, open the Control Panel and then click System and Security and then System. In the resulting System dialog box, click Change Settings to open the Computer Name tab of the System Properties dialog box (see Figure 39.4).

The Computer Name tab shows the current computer name, description, and workgroup name. If the workgroup isn't what you need it to be, click the Change button.

In the resulting Computer Name/Domain Changes dialog box, click the Workgroup option and type the required workgroup name in the Workgroup text box. Then click OK. Click OK again to close the System Properties dialog box.

FIGURE 39.4

The Computer Name tab of the System Properties dialog box.

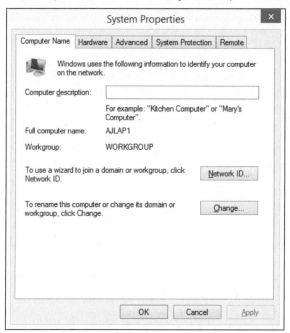

When you've turned on all the Sharing and Discovery options and set the workgroup name, you're ready to move to the next computer in the network and repeat the process. Once all the computers have sharing and discovery enabled and belong to the same workgroup, they'll be able to find each others' shared resources. But it's still up to each user to decide what they want to share. The sections that follow look at techniques for sharing resources.

 You can share media files from Windows Media Library, rather than from the folders in which those files are contained. See Chapter 24 for details.

Windows 8.1 Homegroups

Homegroups are a feature introduced in Windows 7 and carried over to Windows 8 and Windows 8.1 that simplify setting up a home network and sharing resources on the network. When you set up a Windows 7 or Windows 8.1 computer, Windows creates a homegroup automatically if one doesn't already exist and generates a network password for the homegroup. With that network password, other Windows 7 and Windows 8.1 computers on the network can join the homegroup, and users on those computers can access resources that are shared by other computers in the homegroup.

> **TIP**
>
> Computers must be running Windows 7, Windows 8, or Windows 8.1 to participate in a homegroup, and support for homegroups is included in all editions of Windows 7 and Windows 8.1. However, Windows 7 Starter and Windows 7 Home Basic can participate in a homegroup but cannot create one.

Finding or changing the homegroup password

If Windows 8.1 doesn't find an existing homegroup, it creates one. From that point on, you can add other Windows 7 or Windows 8.1 computers to that existing homegroup. All you need is the homegroup password, which Windows creates automatically when it creates the homegroup.

If you don't already know the homegroup password, open the Control Panel and under Network and Internet, click Choose Homegroup and Sharing Options. In the Homegroup applet, click View and Print Your Homegroup Password. A dialog box opens (see Figure 39.5) and displays the password. Click Print This Page if you need a printed copy.

FIGURE 39.5

View or print your homegroup password.

As mentioned previously, Windows sets the homegroup password when it sets up the homegroup. If needed, you can change the password. To do so, first make sure all the computers in the homegroup are turned on. Then open the Homegroup applet as explained previously and click Change the Password. In the resulting dialog box, click Change the Password. Windows generates a new password that you can use, or you can type your own password. In either case, click Next when you're satisfied with the new password.

Next, go to each of the other computers on the homegroup and open the Homegroup applet from the Control Panel. Windows detects that the password has changed and gives you the opportunity to change it. Click the Type New Password button, type the new password, and click Next. After the password has been changed, click Finish.

Joining a homegroup

When you add a new Windows 8.1 computer to your network, you can add it to your homegroup (although you don't have to unless you want the computer to participate in the homegroup). To add a computer to the homegroup, boot the computer and make sure the computer is on the network. (See Chapter 38 if you need help with that.)

Next, open the Control Panel and then open the Homegroup applet. Click the Join Now button (see Figure 39.6); then, in the resulting Join a Homegroup dialog box, click Next and choose which items you want to share (see Figure 39.7). Then click Next. Type the homegroup password, click Next, and click Finish.

FIGURE 39.6

Click Join Now to join the homegroup.

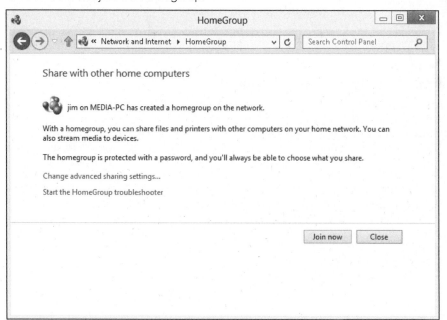

39

FIGURE 39.7

Choose the items to share with the homegroup.

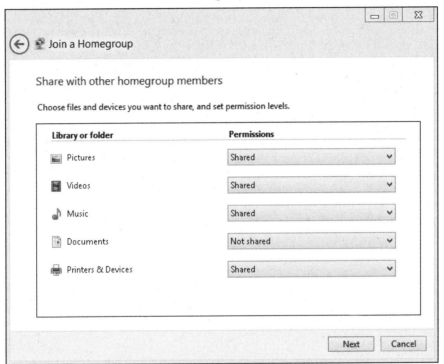

Sharing items with the homegroup

If you change your mind about what you want to share with the homegroup, you can change sharing options accordingly. To do so, open the Homegroup applet from the Control Panel (see Figure 39.8). If you just want to choose which items to share, place a check beside those you want to share and deselect the check box by those you don't want shared.

You can easily share other items with your homegroup. To do so, open the folder containing the item you want to share. For example, if you want to share a folder in the Documents folder, open Documents, click the folder, and select the Share tab of the ribbon; then choose Homegroup (View) to give others the capability to read items in the folder, Homegroup (View and Edit) to enable them to also write to the folder, or Stop Sharing to remove the folder from sharing (see Figure 39.9).

FIGURE 39.8

The HomeGroup dialog box.

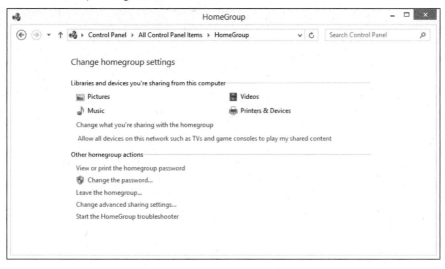

FIGURE 39.9

Sharing a folder.

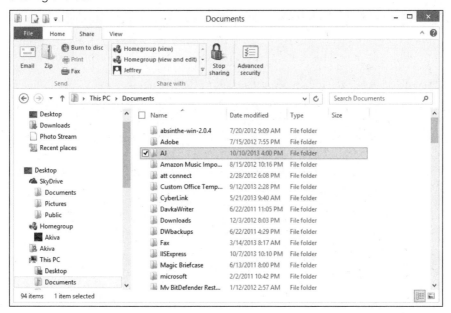

Excluding items from sharing

In some situations, you might want to share a folder or library but exclude access to certain folders or even individual files. Excluding a folder or file is simply a matter of selecting the item and clicking Stop Sharing. Open the folder containing the folder you want to exclude, or in the case of an individual file, open the folder containing the file. Click the item you want to exclude, and click Stop Sharing in the ribbon. That library, folder, or file will not show up when others browse the homegroup.

Sharing with individual users

You can also share folders and files with individual users, but those users must have an account on your computer and access the files from that same computer. For example, if you have a single home computer you share with your spouse and children, you might want to share a folder with only your spouse and not the children. To share the folder or file, open the folder containing the item to be shared, click it, and select the Share tab in the ribbon. Choose Specific People to open the File Sharing dialog box, choose an account from the drop-down list, and click Add. Then click Share to close the dialog box.

To access a folder or file that has been shared in this way, open the Network folder, and expand the local computer, then the Users folder, and finally the user who is sharing the folder or file.

Using Public Folders

Windows 7, Windows 8, and Windows 8.1 include a public folder from which files are shared automatically. This feature is similar to the Shared Documents folder in Windows XP and Windows Vista. In previous versions of Windows, even as recently as Windows 8, public folders were accessible from the Libraries node, which is no longer supported. You can simply move any files that you intend to share across all user accounts or computers in a private network to that folder. To get to that folder, start by opening File Explorer. Figure 39.10 shows the public folders.

The public folders are actually all contained in a single folder named Public in the Users folder. (The default path is C:\Users\Public.) The Public folder is organized much like your Documents folders. It contains subfolders for storing documents, downloads, music, photos, and videos. If you have Media Center installed, it also contains a Recorded TV folder, in which Media Center–recorded TV files are stored.

Perhaps the easiest way to move files into a Public folder is to open one of its subfolders, like Public Documents or Public Pictures. Then open the folder that contains the files you want to share. Size and position the two windows so you can see both. Then drag files from one folder to the other. See Chapter 21 for more information on moving and copying files.

FIGURE 39.10

Public folders in various libraries.

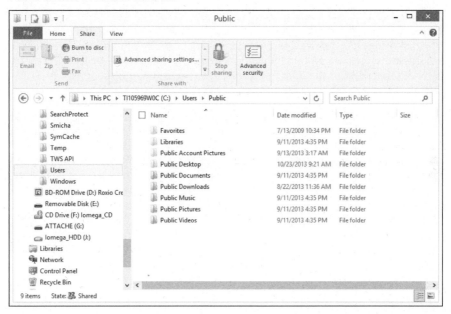

The Public folder is shared in a way where every user on the computer (and in the network) has free reign over its contents. In other words, every user has equal rights to the Public folder. If you have files you want to share more selectively, such as only with certain people or only with certain permissions, use the method described previously in the section, "Sharing with individual users."

Advanced Sharing

Advanced Sharing allows a user with administrative privileges to set custom permissions for multiple users, control the number of simultaneous connections and caching for offline files, and set other advanced properties. Some of these topics require training in or knowledge of network administration. The Public folder and selective sharing methods described in the preceding sections should be adequate for a home network and much easier to work with.

For people who understand the concepts (and potential problems) involved, we'll just quickly run through the process. Locate the folder you want to share, right-click that folder's icon, and choose Properties. Select the Sharing tab and click Advanced Sharing. Elevate your privileges (if prompted) and choose Share This Folder. Then click the Apply button. Set the number of simultaneous users up to a maximum of 20 and (optionally) add a comment.

To configure sharing permissions, click the Permissions button to open the Permissions dialog box for the shared folder. Here, you can view existing sharing permissions and also add and remove users and groups. You'll notice that you're limited to specifying Full Control, Change, or Read permission sharing levels.

If the disk where the shared folder resides is on an NTFS volume, you can also set NTFS permissions, which are more flexible than sharing permissions. To set NTFS permissions, open the properties for the folder and select the Security tab (see Figure 39.11).

On the Security tab, you can add or remove users and groups and specify the permission levels for each one. The available permissions are more granular than the sharing permissions described previously, giving you finer control over what each user or group can do in the folder. As you assign permissions, keep in mind that the most restrictive permissions apply. For example, if you share a folder and apply Full Control for all users, but then set NTFS permissions so that all users have only Read access, then the more restrictive NTFS permissions will apply and users will only be able to read items in the folder, not modify them.

FIGURE 39.11

The Security tab for NTFS permissions.

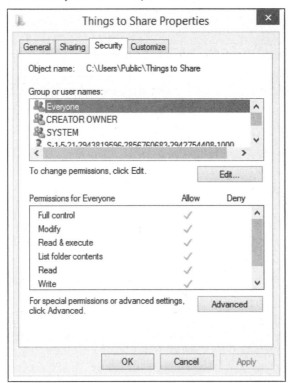

Identifying Shared Folders

In Windows 8.1, you have a few methods for identifying which folders are shared. First, in File Explorer, open a folder. If the folder is shared, you'll see the words "State: Shared" in the status bar at the bottom of the window.

You can also use the Shared Folders snap-in with the Computer Management console to see which folders are shared. To open Shared Folders, click Start, right-click Computer, and choose Manage. When the Computer Management console opens, expand the Shared Folders branch and click Shares. The folders that are shared, whether visible or hidden, appear in the right pane.

You can also use the NET command in a command console to see what is shared. Open a command console and type **NET SHARE** to see a listing of shared resources.

Sharing a Printer

Printers in a LAN are usually connected to one of the computers in that network. To ensure that the printer is shared, so everybody in the network can use it, follow these steps:

> **TIP**
>
> With the right hardware, you can connect a printer directly to a LAN without going through a computer. With that type of arrangement, you need to make sure that the printer is turned on, connected to the network, and configured with network settings appropriate for your network.

1. Go to the computer to which the printer is connected by cable. If either is turned off, turn on the printer first and the computer second.
2. Open Devices and Printers from the Control Panel.
3. Right-click the printer and choose Properties to open the Properties dialog box for the printer.
4. Select the Sharing tab; then select Share This Printer, type a name in the Share Name text box, and choose to render print jobs on the client, as shown in Figure 39.12.

> **NOTE**
>
> The Render Print Jobs on Client Computers option lets each user control print jobs from his or her own computer. In earlier versions of Windows, most print jobs had to be managed from the printer to which the computer was physically attached.

FIGURE 39.12

Sharing a printer.

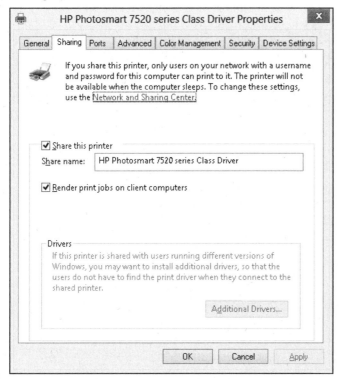

5. Click OK.

When you click the printer's icon in Devices and Printers, the status bar indicates that the printer is shared. The printer should show up automatically in all network computers' Print dialog boxes. If it doesn't show up on a particular computer, see Chapter 25 for information on installing a shared network printer.

What About Sharing Programs?

Although you can share folders and documents freely on a LAN, there's no way to share programs. You can only run programs currently installed on your computer. If you try to open a document on another computer, but you don't have the appropriate program for that document type, you can't open the document.

Don't bother trying to copy an installed program from one computer to another — except in rare cases it won't work. Only programs that you specifically install on your own computer will run on your computer.

The only solution will be to install the necessary program on your own computer.

Wrap-Up

People create computer networks to share resources among computers. Resources include things such as an Internet connection, media files, folders, and printers. Windows 8.1's sharing and discovery makes it relatively easy to share resources and discover them. This chapter has focused on the "sharing" part. The following are some of the key points covered in this chapter:

- To turn on sharing and discovery, open the Network and Sharing Center and choose Advanced Sharing Settings.
- Use a homegroup to easily share resources among Windows 7 and Windows 8.1 computers on a small network.
- To share a printer, use the Sharing tab of the printer's Properties dialog box.
- One way to share files is to move them to the Public folder or one of its subfolders.
- Use the Computer Management console or the NET SHARE command to see which folders are shared.

39

Using Shared Resources

IN THIS CHAPTER

Accessing remote resources

Opening documents from remote computers

Transferring files between networked computers

Using a shared printer

Using shared media

C hapters 38 and 39 covered all the basics of setting up and sharing resources on a private home or small business network. This chapter assumes that you've already done all that. Nothing in this chapter will work until the network is set up, you've turned on network sharing and discovery on each Windows 8 and Windows 8.1 computer, and you've shared some things on the network.

This chapter looks at how you find and use shared resources from computers within the network. It looks at opening documents from remote resources, moving and copying files between networked computers, using remote printers, and ways of using shared media.

UNC Paths

Before diving too deep into methods for accessing network resources, let's take some time to delve into a topic that will help you navigate network resources more easily — UNC paths.

UNC stands for Universal Naming Convention. A UNC path is expressed in the form:

```
\\MachineName\PathName
```

MachineName is the name of the computer and PathName is a folder path on that computer. For example, assume that your network includes a computer named SNOOPY that you use as a file server. On that computer is a folder that you have shared as SharedDocs. Within that SharedDocs folder is a subfolder named Contracts. The UNC path to the Contracts folder would be \\SNOOPY\SharedDocs\Contracts. Note that the UNC path is not case-sensitive.

A UNC path makes it easy to navigate the network, particularly when you know the path name already. Using a UNC path is often quicker than navigating to the Network folder, and then to a remote computer, and drilling down through its shared folders. Instead, you can open the This PC folder, click in the Address bar, and simply type the UNC path to the remote share that you want to use.

Another point to understand is that you can specify the IP address of the remote computer in place of the computer name in the UNC path. So, assuming that our trusty computer named SNOOPY has the IP address 192.168.0.5, the UNC path to the Contracts folder would be \\192.168.0.5\SharedDocs\Contracts.

Now that you're up to speed on UNC paths, let's take a look at how to access network resources.

Accessing Remote Resources

Every Windows 8.1 computer on which you've enabled network sharing and discovery should show up in every computer's Network folder. The same is true of any Windows 8, Windows 7, Vista, and XP computers in the network that have at least one shared resource (such as the built-in Shared Documents folder). To open the Network folder on a Windows 8.1 computer, use whichever technique is most convenient:

- Display the Charms Bar, click Search, type **network**, click Network, and then right-click on the Network node on the tree in the dialog box that opens and select Properties. The Network and Sharing Center app now opens. Information about your network appears in the View Your Active Networks area.
- If you're already in a File Explorer folder, click Network in the Folders list.

The first time you open the Network folder on a computer, it might take a few seconds for it to discover other computers in the network. But within a few seconds you should see an icon for each computer in the network, as in the example shown in Figure 40.1. Notice how each computer is also accessible from the Folders list after expanding the Network category in that list.

Each computer's icon is like a folder in that, when you open it, you see shared resources from that computer. That includes a folder icon for each shared folder and printer icons for any shared printers connected to that computer.

FIGURE 40.1

A Network folder.

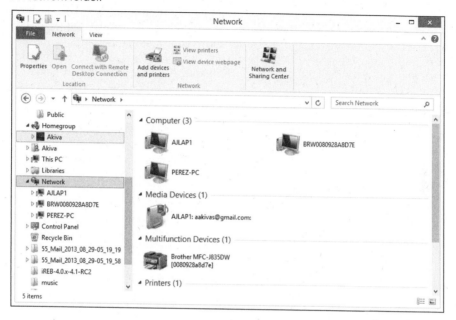

If you use the Network folder often, you'll want to make sure it's easy to find its icon. To put a Network icon on your desktop, right-click the desktop and choose Personalize. In the left column, click Change Desktop Icons. Select the Network check box (and the check boxes of any other icons you want) and click OK.

If you don't have a Network option on the right side of your Start screen, you can add one using methods for customizing the Start screen discussed in Chapter 10.

To add Network to your Favorite Links in File Explorer, open a folder and make sure you can see the Navigation pane. Open the Folders list, and then drag the Network icon in the Folders list into the Favorites Bar.

> **TIP**
>
> Any time you're in File Explorer, clicking the leftmost arrow in the Address bar usually displays a quick link to the Network folder.

40

Opening Remote Documents

One of the advantages to having a network is that you can put documents in shared folders and open them from any computer in the network. For example, you might put all your important work documents in a shared folder on your main work computer. If you also have a portable computer, you can use outside on sunny days (or from the sofa on lazy days), you can work directly with those documents from the remote computer.

The process is really no different from opening a document on a local computer. You could, for instance, just navigate to the folder, via the Network folder, in which the document is stored. Or open the Computer folder, type the UNC path to the shared folder in the Address bar, and press Enter. Then double-click (or click) the document you want to edit, and the document will open from the remote computer (providing that the local computer has the appropriate program installed for working with that type of document).

Optionally, you can go through the program's Open dialog box to get to the document. Here's how:

1. Open the program you want to use and choose File ⇨ Open or the command, link or button to open a file.

2. In the Open dialog box, click Network (if available) at the left side of the dialog box.

3. Select the computer on the network where the document resides. Then navigate to the folder for (or a parent folder to) the document. If you have to open a parent folder, just navigate down through the subfolders until you get to the document's icon.

4. Click or double-click the document's icon.

Once the document is open, you can edit it or print it however you like. When you save the document, your changes will be saved at the original location. If you want to save a local copy of the document to work with, choose File ⇨ Save As within the program, navigate to a local folder such as your Documents folder, and save your copy there.

Opening a read-only copy

If you try to open a document that someone already has open on another computer, you might see a message telling you what your options are. Those options will vary from one program to the next. For example, you might be offered the option to open a read-only copy of the document, or to open an editable copy of the document. If you choose to open a read-only copy, you can then choose File ⇨ Save As in the program and save a local copy that you can modify.

Creating network locations

If you have your own website, or permission to upload to an FTP site, Microsoft SharePoint site, or really anything on the Internet to which you can upload files, you can add an icon for that location to your This PC folder. Doing so will allow you to upload files to that location using the same techniques you use to save a file to your own computer.

You'll need to know the URL (address) to which you can download. Chances are, you'll need a username and password as well. The people who own the site to which you'll be uploading will provide that information when you set up your account. They might also provide upload instructions. But as long as you know the URL and your username and password, you should be able to use the technique described here in addition to whatever method they provide.

To create a link to the Internet location, follow these steps:

1. Open your computer folder, named This PC in Windows 8.1.

2. Right-click any unused space in the window and choose Add a Network Location.

3. Click Next on the first wizard page.

4. Click Choose a Custom Network Location and click Next.

5. Type the complete URL of the remote site. For example, if it's a website you own, include the `http://`. In Figure 40.2, we're about to create a shortcut to the `ftp://ftp.akivajoseph.com` site. If the shortcut is to an FTP site for which you have upload permissions, use the `ftp://` prefix on the URL. Click Next. To see a list of examples, click the View Examples link in the middle of the window.

6. If the remote resource requires a username and password, you'll be prompted to enter your credentials. Enter the credentials and click OK.

7. The next wizard page will suggest the URL (without the `http://` or `ftp://` prefix) as the name of the shortcut icon. You can replace that with any name you like because it's used only as the label for the shortcut. Type the desired name and click Next.

8. On the last wizard page, you can select (check) the check box Open This Network Location When I Click Finish if you want to see the remote folder immediately. Or clear the check box if you don't want to see that right now. Then click Finish.

When you double-click the icon for the remote site, it will open in File Explorer, looking much the same as any local folder on your own hard disk. You may not have quite as many options to choose from in the Explorer bar. In Figure 40.3, we've opened an FTP site.

40

FIGURE 40.2

Providing the URL of an Internet resource.

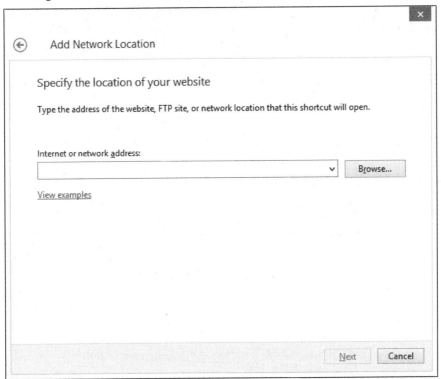

You can treat the folder as you would any other, provided you have the credentials, permissions, and authority. For example, you can create a new folder, or rename or delete existing files and folders by right-clicking, just as you would in any folder on your c: drive. You can also move and copy files to/from the site. Things will be slower than on your own computer because the remote resource could be thousands of miles away, but the techniques should all be the same.

TIP

You can rename any icon, at any time, under Network Locations just as you would any other icon. Just right-click the icon and choose Rename.

FIGURE 40.3

An FTP site as a folder in File Explorer.

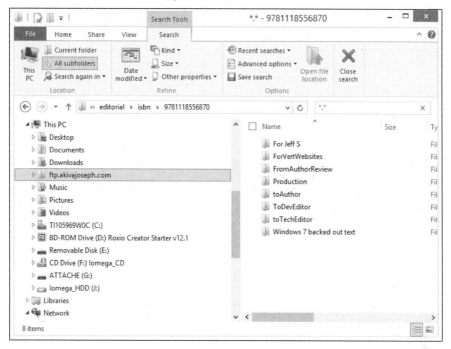

If things don't work as described here, your best resource for getting answers would be the people who provided the site. They're the only ones who know the details of that site. You may have to provide a user ID and password in order to gain access to the location.

Saving to a Remote Computer

Any time you save a new document — whether it's one you've created yourself or something you're downloading — a Save As dialog box (or something similar) will open, enabling you to save the file. The dialog box will have a Folders list so that you can choose where you want to save the document.

As with the Open dialog box, you can choose the Network folder from the Folders list to get to all the locations in your Network folder, and then navigate to wherever you want to save the file from there. Or click in the text box where you would normally enter the filename and instead enter a UNC path to the folder where you want to store the file. After the folder opens in the dialog box, enter the filename.

40

Downloading Programs to a Network Share

If you regularly download programs to install on multiple computers, consider using the folder named Public Downloads within your Public folder. After you save a downloaded program file to that folder, you'll be able to install it on all the computers in the network. You still have to install it on each computer individually, but there is no need to download it on every computer, especially if you're sharing a not-so-speedy Internet connection.

Start by creating the Public Downloads folder in your own Documents folder, or on another shared folder on your network. Then initiate the download as you normally would. When the File Download dialog box appears, click Save or Save As. In the Save As dialog box, navigate to the shared Public Downloads folder and save the file there.

> **TIP**
>
> You can download the file from the computer where the Public Downloads folder resides or from another computer on the network. The advantage of performing the download from the same computer where the file will be stored is that you minimize network traffic. If you're instead saving to a shared folder across the network, the file comes through the network to your computer and then goes across the network to the shared folder, effectively doubling the network traffic and slowing down the process.

After the file has been downloaded, you can access it from any other computer on the network to install the program. Just browse the network from the computer where you want to install the program, open the shared Public Downloads folder, and double-click the file to begin the installation.

> **NOTE**
>
> Some programs need to be installed from a local copy of the file rather than across the network. If you have problems installing across the network, copy the file across the network to the local computer and install from that local copy.

Transferring Files Between Computers

Moving and copying files on a network is virtually identical to doing so on a single computer. You can use any of the techniques described in Chapter 28 to select, move, or copy files from any folder on your own computer to any shared folder or from any shared folder to any folder on your own computer. You can also use those same techniques to move and copy files between shared folders on any two remote computers on the network.

For example, let's say you're sitting at a computer named Hobbes, and you have a bunch of files in a subfolder named Rob-PC\Common Downloads on a computer named Rob-PC. So, the UNC path would be \\Rob-PC\SharedDocs\Common Downloads (where SharedDocs is the name of the shared documents folder). You want to copy one or more files to the Downloads folder of your own user account on HP-Rob. Just open the Network folder. Then open the Rob-PC/SharedDocs/Common Downloads folder. Then open the Documents folder for your user account. It might be easier if you size and position the windows so you can see the contents of both, as in Figure 40.4.

With both folders open, as in the figure, you can select the files you want to copy in the remote folder using any technique you like, as discussed in Chapter 21. To copy (rather than move) the items to the remote folder, right-drag any selected icon to the remote folder and then choose Copy Here after you release the mouse button. (You also can drag using the left mouse button; the files will be copied from the remote location to the local one.) That's all there is to it. As we said, it's no different from moving and copying files between folders and drives on your own computer, except that you have to use the Network folder or a UNC path to open the remote folder.

FIGURE 40.4

Remote shared folder (top) and local folder (bottom).

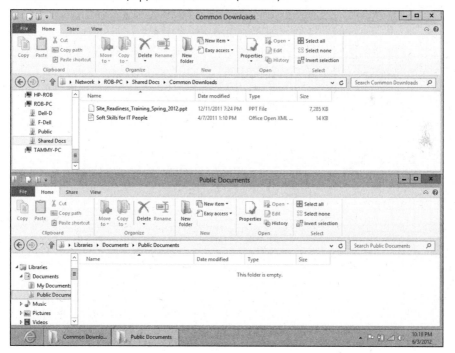

Mapping Drive Letters to Shared Folders

Some programs require that you assign a drive letter to remote resources. You can assign any unused drive letter to a resource. For example, if you already have drives A: through F: in use, you can assign drive letters G: through Z: to any shared resource. Use the following steps to map a drive letter to a shared folder:

1. Go to the computer on which you need to assign a drive letter to a remote shared resource.

2. Open any folder (such as the This PC folder), select the Computer tab, and click Map Network Drive. The Map Network Drive dialog box opens.

3. Click the Browse button to open the Browse for Folder dialog box.

4. In the Browse for Folder dialog box, click the name of the shared resource to which you want to map a drive letter, so its name is selected (highlighted). For example, in Figure 40.5, we're about to map the drive letter Y: to the shared Download folder on a computer named Rob-PC.

FIGURE 40.5

The Map Network Drive dialog box.

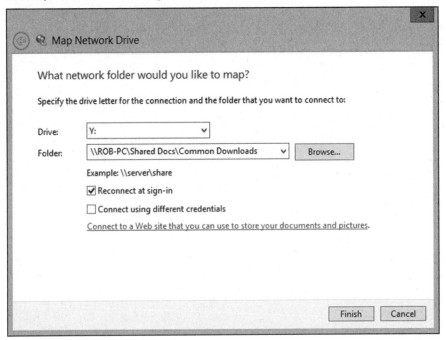

5. Click OK.

6. If you want the drive to be mapped automatically each time you log on, select the Reconnect at Sign-In check box.

7. Click Finish.

The remote resource will open. You can close that folder and also close the Network folder. Because you've mapped a drive letter to the remote resource, it will appear in your This PC folder. In Figure 40.6, we've mapped two resources: Y: is mapped to the Download folder on the computer named Rob-PC, and Z: is mapped to the hidden root share of drive C: on the computer with an IP address of 192.168.0.2.

FIGURE 40.6

Drives Y: and Z: are actually shared resources on other computers.

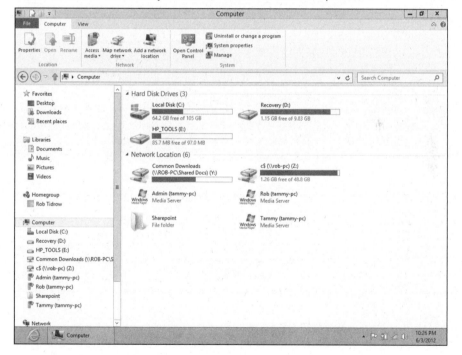

Hidden Shares

Windows creates a hidden administrative share for each drive connected to the computer. These shares, which share the root of the drive, take the name of the drive letter followed by a $ sign. For example, the administrative share for drive C: is C$, for drive E: would be E$, and so on. If you have an administrative account (or have access to the administrative shares) on the remote computer, you can map to its hidden share using the UNC path. For example, to connect to drive C: on a computer named Spock, you would use the UNC path \\Spock\C$.

These shares are called "hidden shares" because they don't appear when you browse the network for resources. For example, you won't see these shares in the Network folder. In addition, you can create your own hidden shares. When you share the resource, just add a $ sign at the end of the share name. See Chapter 39 to learn more about sharing resources on the network.

From that point on, you can access the folder either by going through the Network folder as usual, or just by opening your This PC folder and opening the resource's icon under Network Location.

> **NOTE**
> Even though a mapped network drive shows up as a disk drive in the Computer folder, a shared network resource need not be a disk drive at all. It can be a folder. The term *network drive* just refers to the fact that the shared resource "looks like" a drive, by virtue of the fact that it has a drive letter and icon in your Computer folder.

Disconnecting from a Network Drive

In your This PC folder, you can disconnect from any network drive by right-clicking the drive's icon and choosing Disconnect. If you chose the option Reconnect At Sign-In when you previously mapped the drive, the shared resource will no longer be mapped the next time you log on to the computer.

Using a Shared Printer

You use a shared printer from a remote computer exactly as you use a local printer. Choose File ➪ Print from the program's menu bar. When the Print dialog box opens, look for the shared printer, click it, and click the Print button.

If the shared printer doesn't show up in the Print dialog box, you can either add it right from the Print dialog box or install it from the Devices and Printers applet. To install it from the Devices and Printers Control Panel applet, click Add a Printer to open the Add Printer dialog box. Windows 8.1 automatically searches for all local and shared network printers and displays them in the Select a Printer dialog box (see Figure 40.7).

FIGURE 40.7

Windows 8.1 does a great job finding networked printers.

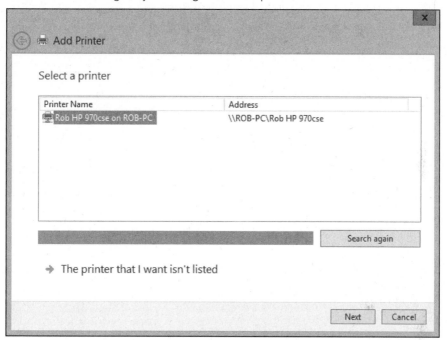

Select the printer you want to add to your list of printers and click Next. Windows 8.1 attempts to install the necessary printer driver for the networked printer. If it does not find one, you're shown a message that Windows could not find a driver. Click OK to manually specify where the necessary drivers are for the printer you want to set up.

After the drivers are installed, you return to the Devices and Printers folder. If that's the printer you'll use most often, make it the default printer as described in Chapter 25.

Whichever method you use to add the printer, after the printer is installed, choose File ⇨ Print, select the newly installed printer, and click Print.

> **CAUTION**
>
> You can play shared media from a Windows 8.1 computer on any other Windows 8.1 computer in the network and on compatible networked digital media players.

40

Using Shared Media

Shared media are different from shared files because they're *streamed* to the local computer when played. This allows you to play the media files on non-computer network devices such as the Xbox 360 or a networked digital media player. Exactly how you work such a device depends on the device. You'll need to refer to the instructions that came with the device for specifics. You also can use the new Windows 8.1 Xbox LIVE Games app from the Windows 8.1 interface to connect your Windows computer or tablet with a Microsoft Xbox device.

You can access the shared media by opening Windows Media Player normally. In the left pane, you should see each of the devices on the network that are sharing their media. Click the arrow next to a device to access its shared music, as shown in Figure 40.8.

You can also browse for media devices (and computers that are sharing their music libraries) from the Network folder. When you open the Network folder, you'll see a section named Media Devices that shows all the streaming media devices on the network (see Figure 40.9). Just double-click a device to open its library in Media Player.

FIGURE 40.8

Accessing a remote shared library.

FIGURE 40.9

Shared media in the Network folder.

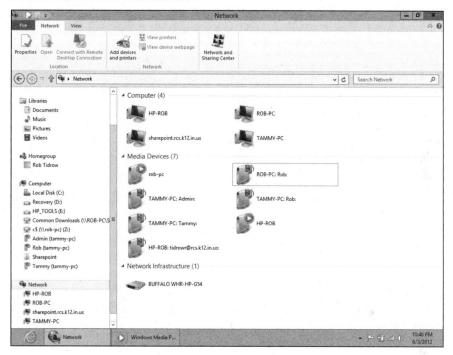

Wrap-Up

This chapter looked at ways to access shared network resources from computers in the same private network.

- To get to shared folders on other computers in the network, first open the Network folder on the computer at which you're sitting.

- To open a remote document from within a program, choose File ⇨ Open from that program, as usual. Then choose the Network folder from the Folders drop-down list in the Open dialog box.

- To save a document to a remote computer, choose File ⇨ Save (or File ⇨ Save As), and choose your Network folder from the Folders drop-down list.

- To create a Network Location link to an Internet site, right-click within your Computer folder and choose Add a Network Location.

40

- To move or copy files between computers in a network, use your Network folder to open the source and/or destination folders. Then use the standard techniques described in Chapter 21 to select, move, or copy the files.

- To use a shared printer, print normally but select the shared printer's name in the Print dialog box.

- If you don't see a shared printer in the Print dialog box, install the printer on the local computer using techniques described in Chapter 25.

- To play shared media using Windows Media Player, open the Network folder and double-click the shared media's icon.

Part X

Appendixes

Upgrading to Windows 8.1

IN THIS APPENDIX

Windows 8.1 system requirements

Pre-installation housekeeping

Installing Windows 8.1

I f you purchased your PC with Windows 8.1 already installed and have no interest in dual-booting, you need to hang a U-turn. There's nothing in this appendix for you. Go straight to the Introduction, or Chapter 1, at the beginning of this book, and forget all about this appendix.

If you purchased an upgrade version of Windows 8.1 to replace your current version of Windows and you haven't yet installed that upgrade, this is the place to be. To tell you the truth, you really don't have to read this entire appendix to install your upgrade. You really just have to do this:

1. Insert the disk that came with your Windows 8.1 upgrade into your computer's disk drive and wait a few seconds.
2. Follow the instructions that appear on the screen to install Windows 8.1 by upgrading your current version of Windows.

When the installation is complete, remove the new disk from your disk drive, put it someplace safe, and ignore the rest of this appendix. If these two steps don't quite get the job done, read on.

> **NOTE**
> There is one point that we need to stress. It's important that you know that Windows 8.1 can upgrade only from Windows 7 or Windows 8. If you have a version of Windows *other than* Windows 7 or Windows 8, you'll need to back up all your data and then perform a "clean install" of Windows 8.1 on the computer. Doing so will cause all the data on your computer to be erased, so you'll need to restore your data after installing Windows 8.1.

Windows 8.1 System Requirements

Windows 8.1 has the same hardware requirements as Windows 7 and Windows 8, but it requires a bit more hardware horsepower than versions of Windows prior to 7. The more hardware capability you have, the better Windows 8.1 will run. The recommended minimum hardware requirements are as follows:

- 1GB of RAM for 32-bit (x86) versions; 2GB of RAM for 64-bit (x64) versions
- A 1.0 GHz 32-bit (x86) or 64-bit (x64) processor
- At least 16GB free space available for 32-bit (x86) versions; 20GB for 64-bit (x64) versions
- DirectX 9–capable GPU with WDDM 1.0 driver or higher
- Screen resolution of at least 1024 x 768 for Windows 8 apps
- Screen resolution of at least 1366 x 768 for the Snap feature

When you run the installation program for Windows 8.1, it automatically runs the Windows 8 Installation Compatibility Advisor tool on your computer. This tool tests to ensure your computer meets minimum requirements for Windows 8.1. It also checks many of your installed programs to see if there are any known problems with those programs running with Windows 8.1.

Pre-Installation Housekeeping

If you've been using your PC for a while with an earlier version of Windows, you'll want to do some things before you begin your upgrade:

- If your computer has any time-out features, such as the power-down features found on some portable PCs, disable those features now.
- If you have an antivirus program handy, run it now to check for, and delete, dormant viruses that may still be lurking on your hard drive.

> **NOTE**
> Disable your antivirus software after you've run the virus check. Leave it disabled until after you've completed the upgrade.

- Make sure that any external devices (printers, external disk drives, and so on) are connected and turned on so that Windows 8.1 can detect them during installation.
- If at all possible, back up the entire hard drive at this point. At the very least, jot down all the information you need to connect to your Internet account. Back up all your documents, e-mail messages, contacts, and anything else you'll need after you complete the upgrade.

Most enterprise IT environments provide at least some mechanism of backing up your documents and other data. There are also services such as Backblaze (www.backblaze. com), Carbonite (www.carbonite.com), and Mozy (www.mozy.com), which enable you to back up your computer outside the enterprise environment (such as at home). But even in the absence of those backup options, you can back up documents, e-mail messages, names and addresses, and so forth. One option for backup that Windows 8 includes is the Windows Easy Transfer.

 See Chapter 24 for some general pointers on backing up documents.

Installing Windows 8.1

To upgrade an existing version of Windows 7, start your computer normally. You'd do well to restart the computer and get to a clean desktop with no open program windows or dialog boxes. Then put the Windows 8.1 disk in your disk drive and wait for the Welcome screen to open. If nothing appears on the screen within a minute or so, follow these steps:

1. Open Computer.

2. Open the icon for your disk drive. If the Welcome screen opens, skip the next step.

3. Click (or double-click) the setup (or setup.exe) file on the disk.

By now, you should definitely see on your screen some options for installing Windows 8.1. To get things rolling:

1. Choose the Install Now option.

2. When the Get Important Updates for Installation window appears, you're able to go online to get the latest updates for your installation of Windows 8.1. If you choose this option, your system needs to stay connected throughout the installation.

 Before clicking Install, you can use Windows Easy Transfer, an application included with Windows 8, for copying your files and settings to a different computer.

The installation procedure begins. You may notice that the screen goes blank once in a while during the installation. Don't be alarmed — that's normal. If the screen goes blank for a long time, try moving the mouse around a bit to bring it back. From here on out, you can just follow the instructions on the screen.

Installation options

The exact procedure from this point on varies a bit, depending on what version of Windows 8.1 you're installing. Also, the specific hardware that's connected to your computer affects the information that the setup procedure requests. Each request is largely self-explanatory, but here's a summary of the items you're likely to encounter along the way.

- **Get updates:** During the upgrade process, you can instruct Windows 8.1 to download and install any updates that Microsoft has released. You need to have an Internet connection for this to take place.

- **Product key:** Type the product key. You should be able to find it on the sleeve in which the Windows 8.1 disk was delivered.

- **License terms:** If you agree with the terms and conditions of the license, select the I Accept the License Terms check box.

- **Upgrade or custom installation:** If you decide that you want to do a fresh installation, choose the Custom option. This will not keep your personal files and programs. The Upgrade option will.

- **Date and time settings:** Set the date and current time, choose your time zone, and decide whether you want Windows to automatically adjust for daylight saving time.

Reenabling old startup programs

You may discover that some of the programs that used to start automatically on your computer don't do so after you've installed Windows 8.1. You can follow these steps to get those programs to start automatically again in the future:

1. Open the Start screen, type **Task Manager**, and click Task Manager in the search results. This runs the Task Manager tool.

2. Select the Startup tab.

3. Right-click a program that shows Disabled in the Status column and click Enable. Or click a program that shows Disabled in the Status column and click the Enable button at the bottom of the Task Manager window.

4. Choose File ⇨ Exit to close the Task Manager.

Windows 8.1 should restart with the programs from your previous version of Windows.

Installing Windows 8.1 on a New System

IN THIS APPENDIX

Gearing up for a clean installation

Doing the clean installation

Completing the installation

I f you've just built a new computer from scratch, or if you've replaced your old drive c: with a new hard drive, you'll have to do a *clean install* of Windows 8.1. From a purely technological standpoint, this is really your best option. You don't have to bring any of the old "baggage" with you, but therein lies an issue.

You can opt to do a clean install even if you already have a version of Windows installed on the hard drive; however, you must realize that doing so is *very* serious business. When you do a clean install, you wipe out everything on your hard drive. And we do mean *everything* — all programs, documents, settings, Internet account information, everything. There's no getting *any* of that stuff back, either. Just to make sure nobody misses this important fact, let us say it with a big Caution.

> **CAUTION**
> The procedures described in this chapter are for advanced users only. You should know your hardware; your system's BIOS setup, all your Internet account information; how to export, back up, and restore messages, contacts, favorites, and the like; and how to find technical information about your hardware components on your own before attempting any of the techniques described in this chapter. Don't confuse a "clean install" with a "clean boot."

Gearing Up for a Clean Install

Most experts prefer to do a clean install when they upgrade to a new version of Windows, largely because it gets everything off to a clean start. Besides, it's a great excuse for upgrading to a bigger and faster hard drive. You can use your original hard drive as a second hard drive and easily transfer documents from that drive to the new drive after you've installed Windows 8.1 on the new drive. However, you'll still need to reinstall all your programs and redo all your settings after you complete the installation.

Back up all your data

If you intend to keep your existing c: as the c: drive after the clean install, it's important that you understand that you will permanently lose everything on that drive during the clean install. Therefore, you should

- Write down all your Internet connection data so that you can reestablish your connection after the clean install.

- Back up or export all your e-mail messages, contacts, favorites, and anything else you'll want after the clean install so that you can recover them. *Remember:* Whatever you don't save will be lost forever. However, this does not apply for web-based e-mail accounts that don't store messages on your computer.

- Back up all your documents because each and every one of them will be wiped out along with Windows and all your programs.

> **CAUTION**
>
> A clean install permanently erases everything on your hard drive, which is basically everything that's "in your computer." Users who don't fully understand the ramifications of this should not attempt to do a clean install of Windows 8.1 or any other operating system. It's extremely difficult to recover data from an erased drive, but if you need that kind of help, you can turn to a data recovery service. Search the web for "hard drive recovery" for resources.

If Windows is currently installed on the c: drive you intend to reuse, you can use the Windows Easy Transfer to back up all your documents and settings. Ideally, you want to back up the data to another computer in the network. Windows Easy Transfer allows you to transfer files and folders, e-mail settings, and many other personal items from your existing computer to the new computer or hard drive. You can do this by using a USB Easy Transfer cable, the network, DVDs or CDs, or external USB devices.

Given that hard drives are so inexpensive these days, it almost seems a shame *not* to start the clean install from a new hard drive. You don't have to worry about losing any data from the old drive if you do a clean install of Windows 8.1 to a new drive. The data from your old drive will stay intact because Windows will be installed on the new drive.

Make sure that you can boot from your DVD

By far, the easiest way to do a clean install on a new drive is to boot from the Windows 8.1 disk. You'll want to make sure that you *can* do this before you do anything inside the computer. Most disks aren't bootable, so you need to insert the Windows disk into the drive and restart the computer. Watch for a message that says, "Press any key to boot from

CD or DVD countdown," and tap the Spacebar before the countdown runs out. (In case you're curious, it's five seconds.)

If you see a message that tells you that Windows is loading files, you know you can boot from a disk. Press Ctrl + Alt + Del to reboot before setup actually starts, and remove the disk from the drive while the system is rebooting. Then shut down the PC altogether.

If you can't boot the system from the Windows disk, you need to adjust your BIOS settings. Again, this isn't something we can tell you how to do specifically because it depends on your system's BIOS. But the usual scenario is to press F2 or Del as the computer is starting up to get to your BIOS setup. After you get into the BIOS settings, make sure that booting from the disk drive is enabled and that the disk drive has a higher priority than the hard drive.

If you'd rather not adjust your BIOS settings, many computers give you the option to select the boot device. Pressing a key during the startup process tells the BIOS that you want to select your boot device this one time. It can be the F10, F11, or F12 key, but you'll want to check your computer's documentation to find out which key it actually is.

If you do opt to change the BIOS settings, put the Windows disk back into the disk drive, save your BIOS settings, and exit so that the computer reboots again. If you got it right, you should see a message that tells you Windows is loading files again on restart, indicating that you've successfully booted from the disk. Cancel that startup as well, by pressing Ctrl + Alt + Del, and remove the disk from the drive before the computer gets another chance to boot from the disk.

Installing a new C: drive

If you're upgrading your c: drive along with your version of Windows, the first step is to hide existing hard drives from the system altogether so that, to the BIOS, the new drive appears to be the only hard drive in the system. Simply disconnecting the power and interface plugs from the backs of the drives will do the trick.

> **CAUTION**
>
> Never do anything inside your system case while the computer is turned on or even plugged into a power outlet. Wear an antistatic wrist strap to prevent static discharge from wiping out components and the warranties that go with them!

The next step involves getting the new drive installed to the point at which it's at least recognized by the BIOS. We can't tell you how to do that because the procedure varies from one drive manufacturer to the next. You must follow the instructions that came with the drive, or the instructions on the drive manufacturer's website, to get to the point at which the system recognizes that drive at startup.

Chances are, the drive manufacturer's instructions will include steps to partition and format the drive. You should probably do so even if you intend to repartition and reformat the drive during the Windows 8.1 clean installation. You still won't be able to boot from the drive, but at least the drive will be recognized as c: during the Windows installation.

It's also important to note which connection architecture your system uses, which determines how the drive plugs into the motherboard. The vast majority of new systems today use a Serial ATA (or SATA) interface. Systems from a couple of years ago used both SATA and the older Parallel ATA (or PATA). SATA cables are thin and have plastic connector tips, somewhat like USB. PATA cables are wide and flat, and the connector blocks have two rows of holes.

The other part of the installation requires knowing how the drive will be powered. If you have a laptop, you need a 1.8-inch or 2.5-inch drive, and it will be bus powered. Desktop drives will either have the older Molex (white-tipped) power adapters or the newer, more common, black- or red-tipped SATA power tips. Most systems have both Molex and SATA power adapters inside, but you need to pay close attention to the power that the drive needs. Some SATA drives come with Molex power ports, and you can find Molex-to-SATA–type adapters online or in certain PC stores.

If you intend to handle the hard drive installation on your own, you need to become familiar with these interfaces and make sure that you get the correct drive to support it.

Doing the Clean Install

When you feel confident that you'll be able to get back everything you want from your hard drive, you're ready to start the clean install. Put the Windows disk in the disk drive and shut down the computer. Then restart the computer and boot from the disk. Your system's screen will go blank with a progress bar across the bottom of the screen while it copies some setup files. After the copy, the screen will change to a blue and green background, and you'll be given a mouse pointer. Follow these steps to continue the installation:

1. At the Install Windows dialog box, select the Language, Time, and Currency format and the type of keyboard; then click the Next button.

2. Click the Install Now link, and you'll be prompted for the product key. After entering the product key, click the Next button.

3. If you accept the license terms, select the I Accept the License Terms box and click the Next button.

4. Select the Custom: Install Windows Only (Advanced) option to continue.

5. The next dialog box lists all the drives and partitions that the installation application sees on your system. Select the partition on which you want to install Windows 8.1 and click Next.

   If you don't see your drive, the controller your hard drive is connected to might require a special driver that the installation application doesn't know about. You can click the Load Driver link to load the driver provided by the controller's manufacturer. Clicking the Drive Options (Advanced) link enables the option to format the drive before installing Windows 8.1. Select the partition on which Windows 8.1 will be installed and click the Format link. The installation application will prompt that the data on the drive will be erased and permanently deleted. Click OK as long as you're sure that your database has been saved elsewhere.

6. After the drive is formatted, the Total Size and Free Space columns will be almost identical. Don't worry about any discrepancies. They're a result of how file systems and the formatting process works. Click the Next button to continue. At this point, the installation application will start copying files.

The Rest of the Installation

Copying the files and installing them to your system takes some time. When the installation continues, follow these steps:

1. You can change the color of the main screen from blue to one you prefer more.

2. Type a name for your computer. You should make it unique in your environment. For example, if you have multiple computers in your home and they're connected to one another by a network (such as a Windows homegroup), make sure you name this computer something different from all your other computers. Click Next.

3. Click Use Express Settings.

4. You're prompted to set up a sign-on name for your computer, which creates a Microsoft account for you. Use an existing e-mail address. Click Next. (Click the Sign Up for a New Email Address link if you need to set up an e-mail account right now.)

5. Enter your Microsoft account password and click Next.

6. Enter a phone number to which a text message and/or phone call can be sent in case you forget your password.

Windows installation will continue for several minutes as it finalizes and prepares your computer to be used. After Windows 8.1 has been installed, you're ready to start using it.

B

Universal Shortcut Keys

IN THIS APPENDIX

General, dialog box, and Explorer shortcut keys

Ease of Access shortcut keys

Text-editing shortcut keys

Internet Explorer shortcut keys

This appendix is a quick reference to shortcut keys that are used throughout Windows 8.1. Many application programs use the same shortcut keys. That's why we've titled this appendix "Universal Shortcut Keys." Of course, any program can have additional shortcuts to its own unique features. For example, the Word 2013 Options window shows underlined characters, denoting them as hotkeys for activating an option. The first option is Typing Replaces Selected Text. The hotkey for this option is T. For programs still using menus, the *key + key* combination to the right of each menu command is the shortcut key for using that command from the keyboard without the menu.

Virtually every program also comes with its own Help. Typically, you get to that by pressing Help (F1) while the program is in the active window. Or you choose the ? or Help from that program's menu bar. Use the Help feature of that program to search for the term "shortcut" or "shortcut keys" to see whether you can find a summary of that program's shortcut keys.

Of course, Windows 8.1 has its own Help, too. To open Windows Help and Support, open the Charms Bar, click Settings, and then click Help. Type **shortcuts keys** as your search text, and press Enter. The search results will include shortcut keys for Windows 8.1 and many programs that are built into Windows 8.1. The following tables provide lots of detail and make a handy reference.

TABLE C.1 **General Shortcut Keys**

To Do This	Press This Key
Copy selected icon(s)	Ctrl+C
Cut selected icons(s)	Ctrl+X
Paste cut or copied text or item(s) to current folder	Ctrl+V
Undo your most recent action	Ctrl+Z

continued

TABLE C.1 *(continued)*

To Do This	Press This Key
Delete selected icon(s) to Recycle Bin	Delete or DEL
Delete selected icons(s) without moving to Recycle Bin	Shift+Delete
Rename selected icon(s)	F2
Extend selection through additional icons	Shift+any arrow key
Select all items in a document or window	Ctrl+A
Search for a file or folder	F3
Display properties for selected icon	Alt+Enter
Close program in the active window	Alt+F4
Open the shortcut menu for the active window	Alt+Spacebar
Close the active document in a multiple-document program	Ctrl+F4
Switch between open programs	Alt+Tab
Cycle through open programs in the order in which they were opened	Alt+Esc
Cycle through screen elements on the desktop or in a window	F6
Display the shortcut menu for the selected item	Shift+F10
Open/close the Start screen	Ctrl+Esc or Windows key
Open menu or perform menu command	Alt+underlined letter
View menu bar in active program	F10 or Alt
Move left or right in menu bar	← and →
Move up or down in menu	↑ and ↓
Select highlighted menu command	Enter
Refresh the active window	F5
View the folder one level up in File Explorer	Backspace
Cancel the current task	Esc
Open Task Manager	Ctrl+Shift+Esc
Copy dragged item to destination	Ctrl+*drag*
Move dragged item to destination	Ctrl+Shift+*drag*

TABLE C.2 Dialog Box Keyboard Shortcuts

To Do This	Press This Key
Choose the option with the underlined letter	Alt+*letter*
Select a button if the active option is a group of option buttons	Arrow keys
Open a folder one level up if a folder is selected in the Save As or Open dialog box	Backspace

TABLE C.2   *(continued)*

To Do This	Press This Key
Go to the previous tab	Ctrl+Shift+Tab
Go to the next tab	Ctrl+Tab
Same as clicking OK	Enter
Same as clicking Cancel	Esc
Help	F1 key
Display the items in the active list	F4 key
Move to the previous option	Shift+Tab
Select or clear the check box	Spacebar
Move to the next option	Tab

TABLE C.3   **Windows 8.1 Start Screen Keyboard Shortcuts**

To Do This	Press This Key
Move Windows 8.1 app down	Arrow key, Alt+↓
Move Windows 8.1 app left	Arrow key, Alt+←
Move Windows 8.1 app right	Arrow key, Alt+→
Move Windows 8.1 app up	Arrow key, Alt+↑
Display unpin option and Advanced Windows 8.1 icons	Arrow key, App key
Select Windows 8.1 apps left, right, up, or down	Arrow keys
Move one page left on the Windows 8.1 UI menu	Ctrl+←
Move one page right on the Windows 8.1 UI menu	Ctrl+→
Return to previous app	Esc
Jump between Windows 8.1 interface and previous app	Windows key
Move Windows 8.1 app split screen right	Windows+period
Launch the desktop	Windows+B
Open the Charms Bar	Windows+C
Launch File Explorer on the classic desktop	Windows+E
Launch Narrator	Windows+Enter
Open File Search	Windows+F
Open the Share Charm	Windows+H
Open Charms settings	Windows+I
Opens the Connect Charm	Windows+K
Lock Screen	Windows+L

continued

C

TABLE C.3   *(continued)*

To Do This	Press This Key
Launch the desktop	Windows+M
Lock the device orientation	Windows+O
Second screen – projector mode	Windows+P
Move tiles to the right	Windows+PgDown
Move tiles to the left	Windows+PgUp
Open the Search window	Windows+Q
Open Run on the desktop	Windows+R
Move the Windows 8.1 app split screen left	Windows+Shift+period
Switch the input language and keyboard layout	Windows+Spacebar
Display the desktop	Windows+T
Start the Ease of Access Center	Windows+U
Open the search settings	Windows+W
Open the Quick Links menu (Advanced Tools menu) on the desktop	Windows+X
Open the App Bar	Windows+Z

TABLE C.4   File Explorer Keyboard Shortcuts

To Do This	Press This Key
Collapse the selected folder	– on the numeric keypad
Display all the subfolders under the selected folder	* on the numeric keypad
Select or collapse the parent folder	←
Expand the current folder or move to the next subfolder	↓
Display the contents of the selected folder	+ on the numeric keypad
Display the bottom of the active window	End
Display the top of the active window	Home
Open the selected folder in a new instance	Shift+*double-click*

TABLE C.5   Ease of Access Keyboard Shortcuts

To Do This	Press This Key
Open the Ease of Access center	Windows+U
Switch the MouseKeys on or off	Left Alt+Left Shift+Num Lock
Switch High Contrast on or off	Left Alt+Left Shift+Print Screen

TABLE C.5   *(continued)*

To Do This	Press This Key
Switch the ToggleKeys on or off	Num Lock for 5 seconds
Switch FilterKeys on or off	Right Shift for 8 seconds
Switch the StickyKeys on or off	Shift five times

TABLE C.6   Windows Help Shortcut Keys

To Do This	Press This Key
Open Windows Help and Support	F1
Display the Connection Settings menu	Alt+N
Display the Help Settings menu	F10
Move back to the previously viewed topic	Alt+←
Move forward to the next (previously viewed) topic	Alt+↓
Display the customer support page	Alt+A
Display the Help home page	Alt+Home
Move to the beginning of a topic	Home
Move to the end of a topic	End
Search the current topic	Ctrl+F
Print a topic	Ctrl+P
Move to the Search box	F3

TABLE C.7   Keyboard Shortcuts

To Do This	Press This Key
Display or hide the Start menu	Windows key
Lock the computer	Windows+L
Display the System Properties dialog box	Windows+Break
Show the desktop	Windows+D
Open the Computer folder	Windows+E
Search for a file or folder	Windows+F
Search for computers	Ctrl+Windows+F
Display Windows Help	Windows+F1
Minimize all the windows	Windows+M
Restore all minimized windows	Windows+Shift+M

continued

TABLE C.7   *(continued)*

To Do This	Press This Key
Open the Run dialog box	Windows+R
Switch apps	Windows+Tab
Open the Ease of Access Center	Windows+U
Open the Windows Mobility Center	Windows+X

TABLE C.8   **Text Navigation and Editing Shortcuts**

To Do This	Press This Key
Move the cursor down one line	↓
Move the cursor left one character	←
Move the cursor right one character	→
Move the cursor up one line	↑
Delete the character to the left of the cursor	Backspace
Move the cursor to the start of the next paragraph	Ctrl+↓
Move the cursor to the start of the previous paragraph	Ctrl+↑
Move the cursor to the start of the previous word	Ctrl+←
Move the cursor to the start of the next word	Ctrl+→
Select all	Ctrl+A
Copy to the Clipboard	Ctrl+C
Copy the selected text to the destination	Ctrl+*drag*
Select to the end of the paragraph	Ctrl+Shift+End
Select to the end of the word	Ctrl+Shift+→
Select to the beginning of the word	Ctrl+Shift+←
Select to the beginning of the paragraph	Ctrl+Shift+↑
Select to the end of the document	Ctrl+Shift+End
Select to the top of the document	Ctrl+Shift+Home
Paste the Clipboard contents to the cursor position	Ctrl+V
Cut to the Clipboard	Ctrl+X
Undo the last action	Ctrl+Z
Delete the selected text or character at the cursor	Del
Cancel the current task	Esc
Select to the character in the line above	Shift+↑
Select to the character in the line below	Shift+↓

TABLE C.8   *(continued)*

To Do This	Press This Key
Select the character to the left	Shift+←
Select the character to the right	Shift+→
Select from the cursor to here	Shift+*click*
Select to the end of the line	Shift+End
Select to the beginning of the line	Shift+Home
Select the text down one screen	Shift+PgDown
Select the text up one screen	Shift+PgUp

TABLE C.9   Microsoft Internet Explorer Shortcuts

To Do This	Press This Key
Add www. to the beginning and .com to the end of the text in the Address bar	Ctrl+Enter
Add the current page to Favorites	Ctrl+D
Click the Information bar	Spacebar
Close the current tab (or the current window if tabbed browsing is disabled)	Ctrl+W
Close other tabs	Ctrl+Alt+F4
Close Print Preview	Alt+C
Close the current window (if you have only one tab open)	Ctrl+W
Copy the selection to the Clipboard	Ctrl+C
Display a list of addresses you've typed	F4
Display a shortcut menu for a link	Shift+F10
Display the first page to be printed	Alt+Home
Display the last page to be printed	Alt+End
Display the next page to be printed	Alt+↓
Display the previous page to be printed	Alt+←
Display zoom percentages	Alt+Z
Find on this page	Ctrl+F
Go to the home page	Alt+Home
Go to the selected link	Enter
Go to the next page	Alt+↓
Go to the previous page	Alt+← or Backspace
Go to the Toolbar Search box	Ctrl+E

C

continued

TABLE C.9   *(continued)*

To Do This	Press This Key
Help	F1
Move back through the items on a web page, the Address bar, or the Links bar	Shift+Tab
Move back through the list of AutoComplete matches	→
Move backward between frames (if tabbed browsing is disabled)	Ctrl+Shift+Tab
Move focus to the Information bar	Alt+N
Move forward through frames and browser elements (if tabbed browsing is disabled)	Ctrl+Tab or F6
Move forward through the items on a web page, the Address bar, or the Links bar	Tab
Move forward through the list of AutoComplete matches	↓
Move the selected item down in the Favorites list in the Organize Favorites dialog box	Alt+↓
Move the selected item up in the Favorites list in the Organize Favorites dialog box	Alt+↑
Move the cursor left to the next punctuation in the Address bar	Ctrl+←
Move the cursor right to the next punctuation in the Address bar	Ctrl+→
Move to the beginning of the page	Home
Move to the end of the page	End
Open a new tab in the foreground	Ctrl+T
Open a new tab in the foreground from the Address bar	Alt+Enter
Open a new website or page	Ctrl+O
Open a new window	Ctrl+N
Open Favorites	Ctrl+I
Open Feeds	Ctrl+J
Open History	Ctrl+H
Open links in a new background tab	Ctrl+*click*
Open links in a new foreground tab	Ctrl+Shift+*click*
Open a search query in a new tab	Alt+Enter
Open the Organize Favorites dialog box	Ctrl+B
Page Setup	Alt+U
Paste the Clipboard contents	Ctrl+V
Print the current page or active frame	Ctrl+P
Refresh the current web page	F5
Refresh the current web page regardless of timestamp	Ctrl+F5

TABLE C.9   *(continued)*

To Do This	Press This Key
Save the current page	Ctrl+S
Scroll down a line	↓
Scroll down a page	PgDown
Scroll up a line	↑
Scroll up a page	PgUp
Select all items on the current web page	Ctrl+A
Select frames to print in framed website	Alt+F
Select the text in the Address bar	Alt+D
Set printing options and print the page	Alt+P
Stop downloading a page	Esc
Switch between tabs	Ctrl+Tab or Ctrl+Shift+Tab
Switch to a specific tab number	Ctrl+n (where n is a number between 1 and 8)
Switch to the last tab	Ctrl+9
Toggle between full-screen and regular views	F11
Toggle Quick Tabs on or off	Ctrl+Q
Type the number of the page you want displayed	Alt+A
Zoom in	Alt+plus sign
Zoom in 10 percent	Ctrl+plus sign
Zoom out 10 percent	Ctrl+minus sign
Zoom to 100 percent	Ctrl+0

C

Windows 8.1 Touch Gestures

IN THIS APPENDIX

Getting acquainted with the touch interface

Exploring Windows 8.1 touch gestures

The Windows 8.1 touch interface is designed to be used on different platforms with different inputs. Users on regular laptops or desktop computers can use keyboard and mouse movements to select, deselect, or move items, resize windows, and perform other tasks. With Windows-based tablets, however, you can use Windows 8.1 touch interface gestures. These are hand gestures you can use instead of relying on simple clicks or requiring that a mouse device performs Windows tasks.

Table D.1 lists touch gestures and a description of those gestures. Keep in mind that other gestures may be available based on a particular Windows 8 app that you're running. Also, not all these gestures are available with every app. It's up to the app developer to program them into their app.

> **TIP**
> Semantic Zoom is used in Microsoft Windows 8.1 apps to allow users to navigate large amounts of data presented in a single view. For example, users can view full-size maps by pinching and zooming into a region on the map or a small location on the map. Conversely, the user can zoom out from a point on a map to a larger view.

TABLE D.1 Windows 8.1 Touch Interface Gestures

This Action	Does This
Slide your finger left or right.	Scrolls through the screens.
Tap once.	Starts an app.
Swipe from the right side of the screen toward the middle.	Displays the Charms Bar, which includes the Search, Share, Start, Devices, and Settings charms. This action also displays a window that shows connection information, battery information (if using a mobile device), the time, and the date.

continued

TABLE D.1 *(continued)*

This Action	Does This
Swipe from the left side of the screen toward the middle.	Launches the last app that was launched.
Swipe down.	Displays additional menus.
Press and hold down on an item and then move it.	Enables you to move an item onscreen.
Tap and hold.	Shows the name of the element or the type of action you can perform with it.
Swipe down on an item.	Selects the item.
Swipe down past an item.	Allows movement of the item so you can move it from its current placement on the screen.
Slide an item from left or right.	Enables you to drag the item across the screen.
Place two or more fingers on an item and rotate your fingers.	Rotates an object.
Pinch inward with two or more fingers.	Zooms in on an item that uses Semantic Zoom, such as an object on an interactive map.
Pinch outward with two or move fingers.	Zooms out from an item that uses Semantic Zoom, such as zooming out on a photo or picture.
Swipe from left edge, hold, release.	Snaps an app on the left side of the screen so that it stays onscreen with another window to the right of it. You must have your screen set to at least 1366 x 768 resolution.
Swipe from left to right or right to left in Internet Explorer.	Enables you to navigate from page to page while web browsing.
Press and hold down on an app, and then drag to the bottom of the screen.	Closes the app.
From the left side of the screen, swipe to the right, hold, and then swipe to the left.	Shows currently running apps.
Swipe from the left and release.	Switches the active app.

Index

Index

005.446 BOYCE
Boyce, Jim,
Windows 8.1 bible /
R2001120621 PALMETTO

ODC

Atlanta-Fulton Public Library